The Markan Matrix

A Literary-Structural Analysis
of the Gospel of Mark

David G. Palmer

Cover photograph: The Arch of Titus, Rome, depicting the spoils which the Romans took from the temple in Jerusalem, in AD70. (Photograph taken by the author, 3rd August 1998.)

British Library Cataloguing in Publication Data.

Palmer, David G.
    The Markan matrix: a literary-structural analysis
    of the Gospel of Mark
    1.Bible. N.T. Mark - Criticism, interpretation, etc.
    I.Title
    226.3'06

ISBN 0 9513661 2 2

Copyright © 1999 Revd. Dr. David G. Palmer, MA, BSc, PhD,
                  DiplArch, RIBA, ARIAS

First published 1999. All rights reserved. No part of this publication may be reproduced, stored in a retrieval system, transmitted, in any form or by any means, without the prior permission of the publisher.

Prepared for printing and published by Ceridwen Press, Moredun House, Stanely Road, Paisley, PA2 6HF.
Web page: www.btinternet.com/~ceridwenpress/

Printed in Great Britain by Bell and Bain Ltd., Glasgow.

Notes on the Author:

David Palmer was born in 1948 in Hull where he was a pupil at the city's Grammar School. After six months at the Hull City Architect's Department and three months extensive travelling around Europe he began a seven-year course in Architecture, based at University College London. During these years he gained practical experience with Costain Construction Ltd., Yorke Rosenberg Mardall, and the Haringey Borough Architect's Service. He registered as an Architect in 1975. Two years after qualifying, he established with a close friend the Pickard and Palmer Partnership, in the City of London.

A seven-year biblical, pastoral and theological training followed. It began at All Nations Christian College in Ware, Hertfordshire, and continued in a Lay Ministerial and Pre-collegiate appointment with the Methodist Church in Lower Holloway and Camden Town in North London. After further studies in Cambridge, at Wesley House and Fitzwilliam College, he was ordained a Methodist Minister in 1983, in Durham.

Following his ordination he served seven years as a Circuit Minister in the Docks, Canton and Fairwater in Cardiff. It was during this time, in 1988, that he self-published his first book, "Sliced Bread (the Four Gospels, Acts and Revelation: their Literary Structures)", ISBN 0-9513661-0-6. For the past nine years he has been resident in Paisley. For six of these years he was the Superintendent Minister of the Paisley Mission Circuit. Currently, he is a Director of the Firehouse, an ecumenical Centre for Youth, and also proprietor of a Home for the Elderly. For the whole of his time in Paisley he has been a post-graduate student of the Department of Theology and Religious Studies, Glasgow University. This book represents the work he has successfully completed for a PhD.

He and his wife Susan have three grown-up children, Gavin, Rosalind and Alice.

To my parents,
Harold and Kathleen Palmer

The Markan Matrix:
A Literary-Structural Analysis of the Gospel of Mark
David G. Palmer

List of Contents 1
Preface 5
Abbreviations 7

Chapter One: Introduction: 8
Methodological Issues in the Study of the Gospel of Mark 8
Fundamental Questions in the Study of Mark's Gospel 10
   his leading idea 10
   his theological, literary and compositional abilities 13
The Cultural and Historical Context of the Gospel 16
An Interest in "Days" 32
A Methodology for identifying "Days", their intra- and
   inter-relationships, and their literary-structures 37
Matrix: a working definition 43

Chapter Two: The Days Beginning the Gospel (1.1-20): 46
The Prologue: 46
Content Considerations 46
Literary-structural Considerations 51

Chapter Three: The First Series of Seven Days (1.21-5.43): 76
   Day One: 1.21-38   76
   Day Two: 1.39-45   84
   Day Three: 2.1-22   91
   Day Four: 2.23-3.6   98
   Day Five: 3.7-4.41   112
   Day Six: 5.1-20   129
   Day Seven: 5.21-43   137
A Summary of the First Series of Seven Days 142
A Tabular Summary of the literary-structure of the First Seven Days 147
Addendum: a summary of studies so far made of Mark's signifiers of form
   and structure, and reflections on his rhetorical method 148

Chapter Four: The Second Series of Seven Days (6.1-8.26): 150
    Day Eight: 6.1-29   150
    Day Nine: 6.30-52   163
    Day Ten: 6.53-7.23   167
    Day Eleven: 7.24-30   174
    Day Twelve: 7.31-37   178
    Day Thirteen: 8.1-21   181
    Day Fourteen: 8.22-26   186
    A Summary of the Second Series of Seven Days   191
    A Tabular Summary of the literary-structure of the Second Seven Days 196
    Addendum: an additional signifier of form and structure, and further
        reflections on Mark's rhetorical method   196

Chapter Five: The Third Series of Seven Days (8.27-10.52): 198
    Day Fifteen: 8.27-9.1   198
    Day Sixteen: 9.2-29   206
    Day Seventeen: 9.30-50   211
    Day Eighteen: 10.1-16   215
    Day Nineteen: 10.17-31   221
    Day Twenty: 10.32-45   224
    Day Twenty-one: 10.46-52   228
    A Summary of the Third Series of Seven Days   233
    A Tabular Summary of the literary-structure of the Third Seven Days 236
    Addendum to the analysis   237
    A Comparison of the Second and Third Series of Seven Days   237

Chapter Six: The Fourth Series of Seven Days (11.1-16.8): 239
    Day Twenty-two: 11.1-11   239
    Day Twenty-three: 11.12-19   242
    Day Twenty-four: 11.20-13.37   246
    Day Twenty-five: 14.1-11   264
    Day Twenty-six: 14.12-72   266
    Day Twenty-seven: 15.1-47   276
    Day Twenty-eight: 16.1-8   284
    A Summary of the Fourth Series of Seven Days   286
    A Tabular Summary of the literary-structure of the Fourth Seven Days 290
    Addendum to the analysis   290
    A Comparison of the First and Fourth Series of Seven Days   291

Chapter Seven: The Days Following (16.9-16, 19-20a): 299
The Longer Ending: 16.9-20: the "Day(s)" following the gospel narrative: 299
   1) The absence from reliable, early manuscripts 299
   2) It does not square with the preceding passage, 16.1-8 303
   3) Its language is different from the rest of the text 308
   4) Dependency 313
A Summary Statement of today's predominating views on 16.9-20 316
Literary-structural Evidence 318
Prologue (1.1-20) and reduced longer ending (16.9-16, 19-20a) compared 322
A Tabular Summary of the literary-structures of the Prologue and the
   revised longer ending 328
Conclusion 328

Chapter Eight: The Gospel Matrix of Days and Series of Days: 332
The Results of Literary-structural Analysis: 332
Including tables:
   1: The Primary Schematic Structure of the Gospel Narrative 332
   2: The Markan Matrix: His Series' Theme Plan and Basic Structure 333
   3: The Gospel's Primary Thematic Scheme 334
   4: Number and Order of Verses of "Days" 335
   5: Number and Order of Verses of sub-Series... 336
   6: Fundamental Correspondences between the Series... 337
   7: The Structures of the Gospel's Component Parts 338
   8: The Gospel's Literary Orders 340
Fundamental Questions in the Study of Mark's Gospel, Re-visited 344
Map: the Days of Jesus' Journeyings 345
   'Invention' 346
   'Arrangement' 348
   'Style' 349
   'Memory' and 'Delivery' 350
Mark's Literary and Compositional Abilities 351
Mark's Theological Abilities 354
The Agenda For Future Work: 358
   1) On Reading Mark now 359
   2) Understanding Mark now 360
   3) Sharing Mark now 361
Artwork of Mark's Gospel 362
Chart: "Days in the Markan Matrix" 363
Chart: "The Four Seven-Day Series of the Markan Matrix" 364

Bibliography: 365
   Texts 373
   Ancient Authors and Writings 373

Preface:

Literary-structural analysis first became an interest of mine while I was preparing for ordination as a Minister of the Methodist Church. As an architect before then, design method had been my stock-in-trade. It surprised me, therefore, to discover that there was still much to be discussed about the 'designs' of the new Testament Books. The 'architect' in me recognised the challenge. Surely? if we were to understand these works, and their writers' intentions, we needed to know how their contents were arranged. That was my view then, and it has not changed since.

I was first attracted to examining the "Central Section" of Luke's Gospel (Lk. 9.43b-19.46). It was the subject of my Cambridge undergraduate dissertation, and it led me into an appreciation of 'design' in Luke's two-volumed work as a whole. In turn, it led me into a design-study of the other Gospels and, at the last, also of the Book of the Revelation to John. Because of my excitement in making many discoveries during the early eighties, and my disappointment in the late eighties at having my work turned down for publication, I self-published my first book, "Sliced Bread" in 1988, for the sake of recording and making available my results. In this book, again self-published for similar reasons, after much more detailed work on Mark's Gospel than I was able to do then, I present not only my findings, but also my reasonings of Mark's method which I think will promote a better understanding of his Gospel's plan and purpose, and of his literary and theological abilities.

The presenting of Mark's literary-scheme clearly requires that his Gospel is reproduced in Greek. It need not, however, prevent the reader who has no Greek from learning Mark's method because the chapter and verse references are given throughout and any bible translation may be read with profit alongside. An interlinear Greek-English translation would, of course, be an even better aid.

From the moment that I started sharing what I was discovering in the Lent Term of 1982, and up to the present time, my work has been viewed with much scepticism. Indeed, it has caused some, at times, to be quite hostile. It is my pleasure below, therefore, to thank a number of people for the encouragement and help they have given me over these years.

For emphatically insisting that I went to Cambridge to study for a theology degree at the age of thirty-three, when all I wanted to do was to continue working as a minister, I warmly thank the Revd. Gerald M. Burt (then Secretary of Candidates for the Ministry). In my Cambridge days I learned much from David M. Thompson (Fitzwilliam College) about studying and writing, and from Professor Morna Hooker (The Lady Margaret's Professor of Divinity in the University of Cambridge) about the synoptic gospels and particularly Mark's. More than anybody else, as I returned to student-life, the Revd. David G. Deeks (then Tutor at Wesley House) steered me through the first difficult terms. A single audience in Birmingham with Michael Goulder, during my Cardiff years, was inspirational in itself. And since coming to Paisley, for the past eight years (part time) I have had the support of the Department of Theology and Religious Studies, at Glasgow University, and in particular that of the Revd. Professor John K. Riches. I thank him for his patient and most helpful supervision of my work on this title for a PhD. I also have to thank Dr. Joel Marcus, another staff member, for his most critical observations on my under-developed first drafts. More recently still I have cause to thank the Revd. Professor Paul Ellingworth and Professor Ron Piper for their critical reading of my work and their many useful suggestions. Needless to say, I can blame no-one but myself for anything that is lacking in my presentation below.

I record my thanks also to the Dr Williams's Trust for help with expenses in the first years of my research in Glasgow, and to Ministerial Further Training of the Methodist Church for its support with academic fees. I am grateful too for my Church's sabbatical system, for the three-month periods I had in 1989 and 1996. Not least, for the present, I am pleased to be released from the demands of 'stationing' and circuit ministry, which gives me the opportunity to continue with this work and do other things too in Paisley.

Lastly, I acknowledge the support of my wife Sue and my children Gavin, Rosalind and Alice who have had to live with me and Mark, and also all those who under my pastoral charge in both Cardiff and Paisley have had to hear me on Mark more times than they may have thought they deserved.

Moredun House, Paisley, August 1999   David G. Palmer

Abbreviations:

AOS	American Oriental Society
AV	Authorized version
Bib	Biblica
BR	Biblical Research
BT	Bible Translator
BThB	Biblical Theology Bulletin
BZNW	Beihefte zur Zeitschrift für die neutestamentliche Wissenschaft
CBQ	Catholic Biblical Quarterly
EKK	Evangelisch-katholischer Kommentar
EphThL	Ephemerides Theological Lovanienses
ER	Epworth Review
EvTh	Evangelische Theologie
ExpT	Expository Times
GNB	Good News Bible
HThR	Harvard Theological Review
IntDB	The Interpreter's Dictionary of the Bible
JBL	Journal of Biblical Literature
JBR	Journal of Bible and Religion
JerB	Jerusalem Bible
JR	Journal of Religion
JSNT	Journal for the Study of the New Testament
LB	Linguistica Biblica
NEB	New English Bible
NIDNTT	The New International Dictionary of New Testament Theology
NIV	New International Version
NovT	Novum Testamentum
NTS	New Testament Studies
ÖTK	Ökumenischer Taschenkommentar
R&E	Review & Expositor
RS	Religious Studies
RSV	Revised Standard Version
SBLDS	Society of Biblical Literature Dissertation Series
SBLMS	SBL Monograph Series
SBLSP	SBL Seminar Papers
StPB	Studia Post Biblica
TU	Texte und Untersuchungen
ZThK	Zeitschrift für Theologie und Kirche

Chapter One
Introduction:

Methodological Issues in the Study of the Gospel of Mark:

Since literary comparison of the Synoptics in the second half of the nineteenth century led to the conclusion that it was the earliest example of the literary genre "gospel", Mark's Gospel has come out from under the shadows of the longer gospels and become a focal point of New Testament study and, therefore, of an ever-increasing volume of monographs and articles. Indeed, it can be stated that the supply of secondary literature on this Gospel is growing so rapidly today that even those who are professionally engaged in Markan studies find it difficult if not impossible to master.

A number of summaries of much effort devoted to understanding and interpreting Mark's work are available[1]. We need not, therefore, see it as a requirement here to rehearse the whole history of the development of approaches to it, for its own sake: rather, I would endeavour to identify, from the methodological approaches that have been and are being made, the key questions that have continued to be raised, and those in particular which patently still require answers, or, at the very least, new attempts at answers.

Over the past one-and-a-half centuries, an appreciation of the three stages in the growth of the Gospels, which focuses on (1) the actual words and deeds of the historical Jesus, (2) a period of oral transmission, and (3) the writings of the evangelists, has led to the development of a multitude of investigative methods. In the nineteenth century, source criticism was developed as New Testament critics were primarily interested in Mark's Gospel as a historical

---

[1] W.G. Kümmel, *Introduction to the New Testament*, SCM Press Ltd, 1979, ch. 6; H. Räisänen, *The "Messianic Secret" in Mark*, T & T Clark, Edinburgh 1990, ch.1; F.J. Matera, *What are They Saying about Mark?*, Paulist Press, New York/Mahwah, 1987; E. Best, *Mark: the Gospel as Story*, T & T Clark, Edinburgh, 1986, ch. XVI; and M.A. Tolbert, *Sowing the Gospel: Mark's World in Literary-Historical Perspective*, Fortress Press, Minneapolis, 1989, p.106.

source for the life of Jesus and his life-setting. At the beginning of the present century, scholars became more interested in the life and life-setting of the early church and began to develop and employ form criticism. Halfway through this century, a new generation turned its attention to the evangelist and his theology and the life-setting of his Christian community and began developing the methodology of redaction criticism.

During the last half of this century, a rash of new methodologies has been developing. Some scholars have begun applying the tools of social science to the text, to understand the social structure and values behind the gospel. Others are reading the text with the assistance of categories learned from anthropology. Structuralists have been entertaining both a philosophy and a critical methodology and they have been developing highly abstract categories based on two presuppositions: that "appearances are not reality"; and that deep structures, below the surface, "express themselves as codes". Also literary-critical study has undergone development[2] and rhetorical criticism has been established. It is these latter two methodologies which many would argue are potentially the most fruitful.

The approach of literary and rhetorical critics begins with seeing the text as a unity. Earlier literary criticism focused on the analysis of texts to establish their structure and composition, their possible use of sources, their integrity and their style. Now much more attention is given to the rhetorical techniques employed by the author to narrate his/her story. We distinguish between two approaches in recent years: some scholars have been attempting to identify the rhetorical genre of the Gospel by comparing it with similar literature of the Greco-Roman world of the first century[3];

---

[2] See the Introduction in particular to *A Complete Literary Guide to the Bible*, eds. Leland Ryken & Tremper Longman III, Zondervan Publishing House, Grand Rapids, Michigan, 1993.

[3] E.g. and so henceforth: G.G. Bilezikian, *The Liberated Gospel: A Comparison of the Gospel of Mark and Greek Tragedy*, Grand Rapids: Baker, 1977; B. Standaert, *L'Évangile selon Marc: Commentaire*, Lire la Bible 61, Les Éditions du Cerf, Paris, 1983; V.K. Robbins, *Jesus the Teacher (A Socio-Rhetorical Interpretation of Mark)*, Fortress Press, Philadelphia, 1984; J. Dewey, *Markan Public Debate: Literary Technique, Concentric Structure, and Theology in Mark 2.1-3.6*, SBLDS 48, Scholars Press, Chico CA, 1980; Tolbert, *Sowing the Gospel...*; John Painter, *Mark's Gospel: Worlds in Conflict*, Routledge, London and New York, 1997; and for an introduction and guide to scholarship in rhetorical criticism, Burton L. Mack, *Rhetoric and the New Testament*, Fortress Press, Minneapolis, 1990.

others have been employing the tools of contemporary literary criticism, arguing that since Mark's Gospel is a narrative, it is capable of being analysed like any other story, in terms of plot, character, development, narrative technique, and so on[4]. Redaction critics, since the beginning of the third quarter of this century, did indeed view Mark as both author and theologian, but they often read the Gospel in a piecemeal fashion by concentrating primarily on the evangelist's supposed additions and alterations to the traditions he received.

The study of Mark's Gospel has never before been so diversified and the questions being put have never before been so wide-ranging. The methodological tool-box is full to over-flowing and specialisms of craftsmanship have grown beyond any early expectation, but the fact remains that fundamental questions, spanning the last century-and-a-half, still remain unanswered to the satisfaction of scholarship in general.

Fundamental Questions in the Study of Mark's Gospel:

Fundamental questions in the study of Mark's Gospel focus upon his leading idea and upon his theological, literary and compositional abilities.

In 1901, Wrede's rigorous historical analysis led him to define Mark's "leading idea" "or purpose" as the constructing of his Gospel on the basis of a dogmatic theory of a messiahship that was to be kept secret until after Jesus' resurrection[5]. He was dissatisfied with his own work, however, because he recognised the limits of his own methodological approach. He identified a need for a literary-critical analysis which would make clear the particular character of the book and the factors which had contributed to its production. In taking

---

[4] E.g. and so henceforth: N.R. Petersen, *Literary Criticism for New Testament Critics*, Fortress Press, Philadelphia, 1978; R.M. Fowler, *Loaves and Fishes. The Function of the Feeding Stories in the Gospel of Mark*, SBLDS 54, Scholars Press, Chico CA, 1981; J.D. Kingsbury, *The Christology of Mark's Gospel*, Fortress Press, Philadelphia, 1983; C.H. Tannehill, "The Disciples in Mark: The Function of a Narrative Role", *JR* 57 (1977); D. Juel, *Messiah and Temple: The Trial of Jesus in the Gospel of Mark*, SBLDS 31, Scholars Press, Missoula, Montana, 1977; and D. Rhoads and D. Michie, *Mark as Story. An Introduction to the Narrative of a Gospel*, Fortress Press, Philadelphia, 1982.

[5] W. Wrede, *The Messianic Secret*, Eng. Tr., James Clarke, Cambridge/London, 1971.

this position, he much anticipated the founding of redaction critical study in the fifties and the more recent literary-critical approaches. The situation today, however, is that we still await sure results from these quarters.

In 1919, K.L. Schmidt raised issues in regard to Mark's "framework" to his history of Jesus. Mark's Gospel, he concluded, stemmed from the linking together of material handed on to him as single units of tradition[6]. He further deduced that Mark's framework was "artificial", but it was still, even then, only loosely and variously describable. Literary-critical analysis has attempted clearer definition, but it has not yet resolved the issue. A framework exists: it is one framework; there are not two or more options. Just as any building has a structure which can be described objectively and in all its detail, so too Mark's Gospel has a single structure which demands definition. When it is revealed, it will be one with which scholarship will be able to work, with a unanimity of a kind which we have not yet seen.

Since Wrede, we have witnessed an ever-growing number of propositions, but "on the basis of which leading idea has the evangelist conceived his blending of material?" asks Kümmel.[7] Best poses a similar question: "What is the glue or cement which holds the material together?"[8] "The question is extremely difficult to answer," says Kümmel, "since it must be answered exclusively on the ground of an analysis of Mark's Gospel itself."

A study of Bultmann's starting point displays one aspect of the problem. He begins with a recognition of Schmidt's "careful analysis", but in freely addressing the issue of the parts, the units of earlier tradition, he fails to address, in as open and critical a manner, the issue of the whole, which to Schmidt is just as important. Bultmann starts with the preconception that "the most ancient tradition consisted of individual sections and that the connecting

---

[6] K.L. Schmidt, *Der Rahmen der Geschichte Jesu, Literarkritische Untersuchungen zur ältesten Jesusüberlieferung*, Trowitzsch & Sohn, Berlin, 1919. For a recent and most comprehensive challenge to Schmidt's methods of argument, see David R. Hall, *The Gospel Framework: Fiction or Fact? (A critical evaluation of Der Rahmen...)*, Paternoster Press, Carlisle, 1998.
[7] Kümmel, *Introduction...*, p.85.
[8] Best, *Mark: the Gospel...*, p.100.

together is secondary"[9]. He falls prey to his second preconception that, "when one tries to determine the leading ideas of Mark's arrangement of his material, one has to take into account the collections of material that he had in front of him."[10] This may sound like good, common sense, but before one can determine Mark's reasons for, and method of organising his material, one has to be able to describe the result, that is, the arrangement itself, of his compositional work. Knowing the shape of the Gospel's presentation is not dependent, in the first instance, on understanding Mark's sources. Bultmann was set on a course, from the beginning, which would lead him inexorably to the conclusion that "Mark is not sufficiently master of his material to be able to venture on a systematic construction himself"[11], apart from a turning point at 8.27ff.[12] A tension is well exhibited here. Mark can be credited with creating a new literary genre, but he lacked both the freedom and ability to create and control it. Bultmann's understanding was that Mark's material controlled him.

Where Bultmann gave up on attempting to define Mark's "leading ideas" others ventured. Dodd sought to show that the order of narratives in Mark's Gospel is basically and essentially the traditional sequence of events of the history of Jesus, as discernible in Acts 10.37-41[13]. Farrer proposed a theological scheme, repetitive of typological fulfilment of Old Testament texts[14]. Carrington proposed that the sequence was the result of a liturgical intention for the Gospel[15] (an idea that Goulder later developed further[16]). Beach identified what he thought were six stages in the revelation of Jesus'

---

[9]   R. Bultmann, *Die Geschichte der Synoptischen Tradition*, Göttingen, 1931; *The History of the Synoptic Tradition*, tr. John Marsh, Basil Blackwell, Oxford, 1972, p.338.
[10]   Bultmann, *The History...*, p.349.
[11]   Bultmann, *The History...*, p.350.
[12]   My analysis below shows that he is at least right about the one "turning point" he recognises.
[13]   C.H. Dodd, "The Framework of the Gospel Narrative", *ExpT* 43 (1932), pp.396ff.
[14]   A.M. Farrer, *A Study in St Mark*, Dacre Press, Westminster, 1951: compare J. Marcus, who confines his study of Old Testament texts to Christological considerations only, *The Way of the Lord: Christological Exegesis of the Old Testament in the Gospel of Mark*, T & T Clark, Edinburgh, 1993.
[15]   P. Carrington, *The Primitive Christian Calendar: A Study in the Making of the Markan Gospel*, Cambridge University Press, Cambridge, 1952.
[16]   M.D. Goulder, *The Evangelists' Calendar (A Lectionary Explanation of the Development of Scripture)*, SPCK, London, 1978.

messiahship[17]. Bowman claimed to have discovered parallels to the Jewish Passover Haggada[18]. And Kümmel despaired, "Close examination of all these schemes leads to no proof based on the text itself"[19]. Again we are presented with the same, basic requirement. The text and the text alone requires analysis. Or, to quote Kümmel once more, the question of Mark's leading idea "must be answered exclusively on the ground of an analysis of Mark's Gospel itself."

On Mark's theological, literary and compositional abilities, not surprisingly we meet with a wide range of opinion too. To Bultmann, Mark was simply a collector or hander on of traditions, not a theologian. On the other hand, Marxsen's pioneering redaction critical studies[20] led him, and Schweizer[21] in turn, to the view that Mark was a profound interpreter, whose theology may also be used on the contemporary scene[22]. Schreiber sees the Gospel as a kind of kerygmatic allegory and that "every line of Mark's Gospel must be explored for its allegorical meaning" (the historical form of the Gospel is but an external wrapping)[23]. Pesch argued that Mark handled the tradition in a very conservative way, that his work was "scarcely governed by any sweeping compositional viewpoint", but is rather "a kind of "unliterary writing", and that he did not attempt to "unify the traditional material"[24]. Pesch's hypothesis that the Gospel is an extended passion narrative has not attracted wide support. Best argues that Mark had "a positive respect for the material which he used" and that he altered the individual units as little as possible. He says, therefore, that "we should not look for a coherent and consistent

---

[17] C. Beach, *The Gospel of Mark: Its Making and Meaning*, Harper & Bros., New York, 1959.

[18] J. Bowman, "The Gospel of Mark: The New Christian Passover Haggada", *StPB* 8 (1965).

[19] Kümmel, *Introduction...*, p.86.

[20] W. Marxsen, *Mark the Evangelist*, Ger. orig. 1956, Eng.tr. J. Boyce, Abingdon, Nashville, 1969.

[21] E. Schweizer, *The Good News according to Mark*, tr. D.H. Madvig, John Knox Press, Atlanta, 1970.

[22] E. Schweizer, "Die Frage nach dem historischen Jesus", *EvTh* (1964), pp.403-419, 411f.: the mystery of Jesus Christ "can always be preached and never really described"; compare also Marxsen, *Mark...*, p.216.

[23] J. Schreiber, "Die Christologie des Markusevangeliums. Beobachtungen zur Theologie und Komposition des zweiten Evangeliums", *ZThK* 58 (1961), pp.154-183.

[24] R. Pesch, *Das Markusevangelium 1. Teil: Einleitung und Kommentar zu Kap. 1.1-8.26*, Herders Theologischer Kommentar zum Neuen Testament II, Herder, Freiburg, 1976.

theology in the Gospel, but be prepared to find unevenness"[25]. Meagher takes the view that Mark's Gospel is "clumsy construction", that it has "an air of great ordinariness" and that it "is not egregiously bad... nor memorably good" as a literary work[26]. Schmithals distinguishes between the work of the final redactor (Mark) and the *Grundschrift*, the bulk of the Gospel: Mark is a very ordinary churchman without literary skill; the author of the believed *Grundschift* is an "excellent theologian[27]. Williams contends that Mark is "hardly a collector or editor", but "a maker, a poet in the strict sense."[28]

Räisänen notes that Williams' work is informed by the new literary approach and that in recent years the focus has turned to Mark's Gospel as a narrative. "Historical or tradition historical questions need not be wholly excluded," he says, "but have to be postponed until a purely literary analysis has been carried out. In such an analysis, the plot and the rhetoric as well as the settings and the characters of the gospel are scrutinised."[29] He refers to the pioneering work of Petersen[30] and to the narrative work of Kingsbury on the "messianic secret"[31]. He quotes from Rhoads' and Michie's work: "The study of narrative emphasises the unity of the final text... A literary study... suggests that the author succeeded in creating a unified narrative."[32] Räisänen confidently states himself that, "Mark does have a plot. He has a point of view of his own. He has composed his work according to a plan. Let there be no doubt about that. The *question remains*, however, just how much skill and

---

[25] E. Best, *Disciples and Discipleship: Studies in the Gospel according to Mark*, T & T Clark, Edinburgh, 1986, pp.46f.
[26] J.C. Meagher, *Clumsy Construction in Mark's Gospel: A Critique of Form and Redaktionsgeschichte*, Toronto Studies in Theology 3, New York, 1979.
[27] W. Schmithals, "Das Evangelium nach Markus", 1-2, ÖTK 2/1-2, Gütersloh (1979).
[28] J.G. Williams, *Gospel against Parable. Mark's language of Mystery*, Sheffield University Press, Sheffield, 1985.
[29] Räisänen, *The Messianic Secret*..., p.14; see also Matera, *What are the saying about...?* p.92 for a similar view and for his reflection on the nineteenth century search for the historical Jesus that investigations would have been more profitable if they had begun with a literary critical study.
[30] N.R. Petersen, *Literary Criticism*...; also, "The Composition of Mark 4.1-8.26", *HThR* 73 (1980), pp.185-217.
[31] Kingsbury, *The Christology*....
[32] Rhoads & Michie, *Mark as Story*...

sophistication does Mark's work display? Just how well did he succeed in creating a unified narrative?"[33]

Again, the requirement of a "purely literary analysis" is called for. If Mark has a plot, what is it? If he has a plan, let it be defined. Only when these things are known will it be possible to proceed with anything like an objective evaluation of Mark's theological, literary and compositional abilities. It follows, that a greater degree of unanimity between scholars would be possible also. It is my essential purpose, therefore, to demonstrate that an analysis of the text and the text alone, with the employment of methodologies appropriate to the task, is able to establish what is the Markan framework and his methods of organisation and presentation.

It may be asked, "If Mark employed both a plan and a method of presentation, why have they not been identified before now?" The answer must lie somewhere between the fact that in the biblical-critical era there has been a loss of contact with first century literary-compositional method[34], and the fact that we have not been employing the right analytical methodologies.

Those who have approached the Gospel text as a unified whole and who have attempted a careful and thoughtful outlining of the overall organisation of Mark's Gospel have had their influence on my thesis. In addition to the work of Williams, Petersen, Kingsbury, Rhoads and Mitchie, as referenced above, I include that of Robbins, Trocmé, Faw, Lang, Scott, Stock, Culpepper, Tolbert and Noble.[35]

---

[33] Räisänen, *The Messianic Secret...*, p.15 (my italics). Further, Robbins, *Jesus the Teacher...*, p.19, identifies with C. H. Holman, when he says, "Virtually every literary document has a formal structure that is a planned framework, and the framework is likely to be a clue to the interrelation of forms in the document."

[34] In his Introduction to *Rhetoric and the New Testament...*, pp.9-11, Mack demonstrates how "the knowledge of rhetoric actually was lost to us in the twists and turns of twentieth-century scholarship. We now know", he writes, "that interest in rhetoric waned around the turn of the century, ushering in approximately four generations of scholarship without formal training in rhetoric and with very little knowledge of the tradition of rhetorical criticism." (p.11).

[35] V. Robbins, *Jesus the Teacher...*, pp.19-51; É. Trocmé, *The Formation of the Gospel According to Mark*, tr. P. Gaughan, London, SPCK, 1975, pp.215-259; C.E. Faw, "The Outline of Mark", *JBR* 25 (1957), pp.19-23; F.G. Lang, "Kompositionsanalyse des Markusevangeliums", *ZThK* 74 (1977), pp.1-24; M.P. Scott, "Chiastic Structure: A Key to the Interpretation of Mark's Gospel", *BThB* 15 (1985), pp. 17-26; A. Stock, "Hinge Transitions in Mark's Gospel", *BThB* 15 (1985), pp.27-31; R.A. Culpepper, "An Outline of the Gospel According to Mark", *R&E* 75 (1978), pp.619-622; M.A. Tolbert, *Sowing the Gospel...*; and D.F. Noble, *An Examination of the Structure of Mark's Gospel*, PhD Thesis,

The rhetorical structure I present, however, runs contrary to all their conclusions. And whilst it adds to the list of potential solutions to the still open, fundamental questions regarding Mark's Gospel, it is offered, nevertheless, as an alternative which meets the challenges of criticism levelled at previous attempts.

The Cultural and Historical Context of the Gospel:

The underlying issues which we recognise at the outset concern the functionings of this new literary genre of "gospel". We necessarily consider the life-setting of the early Christian community and of the Gospel itself.

Readily, we acknowledge that the first audiences of Mark's Gospel shared with him the mind-set of the first century populace in religio-cultural ways. In matters literary-cultural, immediately we note that few first century Christians would possess any literature of their own, sacred or secular, and that the populace, on the whole, would be "un-bookish" and mostly illiterate.[36] Only the wealthy will have possessed their own copies of Biblical books. For one indication of this, according to Luke, an Ethiopian eunuch was in possession of a copy of the book of Isaiah, and he was an important official in charge of all the treasury of the Candace of Ethiopia (Acts 8.27,28). Christians from conscientious Jewish family backgrounds will have memorised the Torah in full, or many of its principal parts, and other scriptures too.[37] Some, indeed, will have been well educated in the

---

University of Edinburgh, 1972.
[36] William Harris has sought to discover the extent of literacy in the ancient world: using a broad definition of literacy as the ability to read and write at any level, he draws on wide and varied evidence - explicit, circumstantial and comparative - and takes some account of the types and the uses of literacy. Granting regional and temporal variations, throughout the entire period of classical Greek, Hellenistic and Roman imperial civilisation, the extent of literacy was about 10 per cent and never exceeded 15 to 20 per cent of the population as a whole (*Ancient Literacy*, Harvard University Press, Cambridge, Mass., 1989).
[37] According to Josephus (*Contra Apion.* 2.204, *Ant..* 4.211; cf. T. Levi 13.2; Philo, *Ad Gaium*, pp.115, 210): in first century Judaism it was a duty, even a religious commandment, that children be taught to read. Instruction may have been given in the home by parents, but rabbinical sources suggest that schools were common in towns and were heavily enrolled. Before its destruction in 70AD, Jerusalem is said to have had 480 synagogues, each with a "house of reading" (*bet sefer*) and a "house of learning" (*bet midrash*) attached. The former provided young children with instruction to read scripture: the latter offered older children

sacred scriptures. Apollos (Acts 18.24) was one who was named. We know that the scriptures were being read aloud in the assemblies (1Tim.4.13)[38]. Such was the practice of the synagogue, in reading from the Law and the Prophets every sabbath (Lk. 4.16,17; Acts 13.15, 15.21). And Luke tells us, indirectly, that Jesus himself was literate (Lk. 4.17 again). The first followers of Jesus we are told, however, were not (Acts 4.13, they were "illiterate and uneducated"), but they need not have been without a good oral education.

Even for the majority of people, who remained illiterate, rhetorical conventions permeated their universe and their culture, the way they heard and the way they spoke[39], for the rhetorical theory of the schools found its immediate application in almost every form of oral and written communication[40], of Jews, Greeks and early Christians alike, with none excepted[41]. In the public place and the place of education, everywhere in the first century, there was a considerable degree of dependence on rhetorical conventions for transmitting and for memorising information[42]. A widespread,

---

instruction in the oral Torah. The capacity to read and understand scripture, especially the Torah, stood at the centre of instruction. For the development of Jewish schools, see M. Hengel, *Judaism and Hellenism*, Fortress Press, Philadelphia, 1974.

[38]   For extra-biblical evidence, we might turn to Justin Martyr (*Apology*, 1.67) who describes the procedure of Christian assemblies in the middle of the second century (this dating itself, of course, limits this as "evidence"): "And on the day which is called the day of the sun there is an assembly of all those who live in the towns or in the country, and the memoirs of the apostles or the writings of the prophets are read as long as time permits. Then the reader ceases, and the president speaks, admonishing and exhorting us to imitate these excellent examples..."

[39]   Tolbert, *Sowing the Gospel...*, p.41.

[40]   G.A. Kennedy,   *New Testament Interpretation through Rhetorical Criticism*, University of North Carolina Press, Chapel Hill, N.C., 1984, p.10.

[41]   Burton L. Mack, *Rhetoric...*, pp.12-17.

[42]   Ian H. Thomson, *Chiasmus in the Pauline Corpus*, JSNT, Sheffield Academic Press, Sheffield, 1995, p.17: he writes, "Throughout classical education, learning by heart was given a prominent role. As the pupils progressed through stages of schooling, ever-increasing attention had to be devoted to the *scriptio continua*." And he quotes from A. Stock: "Chiastic Awareness and Education in Antiquity", *BThB* 14 (1984), pp.23-27, p.24. "Thus, in the Greek system, for those 14-21 years, the grammarian based his instruction on poetry, with Homer in the first place. At the beginning of the Christian era, the treatment of an author had four stages: textual criticism; expressive reading (for this the *scriptio continua* had to be broken down: words separated, punctuation determined, phrases and sentences found, questions distinguished, lines made to scan); literal and literary explanation of both form and content; and ultimately moral judgement of the text. Effectively, to sustain this level of attention to the text, it was learned by heart."

"The ancient educational system, both Greek and Roman, made even its youngest customary use of rhetorical figures and patterns of argumentation had established itself cross-culturally. Perelman and Olbrechts-Tyteca[43] in their research on ancient rhetoric re-established its classical definition as "the art of persuasion", described a logic of communication that could be applied to widely ranging modes of human discourse, and immersed the study of speech events in social situations. They well demonstrated the importance of the situation or speech context when calculating the persuasive force of an argumentation. And they well rescued the understanding of rhetoric from that of mere ornamentation, or embellished literary style, or extravagance in public oratory, and placed it at the centre of a social theory of language. Like grammar in culture and language, rhetoric in an ancient society and in its discourse had its rules which developed over centuries and which by trial and error and usage became acceptable. It was, therefore, identified, studied and re-applied in succeeding generations.

A full treatise on what features of literacy and methods of learning characterised the early Christian community may not be possible today[44], but we now know that certain common patterns of interaction, communication and education existed throughout the cultural milieu in which Christianity was born, despite the variations within Mediterranean culture. Robbins informs us that "rhetorical forms and the figure and concept of the sage intersected with established traditions to provide a common cultural base for Greek, Roman, Jewish and Christian communities. Within this setting small forms like the proverb, the apophthegma, and the chreia provided a

---

pupils much more aware of the movement and structure of a passage than moderns are. Thus in both systems, a child was not deemed to have learned the alphabet until it could be recited both from alpha to omega (A to X in Latin - Y and Z were looked on as "foreign"), and also from omega to alpha, and then both ways at once, alpha-omega, beta-psi... mu-nu." Thomson suggests that "this approach to the alphabet could not but help contribute to chiastic awareness."

[43] Chaim Perelman, and L. Olbrechts-Tyteca, *The New Rhetoric: A Treatise on Argumentation*, University of Notre Dame Press, Notre Dame, Ind., 1969.

[44] In his book, *Books and Readers in the Early Church: A History of Early Christian Texts*, Yale University Press, New Haven and London, 1995, Harry Y. Gamble gathers some evidence on the subject of education and social class, and recognises also the influence of the multicultural and multilingual settings of the church: for instance, a Christian in Palestine would be well versed in Aramaic, less so in Hebrew, in Greek only a little, and in Latin probably not at all; a Christian in Rome would likely know no Aramaic or Hebrew, but would be well-versed in Greek and best of all in Latin.

bridge between oral and written culture."⁴⁵ Of the larger literary forms, of oration, diatribe, essay, symposium, epistle, biography and novel, Robbins suggests that they "represented the meeting ground for rhetorical forms and patterns of influence from the wise personages in the culture."⁴⁶

Identifying conventional repetitive and progressive forms in Mark's Gospel, Robbins[47] viewed Mark's accomplishment as that of adopting and modifying such forms as were present in prophetic biblical literature and in non-biblical literature associated with Greco-Roman religio-ethical teachers who gathered disciple-companions.

In terms of 'biblical form' sources, he particularly discovered in 1 and 2 Kings (concerning Elijah and Elisha) and Jeremiah a socio-rhetorical pattern containing three essential elements:

1. the word of the Lord comes to the prophet;
2. the prophet does and says the word of the Lord;
3. events occur according to the word of the Lord as pronounced by the prophet.

In terms of extra biblical material, Robbins sees Xenophon's *Memorabilia* (dating: 390-355BC) as the most informative document. Other similar documents from the second and third centuries AD are known which similarly tell of people possessing wisdom who gathered disciple-companions. The socio-rhetorical pattern he discerns contains, again, three essential elements:

1. the teacher himself does what he teaches others to do;
2. the teacher interacts with others through speech to teach the system of thought and action he embodies;
3. through his teaching and action the teacher transmits a religio-ethical system of thought and action to later generations through his disciple-companions.

---

[45] Robbins, *Jesus the Teacher...*, p.2.
[46] Robbins, *Jesus the Teacher...*, p.2; H.A. Fischel, "Story and History: Observations on Greco-Roman Rhetoric and Pharisaism", *AOS* (1969), pp.59-88, see pp.61-63; and Tolbert, *Sowing the Gospel...*, pp.81-83.
[47] Robbins, *Jesus the Teacher...*, chapters 3 to 6.

Additionally, Robbins usefully notes how early Christian writers during the second century referred to the gospels as Ἀπομνημονεύματα (Latin: *Memorabilia*)[48]. In Mark's Gospel he discerns a shift in terminology from the Old Testament 'word' to 'gospel' and a development by Mark of what in the biblical material is often only simple repetition, but after the Greco-Roman method is progressive repetition (by which minor changes are introduced). He discerns a three-step pattern that dominates the narrative, as follows:

1. Jesus comes into a place accompanied by his disciples;
2. people interact both positively and negatively with the action and speech of Jesus;
3. Jesus summons his disciple-companions to transmit features of his action and thought that he has enacted before them.

And based on this, he argues that the formal structure of Mark's Gospel as a whole is established on such three-step progressions as he identifies.

For Tolbert, the two major formative influences on Mark's stylistic development were Greco-Roman rhetoric and popular culture. To the evidence of élite, first century Greco-Roman literature[49] which has been much studied already for its Gospel links in terms of aretalogy, biography and memorabilia, Tolbert usefully draws in a consideration of early examples of the ancient popular novel[50]. Whilst she acknowledges that Mark's Gospel does not share with them the same story line, she demonstrates that the similarities, nevertheless, between their rhetorical, stylistic and linguistic features are conspicuous. She writes, "Both are synthetic, conventional narratives that combine historiographic form with epic and dramatic

---

[48] Robbins, *Jesus the Teacher...*, p.65.
[49] E.g. *The Histories* of Herodotus; also Virgil's *Eclogues, Georgics* and *Aeneid*; Homer's *Iliad* and *Odyssey*; Xenophon's *Memorabilia*; the works of Plutarch, Catullus and Thucydides.
[50] Gamble (*Books and Readers...*, p.39) raises the question, "In what sense may we speak of there having been a popular literature in the Roman empire?" He argues that the capacity to read, the interest and leisure to do so and the financial means to procure texts, belonged to a few, and this circumstance must limit the idea of popular literature. But, he reminds us that much ancient reading was aloud and occurred in public, quasi-public and domestic settings where those listening might include the semiliterate and illiterate as well as the literate.

substance. Episodic plots, central turning points, final recognition sequences, dialogic scenes with narrative frames, sparing but crucial use of monologue, repetition, narrative summaries, foreshadowing, and monolithic illustrative characters are some of the elements the Gospel and ancient novels have in common - and all of these are presented in a simple, crude, conventional style suitable to popular dissemination across a broad spectrum of society."[51]

For Hooker, Mark's Gospel functions *like* a drama, after the manner of a contemporary Greek drama as described by Aristotle (in *Poetics* 10-12,18 and *Rhetoric* III.14). Following the basic pattern of a tragedy, after the 'prologue' (which in practice provides the audience with whatever they need to understand the play), the Gospel presents firstly the 'complication', secondly the 'turning point' or 'reversal', and thirdly the 'dénouement' (lit. 'untying'). Hooker identifies 8.27 to be the likely candidate for such a 'turning point'. Without conviction, she writes that an Aristotelian Greek tragedy "*may* be rounded off with an epilogue"[52]. In her commentary[53] she identifies 16.1-8 as 'the last section of the Gospel', but titles it 'the Epilogue' as many other commentators do. My reading, however, is that 16.9-20, although generally considered an addition to Mark's writing, appears more separated from the preceding text[54], and exhibits more the qualities, therefore, of an 'epilogue' after the manner of a Greek tragedy.

Mack's interesting observations, about the historical probability of New Testament writers and even bearers of Palestinian traditions being influenced by Greco-Roman rhetorical theory and practice, fuel the argument that Mark deliberately and understandably employed literary conventions available to him from the cultural milieu of his age. In referring to the classical handbooks[55] he summarises the five aspects of the practice of rhetoric that were, in general, addressed[56]:

---

[51] Tolbert, *Sowing the Gospel...*, p.78.
[52] Morna D. Hooker, *Beginnings: Keys that open the Gospels*, SCM Press Ltd., London, 1997, p.4.
[53] Morna D. Hooker, *The Gospel according to St Mark*, Black's New Testament Commentaries, A & C Black, London, 1991, p.382.
[54] See most commentaries for arguments of dislocation between 16.8 and v.9.
[55] Principally: Aristotle's *Ars Rhetorica*, Cicero's *De inventione*, the *Rhetorica ad Herennium* and the Progymnasmata of Theon and Hermogenes.
[56] Mack, *Rhetoric...*, pp.32-34.

a) Invention (*heuresis, inventio*): the conceptual process of deciding on the subject to be elaborated, the position one would take on an issue of debate, or the thesis one wished to propose. It also referred to the search for materials one might use which was more a matter of finding or discovering the right material for making a point, and less a matter of creating a brand-new idea (for a 'clever' example, he turns to Mk.2.23-28, because it is taken from the objectors' own literary tradition and used against them[57]).

b) Arrangement (*taxis, disposito*): the work of ordering material into an outline, paying attention to such things as the best sequence to use, or whether one should expand on this or that point, or how best to develop a sub-theme. Skeletal outlines were standard and in crafting a speech in particular, rhetors were expected to "hide the standard outline" (an example of this is possibly the 4-8-4-8-4 scheme of Luke's Sermon on the Plain[58]). Arrangement was as important and creative a process as invention.

c) Style (*lexis, elocutio*): the way in which material was handled in the process of composition. Grammar, syntax, rhythm and the selection and repetition of words were matters of importance. Style was a matter of aesthetic effect and an important factor in persuasion; it also had a mnemonic function.

d) Memory (*mnēmē, memoria*): the process of memorising the speech so that delivery would be natural. Techniques in writing were devised: the most interesting is the imaginative creating of a scene in which vivid and striking images of persons, objects and events would be set by association with the points, words and figures of speech one wished remembered (*Ad Herennium* III.xvi.28 to xxiv.40).

e) Delivery (*hypocrisis, pronunciato*): it referred to voice, pauses, and gestures appropriate to a speech occasion.

With Robbins, in the literary-structural analysis I present, I will agree on the importance of three-step progressions in the Markan text, but not with his thematic description of the three steps. Rather, I will show that the three-step progressions are of a purely literary-structural kind. Based on syntax, grammar and word

---

[57] Mack, *Rhetoric...*, p.52.
[58] David G. Palmer, *Sliced Bread: The Four Gospels, Acts and Revelation: Their Literary Structures*, Ceridwen Press, Cardiff, 1988, p.70.

INTRODUCTION 23

repetition, the three steps read as 'introductory', the 'first development', and the 'second and completing development'. I will agree with Robbins that three-step progressions indicate the nature of the structure and plan of the Gospel as a whole, but I will not be found to be agreeing with him on his outline of Mark's Gospel. Fundamentally it is because many more three-step progressions exist by this definition than by his. The interest he shows in 1 and 2 Kings and Jeremiah appears justified. A few of the three-step progressions I define do correspond to his. It may well be the case that Mark was influenced by the forms of prophetic biblical literature. Additionally, however, there is the possibility that Mark was also influenced by the methodology and content of the first Priestly document of the Pentateuch (Genesis 1.1-2.4a, dated 538-450BC) and the compositional method of the editors of the Pentateuch (of only a slightly later period).

On the structural parallelism of the first eleven chapters of Genesis, 1.1-7.24 and 8.1-11.26, for parallels between 'creation' (chs.1,2) and 're-creation' (8.1-9.17), and further meaningful parallels, see Barry L. Bandstra[59]. We will see that Mark displays similar sectional, simple parallelism, denoted A:A'. And specifically on the structure of Gen. 1.1-2.4a, Bandstra discerns two three-day sub-series[60]. My literary-structural analysis will demonstrate that Mark repeatedly employs a 'seven day' scheme, and we will see that each of Mark's seven-day schemes (four in all) exhibit similar three-day sub-series, though, in Mark's case, each side of a central day's telling. (Day seven of the Priestly 'creation story' is included in the Epilogue.)

Attention is attracted also to the fact that Mark opens his Gospel Prologue with the words "The *beginning* of the Gospel..." (see Gen. 1.1) and the longer ending includes a reference to "creation" too (Mk. 16.15). Further to this, I observe, as does Painter, that Mark quotes from Gen. 1.27 in Mk. 10.6. In my presentation of my structural analysis, we will see that it significantly falls in the central Day's telling of Mark's third series of seven days, the turning point of the series. Painter's contribution is important and worth mention here: to

---

[59] Barry L. Bandstra, *Reading the Old Testament: An Introduction to the Hebrew Bible*, Wadsworth Publishing Co., International Thomson Publishing Inc., 1995, p.72.
[60] Bandstra, *Reading the Old Testament...*, p.62.

him, Mark's Gospel "is... an attempt to proclaim the good news of God in a world dominated by evil... While Mark lacks a full account of creation of the world by God, 10.6, 'From the beginning of the creation male and female he made them', is enough to show full dependence on the Genesis account... In earlier Jewish historical writings all being and action were understood as expressions of the will of God, and if Israel suffered it was understood to be a consequence of disobedience to God."[61] We may observe also that in the accounts of the flood, by which God is said to have first dealt with all the evil in the world, there are other references to seven-day passages of time (Gen. 8.10,12), and references also to forty-day periods (Gen. 7.12,17; 8.6; cf. Mk. 1.13) and a twenty-seventh day (Gen. 8.14, the day that "the earth was completely dry"; cf. Day 27 in Mark's account, the day of Jesus' death and burial). Another possible point of contact is Mark's identification of the Spirit as coming down on Jesus as a "dove" (Mk. 1.10; cf. Gen. 8.8-12).

My reading of Gen. 1.1-2.4a, in brief, is as follows:

		Prologue:	1.1,2	God created the heavens and the earth
A A		Day One:	1.3-5	light; day and night
	B	Day Two:	1.6-8	water/water; sky
	B'	Day Three:	1.9-13	water/land, vegetation
A'A		Day Four:	1.14-19	lights; day and night
	B	Day Five:	1.20-23	water/sea - creatures; sky - birds; "be fruitful..."
	B'	Day Six:	1.24-31	land; creatures; man; "be fruitful..."; vegetation
		Epilogue:	2.1-4a	(including Day Seven) the heavens and the earth... created

ABB' is a denotation which I deem reflects the relationship of the contents of the days within each of the two three-day sub-series, where A is 'introductory', B is the 'first development', and B' is the 'second and completing development'. We will discover similar three-day arrangements in Mark's Gospel, A(ABB'):A'(ABB'), but with an inserted middle day, B, hence A(ABB'):B:A'(ABB'). Further, a literary-structural analysis of Gen. 1.1-2.4a, as a whole, demonstrates AA' formations (in the structures of the contents of the parts) and ABB' formations (in the structures of the sub-parts). We will see how Mark employs these forms.

---

[61] Painter, *Mark's Gospel...*, pp.19,20.

From the Prologue:
- A a In the beginning
-   b God created the heavens
-   b' and <u>the earth</u>.
- A' a <u>The earth</u> was without form
-   b and darkness was upon the <u>face of the deep</u>
-   b' and the Spirit of God was moving over the <u>face of the waters</u>.[62]

From the First Day:
- A a And God said, "Let there be <u>light</u>."
-   b And there was <u>light</u>.
-   b' And God saw that the <u>light</u> was good.
- A' a And God separated the <u>light</u> from the <u>darkness</u>.
-   b God called the <u>light</u> "day"
-   b' and the <u>darkness</u> he called "night".

And there was evening/ and there was morning/ one day.
(*a repeating, concluding formula*)

Tolbert, we note, omits to give consideration to this or any other possible, third formative influence on Mark's style, that is of Old Testament composition. And such composition, as I demonstrate above, itself exhibits a possible 'Greco-Roman' influence. It need not be considered 'out of the question': clearly Homer was being read from the eighth century BC, and his *Iliad* pre-dated the completion of the Pentateuch by several centuries.

Fascinatingly, we will see that the 'arrangement', the skeletal outline of Homer's *Iliad* finds a parallel of a kind, like that of the creation account in Genesis, with that of Mark's Gospel. The whole tale, of the beginnings of Greek civilisation (compare the beginnings of Christian civilisation in Mark's Gospel), is told in fifty-two "days". We will compare Mark's twenty-eight "Days", in his telling, of Gospel Narrative, and other days in its framing, that is in both Prologue and Epilogue. Book one of the *Iliad* covers the following in order: one day, an interval of nine days, one day and an interval of twelve days; the last book (twenty-four) covers the following: an interval of twelve days, one day, an interval of nine days and one day. It is the first book's scheme in reverse. In other words the epic both begins and ends with episodes covering twenty-three days each. The

---

[62] It is interesting to note that Luke, writing about twenty years after Mark, opens his Gospel with a threefold protasis and threefold apodosis which can be described similarly, in broad terms, by A:A', and in its more detailed form as abb':abb'. Lk. 1.1-4, however, is significantly longer than Gen. 1.1,2.

six remaining days of Homer's scheme, that is the main days of his telling, are arranged around a central episode (book nine), the envoy's visit to Achilles, which is the turning point in the whole epic. The first 'three days' are told in books 2-8 (seven in all) and the second 'three days' in books 10-23 (fourteen in all). The scheme, according to my own summary, is:

3 days	Book 1	Days 1, 9, 1, 12	
3 days	Books 2-8	Books 2,3	Day 1 beginning with night
		Books 4-7	Day 2 beginning with Zeus & Hera
		Book 8	Day 3 beginning with dawn
X	Book 9	the turning point	
3 days	Books 10-23	Books 10-14 Day 1 beginning with night	
		Books 15-18 Day 2 beginning with Zeus & Hera	
		Books 19-23 Day 3 beginning with dawn	
23 days	Book 24	Days 12, 1, 9, 1	

We will observe Mark's employment of a similar 'skeletal outline'/'arrangement' for each of his four Gospel Series which is very similar to the above: that is 'three: one: three', where at the centre of each of Mark's seven-day schemes, he has a day's telling (in distinction to Homer's separated 'heavenly' scene of a turning point) which acts as a fulcrum, hinge or turning point to the two sub-series of three days around it.

On the issue of 'style', we will discern only a vague similarity between 'sixes' and 'threes'. In the epic poem it is a hexameter with rich and subtle cadences, and in the 'epic gospel' it is fundamentally a three-piece, ABB' presentation, which we will identify as simultaneously employed at a number of literary levels. Lastly, in this much abbreviated comparison, in terms of 'delivery', the meter of Homer's poetry is based on pronunciation time and not, as in our language, on stress[63], whereas Mark's prose for its clausal constructions will be shown to reflect a breathing rhythm.

---

[63] Bernard Knox, "Introduction" to Robert Fagles' translation, *The Iliad: Homer*, Viking Penguin, 1990, p.12.

The histories of criticism of both 'epics' demonstrate similarity, in consideration of the parts played by oral and written tradition, and of the freedom of the author to control his production and create something new. The uncovering of Homer's structure leads his critics and myself on Mark to similar convictions too: consider Sinclair's two summaries: "the use of words in subtle and recurrent patterns as well as the complex formation of the whole point irresistably to the genius of one man"[64], and "without understanding the complexity of the *Iliad* there can be no understanding of Homer himself"[65]. I am happy to say the same of Mark's work. But I am not saying that Mark modelled his work expressly on Homer's. My understanding is simply this, that the Homeric presentational methods[66] were known in Mark's day and to Mark himself, as likely in the day of the Pentateuch's completion. His rhetorical conventions were learned, imitated and built upon over the centuries, over which time they gained and maintained an acceptance cross-culturally. It may be that we will not be able to identify with certainty the link specifically between Mark's Gospel and any one work, or the collected works of an ancient rhetor, either as reviewed here, or above. It is a matter more of understanding the background literary culture in which Mark's Gospel was fashioned. In Genesis, 1 and 2 Kings, in Tolbert's identification with the ancient popular novel, in Hooker's reference to form in Aristotelian Greek tragedy, and in Mack's specific reference (as with others) to Xenophon's *Memorabilia*, I do find parallels in Mark's Gospel which will be identified in the following chapters.

It is accepted that structure and organisation, of that which was written to be read aloud, had an immediate, two-fold practical purpose of aesthetic[67] and mnemonic[68]. The memorising of texts, by

---

[64] Andrew Sinclair, "Appreciation", *Homer's Iliad*, tr. W.H.D. Rouse, Thomas Nelson & Sons Ltd., London/Heron Books, undated, p.503.
[65] Sinclair, "Appreciation", *Homer's Iliad*, p.496.
[66] See again Introduction, note 42. Further, the chronological scheme for Homer's *Iliad* is interpreted by some, by 'day-reports' (i.e. two in both Prologue and Epilogue), as an eleven-section chiasm (so also *Odyssey*). In my book, *Sliced Bread...*, I present eleven-sectioned chiasms for Matthew's Gospel and for Luke's two books. The case may be put, therefore, that these writers too followed Homeric methods of ancient rhetoric.
[67] We observe that the aesthetic component, in interior design, artefact, architecture and town-planning today, is often considered separately from function: in first century literature, created for reading aloud, function and aesthetic could not be so separated. Literature functioned through its aesthetic.
[68] See: C.H. Talbert, *Literary Patterns, Theological Themes, and the Genre of*

listening to what is read aloud, is in any culture or civilisation assisted and enhanced by rhetorical conventions. It was especially so in the first centuries BC and AD. Examples of these include the organisation of information in listings, acrostics and symmetries of presentation by both simple parallelism and chiasm, also the exercise of rhythm and the repetitions of words, phrases, sentence-constructions, paragraph-forms, and so on. The fact that we are discovering applications of all of these methods and such characteristics within the Biblical corpus (both Old and New Testaments) should not be a surprise to us. Literature which is structured at every level, and which has its repetitions and its rhythms of themes and details, assists not only the process of oral education and clear communication but also the memorising of it, for private recall, at one end of the scale, and for a perfect, public re-presentation, at the other end of the scale.

No literature of the first century will have been without an 'arrangement', a plan and framework[69], nor, we add, its detailed presentational system which is the rhetorical method/'style' the writer employed to construct his sentences and paragraphs[70]. It simply would not have functioned without it. It is difficult to argue otherwise therefore, than that the first requirement of a gospel was that it needed a simple, memorable, rhythmic structure for the whole, and a system, or method of presentation used throughout, for its parts. My analysis of Mark's Gospel will show that its author well met these requirements, and that he did so by employing rhetorical conventions in use in his day. If the new literary genre of gospel was to function well, it had to be compiled and composed to fit its life-setting of the first century.

We turn now to a brief consideration of the likely historical context to Mark's writing of his Gospel. The first issue focuses on the tradition which is judged to link the writing of Mark's Gospel with

---

Luke-Acts, SBLMS 20, Scholars Press, Missoula, Montana, 1974, p.81, (in regard to Homer); Birger Gerhardsson, *Memory and Manuscript* (tr. Eric J. Sharpe), C.W.K. Gleerup, Uppsala, 1961, p.147 (in regard to Jewish haggadah).

[69] See note 33 above.

[70] Barthes says: "...there does, of course, exist an 'art' of the storyteller which is the ability to generate narratives (messages) from the structure (the code)." Roland Barthes, "Introduction to the Structural Analysis of Narrative", *Image - Music -Text*, ed. & tr. Stephen Heath, Hill and Wang, New York, 1977, p.80.

the time of the death of Peter (in AD64). According to the tradition of John the elder and passed on (in about AD130) by Papias, Bishop of Hierapolis, and recorded by Eusebius in his *Ecclesiastical History*[71], we can read the following, that:

"...Mark became the the interpreter of Peter and he wrote down accurately, but not in order, as much as he remembered of the sayings and doings of Christ. For he was not a hearer or a follower of the Lord, but afterwards, as I said, of Peter, who adapted his teachings to the needs of the moment and did not make an ordered exposition of the sayings of the Lord. And so Mark made no mistake when he thus wrote down some things as he remembered them; for he made it his especial care to omit nothing of what he heard, and to make no false statement therein."

Those who wish to affirm the historical reliability of Mark's Gospel frequently appeal to this testimony, though there is much that can be discussed about its reliability:

1) it is likely that after the first sentence everything else is what Papias has added;

2) Papias may have identified Mark with Peter's companion on the basis of 1 Peter 5.13 (compare other references to a John Mark in Acts 12.12,25; 15.37-39; and presumably the same person in Col. 4.10, Philemon 24 and 2 Tim. 4.11);

3) though dependency may have been upon Papias, we may still consider the support for the linking of Mark with Peter: of Justin Martyr who refers to the 'memoirs of Peter' (*c.* 150); of the Anti-Marcionite Prologue (*c.* 160-180) which tells us that Mark was the interpreter of Peter and that he wrote his Gospel after Peter's death in Italy; of Irenaeus (*c.* 180-200) who describes Mark as the disciple and interpreter of Peter, who wrote after the deaths of both Peter and Paul; of the several records of Clement of Alexandria (*c.* 180) which tell of Mark's writing down the words of Peter, but in contrast to the former support, during the latter's lifetime; and of Origen (*c.* 200) likewise, who tells how Peter instructed Mark.

We cannot here develop the discussion; space does not allow. But it is clear that the tradition that Mark was a "disciple of Peter"

---

[71] Eusebius, *HE*, iii.39.15, also reproduced in Henry Bettenson, *Documents of the Christian Church*, Oxford University Press, 2nd Ed., 1963, p.27, from which the translation quoted is taken.

could have been either the cause or the result of the early church's view that all the canonical gospels required apostolic authentication. We cannot be certain either way. And the debate about whether or not Mark's Gospel really connects with Peter is an open question too. Nevertheless, we can deduce simply that it is most likely that the 'Gospel' was required because the eye-witnesses of the life of Jesus were dying out. Thus, the church will have had a justifiable need for written material, or written record of the 'beginnings' of the faith. The deduction is that this need did indeed lead Mark to write, and did lead, in turn, to the contributions of the other three evangelists.

Equally, other questions arise and they are still open too. Where was the Gospel written? And what was the date of its writing? (Or given the above: How long after the death of Peter was it written?) They are recognised as important, but they are not best addressed separately at this juncture[72]. Rather, we ask, "Was Mark motivated to write his Gospel because of a significant historical event which marked an upheavel that was both political and religious?" We consider what may have been the possible reaction of Mark and the early church to the fall of Jerusalem and the destruction of its temple in the year 70, because of which the Jewish revolt which began in 66 was coming to its end in 73. If Mark had been in Rome around that time[73], he would have seen for himself the victorious Titus return with the spoils from the temple; if he had been other than in Rome, he would certainly have heard about it.

---

[72] All commentaries raise these issues and present the evidence for different options. We note that Gamble (*Books and Readers...*, p.102) says of Mark's Gospel that "wherever it was composed, it must have circulated widely within ten to twenty years of its origin. How else might it have come independently into the hands of... Matthew and... Luke...?" Étienne Trocmé, *The Formation of the Gospel according to Mark*, SPCK, London, 1975 (first publ. in Fr. 1963), p.242, asks, "How could a work as distinguished as Mark have circulated widely and enjoyed a measure of authority... despite the competition of Matthew, Luke and John and of its distant claim to descent from an apostolic source? The only plausible explanation is that it was covered by the prestige of a very important church which gave special credit to it, no doubt because the book was written by one of its members and for its own use. All things considered, this important church could only have been the Church of Rome, as ancient tradition suggests."

[73] According to Clement of Alexandria, Mark wrote his Gospel in Rome; the Anti-Marcionite Prologue says he was in "the regions of Italy"; and Irenaeus implies that the Gospel was written in Rome. See note 72 also for Trocmé's view. But the belief that he wrote there could have been attributed to the link between Mark and Peter. Further, Chrysostum (in the fourth century) said he wrote in Egypt, and others have suggested Antioch, and still others (ref. Marxsen) Galilee.

Clearly, the defeat of the Jews, the destruction of the temple, and the re-occupation of Jerusalem by the Roman legions will have spelt, somewhat emphatically to early Christians and to both insiders and outsiders of the Jewish faith, the end of Judaism, the end of the era of the 'Old Covenant'. We will see from literary-structural analysis that there is in Mark's 'arrangement' of his Gospel an important emphasis on 'good news'. 'Good news' is, of course, a counter to 'bad news'. We properly ask, therefore, "Might the 'bad news' that was countered with 'good news' have been, more than anything else, the considered demise of the Old Covenant?" If so, the 'good news' was fundamentally God's establishing of a New Covenant, to replace the Old. We will see from literary-structural analysis that Mark's 'arrangement' does indeed place a strong emphasis on the role of Jesus in establishing a New Covenant, and replacing the Old. Indeed, given what we shall see of the ordering of the contents of his Gospel, we will be able to picture Mark writing at a time when the nationalistic religion of Old Israel was already in ruins, literally in terms of its temple, but also morally- and spiritually-speaking. And his 'good news' about the new, universal faith of a New Israel, in which both Jew and Gentile would share, simply had its focus on the one who, by his call, mission, death, resurrection and ascension, had been demonstrating God's new way of dealing with evil in the world (an evil which was bringing down/had already brought down the Old Covenant); one who was establishing a new kingdom, the Kingdom of God, which would have no boundaries either in creation, or, for that matter, even between heaven and earth.

To summarise at this point, we may simply state that the immediate requirement of the new literary genre of gospel was to fill a vacuum created by the decease of the first witnesses, and to provide for the church a mission statement for a new age that was born of the greatest upheaval the world had ever seen[74]. We will return to such matters when we have a surer understanding of the primary document itself.

---

[74] "The war of the Jews against the Romans was the greatest of our time; greater too, perhaps, than any recorded struggle whether between cities or nations... This upheaval, as I said, was the greatest of *all* time...", so wrote Josephus in his Preface, 1,7, *The Jewish War*, tr. G.A. Williamson, Rev. Ed., Penguin Books, Harmondsworth, 1980.

There remain many other, open questions. Those which impinge on the actual process of producing the first Gospel, and on the functions for which the Gospel was intended, as well as its status in the church, are numerous indeed. There is every reason to rehearse some of them here. Was the Gospel simply completed in one operation, or was it first written and then re-written by the same person after input or reflective comments from others? Did it attempt to satisfy requirements laid down by any other, or others, than the writer? When it was first read was it publicly or privately? Did it need approval? Or did it attract approval? And when it was first circulated was it as one manuscript, only? When were copies first made? And how many copies...? For what purpose might they have been made? To whom was the task given to read it aloud publicly? Or was it first circulated by being committed to memory for recital in Christian or other gatherings? How many people would have been appointed initially to "present" it? Would they have had training in its presentation, both in how it was composed and how it was to be read? Was it to be read, or presented in one sitting? Or, was it to be serially presented or read over a number of meetings? And when it was read or presented whole, or in parts at a time, what was then expected to follow? Were questions invited and discussion encouraged? Did its reading in public lead to people making commitments, or re-commitments to Jesus? Did it have a mission effect?

Accessibility to the answers to all these and similar questions is not ours today, but they are posed here simply because they need to be asked. In some way or another, the church chose to "own" the Gospel of Mark, to show it respect, to use it for its own purposes, and to preserve it. That it was later re-written by Matthew and Luke in turn and added to for other purposes by them is another, though much associated matter.

An Interest in "Days":

A number of readers of Mark's Gospel have identified, almost in a cursory manner, the presence of days. Bultmann[75], whose focus is the

---

[75] Bultmann, *The History...*, p.341.

first century Hebrew/Palestinian Day which begins and ends with sunset, says, "Jesus' last ministry in Jerusalem is somewhat awkwardly compressed along with the Passion itself into a sequence of seven days, and the components of the last act are divided among the hours of the day: the first watch of the night starts at 14.17...". For Drury, "at both the beginning and the end of the book, days are marked out, together with times of day, with a precision lacking elsewhere. And in both the familiar pattern is discernible." (He sees the correspondence between Jesus' rising up a great while before day, 1.35, "prophesying" his early morning resurrection, 16.2ff. The pattern in both is "action followed by withdrawal leading to further action".) He writes, "The early passage 1.21-38 covers some twenty-four hours from morning to morning...."[76]. As such, Drury shows an interest in what is termed the "civil day" (see my note 82) which can be qualified either as beginning at sunset, or as beginning at sunrise, but which is identified by Drury here as beginning with sunrise. "The last chapters cover a series of days and of times within them, beginning at 14.1," he says.

Drury's list includes 1.21-38 and, it might be deduced (because he does not state), 14.1-11, 14.12-72, 15.1-47 and 16.1-8. These limits satisfy the criterion of the "civil day" as beginning at sunrise. We can add others, on the same principle: 11.1-11; 11.12-19 and 11.20-13.37. (This makes initially eight days in all, by simple reading.) In a number of commentaries[77] these last three days are discerned, and Hooker notes that they are "three successive days". Schweizer, however, fails to discern any of these day-divisions in chapter 11. It would appear from his notes on 11.12-26 that he is distracted fully by the so-called Markan preference (he cites only 5.21-43 as another example at this point) for sandwich construction. Indeed, many scholars see the two-part story of Jesus' withering of the fig tree as a whole (11.12-14 and vv.20-26), enveloping a central part, telling of Jesus' action in the temple (11.15-19)[78]. The arrangement

---

[76] J. Drury, "Mark", *The Literary Guide to the Bible*, eds. R. Alter & F. Kermode, Collins, London, 1987, p.410.
[77] E.g. D.E. Nineham, *Saint Mark*, The Pelican Gospel Commentaries, Penguin Books Ltd., Harmondsworth, 1963, pp.303 and 305; also M.D. Hooker, *The Gospel...*, p.255.
[78] Compare: Eduard Schweizer, *The Good News according to Mark*, tr. Donald H. Madvig, John Knox Press, Atlanta, 1970, pp.229-236; Nineham, *Saint Mark*, pp.297ff.; and Hooker, *The Gospel...*, pp.260ff.

and the possible significance of the arrangement of Markan "Days" is lost on them: their interest is in other matters.

Elsewhere in the Gospel "Days" *seem* not to be important beyond mention of other sabbaths in 2.23 (possibly 3.1) and 6.2, and references to the passing of days in 2.1, 8.1,2 and 9.2. To the eight "Days" discerned already above we add two sabbaths (I judge 2.23-3.6 to be one sabbath day) making now ten "Days" in all. To these ten we now add the three "Days" which, as my analysis will show, begin at 2.1, 8.1 and 9.2. These "Days" begin with summary tellings of other days that are otherwise left unreported. (In this way Mark makes it perfectly clear that he is not reporting every day in the mission of Jesus.) The tally of defined "Days" in Mark's telling is now thirteen. Additionally in the Gospel we discover references to times or periods of days: 1.32, 35; 4.35; 6.35, 47, 48; 11.11, 19, 20; 14.17, 72; 15.1, 25, 33, 34, 42; 16.2 (also 16.9, 14). Given the references to 'evenings' in 4.35 and 6.47 we can discern two more days to add to the list. The first of these can be deduced to begin at 3.7 and the second of these to begin at 6.30. Fifteen "Days" are definable simply from the text.

It is the case that other "Days" are less clearly delineated by Mark. Good story-telling requires no continuing repetition of detail to establish a rhythm, a pattern or a sequence. It is, therefore, most significant that the first "Day" of Mark's narrative (1.21-38) covers a twenty-four hour period from sunrise to before sunrise the following day. He clearly presents it as one which begins with the beginning of daylight, proceeds through the daylight hours and the sunset into the evening, and ends in the night before the new dawn. It acts as a model, a type, a pattern. Mark presents it as an indication of what he has in mind for his narrative presentation and the form it will take - a presentation of "Days" - and he establishes it right at the beginning. All other "Days", that is reportings of events and teachings, will fall into the same temporal mould. They will not, indeed they cannot extend beyond the twenty-four hour period defined by Day One. What is reported as an event or succession of events or teachings will be told within the parameters of a twenty-four hour day which begins with sunrise.

It follows, therefore, that other "Days" are inferred, and that they can be deduced from the text. Simple deduction is possible by giving consideration to "Days" which stand in juxtaposition, for instance where a sabbath day precedes a "Day" in sequence and where the activities of the "Day" following are non-sabbatical. An example of this is the "Day" of 3.7-4.41 which follows that of 2.23-3.6. The "Day" of 3.7-4.41 is the fourteenth "Day" added to the list (see above). The activities described in the introductory passage, 3.7-12, are clearly not introductory activities to a Day's telling which has its beginning in the evening of a Hebrew/Palestinian Day, which begins with sunset. They are the introductory activities with which Mark begins a new Day's telling at a time after sunrise, hence within the temporal parameters of the Civil Day defined as beginning at sunrise. This particular Day's telling takes us to the evening and night-time event (4.35: "And he says to them on that day, evening having come..."). The story which follows, of 5.1-20, is one that is set in the day-time: it allocates to another "Day", the sixteenth for the list.

Other deductions are based on phrases which speak of Jesus' "rising" (see 7.24 and 10.1) meaning "getting up from sleep"[79]; on new journey beginnings (as in 9.30, "And thence, going forth...") or on new arrivals (as at 5.1, "And they came to the other side of the sea..."; or as at 10.46, which is a most interesting juxtaposition of statements, literally, "And they come to Jericho. And as he was going out from Jericho..."). For Bultmann, "the spatial link is also a *temporal* one. This expresses the temporal sequence..."[80] In the presentation of my analysis, in which the Markan "Days" and Series of "Days" are established, these matters are fully presented and discussed. We will see many times over, in his opening pieces to new "Days", and simply nowhere else in his "Day" presentations, that Mark references other days which pass between his formal tellings of "Days", either specifically (by number or dating), or by inference (with brief journey details which suggest numbers of days which are taken up with travel, which are otherwise not reported).

In his discussion of the Markan outline, Taylor makes comment: "It is soon manifest that he (Mark) has no day to day account of the

---

[79] In 1.35, Jesus' rising is 'from sleep'; it is judged that there is no good reason for changing the meaning for 7.24 and 10.1. Further, we observe that the rising of Jairus' daughter in 5.42 is also from 'sleep', see 5.39.
[80] Bultmann, *The History...*, p.340.

progress of the mission, but he shows a good historical judgement in using an impressive record of a typical day in the life of Jesus (1.21-39)... There is little ordered sequence but *it is notable how particular days stand out*"[81]. He sees 4.1-5.43 as one day, "remembered not only for its teaching but also for its crossing and re-crossing of the lake and a series of events perhaps telescoped, but given in chronological order." A number of issues are raised here. What are the other days that "stand out" for Taylor? Is the 'day' really 1.21-39? And is it really part of the tradition? Or was it compiled, or even created by Mark? Further, could the passage 4.1-5.43 possibly be only one day? We read at 4.35 that evening had come. Is it possible that the stories of 4.35-5.43 were set in the night watches, with so many people about, and without Mark telling us which watch? Or, rather are there not three days of activities told in these verses, so deduced because there is one night-crossing of the lake and one return crossing at the end of another day's episodes?

Clearly, an examination of the whole text of Mark's Gospel, for "Days", was an exercise waiting to be done. The possibility did indeed exist, contrary to what Taylor understood, as recorded above, that the Gospel Mark created consisted of reports of "Days". Another distinct possibility also existed, that the Gospel outline combined both Days and Series of Days in a framework or matrix, artificial or otherwise. In my analyses of Chapters 3 to 6, I present the arguments which support my view that the main Gospel Narrative, from 1.21 to 16.8, consists of twenty-eight Days, in Mark's telling, and that these Days are arranged in four Series each of seven Days. The definition of "Day" which Mark employs consistently, for the purpose of his presentation, as defined by Day One, 1.21-38, is the period from the dawn of one day to the beginning of dawn the next day, that is from sunrise to just before sunrise[82]. I will argue that clear

---

[81] V. Taylor, *The Gospel according to St Mark*, MacMillan, London, 1952, p.146: my italics.

[82] From *IntDB*, Vol. 1, (1962) Abingdon, Nashville, 1981, p.783, S.J. De Vries: The civil day can be a space of twenty-four hours, extending from sunrise to sunrise or from sunset to sunset. Early Hebrews reckoned the civil day from one dawn to the next. Gradually, they began to count from sunset to sunset in accordance with the rising importance of their lunar festivals.

We observe that, while we define a 'day' in the world today as being from just after midnight to the next midnight, we now have a 'TV Day' of twenty-four hours which begins with dawn, or thereabouts (see any programme chart). We also often talk of "tomorrow"

INTRODUCTION 37

correspondences between Days and Series of Days are evident, with the result that the Markan matrix can be defined in some detail. In Chapters 2 and 7 I give careful consideration also to the "Days preceding" and "following" the main Gospel Narrative, which I define in turn as the Prologue, for which read 1.1-20, and a near representative form of the original Epilogue, for which read 16.9-16, 19-20a.

A Methodology for identifying "Days", their intra- and inter-relationships, and their literary-structures:

It may be that some days do "stand out" more than others but, as we have seen above, any definition of a "Day" needs testing. Fundamental to establishing that the text is actually structured in "Days" is the defining of the beginnings and the endings of the "Days" themselves. Temporal, geographical and place-defining terms all have value and all such references have to be weighed carefully. Arguments based on vocabulary, syntax and style have their value for not only are there Markan introductory formulae to be defined, but also there is a Markan method (of writing) to be understood. Further, a structural relationship exists between Series of Days, Days, their sections, their parts, their sub-parts and their sub-sub-parts, and it requires description. Points in the text where Mark introduced new themes require identifying. And his development of his themes, as also his repetitions of keywords and phrases, needs to be understood for the ways in which they locate within any particular "Day" or within associated "Days" (either in juxtaposition, or in balance through a vertical reading or a horizontal reading of the Gospel's Series).

During the early stages of analysis, because nothing was known with any certainty about Mark's framework and plan, and nothing at all about either Mark's framework of "Days" and his "Series of Days", and further, because so very little was known with any certainty about

---

(even after midnight) as meaning when we wake from sleep. Mark was as aware as we are today of different reference points to the start of the day, for he shows that, while he plans his Days to a dawn beginning, as when Jesus "rises" from sleep, he also understands the other, alternative civil day definition, which is the Hebrew/Palestinian Day, whereby when evening comes prior to a sabbath, see 15.42, the new day's own particular obligations begin.

his rhetorical method (beyond the possibilities of limited chiastic arrangements, his threesomes of details, and some threesomes of construction), it was simply a case of trial and error, of attempt and renewed attempt, of developing one hypothesis after another and putting each to the test. It was a "messy" but most important stage in the process of analysis.[83] But once a focus began to be secured upon the signifiers of Mark's primary-structure of "Days" and "Series of Days", and upon meaningful and significant correspondences between these elements, the process of literary-structural analysis became more methodical. To meet the need of a purely literary-structural analysis of the Markan text in the beginning no single methodology on its own was sufficient to the task. Not until 1.1-16.8 disclosed its Prologue (1.1-20) and its Gospel narrative of Four Series of Seven Days (1.21-16.8) did it appear pertinent to examine Mark's work for any systematic presentational-method he may have used to form the elements of his work. In other words, the basic 'structure' of the book had to be discovered first; it was only then that the question could be asked if Mark had a 'construction method' too. For the purpose of presenting the analysis, it was deemed sensible to present the disclosures of these characteristics of his composition simultaneously. The discovery of Mark's repeated use of the same, complete rhetorical constructions qualifies not only the nature of the structural organisation of 1.1-16.8, but also facilitates a new reading of 16.9-20.

That this analysis has been carried out at a time when more methodologies exist than could ever have been dreamed of in ancient times means that it can be well-tested against the propositions which have resulted from many other lines of enquiry. Clearly, commentaries and studies are available for comparisons to be made between my findings and those of others who, through source, form, redaction and, principally, rhetorical criticism, have been exploring for possible answers to age-old questions. The commentaries which

---

[83] The similarities between the first stage in the process of examining the 'design' of a text, for its structure and its construction-method, and the first stage of designing a building are worth paralleling. In both it is the most demanding stage. The scheme-design stage (of a building) is literally the most mind-bending and yet the most exciting. Further, it is the stage which is most influential upon the end-outcome. It is typically one in which no single methodology is sufficient to the task, for it is a time for discerning all the influential factors and for considering all the possibilities.

we employ include principally four: that of Taylor, which is typical of the British scholars of his period, approaching the Gospel from the stand-point of source critics (the commentary was first published in 1952 and has been judged "a classic" by other commentators); that of Nineham, published in 1963, reflective of the position form critics were then taking; that of Schweizer, published in 1967, which is the first recognised commentary based on the redaction critical method[84]; and that of Hooker, published in 1991, which takes account of many late twentieth-century Markan studies and represents a work of scholarship which is the result of many years of teaching, much valued by her students. In the discussions, we also draw on traditional and contemporary studies for the valuable insights of those who have practised an openness to possibilities, holding at the same time to sound exercise of reason and scholarship.

In Chapters 2 to 7, during the course of our examination of the Gospel's component parts, I re-present the Nestle-Aland text, which, with annotations and underlinings, demonstrates what I discern to be the literary-structure of each. For each Day's presentation, Mark employs, in simple form or composite forms, an A,B,B' structure, whereby A is introductory, B is the first development, and B' is the second and concluding development. This phenomenon can be observed throughout the Gospel at several different levels of literary order.

As an example, I present my analysis of the first two verses of Day One, 1.21,22:

A α ²¹ Καὶ εἰσπορεύονται εἰς Καφαρναούμ.
   β   καὶ εὐθὺς τοῖς σάββασιν εἰσελθὼν εἰς τὴν συναγωγὴν <u>ἐδίδασκεν</u>.
   β' ²² καὶ ἐξεπλήσσοντο ἐπὶ <u>τῇ διδαχῇ</u> αὐτοῦ, ἦν γὰρ <u>διδάσκων</u> αὐτοὺς ὡς ἐξουσίαν ἔχων καὶ οὐχ ὡς οἱ γραμματεῖς.

In Chapter Three we will sift the evidence for concluding that Day One (1.21-38) comprises two halves, each containing three main parts A,B,B'. Here A denotes 1.21,22 as the first and introductory part of the three parts which make up the first half's telling. B is the

---

[84] John K. Riches, *A Century of New Testament Study*, The Lutterworth Press, Cambridge, 1993, pp.153f.: Schweizer's commentary on Mark "remains one of the most balanced examples of redaction critical work, even if there is never any real doubt about his commitment to a broadly Barthian conception of the freedom and radical grace of God."

first development, which is vv.23-25. And B' is the second and completing/concluding development, which is vv.26-28. (The second half's telling of the Day comprises A which is 1.29-31; B which is vv.32-34; and B' which is vv.35-38.) Here in A (1.21,22), part α is the introductory part at this level of literary order. In it Mark establishes the geographical place. In part β, his first development, he details the day and the time of day (καὶ εὐθὺς τοῖς σάββασιν), movement into the locality of the event, and the activity (teaching) of the subject who is Jesus, un-named here, as in many other similar occurences. In part β', his second and completing development of this construction, Mark reports the response of the people to Jesus' activity (teaching) as well as the reason for their response, in two balancing parts ("for he was teaching them as having authority", "and not as the scribes."). The key words which suggest balance between parts β and β' are underlined.

Further detailed breakdown, at the next level of literary order, can be exhibited:

A α ²¹[α] Καὶ εἰσπορεύονται [α'] εἰς Καφαρναούμ.
   β [α] καὶ εὐθὺς τοῖς σάββασιν [β] εἰσελθὼν εἰς τὴν συναγωγὴν
      [β'] ἐδίδασκεν.
   β' ²²[α] καὶ ἐξεπλήσσοντο ἐπὶ τῇ διδαχῇ αὐτοῦ, [α'] ἦν γὰρ διδάσκων
      αὐτοὺς ὡς ἐξουσίαν ἔχων καὶ οὐχ ὡς οἱ γραμματεῖς.

Part α breaks down into sub-parts [α] and [α']. Part β breaks down into sub-parts [α], [β] and [β']. (In this case the [β] [β'] relationship holds: [β'] completes [β].) And part β' breaks down into sub-parts [α] and [α'], where [α'] explains or completes [α].

It may be judged, quite properly, from these analyses that Mark's rhetorical method at this level of literary-structural order, αββ', does not require that these parts are equal either in their number of words or in their more detailed structural compositions.

Lastly, further detailed breakdown is possible in β', and it can be annotated as follows:

   β' ²²[α] [.α] καὶ ἐξεπλήσσοντο [.α'] ἐπὶ τῇ διδαχῇ αὐτοῦ,
      [α'] [.α] ἦν γὰρ διδάσκων αὐτοὺς [.β] ὡς ἐξουσίαν ἔχων [.β'] καὶ οὐχ
      ὡς οἱ γραμματεῖς.

In [α]: [.α] and [.αʻ] are in balance; [.αʻ] completes [.α]. In [ἀʻ]: [.α] is introductory; [.β] is the first development; and [.βʻ] is the second and completing/concluding development.

In this way all the clauses of these verses, 1.21,22, are identified and defined for their settings and their relationships in the complete presentation. We observe here four levels of literary-structural order in all, as annotated by A, α, [α] and [.α] (B, B' and so on). The annotational method itself may be deemed somewhat cumbersome, but it is my best approach. Hence, in the following chapters this kind of detailed analysis which is here presented in stages will appear as a composite, as presented below:

A α ²¹[α] Καὶ εἰσπορεύονται [αʻ] εἰς Καφαρναούμ.
   β   [α] <u>καὶ εὐθὺς</u> τοῖς σάββασιν [β] εἰσελθὼν <u>εἰς τὴν συναγωγὴν</u>
       [βʻ] <u>ἐδίδασκεν</u>.
   βʻ ²²[α] [.α] καὶ ἐξεπλήσσοντο [.αʻ] ἐπὶ <u>τῇ διδαχῇ</u> αὐτοῦ, [αʻ] [.α] ἦν γὰρ
      <u>διδάσκων</u> αὐτοὺς [.β] <u>ὡς</u> ἐξουσίαν ἔχων [.βʻ] καὶ οὐχ <u>ὡς</u> οἱ
      γραμματεῖς.

All the words which are underlined will have significance in one way or another in the whole scheme of Mark's telling of a "Day". Clearly, explication of all these and of all the detailed arguments by which I determine my view of Markan organisation at the lower levels of literary order will not be possible. Limited space simply does not allow such a luxury. In one sense they will have to be viewed as *unsupported* evidence because their presentations will have to be interpreted by the reader in the same way as the higher levels of literary ordering, which are discussed. What can be stated, however, is that the full, detailed structural breakdown which I present has been fully checked against Neirynck's most detailed and most helpful analysis[85]. A reading of his work, to which I was referred after making my initial analysis, confirmed much of what I had found at the higher levels of literary order. It did lead me to revise, nevertheless, significantly more than I might have been prepared to believe was required in the middle and lower orders.

---

[85] Frans Neirynck, *Duality in Mark: Contributions to the Study of the Markan Redaction*, Rev. Ed., Leuven University Press, Leuven, 1988.

Of particular value in Neirynck's analysis is his Part II where he tabulates all references to "dualities" (and *other repetitions*) under a total of thirty separate headings. By this method he ably draws attention to dualities and repetitions that otherwise might be overlooked. The chief categories are listed below:

Compound verb followed by the same preposition; Multiplication of cognate verbs; Double participle; Double imperative; Double negative; Double statement: negative-positive; Double statement: temporal or local; Double statement: general and special; Synonymous expression; Translation; Double Group of persons; Series of three; Correspondence in narrative; Command and Fulfilment; Request and Realization; Double question; Correspondence in discourse; Sandwich arrangement; Parallelism in sayings; and Doublets.

In his Part III, Neirynck presents "Mark in Greek" and so displays a synthesis of the data in lines and spaces (the latter vertically to portray sections, and horizontally to portray sub-sections and parts). Whilst it is not the case that I can agree with his synthesis, for the reason that he does not discern what to me is the fundamental 'arrangement' by Mark of material in Days and Series of Days, in the higher orders of Mark's literary structure, I do find myself agreeing significantly, nevertheless, with his detailed correspondences, in the middle and lower levels of literary order. As will be demonstrated, in a case study, in my evaluation of my synthesis of Mark's Prologue (in chapter 2), the dual expressions that Neirynck discerns, in the majority of usages, fall into the B and B' parts of Mark's ABB' structures, in the middle and lower orders. They do also significantly fall in the introductory pieces of balancing halves of Day-structures (as in Day One: 1.21,29; and as in Day Three: 2.1,13); in the introductory pieces of Days beginning balancing three-day sub-series (as between Days Twenty-two and Twenty-six: 11.1-6 and 14.12-16); in the introductory (first) Days of new Series (as between Days One and Twenty-two: 1.21 and 11.11; and as between Days Eight and Fifteen: 6.1 and 8.27, see also here: 6.14,15 and 8.28); and in the final Days of Series (as between Days Fourteen and Twenty-one: 8.22-26 and 10.46-52; and as between Days Seven and Twenty-eight: 5.22,23,35-43 and 16.1-8).

INTRODUCTION

Matrix: a working definition:

In turning to any commmentary, we usually look to the contents' page or to some presentation in the introduction to see what understanding the writer might have concerning the composition of the book under examination. The very positioning of this listing or table and the designation which is given to it seem to say as much about the commentators and their attitude to their work as about the biblical text they are handling. Their terms include: contents, structure, analysis, plan, arrangement, outline, plot and framework.

In a publication, a few years ago, I was content to apply the term "infra-structure" to the study of Mark's Gospel arrangement[86]. An architect is pleased to use a term with which he is familiar. It is a perfectly good planning, engineering and architectural term which describes a basic structure, to which attach other sub-structures and into which all other services and provisions, parts and details connect. I am not suggesting that Best's use of "cement" (if he really means "mortar") makes him out to be a bricklayer[87], but we are here talking about more than what is the glue or mortar which holds Mark's work together.

My choice of "matrix" was not consciously stirred by "structuralists'" use of the term; but it is useful because it holds in one, single term the two aspects of whole design on the one hand and detailed construction on the other.

A "matrix", according to the Concise Oxford Dictionary[88], has six definitions:
1) a mould in which a thing is cast or shaped, e.g. gramophone record;
2a) an environment or substance in which a thing is developed;
2b) a womb;
3) a mass of fine-grained rock in which gems, fossils, etc. are embedded;
4) *(Math.)* a rectangular array of elements in rows and columns that is treated as a single element;
5) *(Biol.)* the substance between cells or in which structures are embedded;
6) *(Computing)* a gridlike array of interconnected circuit elements.

---

[86] David G. Palmer, *Sliced Bread...*, p.22.
[87] Best, *Mark: the Gospel...*, pp.100ff.
[88] R.E. Allen (ed.), *Concise Oxford Dictionary of Current English*, Clarendon, Oxford, 8th ed. 1990.

All may be considered to have illustrative and metaphorical value, but it is definition four I have in mind. Structuralists[89] establish charts and "sets", for example, for parables, or sayings, and then determine their meaning by both a "serial reading" (horizontal: across, say, listings of meaningful units of each parable) and a "formal reading" (vertical: down the list of parables and their meaningful units), thus proceeding to a definition of the "generative matrix" (out of which, in this illustration, all parables come by means of certain laws of transformation). As we discuss the "Days" and their Series and Sub-Series, also the linkages between the "Days", that is the correspondences between the "Days" and their Series in regard to the distribution of themes and details throughout the whole of the gospel, it will be seen that "matrix" is an apt, current term to apply to a piece of literature which demands to be appreciated as much for its overall unity and plan as for its systematic arrangement of themes and details.

An identification is made between the "generative matrix" of Mark's Gospel and the framework which is revealed, which can be read at once both horizontally, across a charting of each Series of seven Days, and vertically, down through the charting of the four Series of Gospel Narrative, and which plots also the Prologue at its beginning, and the near original Epilogue at its end. For examples of horizontal readings in the second Series, the feeding of the five-thousand lies diametrically opposite the feeding of the four-thousand, and in the third Series, in the same positions (as the above) stand the transfiguration-glory accompaniment of Jesus by 'two' and opposite, the request of 'two' to be each side of Jesus in his future glory. For examples of vertical readings, the last Days of the middle two Series end with the only descriptions in the Gospel of healings of blind people, and the last Days of the outer two Series end with the Gospel's two only "raisings from the dead". In Chapter 8, we

---

[89]   E.g. and so henceforth: R. Funk, *Language, Hermeneutic, and the Word of God*, Harper & Row, New York 1966; E. Güttgemanns, *Offene Fragen zur Formgeschichte des Evangeliums*, Christian Kaiser Verlag, München, 1970; E. Leach, *Genesis as Myth and Other Essays*, Cape, London, 1969; E. Leach & D.A. Aycock, *Structuralist Interpretations of Biblical Myth*, Cambridge University Press, 1983 (reviewed by R.Carroll, *Religious Studies*, 21/1 (1985), pp.116-118); D.O. Via, *The Parables: Their Literary and Existential Dimension*, Fortress Press, Philadelphia, 1974; and *Kerygma & Comedy in the New Testament: A Structuralist Approach to Hermeneutic*, Fortress Press, Philadelphia, 1975.

take the results of Chapters 2 to 7 and re-construct what was Mark's overall plan and matrix.

The conclusion to the presentation, as a result of the findings of literary-structural analysis, necessarily begins over again a discussion of Mark's leading idea, and of his theological, literary and compositional abilities. At the last, I draw up an agenda of further work which is needing to be done if we are to be respecting Mark's intentions for the reading, understanding and sharing of his Gospel.

Chapter Two
The Days Beginning the Gospel (1.1-20):

The Prologue:

Throughout the years of biblical criticism, the question has been, "Is the prologue the first eight verses, the first thirteen, the first fifteen, or the first twenty verses?"

In recent times, a great many scholars and commentators have thought it is the second option[1]; a few the third[2]; and a very few the fourth (and one of these, likely by default, argues for vv.1-15 and attaches vv.16-20 without comment[3]). Which choice does the weight of evidence and argument support, as being the introduction Mark had in mind? Clearly, if the Gospel narrative is arranged in "Series" of individual presentations of "Days" from 1.21, as I state in my Introduction, then there is a literary-structural argument for the Prologue being twenty verses. In Chapter Three, Day One (1.21-38) will be examined; here, we rehearse the now traditional arguments and sift new, literary-structural evidence.

Content Considerations:

A glance at the New English Bible will show that the translators who were responsible for it viewed the first thirteen verses of Mark's Gospel as his Introduction. The belief that a division should be made at this point, after v.13, goes back to R.H. Lightfoot[4]. He argued that the printed Greek texts of his day were wrong to leave a gap after v.8; rather, it should be after v.13. Lightfoot's influence has been of great

---

[1] Lightfoot, Wilson, Cranfield, Schweizer, Hooker, Nineham, English, Standaert, Robbins, Kümmel, Farrer, Matera, Hengel, Tolbert and Painter.
[2] Keck, Pesch, Drury, Best and Dewey.
[3] Goulder, *The Evangelists' Calendar...* (by default); F. Belo, *A Materialist Reading of the Gospel of Mark*, Maryknoll, New York, 1981: he supports 1-21a.
[4] R.H. Lightfoot, *The Gospel Message of St Mark*, Clarendon Press, Oxford, 1950.

importance; few commentators have ignored his insight that these thirteen verses form a closely connected section. For him, this re-created gap defined the limits of an opening, christological section which provides the key to understanding the rest of the Gospel. The introduction was not just two or three incidents leading up to the ministry of Jesus.

Possibly following Lightfoot's argument, Nineham understood the "prologue" to be vv.1-13, and that it is "what the reader learns about the secret about Jesus before the story of the ministry begins." He argued that the incidents of these verses, from the evangelist's view, formed a fully coherent unity; that the passage stands apart from the rest of the gospel as a sort of curtain-raiser; and that "the curtain goes up" at v.14.[5] Nineham argued that the Gospel is written from the viewpoint of Jewish eschatological hope and that for Mark this hope found fulfilment in Jesus; that in his life we see the beginnings of God's final intervention in history, the first, but decisive, stage in the overthrow of the powers of evil and the establishment of God's sovereign rule. He further observed that the introduction establishes the identity and authority of Jesus beyond any doubt.

To Hooker also, the "first thirteen verses stand apart from the rest of the gospel and provide the key for what follows".[6] Following Nineham, she sees the similarity between Mark's introduction and that of John (John 1.1-18). Though different in character they both, nevertheless, set out to give information about Jesus which will provide the key to understanding the rest of the gospel. Both prologues explain who Jesus is by comparing him with the Baptist and by stressing Jesus' superiority. For Hooker, the first thirteen verses describe events "different in character from those that take place in most of the remaining pages of the gospel", though she has to recognise some parallels: with chapter 9, for visions and voices (9.2-7), and chapter 3, for mention of the activities of the Holy Spirit and Satan (3.23-29). We are "allowed to view the drama from a heavenly vantage-point before Mark brings us down to earth."

Where the supporters of a thirteen-verse Prologue discuss their case, we observe the similarity of their appeal to evidence. A

---

[5] Nineham, *Saint Mark*, p.55.
[6] Hooker, *The Gospel...*, p.31.

common argument is that vv.14 and 15 are separate from the Prologue because these verses introduce the first major section of the Gospel, which is Jesus' Galilean Ministry (e.g. see Nineham and Tolbert)[7]. Hooker recognises that other scholars argue that vv.14-15 should be included. "But," she says, "vv.14-15 lead us into the story of the ministry of Jesus with a summary of his proclamation of the Kingdom, whereas vv.1-13 provide us with the key to understanding that story, and the basis for his declaration that the Kingdom is at hand." Later, however, she argues that according to Mark's summary in 1.15, the Kingdom of God was the central theme of Jesus' teaching, borne out by the rest of the gospel. It is exactly this kind of consideration which suggests to me its inclusion in Mark's introduction. For both Drury and Best, vv.14-15 "conclude" the prologue. For Drury, it is an "active" ending, the announcement of "the Gospel" of the first verse of the book, and "the story is set on its way"[8]. For Best, the prologue concludes with an amalgam and summary of terms Jesus himself used ("the Kingdom of God is at hand") and terms the church used ("repent and believe the gospel")[9].

On 1.16-20, Hooker argues that "the theme of discipleship is prominent in Mark's gospel". It may be considered also, therefore, as appropriate for inclusion in the introduction. An introduction, even in much biblical and other ancient literature, opens up a consideration of themes that the book is to address. John 1.1-18 for example does. Hooker argues that the impression given by Mark is that the personality and authority of Jesus were such that four men responded to his call at their first meeting. Mark impresses his readers with Jesus' authority. And for both Nineham and Hooker this authority of Jesus is one of the insights we are given in the introduction, vv.1-13. Vv.16-20 arguably, therefore, extend the introduction. It is this that Belo sees, in judging that the narrative of Mark actually begins at 1.21b. And for him, the story proper begins in Capernaum, with the sabbath[10]. Goulder's support for 1.1-20 being a whole is based on his interest in possible lectionary parallelism: but, he covers only vv.1-15 in his argument[11].

---

[7] E.g. Nineham, *Saint Mark*, p.67; also Tolbert, *Sowing the Gospel...*, pp.113ff.
[8] Drury, *The Literary Guide...*, p.409.
[9] Best, *Mark: the Gospel...*, p.129.
[10] Belo, *A Materialist Reading...*
[11] Goulder, *The Evangelists' Calendar....*, p.246.

Continuing our discussion centred on matters of content, we might consider the repentance that John looked for (1.4) and the extension of this theme, the repentance which Jesus looked for (1.15). Further, John preaches a "baptism of repentance for the forgiveness of sins", also that the one who is coming is "stronger.....": we observe that Jesus preaches, in addition to repentance (and the Kingdom...) "belief - in the Gospel". Additionally, there is the theme of "attraction", in 1.5, of John, and of "greater attraction", in 1.18 and v.20, of Jesus, for there is not only a going to Jesus, as to John, but a following and a giving up of life as it had been, which is a fuller expression of the repentance which John the Baptist was preaching. If as both Hooker and Nineham say, the introduction compares and contrasts John and Jesus, then the introduction cannot be concluded at 1.13, leaving such an issue incomplete. 1.14 makes the link so strongly anyway: John's ministry is over, Jesus' is beginning. There is an argument, on content consideration alone, for understanding Mark's Prologue to be the first twenty verses.

We may consider another line of argument, based on contents: the Gospel of Mark, as a single whole, not only presents the story of Jesus, but also includes a call to its reader/its listeners. No-one can just sit there: there are things to be done! Repenting, believing and following are stated early on (1.15,17,20). These are in addition to being "baptised in/with the Holy Spirit" (1.8) and becoming "fishers of men" like the first disciples (1.17). To the introductory content of verses 1.1-13, therefore, we may properly consider adding the contents of vv.14-20[12]. It may well have been in Mark's mind that his Prologue had a two-fold purpose: to present information about Jesus that those who were there around him did not know at first, and to lay down at the outset issues of discipleship and matters which will need to be addressed in future generations.

Content-wise, the first thirteen verses link (according to Schweizer's summary, for example) a resumé of the story of John the Baptist with both the Baptism of Jesus and the Temptation of Jesus. Schweizer sets these under the title of "The Beginning"[13]. The verses

---

[12] To the arguments above, of Hooker, Nineham and Tolbert, that vv.14-20 represent a second, separate Introduction to the Galilean Mission, we can also add those of Painter, from his most recent commentary, *Mark's Gospel*, 1997..., pp.33-37.
[13] Schweizer, *The Good News...*, pp.28ff.

which follow are placed under a new, sectional title, "The Authority of Jesus and the Blindness of the Pharisees" (1.14-3.6) and a sub-title, "The Authority over Demons and Illness" (1.14-45) and then the descriptive titles of "Jesus proclaims the Kingdom of God" (1.14-15) and "The Call to Discipleship" (1.16-20). That is a lot of titling, and it is not all helpful. The passages of 1.14-15 and 1.16-20 sit comfortably under the specific headings but uncomfortably under the larger headings. The "blindness of the Pharisees", it may be noted, is not specifically an issue, until 3.5[14]; Jesus' "authority over demons and illness" appears first in 1.23ff.; and the issue of Jesus' "authority" is not verbalised until 1.22. For Schweizer, "The Demonstration of the Authority of Jesus" does come with 1.21-28. Almost as if she were paraphrasing Schweizer, Hooker titles 1.14-3.6, "Authority at work: success and opposition in Galilee." Again, "authority", considering simply her own references, comes into her titling of the piece beginning only at 1.21.[15] The case is similar with Nineham, who identified the section "The Galilean Ministry" as beginning at 1.14 but continuing to 8.26. For Tolbert, Jesus' Galilean Ministry extends from its specific introduction in vv.14,15, from 1.14 to 10.52.[16] It is true that Mark's grasp of Palestinian geography is suspect, but would he have thought that the country of the Gerasenes (5.1) and Tyre and Sidon (7.24 and v.31) were all in Galilee? Clearly, Nineham, ending this section at 8.26, was convinced that Mark did not think that Caesarea Philippi (8.27) was in Galilee. These things, and the fact that Mark himself introduces at 10.1 the Judaean element of Jesus' journeying, bring into question Tolbert's bi-sectionalising of the Gospel into a Galilean Ministry and a Jerusalem Ministry only. These and other attempts to separate vv.14,15 and vv.16-20 from the earlier verses of 1.1-13 are wholly problematic.

---

[14]   In 2.6, what is raised is the "blindness" of the scribes; in 2.16, the scribes of the Pharisees question only, and in 2.18 the same (it may be judged) question Jesus about fasting only; and in 2.24, the Pharisees question only.
[15]   Hooker, *The Gospel...*, pp.52ff.,61.
[16]   For Tolbert, following the arguments of R.H. Lightfoot, *Locality and Doctrine in the Gospels*, Hodder & Stoughton, London, 1938, and E.S. Malbon, "Galilee and Jerusalem: History and Literature in Marcan Presentation", *CBQ* 44 (1982) pp.242-248, the Galilean Section of the Gospel extends to 10.52.

Literary-structural Considerations:

We consider now the contributions of literary-structural evidence to the debates over the opening verses of the Gospel, and we begin with Robbins, who identifies three-step progressions in relation to the formal structure of Mark. His "Introduction" is 1.1-13. He says, "The first three-step progression in the narrative... is 1.14-15, 16-18 and 19-20"[17] (he explains: Jesus came...; and passing along...; and going on a little further...). His structural understanding of these verses is one to which I hold, but it is not the earliest three-step progression. An earlier structural threesome can be observed in 1.9, 10-11 and 12-13 (And it came to pass, Jesus....; and immediately... the Spirit...; and immediately... the Spirit....). The earliest, structural threesome of the Gospel, of such scale, however, is that of 1.1-3, 4-5 and 6-8 (The beginning of the gospel of Jesus...; it came to pass, John....; and there was John....). In each of these cases, a structure is identified which might be described by α, β, β', that is where α is the introductory piece, β is the first development and β' is the second and completing development, where β and β' balance and parallel each other. Simple, literary-structural analysis does indeed suggest that the Prologue *is* the first twenty verses of the Gospel. It suggests that the Prologue itself is a three-step progression, of vv.1-8, 9-13 and 14-20. We will return to a consideration of this after we have reviewed the literary-structural propositions of others.

It is presently the case that published structural-analyses of pieces of Mark's writing concentrate much upon his possible chiastic organisation of material. We consider three such serious analyses of the Prologue: Dewey's (1.1-8 of 1.1-15)[18], Drury's (1.1-15)[19] and Tolbert's (1.1-13)[20]. It may be argued straightway, because they all differ appreciably, that they cannot all be what Mark had in mind. Chiasm, it is noted, is the simplest thing to argue wrongly[21]. In the attempt to establish any pattern by one set of criteria, another set of

---

[17] Robbins, *Jesus the Teacher*..., pp.27ff: for Robbins, three-step progressions begin all the sections of the Gospel's formal structure.
[18] Dewey, *Markan Public Debate*..., pp.144ff.
[19] Drury, *The Literary Guide*..., p.408; and in "Mark 1.1-15: An Interpretation", *Alternative Approaches to New Testament Study*, ed. A.E. Harvey, SPCK, London, 1985.
[20] Tolbert, *Sowing the Gospel*..., pp.108-113.
[21] See Thomson, *Chiasmus*..., pp.290-292.

criteria either is rejected, or simply unidentified. A later and simple illustration of this, chosen particularly because it arose in my search for Mark's 'design criteria', is found in 11.12-25. For many scholars it is a typical example of Markan envelope-structuring (11.12-14, the first part of the fig-tree incident; vv.15-19, Jesus' clearing of the Temple; vv.20-25 the second part of the fig tree episode). The "Day"-division at 11.19,20, however, which to me is Mark's clearest signal of his structural method, slashes right through such a scheme.[22]

In presenting her scheme, Dewey[23] first describes the larger rhetorical unit of the prologue as 1.1-15 and as delimited by the *inclusio* of the word "gospel". For her the prologue divides into two parts, vv.1-8 which is concerned with John, and vv.9-15 which is concerned with Jesus. The second part, vv.9-15, is marked off by its own *inclusio*, "came Jesus", vv.9, 14. Further, the conclusion of the first part, "John's preaching concerning the coming of Jesus" (vv.7,8), parallels the conclusion of the second part, "Jesus' preaching concerning the coming of the kingdom of God" (vv.14,15). She sees the two parts as closely interrelated by extensive and varied use of word repetitions (e.g., wilderness, baptism, spirit, preaching, repentance and messenger). She restricts her analysis after this to vv.1-8 and presents a five-part chiasm for the first eight verses:

> A   1,2a   Jesus
>   B   2b,3   description of John
>   C   4,5   a pair of presentations on John's ministry
>   B   6   description of John
> A   7,8   Jesus.

The symmetrical rhythm is indicated by the content. She sees it as significant that in the opening verses of the Gospel, "Mark's audience is alerted from the very beginning to Mark's use of symmetrical and chiastic patterns"[24].

At first sight, it appears a most promising analysis of not only vv.1-8, but also of vv.1-15. Yet it begs several questions: can we really say that A parallels A (when v.2 might connect better with v.3,

---

[22] Refer to Chapter Six, The Fourth Seven-Day Series, and the discussions on Days Twenty-three and Twenty-four.
[23] Dewey, *Markan Public Debate...*, pp.144ff.
[24] *ibid.*

and Jesus' name is missing in vv.7,8), that B parallels B (when the issues regarding John are so different, and when v.4 and v.6 mention John only, and in their opening phrases), and that C is a pair of central statements (when there are really more than two statements, and the ministry of John well covers vv.4-8, in all)? Further, given that her basic contents' reason, for her identification of two parts to the Prologue, is that the first is concerned with John and the second with Jesus, she does seem to be simplifying the argument too much as Jesus and John are mentioned in both. We move on, but we will continue to consider her case.

When Drury's analysis was first published[25], he claimed that the first fifteen verses of the gospel were set in a four-part chiasm, ABBA: where in the outer pieces, Jesus is announced in the first and arrives in the last; and where in the inner pieces, John is announced in the first and arrives in the second. It is left to his readers to unravel. It may be read as: A: v.1, B: vv.2,3, B: vv.4-8 or vv.4-13 and A: vv.9-15 or vv.14,15. Drury's second attempt[26] describes a six-part chiasm of ABCCBA:

A	1	(Gospel)
B	2,3	Wilderness
C	4-8	Jordan
C	9-11	Jordan
B	12,13	Wilderness
A	14,15	(Gospel).

Immediately, comparison with Dewey's chiasm demonstrates that Drury and she are identifying different content criteria (to which problem for defining chiasm, refer above). Drury's focus for his middle four pieces is on 'place'; Dewey's is on 'persons'; though they both refer to the locating of the word 'gospel' in similar ways. We consider Tolbert's analysis.

Tolbert's contribution to the debate is that of a four-part chiasm for the first thirteen verses. For her, the first thirteen verses comprise the prologue, and the prologue she argues is "carefully organised rhetorically into four sections by patterns of word repetition". Her sections are:

---

[25] Drury, *The Literary Guide...*, p.408.
[26] Drury, "Mark 1.1-15...".

A   1-3   Ἀρχὴ Jesus, Son of God, messenger, voice, in the wilderness
B   4-8   ἐγένετο John, baptising, Jordan
B'   9,10   καὶ ἐγένετο Jesus, baptised, John, Jordan
A'   11-13   καὶ φωνὴ ἐγένετο Jesus, beloved Son, voice, in the wilderness, Angels.

She identifies that, after the opening three verses, an anaphoric[27] use of the impersonal ἐγένετο begins each section. (Immediately, we see that her criteria for delimiting the parts are different again from Dewey and Drury.) Additionally, she identifies that the four sections are related to each other by an anastrophe, whereby a keyword or hook word[28] near the end of each section is repeated near the beginning of the next: that is, between sections A and B: ἐν τῇ ἐρήμῳ ; between B and B': ἐβάπτισα, βαπτίσει and ἐβαπτίσθη; and between B' and A': οὐρανοὺς, τὸ πνεῦμα and ἐκ τῶν οὐρανῶν, τὸ πνεῦμα.

She says, "The tendency to supply linking words or phrases, often but not always indicative of major themes, close to the end of one division and near the beginning of the next, is a very common practice. It serves to alert the reader to the shift in material while at the same time smoothing the transition." She further recognises that this type of stylistic feature is what Lucian, writing in about 165AD, had in mind on a grander scale in recommending that the historian adopt a smooth, even style of narration. He wrote: "Only when the first point has been completed should it lead on to the next, which should be, as it were, the next link of the chain. There must be no sharp break, no multiplicity of juxtaposed narratives. One thing should not only lie adjacent to the next, but be related to it and overlap it at the edges."[29] Tolbert views her four sections of the prologue as distinct but that "they overlap one another at the edges".

---

[27] Anaphora (or epanaphora) is the repetition of the same word or phrase at the beginning of successive clauses, sentences or sections. See, eg., Demetrius, *On Style*, pp.59-62; and *Rhetorica ad Herrenium* 4.13.19.

[28] She agrees with Dewey (*Markan Public Debate*. p.32) that "hook word" is probably a better term for this type of repetition, because it is more neutral. See also H. Parunak, "Oral Typesetting: Some uses of Biblical Structure", *Bib* 62 (1981): pp.153-168.

[29] Lucian, *De conscribenda historia* p.55 (tr. D.A. Russell in *Ancient Literary Criticism: The Principal Texts in New Translations*, eds. D.A. Russell and M. Winterbottom, Clarendon Press, Oxford, 1972, p.545.

She rightly sees further thematic and verbal correspondences between the sections, which I have included in the above summary presentation of her work. We can observe some problems, however. Whilst her fourth section, 1.11-13, is about "Jesus" it does not mention his name. Further, her section B is twice as long as her other sections; it mentions John twice. In regard to anastrophes, the matter of "baptism" is rehearsed more times than she acknowledges. And much more material is found here which does not connect with any in section B'. Further, her appeal to anastrophes is unconvincing. Besides the problem of the link between sections B and B' on "baptism", there is mention of the "spirit" at the end of B, but not at the beginning of B'. If it is that a keyword is identified in one section, the same *key*-word cannot, surely, be identified as a 'non-keyword' (such as "spirit", in B, v.8) in another section within the same construction.

Reviewing these three proposals for chiasm, we expose the difficulties which are always faced when attempts are made to define structure from such a mix and repetition of themes, details and words. To these proposals, and to Dewey's additional proposal for 2.1-3.6[30], I will present counter arguments that lead me to the view that the first detailed chiasm in the gospel appears only at 5.3-5.[31] Literary-structural analysis of the first twenty verses of the Gospel pursuades me that chiasm was not in Mark's mind as he composed his Prologue. To this method of analysis we now return.

While reviewing Robbins' analysis I stated that the evidence suggested that the Prologue comprises the first twenty verses of the Gospel, on the grounds that it is a three-step progression itself of vv.1-8, 9-13 and 14-20. Below we annotate these A, B and B' in turn, because step A may be considered introductory, step B may be considered to be the first development, and step B' may be considered to be the second and concluding/completing development. We identified above that each of these steps were themselves three-step progressions: vv.1-3,4-5,6-8; vv.9,10-11,12-13; and vv.14-15,16-18,19-20. I present below the full results of

---

[30] Dewey, *Markan Public Debate...*, pp.109ff., which we discuss under The First Seven Days.
[31] We discuss this under The First Series of Seven Days, and Day Six.

literary-structural analysis on the first twenty verses of the Gospel, which may be judged to be the Markan Prologue:

Αα [α]¹ [.α] [..α] Ἀρχὴ τοῦ εὐαγγελίου [..β] Ἰησου Χριστοῦ [..β'] [υἱου θεοῦ].
    ²[.α'] [..α] καθὼς γέγραπται [..β] ἐν τῷ Ἠσαΐᾳ [..β'] τῷ προφήτῃ,
  [β] [.α] Ἰδοὺ [.β] [..α] ἀποστέλλω τὸν ἄγγελόν μου [..α'] πρὸ προσώπου σου, [.β'] ὃς κατασκευάσει τὴν ὁδόν σου·
  [β']³[.α] [..α] φωνὴ βοῶντος [..α'] ἐν τῇ ἐρήμῳ, [.β] Ἑτοιμάσατε τὴν ὁδὸν κυρίου, [.β'] εὐθείας ποιεῖτε τὰς τρίβους αὐτοῦ.
β [α] ⁴ [.α] Ἐγένετο Ἰωάννης [.β] [..α] [ὁ] βαπτίζων [..α'] ἐν τῇ ἐρήμῳ [.β'] [..α] καὶ κηρύσσων [..β] βάπτισμα μετανοίας [..β'] εἰς ἄφεσιν ἁμαρτιῶν.
  [β] ⁵[.α] καὶ ἐξεπορεύετο πρὸς αὐτὸν
    [.β] πᾶσα ἡ Ἰουδαία χώρα
    [.β'] καὶ οἱ Ἱεροσολυμῖται πάντες,
  [β'] [.α] [..α] καὶ ἐβαπτίζοντο [..α'] ὑπ' αὐτου
    [.β] ἐν τῷ Ἰορδάνῃ ποταμῷ
    [.β'] ἐξομολογούμενοι τὰς ἁμαρτίας αὐτῶν.
β'[α] ⁶[.α] Καὶ ἦν ὁ Ἰωάννης
    [.β] [..α] ἐνδεδυμένος τρίχας καμήλου [..α'] καὶ ζώνην δερματίνην περὶ τὴν ὀσφὺν αὐτοῦ,
    [.β'] [..α] καὶ ἐσθίων ἀκρίδας [..α'] καὶ μέλι ἄγριον.
  [β] ⁷[.α] [..α] καὶ ἐκήρυσσεν [..α'] λέγων,
    [.β] Ἔρχεται ὁ ἰσχυρότερός μου [.β'] ὀπίσω μου,
  [β'] [.α] [..α] οὗ οὐκ εἰμὶ ἱκανὸς [..β] κύψας [..β'] λῦσαι τὸν ἱμάντα τῶν ὑποδημάτων αὐτοῦ·
    ⁸[.β] [..α] ἐγὼ ἐβάπτισα ὑμᾶς [..α'] ὕδατι,
    [.β'] [..α] αὐτὸς δὲ βαπτίσει ὑμᾶς [..α'] ἐν πνεύματι ἁγίῳ.

Βα [α]⁹[.α] Καὶ ἐγένετο [.α'] ἐν ἐκείναις ταῖς ἡμέραις
  [β] [.α] ἦλθεν Ἰησοῦς [.β] ἀπὸ Ναζαρὲτ [.β'] τῆς Γαλιλαίας
  [β'] [.α] καὶ ἐβαπτίσθη [.β] εἰς τὸν Ἰορδάνην [.β'] ὑπὸ Ἰωάννου.
β [α] ¹⁰[.α] Καὶ εὐθὺς [.β] ἀναβαίνων [.β'] ἐκ τοῦ ὕδατος
  [β] [.α] εἶδεν σχιζομένους τοὺς οὐρανοὺς
    [.β] καὶ τὸ πνεῦμα ὡς περιστερὰν
    [.β'] καταβαῖνον εἰς αὐτόν·
  [β'] ¹¹[.α] [..α] καὶ φωνὴ ἐγένετο [..α'] ἐκ τῶν οὐρανῶν,
    [.β] [..α] Σὺ εἶ ὁ υἱός μου [..α'] ὁ ἀγαπητός,
    [.β'] ἐν σοὶ εὐδόκησα.
β'[α] ¹²[.α] Καὶ εὐθὺς [.β] τὸ πνεῦμα αὐτὸν ἐκβάλλει [.β'] εἰς τὴν ἔρημον.
  [β] ¹³[.α] καὶ ἦν ἐν τῇ ἐρήμῳ [.β] τεσσεράκοντα ἡμέρας
    [.β'] πειραζόμενος ὑπὸ τοῦ Σατανᾶ.
  [β'] [.α] καὶ ἦν μετὰ τῶν θηρίων, [.α'] καὶ οἱ ἄγγελοι διηκόνουν αὐτῷ.

Β' α [α]¹⁴[.α] Μετὰ δὲ [.α'] τὸ παραδοθῆναι τὸν Ἰωάννην
  [β] [.α] [..α] ἦλθεν ὁ Ἰησοῦς [..α'] εἰς τὴν Γαλιλαίαν
    [.β] [..α] κηρύσσων [..α'] τὸ εὐαγγέλιον τοῦ θεου
    ¹⁵[.β'] [..α] καὶ λέγων [..α'] ὅτι Πεπλήρωται ὁ καιρὸς
  [β'] [.α] καὶ ἤγγικεν ἡ βασιλεία τοῦ θεοῦ· [.β] μετανοεῖτε [.β'] καὶ
    πιστεύετε ἐν τῷ εὐαγγελίῳ.
β [α]¹⁶[.α] [..α] Καὶ παράγων [..β] παρὰ τὴν θάλασσαν [..β'] τῆς Γαλιλαίας
    [.β] [..α] εἶδεν Σίμωνα [..β] καὶ Ἀνδρέαν [..β'] τὸν ἀδελφὸν Σίμωνος
    [.β'] [..α] ἀμφιβάλλοντας [..β] ἐν τῇ θαλάσσῃ· [..β'] ἦσαν γὰρ ἁλιεῖς.
  [β]¹⁷[.α] [..α] καὶ εἶπεν [..β] αὐτοῖς [..β'] ὁ Ἰησοῦς,
    [.α'] [..α] Δεῦτε ὀπίσω μου, [..β] καὶ ποιήσω ὑμᾶς [..β'] γενέσθαι
    ἁλιεῖς ἀνθρώπων.
  [β']¹⁸[.α] καὶ εὐθὺς [.β] ἀφέντες τὰ δίκτυα [.β'] ἠκολούθησαν αὐτῷ.
β'[α]¹⁹[.α] Καὶ προβὰς ὀλίγον
    [.β] [..α] εἶδεν Ἰάκωβον τὸν τοῦ Ζεβεδαίου [..β] καὶ Ἰωάννην
    [..β'] τὸν ἀδελφὸν αὐτοῦ,
    [.β'] [..α] καὶ αὐτοὺς [..β] ἐν τῷ πλοίῳ [..β'] καταρτίζοντας τὰ δίκτυα.
  [β] ²⁰[.α] καὶ εὐθὺς [.α'] ἐκάλεσεν αὐτούς.
  [β'] [.α] [..α] καὶ ἀφέντες τὸν πατέρα αὐτῶν Ζεβεδαῖον [..β] ἐν τῷ
    πλοίῳ [..β'] μετὰ τῶν μισθωτῶν
    [.α'] [..α] ἀπῆλθον [..α'] ὀπίσω αὐτοῦ.

In this literary-structural presentation, I have underlined not only the significantly repeated name of "Jesus" but also what is likely an equally important signifier of the structure and, therefore, of the literary-structural completeness of his introduction. Mark's use of ἔρχομαι, apparently so strategically[32], warrants close attention. In A, starting with "the beginning of the gospel", the focus begins on Jesus, moves on to John, and then returns to Jesus, the one who "is coming" (Ἔρχεται). In B, he has come: Jesus came (ἦλθεν) to John. And in B', Jesus came (ἦλθεν) into Galilee to begin his ministry, according to Mark, after John was imprisoned. The overall structure of the Prologue is expressed, therefore, by ABB'.

The analysis breaks down the text of the Prologue into five different levels of literary order expressed in turn by: ABB', αββ', [α] [β] [β'], [.α] [.β] [.β'] and [.α] [.α'], [..α] [..β] [..β'] and [..α] [..α']. We may discern Mark's use of his literary-structural three-part presentational principle at each of these levels, and note at the lower and, therefore, more detailed levels only, a use also of an alternative 'two-part' construction-method. The basic principle of his writing method is

---

[32] See under Day Two for further examples of the importance to Mark of ἔρχομαι.

that he establishes an introductory part, follows it with a first development, and then completes the whole piece with a second development, whereby the first and second developments balance each other. By employing this method throughout his Gospel presentation (at every level of literary order) he signals his definition of sections, parts, sub-parts, etc. This uncovering of his rhetorical method is of fundamental assistance in the establishing of his framework and plan for the Gospel as a whole, as well as in the defining of its constituent parts. In the larger constructions (of ABB', αββ' and [α] [β] [β']) his presentations balance for content and detail, and in the smaller constructions (of [.α] [.β] [.β'], [.α] [.α'] and [..α] [..β] [..β'], [..α] [..α']) the parts and sub-parts balance by reason of their detail and their function in the text (for qualifying and completing purposes).

In analysing the Gospel text, the question arose as to how far the analysis of the detailed presentations was going to be meaningful. Simply, it is the case that as the analysis was once begun it developed its own momentum and could not be stopped. As a result, it demonstrates how much the three-part presentational method of Mark's choice governed his writing effort. The breaking down of the text into clauses and words has its purpose.

The literary-structural/rhetorical analysis of the Gospel's Prologue provides, then, an excellent example of how Mark's rhetorical method signals the delimiting of his Gospel sections. It is a method, as we will see, which he applies consistently from beginning to end of his Gospel. Not only is his method, on discovery, a cause of some amazement, but also is his ability to work it at so many levels of literary order simultaneously.

In the Introduction, page 42, I promised a case study which would determine whether or not there was a meeting point between Neirynck's analysis[33] and mine. It is judged a good moment to present it. The apparent difference between our findings is that he discerns dualities and I discern three-part presentations. In all he discerns forty-six dualities in the verses which make up Mark's Prologue. They are to be found under nineteen of his thirty Group headings. We examine them group by group:

---

[33] Neirynck, *Duality...*, Part II, pp.73-135.

THE DAYS BEGINNING 59

Group 1, Compound Verb Followed by the Same Preposition:

1.16 παράγων παρά I read: [..α] Καὶ παράγων [..β] παρὰ τὴν θάλασσαν [..β'] τῆς Γαλιλαίας; παράγων is introductory; παρὰ τὴν θάλασσαν is the first development, and τῆς Γαλιλαίας is the second and completing development.

Group 4, Multiplication of Cognate Verbs:

1.4,9 ἐγένετο ἐγένετο I read a third in 1.11, and hence discern no 'duality' as such. Their employments at vv.4,9 are not structurally significant.

1.8 ἐβάπτισα ὑμᾶς I read:[.β] [..α] ἐγὼ ἐβάπτισα ὑμᾶς [..α'] ὕδατι,
  βαπτίσει ὑμᾶς   [.β'] [..α] αὐτὸς δὲ βαπτίσει ὑμᾶς [..α'] ἐν πνεύματι ἁγίῳ.
Hence, they are the second and third parts of a three-part construction.

1.10 ἀναβαίνων ἐκ I read: [α][.α] Καὶ εὐθὺς [.β] ἀναβαίνων [.β'] ἐκ τοῦ
  καταβαῖνον εἰς   ὕδατος
        [β] [.α] εἶδεν σχιζομένους τοὺς οὐρανοὺς
         [.β] καὶ τὸ πνεῦμα ὡς περιστερὰν
         [.β'] καταβαῖνον εἰς αὐτόν·
        [β'][.α] [..α] καὶ φωνὴ ἐγένετο [..α'] ἐκ τῶν οὐρανῶν,
         [.β] [..α] Σὺ εἶ ὁ υἱός μου [..α'] ὁ ἀγαπητός,
         [.β'] ἐν σοὶ εὐδόκησα.
Hence, ἀναβαίνων ἐκ is part of the introductory clause, and καταβαῖνον εἰς is simply included in the first of two balancing and completing clauses.

1.13 ἦν ἦν I read:[β][.α] καὶ ἦν ἐν τῇ ἐρήμῳ [.β] τεσσεράκοντα ἡμέρας [.β'] πειραζόμενος ὑπὸ τοῦ Σατανᾶ.
[β'] [.α] καὶ ἦν μετὰ τῶν θηρίων, [.α'] καὶ οἱ ἄγγελοι διηκόνουν αὐτῷ.
Hence, they are to be found introducing the second and third parts of a three-part construction.

Group 5, Double Participle:

1.4 [ὁ] βαπτίζων
καὶ κηρύσσων

I read: [.α] [..α] 'Εγένετο 'Ιωάννης
[.β] [..α] [ὁ] βαπτίζων [..α΄] ἐν τῇ ἐρήμῳ
[.β΄] [..α] καὶ κηρύσσων [..β] βάπτισμα
μετανοίας [..β΄] εἰς ἄφεσιν ἁμαρτιῶν.
Hence, they are to be found introducing the second and third parts of a three-part construction.

1.6 ἦν
ἐνδεδυμένος
καὶ ἐσθίων

I read: [.α] Καὶ ἦν ὁ 'Ιωάννης
[.β] [..α] ἐνδεδυμένος τρίχας καμήλου
[..α΄] καὶ ζώνην δερματίνην περὶ τὴν ὀσφὺν αὐτοῦ,
[.β΄] [..α] καὶ ἐσθίων ἀκρίδας [..α΄] καὶ μέλι ἄγριον.
Hence, they are to be found introducing the second and third parts of a three-part construction.

1.14,15 κηρύσσων
καὶ λέγων

I read: [α][.α] Μετὰ δὲ [.α΄] τὸ παραδοθῆναι
τὸν 'Ιωάννην
[β] [.α] [..α] ἦλθεν ὁ 'Ιησοῦς [..α΄] εἰς τὴν
Γαλιλαίαν
[.β] [..α] κηρύσσων [..α΄] τὸ εὐαγγέλιον τοῦ
θεου
[.β΄] [..α] καὶ λέγων [..α΄] ὅτι Πεπλήρωται ὁ
καιρὸς
[β΄] [.α] και ἤγγικεν ἡ βασιλεία τοῦ θεοῦ·
[.β] μετανοεῖτε
[.β΄] και πιστεύετε ἐν τῷ εὐαγγελίῳ.
Hence, they are to be found introducing the second and third parts of a three-part construction.

Group 6, Double Imperative:

1.3   see Group 13, 1.3
1.15   see above, for 1.14,15, μετανοεῖτε , και πιστεύετε: they are to be found in the second and third parts of a three part construction.

THE DAYS BEGINNING

Group 7, Repetition of the Antecedent:

1.7 <u>ου</u> <u>αὐτοῦ</u>·
I read: [..α] <u>ου</u> οὐκ εἰμὶ ἱκανὸς [..β] κύψας [..β'] λῦσαι τὸν ἱμάντα τῶν ὑποδημάτων <u>αὐτοῦ</u>: it is a resumptive pronoun preceded by the relative; see also only 7.25, 9.3,and 13.19. In this instance, the words introduce and complete the clause.

1.11,10
ἐκ τῶν οὐρανῶν,
σχιζομένους <u>τοὺς</u>
<u>οὐρανοὺς</u>
See under Group 4 above, 1.10: they are both to be found in the first lines of the second and third parts of a three part construction.

1.16 <u>Σίμωνα</u> <u>Σίμωνος</u>
I read: [..α] <u>εἶδεν</u> <u>Σίμωνα</u> [..β] καὶ 'Ανδρέαν
[..β'] <u>τὸν ἀδελφὸν</u> <u>Σίμωνος</u>
The first use is introductory; the second use is qualifying in the third part what is stated in the second part of a three-part construction.

1.16
παρὰ τὴν θάλασσαν
ἐν τῇ θαλάσσῃ·
I read: [.α] [..α] <u>Καὶ παράγων</u> [..β] <u>παρὰ τὴν</u>
<u>θάλασσαν</u> [..β'] <u>τῆς Γαλιλαίας</u>
[.β] [..α] <u>εἶδεν</u> <u>Σίμωνα</u> [..β] καὶ 'Ανδρέαν
[..β'] <u>τὸν ἀδελφὸν</u> <u>Σίμωνος</u>
[.β'] [..α] ἀμφιβάλλοντας [..β] ἐν τῇ θαλάσσῃ·
[..β'] ἦσαν γὰρ <u>ἁλιεῖς</u>.
The first use is introductory; the second use in the third part is qualifying what is stated in the second part of a three-part construction.

1.19 αὐτοὺς
'Ιάκωβον...'Ιωάννην
I read: [α] [.α] <u>Καὶ προβὰς ὀλίγον</u>
[.β] [..α] <u>εἶδεν</u> 'Ιάκωβον τὸν τοῦ Ζεβεδαίου
[..β] καὶ 'Ιωάννην [..β'] <u>τὸν ἀδελφὸν</u>
αὐτοῦ,
[.β'] [..α] καὶ αὐτοὺς [..β] <u>ἐν τῷ πλοίῳ</u>
[..β'] καταρτίζοντας <u>τὰ δίκτυα</u>.
αὐτοὺς may be "a redundant pronoun", but it does seem to have literary-structural significance here in strengthening the balance between the second and third parts of a three-part construction.

1.20	I read: [β] [.α] καὶ εὐθὺς [.α´] ἐκάλεσεν αὐτούς.
τὸν πατέρα αὐτῶν	[β´] [.α] [..α] καὶ ἀφέντες τὸν πατέρα αὐτῶν
Ζεβεδαῖον	[..β] ἐν τῷ πλοίῳ
τὸν τοῦ Ζεβεδαίου	[..β´] μετὰ τῶν μισθωτῶν
(1.19)	[.α´] [..α] ἀπῆλθον [..α´] ὀπίσω αὐτοῦ.

For the full three-part construction read the above with this, i.e. vv.19 and 20 together. The first use is introductory; the second use is in the third part, and bonds the whole rhetorical unit firmly together.

Group 10, Double Statement: Temporal or Local:

1.12,13	I read: [α] [.α] Καὶ εὐθὺς [.β] τὸ πνεῦμα αὐτὸν
εἰς τὴν ἔρημον	ἐκβάλλει [.β´] εἰς τὴν ἔρημον.
ἐν τῇ ἐρήμῳ	[β] [.α] καὶ ἦν ἐν τῇ ἐρήμῳ [.β] τεσσεράκοντα
	ἡμέρας [.β´] πειραζόμενος ὑπὸ τοῦ Σατανᾶ.
	[β´] [.α] καὶ ἦν μετὰ τῶν θηρίων, [.α´] καὶ οἱ ἄγγελοι διηκόνουν αὐτῷ.

The first use is introductory; the second use is in the first of the two completing parts (regarding which, see Group 4 above).

Group 11, Double Statement: General and Special:

1.5	I read: [.α] καὶ ἐξεπορεύετο πρὸς αὐτὸν
πᾶσα ἡ 'Ιουδαία χώρα	[.β] πᾶσα ἡ 'Ιουδαία χώρα
καὶ οἱ 'Ιεροσολυμῖται	[.β´] καὶ οἱ 'Ιεροσολυμῖται πάντες
πάντες	Hence, they are the second and third parts of a three-part construction.

1.5,9 V.5 tells how those who came to John were baptised by him in the Jordan river;
v.9 tells how Jesus was baptised in the Jordan river by John.

They fall in sections one and two (A and B) of the Prologue. Section A is introductory. Sections B and B' complete the three-section Prologue focusing on Jesus who "came" (in vv.9 and 14, compare Bα[β] and B´α[β]).

THE DAYS BEGINNING 63

Group 12, Double Statement: Repetition of the Motif:

1.2,3	I read: [α] [.α] [..α] Ἀρχὴ <u>τοῦ εὐαγγελίου</u>
ὃς κατασκευάσει	[..β] <u>Ἰησου</u> Χριστοῦ
<u>τὴν ὁδόν</u> σου·	[..β‘] [<u>υἱου θεοῦ</u>].
Ἐτοιμάσατε <u>τὴν ὁδὸν</u>	[.α‘] [..α] καθὼς γέγραπται
κυρίου	[..β] ἐν τῷ Ἠσαΐᾳ
	[..β‘] τῷ προφήτῃ,
	[β] [.α] Ἰδοὺ
	[.β] [..α] ἀποστέλλω τὸν ἄγγελόν μου
	[..α‘] πρὸ προσώπου σου,
	[.β‘] ὃς κατασκευάσει <u>τὴν ὁδόν</u> σου·
	[β‘] [.α] [..α] <u>φωνὴ</u> βοῶντος [..α‘] <u>ἐν τῇ ἐρήμῳ</u>,
	[.β] ‘Ετοιμάσατε <u>τὴν ὁδὸν</u> κυρίου,
	[.β‘] εὐθείας ποιεῖτε τὰς τρίβους αὐτοῦ.

They are found in the second and third parts of the three part construction, 1.1-3.

1.7	
Ἔρχεται ὁ	These occupy the second and third parts of the
ἰσχυρότερός μου	three-part construction, 1.6-8.
ὀπίσω μου,	
<u>οὗ</u> οὐκ εἰμὶ ἱκανὸς κύψας	
λῦσαι τὸν ἱμάντα τῶν	
ὑποδημάτων <u>αὐτοῦ</u>·	

1.17	I read: [.α] [..α] καὶ εἶπεν [..β] <u>αὐτοῖς</u> [..β‘] ὁ Ἰησοῦς,
καὶ ποιήσω ὑμᾶς	[.α‘] [..α] <u>Δεῦτε ὀπίσω μου</u>,
γενέσθαι (<u>ἁλιεῖς</u>	[..β] καὶ ποιήσω ὑμᾶς
ἀνθρώπων)	[..β‘] γενέσθαι <u>ἁλιεῖς</u> ἀνθρώπων.

These occupy the second and third parts of a three-part construction.

Group 13, Synonymous Expression:

1.	These are found in the second and third parts of a three
Ἑτοιμάσατε <u>τὴν ὁδὸν</u>	part construction. See Group 12, 1.2,3.
κυρίου,	
εὐθείας ποιεῖτε	
τὰς τρίβους αὐτοῦ.	

1.4 μετανοίας I read: [..α] καὶ κηρύσσων
εἰς ἄφεσιν ἁμαρτιῶν [..β] βάπτισμα μετανοίας
  [..β'] εἰς ἄφεσιν ἁμαρτιῶν.
  These occupy the second and third parts of a three-part construction.

1.13 ἦν ἐν τῇ ἐρήμῳ I read: [β] [.α] καὶ ἦν ἐν τῇ ἐρήμῳ ...
καὶ ἦν μετὰ τῶν [β'] [.α] καὶ ἦν μετὰ τῶν θηρίων
θηρίων These occupy the second and third parts of a three-part construction.

1.15 For presentation, see Group 5, 1.14,15. These occupy
Πεπλήρωται ὁ καιρὸς [β] [β'] positions.
καὶ ἤγγικεν ἡ
βασιλεία τοῦ θεοῦ·

1.15 μετανοεῖτε For presentation, see Group 5, 1.14,15. These occupy
καὶ πιστεύετε ἐν [.β] [.β'] positions.
τῷ εὐαγγελίῳ.

Group 15, Substantive followed by Apposition:

1.1 Ἰησοῦ Χριστοῦ I read: [α] [.α] [..α] Ἀρχὴ τοῦ εὐαγγελίου
   [υἱοῦ θεοῦ]. [..β] Ἰησοῦ Χριστοῦ
  [..β'] [υἱοῦ θεοῦ].
  These occupy [..β] [..β'] positions.

Group 16, Double Group of Persons (Two Individuals):

1.16 See Group 7, 1.16;
1.19 See Group 7, 1.19.   (And an additional note:
  in the Prologue, we observe two calls of two named individuals, four in all;
  in the first Series, they are named again in the first day, Day 1, 1.29;
  in the second Series, the first day, Day 8, the disciples are sent out "two by two", 6.7;
  in the third Series, 'two', who are named, meet with Jesus at his transfiguration on the second day, Day 16, 9.4; and in the balancing day of the series, Day 20, 'two', who are named, ask to sit either side of Jesus in his glory, 10.37;
  in the fourth Series, on the days beginning both sub-series of three days, Days 22 and 26, 11.1 and 14.13, Jesus sends 'two' (not named), each time, to make preparations for him;
  and in the longer ending, Jesus appears to 'two' (not named), 16.12.

That is a lot of 'twos', and it is also a reasonably well balanced distribution of the same. For a possible significance, we need to return to the Introduction, and to matters raised on page 24 in regard to the motif of the flood which we observed might have had an influence on Mark's compositional arrangement. Clearly, in the flood story, it is animals which go into the ark and are saved from God's judgement in order that they might "multiply on the earth and be fruitful and increase in number upon it" (Gen. 8.17). The story-line does appeal, nevertheless, as a parallel to judgement and salvation, and to mission, as they pertain to followers of Jesus. We shall return to such matters.)

Group 18, Correspondence in Narrative:

1.4,5
Ἐγένετο Ἰωάννης
[ὁ] βαπτίζων
κηρύσσων βάπτισμα
εἰς ἄφεσιν ἁμαρτιῶν

καὶ ἐβαπτίζοντο ὑπ' αὐτοῦ...
ἐξομολογούμενοι
τὰς ἁμαρτίας αὐτῶν

I read: [α] [.α] <u>Ἐγένετο Ἰωάννης</u>
       [.β] [..α] <u>[ὁ] βαπτίζων</u> [..α'] <u>ἐν τῇ ἐρήμῳ</u>
       [.β'] [..α] καὶ <u>κηρύσσων</u> [..β] <u>βάπτισμα</u>
                                  <u>μετανοίας</u>
       [..β'] εἰς ἄφεσιν <u>ἁμαρτιῶν</u>.
     [β] [.α] καὶ ἐξεπορεύετο πρὸς αὐτὸν
       [.β] πᾶσα ἡ Ἰουδαία χώρα
       [.β'] καὶ οἱ Ἱεροσολυμῖται πάντες,
     [β'] [.α] [..α] <u>καὶ ἐβαπτίζοντο</u> [..α'] <u>ὑπ' αὐτου</u>
       [.β] ἐν τῷ Ἰορδάνῃ ποταμῷ
       [.β'] ἐξομολογούμενοι τὰς <u>ἁμαρτίας</u>
             αὐτῶν.

These occupy [α] and [β'] positons. This rhetorical unit is introduced and concluded with the same material, but it is still a three-part unit, where the *first part* introduces the subject, the *second* develops it, and the *third* completes it, by completing the second. Mark follows his usual *three-step* principle; he is not intentionally creating a chiasm, [α] [β] [α'].

1.16,18
ἀμφιβάλλοντας
καὶ... ἀφέντες τὰ δίκτυα

I read: [α] [.α] [..α] <u>Καὶ παράγων</u>
         [..β] <u>παρὰ τὴν θάλασσαν</u> [..β'] <u>τῆς</u>
                           <u>Γαλιλαίας</u>
       [.β] [..α] <u>εἶδεν Σίμωνα</u>
         [..β] καὶ Ἀνδρέαν [..β'] <u>τὸν ἀδελφὸν</u>
                   <u>Σίμωνος</u>
       [.β'] [..α] ἀμφιβάλλοντας
         [..β] ἐν τῇ θαλάσσῃ· [..β'] ἦσαν γὰρ
               <u>ἁλιεῖς</u>.

THE MARKAN MATRIX

[β] [.α] [..α] καὶ εἶπεν [..β] <u>αὐτοῖς</u> [..β'] ὁ
    Ἰησοῦς,
  [.α'] [..α] <u>Δεῦτε ὀπίσω μου,</u>
    [..β] καὶ ποιήσω ὑμᾶς
    [..β'] γενέσθαι <u>ἁλιεῖς</u> ἀνθρώπων.
[β'] [.α] <u>καὶ εὐθὺς</u>
  [.β] <u>ἀφέντες τὰ δίκτυα</u>
  [.β'] <u>ἠκολούθησαν</u> αὐτῷ.

These occupy [α] and [β'] positons. This rhetorical unit as above, is introduced and concluded with the same material, but it is still also a typical/standard three-part unit. Again, Mark follows his usual *three-step* principle; he is not intentionally creating a chiasm, [α] [β] [α']. The *third* part follows, story-wise, the *second* part. The *first* is introductory.

1.19,20
καὶ αὐτοὺς <u>ἐν τῷ πλοίῳ</u>
καὶ <u>ἀφέντες</u> τὸν πατέρα αὐτῶν Ζεβεδαῖον <u>ἐν τῷ πλοίῳ</u>

See Group 7, 1.19 and 1.20, for my reading. As the other two examples in Group 18 demonstrate, so here too these correspondences occupy [α] and [β'] positions, in linear three-step progressions.

Group 19, Exposition and Discourse:

1.16,17
ἦσαν γὰρ <u>ἁλιεῖς</u>

ποιήσω ὑμᾶς γενέσθαι
<u>ἁλιεῖς</u> ἀνθρώπων

See Group 18, 1.16,18, for my reading. These occupy parts [α] and [β], that is the introductory part and the second and first developing part of the three-part construction, 1.16-18.

Group 20, Narrative and Discourse:

1.5,8
<u>καὶ ἐβαπτίζοντο ὑπ'</u>
<u>αὐτοῦ ἐν τῷ Ἰορδάνῃ</u>
ποταμῷ ἐγὼ ἐβάπτισα
<u>ὑμᾶς ὕδατι</u>

These occupy β[β'] and β'[β'] parts. See the Prologue in full.

1.7,14
Ἔρχεται ὁ
ἰσχυρότερο
μου ὀπίσω μου,
Μετὰ δὲ τὸ
παραδοθῆναι τὸν
Ἰωάννην
ἦλθεν ὁ Ἰησοῦς

My reading is that the first occupies Aβ', the third part of the first section, and the second occupies B'α, the first part of the third section. See the Prologue in full. No chiasm should be read here, even though section A *begins* with reference to "gospel", as does B' twice-over. All Mark's sections are linear ABB'. B' simply completes the whole construction which is begun in A and first developed in B. B' will, therefore, by Mark's method, connect regularly with A in one way or another.

1.8,10
ἐγὼ ἐβάπτισα ὑμᾶς
ὕδατι, αὐτὸς
δὲ βαπτίσει ὑμᾶς
ἐν πνεύματι ἁγίῳ.
ἀναβαίνων ἐκ τοῦ
ὕδατος..
καὶ τὸ πνεῦμα ...
καταβαῖνον εἰς αὐτόν·

Refer to the Prologue in full. The first occupies the closing lines of the first section; the second occupies the second part of the second section. I discern no detailed structural relationship between the two, save that section B well develops from the introductory section A and its own concluding piece.

Group 21, Command and Fulfilment:

1.17,18,20   The call of Jesus, and the response of each pair of brothers, in each presentation, 1.16-18 and 1.19,20, both significantly occupy [β] and [β'] positions in turn.

Group 23, Direct Discourse Preceded by Qualifying Verb:

1.14,15   See Group 5, 1.14,15
κηρύσσων τὸ εὐαγγέλιον
  τοῦ θεου
καὶ λέγων ὅτι Πεπλήρωται
  ὁ καιρὸς

Group 24, Quotation and Comment:

1.2,14
Ἰδοὺ ἀποστέλλω τὸν
ἄγγελόν μου πρὸ
προσώπου σου,
Μετὰ δὲ τὸ
παραδοθῆναι
τὸν Ἰωάννην
ἦλθεν ὁ Ἰησοῦς

The first occupies the opening part of section A; the second occupies the opening part of section B'. See the Prologue in full. I note how both sections B and B' include ἦλθεν [ὁ] Ἰησοῦς in the same position, α[β]. As developing and completing sections they both relate to the introductory section A, but more specifically to each other, in an ABB' scheme.

1.3,4
φωνὴ βοῶντος
ἐν τῇ ἐρήμῳ
Ἐγένετο Ἰωάννης
[ὁ] βαπτίζων ἐν τῇ
ἐρήμῳ καὶ κηρύσσων

Refer to the Prologue in full. The first completes the first part which *is* introductory; the second begins the second part which is the first development.

Group 27, Inclusion:

1.1,15 εὐαγγελίου
εὐαγγελίῳ

For references to "gospel", see not only 1.1,15, but also 1.14. See notes under Group 24, 1.2,14. All sections are linear ABB'; and section A begins with reference to "gospel", as does section B' twice-over; the two connect strongly and so help to define the limits of the Prologue itself. The opening of the closing Section B' echoes the opening of the introductory section A.

1.9,14
ἦλθεν [ὁ] Ἰησοῦς

Refer to Group 24, 1.2,14. The positionings of these two usages are a clear indication of B and B' sectional beginnings. When read with the opening of Section A, we then discover a significant mention of "Jesus" very near the beginnings of all three sections.

Group 30, Doublets:

1.11 and 9.7   We compare:

καὶ φωνὴ ἐγένετο ἐκ τῶν οὐρανῶν, Σὺ εἶ ὁ υἱός μου ὁ ἀγαπητός, ἐν σοὶ εὐδόκησα.
and
καὶ ἐγένετο φωνὴ ἐκ τῆς νεφέλης, Οὗτός ἐστιν ὁ υἱός μου ὁ ἀγαπητός, ἀκούετε αὐτοῦ.

The common words are underlined. In the first, the voice addresses Jesus at his baptism. In the second the voice addresses the disciples present at the transfiguration. Clearly, it may be simply stated that what Mark included in his three-section Prologue cannot have a literary-structural correspondence with anything that is written in any of his four main series. It could only have correspondence with material in an Epilogue, as both Prologue and Epilogue in ancient rhetoric frame the main presentation. We might rather compare 1.10,11 and 16.19. In the first, the heavens are opened and the Spirit descends on Jesus; in the second, from the longer ending, Jesus is taken up into heaven. Herein is a possibility of structural relationship to which we shall return.

1.16-18,19-20 and 2.(13)-14   The calls of the two pairs of brothers and the call of Levi do display common words and other details (that they were each at their work and were called to follow):

Καὶ παράγων παρὰ τὴν θάλασσαν ... εἶδεν ... καὶ εἶπεν αὐτοῖς ... Δεῦτε ὀπίσω μου ...
καὶ εὐθὺς ... ἀφέντες ... ἠκολούθησαν αὐτῷ.

Καὶ ... εἶδεν ... τὸν τοῦ Ζεβεδαίου ... καὶ εὐθὺς ἐκάλεσεν αὐτούς.
καὶ ἀφέντες ... ἀπῆλθον ὀπίσω αὐτοῦ.

Καὶ ἐξῆλθεν πάλιν παρὰ τὴν θάλασσαν· ... καὶ παράγων εἶδεν ... τὸν του Ἀλφαίου ...
καὶ λέγει αὐτω, Ἀκολούθει μοι... καὶ ἀναστὰς ἠκολούθησεν αὐτῷ.

The three stories are clearly closely related. But again, while the first two stories are structurally related in their setting in the Prologue as β and β' sub-sections, because they are included in the Prologue, and the third story is not, the three stories cannot and indeed do not share a structural relationship. Again we have to look to a possible Epilogue for any balance with the Prologue, and in the longer ending there is found in the closing scene several points of contact: Jesus talks with "the eleven" and sends them out into the world to preach the gospel. My reading of the reduced longer ending's conclusion at 16.20a, is emphatic: they went out "and preached everywhere". That is the call and the promise attached ("I will make you fishers of men") become the commission and an actuality.

My case study based on Neirynck's correspondences must now be concluded. Of his forty-six 'dualities', when compared with the structural breakdown of the Prologue which I present:

- 25 link first and second developments, hence they have A<u>BB</u>' relationship;
- 9 link introduction and first development, hence A<u>BB</u>';
- 9 link introduction and second development, hence A<u>BB</u>';

and 3 only display no structural relationship (of which two are *extra* to the Prologue).

It is, of course, particularly telling that over one half of Neirynck's identified dualities correspond in simple BB' relationship. The remainder which link introduction and first development, and introduction and second/completing development are positively significant also. Indeed all three identifications of relationship serve to demonstrate that Mark is creating three-part wholes. This identification of his 'style' of presentation in his Prologue is important. It is the writing method which he adopts for the whole of his Gospel.

We can now review my presentation of the literary-structure of the first twenty verses, in the rhetorical terms in which Tolbert presents her own.

At the beginning of each of the three sections, we identify the anaphora of "Jesus'" name: consider 1.1, annotation Aα[α][.α][..β], 1.9, annotation Bα[β][.α] and 1.14, annotation B'α[β][.α][..α]. We observe that the anaphora is strengthened at 1.9 and 1.14 by the common application of ἦλθεν. The name of Jesus is given the definite article, in the third and final case, and its use suggests emphasis. The name of "Jesus", at the beginning of all three sections in our literary-structural analysis, would appear to be more convincing than the ἐγένετο of Tolbert's three of four sections. "Jesus" is the central figure of Mark's work, beyond any question.

THE DAYS BEGINNING

The relationship between the three sections of the analysis, A, B, Bʿ, can be described. A introduces literally "the beginning" of the Gospel, which is developed by descriptions of John the Baptist's ministry, as it fulfils the scriptures. B continues the story with Jesus coming to John from Galilee: his baptism at the hands of John leads on to the heavenly disclosures and his John-/Moses-/Elijah-like time in the desert. And Bʿ completes the introduction and Prologue: John's imprisonment marks the time of Jesus' return to Galilee and the beginning of his preaching the 'Gospel' (linking back to the opening of A) and his calling followers. A is introductory; it is developed by B, and in turn Bʿ develops B, completing the whole.

Anaphoras are in evidence also at the next level of literary order, in sections β and βʿ: in A, at 1.4 and 1.6, the name, Ἰωάννης; in B, at 1.10 and 12, in the term, Καὶ εὐθὺς; and in Bʿ, at 1.16 and 19, in repetitions: of place; of εἶδεν; and of pairs of brothers who immediately repond to Jesus' call. Close investigation of the lower literary orders shows also, at their levels, many verbal correspondences, hence other anaphoras. At all levels, what is discerned, is the paralleling of β and βʿ, the second two parts, over and against the introductory role of α, the first part of the construction. These are not heavily dependent on verbal paralleling: rather, at the more detailed scales of presentation, [..α] [..β] [..βʿ] and [..α] [..β] [..βʿ], they are more dependent on meaning, syntax and balance. We use the first two full examples at the lowest order, 1.1,2a, to demonstrate this:

Aα [α]¹ [.α] [..α] Ἀρχὴ τοῦ εὐαγγελίου [..β] Ἰησοῦ Χριστοῦ [..βʿ] [υἱοῦ θεοῦ].
²[.αʿ] [..α] καθὼς γέγραπται [..β] ἐν τῷ Ἡσαΐᾳ [..βʿ] τῷ προφήτῃ,

The introductory parts in both lines, parts [..α], are first qualified by [..β] which are, in turn, qualified by [..βʿ]. We could say that [..α] is completed by both [..β] and [..βʿ], though without any repetition of words. Two additional points are worth making as we look at the opening verse. Manuscript evidence for υἱοῦ θεοῦ is by no means unanimous, but literary-structural analysis does strongly suggest it is Markan. Here, we might argue, is indicated the potential of literary-structural analysis for helping settle disputes of this nature.

Additionally, we identify a fine example of parechesis, in line one, a repetition of the same sound in immediately following words. In fact, a welter of them can be identified in the opening piece, and many of them conclude clauses:

Αα [α]¹ [.α] [..α] ᾽Αρχὴ τοῦ εὐαγγελίου [..β] ᾽Ιησοῦ Χριστοῦ [..β'] [υἱοῦ θεοῦ].
    ²[.α'] [..α] καθὼς γέγραπται [..β] ἐν τῷ ᾽Ησαΐᾳ [..β'] τῷ προφήτῃ,
  [β] [.α] ᾽Ιδοὺ [.β] [..α] ἀποστέλλω τὸν ἄγγελόν μου [..α'] πρὸ προσώπου σου, [.β'] ὃς κατασκευάσει τὴν ὁδόν σου·
[β']³[.α] [..α] φωνὴ βοῶντος [..α'] ἐν τῇ ἐρήμῳ, [.β]῾Ετοιμάσατε τὴν ὁδὸν κυρίου, [.β'] εὐθείας ποιεῖτε τὰς τρίβους αὐτοῦ.

It would appear that Mark has given thought not only to what he was going to write, but also to how it was going to sound. Reworking the LXX and MT versions of scriptures, which he chose to knit together and to ascribe to Isaiah, he has also applied a rhetorical device which would enhance, for his audience, his opening presentation.

Another feature we observe here in this Prologue is that at the beginnings and endings of the sectional constructions are shortened presentations, at the fourth level of literary order, either of one part or two parts. We first consider those at the beginnings of the sections, which attract the annotations α[α][.α] and [.α']:

1.1,2a: Αα[α]¹[.α] [..α] ᾽Αρχὴ τοῦ εὐαγγελίου [..β] ᾽Ιησοῦ Χριστοῦ
          [..β'] [υἱοῦ θεοῦ].
          ²[.α'] [..α] καθὼς γέγραπται [..β] ἐν τῷ ᾽Ησαΐᾳ [..β'] τῷ προφήτῃ,
1.9:   Βα[α]⁹[.α] Καὶ ἐγένετο [.α'] ἐν ἐκείναις ταῖς ἡμέραις
1.14:   Β'α[α]¹⁴[.α] Μετὰ δὲ [.α'] τὸ παραδοθῆναι τὸν ᾽Ιωάννην

At the conclusions of the first two sections, which attract the annotations β'[β'][.α] and [.α'], we consider the following shorter presentations:

1.8   [β']⁸[.β] [..α] ἐγὼ ἐβάπτισα ὑμᾶς [..α'] ὕδατι,
        [.β'] [..α] αὐτὸς δὲ βαπτίσει ὑμᾶς [..α'] ἐν πνεύματι ἁγίῳ.
1.13b [β'] [.α] καὶ ἦν μετὰ τῶν θηρίων, [.α'] καὶ οἱ ἄγγελοι διηκόνουν αὐτῷ.

(We note also at the beginning of both [β] and [β'], in 1.13a and b, the common use of καὶ ἦν.)

THE DAYS BEGINNING

And at the completion of the third section and of the Prologue itself, we actually discover a double-use of [.α] [.αˊ] presentation, which we might describe as emphatic of the end of the presentation, beginning at both βˊ[β][.α] and βˊ[βˊ][.α]:

1.20a [β] ²⁰[.α] καὶ εὐθὺς [.αˊ] <u>ἐκάλεσεν αὐτούς</u>.
1.20b [βˊ] [.α] [..α] καὶ <u>ἀφέντες</u> τὸν πατέρα αὐτῶν Ζεβεδαῖον
       [..β] ἐν τῷ πλοίῳ [..βˊ] μετὰ τῶν μισθωτῶν
       [.αˊ] [..α] ἀπῆλθον [..αˊ] ὀπίσω αὐτοῦ.

At 1.17, we observe the only, other [.α] [.αˊ] presentation, that is at the fourth level of order in the Prologue. Everywhere else, we otherwise discern an [.α] [.β] [.βˊ] structure. It would seem that in place of the anastrophe for which Tolbert looked, at the conclusions and beginnings of sections in juxtaposition, is generally a structural adjustment that would "sound" (without repetitions of words, but by changes of rhythm) the conclusion of one section and the opening of the one following. The rhyming of lines at the closures of Acts in Shakespearean plays might be representative of another, similar rhetorical style which has survived from Greco-Roman literature.

At the second level of literary order, of the Prologue's sections, concerning the parts: α,β,βˊ, we can now record what we observe of the balance of content in the sections:

In the first section, 1.1-8: in α, it is the prophetic scriptures which find their fulfilment; in β, it is through John's baptising and preaching work; and in βˊ, it is in his pointing beyond himself to another.

In the second section, 1.9-13: in α, it is Jesus' baptism which leads, in the first place, to β's heavenly disclosures and Jesus' receiving of the Spirit and, in the second, in βˊ, to the Spirit's sending Jesus into the desert.

In the third section, 1.14-20: in α, it is Jesus' arrival in Galilee and the beginning of his mission which leads, in the first place, in β, to his calling two brothers by the lakeside, and in the second, in βˊ, a little further, along the shore, to calling two more brothers.

In summary, the contents of the introduction's three sections hold together, on the theme of beginning(s). Further, John and Jesus are fully compared and contrasted. It is the beginning of Jesus' mission, after the imprisonment of John, which completes this beginning of the gospel. He is preaching the Gospel of God (1.14) and is calling followers. Repentance and belief, immediacy of following, these are the true responses. The first twenty verses, we may conclude therefore, describe fully and adequately for Mark (and presumably, therefore, for his Church) the background and beginning to the Days of Jesus' messianic mission: "the time is fulfilled", the waiting is over.

We refer to a classic essay on stylistics, in which Ian Watt demonstrated that all of the major themes in Henry James's "The Ambassadors" could be found in its first paragraph alone. As many commentators have pointed out, finding the themes depended upon having read all of "The Ambassadors" and not just the first paragraph.[34] It is also the case with Mark's Prologue, but not only for identifying the main themes: the Prologue demonstrates also Mark's presentation style which he applies throughout his gospel. Whether in its ABB', simple form, or in compounds of the same, ABB'/ABB', ABB'/ABB'/ABB', etc., he uses the same basic method of writing for his individual "Days", and he always completes his successions of three-part wholes before proceeding to another "Day's" telling.

And finally, completing the structural argument, we note that one of the earliest manuscripts lends some support also to the view that 1.1-20 is Mark's opening presentation. Codex Vaticanus (B) clearly exhibits its first edentation[35], a sure sign of a recognised break in the text, at 1.21. This edentation is a single protruding letter in the left hand margin (which has its parallel in our traditional, paragraph signifying indentation, from the left hand margin); it is also preceded in the line above, by a large space, in an incomplete line of characters. Furthermore, other spaces (much smaller) appear prior to 1.4, 9, 14, 16 and 19, that is, at each of the major sub-divisions of the text as we identify (1.1, 9 and 14) and at three of the six minor sub-divisions (1.4, 16 and 19). Codex Vaticanus, it might be argued, has preserved a number of Mark's signifiers of structure, but demonstrates, nevertheless, a stage in the process of loss of his

---

[34] I. Watt, "The First Paragraph of *The Ambassadors*: An Explication", in *Contemporary Essays on Style: Rhetoric, Linguistics, and Criticism*, eds. G. Love and M. Payne, Scott, Foresman and Co., Glenview, Ill., 1969, pp.266-283.

[35] Codex Vaticanus displays only nine edentations in all: compare: Sinaiticus which has 319 and Alexandrinus which has 316.

signifiers, as one copy after another was made from the one which preceded it.

This basically three-section, twenty-verse introduction, it may be judged only very broadly, covered a minimum of fifty days. To the forty days of Jesus' sojourn in the desert we add the days (unstated by Mark) which John spent in the desert before Jesus, and the days (also unstated) between the end of Jesus' forty days in the desert and John's arrest. What follows thereafter, from 1.21, is a narrative which has as its framework a presentation of twenty-eight individual "Days", through the telling of which Mark captures the full extent and implication of Jesus' mission, for those who read and those who hear his gospel. It is not as such a day-to-day account (in consecutive terms) as we shall see; Jesus is no 'twenty-eight day wonder'. In Mark's reporting of "Days" he makes reference to many more days than he actually tells, by report and by suggestion. In his introductory pieces to three of his tellings of "Days" in particular (at 2.1ff, 8.1ff. and 9.2ff), he makes it plain that there are other days to Jesus' mission which he does not report. Simply, Mark adopts, from 1.21, a particular method of presentation, which he employs to the end of his narrative, 16.8. We will discuss these matters much more, as I present the evidence.

Chapter Three
The First Series of Seven Days (1.21-5.43):

Day One: 1.21-38:

Arguably, the Day is 1.21-34, 1.21-38 or 1.21-39.

Drury[1] sees the day, 1.21-38, as "some twenty-four hours from morning to morning". Nineham[2] writes of 1.21-34 as "a specimen day" and of vv.35-39 that "we are meant to take this incident closely with what precedes - as a sort of appendage to the "specimen day"[3]. Wilson titles the day, 1.21-39, "A Day in the Life of Jesus"[4]. Hooker speaks of 1.21-39 as a "closely knit series of events"[5] (but see below). Schweizer treats 1.21-28, 29-31 and 32-39 as separate stories[6], though he suggests that it is likely "that vv.23-26, 29-32, 34a, 35-38 had been told in a connected form before Mark"[7]. Pesch discerns a pre-Markan tradition also, and terms it "a day in Jesus' ministry at Capernaum"; though he estimates that it is 1.21a, 29-39[8]. Kuhn sees 1.16-39 as pre-Markan[9].

The Day begins: Καὶ εἰσπορεύονται εἰς Καφαρναούμ. καὶ εὐθὺς τοῖς σάββασιν εἰσελθὼν εἰς τὴν συναγωγὴν ἐδίδασκεν. The day's telling begins with an introductory, 'dramatic' historical present tense[10]. For Nineham[11], "the day opens after an unspecified

---

[1] Drury, *The Literary Guide...*, p.410.
[2] Nineham, *Saint Mark*, pp.73,82.
[3] Nineham, *Saint Mark*, p.83.
[4] R McL. Wilson, "Mark", *Peake's Commentary on the Bible*, Eds. Black & Rowley, Nelson, Sunbury-on Thames,1977, p.801; see also Taylor, *The Gospel...*, p.146.
[5] Hooker, *The Gospel...*, p.77.
[6] Schweizer, *The Good News...*, pp.49-56.
[7] Schweizer, *The Good News...*, p.50.
[8] Pesch, *Das Markusevangelium...*, p.67.
[9] H-W. Kuhn, *Ältere Sammlungen im Markusevangelium*, Studien zur Umwelt des Neuen Testaments No. 8, Vandenhoeck & Ruprecht, Göttingen, 1971.
[10] H. St. John Thackeray, *The Septuagint and Jewish Worship: A Study in Origins*, 2nd Edn., The Schweich Lectures, Oxford University Press, London, 1923, pp.20-22: speaking of the dramatic type of historical present, he says (p.21), "The tense as a rule is ... "dramatic" in the sense that it serves to introduce new scenes in the drama. It heralds the arrival of a new character or a change of locality or marks a turning-point in the march of events... The main

interval." For Schweizer[12], Mark here begins a new unit (i.e. vv.21-28); "not only is nothing said of any disciples accompanying Jesus, but most important is the fact that the events in vv.16-20 could not have happened on the Sabbath, when fishing and the repairing of nets were strictly forbidden." Schweizer's method of argument may be correct in terms of distinguishing the break between vv.20 and 21, but as all four disciples (who are called in 1.16-20) make their re-appearance in 1.29-31, the first part of his argument appears too strong. Also we may note that he undermines his own argument somewhat, and shows perhaps a little too much confidence, in considering v.32. He says of the verse that it "has little significance unless the setting sun marks the end of the Sabbath, so that from that time on it was permissible, once more, to carry the sick." He says, "It does not have this meaning for Mark, since whenever he refers to Jewish customs he explains them to his readers (7.3f.)" We note, nevertheless, that at 1.32 Mark has at least defined "evening" for his audience by the phrase, "when the sun set". One might deduce from this that Mark assumed his audience would understand the significance of this moment of the day, for the Jew.

Contrary to what Schweizer suggests, Mark does have an understanding of the Hebrew/Palestinian Day which begins with *sunset* and which in the case of the *beginning* of a sabbath involves new obligations for the Jews (see 15.42). He would seem to have a comprehensive grasp of its structure. He is informed about the four watches of the night and the twelve hours of daylight, for on the third day on which Jesus is in the Temple, Mark records all four watches: late, midnight, cock-crowing and early (13.35), and on the day of Jesus' crucifixion, he refers to the third, the sixth and the ninth hours of daylight (15.25, 33 and 34). Bultmann[13] may think that Mark begins a new day at 14.17 with the first watch of the night, that 14.27-65 takes up the second, 14.66-72 the third, and the fourth (πρωΐ) begins at 15.1, but, given Mark's own evidence, while he understands the Hebrew/Palestinian Day to begin with *sunset*, he

---

function is... to introduce a date, a new scene..., in other words a fresh paragraph in the narrative." For a discussion of the historical present, see under Day Two.
[11] Nineham, *Saint Mark*, p.73.
[12] Schweizer, *The Good News...*, p.502.
[13] Bultmann, *The History...*, p.341.

chooses to present his gospel scheme of "Days" in terms of the civil day which is qualified as from *sunrise* to (just before) *sunrise*[14].

The key question is then, what does Mark mean by καὶ εὐθὺς τοῖς σάββασιν, in 1.21? Does he mean 'from the evening of the day' (thus following the Jewish Day, as beginning with sunset), or does he mean 'beginning with daylight' (i.e. from sunrise, so following the "civil day" as qualified by beginning with sunrise)? It is clearly the second of these; the contents of 1.21-38 demand this understanding because the action is continuous through the daylight hours to the evening and the hours of darkness (1.32, Ὀψίας δὲ γενομένης) and well into the night (1.35, Καὶ πρωῒ ἔννυχα λίαν). As was stated in the Introduction, Mark chose to present *all* his Days' reports for his Gospel according to the "civil day" which is qualified as beginning with sunrise and ending just before the following sunrise. We will keep on returning to this matter because it is a most important feature in the literary-structural analysis of Mark's Gospel.

Linking the first two sentences of this Day's report, Hooker[15] expunges any possible reference to 'the disciples' by her translation "And he entered Capernaum", so substituting "he" for "they" for which there is no textual support. (She sees vv.21-28 as a separate unit, also vv.29-31, 32-34, 35-39, 40-45, and so on: twelve units in all from 1.14 to 3.6.) The literal translation "And they entered into Capernaum" in itself points to the coupling of 1.21-28 to what follows from 1.29. This coupling can be suggested because the four who were called by Jesus to follow him (in 1.16-20), who together with Jesus justify the "they" of 1.21, are all named in vv.29-31. In 1.32-34 no disciples are mentioned, but in 1.35-38 Simon is. It is not until 3.16, on Day Five, when Jesus is choosing the twelve, that Simon is mentioned again.

Mark may well have "revised extensively the style of the tradition he received"[16], for the overall outcome of his presentation has its unity as a Day primarily in the temporal references at 1.21 ("And immediately on the sabbath"), at 1.32 ("And when evening came") and at 1.35 ("And rising very early in the night"). Consider also Mark's references to 'place': in 1.21 ("And immediately on the

---

[14] See note 82, in the Introduction.
[15] Hooker, *The Gospel...*, p.61.
[16] Schweizer, *The Good News...*, p.54.

sabbath entering into the synagogue"), in 1.23 ("And immediately there was in their synagogue") and in 1.29 ("And immediately leaving the synagogue"). References to both time and place bind the separate units into a whole. Consider also the day-time exorcism and the day-time healing and the night-time multiplications of both, and the common emphatic editorial record of Jesus' commands to the demons to silence (1.24 and v.34) because "they knew" him. The presentation following, of the literary-structure of Day One, shows how well Mark created a balanced structure of two halves. At the beginning of the first half Jesus enters the synagogue: at the beginning of the second Jesus leaves the synagogue. We will discuss these balancing features below after we have rehearsed the arguments for establishing Mark's first day's conclusion.

1.35a requires discussion: Καὶ πρωῒ ἔννυχα λίαν ἀναστὰς ἐξῆλθεν... Schweizer uses the Good News translation "Very early the next morning, long before daylight, Jesus got up and left the house..." Hooker translates similarly, "And early in the morning, while it was still dark, he got up, left the house..."[17]. Clearly, both Schweizer and Hooker (and others), on this basis, appear to argue that a new day starts at this juncture. In our normal, Western parlance it is surely the case, because for us a new day starts at midnight, but in Mark's terms a new Day of his reporting does not start until dawn. We ask then, how should we translate and interpret πρωῒ ἔννυχα λίαν, which Cranfield characterises as "odd but vivid"[18] and which Drury, as above mentioned, sees as prefiguring 16.2?[19]

Problems of translation and, therefore, of interpretation, in these matters, are not solved simply by recourse to Greek, which here is ambiguous in its use of πρωῒ. The word can mean "early", but it can also be understood to be the technical term for the fourth watch of the night. The problem occurs most acutely for Hooker at 16.2. Here, she translates καὶ λίαν πρωῒ τῇ μιᾷ τῶν σαββάτων ἔρχονται ἐπὶ τὸ μνημεῖον ἀνατείλαντος τοῦ ἡλίου, "And very early in the morning on the first day of the week they came to the tomb just after

---

[17] Hooker, *The Gospel...*, p.75.
[18] C.E.B. Cranfield, *The Gospel according to St Mark*, gen. ed. C.F.D. Moule, The Cambridge Greek Testament Commentary, Cambridge University Press, Cambridge, 1959, rev. 1977, p.88.
[19] Drury, *The Literary Guide...*, p.410; see also Hooker, *The Gospel...*, p.76.

sunrise"[20]. She points out an inconsistency between the first and last temporal parts of the sentence. For her, the first means "in the early hours before dawn". She is determined to see the expression in its technical usage, but it cannot be squared with "just after sunrise". She notes that attempts were made "at an early stage to tidy up this anomaly by altering one phrase or the other" but explains weakly, "probably Mark was not being as precise as his critics". Rather, the explanation would seem to be that nowhere outside of 6.48 and 13.35 does Mark appear to have written about the fourth watch, and nowhere outside of 13.35, in a listing of the night watches, does he use πρωΐ in the technical sense. We note that at 6.48 he might have written πρωΐ, but he in fact writes, "at about the fourth watch of the night...". His use of πρωΐ elsewhere (in 11.20; 15.1; and 16.2) describes the time soon after dawn and, therefore, defines the beginning of new days.

1.35a may translate literally and perfectly acceptably therefore, in Mark's terms, as "And very early in the night...". Mark makes no reference to any watch; it may have been the fourth watch or it may have been the third. (It is unlikely that any implication is intended of either the second or the first: 1.32-34 records Jesus beginning his healing-work at sunset, and he healed many; and when he rises (1.35) it is surely from sleep.) Rather, Mark qualifies πρωΐ by ἔννυχα λίαν. Compare then 16.2 καὶ λίαν πρωΐ, but note the contrast: there is no reference to "night" in this verse. In the telling of the Gospel's last Day, the "night" lies between 16.1 and 16.2; Mark's report of the Day is 16.2-8. 16.1 is purely introductory to that report, in that it gives the names of the women, and the reason for their going to the tomb.

We continue with our consideration of the text, and note that Schweizer[21] sees vv.32-39 as a whole: it is surely the case as Mark presents, that knowing who Jesus was (v.34) and what he was present to do (v.38) are issues which are indissolubly joined. (See also, as above, Schweizer's suggestion that vv.23-26, 29-32, 34a, 35-38 were connected before Mark edited them.) Concerning verses 1.35-39, Taylor[22] says the passage "derives its significance from (the) three

---

[20] Hooker, *The Gospel...*, pp.382-384.
[21] Schweizer, *The Good News*, p.54.
[22] Taylor, *The Gospel...*, p.182, my italics.

preceding stories... *The story ends* with the words of Jesus, 'Let us go elsewhere into the neighbouring towns, that I may preach there also, for to this end came I forth' (1.38)." The case can be put, therefore, in terms of temporal connections (1.21, 32 and 35) and in matters of place and related content, for understanding Mark's First Day as continuous from 1.21 to 38/39. And Taylor himself thinks there is a good case for ending the passage at 1.38.

Where does 1.39 belong, at the end of the first Day, or the beginning of the following Day? We refer to Taylor again, who appears to be contradicting himself: "The statement in v.39 is a summary passage which rounds off the section and prepares the way for what follows." We have three choices before us: it may have been in Mark's mind that it performed as a conclusion to his First Day; it may have been in his mind that it was introductory to the second; or it may have been his deliberate link between the two. Both Hooker[23] and the Good News Version which Schweizer uses read, "So he travelled... " Nineham uses the RSV, "And he went throughout ..." Hooker and Schweizer have strengthened the link between 1.38 and 39 by their acceptance of a looser translation of καί. And there is another consideration: the verb is either ἦλθεν or ἦν. The latter has the support of ACDW and the great majority of MSS. Cranfield[24] suggests that ἦν is probably to be preferred. It is "supported by the Lukan parallel; the periphrastic imperfect is characteristic of Mark; and ἦλθεν looks like a grammatical improvement due to εἰς (which if ἦν is read, is equivalent to ἐν)." The choice is an awkward one. On balance, as the earlier and more reliable witnesses read καὶ ἦλθεν and other new days begin similarly (5.1 and 9.33, καὶ ἦλθεν; 6.1 and 8.27, καὶ ἐξῆλθεν; 8.22 and 10.46, καὶ ἔρχονται), v.39 more likely begins the next Day in Mark's telling, and v.38 does more likely end the telling of this first Day, with Jesus speaking (as in the days ending at 2.22, 8.20, 26, 9.1, 50, 10.31, 45 and 13.37) and with emphasis (as in the days ending at 3.6, 4.41, 5.20, 43, 6.52, 7.30, 37, 9.29, 10.52, 14.11, 72 and 16.8). Additionally, 1.35-38 (the ending of Day One) compares for content

---

[23] Hooker, *The Gospel...*, p.75.
[24] Cranfield, *The Gospel...*, p.90.

with 1.45 (the ending of Day Two): this will be presented under the examination of Day Two, 1.39-45.

We come to the point now where the literary-structure of Day One as a whole can be presented. We first summarise the literary-structure of Day One as we will do for each Day. It is properly described as having an ABB /ABB ʽ form. Mark well created a balanced structure of two halves: in part A of the first, Jesus enters the synagogue; in part A of the second, Jesus leaves the synagogue. In the first half, and series ABBʽ, part A (1.21,22) is introductory of geographical place, day and time of day (καὶ εὐθὺς τοῖς σάββασιν), movement into locality, the activity of the main character, Jesus, and the response of the people and their reason for their response. Part B (1.23-25), in the same setting (and connected by Καὶ εὐθὺς), first introduces a new character into the scene who because of what he says evokes a response from Jesus. Part Bʽ (1.26-28) completes B by first reporting the effect of Jesus' response and then two outcomes. In the second series ABBʽ, part A (1.29-31), linking with the setting of the first series (by reference to 'synagogue' and by καὶ εὐθὺς), establishes the new setting and introduces a new character to whose need Jesus responds. Part B (1.32-34), in the same setting, first establishes the new time of the day and then introduces new characters to whose needs Jesus responds. Part Bʽ (1.35-38) first establishes the new time, the movement to a new locale of the principal character, his being sought, and his response to those who find him.

The first half (and three-part series) concludes with Jesus' being reported in all Galilee (1.28); the second half (and three-part series) establishes that Jesus is then known by everyone in Capernaum because of what he had been saying and doing (see 1.33 and 37), but his purpose was in other local towns too.

The literary structure of Day One is viewed as:

A α ²¹[a] Καὶ εἰσπορεύονται [α'] εἰς Καφαρναούμ.
β [a] καὶ εὐθὺς τοῖς σάββασιν [β] εἰσελθὼν εἰς τὴν συναγωγὴν [β'] ἐδίδασκεν.
β' ²²[a] [.α] καὶ ἐξεπλήσσοντο [..α'] ἐπὶ τῇ διδαχῇ αὐτοῦ, [α'] [.α] ἦν γὰρ διδάσκων αὐτοὺς [.β] ὡς ἐξουσίαν ἔχων [.β'] καὶ οὐχ ὡς οἱ γραμματεῖς.
B α ²³[a] Καὶ εὐθὺς [β] ἦν ἐν τῇ συναγωγῇ αὐτῶν [β'] ἄνθρωπος ἐν πνεύματι ἀκαθάρτῳ.
β [a] [.α] καὶ ἀνέκραξεν [.α'] ²⁴λέγων, [α'] [.α] [..α] Τί ἡμῖν [..β] καὶ σοί, [..β'] Ἰησου Ναζαρηνέ; [.β] ἦλθες ἀπολέσαι ἡμᾶς; [.β'] [..α] οἶδά σε τίς εἶ, [..α'] ὁ ἅγιος τοῦ θεοῦ.
β' ²⁵[a] [.α] καὶ ἐπετίμησεν αὐτῷ ὁ Ἰησοῦς [.α'] λέγων, [β] Φιμώθητι [β'] [.α] καὶ ἔξελθε [.α'] ἐξ αὐτοῦ.
B' α ²⁶[a] καὶ σπαράξαν αὐτὸν τὸ πνεῦμα τὸ ἀκάθαρτον [β] καὶ φωνῆσαν φωνῇ μεγάλῃ [β'] [.α] ἐξῆλθεν [.α'] ἐξ αὐτοῦ.
β ²⁷[a] [.α] καὶ ἐθαμβήθησαν ἅπαντες, [.β] ὥστε συζητεῖν πρὸς ἑαυτοὺς [.β'] λέγοντας, [α'] [.α] Τί ἐστιν τοῦτο; [.β] [..α] διδαχὴ καινὴ [..α'] κατ· ἐξουσίαν· [.β'] [..α] καὶ τοῖς πνεύμασι τοῖς ἀκαθάρτοις ἐπιτάσσει, [..α'] καὶ ὑπακούουσιν αὐτῷ.
β' ²⁸[a] καὶ ἐξῆλθεν ἡ ἀκοὴ αὐτοῦ [β] εὐθὺς πανταχοῦ [β'] εἰς ὅλην τὴν περίχωρον τῆς Γαλιλαίας.

A α ²⁹[a] Καὶ εὐθὺς [β] ἐκ τῆς συναγωγῆς ἐξελθόντες [β'] [.α] ἦλθον [.β] εἰς τὴν οἰκίαν Σίμωνος καὶ Ἀνδρέου [.β'] μετὰ Ἰακώβου καὶ Ἰωάννου.
β ³⁰[a] ἡ δὲ πενθερὰ Σίμωνος κατέκειτο [β] πυρέσσουσα, [β'] καὶ εὐθὺς λέγουσιν αὐτῷ περὶ αὐτῆς.
β' ³¹[a] [.α] καὶ προσελθὼν [.β] ἤγειρεν αὐτὴν [.β'] κρατήσας τῆς χειρός· [β] [.α] καὶ ἀφῆκεν αὐτὴν [.α'] ὁ πυρετός, [β'] καὶ διηκόνει αὐτοῖς.
B α ³² [a] Ὀψίας δὲ γενομένης, [β] ὅτε ἔδυ ὁ ἥλιος, [β'] [.α] ἔφερον πρὸς Αὐτὸν [.β] πάντας τοὺς κακῶς ἔχοντας [.β'] καὶ τοὺς δαιμονιζομένους.
β ³³[a] καὶ ἦν ὅλη ἡ πόλις [α'] ἐπισυνηγμένη πρὸς τὴν θύραν.
β' ³⁴[a] καὶ ἐθεράπευσεν πολλοὺς κακῶς ἔχοντας ποικίλαις νόσοις, [β] καὶ δαιμόνια πολλὰ ἐξέβαλεν, [β'] [.α] καὶ οὐκ ἤφιεν λαλεῖν τα δαιμόνια, [.α'] ὅτι ᾔδεισαν αὐτόν.
B' α ³⁵[a] [.α] Καὶ πρωῒ ἔννυχα λίαν [.β] ἀναστὰς [.β'] ἐξῆλθεν [β] [.α] καὶ ἀπῆλθεν [.α'] εἰς ἔρημον τόπον [β'] κἀκεῖ προσηύχετο.
β ³⁶[a] [.α] καὶ κατεδίωξεν αὐτὸν Σίμων [.α'] καὶ οἱ μετ᾿ αὐτοῦ, ³⁷[β] καὶ εὗρον αὐτὸν [β'] [.α] καὶ λέγουσιν αὐτῷ [.α'] ὅτι Πάντες ζητοῦσίν σε.
β' ³⁸[a] καὶ λέγει αὐτοῖς, [α'] [.α] Ἄγωμεν ἀλλαχοῦ εἰς τὰς ἐχομένας κωμοπόλεις, [.β] ἵνα καὶ ἐκεῖ κηρύξω· [.β'] εἰς τοῦτο γὰρ ἐξῆλθον.

where: A, B, B˖ and in turn, α, β, β˖, [α], [β], [β˖], and so on, denote three-part series and where the annotation α, β, β˖ is deliberately preferred to the possible α, β, γ for the reason that the first part is introductory, the second is the first development and the third part is the second and concluding development, whereby the third part qualifies and completes the second part, and so completes the whole. At the lower levels of literary order, as was stated in the Introduction, there are also parallelisms to identify, represented by [α] [α˖] and [.α] [.α˖]. The most significant words, for the purpose of structural analysis, are underlined.

Further, in the Introduction is a preview of the more detailed structural breakdown and method of annotation; 1.21-22 provided the example.[25] All the parts which make up the whole of this Day's report perform in very similar ways. To present detailed arguments for them all, and for all the constructions of all the Days of Mark's narrative, is judged impossible; it would require much more space than is available. However, further explications will be shared as we proceed, as evidence of Mark's consistency and as an aid to understanding his rhetorical method.

Mark's rhetorical style is simple, tightly-controlled and rhythmic. It will be demonstrated that he repeats it consistently for all his presentations of the "Days". Here, it can be stated that this discovery of his "compositional-structure", because it confirms "Day" presentation completion (in this case, in the completed composite form of ABB /ABB˖), is as important a signifier in the setting of the parameters of "Days" as the temporal, geographical, locational, verbal and material evidence, which Mark also supplies.

Day Two: 1.39-45:

We begin with the consideration that the Day's telling which follows that of Day Two clearly begins at 2.1, Καὶ εἰσελθὼν πάλιν εἰς Καφαρναοὺμ δι᾿ ἡμερῶν. It follows, therefore, that 1.45 ends Mark's telling of Day Two. In this closing verse to his second Day we see features as found in 1.35-38, the closing verses to the first

---

[25] See pages 39-41.

Day. In both, Jesus chooses "desert places", and just as he was known by "everyone" in Capernaum (at the end of the first Day) so he is now known in "all" Galilee (at the end of the second Day). Day One tells both where and how Jesus first became known and where and how popular knowledge of him increased; Day Two continues the telling, presenting a further stage in the same process. The incident of the healing of the leper and the leper's disobedience in telling all, added to the summary account of Jesus' continuing work in Galilee (1.39), leads to the result described in v.45.

We continue with consideration of 1.39. In this opening verse to the second Day, we see that what Mark says took place in Capernaum is what all of Galilee experienced in turn: previously they had only heard (see 1.28). Hooker writes, "It matters little, therefore, whether the closely knit series of events from v.21 to v.39 are understood as they have often been understood, as the recollection of the first sabbath that the (four) disciples spent with Jesus, or whether we interpret the links as artificial, and see the narrative as an account of a typical sabbath; whether or not this particular series of events took place in Capernaum during one particular period of 24 hours, Mark uses them to present to us the impact Jesus made, not only there, but in the whole of Galilee."[26]. This comment, of course, bridges both Days One and Two: it is in the report of Day Two that we learn how it is that people came to Jesus from all over Galilee. 1.39 summarises Jesus' mission in Galilee and v.45 details the outcomes of the Day's specific incident. But, how is 1.39 to be viewed as introductory to vv.40-45?

Clearly 1.39 describes activities over many days, even maybe several weeks (κηρύσσων εἰς τὰς συναγωγὰς αὐτῶν suggests the possibility of a number of sabbaths). The verse is a summary with which Mark defines the context for this new Day's report. At the beginnings of other days Mark also defines or infers a passage of time between his last Day's report and his next Day's report in his introductory, scene-setting, context-establishing opening pieces. We note the temporal links which he defines clearly: 2.1 "after some days"; 2.23 "And it came to pass on the sabbath" (we note, it is likely not consecutive with the Day before); 8.1,2 "In those days.... three

---

[26] Hooker, *The Gospel...*, p.77.

days"; 9.2 "And after six days" (we list further examples: 11.12; 11.20; 14.1; 14.12; 15.1 and 16.1,2).

Further, Bultmann noticed how Mark employs geographical links which behave temporally[27]: all these that are of my listing below begin new Days of Mark's telling:

1.21 "And they entered Capernaum" (we have noted above its disjunction with preceding verses, for reasons of sabbath prohibitions);

6.30 "And the apostles assemble to Jesus" (they have been places and carried out their mission - the whole verse behaves like that of 1.39; the parenthetical placing of the story about John's death, from 6.14-29, strengthens the impression that days have passed[28]);

7.24 "And from there rising up he went away" (see 10.1, which is very similar: notably, these begin the middle Days of the two middle Series of seven Days, 7.24-30 and 10.1-16); one was written with the other to hand/in mind);

7.31 "And again, going out of the city of Tyre he came through Sidon to the sea of Galilee";

8.22 "And they came to Bethsaida";

8.27 "And Jesus went forth and his disciples to the villages of Caesarea Philippi";

9.30 "And from there going forth they passed through Galilee";

9.33 "And they came to Capernaum";

10.1 "And from there rising up he went into the territory of Judaea and beyond the Jordan";

10.17 "And as he went forth into the way"; and

10.46 "And they came to Jericho. And as he was leaving Jericho".

And at the beginning of other Days, we note that Mark employs a combination of geographical and temporal links:

1.21 "And they entered Capernaum. And immediately on the sabbath";

3.7 "And Jesus with his disciples departed to the sea and a large crowd from Galilee followed" (a temporal change is inferred, for

---

[27] Bultmann, *The History...*, p.340.
[28] Inserting a unit of tradition "within another" is said to be a particularly Markan feature, found elsewhere: see 3.22-30; 5.25-34; 11.15-19; 14.3-9, but see our discussions on these matters, under the appropriate "Days".

with 3.6 the sabbath day's activities conclude. Compare Schweizer's argument on the temporal change between 1.20 and 21 above);

5.1 "And they came to the other side of the sea into the country of the Gerasenes" (after a "night crossing"); 5.21 and 6.53 are similar to 5.1; and

6.1f. "And he went from there and came into his own country... and when the sabbath came".

The content of 1.39, reflective of many of Mark's opening verses of accounts of Days, gives both a temporal and a geographical context to the content which begins at 1.40. The verse also provides a material context for the record of a new day, for Jesus is journeying and missioning as he goes. Hooker is surely mistaken in saying that this episode is "introduced abruptly into the narrative"[29], though she is correct in saying that "it is not part of the close complex of stories which is just ended". Clearly, she does not see the significance of 1.39 as introductory to 1.40-45.

We consider also the further matter of Mark's predilection for a compositional/grammatical feature much repeated in the openings to his presentations of Days[30]. 1.39,40 reads:

<u>καὶ ἦλθεν</u> κηρύσσων εἰς τὰς συναγωγὰς αὐτῶν εἰς ὅλην τὴν Γαλιλαίαν καὶ τὰ δαιμόνια ἐκβάλλων.
<u>καὶ ἔρχεται</u> πρὸς αὐτὸν λεπρὸς παρακαλῶν αὐτὸν [καὶ γονυπετῶν] καὶ λέγων αὐτῷ ὅτι 'Εὰν θέλῃς δύνασαί με καθαρίσαι...

We observe: 1.39 "And he went..."/1.40 "And comes to him a leper...", which in 1.40 is a literal translation of a historical present. In the whole of the Gospel, we encounter in all 151 historical presents.[31] Because they are "highly characteristic of Mark's style"[32], we devote a little space to considering them.

In note 10 above, in our discussion of Day One, we referred to Thackeray's observation that the "tense as a rule is... 'dramatic' in the sense that it serves to introduce new scenes in the drama. It heralds the arrival of a new character or a change of locality or marks a

---

[29] Hooker, *The Gospel...*, p.78.
[30] Best, *Disciples...*, p.50, and note 10.
[31] J.C. Hawkins, *Horae Synopticae*, Clarendon Press, Oxford, 2nd edn. 1909, pp.143-149.
[32] See Taylor, on vocabulary, syntax and style, *The Gospel...*, item 5, pp.46f.

turning-point in the march of events... The main function is... to introduce a date, a new scene..., in other words a fresh paragraph in the narrative." Writing specifically on Mark, he says, "(λέγει excluded) they are used in a precisely similar way to introduce new scenes and characters... *They are a feature which to the observant reader serves to divide the gospel* into rough paragraphs."[33] Standard grammars and recent writers describe this as part of the "discourse function" of the historical present.[34] For Fanning, historical presents are used in the New Testament on the whole "to bring a past occurrence into immediate view, portraying the event as though it occurs before the readers' eyes." He adds, "Although the historical present appears in different specific patterns of usage through ancient Greek literature, it does appear that *vivid or dramatic narration* of past events is the common characteristic of its use."[35]

Osburn (see Taylor, note 32) instances examples of historical presents signalling a "shift from background matters to principal action" (e.g. 1.30, with λέγουσιν; also 4.13, with λέγει).[36] It is most surely the case that καὶ ἔρχεται at 1.40 behaves this way, by introducing principal action against the background which Mark gives in his introductory verse of v.39.

The historical present, as we find at 1.40 for Day Two, and at 1.21 for Day One, features strongly in many of the verses of Mark's opening passages to his Days and at the beginnings of new sections in his reporting of those Days: in Days 1, 2, 3, 4, 5, 7, 8, 9, 10, 12, 14, 16, 20, 21, 22, 23, 24, 26, 27 and 28 (that is, twenty out of the total number of twenty-eight days). They are, with the first reference being the beginning of the Day:

---

[33] Thackeray, *The Septuagint...*, p.22; my italics.
[34] Cf. Ernest DeWitt Burton, *Syntax of the Moods and Tenses in New Testament Greek*, 3rd ed., T. & T. Clark Edinburgh, p.271; F. Blass & A. Debrunner, *A Greek Grammar of the New Testament and other Early Christian Literature*, tr. & rev. R.W. Funk, University of Chicago Press, Chicago, 1957, para.321; Randy Buth, "Mark's use of the Historical Present", *Notes on Translation*, 65 (1977), pp.7-13; Carroll D. Osburn, "The Historical Present in Mark as a Text-Critical Criterion", *Bib* 64 (1983), pp.486-500.
[35] B. M. Fanning, *Verbal Aspects in New Testament Greek*, Clarendon Press, Oxford, 1990, p.226; my italics.
[36] It is Hawkins (*Horae Synopticae*) who discerns, from his study of the Westcott-Hort text, not only the number of historical presents in Mark's Gospel but also that 72 are λέγει/λέγουσιν.

1.21/21; 1.39/40*; 2.1/3*/15/18b*/...18c; 2.23/25/3.3.&4; 3.7/13/20*/31*; 5.21/22*/38*; 6.1/1b*; 6.30/30; 6.53/7.1; 7.31/32 (cf. 2.3); 8.22/22a*/22b (see 7.32); 9.2/2; 10.32/35; 10.46/46a*/46b; 11.1/1a/1b/7a/7b; 11.12/15*; 11.20/27*/12.13/18*; 4.12/12/13/17*/32*/37*/41*/41/43; 15.1/20b/21/22/... 24/27; 16.1/2*.

In this list, we include some present participles (e.g. 10.46b) and some λέγει references (e.g. 2.25 and 3.3,4), which are found to introduce new paragraphs. The eighteen examples which are marked* are the present middle historical present, καὶ ἔρχεται or καὶ ἔρχονται. They are worth singling out because Mark shows a particular preference for these.

Twice only in Mark's Gospel do they begin new Days: at 8.22a and at 10.46a, where their use may be described as 'dramatic' ("as they serve to introduce new scenes", ref. Thackeray). In both instances Καὶ ἔρχονται εἰς is found; it is followed in the first of these by "Bethsaida", and in the second by "Jericho". 8.22b and 10.46b can also be compared: in their different ways they both introduce blind men into the reportings of the Days. In 8.22b we read "and they bring to him a blind man". Significantly it is another historical present which follows the one in 8.22a; it behaves like καὶ ἔρχεται at 1.40 by introducing principal action against the background just previously stated (following Osburn's argument), and it behaves also like καὶ ἔρχεται at 1.40 by introducing the principal character of the report of the Day (in a 'dramatic' way, after Thackeray's understanding). In 10.46b Mark employs a present middle participle to introduce the principal action (against the background of v.46a) and then proceeds to introduce blind Bartimaeus who is the principal character of the report of this Day. (Notably, these Days of Mark's telling are the last Days of his two middle Series of seven Days, 8.22-26 and 10.46-52; again[37] one was written with the other to hand.) Mark's employment of the historical present in the general sense, his use of καὶ ἔρχεται also in the general sense, and his exceptional use of ἔρχονται in two introductory settings, in one followed by a further historical present and in the other by a present middle participle, all support the

---

[37] See above, for reference to the two middle Days of the two middle Series of seven Days, 7.24-30 and 10.1-16, where also one was written with the other in mind.

conclusion that 1.40-45 continues a Day's telling which is introduced in 1.39.

The literary structure of Day Two is as follows:

A α ³⁹[α] <u>Καὶ ἦλθεν</u> [β] [.α] κηρύσσων [.β] εἰς τὰς συναγωγὰς αὐτῶν
[.β'] εἰς ὅλην τὴν Γαλιλαίαν [β'] καὶ τὰ δαιμόνια ἐκβάλλων.
  β ⁴⁰[α] <u>καὶ ἔρχεται πρὸς αὐτὸν</u> λεπρὸς [β] [.α] παρακαλῶν αὐτὸν [.β] καὶ
γονυπετῶν [.β'] καὶ <u>λέγων αὐτω</u> [β'] [.α] ὅτι Ἐὰν <u>θέλης</u>
[.α'] δύνασαί με <u>καθαρίσαι</u>.
  β' ⁴¹[α] [.α] καὶ σπλαγχνισθεὶς [.β] ἐκτείνας τὴν χεῖρα [.β'] αὐτοῦ
ἥψατο. [α'] [.α] καὶ <u>λέγει αὐτῷ</u>, [.β] <u>Θέλω</u>, [.β'] <u>καθαρίσθητι</u>·

B α ⁴²[α] <u>καὶ εὐθὺς</u> [β] ἀπῆλθεν ἀπ' αὐτοῦ ἡ λέπρα, [β'] καὶ <u>ἐκαθαρίσθη</u>.
  β ⁴³[α] καὶ ἐμβριμησάμενος αὐτῷ [β] εὐθὺς ἐξέβαλεν αὐτόν.
⁴⁴[β'] [.α] καὶ <u>λέγει</u> αὐτῷ, [.α'] Ὅρα μηδενὶ μηδὲν εἴπῃς
  β' [α] ἀλλὰ ὕπαγε [β] σεαυτὸν δεῖξον τῷ ἱερεῖ [β'] [.α] καὶ προσένεγκε
περὶ τοῦ καθαρισμοῦ σου [.β] ἃ προσέταξεν Μωϋσῆς [.β'] εἰς
μαρτύριον αὐτοῖς.

B' α ⁴⁵[α] Ὁ δὲ ἐξελθὼν [β] ἤρξατο κηρύσσειν πολλὰ [β'] καὶ διαφημίζειν
τὸν λόγον,
  β [α] ὥστε μηκέτι [β] αὐτὸν δύνασθαι φανερῶς [β'] εἰς πόλιν
εἰσελθεῖν,
  β' [α] [.α] ἀλλ' ἔξω [.α'] ἐπ' ἐρήμοις τόποις ἦν· [α'] [.α] καὶ ἤρχοντο
<u>πρὸς αὐτὸν</u> [.α'] πάντοθεν.

Again, the reasons for the annotations and underlinings are as for the Prologue and for Day One.

The literary structure of Day Two may be described, therefore, as having a simple ABB' form: A introduces the Day's principal event (in α, with a contextualising report of Jesus' activity in Galilee; in β, with an introduction of the new character, the leper, with his request to Jesus; and in β', with the active response of Jesus); B is the first development of the Day's story (in α, the leper is cleansed; in β, Jesus takes further action and casts the leper out; and in β', Jesus gives the leper orders); and in B' the Day's report concludes B (in α, with the leper's ignoring of Jesus' command; in β, with the result of the leper's misdeed; and in β', with a qualification of that result). As we have observed above (in the opening paragraphs) Day Two is in sequence with Day One. We will see below how Day Three is in sequence with Day Two and how the first three Days are a three-step progression in Mark's Day-presentational scheme.

Day Three: 2.1-22:

In considering Day Two we identified Day Three as clearly beginning at 2.1. The opening phrase is Καὶ εἰσελθὼν πάλιν εἰς Καφαρναοὺμ δι' ἡμερῶν. A passage of "some days" between Days Two and Three of Mark's telling is clearly established by Mark, if a little unusually[38]. As stated in the Introduction, he tells us that he is not reporting all the Days of Jesus' mission: here he gives clear indication of that.[39] Within the gospel context, this introduction, of 2.1, informs us that Jesus re-enters Capernaum for a second time, that is for a return visit[40]. It recalls the material of Day One (1.21-38). The opening participle is singular but at 2.13 and v.18 the disciples have their place within the linked stories of this Day, as they did in Day One.

Necessarily we refer to the identification of the importance and the purposes for Mark of historical presents (presented as part of Day Two's analysis) and here in this instance to 2.3, to the words Καὶ ἔρχονται (historical present) φέροντες (present participle) with which Mark begins the telling of this Day's first specific event by introducing its principal character. The purpose of 2.1,2 is to establish the setting for the event of the telling of the Day's first half. The content of 2.3-7 is the first development of the event itself, and that of 2.8-12 is the second and completing development. But before we discuss this further, we note a particular constructional feature. Just as there is the geographical link with the beginning of Day One (Capernaum) we find also a verbal link with the ending of Day Two: see 1.45: τὸν λόγον, ὥστε μηκέτι..... εἰσελθεῖν. In 2.1,2 they are found in reverse order. Properly, they may be identified as anastrophes: Dewey sees these as "hook words, reverse repeated,

---

[38] The preposition with the genitive has the idea of "through" but is used here temporarily as "after", F. Blass & A. Debrunner, *A Greek Grammar of the New Testament and other Early Christian Literature*, tr. & rev. R.W. Funk, University of Chicago Press, Chicago, 1957.

[39] For a discussion of 2.1, 8.1,2 and 9.2, the introductory passages to Days which speak clearly of other days untold by Mark, see under "An Interest in Days" in the Introduction.

[40] It is not until 9.33 that we have a report of Jesus being in Capernaum again.

which link the two stories"[41] (according to our designation of 1.39-45 and 2.1-12). Rather, the point may be made, because of the geographical links between 1.21 and 2.1, and the verbal links between 1.45 and 2.1,2, that the first three Days (of Mark's telling), 1.21-38, 1.39-45 and 2.1-22 are held together as a threesome of days in the telling. A case may be built on these connections, but not only these.

Days One and Two lend credence to the expressive second verse of this third Day's setting: καὶ συνήχθησαν πολλοὶ ὥστε μηκέτι χωρεῖν μηδὲ τὰ πρὸς τὴν θύραν. We have already compared the endings of Days One and Two above for indication of Jesus' rapidly growing popularity. Now the people of Capernaum are gathered where they have been before, at the door of Simon's house (1.33, Day One), only now there is no longer space for everyone! Further to this, people have come to Jesus before "carrying" their sick (see 1.32). In Day Three we are presented with a specific healing episode, rather like Days One and Two (Simon's mother-in-law and the leper), and just as it can be said that the earlier healings lead to other matters, here specifically it is to the issue of Jesus' authority to forgive sins (sinners), a presentation which concludes at 2.12, with "all" being astonished and glorifying God. This ending of the first half of this Day is reason in itself for Mark's reference in 2.13 to "all the crowd" gathering to Jesus, which is the way the second half of the Day begins, in the new setting.

We complete our reading of 2.1-12. Vv.1,2 are introductory and establish the setting, the audience, and the principal character's role in regard to the audience; vv.3-7 begin the telling of the first specific event of the day (with a Markan historical present, which introduces new characters and so establishes a new "paragraph": see again note 10); and vv.8-12 complete the story begun in vv.3-7 (the passage opens with a typically Markan Καὶ εὐθὺς). The balance between vv.3-7 and vv.8-12 (parts B and B' of the ABB' construction, as presented at the conclusion of this Day's examination) is evidenced by the αββ' structures and their correspondences of detail. We observe how, in particular, the two uses of λέγει τῷ παραλυτικῷ

---

[41] Dewey, *Markan Public Debate...*, pp.117f.

are found in exactly the same literary-structural location, β [β] [.α], in both parts B and B'.

Now we will see how 2.13-22 connects with 2.1-12. We discuss firstly the temporal reference at 2.13 which is worthy of close attention. We read, Καὶ ἐξῆλθεν πάλιν <u>παρὰ τὴν θάλασσαν</u>. At this point, many commentators see a clear correspondence with 1.16-20, Jesus' calling of two pairs of named brothers by the sea[42] (see page 69 for an earlier discussion on the common words and details of these passages). As a result, the Greek word πάλιν (found 28 times in the Gospel) is simply translated "again". Hence, πάλιν enjoys its *rursus* (*Latin:* back, return) usage. Without taking anything away from this, the case can be put, however, for πάλιν here at 2.13 to mean also "thereupon" or "immediately after".

We turn firstly to Taylor: he records that the word originally meant "back", but that in later Greek it came to be used in the sense of "again"[43]. He recognises also that it is used as an inferential conjunction with the meaning, "further", "thereupon". Bultmann previously noted, "Sometimes πάλιν is added... simply as a succession formula", as translated from the Aramaic[44]. But, Taylor notes Howard's belief that in many of the Markan instances, the meaning of πάλιν is really iterative, and that where it is inferential it is unnecessary to go back to the Aramaic. Bultmann discerns the following possible candidates: 2.1,13; 3.1; 4.1 and 11.27. He omits consideration of 15.13: here we might read, "And they again cried out, 'Crucify him!'" But, this, according to Mark, is the first time the crowd so shouted. "And they immediately cried out...", might be considered the more literal rendering. (The N.I.V. records simply, "'Crucify him!' they shouted.") It may be argued, against Bultmann, that 2.1 and 11.27 best reflect *rursus* usage. In the case of 2.1, the temporal reference suggests no *immediacy* of return (consider "after some days") and at 11.27 we are reading about Jesus' visiting Jerusalem for the third day in a row (see Days Twenty-two, Twenty-three and Twenty-four which are all consecutive in Mark's telling: 11.1-11; vv.12-19; and vv.20-13.37).

---

[42] Nineham, *Saint Mark*, p.95; Schweizer, *The Good News...*, p.63; Hooker, *The Gospel...*, p.94.
[43] Taylor, *The Gospel...*, p.192.
[44] Bultmann, *The History...*, p.339.

The possibility that πάλιν is used as a succession formula at 2.13, 3.1 and 4.1, is particularly interesting because in these positions it appears three "Days" in succession (in Mark's telling) and at the very same point in each Day's reporting, between the first and the second halves. We will see below how these three "Days" are the three central days of this first Series of seven Days. In each of these Days, Days Three, Four and Five, πάλιν may indeed best be rendered, "thereupon" or "immediately after"[45], thus cementing together most strongly the two halves of each of the Days' presentations. In the case of this Day Three, compare especially the beginnings of the two halves, 2.1 and 2.13: Καὶ εἰσελθὼν πάλιν and Καὶ ἐξῆλθεν πάλιν. They do have the appearance of a deliberate match. The first half of the day is set in Simon's house: the second half begins by the sea but settles in Levi's house. What contrasts is the meaning of πάλιν which at 2.1 cannot be inferential, given the summary of 1.45, but which at 2.13 is more likely to be inferential than iterative, given that "all the crowd" of 2.1-12 come to Jesus.

We continue with our examination of 2.13-22. Below, we discover further "paragraph" defining, structurally significant use by Mark of the historical present, the kind we have observed already, in Days One and Two: they are at 2.14, 15,16,18b and 18c. This list includes καὶ ἔρχονται at v.18b, and present participles at vv.14 and 16. We note that Nineham, Schweizer and Hooker[46] all see 2.13-17 as a Markan whole because of the linkage between vv.13,14 and vv.15-17 of "outcasts", but below, I present the introductory piece to the second half's telling of the "Day" as v.13. It is a typical, Markan, three-part opening and introduction to the two presentations following. It describes the change of setting for the telling of the Day's initial, repeating activity of Jesus' teaching (cf. vv.1,2). In vv.14-17 Jesus calls Levi, and eats with tax collectors and sinners which provokes a challenge to Jesus and his response. We may observe that in its third part, vv.16,17, Mark introduces "scribes" for their response to Jesus' activity just as he did in vv.6,7 (significantly,

---

[45] See Alexander Souter, *A Pocket Lexicon to the Greek New Testament*, Clarendon Press, Oxford, 1976.
[46] Nineham, *Saint Mark*, pp.94f.; Schweizer, *The Good News...*, pp.62f.; and Hooker, *The Gospel...*, pp.93f.

both occupy the same structural positions Bβ'[α] [.α]). In vv.18-22 Jesus has to answer challenges as his disciples are eating when others are fasting.

Again, we discover αββ' presentations. In vv.20-22, for example, in the [β] [β'] positions, vv.21,22, we have a pair of presentations beginning in turn with οὐδεὶς and καὶ οὐδεὶς which illustrate Jesus' introductory statement, of part [α], v.20 (structural discoveries of this kind do aid exegesis). And again, a second half three-part presentation is defined which can be characterised as an introduction followed by two stories which connect. Further, these second and third parts in this second half of the Day's telling continue the theme of the second and third parts of the first half, of Jesus' ministry to sinners, "so demonstrating again his authority to forgive sinners"[47] (see v.17b). The second and third parts may be considered representative of Mark's predilection for linking like units of tradition, here, of 'eating and fasting' (though they may have been linked already in earlier oral or written tradition)[48]. The ending of Day Three is at 2.22 because at 2.23 Mark turns the focus onto a sabbath day.

I present the literary structure of Day Three (with annotations as before) which, in the composite form of ABB /ABB', repeats the structure of Day One:

---

[47] Hooker, *The Gospel...*, pp.93,94.
[48] See for another example 2.23-28 and 3.1-6, for what is 'not lawful on the sabbath'.

A α ¹[α] [.α] Καὶ εἰσελθὼν [.β] πάλιν [.β´] εἰς Καφαρναοὺμ
     [α´] [.α] δι' ἡμερῶν, [.β] ἠκούσθη [.β´] ὅτι ἐν οἴκῳ ἐστίν.
  β ²[α] καὶ συνήχθησαν πολλοὶ [β] ὥστε μηκέτι χωρεῖν [β´] μηδὲ τὰ
     πρὸς τὴν θύραν.
  β´ [α] καὶ ἐλάλει [β] αὐτοῖς [β´] τὸν λόγον.

B α[α] ³[.α] Καὶ ἔρχονται [.β] φέροντες πρὸς αὐτὸν παραλυτικὸν
     [.β´] αἰρόμενον ὑπὸ τεσσάρων.
     [β] ⁴[.α] [..α] καὶ μὴ δυνάμενοι [..β] προσενέγκαι αὐτῷ [..β´] διὰ τὸν ὄχλον
     [.α´] [..α] ἀπεστέγασαν [..β] τὴν στέγην [..β´] ὅπου ἦν,
     [β´] [.α] καὶ ἐξορύξαντες [.β] χαλῶσι τὸν κράβαττον [.β´] ὅπου ὁ
     παραλυτικὸς κατέκειτο.
  β [α] ⁵[.α] καὶ ἰδὼν ὁ Ἰησοῦς [.α´] τὴν πίστιν αὐτῶν
     [β] [.α] λέγει τῷ παραλυτικῷ, [.α´] Τέκνον,
     [β´]   ἀφίενται σου αἱ ἁμαρτίαι.
  β´[α] ⁶[.α]   Ἦσαν δέ τινες τῶν γραμματέων [.α´] ἐκεῖ καθήμενοι
     [β] [.α] καὶ διαλογιζόμενοι [.α´] ἐν ταῖς καρδίαις αὐτῶν,
     [β´] ⁷[.α] [..α] Τί οὗτος [..α´] οὕτως λαλεῖ; [.β] βλασφημεῖ · [.β´] [..α] τίς
     δύναται ἀφιέναι ἁμαρτίας [..α´] εἰ μὴ εἷς ὁ θεός;

B´α[α] ⁸[.α] Καὶ εὐθὺς [.β] [..α] ἐπιγνοὺς ὁ Ἰησοῦς [..α´] τῷ πνεύματι αὐτοῦ
     [.β´] [..α] ὅτι οὕτως διαλογίζονται [..α´] ἐν ἑαυτοῖς
     [β] [.α] λέγει αὐτοῖς, [.β] Τί ταῦτα διαλογίζεσθε [.β´] ἐν ταῖς καρδίαις
     ὑμῶν;
     [β´] ⁹[.α] τι ἐστιν εὐκοπώτερον,
          [.β] [..α] εἰπεῖν τῷ παραλυτικῷ, [..α´] Ἀφίενται σου αἱ ἁμαρτίαι,
          [.β´] [..α] ἢ εἰπεῖν, [..α´] [...α] Ἔγειρε [...β] καὶ ἆρον τὸν κράβαττόν
     σου [...β´] καὶ περιπάτει;
  β[α] ¹⁰[.α] ἵνα δὲ εἰδῆτε [.α´] [..α] ὅτι ἐξουσίαν ἔχει ὁ υἱὸς τοῦ ἀνθρώπου
     [..β] ἀφιέναι ἁμαρτίας [..β´] ἐπὶ τῆς γῆς
     [β] [.α] λέγει τῷ παραλυτικῷ, ¹¹[.α´] Σοὶ λέγω,
     [β´] [.α] ἔγειρε [.β] ἆρον τὸν κράβαττόν σου [.β´] καὶ ὕπαγε εἰς τὸν
     οἶκόν σου.
  β´[α]¹²[.α] καὶ ἠγέρθη [.β] καὶ εὐθὺς ἄρας τὸν κράβαττον [.β´] ἐξῆλθεν
     ἔμπροσθεν πάντων,
     [β] [.α] ὥστε ἐξίστασθαι πάντας [.β] καὶ δοξάζειν τὸν θεὸν [.β´]
     λέγοντας
     [β´] [.α] ὅτι Οὕτως [.β] οὐδέποτε [.β´] εἴδομεν.

Α α ¹³ [α] Καὶ ἐξῆλθεν [β] πάλιν [βʹ] παρὰ τὴν θάλασσαν·
β   καὶ πᾶς ὁ ὄχλος ἤρχετο πρὸς αὐτόν,
βʹ   καὶ ἐδίδασκεν αὐτούς.

Β α[α] ¹⁴[.α] καὶ παράγων [.β] εἶδεν Λευὶν τὸν τοῦ ʽΑλφαίου [.βʹ] καθήμενον
           ἐπὶ τὸ τελώνιον,
   [β]   [.α] καὶ λέγει αὐτῷ, [.αʹ] ʼΑκολούθει μοι.
   [βʹ]   [.α] καὶ ἀναστὰς [.αʹ] ἠκολούθησεν αὐτῷ.
  β[α] ¹⁵[.α] καὶ γίνεται [.β] κατακεῖσθαι αὐτὸν [.βʹ] ἐν τῇ οἰκίᾳ αὐτοῦ,
   [β]   [.α] καὶ πολλοι τελῶναι καὶ ἁμαρτωλοι [.β] συνανέκειντο τῷ ʼΙησοῦ
           [.βʹ] καὶ τοῖς μαθηταῖς αὐτοῦ·
   [βʹ]   [.α] ἦσαν γὰρ πολλοι [.αʹ] καὶ ἠκολούθουν αὐτῷ.
  βʹ[α] ¹⁶[.α] [..α] Καὶ οἱ γραμματεῖς τῶν Φαρισαίων [..β] ἰδόντες ὅτι ἐσθίει
           [..βʹ] μετα τῶν ἁμαρτωλῶν καὶ τελωνῶν
   [β]   [.α] ἔλεγον τοῖς μαθηταῖς αὐτοῦ, [.β] ῞Οτι μετὰ τῶν τελωνῶν καὶ
           ἁμαρτωλῶν [.βʹ] ἐσθίει;
   [βʹ] ¹⁷[.α] [..α] καὶ ἀκούσας [..αʹ] ὁ ʼΙησοῦς λέγει αὐτοῖς [ὅτι]
           [.β] [..α] Ου χρείαν ἔχουσιν οἱ ἰσχύοντες ἰατροῦ [..αʹ] ἀλλʼ οἱ κακῶς
           ἔχοντες·
           [.βʹ] [..α] οὐκ ἦλθον καλέσαι δικαίους [..αʹ] ἀλλα ἁμαρτωλούς.

Βʹα[α]¹⁸[.α] Καὶ ἦσαν οἱ μαθηταὶ ʼΙωάννου καὶ οἱ Φαρισαῖοι νηστεύοντες.
           [.β] και ἔρχονται [.βʹ] καὶ λέγουσιν αὐτῷ,
   [β]   Διὰ τι οἱ μαθηταὶ ʼΙωάννου καὶ οἱ μαθηται τῶν Φαρισαίων
           νηστεύουσιν,
   [βʹ]   οἱ δὲ σοὶ μαθηται οὐ νηστεύουσιν;
  β[α] ¹⁹ καὶ εἶπεν αὐτοῖς ὁ ʼΙησοῦς,
   [β]   [.α] Μὴ δύνανται οἱ υἱοὶ τοῦ νυμφῶνος [.β] ἐν ᾧ ὁ νυμφίος μετ᾽
           αὐτῶν ἐστιν [.βʹ] νηστεύειν;
   [βʹ]   [.α] ὅσον χρόνον ἔχουσιν τὸν νυμφίον μετ᾽ αὐτῶν [.αʹ] οὐ δύνανται
           νηστεύειν·
  βʹ[α]²⁰[.α] [..α] ἐλεύσονται δὲ ἡμέραι [..αʹ] ὅταν ἀπαρθῇ ἀπ᾽ αὐτῶν ὁ
           νυμφίος,
           [.αʹ] [..α] καὶ τότε νηστεύσουσιν [..αʹ] ἐν ἐκείνῃ τῇ ἡμέρᾳ.
   [β] ²¹[.α] [..α] οὐδεὶς ἐπίβλημα ῥάκους ἀγνάφου ἐπιράπτει [..αʹ] ἐπὶ
           ἱμάτιον παλαιόν·
           [.β] [..α] εἰ δὲ μή αἴρει τὸ πλήρωμα ἀπ᾽ αὐτοῦ τὸ καινὸν τοῦ παλαιου
           [.βʹ] καὶ χεῖρον σχίσμα γίνεται.
   [βʹ] ²²[.α] καὶ οὐδεὶς βάλλει οἶνον νέον εἰς ἀσκοὺς παλαιούς
           [.β] [..α] εἰ δὲ μη ῥήξει ὁ οἶνος τοὺς ἀσκούς, [..β] καὶ ὁ οἶνος
           ἀπόλυται [..βʹ] καὶ οἱ ἀσκοί.
           [.βʹ] [..α] ἀλλὰ οἶνον νέον [..αʹ] εἰς ἀσκοὺς καινούς.

Clearly, the first three Days tell where and how Jesus first became known and where and how his fame spread. The first Day (1.21-38) speaks of Jesus in Capernaum, the second Day (1.39-45) of Jesus in Galilee after a number of days (or weeks), and the third Day (2.1-22) of his return to Capernaum also after some days, and his attracting his biggest crowd so far. This is the first threesome of Days in Mark's Gospel narrative presentation. Mark has made it very clear that many other days could have been reported, but he has chosen to tell this first phase of Jesus' mission in only three reported Days. On the grounds of geographical place consideration alone, Capernaum/Galilee/Capernaum, it would be tempting to view this sub-Series of Days as being an ABA' scheme. But when we take into acccount the verbal links (for example, as identified between the ending of Day Two and the beginning of Day Three) an ABB' scheme is suggested. I judge that the thrust of Mark's three-Day story-line is the most important signifier of what he intended. On the grounds of Jesus' rising popularity, I view this sub-Series to be an ABB' rhetorical scheme because this best expresses the progression of these three Days' tellings (given the definition above of his rhetorical style, ABB', whereby A is introductory, B is the first development, and B' is the second and concluding development which completes, therefore, the whole). I hold the view that this is what Mark had in mind, and that he chose to write systematically to these levels of literary order, composing consistently to his early-adopted rhetorical method and 'style'.

Day Four: 2.23-3.6:

The Day begins: Καὶ ἐγένετο αὐτὸν ἐν τοῖς σάββασιν παραπορεύεσθαι διὰ τῶν σπορίμων... The sabbath day is the setting: the plural is used with a singular meaning as in 1.21, in Day One[49]. A number of translations begin reading, "One sabbath..." and so the hint is made by translators that Mark's presentation is not necessarily chronological in presentation, that it is a separate story only, simply set in an artificial framework. This hint, or mild

---

[49] Cranfield, *The Gospel...*, pp.71,72,114.

suggestion may be judged to undermine what is Mark's effort in treating the reader/the listener to a created, connected narrative, be it still an artificial framework.[50] The Greek requires something a little more sympathetic, such as "On the sabbath...". Both Mark's framework of Days and his connections between his reportings of Days are expressive of continuity.

We may refer here to Mark's use of καί, to parataxis, which is one of the most noticeable characteristics of Mark's style, whereby he sustains a connectedness of the parts and achieves a unified whole. Hawkins points out that of the 88 sections in the Wescott-Hort text 80 begin with καί and only 6 have δέ as the second word.[51] For comparison, Matthew has 159 sections and the numbers are 38 and 54 respectively, and Luke has 145 sections and 53 and 83 respectively. In fact δέ is found in all in Mark's Gospel only about 156 times which is less than half the number we should expect to find if it was used as freely as in Matthew or Luke. The possibilities that LXX-use or Aramaic-use had an influence on Mark have been entertained[52] but Moulton thinks that "in itself the phenomenon proves nothing more than would a string of "ands" in an English rustic's story." To Taylor too, it is "elementary culture".[53] To Tolbert, however, parataxis, also asyndeta (the absence of the connecting links supplied by particles and conjunctions), as well as ordinary diction and brevity of narration, which are all striking features of Mark's style, all "find a home in Greek rhetorical theory".[54] "In Demetrius' terms," she writes, "the Gospel's style attempts to blend the clarity and simplicity of ordinary speech with the emotion of dramatic delivery."[55]

Literary-structural analysis does demonstrate that καί dominates the opening of the lines of literary order at many levels. Its *absence* from such positions, interestingly, is illuminating also. In a

---

[50] K.L. Schmidt, *Der Rahmen...* In his penetrating investigation in 1919, he may have claimed correctly that as a whole the outline of Mark's Gospel was a purely artificial construction, but too sweeping, surely, is his conclusion that it *reduced* to "only single stories, *pericopae*, which are put into a framework."
[51] Hawkins, *Horae Synopticae*, p.151.
[52] J.H. Moulton & G. Milligan, *The Vocabulary of the Greek Testament* (London, 1914-29), Eerdmans, Grand Rapids, 1972, pp.57-58,314.
[53] Taylor, *The Gospel...*, p.49.
[54] Tolbert, *Sowing the Gospel...*, pp.42,43.
[55] See: Demetrius, *On Style*, pp.221-222.

valuable study, Paul Ellingworth[56] shows how the *absence* of καί functions in Mark's work, particularly: how it features frequently in direct speech; how it marks new pericopae or paragraphs ("thus a new narrative or a new stage in the narrative"); where sentences begin with a pronoun followed by δέ (in several passages, "where chains of such sentences have the apparent effect of heightening the cut and thrust of dialogue"); also, in three places, how it indicates that Mark takes up the thread of his narrative again after a digression; and in other cases how it tends to mark some kind of new phase or step within a narrative[57]. In this Day's account καί introduces all the major sectional and part divisions (the first and second halves, and parts A, B and B'), and of the twelve sub-parts, five of the six β sub-parts and three of the six β ʿ sub-parts. We examine those instances where καί is *absent* in this Day's reading:

1) 2.25 β   ὅτε χρείαν ἔσχεν 2) 2.26 βʿ πῶς εἰσῆλθεν
3) 2.28 βʿ ὥστε κύριός ἐστιν 4) 3.4b βʿ οἱ δὲ ἐσιώπων.

Examples 1), 2) and 3) all occur in direct speech. In 1) and 2) they give the "when" and the "how" to the opening, "what David did." In 3) it introduces the consequence clause, the third and concluding part of Jesus' argument of vv.27,28. Example 4) is a clear case of a pronoun followed by δὲ. And though it stands individually here, it still has dramatic "effect".

We have to look beyond this Day's report for other examples of Ellingworth's listing. They are best raised now, nevertheless, as we here address this matter of the non-καί sentence. We will consider *his own samples* under *his own group headings*, but as they may be judged to function given my literary-structural analysis:

1) How the non-καί sentence marks new pericopae or paragraphs (and "thus a new narrative or a new stage in the narrative"): we consider those at:

1.14 - it opens the third section, B', of the Prologue; 5.11 - it opens the second half of the telling of Day Six; 5.35 - it opens the

---

[56] Paul Ellingworth, "The Dog in the Night: A Note on Mark's non-use of KAI", *BT* 46 (1995) pp.125-128.

[57] I here consider five of Ellingworth's eight categories only. Space does not allow a complete presentation. For a full listing of his groups of non-καί sentences, see his article, "The Dog in the Night...".

last section of Day Seven; 7.24 - it opens Day 11; 8.1 - it opens Day 13; 9.30 - it opens Day 17; 10.32 - it opens Day 20; 9.38 - it opens part B in the middle section of Day 17; 13.14, 24, 28, 32 ("distinct phases in the eschatalogical discourse: all in direct speech") - to these, I add 13.7 which opens 'B' Section A; 13.14 - it opens 'B' Section B'; I add 13.18 which opens 'B" Section A; 13.24 - it opens 'B" Section B; 13.28 - it opens 'B" Section B, part β; and 13.32 - it opens the concluding section 'B" Section B'; 14.1 - it opens Day 25; and 15.6 - it opens 'A' Section B of Day 27.

To the fourteen examples which Ellingworth gives, I have added two. Five begin Days; nine begin Sections (four of which are in the eschatalogical discourse); and two begin major parts of sections. None are found in my analysis which do not hold structural significance. There is reason here to record agreement on our findings.

2) In three places, how the non-καί sentence indicates that Mark takes up the thread of his narrative again after a 'digression':

6.16: given my analysis the non-καί beginning most certainly follows a three-part whole (6.14b, 15a, 15b) and so opens another three-part whole (another *new section*). Ellingworth says of v.16, "When Herod heard it", that it recalls v.14a, "Now King Herod heard about all this". He describes, therefore, vv.14b,15 (these verses "record various opinions about Jesus") as a "digression"[58]. But my reading is that there is no "digression" as such. 6.14a records Herod's *hearing* about Jesus' *disciples' mission*; it ends the telling of the first half of Day Eight's account. 6.16 represents the *particular view of Herod*, against 16.14b,15 which begins the second half with the introductory *views of the people*.

7.20: the non-καί sentence here does follow what may be termed a 'digression' ("In saying this, Jesus declared that all foods are fit to be eaten", GNB). But in my analysis 7.20 opens another *new section*, the last section of Day Ten.

8.25: if the man's comment that he sees "people... like trees walking about" is a 'digression' from the action, then here again the non-καί sentence following a digression opens another *new section* in my analysis.

---

[58] Ellingworth, "The Dog...", p.126.

On the evidence of these three samples, the issue of 'digressions' would appear to be less important than the fact that all three non-καί sentences open new sections and so *mark new pericopae or paragraphs*. It appears that these might be best placed under a sub-category of category 1).

3) How the non-καί sentence tends to mark some kind of new phase or step within a narrative:

1.32: Ellingworth argues that it represents "a transition from a particular healing to a general statement". In this fashion, in Day One of my analysis, this non-καί sentence opens another *new section*. Whether it belongs in this category, or in category 1) is debatable. There is certainly little to separate 1's "new stage" from 3's "new phase or step". If scale *is* the point of difference, then 1.32 does belong under category 1.

9.24a: in my analysis of Day 16, I find that six of the nine parts in the closing section open with non-καὶ beginnings (that is Aαββ', β' here being 9.24a, Bαββ and B'αββ', as underlined). They are each classifiable under Ellingworth's (eight) groupings. We may note that although 9.24a is not classifiable elsewhere under any of his other headings, it does not *alone* of these mark a "new step" as such in the narrative: see 9.22b,25 and v.27. Again as above, if it is scale that separates categories 1) and 3), then 9.24a and those like it that are not classifiable elsewhere can be identified as "marking some kind of *new step* within a narrative".

Further to the issues, for literary-structural analysis, of καί and non-καί sentences, we observe that Mark frequently adds εὐθύς to καί. We may observe that it intensifies Mark's simple linking of parts in succession, and that it is frequently to be found at the beginning of new lines, and we note, at the more significant levels of literary order. Again Paul Ellingworth supplies a useful study[59]. We review his major points. To him, the use of "Immediately" at the beginning of a section shows that Mark is moving "from one story to a closely related one" (he cites 1.12 as an example). In my analysis of the Prologue, 1.12 does link *closely* sub-sections β and β', 1.10,11 and 1.12,13 (see page 56). The use of "and immediately" can show also that Mark is moving "from one stage in a longer story to the

---

[59] Paul Ellingworth, "How Soon is 'Immediately' in Mark?", *BT* 29 (1978) pp.414-419.

next" (for which he cites 6.45; 14.43 and 15.1). In my analysis of Day Nine, 6.45 marks the beginning of the Day's third and final main section. In my analysis of Day 26, 14.43 begins 'B' Section B'. In my analysis of Day 27, 15.1 begins the Day's telling, "And immediately early" ("early" is qualified by "immediately"; Mark provides an immediate and dramatic quickening of the pace of events, for this Day's telling). In the analysis of the Prologue, we further saw how "and immediately" can be used twice to introduce a pair of stories: we observed these links between sub-sections α, β and β ʽ, 1.9 with 1.10,11 and 1.12,13.

We have discussed already πάλιν and seen it function as a strong succession formula[60]. We remind ourselves that it is discovered at the level of literary order whereby it connects two halves of a Day's report, in the middle days, Days Three, Four and Five, of this first Series of seven Days. It would seem that we are beginning to identify a Markan hierarchy of succession formulae, and that his use of καί (and non-καί), καὶ εὐθύς and καὶ πάλιν are to be taken seriously.

We return to our examination of Day Four. The introduction to the Day recalls Day One (see 1.21), though the Day's focus is different from anywhere else in the Gospel: only here is the subject of conflict over the Sabbath addressed. Likely, both stories of the Day, 2.23-28, "doing what is unlawful: plucking ears of corn", and 3.1-6, "doing what is unlawful: healing", were at one time separate units of tradition. Or alternatively, of course, Mark may have created either one or both of these stories to construct this Day's report. What is certain is that the conjunction of Καὶ... πάλιν at 3.1a is Mark's. There may be little doubt, therefore, at the very least that Mark brought these stories together.

At this point, regarding 3.1a we should note that a number of translations waver. For example, the N.I.V. reads, "Another time he went in to the synagogue...", and the N.E.B. reads, "On another occasion when he went to the synagogue..." Both bring disjunction into the Markan text. In the Jer.B. and the R.S.V., πάλιν is translated simply, "again" and the connection is still made between the two episodes. In the G.N.B. the link is strengthened with "Then Jesus

---

[60] See under my examination of Day Three

went back to the synagogue..." It is judged that this is nearer to Mark's intention because of its use of "Then" as a succession formula and because it says also that he "went back" (Jesus has been in synagogues before, in 1.21 and 39); πάλιν here may reasonably be judged to retain its common *rursus* usage also[61]. For a simple, literal translation, for reasons already stated above, the following may be suggested too: "And *immediately after this* he entered into a synagogue..."

We continue with our consideration of the linking of the two halves of this Day's telling. It may be judged that the subject of the verb παρετήρουν in 3.2 is the Pharisees of 2.24, for the reasons that the two stories in juxtaposition share the same focus on what is 'lawful on the sabbath' and that the Pharisees were responsible for introducing the question in the first place, in 2.24. Mark does intend the two incidents to be read together as one Day's activities.

The Day clearly ends at 3.6: the content of 3.7-12 and all that follows on Day Five which this summary introduces, is non-sabbatical.[62] Interestingly, arguments vary as to the purpose and the effect of 3.6. Nineham sees it as a clear conclusion "not only to this (second) story (of the day), but also to the whole series of conflicts[63]. Hooker rightly points out, however, that the conflict theme is taken up again at 3.20ff.[64] It is this very fact that undermines somewhat the abiding deduction, which she also makes, that 2.1-3.6 represents a pre-Markan group of conflict stories.[65] It is

---

[61] It is the case also that as 2.13 reflects Jesus' first time "by the sea" in 1.16 the common usage of πάλιν may be retained in addition to its being a succession formula there: so too 4.1 for the same reasons.

[62] See my notes also, under Day One, for the separation of 1.16-20 from 1.21ff. for reasons of the sabbath's obligations. The question, of course, arises in the same way as before: does the new Day at 3.7 begin with a new sunrise or at the sunset at which the Jewish sabbath ends? Clearly 3.7-12 describes a new Day's activities as after a sunrise: 1) Mark would have told us if it was evening: see 1.32, 4.35, 6.47, 14.7 and 15.42; or that it was "late": see 6.35, 11.11 and 11.19; and 2) he in fact describes in 3.7-12 the beginning of a succession of events which will lead to an evening (4.35)/night-time event (consider the "boat" of 3.9 which re-appears in 4.1 and 4.36).

[63] Nineham, *Saint Mark*, p.110.

[64] Hooker, *The Gospel...*, p.109.

[65] Since the seventies, a number of scholars have begun to argue against a pre-Markan Galilean controversy collection: G. Minette de Tillesse, *Le secret messianique dans l'Évangile de Marc*, LD 47, Éditions du Cerf, Paris, 1968 (for the reason that the stories reflect Mark's overall theology); A.B. Kolenkow, "Beyond Miracles, Suffering and Eschatology", *1973 Seminar Papers*, ed. G. MacRae, SBLSP 109 (1973), pp.155-202 (on

true that it can be argued that Mark may have added another conflict story to a pre-existent collection, but what more weakens the prevailing view are the literary-structural analyses of each Day (so far presented) and the uncovering of a Markan Series of seven Days which has in the first part of its scheme a threesome of the first three days, followed by a fourth and middle Series pivotal day, prior to a further and final, balancing threesome of days. We will be looking at this after the analysis of Days Five, Six and Seven. Mark appears less a conservative editor with each disclosure of the elements of his framework and the features of his rhetorical style: he appears, rather, more a chronicler or compiler[66], and one who exhibits a good control of his material and of his own presentation methodology.

On 3.6 again, both Taylor and Nineham[67] judge that the allusion to the death plot of the Pharisees and the Herodians appears "too early in the Gospel". But there is a case for supposing that Mark knew exactly what he was doing: this fourth and middle Day of his first Series of seven has its parallel in the fourth and middle Day of the final series (14.1-11). Both speak of the plottings against Jesus' life. We may note now that conflict stories are present in Days Three, Four and Five of the first series of Days; we may note also that these are the middle three days. We will see later that conflict stories, with similar emphases, are present in Days Two, Three, Four, Five and Six, the middle five days, in the final series (11.12-19; 11.20-13.37; 14.1-11; 14.12-72 and 15.1-47).[68] Another possibly significant parallel is seen: just as Judas Iscariot is first introduced in Day Five (last in the listing of the twelve) of the first Series, as being "the one who betrayed" Jesus, so he is presented in Day Five of the final Series, in the very act of betrayal (14.43-46). We will come to such considerations later.

---

form critical and redactional grounds as well as on theological grounds); D.-A. Koch, *Die Bedeutung der Wundererzahlungen für die Christologie des Markusevangeliums*, BZNW 42, Walter de Gruyter, Berlin, 1975 (neither 3.6 nor 2.28 need to be explained as pre-Markan redactional conclusions to a collection; the use of "Son of Man" in 2.10,28 are in conformity with the authority-theme begun at 1.21; to place together related traditions would occur to an evangelist as well as to any other compiler of tradition).

[66] See Farrer, *A Study in St Mark...*, p.4.
[67] Taylor, *The Gospel...*, p.146, and Nineham, *The Gospel...*, p.110.
[68] We note: other days of conflict stories exist too, in the middle two series of seven days.

We may notice that in Day Four there is a total absence of any mention of either crowds, or of Jesus' (growing) popularity (compare the first three Days), but the fact that Day Four climaxes with something of a complete contrast to what we have witnessed up to now, the announcing of a death plot against Jesus, does not mean that it is totally detached from what has preceded it, in terms of its subject matter and content. Jesus' growing popularity in Days Two and Three was accompanied by growing opposition in Days Three and Four. Further, the crowds may not be very far from Mark's mind. The very mention of Herodians at this point[69], in 3.6, may be intended by Mark to suggest that Jesus was being seen, even early on in his mission, not only as a threat to Old Israel's religious leadership, but also as a threat to political order in Palestine. One who was attracting such a popular following was a potential cause of political unrest.

Before I present my literary-structural analysis for this day, Day Four, we consider the construction of 2.1-3.6, concerning which Dewey[70] and others[71] have recognised symmetrical patterning of its *pericopae*, though they differ in their views. Dewey's own proposition, which has attracted much support, is as follows:

A	2.1-12	The healing of the paralytic
B	2.13-17	The call of Levi/eating with sinners
C	2.18-22	The sayings on fasting and on the old and the new
B'	2.23-28	Plucking grain on the sabbath
A'	3.1-6	The healing on the sabbath.

And she adds a qualification, "Further, B is rhetorically related to A, and B' to A', while both B and B' are related to C".[72] This "concentric literary pattern is definitely to be found in the text itself," she says. I cannot agree, for a number of reasons.

---

[69] Though it is not certain who they really were, the usual view is that they were friends and supporters of Herod Antipas, not a religious sect.
[70] Dewey, *Markan Public Debate*...
[71] Giuseppe G. Gamba, "Considerazioni in margine alla poetica di Mc.2.1-12", *Salesianum* 28 (1966), pp.324-349; P. Mourlon Beernaert, "Jésus controversé: Structure et théologie de Marc 2.1-3.6", *NRT* 95 (1973), pp.129-149; David J. Clark, "Criteria for Identifying Chiasm", *LB* 35 (1975), pp.63-72.
[72] Dewey, *Markan Public Debate*..., pp.110 and 116.

Firstly, I *will* agree that chiasm[73] is to be found extensively in the New Testament. I will agree also that it is to be found in Mark's Gospel, but it will be demonstrated that chiasm is to be found only sparingly in the detail of Mark's narrative, and regularly, only in his larger structurings of his Series of seven Days, and in his overall Gospel plan. 2.1-3.6 may have the appearance of chiasm when it is separated from its Gospel context, but when it is set where it should be, between 1.45 and 3.7, it does not work as a chiasm anything like so well: details of 2.1-3.6 have their relationships with the text each side of it and beyond, elsewhere in the Gospel, and some details feature more importantly because it is only in 2.1-3.6 that they appear at all in the whole Gospel.

Dewey's analysis may appear to be complete, but it is not. She shows those passages which seem to parallel, and in many instances do parallel in their details, but she fails, with her overall structure, to take account of those that do not parallel. She lacks a detailed summary which takes account of all the parts that make up her supposed whole. Above all, she has had to select one set of

---

[73] Chiasm or "chiasmus" is not truly a term of ancient rhetoric: the first clear reference to it as a technical term is found around the 4th century AD in Hermogenes (*On Invention*, 4.3, H. Rabe (ed.) Rhetores Graece Vol. 6, in Bibliotheca Scriptorum Graecorum et Romanorum Teubneriana, Leipzig, 1913), who uses it in terms of, but limits it to, the crosswise interchange of the clauses in a four-clause sentence. A. Di Marco, "Der Chiasmus in der Bibel 1. Teil", *LB* 36, 1975, pp.21-97, p.23, suggests that a number of other terms were used instead in ancient rhetoric to describe what is now called chiasmus, but this must be treated with caution. Chiasm, or chiasmus, defines a broad range of literary devices, all of which have their similarity only in that a crossing, or an inversion occurs. We use the term in this way here.

In regard to the Gospels and Acts in particular, there is a case to be put for chiasmus **in Matthew** (J.C. Fenton, "Inclusio and Chiasmus in Matthew", *Studia Evangelica*, International Congress on New Testament Studies, Vol. 73, eds. Kurt Aland, et al.; Akademie-Verlag, Berlin, 1959, pp.174-179; Angelico Di Marco, "Chiasmus: 3. Teil", pp.38-57); **in Luke-Acts** (C.H. Talbert, *Literary Patterns, Theological Themes and the Genre of Luke-Acts*, SBL, Scholars Press, Missoula, Montana, 1974; Craig Blomberg, "Midrash, Chiasmus, and the Outline of Luke's Central Section" pp.217-259, *Gospel Perspectives (Studies in Midrash and Historiography)* Vol. III, eds. France & Wenham, JSOT Press, Sheffield, 1983; M.D. Goulder, "The Chiastic Structure of the Lucan Journey", *TU* 87 (1963), pp.195-202; K.E. Bailey, *Poet and Peasant: A Literary Cultural Approach to the Parables*, Eerdmans, Grand Rapids, 1976; Angelico Di Marco, "Chiasmus: 3. Teil", pp.62-68); **and in John** (David Deeks, "The Structure of the Fourth Gospel", *NTS* 15 (1968-69), pp.107-129; Angelico Di Marco, "Chiasmus: 3. Teil", pp. 69-85). In Matthew, Luke-Acts and John, I contribute to the debate on the Gospels and Acts, adding the Revelation to John, in *Sliced Bread...*

For a classical tretament of chiasmus, see A. Vanhoye's, *La Structure Littéraire de l'Epître aux Hébreux*, Desclée de Brouwer, Paris-Bruges, 1976.

structuralising criteria over and against another, as she tries to establish the overall arrangement in her second reading from information from her first reading. She is led to simplify, erroneously, her argument of arrangement, and reject other correspondences which are equally deserving of as much prominence in any scheme.

I give just one example (and there are a number) which provokes this criticism. Her rhetorical critical analysis leads her to the judgement that 3.1-6 "builds on the narrative of" 2.23-28, yet she *chooses* to parallel 2.1-12 with 3.1-6, because "they show a striking similarity" for their rhetorical pattern: the miracle is begun, then interrupted, then completed, in both. She defines their similar frames: she says, "As the debate section in 2.1-12 is framed by Jesus' two addresses to the paralytic" (compare my presentation of my analysis: in both parts, B and B', 2.5 and v.10, at the exact same points we read, at β [β] [.α] λέγει τῷ παραλυτικῷ,...) "...here (in 3.1-6) Jesus' answer to the opponents is framed by his two commands to the sick man..." (compare here my presentation again: in both parts, B and B' (3.3 and v.5), we read in the opening lines, denoted by α, λέγει τῷ ἀνθρώπῳ). "Both are clearly delineated ring compositions," Dewey says, "*Unlike 2.6-10a, however*, the central portion of 3.1-6 should not be considered an interposition. It is not sufficiently set off from the outer ring in which the opponents also feature strongly." This point of difference, identified in her first reading, is important. In her second reading, she summarises an impressive number of parallels, but the counter-logic is not there summarised as well. The point of difference itself is explicable: we note that Dewey is attempting to parallel two sections, the first of which is twelve verses and contains much content that is not matched in the second which is only six verses, that is half the size[74]. The clearest undermining of Dewey's scheme is that in their Gospel context, 2.23-28 and 3.1-6 are the only passages which focus on what is 'lawful on the sabbath' (see 2.24 and 3.4 in particular): they are parallels of each other above all else, and if they were part of a chiasm this would be indicated by their parallel positioning.

---

[74] So far in my presentation of the literary-structural analyses of the Days I discern balance where in Mark's ABB' scheme balance is required, that is between his two parts, B and B' which complete his constructions.

The difference between Dewey's approach and mine is fundamental. Dewey's parts A, B and C by my analysis are one Day's telling and her parts B' and A' are another Day's telling. The two most important signifiers of Markan structure are his rhetorical style of ABB' employed from beginning to end of his Gospel in his constructing of his Prologue and his Days, and his determinative matrix of Series of seven Days. They govern all his work of arrangement. Due to the uncovering of these, I cannot support Dewey's method of analysis of what is at best, even on form-critical grounds[75], an arbitrarily-defined Gospel piece.

Another approach to analysing the text of Mark is that of 'rhetorical analysis' as exemplified by Mack[76], on 2.23-28. The chreia[77] as it stands now, he says, "is elaborated as if the objection were to eating on the Sabbath." (We note the scholarly debate about the issue, whether it focuses upon working (plucking) or eating.) The question is whether the action was a violation of the law. The argument unfolds, for Mack, in this way:

Narrative:	Plucking grain on the Sabbath (v.23)
Issue:	It is not lawful (v.24)
Argument (Rebuttal):	
Citation:	Read the scriptures (v.25)
Example:	What David did (vv.25,26)
Analogy:	Eating when hungry (v.25)
Maxim:	Sabbath made for people (v.27)
Conclusion:	The Son of man is Lord even of the Sabbath (v.28).

This format, he says "gives the impression that the argument unfolded inductively when, as a matter of fact, the elaboration had to be crafted with the 'pronouncement' (v.28) in mind all along. One sees from this that the construction of a pronouncement story (like this one) was an exercise in thinking backward, starting with the

---

[75] 'Conflict stories' are present elsewhere in the Gospel, in Days delimited by 3.7-4.41, 6.53-7.23, 8.1-21, 10.1-16, 11.12-19, 11.20-13.37, 14.1-11, 14.12-72 and 15.1-47.
[76] Mack, *Rhetoric...*, pp.52,53.
[77] Chreia is defined in very similar ways in the ancient handbooks. For Theon, it is "a concise statement or action which is attributed with aptness to some specified character or to something analogous to a character." For Hermogenes it is "a reminiscence of some saying or action or a combination of both which has a concise resolution..."

conclusion and then crafting an inductive approach to it." These comments are helpful to understanding Mark's work of compositon. What we see below, however, is how literary-structural analysis suggests Mark structured his presentation. He presented the narrative and the issue in the introductory part, the argument (the citation, example and analogy) in the second, but the 'maxim' he plainly attached to the 'conclusion'/'pronouncement' in the third part. (We note how both parts B and B' begin similarly.)

I present the literary structure of Day Four:

A α   ²³[α] <u>Καὶ ἐγένετο αὐτὸν</u> [β] <u>ἐν τοῖς σάββασιν</u> παραπορεύεσθαι
       [β'] διὰ τῶν σπορίμων,
  β   [α] καὶ οἱ μαθηταὶ αὐτοῦ ἤρξαντο ὁδὸν ποιεῖν [α'] τίλλοντες τοὺς
       στάχυας.
  β' ²⁴[α] καὶ <u>οἱ Φαρισαῖοι</u> ἔλεγον αὐτῷ, [α'] [.α] Ἴδε [.β] τί ποιοῦσιν τοῖς
       σάββασιν
       [.β'] ὃ <u>οὐκ ἔξεστιν</u>;

B α   ²⁵[α] <u>Καὶ λέγει αὐτοῖς,</u> [β] Οὐδέποτε ἀνέγνωτε [.β'] τί ἐποίησεν
       Δαυίδ,
  β   [α] ὅτε χρείαν ἔσχεν [β] καὶ ἐπείνασεν αὐτὸς [β'] καὶ <u>οἱ μετ' αὐτοῦ</u>;
  β' ²⁶[α] [.α] πῶς εἰσῆλθεν [.β] εἰς τὸν οἶκον τοῦ θεοῦ [.β'] ἐπὶ Ἀβιαθὰρ
       ἀρχιερέως
       [β] [.α] καὶ τοὺς ἄρτους τῆς προθέσεως <u>ἔφαγεν</u>, [.β] οὓς <u>οὐκ</u>
       <u>ἔξεστιν φαγεῖν</u> [.β'] εἰ μὴ τοὺς ἱερεῖς,
       [β'] καὶ ἔδωκεν καὶ <u>τοῖς σὺν αὐτῷ οὖσιν</u>;

B' α ²⁷[α] <u>Καὶ ἔλεγεν αὐτοῖς,</u> [α'] Τὸ <u>σάββατον</u> δια <u>τὸν ἄνθρωπον</u> ἐγένετο
  β   καὶ οὐχ <u>ὁ ἄνθρωπος</u> δια <u>τὸ σάββατον</u>·
  β' ²⁸[α] ὥστε κύριός ἐστιν ὁ υἱὸς <u>τοῦ ἀνθρώπου</u> [α'] καὶ <u>τοῦ σαββάτου</u>.

A α ¹[α] Καὶ εἰσῆλθεν [β] πάλιν [β'] εἰς τὴν συναγωγήν.
 β   [α] καὶ ἦν ἐκεῖ ἄνθρωπος [α'] ἐξηραμμένην ἔχων τὴν χεῖρα·
 β' ²[α] καὶ παρετήρουν αὐτὸν [β] εἰ τοῖς σάββασιν θεραπεύσει αὐτόν,
     [β'] ἵνα κατηγορήσωσιν αὐτοῦ.

B α ³[α] Καὶ λέγει τῷ ἀνθρώπῳ τῷ τὴν ξηρὰν χεῖρα ἔχοντι, [α'] Ἔγειρε
     εἰς τὸ μέσον.
 β   ⁴[α] καὶ λέγει αὐτοῖς, [α'] [.α] Ἔξεστιν τοῖς σάββασιν [.β] [..α] ἀγαθὸν
     ποιῆσαι [..α'] ἢ κακοποιῆσαι, [.β'] [..α] ψυχὴν σῶσαι [..α'] ἢ
     ἀποκτεῖναι;
 β' οἱ δὲ ἐσιώπων.

B' α ⁵[α] Καὶ περιβλεψάμενος αὐτοὺς μετ' ὀργῆς, [β] συλλυπούμενος ἐπὶ
     τῇ πωρώσει τῆς καρδίας αὐτῶν, [β'] [.α] λέγει τῷ ἀνθρώπῳ,
     [.α'] Ἔκτεινον τὴν χεῖρα.
 β   [α] καὶ ἐξέτεινεν, [α'] καὶ ἀπεκατεστάθη ἡ χεὶρ αὐτοῦ.
 β' ⁶[α] καὶ ἐξελθόντες [β] οἱ Φαρισαῖοι εὐθὺς μετὰ τῶν Ἡρῳδιανῶν
     Συμβούλιον ἐδίδουν κατ' αὐτοῦ [β'] ὅπως αὐτὸν ἀπολέσωσιν.

It is properly described, like Days One and Three, as having the form ABB'/ABB'. The verbal linkage between the two halves is as for Day Three, Καὶ..... πάλιν. The linking theme of the two halves is to do with what is "unlawful on the sabbath". Again, we find that Mark has created a well-balanced structure. In the first series, ABB', A (2.23,24) introduces the new day, the sabbath, and begins reporting also the first event of the Day; B (vv.25,26) beginning with a 'dramatic' historical present records Jesus' first response, which is his reply to the Pharisees' question; and B' (vv27,28) gives Jesus' second response (exegetically, here the two responses beg comparison because, for the first time in the Gospel, the potential for associating Jesus with David is raised). In the second series, ABB', A (3.1,2) records the change of setting and begins reporting the second event of the Day, a new challenge to Jesus; B (vv.3,4) beginning with a 'dramatic' historical present, records Jesus' first response and the silence of the Pharisees: and B' (vv.5,6), in its beginning, including the same words as in B, λέγει τῷ ἀνθρώπῳ, gives Jesus' second response which is to heal, which in turn provokes the opposition to plot against him. This middle day's telling of Mark's first Series of seven Days ends on a highly dramatic note.

Day Five: 3.7-4.41:

Several propositions are presented: that Day Five has the limits of 3.7 and 4.41, and that it comprises four sections (3.7-19; vv.20-35; 4.1-32 and vv.33-41) which are each created by Mark according to his ABB' rhetorical method; that with Day Five Mark begins his second sub-Series and threesome of Days (Day Five, 3.7-4.41; Day Six, 5.1-20; and Day Seven, 5.21-43); and that Mark uses this sub-Series (3.7-5.43) to conclude his first Series of seven Days (1.21-5.43) for which Mark's focus is "Jesus' first days of mission (in Galilee and in particular, the region of its Sea)". We rehearse the pertinent judgements and arguments of others as we examine the text.

Hooker notes that most commentators make a major break and, therefore, a new beginning at 3.7, but she says, "such divisions are largely arbitrary". She points out two links with previous material; stories of conflict (2.1-3.6 and 3.21-35) and the injunction of Jesus to silence unclean spirits (1.25, 34 and 3.12).[78] Yet, she notes too the change to a new theme, which she calls "the commissioning of the twelve" (later, "the appointment of the twelve"[79]). She observes also the important theme which is sustained throughout the next three chapters (we note: Days Five, Six and Seven); it is "the response which men and women make to Jesus: the truth about him is spelt out in a series of parables and miracles, but this truth is hidden from the majority of those in the story, who hear and see but fail to comprehend".[80]

We observe also that Jesus' exercise of great authority binds these three days into a threesome. At the end of the first (Day Five, 3.7-4.41) he displays his power over the wind and waves. In the second (Day Six, 5.1-20), after an extravagantly detailed description of a demoniac's possession by evil spirits and the attempts by others to restrain him, he demonstrates his power over immense evil. And in the third (Day Seven, 5.21-43) he shows his power to heal an incurable (whose ailment and whose attempts to find a cure are again spelt out in much detail), and at the climax of the Day's report shows his power to raise even the dead. Nineham argues similarly, and we

---

[78] Hooker, *The Gospel...*, p.109.
[79] Hooker, *The Gospel...*, p.110.
[80] Hooker, *The Gospel...*, p.109.

agree with him, that these stories make up "one of the groups of three of which Mark is so fond".[81]

On 3.7-12, both Nineham and Hooker view the passage as a major editorial summary statement of Jesus' activity[82]. And they compare it with those of 1.14,15 and 1.32-34. For Nineham the question arises, "Why here?" Schweizer's answer to this is simple; he sees 3.7-12 as introductory to part III of the Gospel 3.7-6.6a, on "Jesus' ministry in parables and signs and the blindness of the world"[83]. Contrary to Schweizer, I would argue that the summary introduced at 3.7 is included in the text by Mark at this point as a beginning to his new three-day presentation with which he concludes his first Series of seven Days, 1.21-5.43. At the end of the first of these days, Day Five, there is a night-crossing of the lake, and at the end of the second day's activities (Day Six)[84] there is a return crossing, with the result that the last of the three days, Day Seven, tells what then takes place at, or near the same setting of the first of these three days. It would appear that Mark has deliberately created a geographical scheme which echoes that of the first threesome of days, 1.21-2.22, where the first and last days of that series also have a common setting (which is Capernaum).

Taylor's estimate that 4.1-5.43 is one day's telling[85] is challenged for the reason, as stated in the Introduction, that all that Mark tells us about, in 4.35-5.43, cannot have happened in one day: fundamentally the argument against his proposition has much to do with the fact that 4.35 tells us that 'evening had come'. The content of 4.35-5.43 could not all have taken place in one day, in night-watches; much occurs in successive daylight periods. Other reasons, not raised in the Introduction, are added below. My first point of difference with Taylor is that this Day's telling begins at 3.7 and not at 4.1. As presented under Day Four, the content of 3.7-12 is non-sabbatical and so separates from 3.6 and what precedes it. In my note 62, the notion that the new Day might begin at 3.7 with the sunset at which the Jewish sabbath ends is untenable fundamentally because the reportings of the Day's activities continue to evening

---
[81] Nineham, *Saint Mark*, p.157.
[82] Nineham, *Saint Mark*, p.112; Hooker, *The Gospel...*, p.109.
[83] Nineham, *Saint Mark*, pp.78ff.
[84] See in the discussion on this day, a more detailed consideration of "night-crossings".
[85] Taylor, *The Gospel...*, p.146; see my Introduction, p.36.

(4.35) and beyond, without any hint of a night disrupting the flow of events. (See note 62 for other reasons.)

We continue with a consideration of 3.7-12. Nineham's interest in the first instance is as with Lightfoot[86] in the relationship between 3.7-12 and vv.13-19. As "a typical Markan insertion" (between 2.1-3.6 and 3.20ff. which are stories of conflict) these verses, he says, "provide a foil to the dark picture of mounting misunderstanding and hostility"[87]. Given the appointing of the "twelve" (in vv.13-19), against the description of 'all Israel' gathered to him (in vv.7,8) and the frenzy of an enthusiastic and excitable crowd (in vv.9-12), with Nineham and Lightfoot we may see here "the foundation of the new Israel"[88]. The Day begins, certainly, with the most extended list yet of peoples present, from every part of the Holy Land inhabited by Jews. All "old Israel" gathers to Jesus.

We may judge, therefore, that 3.7-19 is the opening presentation (section) of this Day's telling and that it comprises the three parts Nineham suggests: vv.7,8; vv.9-12; and vv.13-19. Robbins also identifies the same divisions. For him 3.7-19 represents the first three-step progression since 1.14-20:[89] the first unit of the progression, vv.7,8, he calls a "re-statement" of 1.14-20; the second unit, vv.9-12, he says, is a "re-statement" of 1.21-3.6, with the addition of new features; the third and final unit, vv.13-19, he says, parallels units two and three in the first progression, that is 1.16-18 and vv.19f. and "establishes expectations that were not explicit there"[90]. He identifies what will be the three roles of the "twelve" at

---

[86] R.H. Lightfoot, *The Gospel Message...*
[87] Nineham, *Saint Mark*, p.112.
[88] Lightfoot, *The Gospel Message...*, p.39.
[89] Vernon K. Robbins, *Jesus the Teacher...*: Essentially, Robbins identifies three-step progressions in ways similar to myself. But in all the Gospel, he identifies only six possibilities: at 1.14-20; 3.7-19; 6.1-13; 8.27-9.1; 10.46-11.11 and 13.1-37. Upon these six three-step progressions alone, he attempts to build a case for his presentation of the formal structure of the Gospel. Because his next three-step progression after 3.7-19 is at 6.1-13, he argues the new section of material introduced by 3.7-19 ends at 5.43, our three days, Days Five, Six and Seven. We may value Robbins' analysis so far as it goes. His identification of three-step progressions and his judgement that they are a clue to the formal structure of Mark's Gospel is close to what is being uncovered here in this analysis. That he argues the limits of gospel-sections on the grounds that no other than these six three-step progressions exist, which is really what he does, is an argument, of course, with which I cannot agree. Neither can I agree with him on all his identified progressions.
[90] Robbins, *Jesus the Teacher...*, see pp.31-33.

3.14,15: they are: "to be with him", "to be sent out to preach" and "to have authority to cast out demons". Robbins develops this: "the expectation to 'be with' Jesus was evident from 1.16-20 where the men were asked to leave everything and follow; the expectation to be 'sent out to preach' was probably implicit in the promise that the disciples would be made 'fishers of men'. The assertion that the disciples would acquire 'authority to cast out demons' is new information". I would only question, why separate the two mission activities in this way? Preaching and casting out demons were Jesus' own two mission activities, as we read in 1.39. As it is, Mark presents them together, consider: [.α] και ἵνα ἀποστέλλη αὐτοὺς [.β] κηρύσσειν [.βʹ] ¹⁵ καὶ ἔχειν ἐξουσίαν ἐκβάλλειν τὰ δαιμόνια. Again we discern an [.α] [.β] [.βʹ] sequence.

Robbins' references to chapter one have their parallels in the writing of most commentators on 3.7-12. Likewise, his designation of gospel sections, 1.14-3.6 and 3.7-5.43 has the near agreement of a number of commentators (compare 1.14-3.6 and 3.7-6.6a/.13 of Taylor, Schweizer and Hooker). I take a contrary view for the reason stated above, that the evidence points to Mark's creation of two sub-Series of three Days in balance around a middle Day, to form his first Series of seven Days. Other support will be given to this after the completion of the examination of the first seven Days.

As 3.7-19 is the opening section of Day Five, it is not surprising to find within it a particular detail of important literary-structural significance for the construction of the Day as a whole. The 'boat' of 3.9 is an important linkage, because it re-appears in 4.1 and again at 4.36 (though the Greek differs a little: compare: πλοιάριον, εἰς πλοῖον and ἐν τῷ πλοίῳ). It links the first, third and fourth sections of the Day (3.7-19; 4.1-32 and 4.33-41). The strong link at 4.1, Καὶ πάλιν ἤρξατο διδάσκειν παρὰ τὴν θάλασσαν, has been discussed under Day Three, above: in this Day's tellings it links the first and second halves (the first being sections one and two, 3.7-35; the second being sections three and four, 4.1-41). It may be translated: "And immediately afterwards, he began to teach by the sea..." The same verse 'sits' Jesus in 'the boat' as he begins his teaching. 4.35 connects with v.36 as it describes the onset of evening and so 'works' to introduce the final section of the Day's report, Jesus' stilling of the storm.

The second section, 3.20-35, is also a 'whole' presentation. To Best, the opening phrase is attributable to Mark since he regularly introduces "the house" as a place where instruction is given[91]. Hooker sees its connection with what precedes by translating 3.20a Καὶ ἔρχεται εἰς οἶκον as "Then he went indoors...". With this section, she says, "we move back into the atmosphere of conflict... but move another step forward in the development of this theme, since now Jesus' opponents do not merely watch him and criticize, but offer their own - utterly false - interpretation of the source of his authority and power."[92] With regard to this section's form, she argues that a number of stories have been woven together, probably by Mark, and she sees another example of intercalation of incidents "of which he is so fond", describing the structure as 3.20,21, vv.22-30 and vv.31-35 (i.e. material about the scribes is "sandwiched" between material about his relatives and friends). While I can agree with the limits of this section, I cannot agree with Hooker in the other matters. Understanding Mark's rhetorical method differently, for its ABB' form, it can be argued that the compositional work of Mark was to bring only two stories together, and that this is expressed by the following divisions: vv.20-22 (the opening part, introducing firstly the setting, and secondly the two sets of people who are raising issues: in the first place Jesus' family, and in the second, scribes from Jerusalem), vv.23-30 (the first development: Jesus anwering the scribes) and vv.31-35 (the second and completing development: Jesus speaking about 'family'). Mark's literary-constructional method of αββ' is evidenced again, both in the overall scheme to this section, and also in his treatment of its parts and sub-parts.

The first half of Mark's Day Five is reviewed. For the second half (4.1-41) and for our examination of the third section of the Day's telling (4.1-32) we will draw in the efforts of Dewey and Fay on 4.1-34, and we will rehearse the challenge of Räisänen, for whom chapter 4 is a suitable test-case for any theory about the nature of Mark's composition. We will then examine the fourth section, 4.33-41. We discuss firstly the efforts of Dewey and Fay on 4.1-34.

---

[91] Best, *Disciples...*, p.50.
[92] Hooker, *The Gospel...*, p.114.

For Dewey these verses are a five section concentric structure[93]; for Fay, they are a seven section scheme[94].

Dewey:
A vv.1,2a Introduction X
B vv.2b-20 Parable material

C vv.21-25 Sayings material
B' vv.26-32 Parable material
A' vv.33,34 Conclusion

Fay:
A vv.1,2a Introduction X
B vv.2b-9 Parable material
C vv.10-13 Parabolic method
D vv.14-20 Interpretation (the Sower)
C' vv.21-25 Parabolic method
B' vv.26-32 Parable material
A' vv.33,34 Conclusion

The first difficulty encountered is with vv.1-2a which they both view as a chiasm. They present:

α   Καὶ πάλιν ἤρξατο <u>διδάσκειν</u> παρὰ τὴν θάλασσαν.
β   καὶ συνάγεται πρὸς αὐτὸν ὄχλος πλεῖστος,
γ   ὥστε αὐτὸν εἰς πλοῖον ἐμβάντα καθῆσθαι ἐν τῇ θαλάσσῃ,
β' καὶ πᾶς ὁ ὄχλος πρὸς τὴν θάλασσαν ἐπὶ τῆς γῆς ἦσαν.
α' καὶ <u>ἐδίδασκεν</u> αὐτοὺς ἐν παραβολαῖς πολλά.

The notion that this is a five-part chiasm does not reflect the three sentence structure of this opening piece, and it takes no account of the way, therefore, how Mark built up his introductory piece (to 4.1-9). For this reason it might have been more satisfactorily presented as a three-part chiasm: [α] [βγβ'] [α']; but most typically in defining would-be chiastic structures it depends on selecting one set of criteria over and against the selecting of another. The choice of <u>διδάσκειν</u> and <u>ἐδίδασκεν</u> as key words defining the outer framing sentences is a 'choice': choose θάλασσαν and the other two uses of the word, in all in lines α, γ and β', and no chiasm is suggested. One would have to say that Mark overlooked what might be read as other hook words if he did intend the chiastic arrangement as Dewey and Fay suggest.

---

[93] Dewey, *Markan Public Debate...*, pp.147-152,167, after Jan Lambrecht, *Marcus Interpretator: Stijl en Boodschap in Mc.3.20-4.34*, Desclée de Brouwer, Brugge-Utrecht, 1969.
[94] Greg Fay, "Introduction to Incomprehension: The Literary Structure of Mark 4.1-34", *CBQ* 51 (1989), pp.65-81.

I present below my analysis which to me demonstrates another αββ' form:

A α [α] ¹[.α] Καὶ πάλιν [.β] ἤρξατο διδάσκειν [.β'] παρὰ τὴν θάλασσαν.
   [β] [.α] καὶ συνάγεται πρὸς αὐτὸν ὄχλος πλεῖστος,
      [.β] ὥστε αὐτὸν εἰς πλοῖον ἐμβάντα καθῆσθαι ἐν τῇ θαλάσσῃ,
      [.β'] καὶ πᾶς ὁ ὄχλος πρὸς τὴν θάλασσαν ἐπὶ τῆς γῆς ἦσαν.
   [β'] ²[.α] καὶ ἐδίδασκεν αὐτοὺς [.α'] ἐν παραβολαῖς πολλά.

It may be said at the outset that we do at least all identify the same five lines. But my reading is that [α] is 'introductory' not only to the second half of the Day's telling with Καὶ πάλιν (see my earlier arguments for the role of Καὶ πάλιν binding the two halves of the tellings of Days Three, Four and Five), but also to describing the new scene. It is the first full sentence. It may be stated that [β] and [β'] in turn, which are full sentences, develop the scene in the first, and complete the scene in the second. Further, the first of these, [β] begins with a typically Markan historical present so positioned in the [β] part (see my earlier arguments for this, especially under Day Two). It may be pointed out that [β] first develops the scene by picking up on παρὰ τὴν θάλασσαν in [α] [.β']: a crowd gathers to Jesus in [.α], and in [.β] and [.β'] the setting of Jesus and the crowd is further qualified by the balancing pair of statements which include ἐν τῇ θαλάσσῃ and πρὸς τὴν θάλασσαν, following ὥστε (these are typically [.β] and [.β'] paralleling pieces). It may also be pointed out that [β'] in the second case picks up on διδάσκειν in [α] [.β], and qualifies it with καὶ ἐδίδασκεν αὐτοὺς ἐν παραβολαῖς πολλα, so completing the opening piece of 4.1,2a. It is a classically Markan αββ' structure.

Yes, it may be said that Dewey's and Fay's chiasm is simpler and more balanced, but that does not make their analysis right. For Mark, balance is achieved by his basic construction-use of αββ'; he many times demonstrates freer control when it comes to his detailing of their component parts.

As a result of this, I view the larger concentric arrangements of Dewey and Fay with a little scepticism. If they discern chiasm where there is no chiasm in just one-and-a-half verses only, how can we judge they are able to see the chiastic structure of thirty-four verses? Further, if Fay can propose an expanding of Dewey's pattern, to bring different passages into new parallelisms, he raises doubts in my mind that any paralleling can be established at all, on the basis of a concentric pattern. It is judged that his 'centring' of the interpretation of the 'sower' parable is a bad move, as it clearly belongs with the parable. Because of all their many points of detailed contact, in a concentric pattern the two pieces must occupy some kind of α: α˝ setting which expresses their parallelism. This indeed is what we observe in Dewey's chiasm within a chiasm, of 4.2b-20:

α, vv.2b-9; β, v.10; γ, vv.11,12; β˝, v.13; α˝, vv.14-20.

The key to this scheme is what happens between vv.10-13. I present my analysis of these verses:

Listed firstly are the divisions and sub-divisions of my scheme for 4.1-32. In outline it is as follows: where

A is 4.1-9; B is vv.10-23; and B' is vv.24-32,

and where A is introductory, B is the first development, and B' is the second and concluding development, and where part B sits in Mark's scheme as if in parenthesis because of its interrupting setting. The part we are examining is this part B α and the beginning of part B β:

B α [α]¹⁰[.α] Καὶ ὅτε ἐγένετο κατὰ μόνας,
    [.β] [..α] ἠρώτων αὐτὸν [..β] οἱ περὶ αὐτὸν [..β˝] σὺν τοῖς δώδεκα
    [.β˝] τὰς παραβολάς.
  [β] ¹¹[.α] <u>καὶ ἔλεγεν αὐτοῖς</u>,
    [.β] [..α] ʽΥμῖν [..β] τὸ μυστήριον δέδοται [..β˝] <u>τῆς βασιλείας τοῦ θεοῦ</u>·
    [.β˝] [..α] ἐκείνοις δὲ τοῖς ἔξω [..β] <u>ἐν παραβολαῖς</u> [..β˝] τὰ πάντα γίνεται,
  [β˝]¹²[.α] [..α] ἵνα βλέποντες [..β] βλέπωσιν [..β˝] <u>καὶ μὴ</u> ἴδωσιν,
    [.β] [..α] καὶ ἀκούοντες [..β] ἀκούωσιν [..β˝] <u>καὶ μὴ</u> συνιῶσιν,
    [.β˝] [..α] <u>μήποτε</u> ἐπιστρέψωσιν [..α˝] καὶ ἀφεθῇ αὐτοῖς.

β [α] ¹³[.α] <u>Καὶ λέγει αὐτοῖς</u>,
    [.β] Οὐκ οἴδατε <u>τὴν παραβολὴν</u> ταύτην,
    [.β˝] καὶ πῶς πάσας <u>τὰς παραβολὰς</u> γνώσεσθε;

We may interpret that vv.10-12 is the introductory passage to vv.13-20 *and* vv.21-23. That is, part B subdivides as follows: where

α is vv.10-12; β is vv.13-20; and β' is vv.21-23.

The B' part, vv.24-32, is the second development, and we may interpret Mark to mean that these tellings are in the company of the crowd, again, because none of these parables are 'explained'. (See below for the discussion of the full literary-structural analysis of the Day, which shows how 4.33-36 is judged the introductory part α to parts β, vv.37-39b, and β', vv.39c-41. Clearly, literary-structural analysis demonstrates a Markan division between 4.32 and 33 where we would not have been expecting one. Mark's *process* of composition cannot be adumbrated, without a recognition and an examination of his rhetorical method.)

In the introductory piece, B α, vv.10-12, we discern again Mark's predilection for $\alpha\beta\beta'$ structuring. Vv.10-13 do not form a chiasm. Neither, therefore, do vv.2b-20. No concentric structure, on Mark's part is intended anywhere, here in 4.1-32/34. His controlling method is his rhetorical method of $\alpha\beta\beta'$.

We turn briefly to the challenge of Räisänen. In his study on the "Messianic Secret" in Mark's Gospel[95] he says, "Any theory about the nature of Mark's composition must prove good in practice. A theory must be capable of making sense of crucial passages in the gospel. For such a test, the parable chapter of Mk. 4 is as suitable a section as any." Clearly, our tasks are different: he is seeking to describe the process of how the chapter has come to be composed; I am simply trying to establish a description of how the chapter and the Gospel as a whole are composed as they are now.

What I present has to be measured against Räisänen's correct challenge. In answering, it needs to be stated that it was easier to establish the structures of the first, second and fourth sections of this Day Five than it was the third. The reasons may be twofold. Clearly, section three is much longer than the others and that itself poses its own challenge. Further, up until chapter four the narrative concentrated more on action, incident and response than teaching. 4.1-32/34 is the largest concentrate of Jesus' teaching thus far; it is

---

[95] Heikki Räisänen, *The Messianic Secret...*, p.28.

not until 13.5-37 that we find anything of the same order. 3.23-30 is the largest teaching block prior to chapter four and that too, as we have noted, is within the same day's telling. The possibility, therefore, arises that Mark himself was challenged: he was continuing with a structural presentational method which had yet to prove itself appropriate to teaching presentation.

We continue, and we discuss the three difficulties which have been observed by scholars in regard to 3.23-30, 4.33,34 and 4.10-'?'. It has been said of 3.23-30 that it ends a little clumsily at 3.30: "for they said, 'He has an unclean spirit.'" Taylor calls it "an elliptical passage which is an explanatory Markan comment." It is the evangelist's way of saying, "This is the reply of Jesus to the charge, 'He has Beelzebul' (in 3.22)." Taylor sees 4.33,34 in the same category, as the evangelist's explanation. Just as the Good News Version which Schweizer uses puts 3.30 (see above) in parenthesis, so 4.33,34 may be put in brackets, as Taylor sees it "as similar" to 3.30. The bigger problem, clearly, is with 4.10-'?'. We return to the question asked, at what point, if at all, does Jesus resume his teaching of the crowd, because as 4.36 says, he was still in the boat? As presented above (on page 119) the case can be put for the insertion being 4.10-23. In short all three difficult passages (3.30, 4.33,34 and 4.10-23) may be regarded as set in parentheses as explanations. 3.30 is Mark's explanation for Jesus' teaching on what "will not be forgiven" (3.28,29); 4.33,34 is Mark's explanation of Jesus' use of parables and how he interpreted them for his disciples; and 4.10-23 is Mark's insertion by which he features Jesus' explaining the reason for his speaking in parables, and explaining the first of the parables in his teaching block (4.1-32). All three insertions, however, have their proper place within Mark's systematically presented rhetorical scheme. Mark has built them into this Day's framework: they were not added later.

The literary-structural argument for the ending of the larger parenthetical piece (4.10-23) still requires presenting. The question is: at what point, if at all, in Mark's mind, is Jesus talking again to the crowds[96]? To assist enquiry, we have the evidence of Mark's presentation methodology, though here it *is* tested to the limit. It is

---

[96] Which would also include the disciples, that is the twelve and the others.

certainly extended, though it does retain the ABB' form, overall.[97] Fundamental to the exposing of the rhythm of presentation is Mark's frequent repetition of "And he said...". (See the presentation of the literary-structure of the Day, following these notes.) What establishes 4.23 as the end of the parenthetical piece beginning at 4.10 is the repetition of 4.9, "...has ears to hear let him hear." In commentaries on 4.21-25, the inclusion of 4.23 is given either very little or no consideration at all. Taylor, however, does consider it and ruminates on its linkage initially with vv.21f. and comments too, "but it has the appearance of a connecting link relating the sayings to the parable of the sower"[98]. He does not say if he means all the four sayings of vv.21-25 or just the two with which he thinks it was first associated. Clearly, in 4.24-32, after the introductory piece α (vv.24,25), the pair of "Kingdom of God" parables (vv.26-29 and vv.30-32) fall perfectly into parallel positions (β and β‛) as we should expect them to, after the manner of Mark's rhetorical structuring elsewhere. The literary-structural analysis I present does appear to answer Räisänen's challenge.

We here examine section four, the last of the Day's sections, 4.33-41. This story of Jesus' stilling of the storm is clearly linked to the previous section, 4.1-32. Its three parts are arranged to Mark's αββ‛ rhetorical scheme: part A, vv.33-36, is introductory (in part α, in the αββ‛ style Mark summarises Jesus' teaching method exhibited by 4.1-32; in β, 4.35, "evening having come", Jesus suggests they cross to the other side of the sea; and in β‛, they leave the crowd and begin the crossing...); part B, vv.37-39a, is the first development (in α, a storm develops; in β, they rouse sleeping Jesus; and in β‛, Jesus roused, rebukes the storm); and part B‛, vv.39b-41, is the second and completing development (in α, all is calm; in β, Jesus challenges his disciples; and in β‛, they are afraid and question, "Who then is this...?"). It is another sure example of Mark's rhetorical method.

It remains only to justify the overall sectional-structure of Day Five. Several times already the sections have been listed as 3.7-19; 3.20-35; 4.1-32; and 4.33-41. And twice they have been presented as forming two halves: 3.7-35 and 4.1-41.

---

[97] See also, 3.16-19, where the description of "the twelve" is another extension.
[98] Taylor, *The Gospel...*, p.262.

Firstly, we observe that the similarities betwen sections two (3.20-35) and three (4.1-32) are numerous. In regard to their contents, we observe Mark's first uses in his gospel of the term, "parables" in 3.23 and 4.2, 10, 11, 13 *bis*, 33, 34. In both sections also, he addresses "kingdom" issues by resort to parables, and we note too that the term "kingdom" itself, though introduced in the Prologue at 1.15, has its first use only in the Gospel narrative at this point. An examination of the distribution of the word, "Satan", throughout the gospel reveals also the feature of his mention in the Prologue (1.13) and in the middle two sections of this Day (3.23, 26 and 4.15), and only once elsewhere, in 8.33. These middle two sections have their strong links with each other and with the Prologue, 1.1-20.

The above parallels between sections two and three, it may be argued, suggest that the sectional form of the Day is ABB'A', where the inner two sections parallel each other, and where the outer two sections parallel each other for their 'emphasis' on Jesus and his disciples. The undermining of this possibility is that section one, 3.7-19, like sections two and three, also has its contact with the Prologue, 1.1-20 (for the call and future functions of the disciples, in particular). Further, that there is a contents balance between the outer two sections is not easily defensible. We noted above particularly also how sections three and four (4.1-32 and vv.33-41) connect so strongly through the introductory part to 4.33-41, which is vv.33-36. We discern, further, how sections one and two connect for the challenges which were being put to Jesus (that "he is besides himself", 3.21; and "By the ruler of the demons he casts out demons", 3.22) which have their connections with 3.7-19 (Jesus' attracting frenzied crowds and appointing "twelve" to be with him; and his dealing with unclean spirits). And the case for the link at 4.1 repeating Mark's usage at 2.13 and 3.1 is a strong one. In identifying Καὶ πάλιν as the connection between the two halves of the presentations of Days Three and Four (the other two days of these three middle Days to this Series) it would seeem that the phrase does also connect two halves in the telling of Day Five's presentation. The sectional arrangement is to be represented, therefore, by AA'/AA' in its shorter form, and ABB';ABB'/ABB';ABB' in its longer form, denoting the parts in series which make up the sections. Below is the literary structure of Day Five:

(Note: As discussed in Day Two above, we observe key use again by Mark of historical presents at both A, B, B' and α, β, β' levels of order.)

A α ⁷[α] Καὶ ὁ'Ιησοῦς [β] μετὰ τῶν μαθητῶν αὐτοῦ [β'] ἀνεχώρησεν πρὸς τὴν θάλασσαν·
  β [α] [.α] καὶ πολὺ πλῆθος [.β] ἀπὸ τῆς Γαλιλαίας [.β'] [ἠκολούθησεν],
    [β] [.α] καὶ ἀπὸ τῆς'Ιουδαίας ⁸[.β] καὶ ἀπὸ 'Ιεροσολύμων [.β'] καὶ ἀπὸ τῆς'Ιδουμαίας
    [β'] [.α] καὶ πέραν τοῦ'Ιορδάνου [.β] καὶ περὶ Τύρον [.β'] καὶ Σιδῶνα,
  β' [α] πλῆθος πολύ, [β] ἀκούοντες ὅσα ἐποίει [β'] ἦλθον πρὸς αὐτόν.

B α ⁹[α] [.α] καὶ εἶπεν τοῖς μαθηταῖς αὐτου [.α'] ἵνα πλοιάριον προσκαρτερῇ αὐτῷ
    [β] διὰ τὸν ὄχλον [β'] ἵνα μὴ θλίβωσιν αὐτόν·
  β ¹⁰[α] πολλοὺς γὰρ ἐθεράπευσεν, [β] ὥστε ἐπιπίπτειν αὐτῷ [β'] [.α] ἵνα αὐτοῦ ἅψωνται [.α'] ὅσοι εἶχον μάστιγας.
  β' ¹¹[α] [.α] καὶ τὰ πνεύματα τὰ ἀκάθαρτα, [.β] ὅταν αὐτὸν ἐθεώρουν, [.β'] προσέπιπτον αὐτῷ
    [β] [.α] καὶ ἔκραζον [.β] λέγοντες [.β'] ὅτι Σὺ εἶ ὁ υἱὸς τοῦ θεοῦ.
    ¹²[β'] [.α] καὶ πολλὰ ἐπετίμα αὐτοῖς [.α'] ἵνα μὴ αὐτὸν φανερὸν ποιήσωσιν.

B' α ¹³[α] Καὶ ἀναβαίνει εἰς τὸ ὄρος [β] καὶ προσκαλεῖται οὓς ἤθελεν αὐτός, [β'] καὶ ἀπῆλθον πρὸς αὐτόν.
  β[α]¹⁴[.α] καὶ ἐποίησεν δώδεκα, [.α'] [οὓς καὶ ἀποστόλους ὠνόμασεν],
    [β]   ἵνα ὦσιν μετ' αὐτοῦ
    [β'] [.α] καὶ ἵνα ἀποστέλλῃ αὐτοὺς [.β] κηρύσσειν [.β'] ¹⁵καὶ ἔχειν ἐξουσίαν ἐκβάλλειν τὰ δαιμόνια·
  β'[α] ¹⁶[.α] καὶ ἐποίησεν τοὺς δώδεκα,
    [β] [.α] [..α] καὶ ἐπέθηκεν ὄνομα [..β] τῷ Σίμωνι [..β'] Πέτρον,
    ¹⁷[.β] καὶ'Ιάκωβον τὸν τοῦ Ζεβεδαίου [.β'] καὶ'Ιωάννην τὸν ἀδελφὸν τοῦ'Ιακώβου,
    [β'] [.α] [..α] καὶ ἐπέθηκεν αὐτοῖς ὀνόματα [..β] Βοανηργές, [..β'] ὅ ἐστιν Υἱοὶ Βροντῆς· ¹⁸[.α'] [..α] καὶ'Ανδρέαν [..β] καὶ Φίλιππον [..γ] καὶ Βαρθολομαῖον [..δ] καὶ Μαθθαῖον [..ε] καὶ Θωμᾶν [..ζ] καὶ'Ιάκωβον τὸν τοῦ'Αλφαίου [..η] καὶ Θαδδαῖον [..θ] καὶ Σίμωνα τὸν Καναναῖον ¹⁹[..ι] [...α] καὶ'Ιούδαν'Ισκαριώθ, [...α'] ὃς καὶ παρέδωκεν αὐτόν.

A α ²⁰[α] Καὶ ἔρχεται εἰς οἶκον· [β] καὶ συνέρχεται πάλιν [ὁ] ὄχλος,
      [β'] ὥστε μὴ δύνασθαι αὐτοὺς μηδὲ ἄρτον φαγεῖν.
  β ²¹[α] καὶ ἀκούσαντες οἱ παρ' αὐτοῦ [β] ἐξῆλθον κρατῆσαι αὐτόν,
      [β'] [.α] ἔλεγον γὰρ [.α'] ὅτι ἐξέστη.
  β' ²²[α] καὶ οἱ γραμματεῖς [β] οἱ ἀπὸ Ἱεροσολύμων καταβάντες
      [β'] [.α] ἔλεγον [.β] ὅτι Βεελζεβοὺλ ἔχει, [.β'] καὶ ὅτι ἐν τῷ
      ἄρχοντι τῶν δαιμονίων ἐκβάλλει τὰ δαιμόνια.

B α[α]²³[α] Καὶ προσκαλεσάμενος αὐτοὺς [β] ἐν παραβολαῖς ἔλεγεν αὐτοῖς,
      [β'] Πῶς δύναται Σατανᾶς Σατανᾶν ἐκβάλλειν;
  [β] ²⁴[.α] καὶ ἐὰν βασιλεία ἐφ' ἑαυτὴν μερισθῇ, [.α'] οὐ δύναται
      σταθῆναι ἡ βασιλεία ἐκείνη·
  [β'] ²⁵[.α] καὶ ἐὰν οἰκία ἐφ' ἑαυτὴν μερισθῇ, [.α'] οὐ δυνήσεται ἡ οἰκία
      ἐκείνη σταθῆναι.
  β[α]²⁶[.α] [..α] καὶ εἰ ὁ Σατανᾶς ἀνέστη ἐφ' ἑαυτὸν [..α'] καὶ ἐμερίσθη,
      [.α'] [..α] ου δύναται στῆναι [..α'] ἀλλὰ τέλος ἔχει.
  [β] ²⁷[.α] ἀλλ' οὐ δύναται οὐδεὶς [.β] εἰς τὴν οἰκίαν τοῦ ἰσχυροῦ
      εἰσελθὼν [.β'] τὰ σκεύη αὐτου διαρπάσαι
  [β'] [.α] ἐὰν μὴ πρῶτον τὸν ἰσχυρὸν δήσῃ, [.α'] καὶ τότε τὴν οἰκίαν
      αὐτου διαρπάσει.
  β'[α]²⁸[.α] Ἀμὴν λέγω ὑμῖν [.α] [..α] ὅτι πάντα ἀφεθήσεται τοῖς υἱοῖς τῶν
      ἀνθρώπων, [..β] τὰ ἁμαρτήματα καὶ αἱ βλασφημίαι [..β'] ὅσα ἐὰν
      βλασφημήσωσιν·
  [β] ²⁹ [.α] ὃς δ' ἂν βλασφημήσῃ εἰς τὸ πνεῦμα τὸ ἅγιον [.β] οὐκ ἔχει
      ἄφεσιν εἰς τὸν αἰῶνα, [.β'] ἀλλὰ ἔνοχός ἐστιν αἰωνίου
      ἁμαρτήματος
  [β'] ³⁰ [.α] ὅτι ἔλεγον, [.α'] Πνεῦμα ἀκάθαρτον ἔχει.

B' α[α] ³¹ [.α] Καὶ ἔρχεται [.β] ἡ μήτηρ αὐτου [.β'] καὶ οἱ ἀδελφοὶ αὐτου
      [α'] [.α] καὶ ἔξω στήκοντες [.β] ἀπέστειλαν πρὸς αὐτὸν
      [.β'] καλοῦντες αὐτόν.
  β[α]³²[.α] καὶ ἐκάθητο περὶ αὐτὸν ὄχλος, [.α'] καὶ λέγουσιν αὐτῷ,
      [β] [.α] Ἰδου [.β] [..α] ἡ μήτηρ σου [..β] καὶ οἱ ἀδελφοί σου [..β'] καὶ
      αἱ ἀδελφαι σοῦ [.β'] ἔξω ζητοῦσίν σε.
  [β']³³[.α] καὶ ἀποκριθεὶς αὐτοῖς [.α'] [..α] λέγει, [.β] Τίς ἐστιν ἡ μήτηρ
      μου [.β'] και οἱ ἀδελφοί [μου] ;
  β'[α]³⁴[.α] καὶ περιβλεψάμενος τοὺς περὶ αὐτὸν [.β] κύκλῳ καθημένους
      [.β'] λέγει,
  [β] [.α] Ἴδε [.β] ἡ μήτηρ μου [.β'] καὶ οἱ ἀδελφοί μου.
  [β']³⁵[.α] ὃς [γὰρ] ἂν ποιήσῃ τὸ θέλημα τοῦ θεοῦ,
      [.α'] [..α] οὗτος ἀδελφός μου [..β] καὶ ἀδελφὴ [..β'] καὶ μήτηρ
      ἐστίν.

A α [α] ¹[.α] Καὶ πάλιν [.β] ἤρξατο διδάσκειν [.βʹ] παρὰ τὴν θάλασσαν.
   [β] [.α] καὶ συνάγεται πρὸς αὐτὸν ὄχλος πλεῖστος, [.β] ὥστε αὐτὸν εἰς
       πλοῖον ἐμβάντα καθῆσθαι ἐν τῇ θαλάσσῃ, [.βʹ] καὶ πᾶς ὁ ὄχλος
       πρὸς τὴν θάλασσαν ἐπὶ τῆς γῆς ἦσαν.
   [βʹ] ² καὶ ἐδίδασκεν αὐτοὺς ἐν παραβολαῖς πολλά.
β [α] [.α] καὶ ἔλεγεν αὐτοῖς [.β] ἐν τῇ διδαχῇ αὐτοῦ, [.βʹ] ³ Ἀκούετε.
   [αʹ] [.α] [..α] ἰδοὺ [..β] ἐξῆλθεν ὁ σπείρων [..βʹ] σπεῖραι.
   ⁴[.β] [..α] καὶ ἐγένετο ἐν τῷ σπείρειν [..β] ὃ μὲν ἔπεσεν παρὰ τὴν
        ὁδόν, [..βʹ] καὶ ἦλθεν τὰ πετεινὰ καὶ κατέφαγεν αὐτό.
   ⁵[.γ] [..α] [...α] καὶ ἄλλο ἔπεσεν ἐπὶ τὸ πετρῶδες [...αʹ] ὅπου οὐκ εἶχεν
        γῆν πολλήν, [..β] [...α] καὶ εὐθὺς ἐξανέτειλεν [...αʹ] διὰ τὸ μὴ
        ἔχειν βάθος γῆς· [..βʹ] [...α] ⁶ καὶ ὅτε ἀνέτειλεν ὁ ἥλιος
        ἐκαυματίσθη, [...αʹ] καὶ διὰ τὸ μὴ ἔχειν ῥίζαν ἐξηράνθη.
   ⁷[.δ] [..α] καὶ ἄλλο ἔπεσεν εἰς τὰς ἀκάνθας, [..β] καὶ ἀνέβησαν αἱ
        ἄκανθαι καὶ συνέπνιξαν αὐτό, [..βʹ] καὶ καρπὸν οὐκ ἔδωκεν.
   ⁸[.ε] [..α] καὶ ἄλλα ἔπεσεν εἰς τὴν γῆν τὴν καλήν, [..β] καὶ ἐδίδου
        καρπὸν ἀναβαίνοντα καὶ αὐξανόμενα, [..βʹ] [...α] καὶ ἔφερεν ἓν
        τριάκοντα [...β] καὶ ἓν ἑξήκοντα [...βʹ] καὶ ἓν ἑκατόν.
βʹ ⁹[α] καὶ ἔλεγεν, [β] "Ὃς ἔχει ὦτα ἀκούειν [βʹ] ἀκουέτω.

B α[α]¹⁰[.α] Καὶ ὅτε ἐγένετο κατὰ μόνας, [.β] [..α] ἠρώτων αὐτὸν [..β] οἱ
        περὶ αὐτὸν [..βʹ] σὺν τοῖς δώδεκα [.βʹ] τὰς παραβολάς.
   [β] ¹¹[.α] καὶ ἔλεγεν αὐτοῖς, [.β] [..α] ʽΥμῖν [..β] τὸ μυστήριον δέδοται
        [..βʹ] τῆς βασιλείας τοῦ θεοῦ· [.βʹ] [..α] ἐκείνοις δὲ τοῖς ἔξω
        [..β] ἐν παραβολαῖς [..βʹ] τὰ πάντα γίνεται,
   [βʹ]¹²[.α] [..α] ἵνα βλέποντες [..β] βλέπωσιν [..βʹ] καὶ μὴ ἴδωσιν,
        [.β] [..α] καὶ ἀκούοντες [..β] ἀκούωσιν [..βʹ] καὶ μὴ συνιῶσιν,
        [.βʹ] [..α] μήποτε ἐπιστρέψωσιν [..αʹ] καὶ ἀφεθῇ αὐτοῖς.
β [α]¹³[.α] Καὶ λέγει αὐτοῖς, [.β] Οὐκ οἴδατε τὴν παραβολὴν ταύτην,
        [.βʹ] καὶ πῶς πάσας τὰς παραβολὰς γνώσεσθε;
   [αʹ]¹⁴[.α] ὁ σπείρων τὸν λόγον σπείρει.
   ¹⁵[.β] [..α] οὗτοι δέ εἰσιν οἱ παρὰ τὴν ὁδὸν ὅπου σπείρεται ὁ λόγος,
        [..β] καὶ ὅταν ἀκούσωσιν εὐθὺς ἔρχεται ὁ Σατανᾶς [..βʹ] καὶ
        αἴρει τὸν λόγον τὸν ἐσπαρμένον εἰς αὐτούς.
   ¹⁶[.γ] [..α] καὶ οὗτοί εἰσιν οἱ ἐπὶ τὰ πετρώδη σπειρόμενοι, [..β] οἳ
        ὅταν ἀκούσωσιν τὸν λόγον εὐθὺς μετὰ χαρᾶς λαμβάνουσιν
        αὐτόν, ¹⁷[..βʹ] [...α] καὶ οὐκ ἔχουσιν ῥίζαν ἐν ἑαυτοῖς ἀλλὰ
        πρόσκαιροί εἰσιν· [...β] εἶτα γενομένης θλίψεως ἢ διωγμοῦ διὰ
        τὸν λόγον [...βʹ] εὐθὺς σκανδαλίζονται.
   ¹⁸[.δ] [..α] καὶ ἄλλοι εἰσιν οἱ εἰς τὰς ἀκάνθας σπειρόμενοι·
        [..β] οὗτοί εἰσιν οἱ τὸν λόγον ἀκούσαντες, ¹⁹[..βʹ] [...α] καὶ αἱ
        μέριμναι τοῦ αἰῶνος [.] καὶ ἡ ἀπάτη τοῦ πλούτου [.] καὶ αἱ περὶ
        τὰ λοιπὰ ἐπιθυμίαι εἰσπορευόμεναι [...β] συμπνίγουσιν τὸν
        λόγον, [...βʹ] καὶ ἄκαρπος γίνεται.
   ²⁰[.ε] [..α] καὶ ἐκεῖνοί εἰσιν οἱ ἐπὶ τὴν γῆν τὴν καλὴν σπαρέντες,

[..β] οἵτινες <u>ἀκούουσιν</u> <u>τὸν λόγον</u> καὶ παραδέχονται
[..β'] [...α] καὶ καρποφοροῦσιν <u>ἓν</u> <u>τριάκοντα</u> [...β] καὶ <u>ἓν</u>
<u>ἑξήκοντα</u> [...β'] καὶ <u>ἓν</u> ἑκατόν.
β'[α]²¹[.α] <u>Καὶ ἔλεγεν αὐτοῖς,</u> [.α'] [..α] Μήτι ἔρχεται ὁ λύχνος
[..β] [...α] <u>ἵνα</u> <u>ὑπὸ</u> τὸν μόδιον <u>τεθῇ</u> [...α'] ἢ <u>ὑπὸ</u> τὴν κλίνην;
[..β'] οὐχ <u>ἵνα</u> ἐπὶ τὴν λυχνίαν <u>τεθῇ</u>;
[β] ²²[.α] [..α] <u>οὐ</u> γάρ ἐστιν <u>κρυπτὸν</u> [..α'] ἐὰν μὴ <u>ἵνα</u> <u>φανερωθῇ,</u>
[.α'] [..α] <u>οὐδε</u> ἐγένετο <u>ἀπόκρυφον</u> [..α'] ἀλλ' <u>ἵνα</u> ἔλθῃ εἰς <u>φανερόν.</u>
[β'] ²³[.α] εἴ τις ἔχει ὦτα ἀκούειν [.α'] <u>ἀκουέτω.</u>

B' α[α]²⁴[.α] <u>Καὶ ἔλεγεν αὐτοῖς,</u> [.β] Βλέπετε [.β'] τί <u>ἀκούετε.</u>
[β] [.α] ἐν ᾧ <u>μέτρῳ</u> <u>μετρεῖτε</u> [.β] <u>μετρηθήσεται</u> ὑμῖν [.β'] καὶ
<u>προστεθήσεται</u> ὑμῖν.
[β'] ²⁵[.α] [..α] <u>ὃς γὰρ ἔχει,</u> [..α'] δοθήσεται αὐτῷ· [.α'] [..α] καὶ <u>ὃς οὐκ</u>
<u>ἔχει,</u> [..α'] καὶ ὃ <u>ἔχει</u> ἀρθήσεται ἀπ' αὐτοῦ.
β[α]²⁶[.α] <u>Καὶ ἔλεγεν,</u> [.β] Οὕτως ἐστὶν <u>ἡ βασιλεία τοῦ θεοῦ</u> [.β'] [..α] ὡς
ἄνθρωπος βάλῃ τὸν <u>σπόρον</u> <u>ἐπὶ τῆς γῆς</u> ²⁷[..β] καὶ καθεύδῃ καὶ
ἐγείρηται νύκτα καὶ ἡμέραν, [..β'] καὶ ὁ <u>σπόρος</u> βλαστᾷ καὶ
μηκύνηται ὡς οὐκ οἶδεν αὐτός.
[β] ²⁸[.α] αὐτομάτη <u>ἡ γῆ</u> <u>καρποφορεῖ,</u> [.α'] [..α] πρῶτον χόρτον, [..β] εἶτα
<u>στάχυν,</u> [..β'] εἶτα πλήρη[ς] σῖτον ἐν τῷ <u>στάχυϊ.</u>
[β'] ²⁹[.α] <u>ὅταν δε παραδοῖ ὁ καρπός,</u> [.β] εὐθὺς ἀποστέλλει τὸ δρέπανον,
[.β'] ὅτι παρέστηκεν ὁ θερισμός.
β'[α]³⁰[.α] <u>Καὶ ἔλεγεν,</u> [.β] Πῶς ὁμοιώσωμεν <u>τὴν βασιλείαν τοῦ θεου,</u>
[.β'] ἢ ἐν τίνι αὐτὴν <u>παραβολῇ</u> θῶμεν;
[β] ³¹[.α] ὡς κόκκῳ σινάπεως, [.β] ὃς <u>ὅταν σπαρῇ ἐπὶ τῆς γῆς,</u>
[.β'] μικρότερον ὂν <u>πάντων τῶν</u> σπερμάτων τῶν ἐπὶ τῆς γῆς,
[β'] ³²[.α] <u>καὶ ὅταν σπαρῇ,</u> [.β] ἀναβαίνει καὶ γίνεται μεῖζον <u>πάντων τῶν</u>
λαχάνων [.β'] [..α] καὶ ποιεῖ κλάδους μεγάλους, [..β] ὥστε
δύνασθαι ὑπὸ τὴν σκιὰν αὐτοῦ [..β'] τὰ πετεινὰ τοῦ οὐρανου
κατασκηνοῦν.

A α ³³[α] [.α] Καὶ τοιαύταις <u>παραβολαῖς πολλαῖς</u> [.β] <u>ἐλάλει αὐτοῖς τὸν</u>
<u>λόγον,</u> [.β'] καθὼς ἠδύναντο <u>ἀκούειν·</u>
³⁴[β] χωρὶς δὲ <u>παραβολῆς</u> οὐκ <u>ἐλάλει αὐτοῖς,</u>
[β'] [.α] κατ' ἰδίαν δὲ [.β] τοῖς ἰδίοις μαθηταῖς [.β'] ἐπέλυεν πάντα.
β ³⁵[α] [.α] <u>Καὶ λέγει αὐτοῖς</u> [.β] ἐν ἐκείνῃ τῇ ἡμέρᾳ [.β'] ὀψίας
γενομένης,
[α'] διέλθωμεν εἰς τὸ πέραν.
β' ³⁶[α] καὶ <u>ἀφέντες τὸν ὄχλον</u> [β] παραλαμβάνουσιν αὐτὸν ὡς ἦν <u>ἐν τῷ</u>
<u>πλοίῳ,</u> [β'] καὶ ἄλλα <u>πλοῖα</u> ἦν μετ' αὐτοῦ.

B α ³⁷[α] καὶ γίνεται λαῖλαψ μεγάλη ἀνέμου, [β] καὶ τὰ κύματα ἐπέβαλλεν εἰς τὸ πλοῖον, [β'] ὥστε ἤδη γεμίζεσθαι τὸ πλοῖον.
β ³⁸[α] [.α] καὶ αὐτὸς ἦν ἐν τῇ πρύμνῃ [.β] ἐπὶ τὸ προσκεφάλαιον [.β'] καθεύδων·
[β] [.α] καὶ ἐγείρουσιν αὐτὸν [.α'] [..α] καὶ λέγουσιν αὐτῷ, [..β] Διδάσκαλε, [..β'] οὐ μέλει σοι ὅτι ἀπολλύμεθα;
β' ³⁹[α] καὶ διεγερθεὶς [β] ἐπετίμησεν τῷ ἀνέμῳ [β'] [.α] καὶ εἶπεν τῇ θαλάσσῃ, [.β] Σιώπα, [.β'] πεφίμωσο.

B' α [α] καὶ ἐκόπασεν ὁ ἄνεμος, [α'] καὶ ἐγένετο γαλήνη μεγάλη.
β ⁴⁰[α] καὶ εἶπεν αὐτοῖς, [β] Τί δειλοί ἐστε; [β'] οὔπω ἔχετε πίστιν;
β' ⁴¹[α] [.α] καὶ ἐφοβήθησαν φόβον μέγαν, [.α'] καὶ ἔλεγον πρὸς ἀλλήλους, [β] Τίς ἄρα οὗτός ἐστιν [β'] ὅτι καὶ ὁ ἄνεμος καὶ ἡ θάλασσα ὑπακούει αὐτῷ;

As a final point, we ask, should we be concerned that the numbers of the verses of the sections are not 'too equal'? They number in turn: 13, 16, 32 and 9; or in their halves 29 and 41. It is, of course, the case that this Day's telling, compared with those we have already examined, is exceptional: 1) it is the longest so far (in terms of the whole Gospel it is the second longest report, with 70 verses, after Day Twenty-four, 11.20-13.37, which has 90 verses); and 2) it is the first so far to contain much teaching (Day Twenty-four is the next we encounter and it contains even more).

In the Introduction we looked for possible repetitive and progressive forms in biblical and non-biblical literature which might have influenced Mark in his choice of 'arrangement' and 'style'. It is clearly the case that in the Genesis account of creation, 1.1-2.4a, and in Homer's *Iliad* there is evidence of wide variation in the sizes of the presentations of the Days' accounts themselves. (See page 24, for the verses of the days of the Genesis account which vary widely, and page 26 for the marked differences in the numbers of 'Books' which the Days of the *Iliad* comprise.) The analysis of Mark's work shows it, in this regard, to be no different from these comparable compositions. What seems important, therefore, in the writing of such ancient literature, is that the *constructions* were themselves complete, in their ABB' forms. In regard to Day Five's sectional variation, we might then say simply that it follows earlier precedent, and that the variation in sizes of presentations was less important to ancient writers than the completing of their constructions. And we might say of Mark's rhetorical method, from all that we have seen already: it matters not to him how long the elements are, or how much they vary; it matters only that all the main component parts, A, B, B' and α, β, β', are present.

What I have stated previously though, may be correct. Up till this Day's telling Mark's structural method had not really been put to the test, with teaching blocks to include. His method was surely stretched to the limit, as it clearly shows extensions to his normal forms, in 4.1-32 especially.

Day Six: 5.1-20:

The Day begins: Καὶ ἦλθον εἰς τὸ πέραν τῆς θαλάσσης εἰς τὴν χώραν τῶν Γερασηνῶν...

The point has been made above that Day Five (3.7-4.41) ends with the story of a crossing of the sea; it is a crossing which begins in the evening (4.35,36). Four crossings of the sea, in all, are reported by Mark, and there is reason to see them all as night-crossings which separate the telling of the Day on which the crossing begins from the Day on which the crossing ends, with an arrival in a new place. Bultmann's acknowledgement that "the spatial link (in many of his examples beginning with εἰς) is a temporal one"[99] is supportive of the argument. We examine this feature of the night-time sea-crossing because it is an important indicator Mark uses to help his reader/listeners understand that new Days in his telling begin with new locations and new activities after sunrise.

The first sea-crossing of the Gospel begins on Day Five, at 4.35,36 ("When evening had come"). A storm arises and to the amazement of the disciples travelling with him Jesus stills the storm. The sea-journey is concluded with the words "And they came to the other side of the sea into the country of the Gerasenes", at 5.1 which is the beginning of Day Six of Mark's telling and, therefore, the beginning of a new report. And Day Five's report is concluded with the completing of the story of the stilling of the storm. A 'space' exists, we note, between the ending of Day Five and the beginning of

---

[99] Bultmann, *The History...*, p.340.

Day Six. But it is not incumbent on Mark to fill the void with a Pepysian "and so to bed"[100] kind of comment. Night-time equates with sleep-time, and that may be perfectly understood without any reference to sleep, though in Day Five's closing account of the stormy crossing we are told, of course, that Jesus *was* "sleeping on a pillow".

The second sea-crossing begins on Day Six, at 5.18 ("And as he embarked into the boat..."). It ends at 5.21 ("And when Jesus had crossed over in the boat again to the other side a great crowd..."). Two primary questions need to be put as there is no reference (as there is in the first example of a sea-crossing) to the time of embarkation. Was it a night-time crossing? And was the crossing's completion, therefore, coincident with the beginning of a new Day's telling? Estimates of the timings and the times taken by the events of the proposed Day Six (5.1-20) and/or estimates or information of the timings of the events of the proposed Day Seven (5.21-43) are required.

The events of the proposed Day Six begin with a meeting of Jesus and the man who Mark says called himself "Legion" (there is no mention of it being night-time and the story's events are continuous and suggest that they all occur in daylight). Due to the time-taking episodes, whereby the pig-herders witness the drowning of the two thousand or so pigs, and flee to report "*in the city and in the fields*", and the ones to whom they report come out to Jesus and then beg him to go, it may be judged that Jesus' return crossing began late that day. The events of the proposed Day Seven begin with Jesus and an assembled crowd by the sea. Jesus is there long enough for Jairus to learn where he is and to come to him to beg Jesus to go with him to his home to heal his dying daughter. A land-journey ensues, during which Jesus is delayed (by a woman who takes her healing from him), by which time messengers come with news of Jairus' daughter's death, after which Jesus resumes his land-journey, arrives at the house and gives her back her life. The events of 5.21-43, it may be judged, are themselves sufficient for one Day's telling in Mark's scheme.

Additionally, in estimating the possible time lapse between the proposed Days Six and Seven and given their designations in terms of their chapter and verse, there is the evidence of a sequence of

---

[100] Samuel Pepys, *Diary*, 6 May, 1660, *et passim*.

disclosures of 4.35-41 (at least), 5.1-20 and 5.21-43 which is "one of those groups of three of which Mark is so fond" (according to Nineham: see Day Five's examination). We note too that the two other night crossings, of Days Nine and Thirteen, the case for which will be put below, both end the second Day's tellings (underlined) of threesomes of Days in Mark's scheme (the sub-Series are Days Eight, Nine and Ten, and Days Twelve, Thirteen and Fourteen). The proposed night-crossing, beginning (late in the Day) at 5.18 and ending (near the sunrise of the new Day) at 5.21, would play the same role in the telling of Days Five, Six and Seven.

The weight of evidence would seem to suggest that Mark did intend this return crossing as a foil between Days Six and Seven as defined by 5.1-20 and 5.21-43.

The third sea-crossing (of the disciples alone) begins on Day Nine (6.30-52), at 6.45, before sunset: Jesus tells his disciples to embark into the boat and to go ahead of him to the other side, to Bethsaida. "And when evening came the boat was in the middle of the sea and (Jesus) was alone on land" (6.47). The disciples were having trouble with their rowing because the wind was against them. "About the fourth watch of the night" Jesus goes to them "walking on the sea..." (6.48). As he reached them and got into the boat, the wind ceased (6.51). The sea-journey ends on Day Ten (6.53-7.23), at 6.53, "And crossing over onto land they came to Gennesaret and anchored. And as they came out of the boat immediately..." (because it was daylight, we can deduce) people brought to him their sick. This third example of a sea-crossing makes it perfectly clear that a crossing (a maximum eight miles across and sixteen miles from top to bottom) could take all night[101].

The fourth sea-crossing begins on Day Thirteen (8.1-21), at 8.13, "...embarking, he went away to the other side". The sea-journey concludes on Day Fourteen (8.22-26), at 8.22, "And they 'come' to Bethsaida. And they 'bring'...". In this story of a sea-crossing, no time of embarkation is stated in the telling. How are we to estimate it? We may compare Days Nine and Thirteen for some help in the matter, and also examine a detail of the Day itself.

---

[101] Whether rowing or sailing, reasonably short stretches of water, because of wind and storm in the first case and because of a lack of wind in the second, can be perceived to be very long indeed. (I have had the worrying experience of both.)

We consider firstly the parallel contents (pertinent to this issue) of the Days (as proposed) in which these stories of the third and fourth sea-crossings occur. Day Nine (6.30-52) reports the feeding of the five thousand: it records a short sea-journey (not a crossing, in 6.32) to a "solitary place" (which we can assume is just down the coast-line) and records a night-time crossing which was supposed to be to Bethsaida. Day Thirteen (8.1-21) reports the feeding of the four thousand: it records a short sea-journey (not a crossing, 8.10) down the coast to Dalmanutha and records a crossing to Bethsaida. Mark is setting these two tellings of Days in parallel: it is logical to conclude that he intended the crossing of Day Thirteen to behave as for Day Nine, as a Day-separating indicator. We may now see if there is any support for this in the examination of a particular detail of Day Thirteen.

In 8.2, it is reported that the crowd had been with Jesus three "days" and had had nothing to eat. According to rhetorical analysis, the introduction to the telling of the Day's events is 8.1-3: it is the A part of Mark's ABB' construction with which he forms the first half of his whole presentation. It begins reading literally: "In those days there being again a great crowd, and not having anything they might eat, calling to him the disciples he says to them, 'I have compassion on the crowd, because now *three days* they remain with me, and they have nothing they might eat...'" The question arises as to the timing of Jesus' calling his disciples to him. The most likely explanation is that the crowd has been with Jesus all of the day (here reported) and that prior to it they have been with him two days. He, therefore, calls his disciples to him *late on* in the Day being reported. Again we might compare this Day's telling with that of Day Nine. The feeding of the five thousand takes place "late" (6.35) in the Day (when people regularly ate their main meal of the day). The feeding of the four thousand (of Day Thirteen) can be similarly timed, as late in the day, and the timing of Jesus' meeting with the Pharisees would, therefore, have been later, and the crossing later still.

We may assess, therefore, that four times in his gospel narrative, Mark uses the night-crossing of the sea as an important indicator to his audience that new Days in his telling begin with new locations and new activities after (meaning: 'immediately after', 'sometime after', or 'anytime after') sunrise. This exercise establishes the limits of a number of Days in Mark's telling and establishes also the principle that Mark uses new geographical locations to signal his beginning of new Days. We can continue now with our analysis of Day Six (5.1-20).

The Day's story is without exception viewed by commentators as a unity, but over the years attitudes have varied as to how much Mark's hand is evident in the presentation we have here. Bultmann[102] points out that the narrative has the form characteristic of the miracle-story which he suggests is in its original form, save transitional phrases in v.1 and the redactional verse 8. Because of the "unevenness of the narrative", its vivid and emphatic details, and because v.8 "appears to reflect the Evangelist's embarrassment in coping with an excess of material", Taylor explains that the passage was not yet reduced to the rounded form of miracle-stories and was, therefore, a clear piece of oral tradition which is Petrine in origin[103]. Nineham particularly sees its connection with the previous day's story of "the stilling of the storm": the question is posed, he says, "Who then is this that such immense power is at his disposal?" but of its present form, he says, "It has clearly passed through a number of stages" of development[104]. In relation to this, he devotes space to the problem of the setting, "the country of Gerasene", which is thirty miles from the lake shore. Commentators over the years have remarked on Mark's poor geographical knowledge. It is proper to point out, however, in this context, that Mark makes nothing of the fact that this is predominently Gentile country, neither that the man who is healed is a Gentile, nor that those who were attending the pigs were Gentiles, nor those also who then came out to Jesus. No argument from silence is satisfactory, but in contrast, in Day Eleven (7.24-30), Mark spells it out loudly and clearly that Jesus is ministering in Tyre, to "a Greek, a Syrophoenician by race" (7.25) and through her to her daughter. It would seem that in presenting Day Six in the way that he does Mark intends no reader/listeners to dwell on the fact that Jesus' ministry here extends to a Gentile/Gentiles. It is not the issue of the story here, but it is the issue

---

[102] R. Bultmann, *The History...*, p.224.
[103] Taylor, *The Gospel...*, pp.22f.: few commentators today would feel able to write like this.
[104] Nineham, *Saint Mark*, p.152.

in the story of Day Eleven and that is why Mark saves it until then, and deliberately places the telling in the middle Day which marks a turning point in his second Series of seven Days.

Hooker describes *this* day's story as one which contains "an embarrassing amount of detail" [105] and as a "narrative that does not run smoothly". She says that vv.3-5 are "somewhat obtrusive", that v.6 "seems strange" after v.2b, that v.8 is "clumsy", and that we have two proofs of the demoniac's cure, in vv.11-13 and v.15[106]. These are evidences to her of the stages of development the story has gone through, for to her it is possible that two accounts are combined by Mark (5.1-2, 7-8 and 15; and vv.2-6 and 9ff.). According to others[107] it is a combination of a miracle-story and a popular tale about an unknown exorcist who tricked some demons into self-destruction. For the duplicating of v.2 by v.6 she describes one possibility, that Mark "has forgotten what he wrote there"!

The structure of 5.1-20 to Taylor is expressed as an arrangement of scenes, four in all: vv.1-10 the man; vv.11-13 the swine; vv.14-17 the townspeople; and vv.18-20 back to the man by the lakeside. To Taylor, it is a four-act drama "and yet we do not receive the impression of imaginative artistic creation"[108]. But the story's analysis presented below demonstrates well the Markan style, α, β, β^c: it is a story told in two halves (compare Days One, Three and Four, so far) in which the rhythm of presentation is most easily identifiable because of Mark's usage of the non-καὶ sentences at 5.3 and 5.11 (for the latter, refer to page 100) and his favourite historical present at 5.15, and because of other signifiers, principally the balancing parts and sub-parts denoted by β, β^c and $[\beta]$, $[\beta^c]$. Mark's presentational method results in repetitions; there is no need to look for two stories behind his presentation. Both drama and clarity are the product. Verse 8, in many respects like 3.30 in the previous Day's telling, is a Markan parenthetical explanation.

What *is* new, according to literary-structural analysis, in this Day's presentation, is Mark's use of chiasm. For the first time in the Gospel we encounter this literary form much re-discovered in recent

---

[105] Perhaps suggested to her by Taylor's comments recorded above.
[106] Hooker, *The Gospel...*, p.141.
[107] Hooker, *The Gospel...*, p.142.
[108] Taylor, *The Gospel...*, p.277.

years: it is a Greco-Roman rhetorical device[109]. 5.3-5 comprises a six-part chiasm, which is in the first half of his presentation, in B, and which is annotated as: α, β, γ, γ˚, β˚, α˚. The "embarrassing amount of detail" Hooker speaks about has been given its chiastic presentation for maximum effect it would seem. Both reader and audience in the first century would likely recognise the change of rhythm.[110] The man's problems are severe indeed and the parallel part B˚ strengthens further the 'impossibility' of Jesus being able to do anything for the man. We note that the description of the 'incurable' woman with the "issue of blood" (5.25) in the next Day's telling is similarly deliberately full in detail, though non-chiastic. In Day Six, Jesus works such amazing power against the forces of evil, that Nineham is right that it raises again the question posed by Jesus' stilling of the storm in Day Five, "Who then is this that such immense power is at his disposal?" In Day Seven, Mark tells us that Jesus can heal the incurably sick, but more than that, Jesus has the power even to raise the dead.

The literary structure of Day Six may be characterised as an A:A' construction in its shorter form, and as an ABB'/ABB' construction in its longer form, which takes into account the major parts of the Day report's two halves. The literary structure of Day Six is viewed as follows:

---

[109] Consider, for Markan composition: Joanna Dewey, and Benoît Standaert, *L'Évangile...*; and for pre-Markan: Rudolf Pesch *op.cit.* and Paul J. Achtemeier, *Toward the Isolation...*, pp.265-291 and *The Origin...* pp.198-221; see above, under Day Four, for a fuller discussion.

[110] For a discussion of such matters, refer to the Introduction, to the section "The Cultural and Historical Context of the Gospel", and specifically footnote 42.

A α ¹ [α] Καὶ ἦλθον εἰς τὸ πέραν τῆς θαλάσσης [α'] εἰς τὴν χώραν τῶν Γερασηνῶν.
β ²καὶ ἐξελθόντος αὐτοῦ ἐκ τοῦ πλοίου
β' [α] εὐθὺς ὑπήντησεν αὐτῷ ἐκ τῶν μνημείων [α'] ἄνθρωπος ἐν πνεύματι ἀκαθάρτῳ,

B α ³ "Ὃς τὴν κατοίκησιν εἶχεν ἐν τοῖς μνήμασιν·
 β καὶ οὐδε ἁλύσει οὐκέτι οὐδεὶς ἐδύνατο αὐτὸν δῆσαι,
 γ ⁴διὰ τὸ αὐτὸν πολλάκις πέδαις καὶ ἁλύσεσιν δεδέσθαι
 γ' καὶ διεσπάσθαι ὑπ' αὐτοῦ τὰς ἁλύσεις καὶ τὰς πέδας συντετρῖφθαι,
 β' καὶ οὐδεὶς ἴσχυεν αὐτὸν δαμάσαι·
 α ' ⁵[α] καὶ διὰ παντὸς νυκτὸς καὶ ἡμέρας [β] ἐν τοῖς μνήμασιν καὶ ἐν τοῖς ὄρεσιν [β'] ἦν κράζων καὶ κατακόπτων ἑαυτὸν λίθοις.

B' α ⁶ [α] Καὶ ἰδὼν τὸν Ἰησοῦν ἀπὸ μακρόθεν [β] ἔδραμεν καὶ προσεκύνησεν αὐτῷ,
 ⁷[β'] [.α] καὶ κράξας φωνῇ μεγάλῃ [.α'] λέγει,
 β [α] [.α] Τί ἐμοὶ [.β] καὶ σοί, [.β'] [.α] Ἰησοῦ [.β] υἱὲ τοῦ θεοῦ [.β'] τοῦ ὑψίστου;
 [β] [.α] ὁρκίζω σε τὸν θεόν, [.α'] μή με βασανίσῃς.
 [β'] [.α] ⁸ ἔλεγεν γὰρ αὐτῷ, [.α'] Ἔξελθε τὸ πνεῦμα τὸ ἀκάθαρτον ἐκ τοῦ ἀνθρώπου.
 β' ⁹[α] [.α] καὶ ἐπηρώτα αὐτόν, [.α'] Τί ὄνομά σοι;
 [β] [.α] καὶ λέγει αὐτῷ, [.β] Λεγιὼν ὄνομα μοι, [.β'] ὅτι πολλοί ἐσμεν.
 ¹⁰[β'] [.α] καὶ παρεκάλει αὐτὸν πολλὰ [.α'] ἵνα μὴ αὐτὰ ἀποστείλῃ ἔξω τῆς χώρας.

A α ¹¹ [α] [.α] Ἦν δὲ ἐκεῖ [.β] πρὸς τῷ ὄρει [.β'] ἀγέλη χοίρων μεγάλη βοσκομένη·
 ¹²[β] [.α] [..α] καὶ παρεκάλεσαν αὐτὸν [..α'] λέγοντες, [.β] Πέμψον ἡμᾶς εἰς τοὺς χοίρους, [.β'] ἵνα εἰς αὐτοὺς εἰσέλθωμεν.
 ¹³[β'] καὶ ἐπέτρεψεν αὐτοῖς.
 β [α] [.α] καὶ ἐξελθόντα τὰ πνεύματα τὰ ἀκάθαρτα [.α'] εἰσῆλθον εἰς τοὺς χοίρους, [β] [.α] καὶ ὥρμησεν ἡ ἀγέλη κατὰ τοῦ κρημνοῦ [.β] εἰς τὴν θάλασσαν, [.β'] ὡς δισχίλιοι, [β'] καὶ ἐπνίγοντο ἐν τῇ θαλάσσῃ.
 β' ¹⁴[α] καὶ οἱ βόσκοντες αὐτοὺς ἔφυγον [β] [.α] καὶ ἀπήγγειλαν [.β] εἰς τὴν πόλιν [.β'] καὶ εἰς τοὺς ἀγρούς· [β'] [.α] καὶ ἦλθον ἰδεῖν [.α'] τί ἐστιν τὸ γεγονός.

Β α ¹⁵[α] Καὶ ἔρχονται πρὸς τὸν Ἰησοῦν,
   [β] [.α] καὶ θεωροῦσιν τὸν δαιμονιζόμενον [.β] [..α] καθήμενον
   [..β] ἱματισμένον [..β'] καὶ σωφρονοῦντα, [.β'] τὸν ἐσχηκότα τὸν
   λεγιῶνα,
   [β'] καὶ ἐφοβήθησαν.
 β ¹⁶[α] καὶ διηγήσαντο αὐτοῖς οἱ ἰδόντες [β] πῶς ἐγένετο τῷ
   δαιμονιζομένῳ
   [β'] καὶ περὶ τῶν χοίρων.
 β' ¹⁷[α] καὶ ἤρξαντο παρακαλεῖν αὐτὸν [α'] ἀπελθεῖν ἀπὸ τῶν ὁρίων
   αὐτῶν.

Β'α ¹⁸[α] Καὶ ἐμβαίνοντος αὐτοῦ εἰς τὸ πλοῖον [β] παρεκάλει αὐτὸν ὁ
   δαιμονισθεὶς [β'] ἵνα μετ' αὐτοῦ ᾖ.
 β ¹⁹[α] [.α] καὶ οὐκ ἀφῆκεν αὐτόν, [.α'] ἀλλὰ λέγει αὐτῷ,
   [β] [.α] Ὕπαγε [.β] εἰς τὸν οἶκόν σου [.β'] πρὸς τοὺς σούς,
   [β'] [.α] καὶ ἀπάγγειλον αὐτοῖς [.β] ὅσα ὁ κύριός σοι πεποίηκεν
   [.β'] καὶ ἠλέησέν σε.
 β' ²⁰[α] καὶ ἀπῆλθεν
   [β] [.α] καὶ ἤρξατο κηρύσσειν [.β] ἐν τῇ Δεκαπόλει [.β'] ὅσα
   ἐποίησεν αὐτω ὁ Ἰησοῦς,
   [β'] καὶ πάντες ἐθαύμαζον.

Day Seven: 5.21-43:

This third Day of this threesome of Days, Days Five, Six and Seven, begins after Jesus has completed his return night-crossing of the sea[111], and has a similar setting to that of the first of the three days, Day Five. In all three of these Days their stories begin by the sea, though in the second of these it is on the opposite side of the sea.

Day Eight begins at 6.1f.: Καὶ ἐξῆλθεν ἐκεῖθεν, καὶ ἔρχεται εἰς τὴν πατρίδα αὐτοῦ, καὶ ἀκολουθοῦσιν αὐτῷ οἱ μαθηταὶ αὐτοῦ. καὶ γενομένου σαββάτου ἤρξατο διδάσκειν ἐν τῇ συναγωγῃ ... All the underlined words have significance in one way or another in Mark's constructional method for establishing a new Day's telling[112]. Further, the action of 5.21-43 is uninterrupted by a night. The telling of Day Seven, therefore, ends at 5.43.

---

[111] See under the examination of Day Six for the evidence that this is a night-crossing.
[112] Mark's use of historical presents has been discussed under Day Two; his use of καὶ γενομένου σαββάτου is a clear instance of his defining a new Day; his use of εἰς in his introductory passages is highlighted under Day Six as an accessory to the spatial link which expresses a temporal development; and his use of Καὶ ἐξῆλθεν and ἐκεῖθεν will be

5.21-43 is viewed as a unity by all our four commentators, but as we noted in Day Six, they vary in their understanding as to how much of the story's parts and details were connected before Mark came to handle them. Taylor agrees with Bultmann on the classification of this narrative as a miracle-story[113] but totally rejects any suggestion that it is a community-product. Taylor treats this story in the same way as he treated the preceding story of the demoniac, "It is not rounded by repetition but a record based on personal testimony." In this way only, he says, "can we account for its distinctive characteristics: the vivid portraiture of Jairus and his agonized cry for aid, the incident of the woman on the way to his house, the sceptical attitude towards Jesus of the messengers, his refusal to be dissuaded, the picture of the mourners, the saying, 'The child is not dead but sleeps', the mockery thereby provoked, the command in Aramaic addressed to the girl, the compassionate regard for her welfare shown by Jesus."[114] To Taylor, compared with the parallel stories in the Gospels of Matthew and Luke, Mark's account impresses "with its greater originality".

Clearly, however, we have two stories here, the raising of Jairus' daughter and the healing of the woman with the issue of blood. Taylor sees their connection as historical and not merely literary. Schmidt holds also to the view that "the interweaving is due to historical recollection"[115]. With Taylor, we might acknowledge that a story may be told to fill an interval, such as with 6.14-29, but his point that an intercalation of narratives is not a feature of Mark's method is suspect. Hooker would seem to differ from him; see under Day Five for her view on 3.20-35 and, though my sub-dividing differs from hers, I would identify there also Mark's grafting of two stories together. In the case of 5.21-43, Nineham sees 5.25-34 as "more probably a Markan insertion", an insertion with a style "distinctly different in the Greek from that of the rest of the passage."[116] But he does not say in what way it is "distinctly different". We may conjecture that what is "distinctly different" is

---

discussed under Days Eight and Fifteen.
[113] Bultmann, *The History...*, pp.228-230; Taylor, *The Gospel...*, pp.285f.
[114] Taylor, *The Gospel...*, p.285.
[115] Schmidt, *Der Rahmen...*, p.148.
[116] Nineham, *Saint Mark*, p.157.

the specific wording of the woman's medical problem, and not the construction which follows Mark's ABB' form.

Hooker too takes Nineham's position that 5.25-34 is a Markan insertion, but for reasons that the life Jesus restored to the 'twelve-year-old' girl is paralleled in his restoration of the woman who had suffered 'twelve' years.[117] She further notes that the stories are linked by issues of "faith" and that much of the vocabulary would be appropriate to the resurrection hope of the Christian community: consider v.23 "save" and "live"; v.39 the contrast between death and sleep; v.41 "get up" (*cf.* 2.9 and 3.3) and v.40 the mockery of the bystanders ("they laughed at him"). Richardson[118] similarly comments on v.40 as the way in which the world often laughs at Christian hopes of resurrection. That there are correspondences between the last Day of the first Series and the last Day (16.1-8) of the fourth and final Series of Mark's Gospel, the only resurrection accounts in the gospel, is a matter to which we will come as we take these studies of Mark's Days and interpret Mark's Gospel matrix.

Lohmeyer[119] viewed the story of the raising of Jairus' daughter as consisting of four stages: vv.21-24, by the lakeside; vv.35-37 on the road; vv.38-40 in the court of the house; and vv.41-43 in the maiden's chamber. I would agree with his major sub-divisions of the story, on literary-structural grounds, but the arrangement by Mark of the whole of Day Seven is fundamentally another composite of his ABB' tightly organised rhetorical style. The first, introductory (and observably shorter) section A (5.21-24) is followed by the first development B (vv.25-34) and the second and completing development B' (vv.35-43). 5.21-24 and 5.35-43 can hardly be described as an 'envelope structure' to 5.25-34, or 5.25-34 as an 'insertion'.[120] The signifier of the ABB' form is found in the introductory section and at 5.24: it reads, "And he went away with him/and a great *crowd* followed him/and they *pressed upon* him." Both the second and the third section are well introduced by the first section, and there are the verbal links too, as italicised, between 5.24 and 5.31. In regard to the way the text divides up, we may note again

---

[117] Hooker, *The Gospel...*, p.147.
[118] A. Richardson, *The Miracle Stories of the Gospels*, SCM, London 1941.
[119] E. Lohmeyer, *Das Evangelium des Markus*, Meyer K., 11th ed., Vandenhoeck & Ruprecht, Göttingen, 1951, Orig. 1937, p.104.
[120] See Nineham, *Saint Mark*, p.157; and Hooker, *The Gospel...*, p.147.

the use of Καί linked with the historical present and, in particular, Mark's favourites[121] at v.22 (Καὶ ἔρχεται) and v.38 (Καὶ ἔρχονται): both are in the same Bα position, in the first and last sections. In the same Bα position in the second section is another of Mark's favourite signifiers of a new 'paragraph', Καὶ εὐθὺς.[122] And as we observed on page 100, there is also the signifier of a non-καὶ sentence beginning the third section at 5.35.

Sections two and three report amazing changes of state for both the woman and Jairus' young daughter. We observe the detail that the woman has been suffering δώδεκα ἔτη (5.25), and the girl is ἐτῶν δώδεκα (5.42): the two sections are, therefore, further bonded together. And we note for the first time in the Gospel a potential interest of Mark in the significance of numbers[123]. 'Twelve' is a number traditionally associated with the elective purposes of God and, therefore, with Israel[124] (for the obvious link, consider the twelve tribes in O.T. use). We recall Mark's report of Jesus' appointment of 'twelve' disciples (3.14, 16) in Day Five, the first of this sub-Series of Days. We dare, therefore, to interpret Mark's references in these contexts to 'twelve': a new Israel is being established and echoes of Old Israel redound to it.

The literary structure of Day Seven is presented in full:

---

[121] See under Day Two above.
[122] See under Day Four above.
[123] In the reports of Days Nine and Thirteen, on the feedings of the five-thousand and the four-thousand respectively, especially because of 8.19-21, listeners are as challenged as the disciples to understand the significances of "5", "5,000" and "12", and also "7", "4,000" and "7". This will be discussed as we examine Days Nine and Thirteen, and as we review the form of Series Two at the end of chapter Four. We will return to the subject of Mark's possible numerological interest and the possible meanings of "deep" structures in chapter Eight as we resume the discussion of Mark's literary intentions which were introduced in chapter One.
[124] From "Numbers" in *NIDNTT* and *IntDB*.

A α ²¹[a] Καὶ διαπεράσαντος τοῦ Ἰησου [β] [ἐν τῷ πλοίῳ] [βʹ] πάλιν εἰς τὸ πέραν
β συνήχθη ὄχλος πολὺς ἐπ' αὐτόν,
βʹ καὶ ἦν παρὰ τὴν θάλασσαν.

B α ²²[a] Καὶ ἔρχεται εἷς τῶν ἀρχισυναγώγων, [αʹ] ὀνόματι Ἰάϊρος,
β [a] καὶ ἰδὼν αὐτὸν [β] πίπτει πρὸς τοὺς πόδας αὐτοῦ ²³[βʹ] [.a] καὶ παρακαλεῖ αὐτὸν πολλὰ [.αʹ] λέγων
βʹ [a] ὅτι Τὸ θυγάτριόν μου ἐσχάτως ἔχει, [β] ἵνα ἐλθὼν ἐπιθῇς τὰς χεῖρας αὐτῇ, [βʹ] ἵνα σωθῇ καὶ ζήσῃ.

Bʹ α ²⁴Καὶ ἀπῆλθεν μετ' αὐτοῦ.
β καὶ ἠκολούθει αὐτῷ ὄχλος πολύς,
βʹ καὶ συνέθλιβον αὐτόν.

A α ²⁵[a] Καὶ γυνὴ οὖσα ἐν ῥύσει αἵματος δώδεκα ἔτη [β] ²⁶ καὶ πολλὰ παθοῦσα ὑπὸ πολλῶν ἰατρῶν [βʹ] [.a] καὶ δαπανήσασα τὰ παρ' αὐτῆς πάντα [.β] καὶ μηδὲν ὠφεληθεῖσα [.βʹ] ἀλλὰ μᾶλλον εἰς τὸ χεῖρον ἐλθοῦσα,
β ²⁷[a] ἀκούσασα περὶ τοῦ Ἰησοῦ, [β] ἐλθοῦσα ἐν τῷ ὄχλῳ ὄπισθεν [βʹ] ἥψατο του ἱματίου αὐτοῦ·
βʹ ²⁸[a] ἔλεγεν γὰρ ὅτι [β] Ἐὰν ἄψωμαι κἂν τῶν ἱματίων αὐτου [βʹ] σωθήσομαι.

B α ²⁹[a] Καὶ εὐθὺς [β] ἐξηράνθη ἡ πηγὴ τοῦ αἵματος αὐτῆς, [βʹ] [.a] καὶ ἔγνω τῷ σώματι ὅτι [.αʹ] ἴαται ἀπὸ τῆς μάστιγος.
β ³⁰[a] [.a] καὶ εὐθὺς [.β] ὁ Ἰησοῦς ἐπιγνοὺς ἐν ἑαυτῷ [.βʹ] τὴν ἐξ αὐτοῦ δύναμιν ἐξελθοῦσαν [β] [.a] ἐπιστραφεὶς ἐν τῷ ὄχλῳ [.αʹ] ἔλεγεν, [βʹ] Τίς μου ἥψατο τῶν ἱματίων;
βʹ ³¹[a] καὶ ἔλεγον αὐτῷ οἱ μαθηταὶ αὐτοῦ, [β] Βλέπεις τὸν ὄχλον συνθλίβοντά σε, [βʹ] [.a] καὶ λέγεις, [.αʹ] Τίς μου ἥψατο;

Bʹ α ³²Καὶ περιεβλέπετο ἰδεῖν τὴν τοῦτο ποιήσασαν.
β ³³[a] [.a] ἡ δὲ γυνὴ φοβηθεῖσα καὶ τρέμουσα, [.αʹ] εἰδυῖα ὃ γέγονεν Αὐτῇ, [β] [.a] ἦλθεν [.αʹ] καὶ προσέπεσεν αὐτῷ [βʹ] [.a] καὶ εἶπεν αὐτῷ [.αʹ] πᾶσαν τὴν ἀλήθειαν.
βʹ ³⁴[a] ὁ δὲ εἶπεν αὐτῇ, [β] [.a] Θυγάτηρ, [.αʹ] ἡ πίστις σου σέσωκέν σε· [βʹ] [.a] ὕπαγε εἰς εἰρήνην, [.αʹ] καὶ ἴσθι ὑγιὴς ἀπὸ τῆς μάστιγός σου.

A α ³⁵[α] [.α] ῎Ετι αὐτοῦ λαλοῦντος [.β] ἔρχονται ἀπὸ τοῦ ἀρχισυναγώγου
[.βʹ] λέγοντες
[β] ὅτι ʽΗ θυγάτηρ σου ἀπέθανεν·
[βʹ] τί ἔτι σκύλλεις τὸν διδάσκαλον;
β ³⁶[α] [.α] ὁ δὲ Ἰησοῦς [.β] παρακούσας τὸν λόγον λαλούμενον
[.βʹ] λέγει τῷ ἀρχισυναγώγῳ, [β] Μὴ φοβοῦ, [βʹ] μόνον πίστευε.
βʹ ³⁷[α] [.α] καὶ οὐκ ἀφῆκεν [.β] οὐδένα μετ᾽ αὐτοῦ [.βʹ] συνακολουθῆσαι
[αʹ] [.α] εἰ μὴ τὸν Πέτρον [.β] καὶ Ἰάκωβον [.βʹ] [..α] καὶ Ἰωάννην
[..αʹ] τὸν ἀδελφὸν Ἰακώβου.

B α ³⁸[α] [.α] Καὶ ἔρχονται [.β] εἰς τὸν οἶκον [.βʹ] τοῦ ἀρχισυναγώγου,
[β] καὶ θεωρεῖ θόρυβον
[βʹ] καὶ κλαίοντας καὶ ἀλαλάζοντας πολλά,
β ³⁹[α] [.α] καὶ εἰσελθὼν [.αʹ] λέγει αὐτοῖς,
[β] [.α] Τί θορυβεῖσθε [.αʹ] καὶ κλαίετε;
[βʹ] [.α] τὸ παιδίον οὐκ ἀπέθανεν [.αʹ] ἀλλὰ καθεύδει.
βʹ ⁴⁰[α] καὶ κατεγέλων αὐτοῦ.
[β] [.α] αὐτὸς δὲ ἐκβαλὼν πάντας [.αʹ] [..α] παραλαμβάνει τὸν
πατέρα τοῦ παιδίου [..β] καὶ τὴν μητέρα [..βʹ] καὶ τοὺς μετ᾽ αὐτοῦ,
[βʹ] [.α] καὶ εἰσπορεύεται [.αʹ] ὅπου ἦν τὸ παιδίον·

Bʹ α ⁴¹[α] [.α] Καὶ κρατήσας τῆς χειρὸς τοῦ παιδίου [.αʹ] λέγει αὐτῇ,
[β] [..α] Ταλιθα κουμ,
[βʹ] [.α] ὅ ἐστιν μεθερμηνευόμενον [.αʹ] [..α] Τὸ κοράσιον, [..β] σοὶ
λέγω, [..βʹ] ἔγειρε.
β ⁴²[α] [.α] καὶ εὐθὺς [.β] ἀνέστη [.βʹ] τὸ κοράσιον
[β] καὶ περιεπάτει,
[βʹ] ἦν γὰρ ἐτῶν δώδεκα.
βʹ [α] [.α] καὶ ἐξέστησαν [εὐθὺς] [.αʹ] ἐκστάσει μεγάλῃ.
⁴³[β] [.α] καὶ διεστείλατο αὐτοῖς πολλὰ [.αʹ] ἵνα μηδεὶς γνοῖ τοῦτο,
[βʹ] [.α] καὶ εἶπεν [.αʹ] δοθῆναι αὐτῇ φαγεῖν.

A Summary of the First Seven Days:

The literary-structural features of this first Series of the Gospel of Mark are summarised in tabular form, following a synopsis here of what Mark has been telling us.

The first threesome of "days" (Days One, Two and Three, 1.21-2.22) which Mark presents tells where and how Jesus first became known and where and how his fame spread. Capernaum and neighbouring towns in Galilee were the places Jesus ministered. It was his teaching (in the synagogues, Simon's house and by the

THE FIRST SERIES

lakeshore) and expelling of demons and healing of all manner of sick folk which led to people talking about him and an ever-increasing number of people gathering to him. No-one was unreachable by his ministry: the "unclean", sinners and tax collectors feature prominently in the actual stories of his missioning. And Mark demonstrates, so early in his Gospel, that such a ministry leads to a clash (a charge of 'blasphemy' and other challenges) between Jesus, whose ministry is "new", and others, whose "old" positions are being challenged (so expressed at its climax, in 'parables', and attached to a an enigmatic saying about "the time when the bridegroom will be taken..", which will be a "day" of fasting).

The second threesome of "days" (Days Five, Six and Seven, 3.7-5.43) tells firstly how all "old Israel" gathers to Jesus, who lays down the foundations for a "new Israel" (by appointing the twelve). In the course of these days, he exhibits immense power and authority, stilling a raging storm, subduing evil in the form of a 'legion' of spirits, healing a woman with a 'twelve- year' bleeding-problem, and (at its climax) raising a dead 'twelve year old' girl. With parables, 3.20-35 and 4.1-32, Jesus teaches what his actions demonstrate, the coming complete defeat of the kingdom of Satan and the establishment of the kingdom of God on earth. In his mission, Jesus is reaching out to all, but in no way will all have their place in God's kingdom.

The two three-day series have their rich common seams, their many points of contact, and they are arranged around the central, singular and individualistic Day Four which is different from all the other days of this Series, and which in its conclusion and at its climax alludes to the opposition to Jesus (of Pharisees and Herodians) which will result in his death. In the first messianic-type reference of its kind in the gospel narrative, Jesus himself likens his presence and practice to that of King David. In literary-structural terms, this Day Four has a central, pivotal, or fulcrum role between the sub-Series/threesomes of Days.

The short title I suggest for this, Mark's first Series of seven Days is, "Jesus' First Days of Mission, Confined to Galilee and the Region of its Sea."

For the sake of clarity, we rehearse the points made in this chapter concerning the number of days Mark judged his first stage of

Jesus' mission to have covered. In his presentations of only seven Days he has made it plain that there were many more days than these for the telling. His first three Days' reports (in sub-Series, and the first, a sabbath) summarise activity which extended over possibly many weeks (see pages 85 and 98). Further, the sabbath of Day Four is presented as though it were in succession with the previous Day's telling, but it could have been up to six days later. Mark's telling of the beginning of Day Five's report links it to Day Four as consecutive. The second sub-Series, his balancing three Days' reports, are presented as three days runnning consecutively. (Mark's method in his Day-presentations is to give notice, only in his introductory pieces, of other days which he otherwise does not report.) The first Series of seven Days, in the way that Mark tells it, may be judged, therefore, to cover many weeks.

In addition, we consider the role of the "sabbath" in Mark's scheme. Beyond direct mention of the two sabbaths in this Series, there is a hint only that Jesus did preach on other sabbaths. That two sabbaths are reported, one being the first day and the second being at the turning point of the Series, suggests that the "sabbath" was important to Mark. We may judge their significance in this Series: the first with demonstrating that Jesus' mission was firstly to the Jews; and the second which was a most suitable backdrop to a demonstration of conflict over the law. The second Series, on its first day, begins also with a sabbath (see pages 151,194). Though these mentions of the sabbath have their importance in Mark's thematic presentation, they have no importance structurally-speaking beyond these Series' opening days and the middle day of the first Series. Though Mark presents 'seven Day' Series it is not the case that we should interpret them as 'weeks', with each containing a single sabbath. Rather, his use of 'seven' for a format may be interpreted to express "completion"[125], the completion of a 'stage' in the mission of Jesus. In each Series, as we have seen above for the first Series, Mark demonstrates that he covers more than seven days. He chooses simply to report a stage in Jesus' mission by telling the activities of

---

[125] 'Seven' is a sacred number in many of the world's religions, and as it stands for 'fulfilment' or 'completion' in Hebrew usage (*IntDB*, Vol.3, 1961, Twelfth reprinting, p.564), we, who have not been encouraged in the modern Western world to think in these terms, do have to consider seriously this likely reason for Mark's choice of it for his rhetorical plan.

seven days only, as if he were taking them from a diary. The construct is clearly artificial.

The structure of Mark's first Series of seven Days, may now be summarised. Overall, I interpet it to be an ABA' form, where A represents the first threesome of Days and A' represents the second threesome of Days, around a middle, pivotal Day, designated B. It is a three-part chiasm, but which, in terms of the seven Days it comprises, can be expressed by:

$$A(ABB') - B - A'(ABB').$$

A qualification is called for, however. In analysing the middle three Days of the Series, it was observed that their presentations each included Καὶ πάλιν in the same literary-structural positions, at the beginnings of the second halves. The issue of 'conflict' also appeared to bind these three Days together. Additionally, we might consider that these three days similarly report activities of Jesus' disciples (compare 2.16,18-20; 2.23; 3.9,14-19, 4.10-23, 33-41). Further, we can observe some balance of material between Days Three and Five for parables, untitled as such in Three, but present nevertheless (towards its end, 2.19-22). It may be seen also that in the tellings of Days Two and Six, Jesus ministers to male individuals in each (one is 'unclean', the other has 'an unclean spirit'). And in Days One and Seven, Jesus ministers to individual women. Given these kinds of observations the seven day Series could look more like a *seven*-part chiasm.

Several points need to be made. Whilst there may be some evidence of an *inclusio* between Days One and Seven, this may be interpreted only in this way, that the seven Day presentations make a Series. That is, the series could still be chiastic in terms of three parts (three days, one day, three days), or seven parts (the seven Days: 1, 2, 3, C, 3', 2', 1'). In the very same way, the similarities between the second and sixth Days do not help determine the choice, because they still lie symmetrical opposite each other as the middle days of the three-day sub-Series A(ABB') - B - A'(ABB'). To these arguments, we need to introduce other observations: that individuals with 'unclean spirits' appear not only in Days Two and Six, but also in Days One and Five; and that Day One includes much more than Jesus ministering to a woman (Simon's mother-in-law). Most importantly, Days One and Five have been shown to relate firmly to each other. Further, at the beginning of Day Five there is an emphatically clear new stage in the presentation. And for content and theme development, we have seen how Days One to Three connect, and how Days Five to Seven connect as linear, three-day sub-series, each with their own *inclusio* of geographical location (in the first, Capernaum, and in the second, a similar shore of the Sea of Galilee, due to a crossing and a return crossing).

The structural scheme of this Series of seven Days *is* indeed best described by ABA'. And given the above considerations, it is properly stated that the ending of A (Day Three) and the beginning of A' (Day Five) both connect with the turning point B (Day Four) in their structural forms and some of their content. It is a characteristic of ancient rhetoric that one part "should not only lie adjacent to the next, but be related to it and overlap it at the edges" (Lucian[126]). Further, the Series' three-part chiasm well reflects in the first part 'the complication', the second the 'turning point', and the third the 'dénouement' of Greek tragedy (Aristotle[127]). In the first three-day sub-series is the material which sets out the events that will lead inevitably to tragedy (Jesus' mission against evil and sickness leads not only to his rising popularity, but also to a charge of 'blasphemy' and challenges over other issues); at the centre is the turning point when something of the significance of what is taking place is grasped (at its climax, Pharisees and Herodians plot to kill Jesus); and in the last three-day sub-series is a working out of the tragedy (which in this opening series is a prefiguring of the Gospel's final series; it shows that Jesus is effective in dealing with contrary powers, all evil, sickness and even death).

In summary then, we have identified a Series of seven Days, which comprises a three-day series, a middle day and turning point, and another three-day series. We are given reports of seven Days, but they tell (in their opening pieces) that this stage in Jesus' mission covered many weeks. We have titled this stage, "Jesus' First Days of Mission, Confined to Galilee and the Region of its Sea".

---

[126] Lucian, *De conscribenda...*; see my page 54 for a brief discussion of this and particularly, the anastrophe.
[127] Aristotle, *Poetics...*; see my page 21.

THE FIRST SERIES

Superficially, the text gives us the impression that Mark has provided for us a distillation of the main features of the first phase in Jesus' mission, as if he has chosen particular days to report, as from a diary. Rather, what we discover is the first stage of a tale which is both tragic and wondrous. Its meaning focuses clearly upon Jesus, on who he is and the New Covenant which he will establish.

A Tabular Summary of the literary-structure of the First Seven Days:

DAYS: number identified	1	2	3	4	5	6	7
chapters and verses	1.21-38	1.39-45	2.1-22	2.23-3.6	3.7-4.41	5.1-20	5.21-43
SERIES' STRUCTURE	A			B	A'		
DAYS: in literary-terms, in series	A	B	B'		A	B	B'
DAYS' sections	A / A'	A	A / A'	A / A'	AA' / AA'	A / A'	A / B / B'
DAYS' sectional sub-divisions	A B B' A B B'	A B B'	A B B' A B B'	A B B' A B B'	A B B' A B B' A B B' A B B'	A B B' A B B'	A B B' A B B' A B B'
DAYS' number of verses	18	7	22	12	70	20	23
SUB-SERIES' number of verses	47				113		
SERIES' number of verses	172						

Addendum to the analysis of "The First Seven Days":

During the course of this first chapter (of four) on the literary-structural analysis of Mark's gospel narrative, a number of studies and observations have been made of the signifiers of Mark's structure, and of his rhetorical method in organising his contents. Some of these studies were initiated in the Introduction, others were introduced in Chapter Two. They are foundational to the analysis of the three remaining Series, and they are listed here in summary:

Under Day One:	1)	Mark's understanding of the Hebrew/Palestinian day (see also Introduction: An Interest in "Days");
	2)	Mark's definition of "Day" which he uses for the purpose of his presentation: the civil day beginning with sunrise (see also Introduction: An Interest in "Days" and note 82);
	3)	πρωΐ and other times of day;
Under Day Two:	4)	Temporal links;
	5)	Geographical links which behave temporally;
	6)	Historical Presents;
Under Day Three:	7)	Καὶ πάλιν;
Under Day Four:	8)	Καί and parataxis;
	9)	non-καί sentences;
	10)	Καὶ εὐθύς;
	11)	Chiasm: an alternative to it, part I (see also Introduction: The Cultural and Historical Context... and Chapter Two: The Days beginning the Gospel);
Under Day Five:	12)	Three-step progressions and formal structure;
	13)	Sandwich construction: an alternative to it, part I (see also Introduction: An Interest in "Days");
	14)	Chiasm: an alternative to it, part II;
	15)	Numbers of verses;
Under Day Six:	16)	"Night-crossings of the sea of Galilee": new Days begin with new locations and new activities after sunrise;
Under Day Seven:	17)	Sandwich construction: an alternative to it, part II;
	18)	Mark's numerological interest.

What is clear from the analyses of Mark's Prologue and First Series, and what is worth stating here, is that the sizes of Mark's rhetorical units, whether sub-Series of Days, Days, Day-sections, parts, sub-parts, and so on, vary according to the amount of content he wishes to include for each. Consider the Days themselves, from the tabular summary: they vary by a factor of ten (the longest is seventy verses; the shortest is seven verses). It is the general case that Mark's process of composition at every level is not governed by a need to balance his presentations by numbers of verses, lines of text, or numbers of words. What does matter to him (and in ancient rhetoric) is that these constructions, whether ABA', ABB', ABB'/ABB', αββ' or [α] [β] [β'], are in themselves complete.[128]

What we notice also from the table is that Mark's compositional process did not require him to create his Days' tellings to repetitive sectional schemes. We observe four different Day-structures, in their shortened forms of A, A/A', AA'/AA', and ABB', and no particular pattern as to their use. It appears that it was the amount and type of material which he wanted to present that led to his choice of Day structure, and not the other way about.

---

[128] See pages 128, 129 for an introductory discussion of these matters.

Chapter Four
The Second Series of Seven Days (6.1-8.26):

Day Eight: 6.1-29:

The Day begins with a three-part opening:

   A α   ¹ [a] <u>Καὶ ἐξῆλθεν</u> [a´] <u>ἐκεῖθεν</u>,
      β   [a] <u>καὶ ἔρχεται</u> [a´] <u>εἰς τὴν πατρίδα αὐτοῦ</u>,
      β'   [a] <u>καὶ ἀκολουθοῦσιν</u> αὐτῷ [a´] οἱ μαθηταὶ <u>αὐτοῦ</u>.

The first line of Mark's opening construction is introductory; the second line is the first development; and the third is the second and completing development. The plan exhibits his usual method of presentation.

For the first time in the Gospel, we encounter use of ἐκεῖθεν: in all, Mark uses the word six times; significantly three are found in this Day's telling (at 6.1,10 and 11); and the other three are to be found, as at 6.1, introducing new Days (at 7.24, 9.30 and 10.1). Καὶ, ἐξῆλθεν (and variants, in the aorist), ἔρχεται (and variants, all in the historical present) and εἰς[1] are found principally at important turning points in the Markan text, but never before in such close combination as we find here[2]. To these Mark now adds ἐκεῖθεν to signify strongly a new beginning.[3] But that is not all there is to the matter.

---

[1]   Bultmann, *The History...*, p.339, identifies all four words (and others) as significant in Mark's 'editing of traditional material': but because of the pervasive evidence of Mark's rhetorical style in all the units themselves, they may rather be viewed as significant within his work of composition as a whole.

[2]   ἐξῆλθεν: 2.13, 6.34,54, 7.31, 8.27, 9.30, 16.8; and ἔρχεται: 1.40, 2.3, 3.20,31, 5.15,22,38, 8.22, 10.1,46, 11.15,27, 12.18, 14.32,37: see under Day Two, for further discussion on ἔρχομαι, and under Days Six and Eleven for εἰς. See also note 112 in chapter three.

[3]   Nineham, *Saint Mark*, p.165: on v.1, he says, "The connecting formula is vague and no doubt purely conventional." We reflect on his terminology. In one sense, we are identifying a "disconnecting" formula in v.1: that is, that which is presented from 6.1 has its separation from 5.43 and what precedes it. As a "connecting" formula, it is not "vague" for it well forms a link between what has preceded it and what now takes place in a new setting and

To the commonly-used historical present at the beginning of a β line Mark has added another at the beginning of line β ', ἀκολουθοῦσιν. These two 'developing' lines of Mark's introductory piece represent classically Markan story-telling. Further, when these two lines, β and β', are read with the first line of the following section B, that is, Καὶ γενομένου σαββάτου, we observe what can only be a deliberate repeat on Mark's part of parechesis, the ου sound which we identified richly at the beginning of the Prologue. The word ἀκολουθοῦσιν twice also repeats the sound, and this word is first used in 1.18 of the Prologue (though it is also found in the intervening material at 2.14 *bis*, 2.15, 3.7, and 5.24). We observe also the poetic nature of the first line, Καὶ ἐξῆλθεν ἐκεῖθεν. These observations serve to show two things: that Mark was writing his Gospel for the purpose of it being read aloud; and that he was using rhetorical conventions available to him to indicate his rhetorical plan to his audience[4]. This additional identification of the use by Mark of parechesis and the poetic here establish beyond any doubt that at 6.1 a new Series begins.

Again this is not all there is to the matter. Significant correspondences exist between this first Day of Mark's second Series and the Prologue. In 6.1, καὶ ἔρχεταί εἰς τὴν πατρίδα αὐτοῦ has its earlier counterpart in the Prologue, in 1.9 and 14. The content on the telling of how John the Baptist died, in 6.14-29, clearly has its connection too with the Prologue, in 1.14. And the 'calling to repentance', not mentioned anywhere else in the Gospel (except of John in 1.4, and of Jesus in 1.15) is what the disciples do, in 6.12. Further, significant verbal correspondences exist between this first Day of Mark's second Series and the first Day of his first Series: in 6.2, 1.21 σαββάτου, διδάσκειν, συναγωγῃ; in 6.2, 1.22 ἐξεπλήσσοντο; in 6.7, 1.22 ἐξουσίαν; in 6.7, 1.23, 27 τῶν πνευμάτων τῶν ἀκαθάρτων; in 6.13, 1.34 καὶ δαιμόνια πολλὰ ἐξέβαλλον; and in 6.13, 1.34 καὶ ἐθεράπευον. They all follow in exactly the same order.

---

circumstance. If it is that the connecting formula is "purely" conventional then we note the fact in no derisory way, as Nineham does, but with some satisfaction at discerning Mark's method.

[4] For the general use of ancient rhetorical conventions, see Tolbert, *Sowing the Gospel...*, p.41, and Kennedy, *New Testament Interpretation...*, p.10.

Given these features, it can be argued that Mark established this new beginning in his Gospel narrative in parallel to his beginning of the Gospel itself, in the Prologue, and to the beginning of the narrative, in his Day One. It might be argued also that he fashioned this his eighth Day out of material which he had been considering using in his Prologue and his first Day's telling. The Prologue might have included the report that "John the Baptist was beheaded by Herod", and the first Day's telling might have reported that Jesus was "not easily recognised for who he really was in his home town". But we may surmise that he could do neither of these things. He could not have started his Gospel with two negative accounts; rather, he saved these matters for the first Day's telling of his second Series.

Clearly, two fundamental propositions are being raised: 1) that this Day's telling begins a new Series; and 2) that as it begins with a brilliantly fashioned Markan opening its telling will be sectionalised in ways that we have discerned already. We, therefore, consider the contributions of our earlier selected commentators (Taylor for his 'old' literary-critical approach, Nineham for his form-critical sensitive approach, Schweizer for his redaction-critical approach, and Hooker for her more recent overview of all approaches):

	Gospel Section:	6.1-29 sub-divisions:			Gospel section:
		I	II	III	
Taylor:	3.7-6.13	6.1-6a	6b-13 }{	14-29	6.14-8.26
Nineham:	1.14-8.26	6.1-6a	6b-13	14-29	1.14-8.26
Schweizer:	3.7-6.6a	6.1-6a }{	6b-13	14-29	6.6b-8.26
Hooker:	3.7-6.6a	6.1-6a }{	6b-13	14-29	6.6b-8.26
and compare:	(1.21-5.43) }{	6.1-6a	6b-<u>14a</u>	<u>14b</u>-29	6.1-8.26

They are tabulated along with my own which is based on rhetorical/literary-structural analysis:

For Nineham no sectional break appears, but for Taylor there is one and it is between 6.13 and 14. For Schweizer and Hooker a sectional break is discernable between 6.6a and 6b. Our different methodologies lead us to the same view, nevertheless, that 8.26 ends the section[5]. In terms of the verses which the units comprise, the four

---

[5] Though Hooker rightly points out (*The Gospel...*, p.197) that "some commentators" (we find: Trocmé, *The Formation...*, pp.80, 84, and Best, *Disciples...*, p.2), seeing the similarity between 8.22-26 and 10.46-52 for stories (we note: the only such stories in the

commentators all agree with each other. A number of popular editions of the Bible reflect the same[6]. The Jerusalem Bible stands out, however, with an additional and titled division between vv.16 and 17[7], that is vv.14-16 "Herod and Jesus", and a further untitled division at 6.21.[8] It is at vv.14-16 where rhetorical analysis helps. And it will explain my division between vv.14a and 14b.

Taylor reasons that 6.14 begins a new section which he titles "The Ministry beyond Galilee"[9], and that specifically 6.1-6a represents the ending of the period of Jesus' "synagogue preaching".[10] We compare Nineham's titling: for him, the section from 1.14-8.26 is "The Galilean Ministry".[11] The issue of defining geographical place in terms of an overall region is clearly compounded by what appears to be Mark's own lack of geographical understanding[12]. In non-Markan terms, that is, in strictly factual terms, events do take place both in Galilee and outside of Galilee.

All four commentators argue that the division between v.6a and v.6b is justified because v.6a well completes the story of Jesus' rejection in his home town (it is likely that Mark does mean Nazareth). Taylor also rehearses the other argument that v.6b better links Jesus' movement from village to village with the mission on which he sends his disciples (vv.7ff.), than connects Jesus' movement with his rejection at Nazareth (6.1-6a). But what Taylor rejects, Wellhausen[13] and Schmidt[14] support. The position I take is that Mark presents the two passages, 6.2-6a and 6.6b-14a, in the closest possible way, as B and B' Sections, thus demonstrating that the

Gospel) of the healing of blind people, divide the Gospel at 8.22, judging the healings to form an 'inclusio' to the material about the way of the cross and the meaning of discipleship. We will see below that these two stories, the tellings of Days 14 and 21, conclude the two middle Series of the Gospel.

[6] AV, NEB, GNB, NIV; the RSV shows 6.1, 6b, 7 and 14.

[7] To achieve this, is a very loose translation of Αὐτὸς γὰρ ὁ Ἡρῴδης ἀποστείλας ἐκράτησεν τὸν Ἰωάννην...: "Now it was this same Herod who had sent to have John arrested...". Vv.17 and 18 both contain γὰρ as the second word; vv.17 and 18 parallel each other; and they complete v.16 and form a three-verse whole.

[8] V.21, in my judgement, completes a larger three-part whole, vv.16-21: vv.16-18 is introductory and vv.19,20 and in turn v.21 complete the 6 verse whole.

[9] Taylor, *The Gospel...,* p.307.

[10] Taylor, *The Gospel...,* p.298.

[11] Nineham, *Saint Mark*, pp.65-220.

[12] See the same problem above, in Day Six (5.1-20).

[13] Wellhausen, J., *Das Evangelium Marci*, Reimer, Berlin, 2nd Ed., 1909, p.42.

[14] Schmidt, *Der Rahmen...*, pp.158-162.

reports of *the beginnings* of *two new activities*, in B' (vv.6b-14a), have their cause in B (vv.2-6a). We will expound this later.

On 6.1-6, Hooker writes, "It can fairly be seen as the climax to the previous section of the gospel, and as a parallel to 3.1-6. Just as 1.14-3.6 ended with the rejection of Jesus by the Pharisees, so 3.7-6.6 ends with the rejection of Jesus by his neighbours...." Schweizer's presentation is similar and may have influenced Hooker.[15] Clearly, they are both reasonably certain, by their methods of analysis, that Mark has organised his material to a plan, and that they have discerned that plan. But Hooker continues, "This new section of the gospel begins (at 6.6b), like the two previous ones, with a summary of Jesus' activity (this time very brief - 6.6b only!), followed by a section dealing with the disciples..." In her case, following the path she has set herself, she finds herself at a place where she feels uncomfortable, for 6.6b is too brief! So she writes, "Once again, however, we must remember that the divisions we are making are artificial and are not necessarily part of Mark's own understanding. *It is possible to arrange the material differently...*"[16]

Up to this point in the presentation, I have sought to show: that the Prologue is 1.1-20; that the first full section of the narrative is a Series of Seven Days, 1.21-5.43; and that the Series includes two threesomes of days, 1.21-2.22 and 3.7-5.43, around a central Day, 2.23-3.6. Here I am seeking to demonstrate: that 6.1 begins a new Day, with limits of 6.1-29; that here begins a new threesome of Days with limits of 6.1-7.23, and also a new Series of Seven Days, 6.1-8.26 (with which 'section', three of our four commentators so nearly agree[17]), which is the first of two middle Series. The discovery of Mark's rhetorical style, ABB', at many levels of literary order, and his determining his plan to "Days" and "Series of Days" has served us well so far. We will continue, given this understanding, to plot divisions and sub-divisions which are not impositions of mine, but are of Mark's own creation. Mark's arrangement, not mine of Mark, is what I am attempting to present. I proceed gingerly to a presentation of what, in my judgement, is the literary-structure of Day Eight, for I know it is provocative.

---

[15] See Schweizer, *The Good News...*, pp.122,123; Hooker, *The Gospel...*, p.154.
[16] Hooker, *The Gospel...*, p.154, my italics.
[17] Taylor, Schweizer and Hooker: see the tabular summary above.

Literary-structural analysis demonstrates that Day Eight is constructed like Days One, Three, Four and Six (so far), to a composite of ABB'/ABB'. The first of the two halves to the Day's telling is 6.1-14a, whereby: A is v.1 which is introductory; it tells how Jesus has returned to his home town with his disciples, and so establishes the new geographical setting for the day. Section B, 6.2-6a, tells of his rejection; the first line explains that it is the sabbath and the location (for this section alone) is the synagogue; the issue is Jesus' identity. Section B', 6.6b-14a, tells what follows *from it*, not simply *after it*: its setting is no longer in the synagogue, but outdoors, in the immediate region of Jesus' home town[18]. The second half of the Day's telling, 6.14b-29, begins in A, vv.14b,15, and raises immediately again the first half's opening issue of Jesus' identity (see 6.2-6a). Section B, vv.16-21, tells how Herod is caused to reflect on who Jesus is, and on his beheading of John the Baptist. The second half is completed by Section B', vv.22-29, which tells how John actually came to be beheaded.

The two halves compare, as we would now expect it of Mark, for structural similarity, but here also for size (*cf.* thirteen-and-a-half verses with fifteen-and-a-half verses)[19]. Both display short A sections; and their B and B' sections are similarly proportioned in both halves, B' being slightly longer than B in both cases.

The reason I stand out from the commentators with the division between vv.14a and 14b is due primarily to my discernment of Mark's three-part structures of both vv.12-14a and vv.14b,15. In vv.14b,15, we identify an indisputable αββ' construction; the parts begin: α Καὶ ἔλεγον[20] ὅτι...
  β ἄλλοι δὲ ἔλεγον ὅτι ...
  β' ἄλλοι δὲ ἔλεγον ὅτι ...

---

[18] Robbins, *Jesus the Teacher*..., pp.34ff., sees the three-step progression as 6.1-3; 4-6; 7-13. He gives no consideration to the setting in the synagogue and what may be its influence upon the limits of the second 'step'. Though he has identified a few other three-step progressions with which we can agree, we cannot, therefore, begin to agree here with his method of analysis.

[19] See the discussions with which I end the analyses of Day Five, and the First Series: it matters not how the elements of Mark's ABB' scheme weigh with each other in terms of their numbers of verses, but that they weigh with each other in terms of their function, as introductory, of first development and of second.

[20] We recognise the choice here of Nestle-Aland: ἔλεγον is read by B W and some Latin mss.; ἔλεγεν by many mss.

In vv.12-14a, it is less obvious immediately, but the same construction as found everywhere else is discernible, hence the addition of v.14a to vv.12 and 13:

β'[α] ^{12}[.α] Καὶ ἐξελθόντες [.β] ἐκήρυξαν [.β'] ἵνα μετανοῶσιν,
[β] ^{13}[.α] καὶ δαιμόνια πολλὰ ἐξέβαλλον, [.β] καὶ ἤλειφον ἐλαίῳ
        πολλοὺς ἀρρώστους [.β'] καὶ ἐθεράπευον.
[β'] ^{14}[.α] καὶ ἤκουσεν ὁ βασιλεὺς˙ Ἡρῴδης, [.α'] φανερὸν γὰρ
        ἐγένετο τὸ ὄνομα αὐτοῦ.

In both constructions, the first part [α] is introductory; the second [β] is the first development; and the third [β'] is the completing development. The argument of juxtaposition arises also, because v.14a plays no part structurally in 14b-15. Properly, they may be said to relate contents-wise, but Mark did not mean them to be read without a break between them. And I make an observation: no translation of v.14a, or v.14b, or v.15a I have come across reflects either Mark's structure or (as a result of this) his Greek.

The rhetorical function of v.14a is more than that of completing the first half's telling: it is an anastrophe which makes a connection of the first half with the second half. And equally the connection itself is not established by 14a alone. The introductory passage to the second half, vv.14b-15, reports the questioning which results from the success of Jesus' continuing personal mission, and the mission of the disciples, by which Jesus' name is promoted (we note that Jesus was already known in his own native place for his powerful deeds (v.2) performed elsewhere and before his arrival: he was being talked about everywhere: the first Series of Days makes that plain). But contrast Jesus' lack of success in his home town, in 6.2-6a, with the success that is now attributed to him in the much wider area, because of his disciples' mission, 6.6b-14a.

Because the disciples' mission is the cause of Herod's hearing in Jerusalem, Mark links v.14a with vv.12,13 in one of his rhetorical units to show that it is very definitely the case. The Good News Bible translation of v.14a is: "Now Herod heard about all this, because Jesus' reputation had spread everywhere". I would only replace "Now" with "And", and omit "had" in order to maintain Mark's continuity. And Herod, we note, in terms of the drift of the story presented, could only have heard (v.14a) if these mission activities of the disciples, begun on a sabbath, had continued over a number of days, and over a wide area, and been talked about first by the general populace. Vv.14b-15, with which Mark begins the second half of his presentation, do report that "people were saying" who they thought Jesus was (the verbal link between the two halves of προφήτης of v.4 and v.15 is also noted).

The structural significance of vv.14b,15 is very important for two reasons. 1) It well begins vv.14b-29, the second half of the Day's presentation. And 2) it further anchors this Day as the first of a new Series of seven Days.

We take 1) first. On page 101, when we were discussing Mark's 'new section use' of non-καί sentences, we observed that 6.16 so began, after vv.14b,15 (a three part whole). The argument is that, in v.16, the *particular view of Herod* about Jesus' identity is set against, in vv.14b,15, the introductory *views of the people*. With v.16 begins the second half's B section.

In regard to 2), vv.14b,15 has an important doublet in 8.28[21], which in 8.27-9.1 helps establish Day Fifteen as the first of the next Series of seven Days.[22] It is an important, introductory parallel betweeen the two seven-Day Series, 6.1-8.26 and 8.27-10.52, which are the middle two Series of the Gospel. We expose what is common between 6.14b,15 and 8.28:

6.14b,15:

A α   [α] Καὶ ἔλεγον [β] [.α] ὅτι Ἰωάννης ὁ βαπτίζων [.β] ἐγήγερται
        [.β´] ἐκ νεκρῶν, [β´] [.α] καὶ διὰ τοῦτο [.β] ἐνεργοῦσιν αἱ δυνάμεις
        [.β´] ἐν αὐτῷ.
  β   ¹⁵[α] ἄλλοι δὲ ἔλεγον [α´] ὅτι Ἠλίας ἐστίν·
  β´   [α] ἄλλοι δὲ ἔλεγον [β] ὅτι προφήτης [β´] ὡς εἷς τῶν προφητῶν.

---

[21] Our four commentators all observe this doublet, but fail to see any literary-structural significance in it.

[22] On v.15, Schweizer (*The Good News...*, p.132) expresses his opinion, unsupported, that it "originally must have been connected with 8.27f." On vv.14-29, he says, "It is the only story in Mark which is not directly a story about Jesus (most commentators indeed say this) and it is written in a cultured style which shows that it must have been established in written form before Mark." Schweizer displays here no understanding at all of Mark's ability to compose, construct and create both his Gospel to a plan and the pieces he needed to complete it. The text here continues to exhibit Mark's masterful control, and most clearly his αββ´ rhetorical style. In his handling of tradition, either oral or previously written, he is most certainly re-presenting it himself.

8.28:

²⁸[.β] [..α] οἱ δὲ εἶπαν αὐτῷ [..α´] λέγοντες
[.β´] [..α] [ὅτι] Ἰωάννην τὸν βαπτιστήν,
[..β] [...α] καὶ ἄλλοι, [...α´] Ἠλίαν,
[..β´] [...α] ἄλλοι δε [...α´] ὅτι εἷς τῶν προφητῶν.

The corresponding words and annotations (given that 8.28 is set in a different rhetorical context) all follow the same order. We observe what we may call the 'minor difference' of the Greek that qualifies John as "the baptising one" in 6.14 and "the Baptist" in 8.28, for we note that they are both used in the account of Section B', 6.22-29 (see v.24 and v.25).

Mark's creation of 6.1-29 as the presentation of a whole "Day" is not yet addressed. Likewise, the discussion of the division at 6.14b is not yet completed. In order to do both, we have to return to a consideration of 6.1-14a, and focus on the *key literary feature* here of *verbs in the imperfect tense*.

What none of the selected commentators sees is the important presence of a whole rash of imperfects in 6.1-29, which number sixteen in all. (The next rash, of five, appears in the introductory passage, 6.53-56, of the third Day of this Series.) Eleven are found in the first half (6.1-14a) and five in the second (6.14b-29). In the case of the latter, they are all found within the first five verses, and are restricted to ἔλεγον and ἔλεγεν. The three imperfects of vv.14b,15 are clearly continuous[23]. In 6.11-14a they are significantly dispersed and various. It is these which are important for establishing that 6.1-29 is a single "Day" in Mark's scheme.

Strictly speaking, *only* vv.2-11 tell the happenings of this particular, single, sabbath day, but I argue below that vv.12-14a, being basically inceptive, have their place too. V.1 is purely introductory, and in typical Markan fashion it simply, in the opening piece, gives details of a journey which has been made, and the characters who have made it. Vv. 2-14a tell about *two* new activities that were *begun* on that day which would continue for a number of days: 1) Jesus' going round "the villages in circuit teaching" (6.6b); and 2) the disciples' mission (6.7-14a). Part α of section B´,

---

[23] Max Zerwick & Mary Grosvenor, *A Grammatical Analysis of the Greek New Testament*, Biblical Institute Press, Rome, 1981, p.121: ἔλεγον: 3rd pl. impers. meaning "people were saying".

vv.6b-7b, introduces both activities (the reasons for them are found in section B, vv.2-6a). Part β, vv.7c-11, records Jesus' mission instructions. Part β‛, vv.12-14a, completes the three-part presentation and the first half with a report of the beginning of the disciples' mission and its ultimate effect.

The imperfects require to be understood as continuous action or inceptive (they are nowhere here conative). We will not discuss them all. The first, of real significance in my judgement is in 6.6b: I read, "He began to go round..."[24] It is an activity which begins on that day, and continues beyond it. As in v.7b, καὶ ἤρξατο, "and he began..." ("to send them out..."), so also we read in v.7c, "And he began to give them authority..."[25] In v.13, we might read also, "They began to cast out many demons; and they began to anoint many sick with oil; and they began to heal."[26] That is, in terms of the Day's report, these activities and even that of v.12, "they preached" (though here an aorist), began on that day and were to continue beyond it. V.14a alone of vv.12-14a, with two verbs in the aorist, might be said to speak of the mission of the disciples as then concluded, but that is not the case as Mark presents its completion only in 6.30 when the disciples return to Jesus. V.14a is Mark's reporting of the ultimate effect of the disciples' mission.

---

[24] Hooker says (*The Gospel...*, p.162) "Mark does not describe what Jesus did while his disciples were absent: the gap until their return has been filled by the story of the Baptist's death." My argument is that Mark did tell us what Jesus was doing, and that the Baptist's death was not simply a lacuna-filler. For reasons stated above, it would seem that Mark chose not to report the Baptist's death in the Prologue, likely because of its negative tones, but created his moment of opportunity here to include it.

[25] Nineham, *Saint Mark*, pp.167, 168: Nineham admits disappointment, "We should have expected this (the sending out of the twelve) to be a decisive stage in the development of the Gospel, but as Wellhausen points out, it is not... We may say, in fact, that this incident... plays no vital part in the structure and development of the Gospel. And in line with that is the extremely sketchy way in which the story is told. Why did Jesus send the twelve at precisely this point, and what did he do while they were away?" He adds puzzlement to disappointment. But, the truth is that Mark does tell us what Jesus was doing while the disciples were away, and Mark does tell us why Jesus sent them out at this point. Attention to Mark's rhetorical style, his literary-structure, and his verbal tenses repays all effort.

[26] Neither Fritz Rienecker (*A Linguistic Key to the Greek New Testament: Matthew-Acts*, tr & rev. Cleon L. Rogers, Jr., S. Bagster & Sons, London, 1977) nor Max Zerwick and Mary Grosvenor (*A Grammatical Analysis...*) interpret the imperfects (as either inceptive or continuous action). The presence of the aorist in v.12 may support the interpretation of continuous action, but the presence of ἤρξατο αὐτοὺς ἀποστέλλειν and the inceptive of v.7 support the inceptive.

By completing the construction of the first half of the Day's telling in this way, Mark gives himself the opportunity, in a second half presentation, in 6.14b-29: 1) to use material which he could not use in the Prologue, or the First Day of the First Series; 2) to use material which would help him establish a succession of closely-related points in his first three-day sub-series (Days Eight to Ten; see the discussion at the close of Day Ten); and 3) to use material which he could duplicate, in part, and parallel, in part, in the opening Day's telling of his next Series (see Day Fifteen's presentation).

Space allows no further detailed discussion of this Day's telling, beyond an observation. Many commentators and scholars say that the story (with which it concludes) about John the Baptist's death, is the only story in the Gospel which is not directly a story about Jesus.[27] It is, however, a story which is well attached to the issue of who Jesus is. Consider 6.2-6a and vv.14b-15. And as a story in a succession of stories, (as we will see at the conclusion of Day Ten's presentation) Mark does see it, at this point in the Gospel, as prophetic of Jesus' future destiny (see also Day Sixteen, as it follows Day Fifteen which is the parallel day in the following Series). But this Day's telling, in total, is as much prophetic of the disciples' future mission (16.15,16, 20a; ref. 6.14a, kings will hear about Jesus in the future), and their mission will begin ultimately, after Jesus' death, from his own 'native place'[28] (14.28 and 16.7).

The literary structure of Day Eight is as follows:

A α ¹[α] Καὶ ἐξῆλθεν [α´] ἐκεῖθεν,
   β   [α] <u>καὶ ἔρχεται</u> [α´] εἰς <u>τὴν πατρίδα αὐτοῦ</u>,
   β´ [α] <u>καὶ ἀκολουθοῦσιν</u> αὐτῷ [α´] οἱ μαθηταὶ <u>αὐτοῦ</u>.

B α[α]² Καὶ γενομέν<u>ου</u> σαββάτ<u>ου</u>
   [β] [.α] ἤρξατο διδάσκειν [.α´] ἐν τῇ συναγωγῇ·
   [β´] [.α] καὶ πολλοὶ ἀκούοντες [.β] ἐξεπλήσσοντο [.β´] <u>λέγοντες</u>,

---

[27] Nineham, *Saint Mark*, pp.167, 168.
[28] Two points: 1) I risk here a reference to verses from the supposed non-Markan 'longer ending', which will be discussed in Chapter 7; and 2) ref. 6.1: πατρίς may be translated 'native town' (Nazareth) or 'native place' (Galilee) (Souter, *A Pocket Lexicon...*).

β[α] [.α] Πόθεν τούτῳ ταῦτα, [.β] καὶ τίς ἡ σοφία ἡ δοθεῖσα τούτῳ
  [.β'] [..α] καὶ <u>αἱ δυνάμεις</u> τοιαῦται [..α'] <u>διὰ τῶν χειρῶν αὐτου</u>
  γινόμεναι;
  [β] ³[.α] <u>οὐχ</u> οὗτός <u>ἐστιν</u> ὁ τέκτων, [.β] ὁ υἱὸς τῆς Μαρίας [.β'] καὶ
  ἀδελφὸς [..α] Ἰακώβου [..β] καὶ Ἰωσῆτος [..γ] καὶ Ἰούδα [..δ] καὶ
  Σίμωνος;
  [β'] [.α] <u>καὶ οὐκ εἰσὶν</u> αἱ ἀδελφαὶ αὐτοῦ [.β] ὧδε [.β'] πρὸς ἡμᾶς;
β'[α] [.α] [..α] Καὶ ἐσκανδαλίζοντο [..α'] ἐν αὐτῷ.
  [β] [.α] [..α] ⁴καὶ <u>ἔλεγεν</u> αὐτοῖς [..α'] ὁ Ἰησοῦς
  [.α'] [..α] ὅτι <u>οὐκ ἔστιν</u> προφήτης ἄτιμος [..α'] [...α] <u>εἰ μὴ ἐν τῇ
  πατρίδι αὐτοῦ</u> [...β] καὶ <u>ἐν τοῖς</u> συγγενεῦσιν αὐτοῦ [...β'] καὶ <u>ἐν τῇ</u>
  οἰκίᾳ αὐτοῦ.
  [β'] ⁵[.α] [..α] <u>καὶ οὐκ</u> ἐδύνατο [..β] ἐκεῖ [..β'] ποιῆσαι οὐδεμίαν <u>δύναμιν</u>,
  [.β] [..α] <u>εἰ μὴ</u> ὀλίγοις ἀρρώστοις [..β] <u>ἐπιθεὶς τὰς χεῖρας</u> [..β']
  ἐθεράπευσεν·
  ⁶[.β'] [..α] καὶ ἐθαύμαζεν [..α'] διὰ τὴν ἀπιστίαν αὐτῶν.

Β'α [α] [.α] Καὶ περιῆγεν τὰς κώμας [.β] κύκλῳ [.β'] διδάσκων.
  [β] ⁷[.α] <u>καὶ προσκαλεῖται</u> τοὺς δώδεκα,
  [β'] [.α] <u>καὶ</u> ἤρξατο [.β] <u>αὐτοὺς</u> ἀποστέλλειν [.β'] <u>δύο δύο</u>,
β [α] [.α] <u>Καὶ</u> ἐδίδου <u>αὐτοῖς</u> [.β] ἐξουσίαν [.β'] τῶν πνευμάτων τῶν
  ἀκαθάρτων·
  [β] ⁸[.α] <u>καὶ</u> παρήγγειλεν <u>αὐτοῖς</u> [.β] [..α] ἵνα μηδὲν αἴρωσιν εἰς ὁδὸν
  [..α'] εἰ μὴ ῥάβδον μόνον, [.β'] [..α] [...α] <u>μὴ</u> ἄρτον [...β] <u>μὴ</u> πήραν,
  [...β'] <u>μὴ</u> εἰς τὴν ζώνην χαλκόν, ⁹[..β] ἀλλὰ ὑποδεδεμένους
  σανδάλια [..β'] καὶ μὴ ἐνδύσησθε δύο χιτῶνας.
  [β'] ¹⁰[.α] <u>καὶ</u> ἔλεγεν <u>αὐτοῖς</u>, [.β] [..α] Ὅπου ἐὰν εἰσέλθητε εἰς οἰκίαν,
  [..β] ἐκεῖ μένετε [..β'] ἕως ἂν ἐξέλθητε <u>ἐκεῖθεν</u>. [.β'] ¹¹[..α] [...α] καὶ
  <u>ὃς ἂν</u> τόπος [...β] <u>μὴ</u> δέξηται ὑμᾶς [...β'] <u>μηδὲ</u> ἀκούσωσιν ὑμῶν,
  [..α'] [...α] ἐκπορευόμενοι <u>ἐκεῖθεν</u> [...β] ἐκτινάξατε τὸν χοῦν τὸν
  ὑποκάτω τῶν ποδῶν ὑμῶν [...β'] εἰς μαρτύριον αὐτοῖς.
β'[α] ¹²[.α] Καὶ ἐξελθόντες [.β] ἐκήρυξαν [.β'] ἵνα μετανοῶσιν,
  [β] ¹³[.α] καὶ δαιμόνια πολλὰ ἐξέβαλλον, [.β] καὶ ἤλειφον ἐλαίῳ πολλοὺς
  ἀρρώστους [.β'] καὶ ἐθεράπευον.
  [β'] ¹⁴[.α] καὶ ἤκουσεν ὁ βασιλεὺς Ἡρῴδης, [.α'] φανερὸν γὰρ
  ἐγένετο τὸ ὄνομα αὐτοῦ.

A α [α] <u>Καὶ ἔλεγον</u> [β] [.α] <u>ὅτι</u> Ἰωάννης ὁ βαπτίζων [.β] <u>ἐγήγερται</u> [.β'] ἐκ
  νεκρῶν, [β'] [.α] καὶ δια τοῦτο [.β] ἐνεργοῦσιν <u>αἱ δυνάμεις</u> [.β'] ἐν
  αὐτῷ.
β ¹⁵[α] <u>ἄλλοι δὲ ἔλεγον</u> [α'] <u>ὅτι</u> Ἡλίας ἐστίν·
β' [α] <u>ἄλλοι δὲ ἔλεγον</u> [β] <u>ὅτι προφήτης</u> [β'] ὡς <u>εἷς τῶν προφητῶν</u>.

Β α[α]¹⁶ [.α] [..α] 'Ακούσας δε [..α˙] ὁ ˋΗρῴδης ἔλεγεν, [.β] "Ὅν ἐγὼ ἀπεκεφάλισα˙ Ἰωάννην, [.β˙] οὗτος ἠγέρθη.
[β] ¹⁷[.α] [..α] Αὐτὸς γὰρ ὁ ˋΗρῴδης ἀποστείλας [..β] ἐκράτησεν τὸν Ἰωάννην [..β˙] καὶ ἔδησεν αὐτὸν ἐν φυλακῇ [.β] [..α] διὰ ˋΗρῳδιάδα [..β] τὴν γυναῖκα Φιλίππου [..β˙] τοῦ ἀδελφοῦ αὐτοῦ, [.β˙] ὅτι αὐτὴν ἐγάμησεν˙
[β˙] ¹⁸[.α] ἔλεγεν γὰρ ὁ Ἰωάννης τῷ ˋΗρῴδῃ [.β] ὅτι Οὐκ ἔξεστίν σοι [.β˙] ἔχειν τὴν γυναῖκα τοῦ ἀδελφοῦ σου.
β[α] ¹⁹[.α] ˋΗ δὲ ˋΗρῳδιὰς ἐνεῖχεν αὐτῷ [.β] καὶ ἤθελεν αὐτὸν ἀποκτεῖναι, [.β˙] καὶ οὐκ ἠδύνατο˙
[β] ²⁰[.α] ὁ γὰρ ˋΗρῴδης ἐφοβεῖτο τὸν Ἰωάννην, [.β] εἰδὼς αὐτὸν ἄνδρα δίκαιον καὶ ἅγιον, [.β˙] καὶ συνετήρει αὐτόν.
[β˙] [.α] καὶ ἀκούσας αὐτου [.β] πολλὰ ἠπόρει, [.β˙] καὶ ἡδέως αὐτοῦ ἤκουεν.
β˙[α] ²¹ Καὶ γενομένης ἡμέρας εὐκαίρου
[β] [.α] ὅτε ˋΗρῴδης [.β] τοῖς γενεσίοις αὐτοῦ [.β˙] δεῖπνον ἐποίησεν
[β˙] [.α] τοῖς μεγιστᾶσιν αὐτοῦ [.β] καὶ τοῖς χιλιάρχοις [.β˙] καὶ τοῖς πρώτοις τῆς Γαλιλαίας.

Β˙ α[α] ²²[.α] Καὶ εἰσελθούσης τῆς θυγατρὸς αὐτοῦ ˋΗρῳδιάδος [.β] καὶ ὀρχησαμένης,
[.β˙] ἤρεσεν τῷ ˋΗρῴδῃ καὶ τοῖς συνανακειμένοις.
[β] [.α] εἶπεν ὁ βασιλεὺς τῷ κορασίῳ, [.β] [..α] Αἴτησόν με [..α˙] ὃ ἐὰν θέλης, [.β˙] καὶ δώσω σοι˙
[β˙] ²³[.α] καὶ ὤμοσεν αὐτῇ [πολλὰ] [.β] [..α] ῞Ο τι ἐάν με αἰτήσῃς [..α˙] δώσω σοι [.β˙] ἕως ἡμίσους τῆς βασιλείας μου.
β[α] ²⁴[.α] Καὶ ἐξελθοῦσα [.β] [..α] εἶπεν τῇ μητρὶ αὐτῆς, [..α˙] Τί αἰτήσωμαι; [.β˙] [..α] ἡ δὲ εἶπεν, [..α˙] Τὴν κεφαλὴν Ἰωάννου τοῦ βαπτίζοντος.
[β] ²⁵[.α] [..α] καὶ εἰσελθοῦσα εὐθὺς [..β] μετὰ σπουδῆς [..β˙] πρὸς τὸν βασιλέα [.β] [..α] ᾐτήσατο [..α˙] λέγουσα, [.β˙] [..α] Θέλω ἵνα ἐξαυτῆς δῷς μοι [..β] ἐπὶ πίνακι [..β˙] τὴν κεφαλὴν Ἰωάννου τοῦ βαπτιστοῦ.
[β˙] ²⁶[.α] [..α] καὶ περίλυπος γενόμενος [..α˙] ὁ βασιλεὺς [.β] [..α] διὰ τοὺς ὅρκους [..α˙] και τοὺς ἀνακειμένους [.β˙] [..α] οὐκ ἠθέλησεν [..α˙] ἀθετῆσαι αὐτήν˙
β˙[α] ²⁷[.α] [..α] Καὶ εὐθὺς [..β] ἀποστείλας ὁ βασιλεὺς [..β˙] σπεκουλάτορα [.β] [..α] ἐπέταξεν [..α˙] ἐνέγκαι τὴν κεφαλὴν αὐτοῦ. [.β˙] [..α] καὶ ἀπελθὼν [..β] ἀπεκεφάλισεν αὐτὸν [..β˙] ἐν τῇ φυλακῇ
[β] ²⁸[.α] [..α] καὶ ἤνεγκεν τὴν κεφαλὴν αὐτου [..α˙] ἐπὶ πίνακι [.β] και ἔδωκεν αὐτὴν τῷ κορασίῳ, [.β˙] καὶ τὸ κοράσιον ἔδωκεν αὐτὴν τῇ μητρὶ αὐτῆς.
[β˙] ²⁹[.α] [..α] καὶ ἀκούσαντες [..α˙] οἱ μαθηταὶ αὐτοῦ ἦλθον [.β] καὶ ἦραν τὸ πτῶμα αὐτοῦ [.β˙] [..α] καὶ ἔθηκαν αὐτὸ [..α˙] ἐν μνημείῳ.

Day Nine: 6.30-52:

The day begins:
Καὶ συνάγονται οἱ ἀπόστολοι πρὸς τὸν Ἰησοῦν,
καὶ ἀπήγγειλαν αὐτῷ πάντα ὅσα ἐποίησαν καὶ ὅσα ἐδίδαξαν.

Commentators have noticed what must have been a passing of a number of days between Jesus' sending out of his disciples and their return[29]. Consequently, as for 5.25-34 (in Day Seven), they have viewed 6.14-29 as expressive of an interval of time. Day Eight's analysis makes clear, however, that it is not the only reason it is positioned there. In literary-structural and rhetorical terms, given that 6.14-29 is more fully integrated into the presentation than previously discerned, its primary function is re-established: it reflects the issue of Jesus' identity raised in the synagogue scene, 6.2-6a, firstly in vv.14b,15, and then in vv.16ff; and it springs from the mission, in 6.6b-14a, of Jesus' disciples, which enjoys success from the moment it begins. A new Day's telling well begins at 6.30.

In the introduction to this Day, 6.30-33, in the first part (A, v.30) we read of the return and the reporting of the disciples to Jesus; in the second part (B, v.31) we have Jesus' suggestion that they rest somewhere privately; and in the third part (B', vv.32,33) we read of their going there, by boat, but that they were not going to be alone.

The main story of the Day, the Feeding of the Five-thousand, is found in vv.34-44. It is a story which has its parallel in the symmetrically-opposite Day Thirteen (8.1-21), the Feeding of the Four-thousand. Again, we can discern the Markan hand of careful planning.[30] The story of the Feeding is presented in three parts: after

---

[29] It may, of course, have been weeks if Jesus' "teaching in circuit around the villages" (6.6b) included teaching in synagogues on the sabbaths. On this point, consider I. Sonne, *IntDB*, Vol. 4, "Synagogue", pp.481, 487: "Bigger villages must have had some kind of synagogue"; the synagogue had "the character of an educational institution... reading from the Scriptures and exposition of the Law constituted the focal point in the sabbatical gatherings".

[30] The fact that there are two 'feeding stories' has long intrigued interpreters of the Gospel of Mark. They have been viewed as a 'doublet', two variants of a single story. And for some considerable time now, virtually every interpreter has observed material clusterered around the feeding stories that is also similar in content and form. In chs.6-8, they have been viewed as two parallel cycles of stories. Pre-Markan cycles or catenae have been sought out in chs.6-8, 4-6, and even 4-8. To the approaches, in particular, of Fowler, *Loaves and Fishes...*, and Achtemeier, "Towards the Isolation.." and "The Origin and Function...", (in this literary-structural analysis of Mark's second Series) we bring the additional evidence of the

the short introduction (A, v.34) in which Jesus, coming out of the boat, is met by a large crowd, it is said that he has compassion for the crowd. What follows is a miracle event which expresses his compassion. In the two balanced halves (B, vv.35-38 and B', vv.39-44), v.35 first establishes the lateness of the hour, and in v.36 the disciples establish the need of the crowd to eat (they too will have had need, we interpret, see v.31 of the introduction to the Day).

The closing, third section of the Day relates an evening/night-time crossing of the lake and the second miracle of the Day, Jesus' walking on the sea. For a discussion on the ending of this day, Day Nine, at 6.52, see Day Six, for with Days Five and Six we have identified already the importance of the "night-crossing" of the Sea of Galilee in Mark's scheme; that is, how it concludes one day, prior to the beginning of a new one. As in the earlier examples, so here too the night-crossing of 6.45-52 brings Days Nine and Ten into juxtaposition. Given that Days Five, Six and Seven are a threesome of days, this fact alone suggests that Days Eight, Nine and Ten may form another threesome. We will be able to discuss this later, after the presentation of the literary-structure and contents of Day Ten.

The limits of Day Nine are relatively easily defined, so too is the overall structure of the Day which may be described, from the above, as a composite ABB' form. Mark's rhetorical style is clearly identified again. His αββ‛ literary-structural principle is demonstrated consistently at the higher levels of literary order, here at ABB' and αββ‛, and again with variations at the lower orders, [α] [β] [β‛] and [α] [α‛], [.α] [.β] [.β‛] and [.α] [.α‛], [..α] [..β] [..β‛] and [..α] [..α‛].

We observe two comparatively long parts B and B' in the middle section, that is vv.35-38 and vv.39-44, but they are entirely compatible with what we find in other Day's tellings, with the major parts of the Days' contents[31]. We make another observation: compared with 6.1-29, 6.30-52 has not attracted anything like the interest of commentators and scholars, in its divisions and sub-divisions. This may be explained by the fact that there is little that is controversial here about Mark's presentation, unlike the Day prior to it. It is also the case that there is little attention paid by

---

importance of "days" in Mark's scheme, and his ABB' presentational method.
[31] See note 19 on the lengths of parts in Mark's constructions. See Day Five, in section 4.1-32, the parabolic teachings of Jesus, for an example of longer parts.

commentators to the divisions in the text following, and covering a number of the Days which we will be delimiting. One of the reasons for this is that some of these Days are much smaller units than those previousy defined; another reason is that no major divisions, generally speaking, are proposed by commentators up to 8.21. Below, I present the literary structure of Day Nine. Verbal correspondences, significant historical presents, and Markan sectional introductory formulae are all underlined.

A α   ³⁰[α] Καὶ <u>συνάγονται</u> [β] οἱ ἀπόστολοι [βʹ] πρὸς τὸν Ἰησοῦν,
  β   [α] καὶ ἀπήγγειλαν [αʹ] αὐτῷ
  βʹ   [α] πάντα [β] <u>ὅσα</u> ἐποίησαν [βʹ] καὶ <u>ὅσα</u> <u>ἐδίδαξαν</u>.
B α   ³¹[α] καὶ <u>λέγει</u> αὐτοῖς, [β] [.α] Δεῦτε ὑμεῖς αὐτοὶ [.β] <u>κατ' ἰδίαν</u>
    [.βʹ] <u>εἰς ἔρημον τόπον</u> [.βʹ] καὶ ἀναπαύσασθε ὀλίγον.
  β   [α] ἦσαν γὰρ [β] [.α] οἱ ἐρχόμενοι [.αʹ] καὶ οἱ ὑπάγοντες [βʹ] <u>πολλοί</u>,
  βʹ   [α] καὶ οὐδὲ [β] <u>φαγεῖν</u> [βʹ] εὐκαίρουν.
Bʹ α   ³²[α] [.α] καὶ <u>ἀπῆλθον</u> [.αʹ] ἐν τῷ <u>πλοίῳ</u> [β] <u>εἰς ἔρημον τόπον</u> [βʹ] <u>κατ' ἰδίαν</u>.
  β   ³³[α] καὶ εἶδον αὐτοὺς ὑπάγοντας [αʹ] καὶ ἐπέγνωσαν <u>πολλοί</u>,
  βʹ   [α] καὶ πεζῇ ἀπὸ πασῶν τῶν πόλεων [β] συνέδραμον ἐκεῖ [βʹ] καὶ προῆλθον αὐτούς.

A α   ³⁴[α] καὶ ἐξελθὼν [β] εἶδεν [βʹ] πολὺν ὄχλον,
  β   [α] καὶ ἐσπλαγχνίσθη ἐπ' αὐτοὺς [β] ὅτι ἦσαν ὡς πρόβατα [βʹ] μὴ ἔχοντα ποιμένα,
  βʹ   [α] καὶ ἤρξατο [β] <u>διδάσκειν</u> αὐτοὺς [βʹ] πολλά.
B α[α] ³⁵[.α] <u>Καὶ ἤδη ὥρας πολλῆς</u> γενομένης [.β] προσελθόντες αὐτῷ
    [.βʹ] οἱ μαθηταὶ αὐτοῦ ἔλεγον
  [β]   [.α] ὅτι Ἔρημός ἐστιν ὁ τόπος, [.β] <u>καὶ ἤδη ὥρα πολλή</u>·
    [.βʹ] ³⁶ἀπόλυσον αὐτούς,
  [βʹ]   [.α] [..α] ἵνα <u>ἀπελθόντες</u> [..β] εἰς τοὺς κύκλῳ ἀγροὺς [..βʹ] καὶ κώμας
    [.β] <u>ἀγοράσωσιν</u> ἑαυτοῖς [.βʹ] τί φάγωσιν.
β[α] ³⁷[.α] ὁ δὲ ἀποκριθεὶς [.β] εἶπεν <u>αὐτοῖς</u>, [.βʹ] <u>Δότε αὐτοῖς</u> ὑμεῖς φαγεῖν.
  [β]   [.α] καὶ <u>λέγουσιν</u> αὐτῷ, [.β] <u>Ἀπελθόντες</u> [.βʹ] <u>ἀγοράσωμεν</u> δηναρίων διακοσίων <u>ἄρτους</u>
  [βʹ]   καὶ <u>δώσομεν αὐτοῖς φαγεῖν</u>;
βʹ[α] ³⁸[.α] ὁ δὲ <u>λέγει αὐτοῖς</u>, [.β] Πόσους <u>ἄρτους</u> ἔχετε; [.βʹ] [..α] ὑπάγετε
    [..αʹ] ἴδετε.
  [β]   [.α] καὶ γνόντες [.β] <u>λέγουσιν</u>, [.βʹ] <u>Πέντε</u>,
  [βʹ]   καὶ <u>δύο ἰχθύας</u>.

Β' α[α] ³⁹ [.α] καὶ ἐπέταξεν αὐτοῖς ἀνακλῖναι πάντας [.β] συμπόσια συμπόσια
[.β'] ἐπὶ τῷ χλωρῷ χόρτῳ.
[β] ⁴⁰ [.α] καὶ ἀνέπεσαν [.α'] πρασιαι πρασιαι
[β'] [.α] κατα ἑκατὸν [.α'] καὶ κατα πεντήκοντα.
β[α] ⁴¹ [.α] [..α] καὶ λαβὼν τοὺς πέντε ἄρτους [..α'] καὶ τοὺς δύο ἰχθύας
[.α'] ἀναβλέψας εἰς τὸν οὐρανὸν
[β] [.α] [..α] εὐλόγησεν [..α'] καὶ κατέκλασεν τοὺς ἄρτους [.β] καὶ ἐδίδου
τοῖς μαθηταῖς [αὐτοῦ] [.β'] ἵνα παρατιθῶσιν αὐτοῖς,
[β'] [.α] καὶ τοὺς δύο ἰχθύας [.α'] ἐμέρισεν πᾶσιν.
β'[α] ⁴² [.α] καὶ ἔφαγον πάντες [.α'] καὶ ἐχορτάσθησαν·
[β] ⁴³ [.α] καὶ ἦραν κλάσματα [.β] δώδεκα κοφίνων πληρώματα [.β'] καὶ
ἀπὸ τῶν ἰχθύων.
[β'] ⁴⁴ [.α] καὶ ἦσαν οἱ φαγόντες [τοὺς ἄρτους] [.α'] πεντακισχίλιοι
ἄνδρες.

Α α ⁴⁵ [α] [.α] Καὶ εὐθὺς [.β] ἠνάγκασεν τοὺς μαθητὰς αὐτοῦ [.β'] ἐμβῆναι
εἰς τὸ πλοῖον [β] [.α] καὶ προάγειν [.β] εἰς τὸ πέραν [.β'] πρὸς
Βηθσαϊδάν, [β'] ἕως αὐτὸς ἀπολύει τὸν ὄχλον.
β ⁴⁶ [α] καὶ ἀποταξάμενος αὐτοῖς [β] ἀπῆλθεν εἰς τὸ ὄρος
[β'] προσεύξασθαι.
β' ⁴⁷ [α] καὶ ὀψίας γενομένης [β] ἦν τὸ πλοῖον ἐν μέσῳ τῆς θαλάσσης,
[β'] καὶ αὐτὸς μόνος ἐπὶ τῆς γῆς.

Β α ⁴⁸ [α] καὶ ἰδὼν αὐτοὺς [β] βασανιζομένους ἐν τῷ ἐλαύνειν, [β'] ἦν γὰρ
ὁ ἄνεμος ἐναντίος αὐτοῖς,
β [α] περὶ τετάρτην φυλακὴν τῆς νυκτὸς [β] [.α] ἔρχεται πρὸς
αὐτοὺς [.α'] περιπατῶν ἐπὶ τῆς θαλάσσης· [β'] καὶ ἤθελεν
παρελθεῖν αὐτούς.
β' ⁴⁹ [α] [.α] οἱ δὲ ἰδόντες αὐτὸν [.α'] ἐπὶ τῆς θαλάσσης περιπατοῦντα
[β] [.α] ἔδοξαν ὅτι φάντασμά ἐστιν, [.α'] καὶ ἀνέκραξαν·
⁵⁰ [β'] [.α] πάντες γὰρ αὐτὸν εἶδον [α'] καὶ ἐταράχθησαν.

Β' α [α] [.α] ὁ δὲ εὐθὺς ἐλάλησεν μετ' αὐτῶν, [.α'] καὶ λέγει αὐτοῖς,
[α'] [.α] Θαρσεῖτε, [.β] ἐγώ εἰμι· [.β'] μὴ φοβεῖσθε.
β ⁵¹ [α] καὶ ἀνέβη πρὸς αὐτοὺς [β] εἰς τὸ πλοῖον, [β'] καὶ ἐκόπασεν
ὁ ἄνεμος.
β' [α] καὶ λίαν [ἐκ περισσοῦ] ἐν ἑαυτοῖς ἐξίσταντο, ⁵² [β] οὐ γὰρ
συνῆκαν ἐπὶ τοῖς ἄρτοις, [β'] ἀλλ' ἦν αὐτῶν ἡ καρδία
πεπωρωμένη.

Day Ten: 6.53-7.23:

The opening three-part piece is 6.53-56. V.53 reports the landing at Gennesaret, not Bethsaida as was the proposed destination, of 6.45. Mark gives no direct explanation for this fact, though it may be argued reasonably that he leaves us to judge from his report of the storm the night before that a change was necessitated. Alternatively, because the destination is eventually reached, in 8.22, there are those who want to suggest that Mark has split up an earlier collection of narratives and has inserted 6.53-8.21, and forgotten to amend his geographical reference.[32] Literary-structural analysis, however, challenges this opinion. Everywhere in the text, Mark is demonstrating much control of his material and care in presenting his detailed points. The probability is that there is some kind of deliberate compositional intention expressed here.

This Day Ten, we note, is the third day of this Series' first threesome of days. Day Fourteen, which begins with 8.22, is the third day of this Series' parallel threesome of days. Mark's reference to 'Bethsaida' in both sub-Series is just one detail which connects and, therefore, reinforces the balance between his presentations of Days Eight to Ten and Days Twelve to Fourteen. The thrust of these two sub-Series, 6.1-7.23 and 7.31-8.26, is in similar direction. They both include feeding stories, stories of Sea journeyings, and stories of controversy with Pharisees, in the same order[33]. They also both include accounts of healings, but in different literary settings, and in different forms. And the one noticeable point of real contact between

---

[32] E.g. Hooker, *The Gospel...*, p.171.

[33] Ref. Luke H. Jenkins, "A Marcan Doublet", in *Studies in History and Religion: Presented to Dr. H. Wheeler Robinson*, ed. Ernest A. Payne, Lutterworth, London, 1942, pp.87-111. Jenkins describes what he thought was a "sustained doublet": 6.31-7.37 and 8.1-26; Taylor, *The Gospel...*, revised and reduced it to 6.35-56 and 8.1-10, to his own satisfaction. Since then many attempts have been made at defining the Markan, or the Pre-Markan double cycle, but with no certain results. Much more recently, Fowler, *Loaves and Fishes...*, has focused principally on the feeding stories, and he has concluded that the feeding of the four thousand is the tradition and that of the five thousand is Mark's own creation. For an examination of the function of this duality, he turns to 8.4 (which is the "crucial verse for the interpretation of the two stories as a *doublet*", p.93) and the irony of it is that the disciples "have no concept of the self-condemnation implied by their words", p.99. He does not focus on the irony of 8.14,16. And most lacking of all is any consideration of 8.19-21, which are surely the key, as we will see, to understanding the way these stories really do connect and function in their Gospel settings.

the feeding stories is in 8.19-21, which is where Mark shares a conundrum with his audience. We will return to these issues in the summary of this Series.

The proposal that 6.53-56 is the introductory piece to this Day, a single Day's telling, requires examination. It clearly speaks of activities over several days. As under Day Eight (6.1-29) we considered a glut of imperfects (sixteen), so here also we have the next rash of them (five, in vv.53-56) to consider. The imperfect of part B, vv.54,55, may be interpreted as inceptive and, therefore, as descriptive of activity that "began" (only) to take place. As in Day Eight, so also here ἤρξαντο significantly features and suggests this inceptive interpretation of ἤκουον. The four imperfects of part B', v.56, may be interpreted as continuous or repeated action descriptive of the activity that surrounded Jesus, in the general case, "wherever" he went. It is judged, therefore, that 6.53-56 functions as Mark's introduction to his telling of a single day, this Day Ten.

Overall, Day Ten is structured as Day Nine, in an ABB' form (compare also Day Seven, so far). As with the lower levels of literary order, so here too the three parts perform similarly: the first section (6.53-56) introduces the whole by setting the context; the second section (7.1-13) is the first development, and the third section (7.14-23) is the second and completing development.

Day-Section A, 6.53-56, is introductory in that it opens the Day's telling; it defines the place Gennesaret, which neither Taylor nor Nineham appear to appreciate[34]; and it establishes the activity that surrounded Jesus there and 'wherever' he went. The historical present at 7.1 is the link, which Taylor and Nineham miss.

In true Markan fashion (see Thackeray's understanding of the historical present, under Day Two) this historical present of 7.1 introduces a new section, the Day's Section B, 7.1-13, by introducing new characters into the frame who in turn raise the issue for the Day, which is, first of all, to do with the fact that Jesus' disciples "eat bread with unclean/unwashed hands" (v.2)/"unclean hands" (v.5). It is in the repetition of the question, at v.5, that another question is attached,

---

[34] Taylor, *The Gospel...*, p.334, writes, "Unlike the three preceding stories, there is no link between this narrative and the rest, no temporal or local statement which tells us when and where the incident took place." Nineham, *Saint Mark*, p.188, writes, "The evangelist makes no attempt to locate this section either in space or in time."

in regard to the "tradition of the elders". Lambrecht properly points out that vv.1-5, my part A, raises the questions; vv.6-13, my parts B and B', deal with the tradition; and vv.14-23, my Day's Section B', deals with the matter of unclean hands.[35] Part A, vv.1-5, contains a Markan 'aside'[36], vv.3,4. Parts B and B' commence at vv.6 and 9: compare the beginnings of:

v.6 Ὁ δὲ εἶπεν αὐτοῖς, Καλῶς...
and v.9 Καὶ ἔλεγεν αὐτοῖς, Καλῶς...

In the first of these two parts, Mark quotes from Isaiah 29.13 (closer to the LXX than to the Hebrew text), which he fits into his rhetorical style:

B α ⁶[a] Ὁ δὲ εἶπεν αὐτοῖς, [β] Καλῶς ἐπροφήτευσεν Ἡσαΐας [β'] περὶ ὑμῶν τῶν ὑποκριτῶν,
  β [a] ὡς γέγραπται [ὅτι]
    [β] [.a] Οὗτος ὁ λαὸς τοῖς χείλεσίν με τιμᾷ,
    [.a'] ἡ δὲ καρδία αὐτῶν πόρρω ἀπέχει ἀπ' ἐμοῦ.
  ⁷[β'] [.a] Μάτην δὲ σέβονταί με,
    [.a'] διδάσκοντες διδασκαλίας <u>ἐντάλματα</u> <u>ἀνθρώπων</u>.
β' ⁸[a] ἀφέντες τὴν <u>ἐντολὴν</u> τοῦ θεοῦ [a'] κρατεῖτε τὴν παράδοσιν τῶν <u>ἀνθρώπων</u>.

The quotation has its introduction in [a], its first part presentation in [β], and its second part in [β']. Overall, the introduction to part B is in α, the quote is in β, and Jesus' application of the quote is in β'. (In the symmetrically opposite Day, Day Twelve (7.31-37), there appears to be an inclusion of a deliberate parallel to Isaiah 29.13, on Mark's part, which is an allusion to Isaiah 35.5,6.)

Day-Section B', 7.14-23, is equally made up of three parts and the opening part A, vv.14,15, describes Jesus' calling the crowd to him and addressing them on the first issue raised (raised, structurally-speaking in the parallel section B, 7.1-13). Parts B and B' have a new setting, in a house, away from the crowd (vv.17-19 and vv.20-23); here "his disciples begin to question Jesus about the

---

[35] J. Lambrecht, "Jesus and the Law: an Investigation of Mark 7.1-23", *EphThL* 53 (1977), pp.24-79.
[36] See also 7.2b ("this is unwashed"), v.19 ("purging all foods"), in this same Day's telling.

parable". We can see, in vv.21,22, how Mark lists *twelve* examples of 'evil thoughts' in two lists: the first six are in the plural form and the second six are in the singular. At the fifth level of order, [.α] [.α'], he presents two listings, and at the sixth order [..α]...[ζ] the words themselves.

At vv.14,15 the αββ' presentation of the parts clearly suggests the rejection of v.16, "If anyone has ears to hear, let him hear", which is not supported by our principle witnesses, Codices Siniaticus and Vaticanus. The idea expressed by the enthusiastic copyist, that this verse might be included, is an interesting one, however: it comes from Day Five (3.7-4.41) and specifically from the parables-section, from 4.9 and v.23. The explanation of 4.33,34 is well rehearsed in this Day-Section B': in part A, Jesus addresses the crowd with the *parable*; in part B, *in private*, the disciples question Jesus about it and he begins his explanation; and in part B', he completes his explanation.

The literary structure of Day Ten, given the annotations as for Days Eight and Nine, is viewed as:

A α ⁵³ Καὶ διαπεράσαντες ἐπὶ τὴν γῆν
    β ἦλθον εἰς Γεννησαρὲτ
    β' καὶ προσωρμίσθησαν.

B α ⁵⁴[α] Καὶ ἐξελθόντων αὐτῶν [α'] ἐκ τοῦ πλοίου
    β [α[εὐθὺς ἐπιγνόντες αὐτὸν ⁵⁵[β] περιέδραμον [β'] ὅλην τὴν χώραν ἐκείνην
    β' [α] [.α] καὶ ἤρξαντο [.β] ἐπὶ τοῖς κραβάττοις τοὺς κακῶς ἔχοντας περιφέρειν [β'] [.α] ὅπου ἤκουον [.α'] ὅτι ἐστίν.

B' α ⁵⁶[α] Καὶ ὅπου ἂν εἰσεπορεύετο [β] [.α] <u>εἰς</u> κώμας [.β] <u>ἢ εἰς</u> πόλεις [.β'] <u>ἢ εἰς</u> ἀγροὺς [β'] [.α] ἐν ταῖς ἀγοραῖς [.β] ἐτίθεσαν [.β'] τοὺς ἀσθενοῦντας,
    β [α] καὶ παρεκάλουν αὐτὸν [α'] ἵνα <u>κἂν</u> τοῦ κρασπέδου τοῦ ἱματίου <u>αὐτου ἅψωνται</u>·
    β' [α] καὶ ὅσοι <u>ἂν ἥψαντο αὐτου</u> [α'] ἐσῴζοντο.

Α α ¹[α] Καὶ συνάγονται πρὸς αὐτὸν [β] [.α] οἱ Φαρισαῖοι [.α'] καί τινες τῶν γραμματέων [β'] ἐλθόντες ἀπὸ Ἱεροσολύμων
β[α] ²[.α] Καὶ ἰδόντες τινὰς τῶν μαθητῶν αὐτοῦ [.β] [..α] ὅτι κοιναῖς χερσίν, [..α'] τοῦτ' ἔστιν ἀνίπτοις, [.β'] ἐσθίουσιν τοὺς ἄρτους
[β] ³[.α] [..α] οἱ γὰρ Φαρισαῖοι καὶ πάντες οἱ Ἰουδαῖοι [..β] ἐὰν μὴ πυγμῇ νίψωνται τὰς χεῖρας [..β'] οὐκ ἐσθίουσιν,
[.α'] [..α] κρατοῦντες [..β] τὴν παράδοσιν [..β'] τῶν πρεσβυτέρων,
[β'] ⁴[.α] [..α] καὶ ἀπ' ἀγορᾶς [..β] ἐὰν μὴ βαπτίσωνται [..β'] οὐκ ἐσθίουσιν,
[.β] [..α] καὶ ἄλλα πολλά ἐστιν [..β] ἃ παρέλαβον [..β'] κρατεῖν,
[.β'] [..α] βαπτισμοὺς ποτηρίων [..β] καὶ ξεστῶν [.β'] καὶ χαλκίων [καὶ κλινῶν]
β'[α] ⁵καὶ ἐπερωτῶσιν αὐτὸν οἱ Φαρισαῖοι καὶ οἱ γραμματεῖς,
[β] Διὰ τί οὐ περιπατοῦσιν οἱ μαθηταί σου κατὰ τὴν παράδοσιν τῶν πρεσβυτέρων,
[β'] ἀλλὰ κοιναῖς χερσὶν ἐσθίουσιν τὸν ἄρτον;

Β α ⁶[α] Ὁ δὲ εἶπεν αὐτοῖς, [β] Καλῶς ἐπροφήτευσεν Ἡσαΐας [β'] περὶ ὑμῶν τῶν ὑποκριτῶν,
β [α] ὡς γέγραπται [ὅτι]
[β] [.α] Οὗτος ὁ λαὸς τοῖς χείλεσίν με τιμᾷ,
[.α'] ἡ δὲ καρδία αὐτῶν πόρρω ἀπέχει ἀπ' ἐμοῦ·
⁷[β'] [.α] μάτην δὲ σέβονταί με,
[.α'] διδάσκοντες διδασκαλίας ἐντάλματα ἀνθρώπων.
β' ⁸[α] ἀφέντες τὴν ἐντολὴν τοῦ θεοῦ [α'] κρατεῖτε τὴν παράδοσιν τῶν ἀνθρώπων.

Β' α ⁹[α] Καὶ ἔλεγεν αὐτοῖς, [β] Καλῶς ἀθετεῖτε τὴν ἐντολὴν τοῦ θεοῦ, [β'] ἵνα τὴν παράδοσιν ὑμῶν στήσητε.
β ¹⁰[α] Μωϋσῆς γὰρ εἶπεν, [β] Τίμα τὸν πατέρα σου καὶ τὴν μητέρα σου, [β'] καί, Ὁ κακολογῶν πατέρα ἢ μητέρα θανάτῳ τελευτάτω·
β' ¹¹[α] ὑμεῖς δὲ λέγετε, [β] [.α] Ἐὰν εἴπῃ ἄνθρωπος τῷ πατρὶ ἢ τῇ μητρί, [.α'] [..α] Κορβᾶν, [..β] ὅ ἐστιν Δῶρον, [..β'] ὃ ἐὰν ἐξ ἐμοῦ ὠφεληθῇς, ¹²[β'] [.α] οὐκέτι ἀφίετε αὐτὸν οὐδὲν ποιῆσαι τῷ πατρὶ ἢ τῇ μητρί, ¹³[.β] ἀκυροῦντες τὸν λόγον τοῦ θεοῦ τῇ παραδόσει ὑμῶν ᾗ παρεδώκατε· [.β'] καὶ παρόμοια τοιαῦτα πολλὰ ποιεῖτε.

A α ¹⁴[α] [.α] Καὶ προσκαλεσάμενος πάλιν τὸν ὄχλον [β] ἔλεγεν αὐτοῖς,
         [βʹ] [.α] ᾿Ακούσατέ μου πάντες [.αʹ] καὶ σύνετε.
   β ¹⁵[α] οὐδέν ἐστιν ἔξωθεν τοῦ ἀνθρώπου [β] εἰσπορευόμενον εἰς
         αὐτὸν [βʹ] ὃ δύναται κοινῶσαι αὐτόν·
   βʹ   [α] ἀλλὰ τὰ ἐκ τοῦ ἀνθρώπου ἐκπορευόμενα [αʹ] ἐστιν τὰ
         κοινοῦντα τὸν ἄνθρωπον.

B α ¹⁷[α] [.α] Καὶ ὅτε εἰσῆλθεν [.β] εἰς οἶκον [.βʹ] ἀπὸ τοῦ ὄχλου,
         [αʹ] ἐπηρώτων αὐτὸν οἱ μαθηταὶ αὐτοῦ τὴν παραβολήν.
   β ¹⁸[α] καὶ λέγει αὐτοῖς, [β] Οὕτως καὶ ὑμεῖς ἀσύνετοί ἐστε; [βʹ] [.α] οὐ
         νοεῖτε [.β] ὅτι πᾶν τὸ ἔξωθεν εἰσπορευόμενον εἰς τὸν ἄνθρωπον
         [.βʹ] οὐ δύναται αὐτὸν κοινῶσαι,
   βʹ ¹⁹[α] [.α] ὅτι οὐκ εἰσπορεύεται αὐτοῦ εἰς τὴν καρδίαν [.β] ἀλλ᾿ εἰς
         τὴν κοιλίαν, [.βʹ] καὶ εἰς τὸν ἀφεδρῶνα ἐκπορεύεται;
         [αʹ] καθαρίζων πάντα τὰ βρώματα.

Bʹ α ²⁰[α] ῎Ελεγεν δὲ [β] ὅτι Τὸ ἐκ τοῦ ἀνθρώπου ἐκπορευόμενον
         [βʹ] ἐκεῖνο κοινοῖ τὸν ἄνθρωπον·
   β ²¹[α] [.α] ἔσωθεν γὰρ [.β] ἐκ τῆς καρδίας τῶν ἀνθρώπων [.βʹ] οἱ
         διαλογισμοὶ οἱ κακοὶ ἐκπορεύονται,
         [β] [.α] πορνεῖαι, [.β] κλοπαί, [.γ] φόνοι,
         [.δ] ²²μοιχεῖαι, [.ε] πλεονεξίαι, [.ζ] πονηρίαι,
         [βʹ] [.α] δόλος, [.β] ἀσέλγεια, [.γ] ὀφθαλμὸς πονηρός,
         [.δ] βλασφημία, [.ε] ὑπερηφανία, [.ζ] ἀφροσύνη·
   βʹ ²³[α] πάντα ταῦτα τὰ πονηρα [β] ἔσωθεν ἐκπορεύεται [βʹ] καὶ κοινοῖ
         τὸν ἄνθρωπον.

Before we continue with an examination of Day Eleven, we can determine the relationship of Days Eight, Nine and Ten. In a geographical and temporal sense, Nine and Ten are more closely related, by the night crossing, and because there is a passing of days between Eight and Nine. This might suggest an ABB' relationship of the Days, but the first threesome of Days in the Gospel (of Days 1, 2 and 3), if it had been judged on these grounds alone, would have been determined to be in an ABA' relationship. The overriding consideration in that case, as indeed in the second case also (Days 5, 6 and 7), was the linear movement of the three-day story.

Day Eight, we might say, begins low key, with a rejection of *"the prophet"* Jesus by *those who*, we might have thought, *would have been his keenest supporters*. Jesus' sending out of his disciples clearly raises both key and tempo. After instructions, amongst which "take *no bread and no money*" (*God will provide?*), they begin the mission, and many hear and talk about what is happening. Indeed, as a result, "*King*"[37] Herod himself hears about it, and about Jesus. And Herod, like the people, wonders who he is. We are then given a story about Herod's "*banquet*" and that which leads to the beheading of John[38]. (In all, Jesus, the rejected prophet, is *likened to three prophets: John raised from the dead, Elijah and another*.)

On Day Nine, the disciples, tired from their mission, *rejoin Jesus*. Their futile attempt to find a quiet place, because of the growing crowd, leads to them all taking a boat elsewhere. But a large crowd gathered nevertheless. To Jesus they were like "sheep without a shepherd". (There was *no prophet around* who was worthy to be their "*shepherd*".) And then there is the '*banquet in the desert*' for which, in a fashion like that of *Elijah/Elisha*, but much more miraculously (for *Jesus is greater*, he feeds more with less), *bread and fish are multiplied for the five thousand (as God provides/as Jesus provides it; money was not needed*, the disciples *had five loaves...*). Jesus has already *confounded his disciples* with this miracle, but he goes on to "*terrify*" them. After they have struggled at oar in the face of a contrary heavy wind through three watches of the night, Jesus appears to them walking on the sea. *He rejoins them.* And all is calm. But they are not. They still have <u>not understood</u> *about the "loaves":* "<u>*their hearts were hardened*</u>".

Day Ten tells, when Jesus stepped out of the boat, how he was immediately recognised, and how *people ran* through the countryside *to him* bringing their sick wherever they heard he was. In village, town and farm they laid down their sick in open spaces: just a touch of his cloak was all they needed. (It is action-packed, dramatic presentation. *The people needed him*.) And just as his disciples *had gathered round him*, in Day Nine (6.30), so now, in Day Ten, also Pharisees and some scribes who had heard *in Jerusalem*, came and *gathered round him* (7.1). At the last, *those who might have recognised who Jesus really was* demonstrate to Jesus, who quotes from *Isaiah (the prophet)* that "<u>*their hearts were hardened*</u>", that they

---

[37] Herod was no "king", but Mark probably chose to use the title for the purpose of showing Jesus in a still greater light.

[38] Compare: Herod/Pilate, 6.26/15.15; contrast: John/Jesus, 6.29/15.46 (no disciples buried Jesus).

had "let go of the commands of God", holding to man's traditions on what is "*clean*" and "*unclean*". (They are *not true shepherds* of the people; they have no compassion...). *They will not acknowledge Jesus to be greater than John the Baptist, King Herod, Elijah or any prophet.*

This threesome of Days has its many vivid connections. Key words, themes and interpretations are in italics. The first day is clearly introductory; its themes and sub-themes are picked up and developed, in turn, in the two days which follow it. It is indeed arranged to an ABB' scheme. It has its movement of story-line best expressed in this way.

Day Eleven: 7.24-30:

This Day is the middle Day of the first of two middle Series of Seven Days. The Day begins, as we presented under Day Eight, with use of the significant word Ἐκεῖθεν, with which Mark begins the telling of four Days in all.[39] The opening line reads:

Ἐκεῖθεν δὲ ἀναστὰς ἀπῆλθεν εἰς τὰ ὅρια Τύρου.

We may translate literally: "And from there, rising up" (after the night, from sleep) "he went away to the region of Tyre." In 1.35, ἀναστὰς is used for the first time, but there within the context of a pre-dawn activity. Here, at the beginning of Day Eleven, Mark appears to use it, in a post-dawn, pre-journey sense. He does exactly the same in the opening line of the corresponding middle day, Day Eighteen (10.1-16), of the second middle Series of Seven Days, where (at 10.1) he repeats his use of no less than five words in all:

Καὶ ἐκεῖθεν ἀναστὰς ἔρχεται εἰς τὰ ὅρια τῆς Ἰουδαίας [καὶ] πέραν τοῦ Ἰορδάνου...

The corresponding words are all underlined. We note too that ἀπῆλθεν is a variant of ἔρχεται. It may be judged, therefore, that

---

[39] Refer to page 150.

Mark deliberately composed the beginning of one of these two days, both of them significant for their positions, with the other in mind.

We observe that the introductory piece to this Day's telling (and that of Day Eighteen, 10.1, therefore) is similar in structure and content to that of Day Eight (6.1), in that Mark tells us that Jesus left the place of the earlier Day's telling (in the first part) and arrives in another, the place of Mark's new Day's telling (in the second part). It is an introductory formula which he repeats also at 7.31 (the beginning of Day Twelve), at 8.27 (beginning Day Fifteen), and at 9.30/33 (beginning Day Seventeen). Further, the formula is detected at 6.53 (beginning Day Ten): it is only slightly different in that the 'place' left behind is the sea (from the closing section of the previous Day's telling). Interestingly, the last similar example at 10.46 (beginning Day Twenty-one) is a reversal of this form, where the arrival is told first, and the departure second (the Day's main event takes place on Jesus' departure from Jericho). This introductory formula (and its variant) is a development of the one defined (under Day Six) by the analysis of night-crossings of the Sea of Galilee, which is that new Days begin with new locations and new activities after sunrise. What makes this formula (uncovered here) a development therefore, is the additional information of the leaving of the place of the previous Day's telling. Eight Days in Mark's scheme (we include that of the reversal, Day Twenty-one) begin, therefore, in like manner. The common words are as follows:

Ἐκεῖθεν	four times	(6.1, 7.24, 9.30, 10.1);
Καὶ ἐξῆλθεν	four times	(6.1, 7.31, 8.27, 9.30);
ἦλθον, -εν	three times	(6.53, 7.31, 9.33);
ἔρχεται, -ονται	three times	(6.1, 10.1,46);
εἰς	in all eight cases	(6.1,53, 7.24,31, 8.27, 9.33, 10.1,46).

Additional information is provided in each introductory piece regarding place names, or descriptions of place, and in a number of cases the journey between the place left and the place arrived at is suggestive of a day or more between the tellings of Mark's reported Days. For example, for this Day's telling the place of departure is Gennesaret and the destination is the District of Tyre. The only difficulty we might have is that our estimate of the days of the journey might differ from Mark's; his geographical knowledge, as we have now stated twice above, does not seem too accurate.

As the discovery of this introductory formula is helpful to us now for the purpose of discerning the turning points between Mark's Days, it may be judged that it will have been helpful to Mark's first audience. I present the literary structure to Day Eleven:

A α   ²⁴ [α] Ἐκεῖθεν δὲ [β] ἀναστὰς [βʹ] ἀπῆλθεν εἰς τὰ ὅρια Τύρου.
  β   [α] καὶ εἰσελθὼν εἰς οἰκίαν [β] οὐδένα ἤθελεν γνῶναι, [βʹ] καὶ οὐκ ἠδυνήθη λαθεῖν·
  βʹ   ²⁵ [α] [.α] ἀλλ' εὐθὺς ἀκούσασα [.β] γυνὴ [.βʹ] περὶ αὐτοῦ,
    [β] [.α] ἧς εἶχεν τὸ θυγάτριον αὐτῆς [.αʹ] πνεῦμα ἀκάθαρτον,
    [βʹ] [.α] ἐλθοῦσα [.β] προσέπεσεν [.βʹ] πρὸς τοὺς πόδας αὐτοῦ·

B α   ²⁶ [α] [.α] ἡ δὲ γυνὴ ἦν Ἑλληνίς, [.αʹ] Συροφοινίκισσα τῷ γένει· [β] καὶ ἠρώτα αὐτὸν [βʹ] [.α] ἵνα τὸ δαιμόνιον [.β] ἐκβάλῃ [.βʹ] ἐκ τῆς θυγατρὸς αὐτῆς.
  β   ²⁷ [α] καὶ ἔλεγεν αὐτῇ , [β] Ἄφες πρῶτον [βʹ] χορτασθῆναι τὰ τέκνα,
  βʹ   [α] οὐ γάρ ἐστιν καλὸν [β] λαβεῖν τὸν ἄρτον τῶν τέκνων [βʹ] καὶ τοῖς κυναρίοις βαλεῖν.

Βʹ α   ²⁸ [α] [.α] ἡ δὲ ἀπεκρίθη [.αʹ] καὶ λέγει αὐτῷ, [αʹ] [.α] Κύριε, [.β] καὶ τὰ κυνάρια ὑποκάτω τῆς τραπέζης [.βʹ] ἐσθίουσιν ἀπὸ τῶν ψιχίων τῶν παιδίων.
  β   ²⁹ [α] καὶ εἶπεν αὐτῇ, [αʹ] [.α] Διὰ τοῦτον τὸν λόγον [.β] ὕπαγε, [.βʹ] ἐξελήλυθεν ἐκ τῆς θυγατρός σου τὸ δαιμόνιον.
  βʹ   ³⁰ [α] [.α] καὶ ἀπελθοῦσα [.αʹ] εἰς τὸν οἶκον αὐτῆς [β] [.α] εὗρεν τὸ παιδίον [.αʹ] βεβλημένον ἐπὶ τὴν κλίνην [βʹ] καὶ τὸ δαιμόνιον ἐξεληλυθός.

The presentation structure of this Day is a simple ABB' form. Section A, vv.24,25, in three parts, is introductory, in that it establishes the change of geographical place and sets Jesus in a house, seeking privacy; inevitably he is known to be there, and a woman who had a daughter with an unclean spirit comes to him. Section B, vv.26,27, develops the story and Section B', vv.28-30, concludes it. The first of the three parts of B fills out the details of the woman and the reason for her approaching Jesus; she is a Greek, a Syrophoenician and she asks Jesus to cast out the demon from her daughter. The first part of Jesus' reply, part β is balanced by the second, part βʹ: the connection, as frequently elsewhere, is made by γάρ. In B', the first part is the woman's reply, which in part β gains Jesus' approval (parts β in both B and B' begin similarly), and as he says, so in part β' it is done.

The basic reasons for the judgement that 7.30 ends Day Eleven's telling are that 7.31 clearly begins the next new Day's telling in Mark's scheme, see above, and that Mark's three-part rhetorical presentation is complete. Day Eleven, therefore, is equal to the shortest Day in Mark's telling so far encountered (compare Day Two, for the number of verses).

In content terms, as for the middle day of the first Series, 2.23-3.6, whilst the crowds are not very far away, they are only alluded to. The story moves along with Jesus in centre stage, on his own, without even mention of his disciples (who do of course have an introductory part to play in the earlier middle day). In 7.31ff. the crowd features again (in v.33). The story of 7.24-31 paints a 'quieter' scene than the ones before or after it. Furthermore, for the first time in the Gospel, Mark makes plain that Jesus' ministry is to a Gentile (we might deduce that the demoniac of 5.1-20 is a Gentile, but Mark there makes absolutely no reference at all to the matter). This Day's story, with limits of 7.24 and 30, well performs as a hinge or fulcrum to the presentation of this Series of seven Days. Symmetrically balanced around it, in Days Nine and Thirteen are the feedings of the Five-thousand and the Four-thousand, each with their numerical details which are summarised in the presenting of a numerological puzzle, after the telling of the second of the two stories. Clearly, in the conversation between the woman and Jesus is the issue of bread for the Jews and bread for the Gentiles. The Feeding of the Five-thousand, since Augustine's time at least, has been associated with the Jews and the Feeding of the Four-thousand with the Gentiles (for a recent study on this, see Drury[40] and my development, under Day Thirteen). The mention of "bread" or "loaves", in Greek the same, ἄρτος, is found in five of the seven days of this Series: Day Eight, 6.8; Day Nine, 6.36, 37, 38, 41 *bis*, 44, 52; Day Ten, 7.2, 5; Day Eleven, 7.27; Day Twelve, none; Day Thirteen, 8.4, 5, 6, 14 *bis*, 16, 17, 19; and Day Fourteen, none. The only other references to bread in the Gospel are at 2.26 (the shewbread) 3.20 and 14.22: that

---

[40] Drury, *The Literary Guide...*, pp.414-416.

is, nineteen of the twenty-two references are found in this Series. In Day Thirteen's telling, Jesus wants his disciples to 'understand' the significance of the numbers of the loaves and the baskets: Mark wants his readers/listeners to understand too, because he has set the Days of this Series, and their contents, therefore, to disclose that this first of two middle Series of the Gospel marks the extension of Jesus' ministry, which was not to Jews alone, but to Gentiles also.

Given the arrangement of the Days of this Series and these and numerous, additional features (such as the inclusion of disciples in the mission work, the wider geographical area he covers, and the first, *amazing* healing of a blind man) I am titling the Series, "Days of Increase in the Mission of Jesus".

Day Twelve: 7.31-37:

The day begins:

Α α   ³¹[α] Καὶ πάλιν [β] ἐξελθὼν [β'] ἐκ τῶν ὁρίων Τύρου
  β   [α] ἦλθεν διὰ Σιδῶνος [β] εἰς τὴν θάλασσαν τῆς Γαλιλαίας
      [β'] ἀνὰ μέσον τῶν ὁρίων Δεκαπόλεως.
  β' ³²[α] καὶ φέρουσιν αὐτῷ [β] κωφὸν [β'] καὶ μογιλάλον.

Section A, the introductory piece, vv.31,32a, sets the scene for vv.32b-37, and it displays a link with the previous Day's telling by Καὶ πάλιν ἐξελθὼν ἐκ τῶν ὁρίων Τύρου. It is demonstrated under Day Eleven that this content and construction follows the scheme of an introductory formula which Mark uses eight times in all to define the ending of one of his Day's reports and the beginning of a new one. The first line tells of Jesus' going from one place; the second line tells of his arrival in another; and the third line introduces those also in the scene. The beginning of Day Eight, the first Day of this Series, is the first such example in the Gospel (see 6.1 and the rhetorical analysis as presented); others in this second Series of seven Days include the openings of Days Ten (6.53-56) and Eleven (7.24,25). In all, they are the first and the three middle Days.

We observe further, significant correspondence between 6.1 and 7.31,32a. As Day Eight's telling begins, here too we discover a historical present, with καί, in the balancing part β' with which the introductory section to the Day is completed. Again we judge that Mark began composing one of these two Days with the other as his reference. (Days Eight and Twelve have their significance in Mark's seven Day scheme here as the introductory Days of sub-Series/threesomes of Days.)

For a discussion on ἐξῆλθεν and variants, see under Day Eight. In regard to Καὶ πάλιν (see under Day Three), here it might be judged to qualify ἐξελθὼν ἐκ τῶν ὁρίων Τύρου in like manner as in 2.13, 3.1 and 4.1, meaning "immediately after" or "thereupon". It would express an immediacy in Jesus' setting out to return to Galilee. In other words his journeying back would be interpreted as starting, not at or just after dawn as at other times (7.24 and 10.1), but before evening (in the previous Day's telling, 7.24-30). To argue this does not impugn the principle of Mark's presenting his tellings of Days as beginning with sunrise and ending just before the following sunrise, though in this case it is, uniquely in the Gospel, Mark's next reported Day's introduction which tells how the previously reported Day concluded. A passage of days is inferred for the journeying between the earlier Day's report and this (of 7.31-37). The place of departure is Tyre and the place of arrival is mid Decapolis, sixty miles away[41]. We might estimate that the journey would have taken a minimum of three days or so. Mark's method as with other Days' tellings is to give temporal and geographical information which sets his next, new Day's context in the opening lines. Here this information is in the first two lines, in v.31; a new Day's telling is begun with v.31.

The alternative reading of Καὶ πάλιν, as meaning "again", does not fit the verbal context. Jesus' arrival in Tyre (7.24) was his first, according to Mark, so he could not have been leaving there "again". Further, Καὶ πάλιν cannot qualify ἐξελθὼν only: ἐξελθὼν and ἐκ τῶν ὁρίων Τύρου occupy parallel positions in parts [β] and [β']. And the final point must be stated clearly: Καὶ πάλιν here is not used to link 7.24-30 and 7.31-37 as one Day's telling as at 2.13, 3.1 and 4.1, simply because the introductory link here at 7.31 demonstrates that a journey of days separates the two tellings.

---

[41] All my distances of Jesus' journeys are measured from the maps of Aharoni and Avi-Yonah, *The Macmillan Bible Atlas*, Rev. Ed., Macmillan Publishing/New York & Collier Macmillan Publishers/London, 1977.

The Day's presentation is a simple ABB' form. The introductory section, A, vv.31,32a, well establishes the new geographical setting and the new principal character. Again, we see clearly Mark's hand at work composing. And as we see elsewhere, in a simple ABB' formation for a Day's telling, Section B begins the development of the story and Section B' completes it. Section B, vv.32b-34, relates the new and ardent request to Jesus and Jesus' actions in response. Section B', vv.35-37, in three parts, tells of the resulting double healing and what follows. In the first of the two parallel sub-parts Jesus orders the crowd's silence, but it is a futile request. In the second, the reason is given: their excitement is such that they cannot be quiet. (As in Day Eight, at 6.2 (and also Day One, at 1.22), Mark, at 7.37, uses the word ἐξεπλήσσοντο.) The Day is completed with what seems an allusion to Isaiah 35.5,6; the matter of the 'blind seeing' is the subject for Day Fourteen, with which Day Twelve holds many correspondences; and the composition here of one has much influenced the other. These are the first and last Days of a new threesome of Days.

The literary structure of Day Twelve is viewed as:

Α α   ³¹[α] Καὶ πάλιν [β] ἐξελθὼν [β´] ἐκ τῶν ὁρίων Τύρου
  β   [α] ἦλθεν διὰ Σιδῶνος [β] εἰς τὴν θάλασσαν τῆς Γαλιλαίας
      [β´] ἀνὰ μέσον τῶν ὁρίων Δεκαπόλεως.
  β´ ³²[α] καὶ φέρουσιν αὐτῷ [β] κωφὸν [β´] καὶ μογιλάλον.
Β α   [α] καὶ παρακαλοῦσιν αὐτὸν [β] ἵνα ἐπιθῇ αὐτω [β´] τὴν χεῖρα.
  β   ³³[α] [.α] καὶ ἀπολαβόμενος αὐτὸν [.β] ἀπὸ τοῦ ὄχλου [.β´] κατ᾽ ἰδίαν
      [β] [.α] ἔβαλεν τοὺς δακτύλους αὐτοῦ [.α´] εἰς τὰ ὦτα αὐτου
      [β´] [.α] καὶ πτύσας [.α´] ἥψατο τῆς γλώσσης αὐτοῦ,
  β´ ³⁴[α] [.α] καὶ ἀναβλέψας [.β] εἰς τὸν οὐρανὸν [.β´] ἐστέναξεν,
      [β] [.α] καὶ λέγει αὐτῷ, [.α´] Εφφαθα,
      [β´] [.α] ὅ ἐστιν, [.α´] Διανοίχθητι.
Β´ α ³⁵[α] καὶ ἠνοίγησαν αὐτοῦ αἱ ἀκοαί,
      [β] [.α] καὶ εὐθὺς [.α´] ἐλύθη ὁ δεσμὸς τῆς γλώσσης αὐτοῦ,
      [β´] καὶ ἐλάλει ὀρθῶς.
  β ³⁶[α] [.α] καὶ διεστείλατο αὐτοῖς [.α´] ἵνα μηδενὶ λέγωσιν·
      [α´] [.α] ὅσον δὲ αὐτοῖς διεστέλλετο, [.α´] αὐτοὶ μᾶλλον
      περισσότερον ἐκήρυσσον.
  β´ ³⁷[α] [.α] καὶ ὑπερπερισσῶς ἐξεπλήσσοντο [.α´] λέγοντες,
      [α´] [.α] Καλῶς πάντα πεποίηκεν· [.β] καὶ τοὺς κωφοὺς ποιεῖ
      ἀκούειν [.β´] καὶ [τοὺς] ἀλάλους λαλεῖν.

Day Thirteen: 8.1-21:

The day begins Ἐν ἐκείναις ταῖς ἡμέραις...: compare the beginnings of Days Three (2.1-22), Four (2.23-3.6), and Sixteen (9.2-29), for Mark's explicit mention of other days passing between his reports. That days do pass between the tellings of Days Twelve and Thirteen is made clear in v.2, Σπλαγχνίζομαι ἐπὶ τὸν ὄχλον ὅτι ἤδη ἡμέραι τρεῖς προσμένουσίν μοι. Days Twelve and Thirteen are not consecutive, unlike Days Thirteen and Fourteen which are linked by another late-day/night-crossing of the Sea of Galilee, which sees Jesus and his disciples, in this case, arriving at Bethsaida (for our earlier discussions on night-crossings, see Days Six and Nine; and for our earlier discussions on the goal of Bethsaida, see Day Ten).

Day Thirteen, as we have noted above, begs comparison with Day Nine, for Feedings and for many details in the telling (such as Σπλαγχνίζομαι which we have already presented above, in 8.2: compare 6.34), but also for the summaries of the Feedings in 8.16-21, and for night-crossings of the Sea of Galilee. We have observed already that the two days lie symmetrically opposite each other in Mark's scheme for this, his first middle Series of Seven Days. Clearly, one of these two days has been composed by Mark with the other much in mind.

Fowler[42] concludes from his studies that the story of the feeding of the four-thousand is the tradition, and that the story of the feeding of the five-thousand is Mark's own creation. Comparison of the structural forms of the two stories, given my analysis, appears to offer some support to his conclusion. The form of the story of the feeding of the five-thousand is much more balanced, or weighted, and in a fashion which is more regularly found in the Gospel, than that of the feeding of the four-thousand. It appears he constructed the former with greater freedom. This whole issue of the freedom with which Mark wrote is an interesting one. We might wonder how much he was constrained in handling tradition, and whether or not he was more constrained by his own method. Similarly, in his handling of

---

[42] Fowler, *Loaves and Fishes...*, see note 33.

already written tradition and oral tradition, was he constrained by one more than the other? We will return to such matters in chapter Eight.

We have noted that the chreia of 2.23-28 is likely composed backwards, that is from the conclusion and point to be established. This Day's telling ends with 8.16-21. And it is clear that this concluding piece is important to the functioning of the two feeding stories in Mark's scheme. We might judge, therefore, that Mark here too composed back from his conclusion and from the point that he was wishing to make. We go now to the beginning of the Day.

We observe that in the opening section of this Day, A, 8.1-5, Mark records no geographical setting, only a temporal reference, and a qualification of it, in v.2, which helps us determine easily that this is a new Day in his telling (for our discussion on this being a single Day's reporting, see Day Six and the presentations on night-crossings). As we have done before, so we do again, and seek from the preceding passage what is immediately missing. We have to go back to 7.31 to establish the geographical setting (it is not at all unreasonable to do this when it is understood that 7.31 begins a new threesome of Days). And it is an important setting for making sense of Mark's emphasis for the Day, and not only the Day, but also the sub-Series and the Series in full. Jesus and his disciples are in the Decapolis (lit. 'ten cities') which was a confederation of ten Greek cities, on the east of the Jordan, mainly, under the protection of the Roman Governor of Syria, but enjoying a certain degree of independence. In other words, the setting for Days Twelve and Thirteen places Jesus and his disciples among a people who were predominantly Gentile. The man, of Day Twelve, who was deaf and had a speaking disorder whom Jesus healed, is likely, therefore, to have been a Gentile. Who, then, were the four-thousand that Jesus fed this Day? In a very round-about way, in 8.16-21, Mark is telling us that they were Gentiles. We will discuss this after the presentation of the literary-structure for the telling of this Day.

The Day's telling is the composite ABB'/ABB', 8.1-9: vv.10-21. The literary structure of Day Thirteen is viewed as:

A α ¹⁽ᵃ⁾ Εν ἐκείναις ταῖς ἡμέραις ⁽ᵝ⁾ πάλιν πολλοῦ ὄχλου ὄντος
⁽ᵝ'⁾ καὶ μὴ ἐχόντων τί φάγωσιν,
β ⁽ᵃ⁾ ⁽·ᵃ⁾ προσκαλεσάμενος τοὺς μαθητὰς ⁽·ᵃ'⁾ λέγει αὐτοῖς,
²⁽ᵝ⁾ ⁽·ᵃ⁾ Σπλαγχνίζομαι ἐπὶ τὸν ὄχλον ⁽·ᵝ⁾ ὅτι ἤδη ἡμέραι τρεῖς
προσμένουσίν μοι ⁽·ᵝ'⁾ καὶ οὐκ ἔχουσιν τί φάγωσιν·
³⁽ᵝ'⁾ ⁽·ᵃ⁾ καὶ ἐὰν ἀπολύσω αὐτοὺς νήστεις εἰς οἶκον αὐτῶν,
⁽·ᵝ⁾ ἐκλυθήσονται ἐν τῇ ὁδῷ· ⁽·ᵝ'⁾ ⁽··ᵃ⁾ καί τινες αὐτῶν ⁽··ᵃ'⁾ ἀπὸ
μακρόθεν ἥκασιν.
β' ⁴⁽ᵃ⁾ ⁽·ᵃ⁾ καὶ ἀπεκρίθησαν αὐτῷ ⁽·ᵃ'⁾ οἱ μαθηταὶ αὐτοῦ
⁽ᵝ⁾ ⁽·ᵃ⁾ ὅτι Πόθεν τούτους δυνήσεταί ⁽·ᵝ⁾ τις ὧδε χορτάσαι ἄρτων
⁽·ᵝ'⁾ ἐπ' ἐρημίας;
⁵⁽ᵝ'⁾ ⁽·ᵃ⁾ καὶ ἠρώτα αὐτούς, ⁽·ᵃ'⁾ Πόσους ἔχετε ἄρτους;
⁽·ᵃ'⁾ οἱ δὲ εἶπαν, ⁽·ᵃ'⁾ Ἑπτά.

Β α ⁶⁽ᵃ⁾ καὶ παραγγέλλει τῷ ὄχλῳ ⁽ᵃ'⁾ ἀναπεσεῖν ἐπὶ τῆς γῆς·
β ⁽ᵃ⁾ ⁽·ᵃ⁾ καὶ λαβὼν τοὺς ἑπτὰ ἄρτους ⁽·ᵝ⁾ εὐχαριστήσας ⁽·ᵝ'⁾ ἔκλασεν
⁽ᵝ⁾ ⁽·ᵃ⁾ καὶ ἐδίδου τοῖς μαθηταῖς αὐτοῦ ⁽·ᵃ'⁾ ἵνα παρατιθῶσιν
⁽ᵝ'⁾ καὶ παρέθηκαν τῷ ὄχλῳ.
β' ⁷⁽ᵃ⁾ καὶ εἶχον ἰχθύδια ὀλίγα· ⁽ᵝ⁾ καὶ εὐλογήσας αὐτὰ ⁽ᵝ'⁾ ⁽·ᵃ⁾ εἶπεν
καὶ ⁽·ᵃ'⁾ ταῦτα παρατιθέναι.

Β' α ⁸⁽ᵃ⁾ καὶ ἔφαγον ⁽ᵃ'⁾ καὶ ἐχορτάσθησαν,
β ⁽ᵃ⁾ καὶ ἦραν περισσεύματα κλασμάτων ⁽ᵃ'⁾ ἑπτα σπυρίδας.
β' ⁹⁽ᵃ⁾ ἦσαν δὲ ὡς τετρακισχίλιοι. ⁽ᵃ'⁾ καὶ ἀπέλυσεν αὐτούς.

A α ¹⁰⁽ᵃ⁾ ⁽·ᵃ⁾ Καὶ εὐθὺς ⁽·ᵃ'⁾ ἐμβὰς εἰς τὸ πλοῖον ⁽ᵝ⁾ μετὰ τῶν μαθητῶν
αὐτοῦ ⁽ᵝ'⁾ ἦλθεν εἰς τὰ μέρη Δαλμανουθά.
β ¹¹⁽ᵃ⁾ Καὶ ἐξῆλθον οἱ Φαρισαῖοι ⁽ᵝ⁾ καὶ ἤρξαντο συζητεῖν αὐτῷ,
⁽ᵝ'⁾ ⁽·ᵃ⁾ ζητοῦντες παρ' αὐτοῦ σημεῖον ἀπὸ τοῦ οὐρανοῦ, ⁽·ᵃ'⁾
πειράζοντες αὐτόν.
β' ¹²⁽ᵃ⁾ ⁽·ᵃ⁾ καὶ ἀναστενάξας τῷ πνεύματι αὐτοῦ ⁽·ᵃ'⁾ λέγει, ⁽ᵝ⁾ Τί ἡ
γενεὰ αὕτη ζητει σημεῖον; ⁽ᵝ'⁾ ⁽·ᵃ⁾ ἀμὴν λέγω ὑμῖν, ⁽·ᵃ'⁾ εἰ
δοθήσεται τῇ γενεᾷ ταύτῃ σημεῖον.

Β α ¹³⁽ᵃ⁾ καὶ ἀφεὶς αὐτοὺς ⁽ᵝ⁾ πάλιν ἐμβὰς ⁽ᵝ'⁾ ἀπῆλθεν εἰς τὸ πέραν.
β ¹⁴⁽ᵃ⁾ Καὶ ἐπελάθοντο λαβεῖν ἄρτους, ⁽ᵝ⁾ καὶ εἰ μὴ ἕνα ἄρτον ⁽ᵝ'⁾ οὐκ
εἶχον μεθ' ἑαυτῶν ἐν τῷ πλοίῳ.
β' ¹⁵⁽ᵃ⁾ καὶ διεστέλλετο αὐτοῖς λέγων, ⁽ᵃ'⁾ ⁽·ᵃ⁾ Ὁρᾶτε, ⁽·ᵝ⁾ βλέπετε ἀπὸ
τῆς ζύμης τῶν Φαρισαίων ⁽·ᵝ'⁾ καὶ τῆς ζύμης Ἡρώδου.

Β' α [α]¹⁶[.α] [..α] καὶ <u>διελογίζοντο</u> πρὸς ἀλλήλους [..α'] <u>ὅτι Ἄρτους οὐκ ἔχουσιν</u>. ¹⁷[.α'] καὶ γνοὺς <u>λέγει</u> αὐτοῖς,
  [β] [.α] [..α] Τί <u>διαλογίζεσθε</u> [..α'] <u>ὅτι ἄρτους οὐκ ἔχετε</u>; [.β] <u>οὔπω νοεῖτε</u> [.β'] <u>οὐδε συνίετε</u>;
  [β'] [.α] πεπωρωμένην ἔχετε τὴν καρδίαν ὑμῶν; ¹⁸[.β] [..α] ὀφθαλμοὺς <u>ἔχοντες</u> [..α'] <u>οὐ βλέπετε</u> [.β'] [..α] καὶ ὦτα <u>ἔχοντες</u> [..α'] <u>οὐκ ἀκούετε</u>;
 β[α] καὶ οὐ μνημονεύετε,
  [β]¹⁹[.α] [..α] ὅτε τοὺς πέντε ἄρτους ἔκλασα εἰς τοὺς πεντακισχιλίους, [..α'] πόσους κοφίνους κλασμάτων πλήρεις ἤρατε;
  [.α'] [..α] λέγουσιν αὐτω , [..α'] Δώδεκα.
  [β']²⁰[.α] [..α] ὅτε τοὺς ἑπτα εἰς τοὺς τετρακισχιλίους, [..α'] πόσων σπυρίδων πληρώματα κλασμάτων ἤρατε;
  [.α'] [..α] καὶ λέγουσιν [αὐτῷ], [..α'] Ἑπτά.
 β' ²¹[α] καὶ ἔλεγεν αὐτοῖς, [α'] Οὔπω συνίετε;

We examine the structure of the Day's presentation. Clearly, the opening section of the Day's telling introduces the first half's report, of the feeding of the four-thousand, vv.1-9. Sections B and B', vv.6,7 and vv.8,9, complete what A, vv.1-5, introduces. Section B begins the development of the story: section B' completes it. The second half of the Day's telling begins with a typically Markan conjunctive phrase, and section A, vv.10-12, introduces what will be developed in section B, vv.13-15; and what will be completed in section B', vv.16-21. Section A, as usual, comprises three parts: they are: 1) a day-time sea-journey around the coast (not a crossing); 2) on landing, Pharisees, who seek a sign from heaven; and 3) Jesus' response. Section B relates: 1) Jesus and the disciples embarking again and, this time, beginning a crossing to the other side; 2) their lack of loaves; 3) Jesus' response and warning about 'the leaven' (an interesting touch of Mark!) of the Pharisees and Herod (cf. 6.4-29 for the other mention of Herod in the Series). Section B', again clearly in three carefully contrived parts, raises the puzzle of the Day and Series of Days, and one of the most baffling even[43], of the Gospel. How does Mark intend us to interpret the numerological conundrum, which Jesus poses in regard to the feedings of the five... and the four-thousand?

---

[43] Drury, *The Literary Guide*..., p.414.

Though we reckon that the evidence of the structure and the geography of the Days of the Series is sufficient in itself to suggest the first feeding was of Jews and the second was of Gentiles, there is further assistance. We consider, firstly, the three references to bread or loaves which are not included in this Series. The ones in 3.20 and 14.22 lie significantly opposite each other in Mark's scheme, in the fifth Days of the First and the Fourth Series, that is Days Five (3.7-4.41) and Twenty-Six (14.12-72): in the first of these, Jesus was with his disciples in a house, but the crowd was present and "they were not able to eat bread" (v.20 follows directly on from Jesus' choosing the twelve, 3.13-19; in the second of these, the setting is the Last Supper when Jesus is alone with his disciples. It is a correspondence which is one of many which suggest the deliberate creation, on Mark's part, of a paralleling of Series One and Four. The remaining reference to bread, 2.26, to which Drury appears rightly to turn for assistance, is found in the "hinge" day, Day Four, of the First Series. In this present Series, the "hinge" day, Day Eleven, is most significant also in Mark's scheme, as we have already shown in the analysis of that Day's report (for *bread* for Jews and Gentiles). In the summary of this Series it will be further developed and expressed. In Day Four, 2.26, Jesus' reference to what David did with the shewbread (*twelve loaves*) 'gets him off the hook' with the Pharisees, but only for a while on that day, for later they watch him carefully in the synagogue to see if they might find an accusation that 'could stick'.

Drury refers to Leviticus 24 in which are set out the regulations, regarding the *twelve* loaves.[44] David takes *five* of these loaves: *seven* are left. David's story is somewhat fulfilled by the miraculous feeding of *five* loaves to Jews, but Jesus goes further than David: he completes the distribution, by his miraculous feeding of the remaining seven to Gentiles. Thus far, we are with Drury. Clearly, the conundrum is only part answered. What of the numbers five-thousand and four-thousand, and of the baskets twelve and seven? Drury recognises 'seven' to be the sacred number of fulfilment (or completion), but he does not discuss the other numbers in terms of their rhetorical, cultic or symbolic uses, which were common in the

---

[44] Drury, *The Literary Guide...*, pp.414-416.

civilisations and religions of the Ancient near East, and still evident in the then modern world of the first century.[45]

'Twelve', 'five', 'four' and 'a thousand' have their own early numerological significance, but what we cannot be sure of, is their precise meaning to Mark. 'Twelve' has been a number traditionally associated with the elective purposes of God and, therefore, with Israel (for the obvious link, consider: the twelve tribes). 'Five', as half the basic number ten, is frequently referenced in the books of the Bible: we might link it principally with the decalogue and the five books of the Law of Moses. 'Four' is a sacred number the world over and derives its significance from the 'four winds', the four points of the compass: all the world is signified. Multiples of 'a thousand' are used frequently for hyperbole.[46] We may, thus, deduce that: the feeding of the *five-thousand* with *five* loaves and the left-over *twelve* baskets of fragments are all indicative of Jews; and the feeding of the *four-thousand* with *seven* loaves and the left-over *seven* baskets of fragments are all indicative of the Gentiles (the other nations of the world), whose inclusion within the 'new Israel' for its completeness is a fulfilment of the divine purpose.

Day Fourteen: 8.22-26:

The telling of Day Fourteen, we note, is the most concise of all Mark's twenty-eight Days: it is the shortest, in its number of verses. It consists of a simple three-section structure, ABB'. As was stated under Day Twelve, when compared for correspondences with Day Twelve, 7.31-37, we have to see them as a pair, as one has most clearly influenced the other.

The introductory section A comprises three parts which all begin with καί and a historical present. The first part, v.22a, begins with one of Mark's favourite indications of a new turning point, Καὶ ἔρχονται, and establishes the new geographical place (see also 6.45

---

[45] It may be today that we do not think of numbers as having any symbolic significance, but clearly, we do have to consider first century rhetorical uses. In the years since, the church may have been guilty of 'gross excess' in interpreting them, but it is still no reason, for example, for Hooker (*The Gospel...*, p.166) to say, "It is unlikely that Mark saw any such significance in numbers." Vv.16-21 sets a puzzle: there is no way of skirting around it.

[46] We are condensing much information here, on 'numbers', from *NIDNTT* and *IntDB*.

and discussions on Bethsaida). The balancing second and third parts, v.22b and v.22c, in turn introduce the new character on the scene and, as on Day Twelve, another ardent request which is put to Jesus. The two historical presents and pronouns, καὶ φέρουσιν αὐτῷ... and καὶ παρακαλοῦσιν αὐτόν... are exactly the same as in Day Twelve, and are positioned also in exactly the same way, at β and β'.

Sections B and B', vv.23,24 and vv.25,26, relate a two-part healing, which is a unique event in itself in the Gospel. Further, that this is the first healing of a blind person in the Gospel attracts to it special status also. The only other healing of a blind person is recorded in the last Day of the following Series, that is Day Twenty-one, 10.46-52, which I judge to be the parallel seventh Day of the second middle Series, 8.27-10.52.

The first part of section B, v.23a, as in Day Twelve's report, sees Jesus taking the man away, alone (compare here, καὶ ἐπιλαβόμενος and καὶ ἀπολαβόμενος). In the second part, v.23b, Jesus spits in his eyes (in the parallel story, "spitting he touched his tongue"), places his hands on him (cf. "he put his fingers in his ears"), and begins to ask the man if he can see. In the third part, v.24, the man responds: he sees partially. In section B' and the first part, v.25a, which begins with a non-καί sentence, Jesus again places his hands on the man, here expressed, "on his eyes". In the closing, balancing, two parts, v.25b and v.26, in the first, the man begins to see clearly (the imperfect, as in Day Twelve at this point, is again inceptive), and in the second, Jesus sends him to his home, forbidding him to enter the village (cf. the ending of Day Twelve).

The literary structure of Day Fourteen is viewed as:

A α ²²<u>Καὶ ἔρχονται</u> εἰς Βηθσαϊδάν.
   β   <u>καὶ φέρουσιν</u> αὐτῷ <u>τυφλὸν</u>
   β'   [α] <u>καὶ παρακαλοῦσιν</u> αὐτὸν [α'] ἵνα αὐτοῦ <u>ἅψηται</u>.

B α ²³[α] καὶ ἐπιλαβόμενος τῆς χειρὸς τοῦ <u>τυφλοῦ</u> [α'] ἐξήνεγκεν αὐτὸν ἔξω <u>τῆς κώμης</u>,
   β   [α] καὶ πτύσας εἰς τὰ ὄμματα αὐτοῦ, [β] <u>ἐπιθεὶς τὰς χεῖρας αὐτῷ</u>, [β'] [.α] ἐπηρώτα αὐτόν, [.α'] Εἴ τι βλέπεις;
   β' ²⁴[α] καὶ ἀναβλέψας ἔλεγεν, [β] Βλέπω τοὺς ἀνθρώπους, [β'] ὅτι ὡς δένδρα ὁρῶ περιπατοῦντας.

Β´ α ²⁵[α] εἶτα πάλιν [β] ἐπέθηκεν τὰς χεῖρας [β´] ἐπὶ τοὺς ὀφθαλμοὺς αὐτοῦ,
   β   [α] καὶ διέβλεψεν, [β] καὶ ἀπεκατέστη, [β´] καὶ ἐνέβλεπεν τηλαυγῶς ἅπαντα.
   β´ ²⁶[α] [.α] καὶ ἀπέστειλεν αὐτὸν [.α´] εἰς οἶκον αὐτοῦ [α´] [.α] λέγων, [.α´] Μηδὲ εἰς τὴν κώμην εἰσέλθῃς.

Clearly, I judge, because of the story's parallel in Day Twelve, that 8.22-26 attaches to that which precedes it, and that it is the seventh Day of the Gospel's second Series of seven Days, the first of two middle Series. Most commentators indeed do take 8.27 to begin a new section in Mark's Gospel, but a number entertain the possibility that 8.22 begins it.[47] In his discussion of what he calls "the great central section of the Gospel, 8.22-10.52", Best[48] sees the healings of blind men, 8.22-26 and 10.46-52, as the beginning and the ending of the section. He sees the accounts as "transition sections", but fails to support his view when he argues: 1) "To understand them we need to accept the widespread conception that the restoration of sight is a metaphor for the gift of spiritual understanding"; and 2) that the two-stage healing, of 8.22-26, "represents two stages of enlightenment" and that this is reflected in the next account of 8.27ff, which tells of two stages in Peter's enlightenment (I have other alternative interpretations to this which will be explained below as we discuss this threesome of Days, 7.31-8.26, and as we summarise this Series). Best's understanding and his interpretation of the two passages have their supporters, but neither of his arguments supports his positioning of them as an *inclusio* within 8.22-10.52. I judge other issues determine the two passages' true positionings in Mark's scheme: 1) that 8.22-26 clearly reflects 7.31-37 and, therefore, belongs in sub-Series with it; 2) that 8.27-9.1 reflects 6.1-29 (we discuss this under Day Fifteen) with the result that the first Days of the two middle Series correspond; and 3) that 8.22-26 and 10.46-52, the only two stories in the Gospel on the healings of blind people, in turn, complete the two "central sections" (not *one*, as Best says), so that the last Days of the two middle Series correspond. The symmetries of 2) and 3) are compelling evidence of Mark's plan.

---

[47] See note 5 above.
[48] Best, *Disciples...*, pp.2-4.

We consider again the last three Days of this Series, not separately now, but together. Days Twelve, Thirteen and Fourteen appear to form a threesome of Days, in the style, ABA'. The similarity between Days Twelve and Fourteen would seem to require it. But, temporal details suggest otherwise; that it is an ABB' formation. There is a disjunction between Days Twelve and Thirteen: there is a passing of other days between. Between Days Thirteen and Fourteen there is the link of a late/night-crossing; no days between are suggested or inferred. In geographical terms, however, we might judge that Days Twelve and Thirteen are specially linked by the location in the Decapolis, and judge the scheme is AA'B. We ask again, as we did before, in considering the first threesome of Days in this Series, "Is there a 'movement' or a seam running through the telling of these Days, Days Twelve, Thirteen and Fourteen, that suggests a clear intention on Mark's part?"

Day Twelve tells simply of a healing, in the Decapolis, of a deaf man with a speaking difficulty. Jesus is the prophet who fulfils prophecy. But, he has only partially fulfilled it. From the Isaianic allusion, at its conclusion, the healing of the *lame* and the *blind* are missing. In Day Fourteen we *do*, however, find a report of Jesus' healing of a *blind* man, who sees men as trees "*walking*" in the first stage of his cure. Is this at all significant? If it is, then it suggests an ABA' arrangement of this sub-Series.

Day Thirteen, in between, however, raises a number of issues about 'blindness' in terms of a 'lack' or 'a want' of 'understanding'. It tells of the second miracle-feeding of the Gospel, and immediately after it, Pharisees ask for a "sign from heaven". They want, like Mark's audience, to see something from Jesus that will prove to them who he is. To the reader/listeners, of course, the Pharisees' request is incredible. Were the Pharisees *blind* to what was going on, and *deaf* to reports? Hooker helpfully observes that miracles and parables function similarly in Mark's Gospel[49]. "To those who have eyes to see and ears to hear, both miracles and parables demonstrate the power of the Kingdom of God," she says. (For which, compare 8.18.) And in the first sub-Series (in the summary on page 173) we notice the link between 'not understanding' and 'hardened hearts'. Both Jesus' disciples and the Pharisees provide the examples of this. The same is

---
[49] Hooker, *The Gospel...*, p.191.

found in this sub-Series also, at the very point where Mark begs understanding of the feeding miracles, in 8.17. Only now it is the disciples alone who provide the example, and *they are here being challenged by Jesus about it.* It is clearly the case that the disciples provide Mark with the vehicle for this teaching. In Day Thirteen we read that the disciples are amazingly 'blind'. Just before the feeding of the four-thousand, they would appear to have no recollection at all of how Jesus fed the five-thousand. Furthermore, in 8.15, we see a demonstration of Jesus' concern for his disciples (and, therefore, for all who would follow him) that they are not 'taken in' by the Pharisees, or by Herod (8.15 recalls 6.14bff. in the first sub-Series). To Jesus, the disciples demonstrate a worrying 'blindness' to the meaning of the 'feedings' (in 8.16-21). And Best, as we have seen already above, identifies the link in Mark's Gospel between 'restoration of sight' and 'understanding'.

Day Thirteen raises a number of problems and issues. Day Fourteen ends the sub-Series with a resolution to them all for everyone. Day Fourteen tells how Jesus is able to heal even the blind, and so fulfill all the prophecy alluded to earlier. Only now, the healing is not simply a healing. It is a healing of a blind man, uniquely in the Gospel *in two stages*. It is a metaphor, an acted parable, especially so, given the previous Day's issues raisings. The healing in two stages has to be interpreted. Yes, he can heal the blind, but he can give enlightenment too, so that *all* can "see clearly all things".

In this sub-Series, Mark certainly touches a raw nerve in the minds and hearts of his audience. Pharisees and all like them want an easy step to faith. Jesus' denies the Pharisees and those like them such a sign. Signs are not to be relied upon. Our 'hearts' should tell us that Jesus is.

In summary, the introductory Day to the sub-Series, 7.31-37, reports a simple healing miracle, but it does not, in itself, fulfil the whole of the prophecy alluded to. The middle Day, 8.1-21, reports a miracle feeding and raises a number of issues about 'understanding' and the 'feeding of faith'. The concluding Day, 8.22-26, tells of a healing miracle which completes the earlier prophecy, but it fundamentally points beyond itself, in its unique way, to the very means to 'understanding'. The sub-Series exhibits an *inclusio* between the first and the last days, but it is best expressed as an ABB' scheme, like those we have already encountered, 1.21-2.22, 3.7-5.43 and 6.1-7.23.

A Summary of the Second Series of Seven Days:

Again, as for the First Series of Seven Days, the findings of my analysis are summarised and presented in tabular form.

The first threesome of "days" of this second Series, 6.1-7.23, is discussed under Day Ten. It can be summarised, in terms very similar to the first threesome of "days" of the first Series. It tells initially where and how Jesus' fame further spread (through the mission of his disciples and "Jesus' going round in circuit"). Nazareth and neighbouring villages in Galilee were the places of mission, after Jesus' teaching in the synagogue. The disciples' preaching, casting out of demons and healing work led to people talking about Jesus, wondering who he was, and gathering to him in huge numbers. This time, even Herod hears and wonders, as well as reflects on what he had done to John the Baptist. The feeding of the five-thousand is presented, overall in the Markan scheme, as a symbolic and Messianic meal for Jews. Again, as in the first threesome of "days" of the first Series of the Gospel, Mark demonstrates how Jesus' continuing ministry, wherever he went, in villages, towns or countryside, leads to a clash between Jesus, whose ministry is "powerfully new", and Pharisees and scribes, whose "old" positions are being challenged. This sub-Series raises issues of 'understanding' who Jesus is and what he is doing.

The second threesome of "days", 7.31-8.26, likewise compares with the second threesome of "days" in the first Series of seven Days, as well as with the first threesome of "days" of this Series. Given Jesus is in predominantly Gentile territory (compare also 5.1-20, in the first Series and its second threesome) the continuing work of establishing 'new Israel', which will include Gentiles, begins with a healing, and proceeds to a feeding of four-thousand, a symbolic meal for Gentiles, and another clash with Pharisees, before the first account of its kind in the Gospel, an amazing healing, back in predominantly Jewish territory, of a blind man, in *two stages*. This sub-Series raises issues of 'understanding' who Jesus is and what he is doing, and also the source of 'understanding'.

The two three-day sub-Series have their rich common seams, their many points of contact, and they are arranged around a central, singular and individualistic day, Day Eleven. In literary-structural terms, this Day Eleven has a central, pivotal, or fulcrum role between the sub-Series/threesomes of Days, and as we discussed in Day Eleven's analysis it focuses on the issue of the tension between Jesus' mission to Jews and Gentiles: Jews are first in order, but Gentiles are included, and second.

The balance of the Series is clearly evident. The first sub-Series includes Jesus' symbolic meal for Jews (in the telling of the middle day), and after the pivotal Day, the second sub-Series (again, in the telling of the middle day) his symbolic meal for Gentiles. The summary of the structure of Mark's Second Series of Seven Days, therefore, is now presented: it is in an ABA' form, as is the First Series of Seven Days, where A represents the first threesome of Days, B the singular Day Eleven, and A' the second threesome of Days. In examining the first Series, we had to consider the possibility that it was a seven-Day chiasm. Such a possibility has not surfaced in the examination of this Series' structure.

This Series well indicates the steady and inventive control which Mark exercised over the material he had to hand. This material has been variously described as oral or written, as single, independent units of tradition, or as already-linked units. The miracle stories themselves have been viewed as: already-formed, independent cycles of tradition, 6.32-7.37 and 8.1-26[50]; or, by Achtemeier, as a pre-Markan cycle of miracles consisting of two catenae[51], which he incorporated; or as an earlier, original cycle, 6.32-52, 8.22-30[52] which Mark has split up, and into which he has inserted 6.53-8.21, to create his own double cycle. Additional to the material he had to hand, we have to consider the material which he created[53]. All options need to be weighed very carefully against the new evidence of his rhetorical method, his Day-compositional planning, and his creation of a Series

---

[50] Hooker, *The Gospel...*, p.163.
[51] Achtemeier, "Towards the Isolation...".
[52] Hooker, *The Gospel...*, p.171.
[53] Fowler, *Loaves and Fishes...*, p.181.

of seven Days, with limits of 6.1 and 8.26. It never has been an easy task to separate the tradition Mark employs from his editing: it will be no easier now to determine *what material he had to hand* before he began composing, because it would appear that, if he had written tradition in his possession, he has re-written everything to his αββ' presentational method.

As I stated under Day Eleven, given the contents of the seven Days of this Series, in terms of the incidents/events themselves and their interpretations, and the wider geographical area Jesus covers, I am choosing to title this Series simply, "Days of Increase in the Mission of Jesus".

As I did at the conclusion of the analysis of the First Series, so I will do here. For the sake of clarity, the point is emphasised that while Mark chose to report a second stage in the mission of Jesus in seven Days, he intimated that there were other days he was not reporting. Between the telling of the last Day of the first Series and the telling of the first Day of the second Series, Day Eight, a journey took place (of a minimum of about 18 miles) which will itself have taken at least one day; and the story of Day Eight takes place on a sabbath, up to six days later. Between Days Eight and Nine, under Day Nine's analysis, we noted that weeks may have passed. Days Nine and Ten are consecutive. Between Days Ten and Eleven is a 60 mile journey to Tyre which will have taken three days minimum. Between Days Eleven and Twelve a return journey is made taking the same length of time. Between Days Twelve and Thirteen is a passing of three days minimum. Days Thirteen and Fourteen are consecutive. The point is then made, without any attempt to add up the days to establish Mark's understanding of the actual time this stage of Jesus' mission took. Simply, he summarised what to him was a stage in Jesus' mission of possibly several weeks, in only seven Days of reports.

In completing this presentation on the Second Series, we return to the issue of the final Day, 8.21-26, and to how Mark meant us to interpret the healing of the blind man, *in two stages*. I have already nailed my colours to the mast, by interpreting it in its sub-Series context. But it may be that it has significance also in its Series context, or in the Gospel's context as a whole.

To many, as to Best (see above) it appears to look *forward* to the revelation of Peter that Jesus is the Christ, which is completed by Jesus in turn, in terms of the suffering and death he would have to undergo. Given that it concludes the Second Series, it appears much more certain that, for Mark, it initially looks *back*, and completes his Series' presentation. Given the localities mentioned (which include Jerusalem more than once) and the 'feeding of the Jews' in the first sub-Series (6.1-7.23), Jesus' mission is *firstly to the Jews*, and after the turning point of the middle Day (7.24-30), given the localities and the 'feeding of the Gentiles' in the second sub-Series (7.31-8.26), Jesus' mission is *secondly to the Gentiles*. It would appear that Mark wants his audience to interpret the ministry of Jesus in this way, for which purpose 8.21-26 is a more than adequate, though somewhat mysterious conclusion to the Series. (And we note, the ending of his previous Day's telling in (8.17-21) is no less mysterious.)

Additional support for this conclusion comes from reference to the 'sabbath'. In the first Series of the Gospel its two reports were deemed to have significance. The first was that Jesus' ministry was firstly to the Jews (see page 144). This Day is the first Day of that Series. On the first Day of this second Series, it is a Sabbath also. Again, the significance is the same, and it is re-inforcing for its repetition. Sabbaths are not encountered in Mark's Day scheme beyond this point, until 16.1, when one is reported in the introductory piece to the final Day's presentation, which tells of the events of the first day of the week.

Lastly, we ask, "Are Best *et al.* right in seeing the two-stage healing of 8.22-26 as pre-emptive of the two stages of disclosure about Jesus in the following pericope, 8.27ff.?" (For their proposal and for my views about the positioning of the pericope, see page 188.) Clearly, there are arguments for seeing that this unique healing, in two stages, has its interpretation firstly within the three-day sub-Series of its report, and secondly within the Series itself. Whether or not it has its interpretation in the Gospel as a whole, that is outside of the second Series, is judged best by reference to ancient, rhetorical convention.

Best's interpretation is that 8.22-26 and 8.27ff. are structurally related. Literary-structural analysis sees the relationship in this way: 8.22-26 is the last Day of a Series and 8.27ff. is (part of) the first

Day's telling of the next Series. Normally in ancient rhetoric effort is made to "smooth the transition" between the ending of one section and the beginning of the next. Normally this is achieved by a link *word* or *phrase*, an anastrophe (see page 54). There is a clear example of an anastrophe between Series, in the last Day of the third Series and the first Day of the fourth. In 10.46-52, we read "*Son of David*" twice; and in 11.1-11 we read, "Blessed is the coming Kingdom of *our father David*". (These are the first mentions of "David" since 2.25; and the next follow at 12.35,36 and 37.)

Is it then the case that Mark uses a 'link motif' instead of a standard anastrophe to "smooth the transition" between the ending of the second Series and the beginning of the third? If there is clear indication that Mark himself intended a 'two-stage' parallel, the firmest literary-structural evidence (given our findings so far) would be a presentation of the two stages of revelation in the B and B' parts of a three-part whole. An examination of the first Day of the next Series will show that this is in fact the case. Best and others appear, therefore, to be right about the connection, but wrong in their structural argument. We must conclude, therefore, that there is justification for interpreting the 'two-stage' healing of 8.22-26 in three different contexts: in the sub-Series it concludes; in the Series it ends; and in its Gospel setting, where it precedes the telling of the first Day of the next Series.

A Tabular Summary of the literary-structure of the Second Seven Days:

	1	2	3	4	5	6	7
DAYS: number identified in series							
number identified in Gospel	8	9	10	11	12	13	14
chapters and verses	6.1-29	6.30-52	6.53-7.23	7.24-30	7.31-37	8.1-21	8.22-26
SERIES' STRUCTURE	A			B		A'	
DAYS: in literary-terms, in series	A	B	B'	A	B	B'	
DAYS' sections	<u>A</u> A'	A B B'	A B B'	A	A	<u>A</u> A'	A
DAYS' sectional sub-divisions	A B <u>B'</u> A B B'	A B <u>B'</u> A B <u>B'</u> A B B'	A B <u>B'</u> A B <u>B'</u> A B B'	A B B'	A B B'	A B <u>B'</u> A B B'	A B B'
DAYS' number of verses	29	23	27	7	7	21	5
SUB-SERIES' number of verses	79					33	
SERIES' number of verses	119						

Addendum to the analysis of "The Second Seven Days":

During the course of this chapter, a further signifier of literary-structural division between Days has been added to the list of those established in the analysis of the First Series. It is an introductory formula which is basic to understanding eight of the Day-divisions, four in this Series and four in the following Series. It is added to the list of the features of Mark's rhetorical method, for which reason it continues the numbering:

Under Day Eleven: 19) The leaving of the place of the earlier Day's telling and the arriving in another: an introductory formula.

Again as in the first Series, we note in the second Series a wide variation in the sizes of Mark's rhetorical units of Days, sections of Days, and so on. The Days themselves vary between 29 and 5 verses, by a factor of just less than six (which is much less than the factor of ten of the first Series). We observe that each of the Days in the first sub-Series are longer in the telling than each of those in the second. No symmetry of size in the arrangements of the Days of the two sub-Series appears intended by Mark; in the first sub-Series the middle of the three is the shortest; in the second sub-Series the middle Day is the longest in the telling. Similarly, no repetition (or repetition-pattern) of the sectional-structures of the Days appears to govern Mark's compositional efforts. What matters to Mark is that his constructions, whether ABA', ABB', ABB'/ABB', or αββ`, are in themselves complete.

Chapter Five
The Third Series of Seven Days (8.27-10.52):

Day Fifteen: 8.27-9.1:

The Day begins:
    Α α ²⁷ <u>Καὶ ἐξῆλθεν</u> ὁ Ἰησοῦς
       β   <u>καὶ οἱ μαθηταὶ αὐτου</u>
       β'   <u>εἰς</u> τὰς κώμας Καισαρείας τῆς Φιλίπ<u>που</u>·

We compare it with the beginning of Day Eight:
    Α α ¹[α] <u>Καὶ ἐξῆλθεν</u> [α'] ἐκεῖθεν,
       β   [α] <u>καὶ</u> ἔρχεται [α'] <u>εἰς</u> τὴν πατρίδα <u>αυτου</u>,
       β'   [α] καὶ ἀκολουθοῦσιν αὐτῷ [α'] <u>οἱ μαθηταὶ αὐτοῦ</u>.

Significantly, Day Eight begins the first middle Series (6.1-8.26) and Day Fifteen begins the second middle Series (8.27-10.52). Both these Days begin with the introductory formula of leaving one place and arriving in another (found eight times in all: four times in the Series 6.1-8.26, and also at 9.30/33, 10.1 and 10.46 in this Series); see under Day Eleven for a discussion of this. We can observe, in addition to the same detailed structure in each (but with β and β' in reversal, for contents), seven common words between them, and in each the same repeating use of parechesis (the same sounding endings of <u>ου</u> at the endings of the last two lines of each, as discovered in abundance in the opening of the Prologue of the Gospel, 1.1-3)[1]. It is compelling evidence that as Mark composed one of these two opening parts to these Days' tellings, he did so with an eye on the other. I further deduce that the significant positionings and roles of these two Days, at the beginnings of new Series, 6.1-8.26

---

[1] Other examples of parechesis in the Gospel only occur at 13.1, the beginning of a new half in the telling of 11.20-13.37, Day Twenty-four, the longest Day's telling in terms of verses, and in 16.19b,20 in the longer ending. Their likely significance will continue to be discussed.

and 8.27-10.52[2], caused Mark to compose these introductions with even greater attention to detail than elsewhere, by reflecting the clear characteristic of the Prologue's opening parechesis.

Other significant correspondences with Day Eight can be identified. The structure of this Day's telling, is the same composite ABB'/ABB' structure, with a short A section. The primary correspondence in content terms concerns what people were saying about Jesus, 6.14b,15 and 8.28 (see Day Eight's analysis for this, pages 136,137). And a common phrase is ἤρξατο διδάσκειν (compare 6.2 and 8.31) though it is found also in other introductory elements of Mark's rhetorical units, in 4.1 and 6.34.

The disclosures of Day Fifteen are supremely important in Mark's Gospel scheme as a whole, and in this seven Day Series too. They will be presented below, in our discussions on its literary-structure, which we firstly compare with that of Taylor, Schweizer and Hooker, and with which Robbins and Best[3] also agree. (Nineham does not discuss the matter.) We compare the results of analyses:

	I	II	III
as a result of various methodologies:	8.27-30	vv.31-33	vv.34-9.1
and of my literary-structural analysis:	8.27-33		vv.34-9.1

Given the arguments rehearsed above, it is judged that v.27abc is the introduction to this Day's first half's telling, for its mention of the principal characters, Jesus and his disciples, and the new geographical locus. The first of the two completing sections of this half (B by my designation, vv.27d-30) begins with Καὶ ἐν τῇ ὁδῷ as it establishes more specifically (compared with the more general introduction, that is) the setting for the first disclosure that Jesus is the Christ. V.31, beginning B', does not change the setting. It introduces the second stage of the two disclosures, that Jesus will suffer. Vv.27-33, however much others have said otherwise, belong together as a major rhetorical unit.

The second half opens, in v.34, with a change in the characters present: they are Jesus, his disciples, and the crowd. This half

---

[2] Taylor (*The Gospel...*), Nineham (*Saint Mark*), Schweizer (*The Good News...*), Hooker (*The Gospel...*) and myself, all agree on the limits of this section of the Gospel, though we vary in our designation of it, as the second, the third, the fourth or the fifth section.

[3] Robbins, *Jesus the Teacher...*, pp.37-41; Best, *Disciples...*, p.6.

focuses on discipleship: part A is introductory; the completing two parts, B and B‛, begin similarly ὃς γὰρ ἐὰν and parallel each other for sayings, in the first, on the cost of discipleship and ultimate reward, and, in the second, on attitudes to Jesus and his 'words' which will determine his attitude to followers, in its sub-part α. Sub-parts β and β‛ in turn speak of his coming in the father's glory..., and the coming of the kingdom of God in power. 8.34-9.1 is identified as the second major rhetorical unit of this Day's telling, and with this all those to whom I refer agree.

A α   ²⁷ Καὶ ἐξῆλθεν ὁ Ἰησοῦς
   β   καὶ οἱ μαθηταὶ αὐτου
   β‛ [α] εἰς τὰς κώμας Καισαρείας [α‛] τῆς Φιλίππου·

B α   Καὶ ἐν τῇ ὁδω
  β[α] [.α] [..α] ἐπηρώτα τοὺς μαθητὰς αὐτου [..α‛] λέγων αὐτοῖς,
      [.α‛] [..α] Τίνα με [..β] λέγουσιν οἱ ἄνθρωποι [..β‛] εἶναι;
  [α‛] ²⁸[.α] [..α] οἱ δὲ εἶπαν αὐτω [..α‛] λέγοντες
      [.α‛] [..α] [ὅτι] Ἰωάννην τὸν βαπτιστήν, [..β] [...α] καὶ ἄλλοι,
      [...α‛] Ἡλίαν, [..β‛] [...α] ἄλλοι δε [...α‛] ὅτι εἷς τῶν προφητῶν.
  β‛[α] ²⁹ [.α] [..α] καὶ αὐτὸς ἐπηρώτα αὐτούς, [..β] ‛Υμεῖς δὲ [..β‛] τίνα με
      λέγετε εἶναι;
   [β] [.α] ἀποκριθεὶς [.β] ὁ Πέτρος λέγει αὐτῷ, [.β‛] Σὺ εἶ ὁ Χριστός.
   [β‛]³⁰ [.α] καὶ ἐπετίμησεν αὐτοῖς [.β] ἵνα μηδενὶ λέγωσιν [.β‛] περὶ αὐτοῦ.

B‛ α   ³¹ Καὶ ἤρξατο διδάσκειν αὐτοὺς
  β[α] [.α] ὅτι δεῖ τὸν υἱὸν τοῦ ἀνθρώπου [.α‛] πολλὰ παθεῖν
   [β] [.α] καὶ ἀποδοκιμασθῆναι [.α‛] [..α] ὑπὸ τῶν πρεσβυτέρων
      [..β] καὶ τῶν ἀρχιερέων [..β‛] καὶ τῶν γραμματέων
      [.β] καὶ ἀποκτανθῆναι [.β‛] [..α] καὶ μετὰ τρεῖς ἡμέρας
      [..α‛] ἀναστῆναι·
  [β‛] ³²[.α] καὶ παρρησίᾳ [.β] τὸν λόγον [.β‛] ἐλάλει.
  β‛[α] [.α] [..α] καὶ προσλαβόμενος [..β] ὁ Πέτρος [..β‛] αὐτὸν
      [.α‛] [..α] ἤρξατο [..β] ἐπιτιμᾶν [..β‛] αὐτῷ.
   [β]³³[.α] ὁ δὲ ἐπιστραφεὶς [.β] καὶ ἰδὼν τοὺς μαθητὰς αὐτοῦ
      [.β‛] [..α] ἐπετίμησεν Πέτρω [..α‛] καὶ λέγει
   [β‛] [.α] [..α] ῞Υπαγε [..β] ὀπίσω μου, [..β‛] Σατανᾶ, [.β] [..α] ὅτι οὐ φρονεῖς
      [..β] τὰ [..β‛] τοῦ θεου [.β‛] [..α] ἀλλὰ [..β] τὰ [..β‛] τῶν
      ἀνθρώπων.

A α   ³⁴[α] Καὶ προσκαλεσάμενος τὸν ὄχλον [β] σὺν τοῖς μαθηταῖς αὐτοῦ [β´] εἶπεν αὐτοῖς,
  β   Εἴ τις <u>θέλει ὀπίσω μου ἐλθεῖν</u>,
  β´   [α] ἀπαρνησάσθω ἑαυτὸν [β] καὶ ἀράτω τὸν σταυρὸν αὐτοῦ [β´] καὶ <u>ἀκολουθείτω μοι</u>.

B α[α] ³⁵ [.α] <u>ὃς γὰρ ἐὰν θέλῃ</u> [.β] <u>τὴν ψυχὴν αὐτου σῶσαι</u> [.β´] <u>ἀπολέσει αὐτήν</u>·
  [α´]   [.α] <u>ὃς δ' ἂν ἀπολέσει τὴν ψυχὴν αὐτου</u> [.β] ἕνεκεν ἐμοῦ καὶ τοῦ εὐαγγελίου [.β´] <u>σώσει αὐτήν</u>.
  β   ³⁶[α] <u>τί γὰρ</u> ὠφελεῖ **ἄνθρωπον** [β] κερδῆσαι τὸν κόσμον ὅλον [β´] καὶ ζημιωθῆναι <u>τὴν ψυχὴν αὐτοῦ</u>;
  β´   ³⁷[α] <u>τί γὰρ</u> δοῖ **ἄνθρωπος** [β] ἀντάλλαγμα [β´] <u>τῆς ψυχῆς αὐτοῦ</u>;

B´α   ³⁸[α] <u>ὃς γὰρ ἐὰν ἐπαισχυνθῇ</u> με [β] καὶ τοὺς ἐμοὺς λόγους [β´] ἐν τῇ γενεᾷ ταύτῃ τῇ μοιχαλίδι καὶ ἁμαρτωλῷ,
  β [α]   καὶ <u>ὁ υἱὸς τοῦ ἀνθρώπου</u> <u>ἐπαισχυνθήσεται</u> αὐτὸν
  [α´]   [.α] ὅταν <u>ἔλθῃ</u> [.β] ἐν τῇ δόξῃ τοῦ πατρὸς αὐτοῦ [.β´] μετὰ τῶν ἀγγέλων τῶν ἁγίων.
  β´[α] ¹ [.α] καὶ ἔλεγεν αὐτοῖς, [.α´] Ἀμὴν λέγω ὑμῖν
  [β]   [.α] ὅτι εἰσίν τινες ὧδε τῶν ἑστηκότων [.α´] οἵτινες οὐ μὴ γεύσωνται θανάτου
  [β´]   [.α] ἕως ἂν ἴδωσιν τὴν βασιλείαν τοῦ θεου [.α´] <u>ἐληλυθυῖαν</u> ἐν δυνάμει.

The detailed parallels and correspondences which suggest the way Mark intended the church to be reading his composition over the years, are many. Key words and phrases are underlined or emboldened in the above presentation to amplify reason for the annotations. We necessarily now list and discuss these features of this Day's telling. They are important in the Markan scheme of both his Gospel and of this particular Series:

1) The mention of ἐν τῇ ὁδῷ introduces a phrase much in evidence in the Days of this Series. In the Gospel, the word for "way" is found at: 1.2,3; 8.3,27; 9.33,34; 10.17,32,46,52; and 11.8. In the Prologue (see 1.2,3), the term is used in the accusative case, in the manner of "prepare the way".[4] At 10.17, the phrase is εἰς ὁδόν: "into

---

[4] In his discussion on 8.22-10.52, Best refers to the Prologue and Mark's use of O.T. scripture and states, "Mark's Gospel is the.... gospel of The Way. It is a way in which Jesus, the Lord, goes and it is a way to which he calls his followers..." See Best, *Disciples...*, p.5.

Marcus, in fine detail, sifts the arguments for this same proposition and concludes, "It would be no exaggeration... to say that the way of Jesus/the way of the Lord is not only the double theme of Mark's Gospel, but also the controlling paradigm for his interpretation of the

the way", and at 11.8, similarly, εἰς τὴν ὁδόν: "in the way". At 10.46, the phrase is παρὰ τὴν ὁδόν: "by/at the side of the way". The word by itself is also found at 4.4,15, in the parable of the sower and its interpretation, and in 12.14, when Pharisees and Herodians question Jesus, and acknowledge that he teaches "the way of God". A variant use may be recognised in 13.34, in ἀπόδημος: "on a far journey". In all the other cases, the phrase is ἐν τῇ ὁδῷ : "on the way".

Of the fifteen Gospel uses in total, seven are found in this Third Series, in Days 15, 17 *bis*, 19, 20 and 21 *bis*, that is, in the first and third Days of the first threesome of Days, and in all three Days of the second threesome. We note that they are found twice over in the last Days of both threesomes. The much systematic use of the word itself does much to bind these seven Days themselves together, in Mark's scheme.

This Series contributes much to the notion (derived in the first place from consideration of the Prologue) that Mark's Gospel is "the gospel of the Way", but because its final narrative-use is in the first Day's telling of the fourth and last Series of the Gospel, "the Jerusalem Days", at 11.8, it provokes a narrow interpretation, however, that the destination of this "way", in narrative terms alone, is Jerusalem. See also 10.32. Such an argument justifies the first part of the title suitable for this Third Series: "The Days of Jesus' Journeying to Jerusalem, to the Cross and Glory".

2) Ἰωάννην τὸν βαπτιστήν, καὶ ἄλλοι Ἠλίαν, ἄλλοι δὲ ὅτι εἷς τῶν προφητῶν. The comparison between 8.28 and 6.14b,15 provokes a comparison between the functions of the first days of the two middle series of the Gospel. The question of Jesus' identity is firmly raised at the beginning of both. In 6.1-6a it is introduced in the opening scene of Jesus' teaching in the synagogue in his home town, and developed in 6.14bff. in which three possibilities are entertained by the people. Herod thinks he knows which of the choices is to be made. In 8.28-30, much nearer the beginning of this Day's telling than in the previous example, it leads to the correct answer of Peter: Jesus' identity is not any one of the three entertained by the people; he is "the Christ".

---

life of his community." See Marcus, *The Way of the Lord...*, p.47.

3) Σὺ εἶ ὁ Χριστός, 8.29. For the first time, since the opening phrase of the Prologue, "The beginning of the gospel of Jesus Christ...", this status is given Jesus. The term next appears, on Jesus' own lips, at 9.41, noticeably in Day Seventeen, the third day of this Series and of the first sub-Series (the use in these Days suggests that Mark intended an *inclusio* be read). In the Fourth Series, it is applied at 12.35, 13.21, 14.61 and 15.32. Most significantly, in this first Day's telling of this third Series, it is introduced in the first half's section B and then elaborated upon in section B', in the first of three very similar disclosures in the Series, in terms of Jesus' suffering, death and resurrection. Further, we note the link of Peter between the sections: the one who responds in horror, is the one to whom is attributed the knowledge of Jesus' real identity.

At this juncture, it is worth drawing attention to a title for Jesus which suddenly appears in the Gospel for the first time, in the last Day of this Series, Day Twenty-One. Twice over (in 10.47,48) we read that "Son of David" is the cry of the blind beggar Bartimaeus. To our four commentators, it is a messianic title synonymous with "Christ". In Mark's presentation, this Series ends as it begins, and another Markan *inclusio* is observed.

4)   Και <u>ἤρξατο διδάσκειν</u> αὐτούς
    ὅτι δεῖ <u>τὸν υἱὸν τοῦ ἀνθρώπου</u> πολλὰ παθεῖν
    καὶ ἀποδοκιμασθῆναι ὑπὸ
    τῶν πρεσβυτέρων καὶ τῶν ἀρχιερέων καὶ τῶν
      γραμματέων
    καὶ ἀποκτανθῆναι καὶ μετὰ τρεῖς ἡμέρας ἀναστῆναι·

We observed above a parallel of the opening phrase in 6.2, the first Day of the earlier middle Series. Additionally, the view held by many commentators, that Mark intended his report on the death of John the Baptist to be indicative of what would happen to Jesus, is supported by literary-structural analysis. It demonstrates that for the composition of these first Days of the middle Series Mark had the parallel between John the Baptist and Jesus in mind. The next Day's telling, without actual mention of John's name, but of Elijah[5], continues Mark's train of thought, 9.12,13, and expresses another

---

[5] See page 173 for a reference to the Elijah/Elisha like feeding by Jesus of the five-thousand. The second Days of both middle Series have their points of contact as do the first Days: see Days Nine and Sixteen.

prediction much overlooked[6] of a similar kind to the above: compare 8.31 and 9.12:

8.31:   τὸν υἱὸν τοῦ ἀνθρώπου πολλὰ παθεῖν[7]
9.12:   τὸν υἱὸν τοῦ ἀνθρώπου ...πολλὰ πάθῃ.

The first sub-Series of three Days contains a prediction each Day, therefore, because on the third Day, Day Seventeen (9.30-50), the second of what is commonly termed 'three predictions' is found at 9.31 (with the response of the disciples again, in 9.32). At 10.32-34, the middle day of the second threesome of Days of this Series, in the telling of Day Twenty, is the so-called third prediction of 'three'. This Day too contains at its close, another prediction, from Jesus' own lips, and it is another "Son of man" saying, 10.45, ὁ υἱὸς τοῦ ἀνθρώπου οὐκ ἦλθεν.... δοῦναι τὴν ψυχὴν αὐτοῦ... We discern, then, not three only but five such predictions in this Series. After the two very different "Son of man" sayings so far encountered in the Gospel, at 2.10 and v.28, in Series One, the seven which appear in this Series (8.31,38; 9.9,12,31; 10.33,45) are clearly grouped. The next references come at 13.26, 14.21 *bis*, 14.41,62. The "Son of man" predictions continue in 14.21 and v.41: in 13.26 and 14.62, they are, as for 8.38, to do with Jesus' return.

5)   Εἴ τις θέλει ὀπίσω μου ἐλθεῖν,
ἀπαρνησάσθω ἑαυτὸν
καὶ ἀράτω τὸν σταυρὸν αὐτοῦ
καὶ ἀκολουθείτω μοι.

Jesus' journey through suffering to glory is not his alone; it also awaits his disciples. It is a theme which is here introduced, and is pursued in this Day in vv.35-9.1, and in this Series, in 10.35-39 (and in different terms too, of self-denial, in 9.33-37, 10.17-31). It is a subject which will appear again in Series Four, in 13.9-13.

6) ἐν τῇ δόξῃ τοῦ πατρὸς αὐτου... "Glory" is another key word and issue which this Day's telling introduces. For the first time in the Gospel it is found at 8.38. Jesus' transfiguration glory is the first subject of the following Day, Day Sixteen. Though the word is

---

[6] Attention is much more paid by commentators to the so-called "three predictions" (of this Series), 8.31, 9.31 and 10.33,34.

[7] It will be seen above, in the presentation of this Day's structure that I give this a line on its own in the detailed structure. 9.12 justifies this choice as a statement in its own right.

not mentioned there itself, it is indicated in the episode. The chiastically parallel Day of the Series, Day Twenty, 10.32-45 (compare the second day with the sixth, around the fourth, the central day), contains the second use of the word, at 10.37. In the first of these, two chief characters of the Old Covenant appear with Jesus: in the second, two leading characters of the New Covenant express their wish to be seated each side of Jesus in his "glory". Just as in the first of the two middle Series, where days two and six, in the succession of days, parallel each other for feedings of the five- and the four-thousand in symbolically messianic feasts, so too in the second of the two middle Series, in the same locations, are episodes which point to Jesus' messianic status and function. The third use in the Gospel of the word "glory" is found at 13.26,27, in the same teaching as we discerned above which additionally speaks of the sufferings that awaited the disciples. It is a saying which reflects the sayings of 8.38-9.1. It has a clear parallel also in 14.62, but again without use of the word itself.

7) τὴν βασιλείαν τοῦ θεοῦ: up to this point in the Gospel, this phrase is discovered in the Prologue, and in the parables of the first Series only (hence 1.15; 4.11,26,30). On this first Day of this Series it is well introduced again at 9.1: it appears further at 9.47, 10.14,15,23,24,25 (the only other uses are at 12.34, 14.25 and 15.43). In this Series it appears in the telling of the first and third Days of the first sub-Series, the middle day, and the first Day of the second sub-Series, that is in each of the Series' major rhetorical units[8]. Because our focus is on literary-structural issues we restrict discussion here of the term to a summary of Mark's use of it in this Series: "the Kingdom of God" will come with the glorified Jesus and with power (8.38, 9.1) and will only be entered/received by his disciples/followers if they meet certain conditions (9.47 and following, as above).

---

[8] We noted in the first Series' summary that the middle Days of that Series shared similar structurings and contents. We observed that the last Day of the first sub-Series, the middle Day of the Series, and the first Day of the completing sub-Series were characteristic of ancient rhetoric. Whilst they represented separate rhetorical units, they related and overlapped at the edges (page 146). These three middle Days of this Series, likewise, contain similar contents (teachings on the kingdom of God), and relate and overlap as they function in the same way structurally.

This third Series of Seven Days will be shown to be structured like the first and the second. Day Fifteen, therefore, as Day Eight, begins a Series and begins a sub-Series of three Days. The force of the argument Mark presents for this Day can be expressed in terms similar to that of Mack[9] but more fully and more specifically. Jesus is not only the founder teacher, but he is also the crucified and risen Christ, predictive prophet and apocalyptic judge.

Day Sixteen: 9.2-29:

The day begins Καὶ μετὰ ἡμέρας ἓξ. Clearly there can be no argument that a new Day in Mark's telling does not commence here. As at 2.1, and 8.1,2, here for the last time in the Gospel Mark has given explicit information of days passing between the telling of two Days' reports. Indeed this is the clearest reference in the whole Gospel because it numbers them (even at 8.1,2 the matter of the number is open to interpretation[10]). Because it is so specific, some have tried to interpret the reason for the "six". A number of commentators point to Exodus 24.16 which tells how Moses and Joshua went up Mount Sinai, where the glory of the Lord settled, and a cloud covered it for six days.[11] As Taylor points out Ex. 24.15f. may have coloured the account, but the "temporal statement is used differently" (compare the six days that pass *before* the incident, in Mark's account). Day Sixteen's literary structure[12] is:

---

[9] Mack, *Rhetoric...*, pp.80,81: concluding his examination of 8.34-9.1, he summarises the roles of Jesus, as that of "founder teacher, crucified Christ, predictive prophet, and apocalyptic judge". For this summary he appears to be reading Mark's Gospel as a whole, the plot for which he usefully defines as a combination of "martyrological passion narrative with an apocalyptic resolution". I read these roles of Jesus to be the essential disclosures of this Day's telling.

[10] See under Day Six and the discussion of night-crossings, and under Day Thirteen (8.1-21).

[11] Taylor, *The Gospel...*, p.388; Schweizer, *The Good News...*, p.181.

[12] In his Christological exegesis of the Old Testament in the Gospel of Mark, Marcus opens each of his studies with line by line presentations of the texts and an annotation partitioning the verses. Though it appears he has not analysed for structure beyond this, his definitions of 'lines' in the scanning compare well with mine in my analysis of 9.2-8 and 9.11-13. See Marcus, *The Way of the Lord...*, pp.80 and 94.

A α ² Καὶ μετὰ ἡμέρας ἓξ
  β [α] παραλαμβάνει ὁ Ἰησοῦς [αʹ] [.α] τὸν Πέτρον [.β] καὶ τὸν
     Ἰάκωβον [.βʹ] καὶ τὸν Ἰωάννην,
  βʹ [α] καὶ ἀναφέρει αὐτοὺς [β] εἰς ὄρος ὑψηλὸν [βʹ] [.α] κατ' ἰδίαν
     [.αʹ] μόνους.

B α Καὶ μετεμορφώθη ἔμπροσθεν αὐτῶν,
  β ³[α] καὶ τὰ ἱμάτια αὐτοῦ ἐγένετο στίλβοντα [β] λευκὰ λίαν [βʹ] οἷα
     γναφεὺς ἐπὶ τῆς γῆς οὐ δύναται οὕτως λευκᾶναι.
  βʹ ⁴[α] καὶ ὤφθη αὐτοῖς Ἠλίας σὺν Μωϋσεῖ, [α ͵] καὶ ἦσαν
     συλλαλοῦντες τῷ Ἰησοῦ.

Bʹ α ⁵[α] Καὶ ἀποκριθεὶς [β] ὁ Πέτρος λέγει τῷ Ἰησοῦ, [βʹ] ʽΡαββί,
  β [α] [.α] καλόν ἐστιν [.αʹ] ἡμᾶς ὧδε εἶναι, [β] καὶ ποιήσωμεν τρεῖς
     σκηνάς, [βʹ] [.α] σοὶ μίαν [.β] καὶ Μωϋσει μίαν [.βʹ] καὶ Ἠλία μίαν.
  βʹ ⁶[α] [.α] οὐ γὰρ ᾔδει [.αʹ] τί ἀποκριθῇ, [αʹ] [.α] ἔκφοβοι γὰρ
     [.αʹ] ἐγένοντο.

A α ⁷[α] Καὶ ἐγένετο νεφέλη [αʹ] ἐπισκιάζουσα αὐτοῖς,
  β [α] [.α] καὶ ἐγένετο φωνὴ [.αʹ] ἐκ τῆς νεφέλης, [β] Οὗτός ἐστιν ὁ
     υἱός μου ὁ ἀγαπητός, [βʹ] ἀκούετε αὐτοῦ.
  βʹ ⁸[α] [.α] καὶ ἐξάπινα [.αʹ] περιβλεψάμενοι [.β] οὐκέτι οὐδένα εἶδον
     [βʹ] [.α] ἀλλὰ τὸν Ἰησοῦν [.β] μόνον [.βʹ] μεθ' ἑαυτῶν.

B α ⁹[α] Καὶ καταβαινόντων αὐτῶν [.β] ἐκ τοῦ ὄρους [βʹ] διεστείλατο
     αὐτοῖς
  β [α] [.α] ἵνα μηδενὶ [.β] ἃ εἶδον [.βʹ] διηγήσωνται, [αʹ] [.α] εἰ μὴ ὅταν ὁ
     υἱὸς του ἀνθρώπου [.β] ἐκ νεκρῶν [.βʹ] ἀναστῇ.
  βʹ ¹⁰[α] [.α] καὶ τὸν λόγον [.β] ἐκράτησαν [.βʹ] πρὸς ἑαυτοὺς
     [αʹ] [.α] συζητοῦντες
     [.β] τί ἐστιν [βʹ] τὸ ἐκ νεκρῶν ἀναστῆναι.

Bʹ α ¹¹[α] [.α] Καὶ ἐπηρώτων αὐτὸν [.αʹ] λέγοντες, [α] [.α] Ὅτι λέγουσιν οἱ
     γραμματεῖς [β] ὅτι Ἠλίαν [.βʹ] δεῖ ἐλθεῖν πρῶτον;
  β ¹²[α] ὁ δὲ ἔφη αὐτοῖς, [αʹ] [.α] [..α] Ἠλίας [..β] μὲν ἐλθὼν πρῶτον
     [..βʹ] ἀποκαθιστάνει πάντα, [.β] [..α] και πῶς γέγραπται [..αʹ] ἐπὶ τὸν
     υἱὸν τοῦ ἀνθρώπου [.βʹ] [..α] ἵνα πολλὰ πάθη [..αʹ] καὶ ἐξουδενηθῇ;
  βʹ ¹³[α] ἀλλὰ λέγω ὑμῖν [α] [.α] ὅτι καὶ Ἠλίας ἐλήλυθεν, [.β] [..α] καὶ
     ἐποίησαν αὐτῷ [..αʹ] ὅσα ἤθελον, [.βʹ] [..α] καθὼς γέγραπται
     [..αʹ] ἐπ' αὐτόν.

A α ¹⁴[α][.α] Καὶ ἐλθόντες [.α´] πρὸς τοὺς μαθητὰς [β] [.α] εἶδον [.β] ὄχλον πολὺν [.β´] περὶ αὐτοὺς [β´] [.α] καὶ γραμματεῖς [.β] συζητοῦντας [.β´] πρὸς αὐτούς.
β ¹⁵[α] [.α] καὶ εὐθὺς [.β] πᾶς ὁ ὄχλος ἰδόντες αὐτὸν [.β´] ἐξεθαμβήθησαν, [α´] [.α] καὶ προστρέχοντες [.α´] ἠσπάζοντο αὐτόν.
β´ ¹⁶[α] καὶ ἐπηρώτησεν αὐτούς, [α´] Τί συζητεῖτε πρὸς αὐτούς;
B α ¹⁷[α] [.α] Καὶ ἀπεκρίθη αὐτῷ [.α´] εἷς ἐκ τοῦ ὄχλου, [α´] [.α] Διδάσκαλε, [.β] ἤνεγκα τὸν υἱόν μου πρὸς σέ, [.β´] ἔχοντα πνεῦμα ἄλαλον·
β ¹⁸[α] [.α] καὶ ὅπου ἐὰν αὐτὸν καταλάβῃ [.β] ῥήσσει αὐτόν, [.γ] καὶ ἀφρίζει [.δ] καὶ τρίζει τοὺς ὀδόντας [.ε] καὶ ξηραίνεται· [α´] [.α] καὶ εἶπα τοῖς μαθηταῖς σου [.β] ἵνα αὐτὸ ἐκβάλωσιν, [.β´] καὶ οὐκ ἴσχυσαν.
β´ ¹⁹[α] [.α] ὁ δὲ ἀποκριθεὶς αὐτοῖς [.α´] λέγει, [β] [.α] Ὦ γενεὰ ἄπιστος, [.β] ἕως πότε πρὸς ὑμᾶς ἔσομαι; [.β´] ἕως πότε ἀνέξομαι ὑμῶν; [.β´] φέρετε αὐτὸν πρός με.
B´ α ²⁰[α] [.α] Καὶ ἤνεγκαν αὐτὸν [.α´] πρὸς αὐτόν. [β] [.α] καὶ ἰδὼν αὐτὸν [.α´] τὸ πνεῦμα εὐθὺς συνεσπάραξεν αὐτόν, [β´] [.α] καὶ πεσὼν ἐπὶ τῆς γῆς [.β] ἐκυλίετο [.β´] ἀφρίζων.
β ²¹[α] καὶ ἐπηρώτησεν τὸν πατέρα αὐτοῦ, [β] Πόσος χρόνος ἐστὶν [β´] ὡς τοῦτο γέγονεν αὐτῷ;
β´ [α] ὁ δὲ εἶπεν, [α´] [.α] Ἐκ παιδιόθεν· [.β] ²²[..α] καὶ πολλάκις [..β] καὶ εἰς πῦρ αὐτὸν ἔβαλεν [..β´] καὶ εἰς ὕδατα [.β´] ἵνα ἀπολέσῃ αὐτόν·

A α [α] Ἀλλ' εἴ τι δύνῃ, [β] βοήθησον ἡμῖν [β´] σπλαγχνισθεὶς ἐφ' ἡμᾶς.
β ²³[α] ὁ δὲ Ἰησοῦς εἶπεν αὐτῷ, [β] Τὸ εἰ δύνῃ [β´] πάντα δυνατὰ τῷ πιστεύοντι.
β´ ²⁴[α] [.α] εὐθὺς κράξας [.α´] ὁ πατὴρ τοῦ παιδίου ἔλεγεν, [β] Πιστεύω· [β´] βοήθει μου τῇ ἀπιστίᾳ.
B α ²⁵[α] Ἰδὼν δὲ ὁ Ἰησοῦς [β] ὅτι ἐπισυντρέχει ὄχλος [β´] [.α] ἐπετίμησεν τῳ πνεύματι τῷ ἀκαθάρτῳ [.α´] λέγων αὐτῷ,
β [α] [.α] Τὸ ἄλαλον καὶ κωφὸν πνεῦμα, [.α´] ἐγὼ ἐπιτάσσω σοι, [β] ἔξελθε ἐξ αὐτου [β´] [.α] καὶ μηκέτι [.β] εἰσέλθῃς [.β´] εἰς αὐτόν.
β´ ²⁶[α] [.α] καὶ κράξας [.β] καὶ πολλὰ σπαράξας [.β´] ἐξῆλθεν· [β] καὶ ἐγένετο ὡσεὶ νεκρός, [β´] ὥστε τοὺς πολλοὺς λέγειν ὅτι ἀπέθανεν.
B´ α ²⁷[α] Ὁ δὲ Ἰησοῦς κρατήσας τῆς χειρὸς αὐτοῦ [β] ἤγειρεν αὐτόν, [β´] καὶ ἀνέστη.
β ²⁸[α] [.α] καὶ εἰσελθόντος αὐτοῦ [.α´] εἰς οἶκον [β] [.α] οἱ μαθηταὶ αὐτοῦ [.β] κατ'' ἰδίαν [.β´] ἐπηρώτων αὐτόν, [β´] [.α] Ὅτι ἡμεῖς [.β] οὐκ ἠδυνήθημεν [.β´] ἐκβαλεῖν αὐτό;
β´ ²⁹[α] καὶ εἶπεν αὐτοῖς, [β] [.α] Τοῦτο τὸ γένος [.β] ἐν οὐδενὶ [.β´] δύναται ἐξελθεῖν [β´] εἰ μὴ ἐν προσευχῇ.

The second and third lines, β and β', of the Day's introductory part A (9.2abc) exhibit historical presents in a now observed, classically Markan way: see Days Eight (6.1-29), Twelve (7.31-37) and Fourteen (8.22-26). Overall, the Day's telling is structured in two halves; both comprise two balanced sections: the annotation given to the structure is AA'/AA', the same as for Day Five, where AA'/AA' are the four Day's sections which each have three parts, hence otherwise: ABB';ABB'/ABB';ABB'.

The first half, 9.2-13, tells how Jesus took Peter, James and John (compare also 5.37, 13.3 and 14.33 for their participation in special events) from the other disciples and up onto a high mountain to witness his transfiguration. It tells of the ensuing discussion on their way back down. The first half and first section, 9.2-6, begins in A with a temporal clause, a defining of the primary characters and the place they go; B establishes the amazing event in an introductory part and two completing parts: Jesus' transfiguration, the bright whiteness of his clothes, and the appearance of Elijah and Moses; and B' records Peter's response: he addresses Jesus, "Rabbi" (the first mention of the word in the Gospel: for others, see 11.21 and 14.45), and he speaks of erecting three booths for them, not knowing what he was saying, because he and the others were much afraid. We observe the reverse order of Moses and Elijah in B' from B: it is a convention of ancient rhetoric which indicates the author's intention to show that two parts are in correspondence.

Between vv.6 and 7, an anastrophe[13] can be identified (shown in double underline) which connects the first and second sections of the first half and serves to alert the reader to the beginning of a new presentation. The first half's second section, 9.7-13, therefore, continues the story, which tells of a cloud and a voice coming out of it. The scene and the words of the voice are reminiscent of the scene just after Jesus' baptism, told in 1.11[14]. The "Christ" of Day Fifteen (8.27-9.1) is, in this Day Sixteen, the "beloved Son of God" (see also 1.1) who is to be "listened to" (we note: the prophet[15] whom God would raise up like Moses had to be listened to: Deut.

---

[13] See note 28 and the accompanying text under my analysis of the Prologue.
[14] For a discussion of the comparison of 1.11 and 9.7, and as to why they are not in structural relationship in the Gospel, see page 69.
[15] Identification maybe being made by Mark with the prophet of 6.15 and 8.28. See Fowler, *Loaves and Fishes...*, pp.126-128, who thinks "there can be little doubt" about it.

18.14,15,17,18). Suddenly, the cloud, the voice and Moses and Elijah are all gone. Section B reports the descent. Jesus' command to them to be quiet about the event until "the Son of man should rise from the dead" causes the three to debate the meaning of "rising from the dead". Section B' reports the question that they do put to Jesus, concerning Elijah and the necessity of his coming first. In a two part reply, Jesus speaks, in the first (β), not only about Elijah's coming but also about himself (and his own suffering), and, in the second (β‛), about Elijah (John the Baptist is inferred) who has come already and to whom "they did what they wished". Both replies include reference to what "is written".

The first half of the Day's telling, given its variety of subjects and O.T. allusions, is clearly a conflation on Mark's part of several traditions which cover a number of issues. Added to it, in the second half, 9.14-29, is a telling of an exorcism that the other disciples were unable to carry out. At first sight there is little to connect the two halves; nevertheless, the second half begins with the return to the other disciples (*cf.* 9.2b), who are in the company of a large crowd and 'scribes' (see v.11 for this further connection between the two halves of this same Day's telling). Further, something about Jesus, when he was seen, astonished the crowd. The likely interpetation Mark meant his audience to appreciate was the 'identification' of Jesus with Moses (who, in Ex. 34.29f., reflects the 'glory of God' to a 'large crowd' on coming down from the mountain). The first section of the second half, vv.14-22a, tells how the disciples were not able to cast out a dumb spirit (in v.25, it is a 'dumb and deaf spirit'): the second, completing section, vv.22b-29, tells how Jesus was able to heal him and how Jesus teaches his disciples that such healing is a matter of faith and prayer.

The connection between the two sections of the second half, between v.22a and v.22b is an interesting one. The one speaking, the father of the one with the dumb spirit, answers (in vv.21b,22a) Jesus' question (of v.21a) and goes on to put his own (v.22b) which introduces the theme of the second section. The two sections of each half of this Day's telling are well connected, in their different ways: the first by anastophe and continuing story; the second by continuing story and continuing speech.

After the introductory setting-change, in part A, vv.14-16, of place and characters, and its placing of Jesus again firmly in the centre of the new scene, part B, vv.17-19, tells what the issue is, and, as we seen before in Days Six (5.1-20) and Seven (5.21-43) for something very similar, Mark's detail of the boy's sickness is impressive. (V.17, Διδάσκαλε, is an address to Jesus which we find five times in this Series: see also 9.38, 10.17,20 and v.35.) Part B ends with Jesus' lament for their unbelief and a call to "bring" the boy to him. Part B', vv.20-22a, begins with the boy being brought to him and continues with Jesus questioning the father. The concluding section, vv.22b-29, begins in A, vv.22b-24, with the questioning by the father of Jesus' ability to heal the boy and Jesus' raising the matter of believing which evokes from the father the cry, "I believe; help my unbelief!" (It is the cry of a typical disciple.[16]) Part B, vv.25,26, reports the healing; part B', vv.27-29, completes the Day's reports with Jesus' raising the boy and explaining to his disciples that prayer alone succeeds.

The second Day of this Series (Day Sixteen), therefore, as the first (Day Fifteen), for its disclosures of who Jesus is and its disclosures on active discipleship, finds Jesus instructing his disciples. On the soteriological components of the Day's telling, Schweizer is surely right that the story of the transfiguration unites "two expectations which were alive in Judaism: the coming of the prophet of the end-time who is like Moses, and the appearing of Elijah at the dawning of the end-time"[17] The most important Christological disclosure of this Day's telling is clearly that Jesus is the "Son of God".

Day Seventeen: 9.30-50:

The day begins with words featured in the introductions to other Days: see under Day Eight for a brief discussion on 6.1, 7.24, 9.30 and 10.1, and under Day Eleven where Mark's use of an introductory

---

[16] Hooker, *The Gospel...*, p.224.
[17] Schweizer, *The Good News...*, p.183. The other commentators of my selection write similarly.

formula for these and Days beginning at 6.53, 7.31, 8.27 and 10.46 is established. 10.1 clearly begins a new Day, hence the limits of this Day are 9.30 and v.50.

Mark's literary-structural presentation for Day Seventeen is his commonly-used ABB' plan of three sections: it is presented below:

A α   ³⁰[α] [.α] <u>Κἀκεῖθεν</u> [.β] <u>ἐξελθόντες</u> [.β´] παρεπορεύοντο διὰ τῆς
      Γαλιλαίας, [β] [.α] καὶ οὐκ ἤθελεν [.α´] ἵνα τις γνοῖ · ³¹[β´] [.α]
      ἐδίδασκεν γὰρ τοὺς μαθητὰς αὐτοῦ [.α´] καὶ ἔλεγεν αὐτοῖς
  β   [α] [.α] ὅτι ʿΟ υἱὸς <u>τοῦ ἀνθρώπου</u> παραδίδοται [.α´] εἰς χεῖρας
      ἀνθρώπων, [β] <u>καὶ ἀποκτενοῦσιν</u> αὐτόν, [β´] [.α] <u>καὶ ἀποκτανθεὶς</u>
      [.β] μετὰ τρεῖς ἡμέρας [.β´] ἀναστήσεται.
  β´ ³²[α] οἱ δὲ ἠγνόουν τὸ ῥῆμα, [β] καὶ ἐφοβοῦντο [β´] αὐτὸν
      <u>ἐπερωτῆσαι</u>.

B α   ³³Καὶ ἦλθον εἰς Καφαρναούμ.
  β   [α] καὶ ἐν τῇ οἰκίᾳ γενόμενος [β] <u>ἐπηρώτα</u> αὐτούς, [β´] [.α] Τί [.β] <u>ἐν</u>
      <u>τῇ ὁδῷ</u> [.β´] <u>διελογίζεσθε</u>;
  β´ ³⁴[α] οἱ δὲ ἐσιώπων, [β] [.α] πρὸς <u>ἀλλήλους</u> γὰρ διελέχθησαν [.α´] <u>ἐν</u>
      <u>τῇ ὁδῷ</u> [β´] τίς μείζων.

B´ α ³⁵[α] Καὶ καθίσας [β] ἐφώνησεν τοὺς δώδεκα [β´] καὶ λέγει αὐτοῖς,
  α´ [α] [.α] Εἴ τις θέλει [.α´] πρῶτος εἶναι
      [β] ἔσται <u>πάντων</u> ἔσχατος
      [β´] καὶ <u>πάντων</u> διάκονος.

A α   ³⁶[α] [.α] Καὶ λαβὼν <u>παιδίον</u> [.β] ἔστησεν αὐτὸ [.β´] ἐν μέσῳ αὐτῶν
      [β] καὶ ἐναγκαλισάμενος αὐτὸ [β´] εἶπεν αὐτοῖς,
  β   ³⁷[α]ʿʹΟς ἂν ἓν τῶν τοιούτων <u>παιδίων</u> δέξηται [β] <u>ἐπὶ τῷ ὀνόματί</u>
      <u>μου</u>, [β´] <u>ἐμὲ δέχεται</u>·
  β´ [α] καὶ <u>ὃς ἂν ἐμὲ δέχηται</u>, [β] οὐκ ἐμὲ δέχεται [β´] ἀλλὰ τὸν
      ἀποστείλαντά <u>με</u>.

B α   ³⁸[α] Ἔφη αὐτῷ ὁ Ἰωάννης, [β] Διδάσκαλε, [β´] [.α] εἴδομέν τινα
      [.β] <u>ἐν τω ὀνόματί σου</u> [.β´] ἐκβάλλοντα δαιμόνια,
      [.α] και <u>ἐκωλύομεν αὐτόν</u>, [.α´] ὅτι οὐκ ἠκολούθει ἡμῖν.
  β´ ³⁹[α] ὁ δὲ Ἰησοῦς εἶπεν, [α´] Μὴ <u>κωλύετε αὐτόν</u>,

B´ α [α] Οὐδεὶς γάρ <u>ἐστιν</u> [β] [.α] ὃς ποιήσει δύναμιν [.α´] <u>ἐπὶ τῷ</u>
      <u>ὀνόματί μου</u> [β´] [.α] καὶ δυνήσεται [.β] ταχὺ [.β´] κακολογῆσαί με·
  β   ⁴⁰[α] <u>ὃς γὰρ</u> οὐκ <u>ἔστιν</u> καθ᾽ ἡμῶν, [α´] ὑπὲρ ἡμῶν <u>ἐστιν</u>.
  β´ ⁴¹[α] [.α] <u>ὃς γὰρ</u> ἂν <u>ποτίσῃ</u> ὑμᾶς <u>ποτήριον</u> ὕδατος [.β] <u>ἐν ὀνόματι</u>
      [.β´] ὅτι Χριστοῦ ἐστε, [α´] [.α] ἀμὴν λέγω ὑμῖν [.α´] ὅτι οὐ μὴ
      ἀπολέσῃ τὸν μισθὸν αὐτοῦ.

A α ⁴²[α] Καὶ ὃς ἂν σκανδαλίσῃ [.β] ἕνα τῶν μικρῶν τούτων [βʹ] τῶν πιστευόντων [εἰς ἐμέ],
  β [α] καλόν ἐστιν αὐτῷ μᾶλλον [β] εἰ περίκειται μύλος ὀνικὸς [βʹ] περὶ τὸν τράχηλον αὐτοῦ
  βʹ [α] καὶ βέβληται [αʹ] εἰς τὴν θάλασσαν.

B α[α] ⁴³[.α] Καὶ ἐὰν σκανδαλίσῃ σε ἡ χείρ σου, [..αʹ] ἀπόκοψον αὐτήν·
   [β] [.α] καλόν ἐστίν σε [.αʹ] κυλλὸν εἰσελθεῖν εἰς τὴν ζωὴν
   [βʹ] [.α] ἢ τὰς δύο χεῖρας ἔχοντα [.β] ἀπελθεῖν εἰς τὴν γέενναν, [.βʹ] εἰς τὸ πῦρ τὸ ἄσβεστον.
  β[α] ⁴⁵[.α] καὶ ἐὰν ὁ πούς σου σκανδαλίζῃ σε, [.αʹ] ἀπόκοψον αὐτόν·
   [β] [.α] καλόν ἐστίν σε [.αʹ] εἰσελθεῖν εἰς τὴν ζωὴν χωλὸν
   [βʹ] [.α] ἢ τοὺς δύο πόδας ἔχοντα [.αʹ] βληθῆναι εἰς τὴν γέενναν.
  βʹ[α] ⁴⁷[.α] καὶ ἐὰν ὁ ὀφθαλμός σου σκανδαλίζῃ σε, [.αʹ] ἔκβαλε αὐτόν·
   [β] [.α] καλόν σέ ἐστιν [.αʹ] μονόφθαλμον εἰσελθεῖν εἰς τὴν βασιλείαν τοῦ θεοῦ
   [βʹ] [.α] ἢ δύο ὀφθαλμοὺς ἔχοντα [.β] βληθῆναι εἰς τὴν γέενναν,
       [.βʹ] ⁴⁸[..α] ὅπου ὁ σκώληξ αὐτῶν οὐ τελευτᾷ [..αʹ] καὶ τὸ πῦρ οὐ σβέννυται·

Bʹ α ⁴⁹[α] Πᾶς γὰρ [β] πυρὶ [βʹ] ἁλισθήσεται.
  β ⁵⁰[α] Καλὸν τὸ ἅλας· [β] ἐὰν δὲ τὸ ἅλας ἄναλον γένηται, [βʹ] ἐν τίνι αὐτὸ ἀρτύσετε;
  βʹ [α] ἔχετε ἐν ἑαυτοῖς ἅλα, [αʹ] καὶ εἰρηνεύετε ἐν ἀλλήλοις.

The opening section, in its first part, vv.30-32, continues the theme of Jesus' instructing his disciples; together they are again the principal characters of this Day's telling. This opening is a summary of their journeying, in private, and of what "he was teaching" as they passed through Galilee. The teaching is a re-telling of Day Fifteen's predictions of what will happen to him, and again the response of his disciples is one of continuous non-understanding and fear. Parts B, vv.33,34, and Bʹ, v.35, complete the introduction to the Day. Part B establishes the geographical location as Capernaum[18] and the setting "in a house"[19]; and reflecting the earlier journeying (cementing parts B and Bʹ to A) Jesus asks what they were discussing ἐν τῇ ὁδῷ[20], in β; and they do not reply because they had been discussing ἐν τῇ

---

[18] See Days One and Three for earlier references, 1.21 and 2.2.
[19] See also for "in a house": 2.1,15, 3.19, 7.17,24, 9.28 and 10.10.
[20] For a discussion on the importance of ἐν τῇ ὁδῷ in this Series of Days, see 1) under Day Fifteen.

ὁδῷ who was 'the greatest', in β'. Part B' reflects B well: Jesus sits, calls the twelve and what he says about being 'first' is presented in the form of a protasis in [α], and a double apodosis in [β], [β'].

In Section B, vv.36-41, the teaching continues, but with a new beginning: Jesus takes a child and stands him in the midst of them. The child is a 'believer', so v.42 suggests, which verse begins the parallel and concluding section B', vv.42-50. Again, we see Mark's constructive hand so clearly at work. In section B, the first part introduces the phrase ἐπὶ τῷ ὀνόματί μου: this sets up the teaching for the second two parts, both of which include reference to the same. In section B', the opening part introduces ὃς ἂν σκανδαλίσῃ and καλόν: the first of the two completing parts, B, comprises three very similar sayings which in the concluding sub-part climaxes with entry "into the Kingdom of God"[21]; the completing second part, B', links fire (from before) with salt, in its first line, and in its concluding two lines presents the illustration of salt.

With this collection of sayings Mark concludes a sub-Series of three Days of Jesus' teaching addressed to his disciples. Hooker[22] observes that 9.41-50 possesses a unity and an emphasis remarkably close to that of 8.34-38. We draw attention also to the obvious parallel between 8.31 and 9.31. When Mark composed Day Seventeen, he had Day Fifteen (8.27-9.1) in mind. Again, this kind of observation tends to a summarising of Mark's plan for these three Days in terms of an ABA' form. That they are a threesome of Days is well supported, but how did Mark himself view his composition? References to changes in geographical place (that is, as opposed to change of local setting) and to the Days, as to whether or not two of the three are consecutive, have proved futile in all previous cases. We will not be discussing such, therefore. It is the movement of the story-line and the revelations that indicate the form.

The view I take is that Day Fifteen is clearly and emphatically introductory. It introduces new information in the Gospel narrative, both about Jesus and about discipleship. Day Sixteen continues these two themes and develops them. And Day Seventeen in completing the sub-Series returns in part to Day Fifteen's Christological

---
[21] For a discussion on the importance of "the kingdom of God" in this Series of Days, see 7) under Day Fifteen for a brief discussion.
[22] Hooker, *The Gospel...*, pp.230f.

disclosures, thus providing an *inclusio*, but again continues to develop the theme of discipleship. In all three Days, in the first verses the focus is on Jesus, and in the remaining verses the focus is on discipleship.

When we look at the presentations of the Christological disclosures of these three days, we can identify another important link. To the first Day's disclosure that Jesus is the Christ attaches the command to silence, on the part of the disciples, 8.30 (here the Messianic secret, specifically the Messianic secret, is introduced). To the second Day's disclosure of Jesus' transfiguration glory (and his Sonship of God?) attaches a second command to silence, till Jesus was risen from the dead (9.9). (They had to be silent about "what they had seen", and "heard" too, we might add to be consistent.) At the beginning of this third Day's telling (9.30,31), we read that Jesus' teaching of his diciples, about his death and resurrection, was for them only to know, at that time[23]. In contrast to the beginning of the third Day's telling (i.e. Day Seventeen's telling), 9.30, the next (Day Eighteen) begins with reference to "the crowds who go with him again", 10.1. Day Eighteen includes no reference to any Messianic secret. Clearly, Days Fifteen to Seventeen are a sub-Series, and they are arranged as before in the earlier Series, in an ABB' form.

Day Eighteen: 10.1-16:

Commonly, commentators view 10.1 as introductory in geographical terms to a collection of narratives, based on topical arrangement:[24]

10.2-12	on Adultery
10.13-16	on Children
10.17-22	The Rich Man and Eternal Life
10.23-27	The Conversation on Riches
10.28-31	The Question of Rewards.

---

[23] The "Messianic secret" is discussed below, in the summary of this Series and in Chapter 8.
[24] Taylor, *The Gospel...*, p.415. Compare J. Jeremias, *Infant Baptism in the First Four Centuries*, tr. by D. Cairns, SCM Press, London, 1971, p.50: Jeremias sees 10.1-31 as a pre-Markan complex. Kuhn argues that it is 10.1-45 which goes back to an original complex of pre-Markan material containing three pericopae relating to divorce, wealth and position, approx. vv.2-12, 17-32 and 35-45 (H.W. Kuhn, *Ältere Sammlungen im Markusevangelium*, Vandenhoeck & Ruprecht, Göttingen, 1971, pp.146-191).

The reason I break after 10.16, and so discern this Day's telling ends at v.16, is that a new Day's journeying is inferred by the opening of 10.17: Καὶ ἐκπορευομένου αὐτοῦ εἰς ὁδὸν προσδραμὼν εἷς καὶ γονυπετήσας αὐτὸν ἐπηρώτα αὐτόν, Διδάσκαλε ἀγαθέ... It compares with 10.32: ᾽Ησαν δὲ ἐν τῇ ὁδῳ ἀναβαίνοντες εἰς ῾Ιεροσόλυμα... It also compares with 8.27d, καὶ ἐν τῇ ὁδω, (the Day starts at v.27a) and 9.33, Τί ἐν τῇ ὁδω (the beginning of the Day is 9.30-32; 9.33 is reflective of it). To these, we can add 10.46 because the character, whose story is related, sat παρὰ τὴν ὁδόν. Hence, we may discern that the beginnings of five of the seven Days of this Series employ ἐν τῇ ὁδῷ or variants, and that Mark used the term in such a position to signal the beginnings, or to reinforce the beginnings of the tellings of these new Days. The pericopae of 10.17-22, 23-27, 28-31 in the table, so separated from the others by 10.17, are the A, B and B' sections of Day Nineteen's three-part presentation.

Day Eighteen's telling is organised by Mark (here also) to his ABB' scheme. The short introductory section A (compare that of Day Fifteen, and others) establishes the new geographical location in α, the accompaniment of crowds in β, and a common activity of Jesus, which is teaching, in β' (elsewhere in introductory verses: teaching: 1.21, 6.2, (8.2), 9.31; preaching: 1.39; speaking the word: 2.2; telling them: 10.32). Section B commences with introducing Pharisees into the scene who begin to question Jesus about the law and divorce, "testing him". Section B' commences by relating a relocation ("in the house again", v.10), and establishes that it is Jesus and his disciples who are now present only (reminding us of scenes described in the previous three days). Conversation turns to the matter of remarriage, on divorce, which to Jesus is adultery. Into this same setting children are now brought, and they become an illustration (compare Day Seventeen, 9.30-50, v.36) to the disciples of how they must receive the kingdom of God. In the conclusion to the Day's telling, Jesus is "repeatedly blessing" the children.

I present the literary structure of Day Eighteen. The levels of literary order follow again the αββ' presentational approach of Mark at his higher levels: they exhibit again his careful creating of introductory pieces to balancing pairings of contents.

A α ¹[α] Καὶ ἐκεῖθεν [β] ἀναστὰς [β‎ʹ] [.α] ἔρχεται [.β] εἰς τὰ ὅρια τῆς
       Ἰουδαίας
       [.βʹ] [καὶ] πέραν τοῦ Ἰορδάνου,
   β   [α] καὶ συμπορεύονται [β] πάλιν [βʹ] ὄχλοι πρὸς αὐτόν,
   βʹ [α] καὶ ὡς εἰώθει [β] πάλιν [βʹ] ἐδίδασκεν αὐτούς.

B α [α] ²Καὶ προσελθόντες
       [β] [.α] Φαρισαῖοι ἐπηρώτων αὐτὸν [.β] εἰ ἔξεστιν [.βʹ] ἀνδρὶ
       γυναῖκα ἀπολῦσαι,
       [βʹ] πειράζοντες αὐτόν.
   β [α] ³[.α] ὁ δὲ ἀποκριθεὶς [.β] εἶπεν αὐτοῖς, [.βʹ] Τί ὑμῖν ἐνετείλατο
       Μωϋσῆς;
       [β] ⁴[.α] οἱ δὲ εἶπαν, [.αʹ] [..α] Ἐπέτρεψεν Μωϋσῆς [..β] βιβλίον
       ἀποστασίου γράψαι [..βʹ] καὶ ἀπολῦσαι.
       [βʹ] ⁵[.α] ὁ δὲ Ἰησοῦς εἶπεν αὐτοῖς, [.β] Πρὸς τὴν σκληροκαρδίαν ὑμῶν
       [.βʹ] ἔγραψεν ὑμῖν τὴν ἐντολὴν ταύτην.
   βʹ[α] ⁶[.α] ἀπὸ δὲ ἀρχῆς κτίσεως [.αʹ] ἄρσεν καὶ θῆλυ ἐποίησεν αὐτούς·
       [β] ⁷[.α] [..α] ἕνεκεν τούτου [..β] καταλείψει ἄνθρωπος τὸν πατέρα
       αὐτοῦ καὶ τὴν μητέρα [..βʹ] [καὶ προσκολληθήσεταὶ πρὸς τὴν
       γυναῖκα αὐτοῦ]
       ⁸[.β] [..α] καὶ ἔσονται οἱ δύο [..β] εἰς σάρκα [..βʹ] μίαν·
       [.βʹ] [..α] ὥστε οὐκέτι [..β] εἰσὶν δύο [..βʹ] ἀλλὰ μία σάρξ.
       [βʹ] ⁹[.α] ὃ οὖν ὁ θεὸς συνέζευξεν [.αʹ] ἄνθρωπος μὴ χωριζέτω.

Bʹα[α] ¹⁰[.α] Καὶ εἰς τὴν οἰκίαν [.β] πάλιν [.βʹ] [..α] οἱ μαθηταὶ [..β] περὶ
       τούτου [..βʹ] ἐπηρώτων αὐτόν.
       [β] ¹¹[.α] καὶ λέγει αὐτοῖς, [.αʹ] [..α] "Ὃς ἂν ἀπολύσῃ τὴν γυναῖκα αὐτοῦ
       [..β] καὶ γαμήσῃ ἄλλην [..βʹ] μοιχᾶται ἐπʹ αὐτήν,
       [βʹ] ¹²[.α] καὶ ἐὰν αὐτὴ ἀπολύσασα τὸν ἄνδρα αὐτῆς [.β] γαμήσῃ ἄλλον
       [.βʹ] μοιχᾶται.
   β[α] ¹³[.α] Καὶ προσέφερον αὐτῷ παιδία [.αʹ] ἵνα αὐτῶν ἅψηται·
       [β] οἱ δὲ μαθηταὶ ἐπετίμησαν αὐτοῖς.
       [βʹ] ¹⁴[.α] ἰδὼν δὲ [.β] ὁ Ἰησοῦς ἠγανάκτησεν [.βʹ] καὶ εἶπεν αὐτοῖς,
   βʹ[α] [.α] Ἄφετε τὰ παιδία ἔρχεσθαι πρός με, [β] μὴ κωλύετε αὐτά,
       [βʹ] τῶν γὰρ τοιούτων ἐστὶν ἡ βασιλεία τοῦ θεοῦ.
       [β] ¹⁵[α] ἀμὴν λέγω ὑμῖν, [β] [.α] ὃς ἂν μὴ δέξηται τὴν βασιλείαν τοῦ
       θεοῦ [.αʹ] ὡς παιδίον, [βʹ] οὐ μὴ εἰσέλθῃ εἰς αὐτήν.
       [βʹ] ¹⁶[.α] καὶ ἐναγκαλισάμενος [.β] αὐτὰ κατευλόγει [.βʹ] τιθεὶς τὰς
       χεῖρας ἐπʹαὐτά.

Day Eighteen opens, in 10.1, without any reference to ἐν τῇ ὁδῷ (see item 1 on page 201). We can observe the complete absence of this Series' familiar feature in the Day's telling, and also, in this Series of seven Days so far, the absence of any new Christological disclosures or predictions about Jesus. The opening itself is very similar to that of Day Eleven, 7.24-30, which is the middle day of the first of the two middle Series of the Gospel (see under Day Eleven, for a discussion on this). The common opening words are ἐκεῖθεν, ἀναστάς, and εἰς τὰ ὅρια. Clearly, Mark composed one of these two days with the other in mind. That in itself suggests that it was also in his mind that he was composing here the middle Day to his second and corresponding middle Series.

The Day indeed stands alone in this Series: Pharisees are present (in vv.2-9, the first major part of the Day's telling, and nowhere else in the Series) to "test" Jesus by questioning him on *marriage and divorce* (not specifically adultery). In the second and final major part (vv.10-16) in a new setting, "in the house", the disciples question Jesus on the subject which becomes that of *adultery*; they then cause Jesus to be "angry" by turning away those who were bringing children to him. 'Marriage' and 'family' do link the two major sections, and the Day's point ends on discipleship matters again (as in all the Days of this Series).

In the first of these two major sections, vv.2-9, in his reply to the Pharisees, Jesus quotes interestingly from Genesis 1.27 *and* 2.24, connecting them together in a way which to Nineham[25] is reminiscent of rabbinical exegesis. Because of my interest in Genesis 1.1-2.4a, that it had possible influence on Mark's choice of literary structure (see page 24, in my Introduction), I find this matter particularly noteworthy. Its inclusion here, in a Series' middle Day and turning point, does suggest that this reference to the Genesis account of creation is indeed significant. It is especially so, because the middle Day and turning point of the first Series, on 'what is lawful on the sabbath', connects clearly also with the creation story, in Genesis 2.1-4a, its epilogue. This matter will be addressed in Chapter 8.

On the inclusion of vv.13-16, Isaksson is one who prefers to connect it to 10.1-12 and regards the two together, as they are found in Matt. 19.1-15 as a church marriage catechism.[26] My literary-structural analysis establishes this link: 'marriage' (even

---

[25] Nineham, *Saint Mark*, p.265: on "For this reason", v.7, he notes that "Jesus makes it refer to something different - the fact (in Gen 1.27) that the human race was created from the beginning in two sexes", and not 2.23, that woman was created from man.

[26] A. Isaksson, *Marriage and Ministry in the New Temple*, Lund, 1965, pp.119, 121.

marriage stability) and 'children' are the subjects (of sections B and B', in turn) which here seem to be linked in Mark's mind. In regard to the exemplary qualities of children in matters of discipleship many suggestions have been made. They include: a child's innocence, simplicity, ingenuousness, and receptiveness. Barclay's traditional stance[27] that 'a child trusts adults', however, still offers the most strightforward interpretation, that a disciple is to trust God. Entry into/receiving the Kingdom, for the disciple, promises 'repeated blessing'; he/she has simply to allow God continuous rule in his/her life. Moral and salvific issues here combine in Mark's presentation.

The question now put is: how does this middle day of this Series of seven Days function as a pivot to the sub-Series each side of it if, that is, it is any more than just a buffer between them? The middle day, Day Eleven, of the first middle Series looks both ways, that is to what precedes and to what follows it. We might expect this Day, therefore, to perform a similar function, especially as we identify Mark's interest in starting it like Day Eleven.

In terms of the major component, we may identify the subject to be 'discipleship: marriage, divorce and adultry' (not 'parenting' as such). The emphasis is on what is ethical. It is "representative of the kind of controversy in which the church frequently was engaged, as, e.g., in its quarrel with Judaism", says Schweizer[28]. Children then feature in the Day's telling, but as an illustration of a salvific point, which has to do with the Kingdom of God. In the previous Day's telling, Jesus uses a child as an illustration for discipleship teaching. And we note in the day following that Jesus, for the only time in the Gospel, addresses his disciples, "Children..." (10.24).

We may make the observation that this Series re-introduces the concept of the Kingdom of God to the Gospel, in its first Day's telling, at 9.1 (see item 7 on page 205). It is a term not otherwise found in the Series outside of the three middle days. Issues are raised over "entering", or "receiving" the Kingdom of God. In Day Seventeen, there is one reference, at 9.47 (on entry); in the telling of Day Eighteen there are two references, at 10.14,15 ("of such (of children) is..."/receiving, entry); and in Day Nineteen, there are three references, at 10.23,24,25 (on entry, three times). In the handling of

---

[27] Wm. Barclay, *Mark*, Daily Study Bible, St Andrew Press, Edinburgh, 1954, p.251.
[28] Schweizer, *The Good News...*, p.201.

the Kingdom of God concept in the central Day's telling we may note, therefore, a different emphasis from that of the Day preceding and the Day following, which mirror each other. The central day expresses uniquely that the kingdom of God is a gift to be received. The Kingdom of God is to be full of child-like disciples, who receive it as a gift, through trusting God. All discipleship hinges on this. Day Eighteen is a hinge day's telling in itself, therefore, a fulcrum to the presentations of 'teachings on discipleship'. There is more to the argument, however.

The opening reference to the Kingdom of God, in 9.1 which is coupled to 8.38 by Mark, in the first Day's telling of this Series is further illuminating. This first Day establishes that Jesus is the Christ, that he is to suffer, be rejected, be killed and after three days rise again (the Series variously, but consistently reminds the reader/listeners of this: five predictions in all are identified[29]). Further to these things, Jesus is to come in the glory of his father, and the kingdom of God is to come in power with him. These 'Christological-disclosures' link firmly with Jesus' 'teachings on discipleship', but fundamentally they make it plain that the Kingdom of God (God's rule) becomes possible through his suffering, death, resurrection and return. Day Eighteen is pivotal in this Series because it establishes that the Kingdom of God, secured for all by Jesus, is a gift to be received. The Day is central because it calls for this understanding of the two major components which make up the Series, and it gives guidance as to what must be the reader's/listeners' response to these matters.

The contents' repetitions, of 'children' and 'the Kingdom of God' in the middle three Days of this Series, may be judged to be evidence again of what we discovered particularly clearly in the first Series (see page 146), of the characteristic in ancient rhetoric whereby smooth transitions between rhetorical units were established by hook words and phrases.

---

[29] See 4) under Day Fifteen and the features of the Series.

Day Nineteen: 10.17-31:

For the arguments for seeing 10.17 and 10.32 as beginning new Days, refer to the discussions under Day Eighteen.

On the structure of 10.17-31, Taylor, Schweizer, Hooker and Best[30] all agree that these verses form a Markan whole, and that they divide into three parts, vv.17-22, vv.23-27, and vv.28-31. Literary-structural analysis demonstrates that this Day's telling is indeed constructed in these three parts, and that their relationship is best expressed by ABB'. Bultmann's analysis sees the unit, vv.17-22, as the base unit (which I designate A), to which 'supplements' are attached: vv.23-27 (my B), vv.28-30 and v.31 (together, my B').[31]

The literary structure of Day Nineteen is as follows:

A α [α][17][.α] Καὶ ἐκπορευομένου αὐτοῦ [.α'] εἰς ὁδὸν
   [β] [.α] [..α] προσδραμὼν εἷς [..α'] καὶ γονυπετήσας αὐτὸν
      [.α'] ἐπηρώτα αὐτόν,
   [β'] [.α] Διδάσκαλε ἀγαθέ, [.β] τί ποιήσω [.β'] ἵνα ζωὴν αἰώνιον
      κληρονομήσω;
β [α][18][.α] ὁ δὲ Ἰησοῦς εἶπεν αὐτῷ, [.β] Τί με λέγεις ἀγαθόν; [.β'] οὐδεὶς
      ἀγαθὸς εἰ μὴ εἷς ὁ θεός.
   [β][19][.α] [..α] τὰς ἐντολὰς [..α'] οἶδας·
      [.α'] [..α] Μὴ φονεύσῃς, [..β] Μὴ μοιχεύσῃς, [..γ] Μὴ κλέψῃς,
      [..δ] Μὴ ψευδομαρτυρήσῃς, [..ε] Μὴ ἀποστερήσῃς, [..ζ] Τίμα
      τὸν πατέρα σου καὶ τὴν μητέρα.
   [β'][20][.α] ὁ δὲ ἔφη αὐτῷ, [.β] Διδάσκαλε, [.β'] [..α] ταῦτα πάντα
      [..β] ἐφυλαξάμην [..β'] ἐκ νεότητός μου.
β'[α][21][.α] ὁ δὲ Ἰησοῦς ἐμβλέψας αὐτω [.β] ἠγάπησεν αὐτὸν [.β'] καὶ εἶπεν
      αὐτω,
   [β] [.α] Ἕν σε ὑστερεῖ·
      [.β] [..α] ὕπαγε [..β] [...α] ὅσα ἔχεις πώλησον [...α'] καὶ δὸς [τοῖς]
      πτωχοῖς, [..β'] καὶ ἕξεις θησαυρὸν ἐν οὐρανῷ,
      [.β'] [..α] καὶ δεῦρο [..α'] ἀκολούθει μοι.
   [β'][22][.α] [..α] ὁ δὲ στυγνάσας [..α'] ἐπὶ τῷ λόγῳ [.β] [..α] ἀπῆλθεν
      [..α'] λυπούμενος, [.β'] [..α] ἦν γὰρ ἔχων [..α'] κτήματα πολλά.

---

[30] Taylor, *The Gospel...*, p.424; Schweizer, *The Good News...*, p.208f.; Hooker, *The Gospel...*, p.239f.; Best, *Disciples...*, p.17.
[31] Bultmann, *The History...*, p.20. Hooker allows also that the section may originally have been these four separate units, *The Gospel...*, p.240.

Β α[α]²³[.α] Καὶ περιβλεψάμενος [.α´] ὁ ᾽Ιησοῦς λέγει τοῖς μαθηταῖς αὐτοῦ,
[β]   [.α] Πῶς δυσκόλως [.β] οἱ τὰ χρήματα ἔχοντες [.β´] εἰς τὴν
       βασιλείαν τοῦ θεου εἰσελεύσονται.
[β´]²⁴[.α] οἱ δὲ μαθηταὶ ἐθαμβοῦντο [.α´] ἐπὶ τοῖς λόγοις αὐτοῦ.
β[α]   [.α] ὁ δὲ ᾽Ιησοῦς [.β] πάλιν ἀποκριθεὶς [.β´] λέγει αὐτοῖς,
[β]   [.α] Τέκνα,
       [.β] [..α] πῶς δύσκολόν ἐστιν [..α´] εἰς τὴν βασιλείαν τοῦ θεου
       εἰσελθεῖν·
       ²⁵[.β´] [..α] εὐκοπώτερόν ἐστιν
       [..β] [...α] κάμηλον [...β] διὰ [τῆς] τρυμαλιᾶς [τῆς] ῥαφίδος
       [...β´] διελθεῖν
       [..β´] [...α] ἢ πλούσιον [...β] εἰς τὴν βασιλείαν τοῦ θεου
       [...β´] εἰσελθεῖν.
[β´]²⁶[.α] οἱ δὲ περισσῶς ἐξεπλήσσοντο [.β] λέγοντες πρὸς ἑαυτούς,
       [.β´] Καὶ τίς δύναται σωθῆναι;
β´[α]²⁷[.α] ἐμβλέψας αὐτοῖς [.α´] ὁ ᾽Ιησοῦς λέγει,
[β]   Παρὰ ἀνθρώποις ἀδύνατον
[β´]   [.α] ἀλλ᾽ οὐ παρὰ θεῷ, [.α´] πάντα γὰρ δυνατα παρὰ τῷ θεῷ.

Β´ α [α]²⁸[.α] ῎Ηρξατο λέγειν [.β] ὁ Πέτρος [.β´] αὐτῷ,
[β]   [.α] ᾽Ιδοὺ [.β] ἡμεῖς ἀφήκαμεν [.β´] πάντα
[β´]   καὶ ἠκολουθήκαμέν σοι.
β [α]²⁹[.α] ἔφη ὁ ᾽Ιησοῦς, [.β] ᾽Αμὴν λέγω ὑμῖν,
[β]   [.α] [..α] οὐδείς ἐστιν [..α´] [...α] ὃς ἀφῆκεν οἰκίαν [...β] ἢ ἀδελφοὺς
       [...γ] ἢ ἀδελφὰς [...δ] ἢ μητέρα [...ε] ἢ πατέρα [...ζ] ἢ τέκνα
       [...η] ἢ ἀγροὺς
       [.β] ἕνεκεν ἐμοῦ [.β´] καὶ ἕνεκεν τοῦ εὐαγγελίου,
[β´]³⁰[.α] ἐὰν μὴ λάβῃ [.β] [..α] ἑκατονταπλασίονα [..β] [...α] νῦν [...α´] ἐν τω
       καιρῷ τούτῳ [..β´] [...α] οἰκίας [...β] καὶ ἀδελφοὺς [...γ] καὶ ἀδελφὰς
       [...δ] καὶ μητέρας [...ε] καὶ τέκνα [...ζ] καὶ ἀγροὺς [...η] μετὰ
       διωγμῶν,
       [.β´] [..α] καὶ ἐν τω αἰῶνι τῷ ἐρχομένῳ [..α´] ζωὴν αἰώνιον.
β´   ³¹[α] πολλοὶ δὲ ἔσονται [β] πρῶτοι ἔσχατοι [β´] καὶ [οἱ] ἔσχατοι
       πρῶτοι.

Section A, part α, tells how 'on the way' a rich man 'runs' up to Jesus to question him about 'inheriting eternal life'. 'Entry into life' is an issue twice raised by Jesus in Day Seventeen (9.30-50, in 9.43,45), day three of the first sub-Series (of this Series). It is, therefore, one of the correspondences between the first and second sub-Series (of this Series), for this Day begins the second sub-Series. (For references also to the 'Kingdom of God', see the discussion at the end of Day Eighteen's examination.) 'Eternal life' is a phrase which is found again, later in this Day's telling, at v.30 (and nowhere else in the Gospel). In part β, the rich man's address to Jesus, "Good Teacher..." is questioned by Jesus, before he himself questions the man as to his understanding of the law. The part concludes with the man's answer, prefaced now by "Teacher" only. Part β' completes the section: challenged to sell what he has and to give it to the poor, and invited to follow Jesus, the man walks away sad.

Section A (10.17-22) introduces the issues: 1) concerning 'riches' and 'eternal life' (see 10.17,21,22) which is addressed in section B (vv.23-27); and 2) concerning 'giving up what one has and following Jesus' (see 10.21), which is addressed in section B' (vv.28-31). Again Mark's three-part rhetorical method is in evidence, whereby A sets up B and B': it distinguishes vv.17-31 as his own composition. It is difficult to define which if any of these units (but v.31) had an earlier separate existence: I cannot, therefore, agree with Bultmann that sections B and B' are 'supplements' only, nor with Hooker, or others that the parts pre-existed independently.

In Section B, part α, Jesus raises the issue of riches and entry into the kingdom of God (three times in this section: the phrase is synonymous with 'eternal life'). Parts β and β' develop Jesus' teaching on the subject. A unique address by Jesus of the disciples appears, Τέκνα (see the discussion on the role of the central Day of this Series, Day Eighteen). In Section B', part α, Peter raises the issue of leaving "all" and following Jesus, and parts β and β' develop the teaching of Jesus on this: leaving "all" (in part β) is both possessions (house and fields) and family, and (in part β'), additionally status. Giving up the first of these, nevertheless, is rewarded in kind "in this time" (v.30b), and with eternal life "in the age to come" (v.30c).

On 10.17-31, Mack states, "This material belongs to a section of Mark that is notoriously difficult to parse (Mark 9.38-10.31). The section falls between the second and third prediction units, and appears to serve a function similar to that of the "confession of Peter" (for the first prediction unit) and the transfiguration (for the second prediction unit) by preparing for the prediction and for a set of discipleship sayings to follow."[32] My observation is that it is expressedly the function of 10.17-31. Simply, Mark *has* begun his

---

[32] Mack, *Rhetoric...*, p.54.

second sub-Series of this Series in a way that reflects the beginning of his first. (9.38-10.31 is much easier to parse, as other passages too, when one takes account of Mark's Days and his Series of Days.)

Additionally, we may note Mark's reference to "gospel" in both these sub-Series' opening Days, at 8.35 and 10.29. Its mention further links these Days. Altogether the word appears only four times in his Gospel narrative. Outside of this third Series, it is found only in 13.10, where it combines with "the Gentiles", and in 14.9, the middle Day of the final Series, where it is linked with the "world". In the Prologue, it is found three times (1.1,14,15). In the longer ending, it is found once (16.15), where it is linked with "the world" and "all creation"[33]. We will see in Chapter 8 that the word "gospel" has its significance in terms of Mark's overall plan for reasons of its incidence.

For further parallels with the teaching content of this Day, see my presentations on 8.34-37 and 9.35 (in my analyses of Days Fifteen and Seventeen, the first and third Days of the first sub-Series of this Series). We may observe too how Days Seventeen and this Day end with concise sayings, 9.50 (on "salt") and 10.31 (on "first" and "last")[34]. For other reasons as well, such as teachings on "the Kingdom of God", and the setting which after a Day's break (in the middle Day of the Series) is 'on the way' again (as first introduced in Day Fifteen), we may observe that this Day's telling does indeed function in Mark's scheme as the first of a new threesome of Days.

Day Twenty: 10.32-45:

The Day begins, as we observed under Day Eighteen, with another reference to ἐν τῇ ὁδῷ[35], but now 'the way' is qualified, as the way 'to Jerusalem'. This Day is the second Day of this new threesome of

---

[33] See my discussion under Day 18 on Genesis and the creation story, and its possible influence in Mark's arranging of his "Gospel".

[34] 9.34,35; 10.31 and 10.43,44 all beg comparison. 9.34,35 (in Day 17), in response to "greater" has a single saying on "first" and "last", to which "and servant of all" is attached. 10.31 (Day 19) has a double, reverse saying: "first"/"last"; "last"/"first". And 10.43,44 (Day 20), in response to "great" has "servant"; and in response to "first" has "slave of all". They demonstrate a close relationship. They clearly link sub-Series one with sub-Series two, but clearly, in the last of these we discern the Series' final development of such issues.

[35] See 8.27, 9.30/33, 10.17 for similar Day-beginnings.

Days, and as on Days Fifteen (8.27-9.1) and Seventeen (9.30-50), it includes, early in the telling, the third of the three similar 'Son of man' predictions by Jesus, by which he says what is going to happen to him. Only now the earlier predictions are doubly qualified: what will happen to Jesus will happen to him in Jerusalem (vv.33,34); and what will happen to him (in the co-sequent Day of the following and final Series)[36] will be at the hands of the "Gentiles". Section A records these matters, and in part α, expressed by four imperfects expressing continuous action, Jesus leads the way to the astonishment and fear of those behind him[37]. The Day's presentation is another, simple ABB' scheme[38]. The contents set it apart, however. But for the introduction which refers to "the ones following" (v.32), the Day's episodes include only Jesus and "the twelve"[39] in the telling. And here attaches an important point. Just as in the first sub-Series of this Series, in matters of Jesus' disclosures to his disciples of his death and resurrection, (8.30, 9.30,31) and of his Sonship of God (9.9), here also, in the second sub-Series, we see that Jesus' disclosures of his death and resurrection are for a limited audience. Here, expressedly, it is to "the twelve" alone.

This Day's sections are: A, vv.32-34; B, vv.35-41; B', vv.42-45. Taylor, Nineham, Schweizer and Hooker all describe the limits of these units as vv.32-34; vv.35-40; and vv.41-45.[40] The reason for my differing with them again is due, as before, to discerning Mark's rhetorical method. I interpret Mark's method in such a way that v.42 begins section B', with Jesus calling his disciples to him. V.42 (itself an [α] [β] [β'] structure) best introduces the new pericope with a description of the characters present. On the conclusion to section B, I read vv.40 and 41 as performing [β] [β']

---

[36] "... the Gentiles,... will mock him and spit on him, flog him and kill him." cf. Day 27: the Gentiles flog Jesus, mock him, spit on him, and kill him.

[37] We observe in v.32 that these emotions precede the third prediction. Could it be that the disciples have understanding now, *before* Jesus tells them in more detail what is to happen?

[38] For other 'simple' ABB' constructions of Days so far uncovered, see Days Two, Eleven, Twelve, Fourteen, Fifteen, Eighteen and Nineteen. Days Seven, Nine, Ten and Seventeen are the larger 'composite' ABB' constructions.

[39] Day Seventeen, 9.30-50, is the next nearest to telling that only Jesus and the 'twelve' were present (vv.30,35). Jesus sets a child in their midst (v.36), so others are about.

[40] Taylor, *The Gospel...*, pp.436-443; Nineham, *Saint Mark*, pp.277-280 (for Nineham 10.32-52 should be read together); Schweizer, *The Good News...*, pp.216-218; and Hooker, *The Gospel...*, pp.244-246.

functions. What is 'said' by Jesus (in v.40) is 'heard' by the disciples and provokes their angry response to James and John (in v.41) for the question they had put to Jesus (in v.37). Sections B and B' hold together well, because (in B') Jesus speaks to them all as he answered James and John (in B). Discipleship and the want of seats of "lordship" and "authority" (as James and John wanted, each side of Jesus 'in his glory') are not compatible. The concluding verses, vv.43b-45, recall the predictions of the introductory section A: servanthood is expected of disciples, because Jesus himself has come "to serve and to give his life...".

Clearly, this Day's telling, the second of this sub-Series of three, begs comparison with the transfiguration story of Day Sixteen, the second Day of the first sub-Series of three. Day Sixteen tells about two who *meet* with Jesus in his glory. Day Twenty tells about two who would *sit* with Jesus in his glory. The first are Moses and Elijah, representative of the Law and the Prophets, or leaders of the Old Covenant. The second are James and John who, with the other disciples, have been called to leadership under the New Covenant. Specifically, in Day Twenty's telling, the disciples are taught by Jesus about the qualities of leadership which he expects from them. His illustration is not that their leadership must be like that of the leaders of Moses and Elijah. The disciples might not have aspired too easily to such. Rather, it is that their leadership must not be anything like that of the leaders of the "Gentiles" (v.42). In v.33, τοῖς ἔθνεσιν is well translated "to the Gentiles". In v.42, τῶν ἐθνῶν could be translated "of the nations", to include both Israel and Gentile nations, because Jesus nowhere commends Israel's leadership (see 6.34 for an indication of this).

Under the examination of Day Nineteen, on page 224, I drew attention to the importance of Mark's distribution of the word "gospel" in matters of understanding Mark's plan. Outside of the Prologue, it links to "Jesus" (in 8.35, 10.29), "the world" (in 14.9, 16.15), "all creation" (in 16.15) and "the Gentiles" (in 13.10). I here draw attention similarly to the importance of the word meaning either "Gentiles" or "nations". References include the above, 10.33 and v.42, and in addition only: 11.17, 13.8,10. These are found solely in

THE THIRD SERIES

the second and third Days of the final Series. In chapter 8, we will discuss Mark's spared use of both.

The literary structure of Day Twenty, with its many corresponding details, is viewed as:

A α[α]³²[.α] Ησαν δὲ <u>ἐν τῇ ὁδῷ</u> [.α'] <u>ἀναβαίνοντες εἰς Ἱεροσόλυμα</u>,
   [β]   [.α] καὶ ἦν προάγων αὐτοὺς ὁ Ἰησοῦς, [.α'] καὶ ἐθαμβοῦντο,
   [β']   [.α] οἱ δὲ <u>ἀκολουθοῦντες</u> [.α'] ἐφοβοῦντο.
  β[α] καὶ παραλαβὼν πάλιν τοὺς δώδεκα
    [β] ἤρξατο <u>αὐτοῖς λέγειν</u>
    [β'] τὰ μέλλοντα <u>αὐτῷ</u> συμβαί<u>νειν</u>,
  β'[α] ³³[.α] [..α] ὅτι Ἰδοὺ [..α'] <u>ἀναβαίνομεν εἰς Ἱεροσόλυμα</u>,
    [.β] [..α] καὶ <u>ὁ υἱὸς τοῦ ἀνθρώπου</u> παραδοθήσεται
      [..β] τοῖς ἀρχιερεῦσιν [..β'] καὶ τοῖς γραμματεῦσιν,
    [.β'] καὶ κατακρινοῦσιν αὐτὸν θανάτῳ
   [β]   [.α] καὶ παραδώσουσιν αὐτὸν <u>τοῖς ἔθνεσιν</u>
      ³⁴ [.β] καὶ <u>ἐμπαίξουσιν αὐτῷ</u>
      [.β'] καὶ <u>ἐμπτύσουσιν αὐτῷ</u>
   [β']   [.α] καὶ μαστιγώσουσιν αὐτὸν
      [.β] καὶ ἀποκτενοῦσιν,
      [.β'] καὶ μετὰ τρεῖς ἡμέρας ἀναστήσεται.

B α[α] ³⁵[.α] [..α] Καὶ <u>προσπορεύονται</u> αὐτῷ [..β] Ἰάκωβος καὶ Ἰωάννης
   [..β'] οἱ υἱοὶ Ζεβεδαίου [.α'] [..α] <u>λέγοντες</u> αὐτῷ, [..α'] Διδάσκαλε,
   [β]   [.α] <u>θέλομεν</u> [.β] ἵνα ὃ ἐὰν <u>αἰτήσωμέν</u> σε [.β'] <u>ποιήσῃς</u> ἡμῖν.
  [β'] ³⁶[.α] <u>ὁ δὲ εἶπεν αὐτοῖς,</u> [.β] Τί <u>θέλετε</u> [με] [.β'] <u>ποιήσω</u> ὑμῖν;
  β[α] ³⁷[.α] <u>οἱ δὲ εἶπαν αὐτῷ,</u> [.α'] [..α] <u>Δὸς</u> ἡμῖν [..β] [...α] ἵνα <u>εἷς σου ἐκ δεξιῶν</u> [...α'] καὶ <u>εἷς ἐξ ἀριστερῶν</u> [..β'] <u>καθίσωμεν</u> ἐν τῇ δόξῃ σου.
   [β] ³⁸[.α] <u>ὁ δὲ Ἰησοῦς εἶπεν αὐτοῖς,</u> [.β] Οὐκ οἴδατε [.β'] τί <u>αἰτεῖσθε</u>.
    [.β] [..α] <u>δύνασθε πιεῖν τὸ ποτήριον</u> [..α'] <u>ὃ ἐγὼ πίνω</u>,
    [.β'] [..α] ἢ <u>τὸ βάπτισμα</u> [..β] <u>ὃ ἐγὼ βαπτίζομαι</u> [..β'] <u>βαπτισθῆναι</u>;
  [β'] ³⁹[.α] <u>οἱ δὲ εἶπαν αὐτῷ</u>, [.α'] <u>Δυνάμεθα</u>.
  β'[α] [.α] <u>ὁ δὲ Ἰησοῦς εἶπεν αὐτοῖς,</u>
    [.β] [..α] <u>Τὸ ποτήριον</u> [..β] <u>ὃ ἐγὼ πίνω</u> [..β'] <u>πίεσθε</u>
    [.β'] [..α] καὶ τὸ βάπτισμα [..β] <u>ὃ ἐγὼ βαπτίζομαι</u>
      [..β'] <u>βαπτισθήσεσθε</u>,
   [β] ⁴⁰[.α] [..α] τὸ δὲ <u>καθίσαι</u> [..β] <u>ἐκ δεξιῶν μου</u> [..β'] ἢ <u>ἐξ εὐωνύμων</u>
    [.β] οὐκ ἔστιν ἐμὸν <u>δοῦναι</u>, [.β'] ἀλλ' οἷς ἡτοίμασται.
   [β'] ⁴¹[.α] καὶ ἀκούσαντες [.β] οἱ δέκα ἤρξαντο ἀγανακτεῖν [.β'] περὶ Ἰακώβου καὶ Ἰωάννου.

B'α[α]⁴²[.α] Καὶ προσκαλεσάμενος <u>αὐτοὺς</u> [.β] ὁ Ἰησοῦς λέγει <u>αὐτοῖς</u>,
  [.β'] <u>Οἴδατε</u>
 [β] [.α] ὅτι οἱ δοκοῦντες ἄρχειν <u>τῶν ἐθνῶν</u> [.α'] <u>κατακυριεύουσιν</u>
  <u>αὐτῶν</u>
 [β'] καὶ οἱ μεγάλοι αὐτῶν <u>κατεξουσιάζουσιν</u> αὐτῶν.
β[α] ⁴³[.α] οὐχ οὕτως δέ [.β] ἐστιν [.β'] <u>ἐν ὑμῖν</u>·
 [β] [.α] ἀλλ' <u>ὃς ἂν θέλῃ</u> [.β] μέγας γενέσθαι <u>ἐν ὑμῖν</u>, [.β'] <u>ἔσται</u> ὑμῶν
  <u>διάκονος</u>,
 [β'] ⁴⁴[.α] καὶ <u>ὃς ἂν θέλῃ</u> [.β] <u>ἐν ὑμῖν</u> εἶναι πρῶτος, [.β'] <u>ἔσται</u> πάντων
  <u>δοῦλος</u>·
β'[α] ⁴⁵[.α] καὶ γὰρ <u>ὁ υἱὸς τοῦ ἀνθρώπου</u> [.β] οὐκ ἦλθεν [.β'] <u>διακονηθῆναι</u>
 [β] ἀλλὰ <u>διακονῆσαι</u>
 [β'] [.α] καὶ δοῦναι τὴν ψυχὴν αὐτοῦ [.β] λύτρον [.β'] ἀντὶ πολλῶν.

Day Twenty-one: 10.46-52:

This last Day of this second of two middle Series begins in a manner previously much observed: see Days One, Two, Three, Six, Eight and Fourteen. All begin with a clear definition of a new geographical location, and similar presentation. However, none is as similar for its opening line as Day Fourteen (8.22-26) which is the last Day of the first of these two middle Series. We compare the opening lines:

  Day Fourteen: <u>Καὶ ἔρχονται εἰς</u> Βηθσαϊδάν
  Day Twenty-one: <u>Καὶ ἔρχονται εἰς</u> Ἰεριχώ

For a discussion on the other similarities of these two Days, for the only reports of healings of blind people in the Gospel, see Day Fourteen.

Additional to these considerations, there is also the identification of Mark's use of the introductory formula as discussed under Day Eleven, by which he records both the place of departure and the place of arrival, thus signifying a passing of days, untold by him, which the journeys would have covered[41]. What is of particular interest here is that Mark reverses the order: the naming of the place of arrival precedes the naming of the place (the same place, Jericho) of departure:

---

[41] See the Days beginning 6.1, 53, 7.24, 31, 8.27, 9.30/33, 10.1 for their similar introductory pieces.

Καὶ ἔρχονται εἰς Ἰεριχώ.
Καὶ ἐκπορευομένου αὐτοῦ ἀπὸ Ἰεριχω ...

Whether we should interpret days, hours or just minutes between arrival and departure Mark gives us really no clue here. Given the other uses of this introductory formula, however, which infer 'days' spent in journey-time, and given that Jericho was a major town on Jesus' route to Jerusalem and that it is reasonable to consider that he might have stayed there, it may be considered more likely that Mark meant the interpretion to be that he stayed a day or more. It is clearly not an essential detail in the narrative's purpose, but it is an issue Mark himself raises by his construction and one which caused the scribe of Codex Alexandrinus a problem. He was persuaded that Καὶ ἔρχονται εἰς Ἰεριχώ belonged with the contents preceding it, and introduced a space between it and Mark's next line. It is clear, however, from consideration of Mark's rhetorical method (of αββ´, and his repeated use of the introductory formula) that the scene is set in this fashion for the telling of the story of Day Twenty-one. Mark's introduction is 10.46 in full. It is again on "the way"[42], because Bartimaeus is seated παρὰ τὴν ὁδόν.

The literary structure of Day Twenty-one is viewed as:

A α   ⁴⁶Καὶ ἔρχονται εἰς Ἰεριχώ.
  β   [α] Καὶ ἐκπορευομένου αὐτοῦ ἀπὸ Ἰεριχω [β] καὶ τῶν μαθητῶν αὐτοῦ [β´] καὶ ὄχλου ἱκανοῦ
  β´   [α] ὁ υἱὸς Τιμαίου Βαρτιμαῖος [β] τυφλὸς προσαίτης [β´] ἐκάθητο παρὰ τὴν ὁδόν.

B α[α] ⁴⁷[.α] Καὶ ἀκούσας [.β] ὅτι Ἰησοῦς [.β´] ὁ Ναζαρηνός ἐστιν
    [β]   [.α] ἤρξατο κράζειν [.α´] καὶ λέγειν,
    [β´]   [.α] Υἱὲ Δαυὶδ [.β] Ἰησοῦ, [.β´] ἐλέησόν με.
  β[α] ⁴⁸[.α] καὶ ἐπετίμων αὐτῷ πολλοὶ [.α´] ἵνα σιωπήσῃ·
    [β]   [.α] ὁ δὲ πολλῷ μᾶλλον ἔκραζεν,
    [β´]   [.α] Υἱὲ Δαυίδ, [.α´] ἐλέησόν με.
  β´[α] ⁴⁹[.α] καὶ στὰς [β] ὁ Ἰησοῦς εἶπεν, [.β] Φωνήσατε αὐτόν.
    [β]   [.α] καὶ φωνοῦσιν τὸν τυφλὸν [.β] λέγοντες αὐτῷ,
    [β´]   [.α] Θάρσει, [.β] ἔγειρε, [.β´] φωνεῖ σε.

---

[42] See the Days of this Series: the first, third, fifth and sixth days (Days Fifteen, Seventeen, Nineteen and Twenty) and the presentation of the matter under Day Eighteen.

Β‛α ⁵⁰ [α] Ὁ δὲ ἀποβαλὼν τὸ ἱμάτιον αὐτοῦ [β] ἀναπηδήσας [β‛] ἦλθεν
       πρὸς τὸν Ἰησοῦν.
   β[α] ⁵¹ [.α] καὶ ἀποκριθεὶς αὐτῳ [.α‛] <u>ὁ Ἰησοῦς εἶπεν,</u>
     [β] [.α] Τί σοι θέλεις [.α‛] ποιήσω;
     [β‛] [.α] ὁ δὲ τυφλὸς <u>εἶπεν αὐτῷ,</u> [.β] Ραββουνι, [.β‛] ἵνα <u>ἀναβλέψω.</u>
   β‛[α] ⁵² [.α] καὶ ὁ Ἰησοῦς <u>εἶπεν αὐτῷ,</u> [.β] Ὕπαγε, [.β‛] ἡ πίστις σου
       σέσωκέν σε.
     [β] [.α] καὶ εὐθὺς <u>ἀνέβλεψεν,</u>
     [β‛] [.α] καὶ ἠκολούθει αὐτῷ [.α‛] <u>ἐν τῇ ὁδῷ.</u>

Again, the structure is in a simple ABB' form, where A is introductory, B is the first development, and B' is the second and completing development. In literary-structural terms it is a perfect example of how Mark writes, and of how any rhetor might complete a sub-Series and a Series at the same time. The introductory section A begins with an emphatic opening. Jericho is some fifteen miles away only from Jerusalem. (The fact that this geographical disclosure stands alone in α is suggestive of a pause to the reader in his/her reading aloud for Mark's audience. The disclosure itself is surely a matter for contemplation.) The journey to Jerusalem is now so very near to its end. The introductory section completes the details which are essential to the story being told: it takes place when they leave Jericho; the disciples and a "considerable" crowd are present (it is the only time in the Gospel we read ἱκανοῦ), also a blind beggar who is named (unlike the vast majority of the characters in the Gospel to whom Jesus ministers), and who sits παρὰ τὴν ὁδόν (the Day's telling closes with a second mention of this significant Series' phrase, and in a most resonant way).

Section B tells how the blind beggar attracts Jesus' attention. The balance of this presentation of Mark's αββ‛ scheme is impressive indeed. And the Christological disclosure is no less impressive. In part α, we meet firstly with a title for Jesus not used since Day One, 1.24: the blind man hears that "it is Jesus the Nazarene"[43] (v.47); and it is followed by another title not used at all before in the Gospel: in the first public and unrebuked (by Jesus, that is) recognition of its kind, this 'blind' man knows ('sees') who Jesus is: he is the "Son of

---

[43] The term, "Jesus of Nazareth", is used sparingly and, therefore, significantly by Mark, in 1.24, 10.47, 14.67 and 16.6. It is to be found in an introductory sense in 1.9, "Jesus came from Nazareth...". In Chapter 8 we will judge its importance in Mark's presentation.

David". Part β tells how he is "rebuked"[44] by "many" which causes him "the much more to cry out, Son of David...". (Firstly, we note that we have come across something like this before, in 7.36, in the same second sub-Series of the first of these two middle Sections, though there it is Jesus who is ordering silence. Secondly, we note that Mark's audience hear the title twice. Mark is promoting the application of this messianic title to Jesus[45].) Part β' concludes section B with Jesus' response to Bartimaeus who had managed to catch his attention: Jesus said, "Call him"; and in indirect and direct speech (in balancing [β] and [β'] sub-parts) he is called.

Section B' tells how Bartimaeus received his physical sight. In part α, he responds to the call and goes to Jesus; in part β, he tells Jesus that he wants to see again; and in part β', he sees again (*cf.* Ὕπαγε, ἡ πίστις σου σέσωκέν σε with 5.34, the same words of Jesus to the woman who is healed, though ὕπαγε follows ἡ πίστις σου σέσωκέν σε: it is significant because Day Seven is the last Day of the first Series). He also begins to *follow* Jesus (consider the references to "following" in the Series: 8.35, 9.38 *bis*, 10.21, 28 and 32) ἐν τῇ ὁδῷ [46].

As Hooker says, "The story is an appropriate climax to a section which has spelt out the meaning of discipleship... It is a final challenge to his readers to join Bartimaeus in following Jesus on the road (or 'way') of discipleship, even though that road leads to Jerusalem and all that happens there"[47]. It is a fitting climax too to the sub-Series of Days Nineteen, Twenty and Twenty-one which after the middle Day's "testing" of Jesus by Pharisees, and its teaching on "receiving" the kingdom of God as a gift (in Day Eighteen, 10.1-16), returns to Christological matters and teachings on discipleship. This Day's setting well succeeds that of 10.32: Jesus is now only fifteen

---

[44] I agree with Rienecker that the imperfect here represents continuous action, though it is border-line with inceptive. We read: Bartimaeus "begins to cry out and to say...", and judge "the crying out" continues; hence also the rebuking begins and continues too (Fritz Rienecker, *A Linguistic Key...*).

[45] The title, "Son of David" became a familiar title for the messianic king in later Jewish literature (its first known use is in Pss. Sol. 17.21) and would have been understood in that sense by Mark, who nevertheless demonstrates later that it is not a fully adequate title for Jesus (12.35-37).

[46] For a discussion on the importance of ἐν τῇ ὁδῷ see 1) under Day Fifteen.

[47] Hooker, *The Gospel...*, p.252.

miles from Jerusalem and just a short distance, therefore, from his journey's goal.

This sub-Series of Days Nineteen, Twenty and Twenty-One exhibits another ABB' arrangement. Day Nineteen picks up the themes of the first sub-Series, after the Series' middle Day's different emphases. It emphatically makes a new beginning "on the way", which becomes in the second Day (Day Twenty's telling) "the way up to Jerusalem", and in the third becomes "the way out of Jericho" (the last lap of the journey is *already begun*). Days B and B' in turn, in their introductory geographical statements, develop and announce with exactitude what was only an opening generality. I realise that this argument sits uneasily as we have learned previously not to define the structure of a threesome of Days, either by geographical location, or by which Days are consecutive, and not. Nevertheless, it would seem to be the case that Mark has indeed concluded this Series in this manner, simply because the Series itself does report Jesus' journey to Jerusalem, to the cross and glory. Clearly, to be consistent, however, we should look for an accompanying development in his presentation of Jesus' teaching of the disciples It is this that established the ABB' structure of the first sub-Series.

The first day of this threesome establishes that the disciples have already left everything behind to follow Jesus. The rich man was not prepared to do that. The second day begins with Jesus spelling out what is going to happen to him in Jerusalem, but two of his disciples still want "glory" for themselves. Though they say that they are able to drink the same cup and be baptised with the same baptism as Jesus, they show they do not understand what Jesus is asking them. The third Day tells how a "blind man" who knows something of Jesus' status has "faith" to be healed. People with "faith" will have sight. People who understand will follow Jesus' way of suffering to glory. This story of the healing of blind Bartimaeus has the same function as the previous Series' concluding story. Only now it is more simply interpreted; "understanding" comes through "faith". The second and third Days of this Series deal with this issue, and are to be seen as a pair in the sub-Series. The structure is ABB'.

A Summary of the Third Series of Seven Days:

This third Series of Seven Days is structured ABA', where, as before, A represents the first sub-Series/threesome of Days and A' the last sub-Series/threesome of Days around a central, pivotal Day, B. As is discussed under the middle Day, Day Eighteen, this fulcrum to the Series is established neither essentially by absences of Christological statement and oft-repeated phrases in the Series (such as ἐν τῇ ὁδῷ), nor by elements of story-content which are included there and nowhere else in the Series, such as the "testing" of Jesus by Pharisees and the issues of marriage and divorce concerning which Jesus re-interprets the Mosaic Law. The Day is more than a buffer between the two sub-Series of three Days for which Jesus' own Christological statements about his suffering, death and resurrection and his servanthood undergird his teachings on discipleship. The middle Day both interprets and is interpreted by the Sub-Series. The kingdom of God is a gift to be received like a child, who trusts, and it is a gift of Jesus, as a result of his suffering, dying and resurrection, which promises repeated blessings. All discipleship hinges on receiving this gift.

We observe, therefore, in this Series as in the first two, that the 'arrangement' of Days demonstrates application of ancient rhetorical conventions whereby there is a smoothing of the sharp edges of the transitional central turning point and the material around it. The accumulated evidence from the examination of the first three Series of the Gospel suggests the possibility of a modified annotation. Clearly, Mark's 'arrangement' could be summed up as three three-Day sub-Series which overlap, where the first sub-Series is described by ABB', the second by ABA', and the third by ABB':

$$\begin{array}{ccc} A & B & \underline{B'} \\ & & \underline{A} \quad B \quad \underline{A'} \\ & & \underline{A} \quad B \quad B' \end{array}$$

All this is, of course, is an elaboration only of the summary ABA' Series form, but it does perhaps more clearly express Mark's method, that is what he had in his mind as he composed his Series.

Other rhetorical features in this particular Series include the *inclusio* of the first and last Days, of "the Christ" in the first, and of

"Son of David" in the last. We have seen in the summary of the second Series (page 194) already how a link-motif smooths the transition between this Series and the former one (the two-stage healing/the two-stage revelation), and how an anastrophe functions in the same way between the ending of this Series and the beginning of the next ("Son of David"/"our father David").

Clearly the defining of this Series, in literary-structural terms, establishes three points which are important to the assessment of the views of Wrede and many others on what constituted Mark's "leading idea", or purpose in constructing his Gospel. For them, it was on the basis that Jesus' messiahship was to be kept secret until after his resurrection (the key verse for which is 9.9). The three points are: 1) the first Day's telling of this Series, in 8.30, introduces the "*Messianic secret*" (specifically) into the Gospel for the first time; 2) the last Day's telling, in 10.47,48, implies that Jesus' Messianic *status* is a secret no longer (because Jesus himself did not rebuke Bartimaeus for what he was crying out); and 3) between these we read about disclosures which were for the disciples alone, about other aspects of Jesus' divine status, also his suffering, death and resurrection. What Mark has given his audience in his third Series is what Jesus wanted his disciples to know at this stage of his mission, and what at this stage he did not want the crowds to know. The logic Mark demonstrates clearly is that the people could not have been told what was going to happen to him in Jerusalem. And the logic continues surely: it could only be after his death and resurrection that all could know fully who he was and what his purpose had been from the beginning. The people could not have been expected *knowingly* to crucify their Messiah and the Son of God (to which 9.9 specifically refers), in order to establish a new Covenant between God and the world[48].

We will return to these matters in Chapter 8. For the present, my view, shaped by the above and by other information which will be discussed, is that a restricting of public information about Jesus' messiahship, and certain aspects about it, simply *had* to be

---

[48] 14.24 is supremely important in this regard. In the telling of the Passion, in the first Day's telling of the final sub-Series of the Gospel, we find this single, specific, Gospel reference to "the covenant". Jesus fulfils Zech. 9.11. In the first Day's telling of the Series and of the first sub-Series, therefore, Jesus' entry into Jerusalem fulfils Zech. 9.9. We will discuss this and other features of Mark's balance in the following Chapter.

maintained until after Jesus' resurrection. Only then *could there truly be* "good news" for "the world"[49].

The title I give this Series, following the style of my titling of the earlier Series, is "The Days of Jesus' Journeying to Jerusalem, to the Cross and Glory."

Again, last of all in summarising a Series we give consideration to the number of days Mark indicates that have passed, even though he has chosen to report only seven in full in a seven Day Series format. The information, where he supplies it, is exclusive to his Days' introductory pieces. Between the Second and the Third Series there is clearly no information about the number of days Jesus stayed in Bethsaida; he may have left there the day following Day Fourteen of Mark's plan, or he may have stayed some days. Further, the journey between Bethsaida and Caesarea Philippi of about 36 miles may have taken two days. Between the tellings of the first and second days, Mark informs his audience that "six" days passed (9.2). (Though he has been specific here we cannot be sure, however, that the number has not been adopted from Exodus 24.16, and that he used it typologically.) Not knowing where the mount of transfiguration was and not knowing how Mark defined Galilee (refer: 9.30) makes it impossible to assess the days of Jesus' journeying to Capernaum prior to the third Day's telling. The fourth Day's report is prefaced with the journey Jesus made from Capernaum to Judea and beyond the Jordan. He rises (10.1) 'from sleep' and began an 80 mile journey which could have taken him four to five days, or more if he had stayed in each place *en route*. At the beginning of the fifth Day's report Jesus is "on the way", but we are not told where so there is no way of knowing here how many days had passed. The 'way' becomes the 'way to Jerusalem' (in 10.32) at the beginning of the sixth day; again not knowing the place of departure or the place of arrival before the day's report is given we are here stymied too. Because Jesus and his disciples then arrived in Jericho (and maybe stayed a day or two before leaving, at which point the event of the seventh day is told) we may estimate that the miles travelled between the end of day four and the beginning of day seven

---

[49] We note aspects of Jesus' messiahship that *were* told to the crowd: see 8.38-9.1, in the context of 8.34. This verse establishes Jesus' want of the crowd to hear him on the issues too of 8.34-37. For 'the world' and 'the gospel', see 16.15.

were 10 to 15 only, and therefore, that the passing of other, unreported days would have been due more to Jesus staying in places *en route* than on actual travelling.

The impression we gain overall is that Mark viewed this stage in Jesus' mission as covering a number of weeks. It is not so much the total number of days that counts, but the impression Mark gives, by his method of story-telling.

A Tabular Summary of the literary-structure of the Third Seven Days:

DAYS: number identified in series	1	2	3	4	5	6	7
number identified in Gospel	15	16	17	18	19	20	21
chapters and verses	8.27-9.1	9.2-29	9.30-50	10.1-16	10.17-31	10.32-45	10.46-52
SERIES' STRUCTURE	A	A	A	B	A'	A'	A'
DAYS: in literary-terms, in series	A	B	B'		A	B	B'
DAYS' sections	A / A'	AA' / AA'	A / B / B'	A	A	A	A
DAYS' sectional sub-divisions	A B B' A B B'	A B B' A B B' A B B' A B B'	A B B' A B B' A B B'	A B B'	A B B'	A B B'	A B B'
DAYS' number of verses	13	28	19	16	15	14	7
SUB-SERIES' number of verses	60	60	60		36	36	36
SERIES' number of verses	112						

Addendum to the analysis of "The Third Seven Days":

No new signifiers of literary-structural division between Days are identified in this Series' analysis that were not identified in the analyses of the first two Series. On the sizes of Mark's rhetorical units of Days we observe that the range is from 7 to 28 verses, a factor of four only, which may be compared with a factor of ten for the first Series and a factor of just less than six for the second Series. We may surmise that this demonstrates that Mark exercised a greater control over the contents of his Day-presentations here than he did in the first two Series. It begs, of course, the question, "Why?" The answer may be that he *created* more of the contents of these Day's tellings than he did in the earlier Series. His repetitions, and developments of Jesus' predictions about his suffering, death and resurrection may well be said to be one signal that implies that he was short of 'tradition' here.

A Comparison of the Second and Third Series of Seven Days:

Now that we have completed separate examinations of the literary-structures of the two middle Series of the Gospel, we can determine what if any relationship Mark deemed them to have in his overall Gospel scheme. At various points in the presentations of the two Series already we have touched on some clear points of contact between them. Their titles again are: Series Two: "Days of Increase in the Mission of Jesus"; and Series Three: "The Days of Jesus' Journeying to Jerusalem, to the Cross and Glory". As all the Series are structured in the same way as each other (A:B:A', where A and A' represent sub-Series of three Days, around a central pivotal Day, B) there is no structural argument for seeing Series Two and Three in parallel, save that their number of verses overall are 119 and 112 respectively and that they so compare more or less equally for size when seen against Series One which has 172 verses and Series Four which has 239 verses.

Under the examinations of Days Eight and Fifteen, we saw how these first Days of both Series begin remarkably similarly, and how they contain common subject matter on issues raised in regard to the identity of Jesus (*cf.* 6.14b,15 and 8.28) and on the death of John the Baptist, in Day Eight, which prefigures what Jesus discloses for the first time about his own death, in Day Fifteen. Both opening Days introduce issues of 'discipleship' which are developed in the Series. Under the examinations of Days Fourteen and Twenty-one, the last Days of each Series, we noted the fact that nowhere else in the Gospel are there to be found stories of healings of blind people. These also are illustrative of discipleship matters, as many scholars and commentators have judged previously. We note here, further, that these two Days, in their telling, are the shortest in the Gospel. Given that the central, pivotal Days in both Series begin in very similar ways (see under Days Eleven and Eighteen), the two middle Series not only begin and end in like manner but, therefore, also begin 'turning' at their centre in like manner. We observe also that the two middle Days raise issues of Jewish/Gentile tensions.

Further literary-structural contact between the two middle Series is established by the contents of the second and sixth Days of each, in terms of their intra-Series and inter-Series relationships. The two 'feedings' of the Second Series (in Days Nine and Thirteen) and the two 'glory-episodes' of the Third Series (in Days Sixteen and Twenty) provide messianic disclosures of similar kinds. It is apparent that the second days of each Series reveal fulfilments of Jewish expectations, and their parallels, the sixth days, focus on Gentiles.

It is reasonable to conclude, therefore, that Mark composed these two Series each with the other in mind, as parallel, central Series in his Gospel narrative scheme.

Chapter Six
The Fourth Series of Seven Days (11.1-16.8):

Day Twenty-two: 11.1-11:

The literary structure of Day Twenty-two is viewed as:

A α ¹[α] [.α] Καὶ ὅτε <u>ἐγγίζουσιν</u> [.α΄] <u>εἰς</u> Ἱεροσόλυμα [β] [.α] <u>εἰς</u> Βηθφαγὴ
    [.α΄] καὶ <u>Βηθανίαν</u> [β΄] [.α] πρὸς τὸ Ὄρος [.α΄] τῶν Ἐλαιῶν,
  β [α] <u>ἀποστέλλει</u> δύο τῶν μαθητῶν αὐτοῦ [α΄] ²καὶ <u>λέγει</u> αὐτοῖς,
  β΄ [α] Ὑπάγετε [β] <u>εἰς</u> τὴν κώμην [β΄] τὴν κατέναντι ὑμῶν.
B α [α] [.α] <u>Καὶ εὐθὺς</u> [.β] <u>εἰσπορευόμενοι</u> [.β΄] <u>εἰς</u> αὐτὴν
    [β] εὑρήσετε πῶλον <u>δεδεμένον</u>
    [β΄] [.α] <u>ἐφ'</u> ὃν [.β] οὐδεὶς οὔπω ἀνθρώπων [.β΄] <u>ἐκάθισεν·</u>
  β [α] λύσατε αὐτὸν [α΄] καὶ φέρετε.
  β΄ ³[α] [.α] [..α] Καὶ ἐάν τις [..β] ὑμῖν [..β΄] <u>εἴπῃ</u>, [.α΄] [..α] <u>Τί</u> [..β] <u>ποιεῖτε</u>
    [..β΄] τοῦτο;
    [β] [.α] <u>εἴπατε</u>, [.α΄] [..α] Ὁ <u>κύριος</u> [..β] αὐτοῦ [..β΄] χρείαν ἔχει,
    [β΄] [.α] καὶ εὐθὺς [.β] αὐτὸν ἀποστέλλει [.β΄] πάλιν ὧδε.
B΄ α ⁴[α] Καὶ ἀπῆλθον [β] [.α] καὶ <u>εὗρον πῶλον δεδεμένον</u> [.β] πρὸς θύραν
    ἔξω [.β΄] ἐπὶ τοῦ ἀμφόδου, [β΄] καὶ <u>λύουσιν αὐτόν</u>.
  β ⁵[α] [.α] καί τινες [.β] τῶν ἐκεῖ ἑστηκότων [.β΄] <u>ἔλεγον</u> αὐτοῖς, [β] <u>Τί</u>
    <u>ποιεῖτε</u> [β΄] <u>λύοντες</u> τὸν <u>πῶλον</u>;
  β΄ ⁶[α] οἱ δὲ <u>εἶπαν</u> αὐτοῖς [β] καθὼς <u>εἶπεν</u> ὁ Ἰησοῦς· [β΄] καὶ ἀφῆκαν
    αὐτούς.

A α ⁷[α] <u>Καὶ φέρουσιν</u> τὸν πῶλον πρὸς τὸν Ἰησοῦν,
    [β] καὶ <u>ἐπιβάλλουσιν</u> αὐτῳ <u>τὰ ἱμάτια αὐτῶν,</u>
    [β΄] καὶ <u>ἐκάθισεν</u> ἐπ' αὐτόν.
  β ⁸[α] καὶ πολλοὶ [β] <u>τὰ ἱμάτια αὐτῶν</u> [β΄] ἔστρωσαν εἰς τὴν ὁδόν,
  β΄ [α] ἄλλοι δὲ στιβάδας [.β] κόψαντες [.β΄] ἐκ τῶν ἀγρῶν.
B α ⁹[α] [.α] Καὶ οἱ προάγοντες [.α΄] καὶ οἱ ἀκολουθοῦντες [α΄] ἔκραζον,
  α΄ [α]   Ὡσαννά·
    [β] [.α] <u>Εὐλογημένος</u> ὁ <u>ἐρχόμενος</u> [.α΄] ἐν ὀνόματι <u>κυρίου·</u>
    ¹⁰[β΄] [.α] <u>Εὐλογημένη</u> ἡ <u>ἐρχομένη</u> βασιλεία [.α΄] τοῦ πατρὸς ἡμῶν
    Δαυίδ·
    [α΄] [.α] Ὡσαννα [.α΄] ἐν τοῖς ὑψίστοις.
B΄ α ¹¹[α] Καὶ εἰσῆλθεν [β] <u>εἰς</u> Ἱεροσόλυμα [β΄] <u>εἰς</u> τὸ ἱερόν·
  α΄ [α] καὶ περιβλεψάμενος πάντα, [β] ὀψίας ἤδη οὔσης τῆς ὥρας,
    [β΄] [.α] ἐξῆλθεν [.β] <u>εἰς</u> <u>Βηθανίαν</u> [.β΄] μετὰ τῶν δώδεκα.

The first half[1] of the Day's telling, 11.1-6, describes the preparation for Jesus' entry into Jerusalem: the second half, 11.7-11, describes the entry itself, and signals immediately the specific and most important venue, the temple, for the following two days.

The opening part A introduces the Day's initial setting, about two miles from Jerusalem, for the beginning of the preparatory activity. Jesus will enter on a colt. Parts B and B', each in the customary three parts (of α introductory and β and β' as balancing completions), conclude the episode. Zech. 9.9 is clearly the primary Old Testament text in the backgound to this Day's telling. Jesus is Jerusalem's coming King[2]. With this O.T. allusion, the first Day of the final Series begins. Again it is the first Day of a three-day sub-Series. Significantly, in 14.24, in the first Day's telling of the balancing three-day sub-Series, we find an allusion to the same coming King, Zech. 9.11. In the setting of the last supper we read literally, "this is the *blood* of *me* of the (new) *covenant*"[3].

The Entry begins in the Day's second A part with the disciples, in α, bringing the colt to Jesus: part β tells of the preparation of the colt and Jesus' sitting on it, and part β' tells of the preparation εἰς τὴν ὁδόν[4] (the detailed correspondence is τὰ ἱμάτια αὐτῶν). Part B is the part which actually tells the story of the entry: part α reads, "The ones going ahead, and the ones following kept crying out...". But, here, Mark breaks briefly from his usual rhythm: instead of β and β', we denote α' and a four part chiasm, [α] [β] [β'] [α'][5]. The moment is one of major significance in Mark's scheme: the whole of the last Series covers Jesus' journeying to Jerusalem; and the Day's telling so far has been of the preparation for the entry. What the people cried continually, to Mark therefore, warranted a chiasm[6] for

---

[1] We may note now that all Mark's opening Days of his Series are 'arranged' to an AA' (ABB':ABB') form.

[2] For the direct references to "King" in the Gospel, as the title pertains to Jesus, see: 15.2,9,12,18,26,32. All these appear in Day Twenty-seven, the sixth Day of this Series, the Day of Jesus' crucifixion.

[3] The word "covenant" occurs only here in the Gospel, though covenant issues are addressed throughout. We will discuss this later. The word "new" is supported by some mss.

[4] See 1) under Day Fifteen's analysis for discussion of εἰς τὴν ὁδόν.

[5] Neirynck notes the chiasm also: *Duality...*, p.173.

[6] Contrary to many scholars who discern chiasms at sectional levels, I have identified only one chiasm before now: 5.3-5, which is at detail level. Mark clearly knows the technique as he applies it at the higher levels of literary order, but chooses to use it very sparingly indeed

the sake of emphasis. To Ps.118.25, or more particularly to the parallel LXX, Ps.117.26, is added a central paralleling phrase, "Blessed is the coming kingdom of our *father* David". It is a description of David which is unknown in Judaism, but one which, overall, adds a messianic ingredient to the passover greeting. As we have seen also, in the summaries of Series Two and Three, it appears contrived by Mark to function as an anastrophe with "*Son* of David" in the final Day's presentation of the preceding Series. Part B' completes the Day's telling: in α, the momentous words are recorded, "And he entered into Jerusalem, into the temple"; in part a', a big hint of bathos appears to be struck: "looking around at all things, late now being the hour, he went out into Bethany with the twelve", having done no more than this. ('Bethany', in the first and last lines, is an *inclusio* for the Day's telling.) For Matthew this is unacceptable: to his parallel passage, he adds immediately Jesus' clearing of the temple. Luke follows Matthew in this[7]. But for Mark it is not bathos. O.T. prophecy is fulfilled again: see Mal. 3.1 ("Suddenly the Lord... will come to his temple.")[8]. It is a particularly important allusion, considering Mark's use of it in the opening of his Prologue. With the completion of the same he opens his final Series of the Gospel narrative. We will see below that the "temple" is truly the most important venue for the next two Days' presentations[9].

Telford[10] studies particularly the relationship between the temple and the withered fig tree which will both feature in the two Days following. He cites a number of scholars' views concerning the

---

at this lower level.

[7] In my view, Mark's Gospel was the first of the Synoptic Gospels to be written: in turn, Matthew created his, editing Mark and adding his own material; and then Luke created his, based on Mark and Matthew, adding his own material. In *Sliced Bread...* (p.54), I support Farrer who said of Q source that, "To be rid of it we have no need of a contrary hypothesis, we merely have to make St Luke's use of St Matthew intelligible" (A.M. Farrer, "On Dispensing with Q", *Studies in the Gospels*, Ed. Nineham, Blackwell, London, 1955, p.66).

[8] O.T. allusions abound in Mark's Gospel. We noted a number of them in the Series prior to this; and already we have discovered Zech. 9.9 on this first Day of this new Series and Zech. 9.11 to be one of the fifth day's allusions.

[9] Nineham (*Saint Mark*, p.294) considers it likely that the tradition attached 'the cleansing', and that Mark, "in the interests of his time-scheme", and his wish to attach "the fig tree story", created v.11. Clearly, the matter of tradition and source (see note 7) is an open question.

[10] William R. Telford, *The Barren Temple and the Withered Tree*, JSNT Suppl. Series 1, JSOT Press, Sheffield, 1980.

integrity, at the redactional level, of 11.1-13.37, and he says of it that it exhibits "editorial organisation"[11]. He recognises the three-day structure as the chronological framework, and views it as a construct of Mark[12], which begins and ends on the *Mount of Olives*[13]. In my view, Mark does indeed set here for the reader/his audience his limits of this first sub-Series of his final Series, in this way. He has demonstrated to us already in his first three Gospel Series that this is his preferred method. What Telford does not recognise, however, is that Mark's chronological framework is also his literary framework.

Day Twenty-three: 11.12-19:

Days two and three of this Series (this Day Twenty-three and Day Twenty-four of the Gospel) begin with clear references to new Days which follow in sequence. For the first time in the Gospel, at 11.12, Mark uses the phrase, Καὶ τῇ ἐπαύριον. 11.20 sees a further use of the word πρωΐ; compare 1.35 and the discussion and synopsis, under Day One, which notes its other uses at the beginning of Days at 15.1 and 16.2 (Days six and seven of this Series, Days Twenty-seven and Twenty-eight of the Gospel). 11.12 and 11.20 begin reports of Jesus' withering of the fig tree (told by Mark in two stages, but by Matthew in one whole as he likely conflates Mark's material again: compare Matthew's singular presentation above of Jesus' entry and the 'clearing' of the temple).

The literary structure of Day Twenty-three is viewed as:

A α[α] ¹²[..α] <u>Καὶ τῇ ἐπαύριον</u> [.β] ἐξελθόντων αὐτῶν ἀπὸ Βηθανίας
  [.β'] ἐπείνασεν.
 [β] ¹³[.α] [..α] καὶ ἰδὼν <u>συκῆν</u> [..β] ἀπὸ μακρόθεν [..β'] ἔχουσαν <u>φύλλα</u>
  [.β] <u>ἦλθεν εἰ ἄρα</u> [.β'] τι εὑρήσει ἐν αὐτῇ,
 [β'] [.α] καὶ <u>ἐλθὼν ἐπ' αὐτὴν</u> [.β] οὐδὲν εὗρεν εἰ μὴ <u>φύλλα</u>· [.β'] ὁ γὰρ καιρὸς οὐκ ἦν <u>σύκων</u>.
β ¹⁴[α] καὶ ἀποκριθεὶς [β] εἶπεν αὐτῇ, [β'] [.α] [..α] Μηκέτι [..α'] εἰς τὸν αἰῶνα [.α'] [..α] ἐκ σοῦ [..α'] μηδεὶς καρπὸν φάγοι.
β' καὶ ἤκουον οἱ μαθηταὶ αὐτοῦ.

---

[11] Telford, *The Barren Temple*..., p.39.
[12] Telford, *The Barren Temple*..., p.41.
[13] Telford, *The Barren Temple*..., p.39.

Β α ¹⁵Καὶ ἔρχονται εἰς Ἱεροσόλυμα.
  β[α] καὶ εἰσελθὼν εἰς τὸ ἱερὸν
    [β] [.α] ἤρξατο ἐκβάλλειν τοὺς πωλοῦντας [.β] καὶ τοὺς ἀγοράζοντας [.β'] ἐν τῷ ἱερῷ ,
    [β'] [.α] καὶ τὰς τραπέζας τῶν κολλυβιστῶν [.β] καὶ τὰς καθέδρας τῶν πωλούντων τὰς περιστερὰς [.β'] κατέστρεψεν,
  β'[α]¹⁶ καὶ οὐκ ἤφιεν
    [β] ἵνα τις διενέγκη σκεῦος
    [β'] διὰ τοῦ ἱεροῦ.

Β' α[α]¹⁷[.α] καὶ ἐδίδασκεν [.α'] καὶ ἔλεγεν αὐτοῖς,
    [β] [.α] Οὐ γέγραπται [.β] ὅτι Ὁ οἶκός μου [.β'] [..α] οἶκος προσευχῆς κληθήσεται [..α'] πᾶσιν τοῖς ἔθνεσιν;
    [β'] ὑμεῖς δὲ πεποιήκατε αὐτὸν σπήλαιον ληστῶν.
  β[α]¹⁸[.α] καὶ ἤκουσαν [.β] οἱ ἀρχιερεῖς [.β'] καὶ οἱ γραμματεῖς,
    [β] [.α] καὶ ἐζήτουν [.β] πῶς αὐτὸν ἀπολέσωσιν· [.β'] ἐφοβοῦντο γὰρ αὐτόν,
    [β'] [.α] πᾶς γὰρ ὁ ὄχλος ἐξεπλήσσετο [.α'] ἐπὶ τῇ διδαχῇ αὐτοῦ.
  β'[α]¹⁹ Καὶ ὅταν ὀψὲ ἐγένετο,
    [β] ἐξεπορεύοντο
    [β'] ἔξω τῆς πόλεως.

Regularly, scholars speak of 11.12-25 as a Markan whole, with the fig-tree incident sandwiching the clearing of the temple. They cite 3.22-30 and 5.21-43 as other examples of Mark's predilection for sandwiches[14], but I have demonstrated already, in consideration of Days Five and Seven, that to Mark the latter, supposed examples are not 'sandwiches' as such in his rhetorical scheme, because they have their introduction in his introductory sections, A. That is, these units form, in the second of these, one of his B sections, and in the third, one of his B' sections, of his ABB' three-section scheme. Whereas he locates these pericopae in his tellings of individual "Days", here the two stages of the fig tree incident are, significantly, the first episodes of new, successive "Days", in the greater B and B' scheme of his first sub-Series of three Days, ABB'. Days Twenty-two, Twenty-three and Twenty-four form his first full construction of his final Series of the Gospel. As we have already noted, these three Days link by reason of reference to the temple-setting, and the consecutive nature of the

---

[14] Bultmann, *The History...*, pp.232ff.; Taylor, *The Gospel...*, p.465; Nineham, *Saint Mark*, pp.297-303; Schweizer, *The Good News...*, pp.229-232; Hooker, *The Gospel...*, pp.260-266.

three Days. A further significant link between these last two Days of this final Series' first threesome of Days is that in the first of the two, Jesus "clears" the temple, and in the second of the two, Jesus speaks to his disciples of its impending, total destruction.

The detailed structure of this Day can be summarised as follows: section A tells of their leaving Bethany (it becomes clear at the beginning of B that the destination is Jerusalem and the temple again, as the first day of the Series) and the first stage of the acted-out parable of the fig tree; section B tells of Jesus' clearing of the temple of every trading or business activity; and section B' records his explanation which causes the chief priests and scribes to begin seeking how "they might destroy" him. The Day concludes similarly to the Day before it, as it becomes late, ὀψὲ.

We observe the first conflict story of this Series, in this Day's telling. In seeing such episodes grouped in the First Series, in Days Three, Four and Five, I referred then (under Day Four) to those that we would find in Days two to six of this, the final Series. I discern an ordering on Mark's part of these major climaxes in each Day's telling of conflict, in Days two and three (completing the first sub-Series) and in Day four (the middle, pivotal Day of the Series):

Day two	(Twenty-three):	ἐζήτουν πῶς αὐτὸν ἀπολέσωσιν·	11.18[15]
Day three	(Twenty-four):	ἐζήτουν αὐτὸν κρατῆσαι	12.12
Day four	(Twenty-five):	ἐζήτουν... πῶς αὐτὸν ἐν δόλῳ	
		κρατήσαντες ἀποκτείνωσιν·	14.1
		ἐζήτει πῶς αὐτὸν εὐκαίρως	
		Παραδοῖ.	14.11
Day five	(Twenty-six):	παραδίδοται... ὁ παραδιδούς...	14.41,42
		καὶ ἐκράτησαν αὐτόν	14.46
		ἐζήτουν κατὰ τοῦ Ἰησοῦ μαρτυρίαν	
		εἰς τὸ θανατῶσαι αὐτόν,	14.55
Day six	(Twenty-seven):	καὶ ἐσταύρωσαν αὐτόν.	15.25
		Καὶ τὸ καταπέτασμα τοῦ ναοῦ	15.38
		ἐσχίσθη εἰς δύο ἀπ' ἄνωθεν ἕως κάτω.	

---

[15] Stephen H. Smith, "The Literary Structure of Mark 11.1-12.40", *NT* 31 (1989), pp.104-124: he sees the connection between 11.18 and 12.12, but because of the limits of his study, 11.1-12.40, he fails to see the others of our listing, and hence their structural significance. He further identifies the three days, but in the case of the third day (like Dewey, *Markan Public Debate...*, p.152) he wrongly sees it as ending at 12.44. Unless section limits are well set at first, rhetorical analysis can lead, and does lead, to all manner of views.

It would appear that Mark deliberately created a series of conflict climaxes, in Days two, three and four, to connect with Days five and six. An obvious link is made between Days two and six: in the first, they seek to destroy Jesus, and in the second they achieve their aim. In the table I have included another phrase also, 15.38, which would remind the reader/listeners, in Day six, of the temple-clearance of Jesus in Day two, and of the temple-destruction pending, in Day three. 14.58 and 15.29 further make the verbal link between the "temple" and "Jesus". Days three and five have their link too: in the first of these, they seek to seize Jesus, and in the second they achieve their purpose. The turning point in the Series, given these matters, is found in the middle day, Day four. The Day begins and ends with plottings: the chief priests and scribes seek how they may seize and kill Jesus, but the feast and the people are a difficulty to them. Judas' promise of betrayal is that which makes the difference. Particularly stimulating in this Series is the Markan structural and, therefore, rhetorical balance between Jesus' clearing of the temple of all things which pertain to the old sacrificial way of Old Israel, and the establishing of the new sacrificial way for New Israel, through his own sacrifice on the cross.

Under our discussion of the middle Day of the First Series, Day Four, we noted the comments of some scholars that the death plot of the Pharisees and the Herodians, in 3.6, appears "too early in the Gospel". I suggested a correspondence then between the conflict stories of the first Series and those of the last Series. The wording of 3.6 and the key phrase ὅπως αὐτὸν ἀπολέσωσιν compares well with the first phrase of these conflict-climaxes. My case for seeing the First and Last Series of the Gospel in parallel in Mark's scheme is based on just such details, but also on thematic parallels and matters of scale. We will return to such matters once we have completed the literary-structural reading of the remaining chapters.

A note may be added here, however, that the above correspondences in this seven-day Series, between days two and six, and days three and five, around a central turning point, day four, suggest a concentric/chiastic arrangement of the days:

1, 2, 3, 4, 5, 6, 7 *cf.* 1, 2, 3, C, 3', 2', 1'.

It is the very same issue which arose in my summarising of the first Series.

The issue can be resolved fully only when we have looked at the very clear relationships between days one and five of this Series. These suggest emphatically that Mark did in fact create only a three-part chiasm, by beginning two three-day sub-Series in similar ways and placing them around a central turning point, day four. Other common themes and details, of one to three, and five to seven, confirm that these days do form threesomes. I will demonstrate the evidence at the appropriate moments. For now, it may be said that the Series' structure is best described in the following terms:

A(ABB') - B - A'(ABB').

Or in terms of the summary of Series Three, it can be expressed also by:

A B B̲'   A̲ B B'
    A̲ B A̲'

where days three and five again (as underlined) smooth the sharp edges of the transitional central turning point, according to the conventions of ancient rhetoric. I would stress that both these methods of annotation are only elaborations of my summary ABA' annotation for this, and indeed all the Series.

Day Twenty-four: 11.20-13.37:

The Day's telling covers ninety-four verses, more verses than any other Day[16]. The structure of the Day's telling can be represented by A:A': compare Days 1, 3, 4, 6, 8, 13, 15 and 22, so far, for similar structures. The structural annotation computes to an ABB':ABB' scheme, where the A sections are short introductions to the two halves of the Day. I present the outline structure below and we discuss the development of this analysis.

On the αββ' principle of how the text divides, I was led first of all to the judgement that the significant break in the Day's telling lay between 12.34 and 35, with καὶ οὐδεὶς οὐκέτι ἐτόλμα αὐτὸν

---

[16] The Day's telling is twenty-four more verses than the next Day which is Day Five. The third longest is Day Twenty-Six, with sixty-one verses.

ἐπερωτῆσαι which ends 12.34. The first B sections of each half were beginning, and it seemed significantly so, with:

11.27 Καὶ ἔρχονται πάλιν εἰς Ἱεροσόλυμα. καὶ ἐν τῷ ἱερῷ ...
13.1 Καὶ ἐκπορευομένου αὐτοῦ ἐκ τοῦ ἱεροῦ...

I observed, however, a feature in 13.1-3 (which I had come across before), at the beginnings of the Prologue and of the Days' tellings at the openings of the two central Series: the ου sound. Consider:

[.α] Καὶ ἐκπορευομένου αὐτου ἐκ του ἱεροῦ [.β] λέγει αὐτῷ [.β'] εἷς τῶν μαθητῶν αὐτοῦ ./...
³[α] Καὶ καθημένου αὐτου [β] εἰς τὸ Ὄρος τῶν Ἐλαιῶν [β'] κατέναντι τοῦ ἱεροῦ.

In my first description of Mark's scheme for this Day, the ου sound did not begin a new Day, or a new Series, or even a new section, ABB', because it began a B part. The question arose, "Does the repetition here of the ου sound have any significance?" I could hardly claim that it was purely accidental when Mark exercised such great care elsewhere[17]. This one small feature of detail caused me to consider that the ου sound here, even though it is not so fully established (it breaks with v.2), at least located the beginning of a new half in the whole Day's tellings. Several possibilities were entertained but only one alternative to my original proposal commended itself.

In the first instance, I was identifying that neither Dewey nor Smith[18], in their studies on the literary structure of chapters 11 and 12, discerned 'the primary division' between 12.34 and v.35, or the correspondence between 11.27 and 13.1. As a result of my re-assessment I have abandoned these notions myself. I continue to argue, however, that their schemes overlook the primary Markan rhetorical structure of "Days" which delimits this third Day of the Series as 11.20-13.37. Smith and Dewey define "day three" as ending at 12.44. For them there are no 'days' to consider here beyond

---

[17] As found so far in the Prologue, 1.1-3; the beginning of Series Two, 6.1; and the beginning of Series Three, 8.27.
[18] Dewey, *Markan Public Debate*..., pp.152-167; Smith, "The Literary Structure...", pp.104-124.

those at 11.1-11, vv.12-19 and 11.20-12.44. They do not, therefore, have to postulate that 13.1 begins a new day, which, of course, it could not (Jesus would have had to have spent the night in the temple, and Mark says nothing about that.) Rather, literary-structural evidence suggests that 11.20-12.44 is but the first half of the Day's telling, and 13.1-37 is the second half.

I present my earlier proposal alongside the one which I have adopted:

My earlier proposal: The adopted proposal:

A	11.20-25	A	11.20-12.44	A	11.20-25	
B	11.27-33			B	11.27-12.17	A 27-33
B'	12.1-12					B 12.1-12

A	12.13-17					B' 13-17

B	12.18-27			B'	12.18-44	A 18-27
B'	12.28-34					B 28-34

A	12.35-44					B' 35-44
--						
B	13.1-6	A'	13.1-37	A	13.1-6	
B'	13.7-17			B	13.7-17	A 7-10
						B 11-13
						B' 14-17

A	13.18-23			B'	13.18-37	A 18-23
B	13.24-31					B 24-31
B'	13.32-37					B' 32-37

We review another attempt at defining Mark's structuring of these chapters, that of Robbins[19]. I have agreed with him earlier on some of his three-step progressions, but here I cannot agree. He thinks he discerns two such progressions in this section of the Gospel: 10.46-48; vv.49-52; 11.1-11 and 13.1-2; vv.3-4; vv.5-37. For Robbins all such three-step progressions are clues to the formal structure of the Gospel. His analysis, therefore, leads him to the erroneous conclusion that the last two sections of the Gospel are

---

[19] Robbins, *Jesus the Teacher...*, pp.41-47.

10.46-12.44 and 13.1-15.47. (16.1-8 is the Conclusion, to him.) His position gains little support from my selected commentators and it gains no support from this literary-structural analysis which sees Day-presentations as all important in Mark's scheme. In our examination of Series Three, I show conclusively that 10.46-52 ends that Series, and in terms of three-step progressions, I demonstrate that 11.1-11 is the first of three Days, in a specific sub-Series. His three-step progression of 10.46-11.11 is not what Mark had in mind. Neither is his 13.1-2, vv.3-4, vv.5-37 progression. In Markan rhetorical terms (see page 257), 13.1,2 and vv.3,4 are the first two parts of a three-part progression, 13.1-6. The closing part is vv.5,6, not Robbins' vv.5-37.

Lastly, we review the contribution of Painter[20] to the structure and the functioning of 11.1-13.37 in Mark's scheme. His, most recent, commentary begins with his outline of Mark's Gospel. In his introduction, he says that he has given attention "to the arrangement of rhetorically shaped stories into collections which shape the plot of the story"[21]. His sectionalising is as follows:

The coming of the King	11.1-11
A tale within a tale: fig tree and temple	11.12-25
Jesus' authority challenged in Jerusalem	11.27-12.12
Opponents and questions in Jerusalem	12.13-37
The temple and the Son of Man	13.1-37

Firstly, we note that Painter does not divide the material in terms of the 'three-days'. Indeed on this matter he comments on 11.27ff.: "Jesus' return to the temple in Jerusalem is described but without any time reference." He appears not to consider that 11.20-26 is introductory, and continues, "Whether this was a day or days later is not significant for Mark..." It is not a promising start, given the three days that others have identified in 11.1-13.37[22], and

---

[20] John Painter, *Mark's Gospel: Worlds in Conflict*, Routledge, London and New York, 1997, pp.xiii, 154-179.

[21] Painter, *Mark's Gospel...*, p.ix.

[22] See page 212 for Telford, page 218 for Smith and Dewey; also: R. Thiel, *Drei Markus-Evangelien*, (AKG, 26), Walter de Gruyter & Co. Ltd., Berlin, 1938, pp.53-59, 114, 170-175; E. Hirsch, *Frühgeschichte des Evangeliums. Das Werden des Markusevangeliums*, J.C.B. Mohr, Tübingen, (1940) 2nd ed. 1951, pp.121-126; K.L. Schmidt, *Rahmen...*, pp.274-303; M. Dibelius, *Die Formgeschichte des Evangeliums*, 5th ed. ed. G. Bornkamm,

all that I have been uncovering so far of the importance of Days in Mark's scheme. 11.20-25 in my reading is introductory to the first half's telling, 11.20-12.44. The second episode of the fig tree establishes the Day's beginning, just as the first episode does the previous Day's telling (for fig tree and temple, see below).

Secondly, 11.27-33 in my reading is introductory to 12.1-12 *and* 12.13-17, because the link is established by 12.13, "And they sent to him...". 12.1-12 is balanced by 12.13-17: they are B and B' parts of a three-part rhetorical unit, 11.27-12.17.

Thirdly, we may observe that the "questions" cease at 12.34, but Painter continues his "questions" section to 12.37. Rather unusually, we observe that two of his titles append "in Jerusalem". In my reading of the next three-part rhetorical unit 12.18-44, 12.18-27 is introductory; 12.28 makes the connection with it ("...and one of the scribes, hearing..."), so that the B part is 12.28-34; and 12.35-44 completes the unit as a B' part, because Mark presents Jesus' teaching, in turn, about "the scribes".

We consider Painter's outline for 13.1-37:

The Lord abandons the temple and predicts its desolation	13.1,2
"When will these things be?"	13.3,4
Jesus' answer: "Watch out, be alert"	**13.5-37**
A^1 Warning: Don't be led astray, the end is not yet	13.5-8
B^1 Warning: You will be delivered up, betrayed	13.9-13
B^2 Warning: Flee to the mountains	13.14-20
A^2 Warning: False Christs, false prophets, signs and wonders	13.21-23
The end is the end	13.24-27
Learn a parable from the fig tree and other sayings	13.28-31
A parable and sayings about watchfulness	13.32-37

In the first three lines, Painter replicates Robbins (for my response to Robbins, see above). He then presents vv.5-23 as a chiasm, to which three-parts awkwardly attach, vv.24-37. Mark, it appears from literary-structural analysis, has been much more careful in his planning than this. After his introductory piece, A, to this half of this Day's telling, 13.1-6, Mark presents two sections, B and B', which each comprise three parts, with introductory repetitions.

J.C.B. Mohr, Tübingen, 1966, p.225; Bultmann, *The History...*, pp.340-341; J. Schreiber, "Die Christologie des Markusevangeliums", *ZThK*, 58 (1961), pp.161-162; E. Wendling, *Die Entstehung des Marcus-Evangeliums*, J.C.B. Mohr, Tübingen, 1908, pp.144ff.

We turn, therefore, to my presentation of the literary structure of Day Twenty-four, beginning with the opening Section:

A α   ²⁰[a] Καὶ παραπορευόμενοι πρωῒ [β] εἶδον τὴν συκῆν
      [β'] ἐξηραμμένην ἐκ ῥιζῶν.
  β   ²¹[a] καὶ ἀναμνησθεὶς [β] ὁ Πέτρος λέγει αὐτῷ, [β'] ' Ραββί,
  β'   [a] ἴδε ἡ συκῆ [β] ἣν κατηράσω [β'] ἐξήρανται.

B α   ²²[a] καὶ ἀποκριθεὶς [β] ὁ 'Ιησοῦς λέγει αὐτοῖς, [β'] ῎Εχετε πίστιν θεοῦ,
  β   ²³[a] ἀμὴν λέγω ὑμῖν [β] ὅτι ὃς ἂν εἴπῃ τῷ ὄρει τούτῳ,
      [β'] [.a] ῎Αρθητι [.β] καὶ βλήθητι [.β'] εἰς τὴν θάλασσαν,
  β'   [a] καὶ μὴ διακριθῇ ἐν τῇ καρδίᾳ αὐτοῦ [β] [..a] ἀλλὰ πιστεύῃ
      [.β] ὅτι ὃ λαλεῖ [.β'] γίνεται, [β'] ἔσται αὐτῷ.

B' α   ²⁴[a] διὰ τοῦτο λέγω ὑμῖν,
  β   [a] [.a] πάντα [.β] ὅσα προσεύχεσθε [.β'] καὶ αἰτεῖσθε,
      [β] [.a] πιστεύετε [.a'] ὅτι ἐλάβετε,
      [β'] καὶ ἔσται ὑμῖν.
  β'   ²⁵[a] καὶ ὅταν στήκετε προσευχόμενοι,
      [β] [.a] ἀφίετε [.β] εἴ τι ἔχετε [.β'] κατά τινος,
      [β'] [.a] ἵνα καὶ ὁ πατὴρ ὑμῶν [.β] ὁ ἐν τοῖς οὐρανοῖς [.β'] ἀφῇ ὑμῖν τὰ παραπτώματα ὑμῶν.

See Day Twenty-three for a discussion on the two parts and their placings of Jesus' withering of the fig tree. Essentially, this opening section of the Day's telling focuses on a teaching of Jesus on faith and prayer, but the fig tree, now "withered from its roots", is illustrative of Old Israel, its leadership, and even its temple, which are all under judgement for rejecting him[23]. The reason we *can* explain it this way is that 13.1-6, the opening part of the second half of this Day's telling, lies directly opposite[24]. It may be said that the illustration of "this mountain being hurled into the sea" is even comparable, for scale, with the temple which one of Jesus' disciples much admires, for its stones and buildings. It was itself, of course, standing on a mountain.

We now turn to Section B of the Day's first half, 11.27-12.17:

---

[23] Our commentators agree though it is more because they see the so-called 'sandwich' of the fig tree and the temple: Taylor, *The Gospel...*, pp.458-460; Nineham, *Saint Mark*, pp.297-302; Schweizer, *The Good News...*, pp.229-233; Hooker, *The Gospel...*, pp.260-266.
[24] Telford sees the same connection: *The Barren Temple...*, p.59.

A α[α]²⁷ Καὶ ἔρχονται πάλιν εἰς Ἱεροσόλυμα.
[β] [.α] καὶ ἐν τῷ ἱερῷ περιπατοῦντος αὐτοῦ [.β] ἔρχονται πρὸς αὐτὸν
[.β'] [..α] οἱ ἀρχιερεῖς [..β] καὶ οἱ γραμματεῖς [..β'] καὶ οἱ
πρεσβύτεροι
[β'] ²⁸ [.α] καὶ ἔλεγον αὐτῷ, [.β] [..α] Ἐν ποίᾳ ἐξουσίᾳ [..α'] ταῦτα ποιεῖς;
[.β'] [..α] ἢ τίς σοι ἔδωκεν τὴν ἐξουσίαν ταύτην [..α'] ἵνα ταῦτα
ποιῇς;
β[α]²⁹ [.α] ὁ δὲ Ἰησοῦς εἶπεν αὐτοῖς, [.α'] [..α] Ἐπερωτήσω ὑμᾶς ἕνα
λόγον, [..β] καὶ ἀποκρίθητέ μοι, [..β'] [...α] καὶ ἐρῶ ὑμῖν [...β] ἐν ποίᾳ
ἐξουσίᾳ [...β'] ταῦτα ποιῶ·
[β] ³⁰ [.α] τὸ βάπτισμα τὸ Ἰωάννου [.β] ἐξ οὐρανοῦ ἦν [.β'] ἢ ἐξ
ἀνθρώπων;
[β'] ἀποκρίθητέ μοι.
β'[α] ³¹ [.α] καὶ διελογίζοντο πρὸς ἑαυτοὺς λέγοντες,
[.β] [..α] [...α] Ἐὰν εἴπωμεν, [...α'] Ἐξ οὐρανοῦ, [..α'] [...α] ἐρεῖ,
[...α'] Διὰ τί [οὖν] οὐκ ἐπιστεύσατε αὐτῷ;
³² [.β'] [..α] [...α] ἀλλὰ εἴπωμεν, [...α'] Ἐξ ἀνθρώπων;
[..α'] [...α] ἐφοβοῦντο τὸν ὄχλον, [...β] ἅπαντες γὰρ εἶχον τὸν
Ἰωάννην ὄντως [...β'] ὅτι προφήτης ἦν.
[β] ³³ [.α] καὶ ἀποκριθέντες τῷ Ἰησοῦ [.β] λέγουσιν, [.β'] Οὐκ οἴδαμεν.
[β'] [.α] καὶ ὁ Ἰησοῦς λέγει αὐτοῖς, [.β] Οὐδὲ ἐγὼ λέγω ὑμῖν [.β'] [..α] ἐν
ποίᾳ ἐξουσίᾳ [..α'] ταῦτα ποιῶ.
B α[α] ¹ [.α] [..α] Καὶ ἤρξατο [..β] αὐτοῖς ἐν παραβολαῖς [..β'] λαλεῖν,
[.α'] [..α] Ἀμπελῶνα [..β] ἄνθρωπος [..β'] ἐφύτευσεν,
[β] [.α] καὶ περιέθηκεν φραγμὸν [.β] καὶ ὤρυξεν ὑπολήνιον [.β'] καὶ
ᾠκοδόμησεν πύργον,
[β'] [.α] καὶ ἐξέδετο αὐτὸν γεωργοῖς, [.α'] καὶ ἀπεδήμησεν.
β[α] ² [.α] καὶ ἀπέστειλεν πρὸς τοὺς γεωργοὺς τῷ καιρῷ δοῦλον,
[.β] [..α] ἵνα παρὰ τῶν γεωργῶν λάβῃ [..α'] ἀπὸ τῶν καρπῶν τοῦ
ἀμπελῶνος·
³ [.β'] [..α] καὶ λαβόντες αὐτὸν [..β] ἔδειραν [..β'] καὶ ἀπέστειλαν
κενόν.
[β] ⁴ [.α] [..α] [...α] καὶ πάλιν [...β] ἀπέστειλεν πρὸς αὐτοὺς [...β'] ἄλλον
δοῦλον· [..β] κἀκεῖνον ἐκεφαλίωσαν [..β'] καὶ ἠτίμασαν.
⁵ [.β] [..α] καὶ ἄλλον ἀπέστειλεν, [..α'] κἀκεῖνον ἀπέκτειναν,
[.β'] [..α] καὶ πολλοὺς ἄλλους, [..β] οὓς μὲν δέροντες [..β'] οὓς δὲ
ἀποκτέννοντες.
[β'] ⁶ [.α] [..α] [...α] ἔτι ἕνα εἶχεν, [...α'] υἱὸν ἀγαπητόν·
[..β] [...α] ἀπέστειλεν αὐτὸν ἔσχατον [...β] πρὸς αὐτοὺς [...β'] λέγων
[..β'] ὅτι Ἐντραπήσονται τὸν υἱόν μου.
⁷ [.β] [..α] [...α] ἐκεῖνοι δὲ [...β] οἱ γεωργοὶ [...β'] πρὸς ἑαυτοὺς εἶπαν
[..α'] [...α] ὅτι Οὗτός ἐστιν ὁ κληρονόμος· [...β] δεῦτε ἀποκτείνωμεν
αὐτόν, [...β'] καὶ ἡμῶν ἔσται ἡ κληρονομία.
⁸ [.β'] [..α] καὶ λαβόντες [..β] ἀπέκτειναν αὐτόν, [..β'] [...α] καὶ
ἐξέβαλον αὐτὸν [...α'] ἔξω τοῦ ἀμπελῶνος.

THE FOURTH SERIES

β'[α] ⁹[.α] τί [οὖν] ποιήσει ὁ κύριος τοῦ ἀμπελῶνος;
 [.α'] [..α] ἐλεύσεται [..β] καὶ ἀπολέσει τοὺς γεωργούς,
  [..β'] καὶ δώσει τὸν ἀμπελῶνα ἄλλοις.
 [β] ¹⁰[.α] οὐδὲ τὴν γραφὴν ταύτην ἀνέγνωτε,
  [.β] [..α] Λίθον ὃν ἀπεδοκίμασαν οἱ οἰκοδομοῦντες, [..α'] οὗτος ἐγενήθη εἰς κεφαλὴν γωνίας·
  ¹¹[.β'] [..α] παρὰ κυρίου ἐγένετο αὕτη, [..α'] καὶ ἔστιν θαυμαστὴ ἐν ὀφθαλμοῖς ἡμῶν;
 [β'] ¹²[.α] Καὶ ἐζήτουν αὐτὸν κρατῆσαι,
  [.β] [..α] καὶ ἐφοβήθησαν τὸν ὄχλον, [..β] ἔγνωσαν γὰρ [..β'] ὅτι πρὸς αὐτοὺς τὴν παραβολὴν εἶπεν.
  [.β'] [..α] καὶ ἀφέντες αὐτὸν [..α'] ἀπῆλθον.

B'α[α] ¹³[.α] Καὶ ἀποστέλλουσιν πρὸς αὐτόν [.β] [..α] τινας [..β] τῶν Φαρισαίων [..β'] καὶ τῶν Ἡρῳδιανῶν [.β'] [..α] ἵνα αὐτὸν ἀγρεύσωσιν [..α'] λόγῳ.
 [β] ¹⁴[.α] [..α] καὶ ἐλθόντες [..β] λέγουσιν αὐτῷ, [..β'] Διδάσκαλε,
  [.β] [..α] οἴδαμεν ὅτι ἀληθὴς εἶ [..β] καὶ οὐ μέλει σοι [..β'] περὶ οὐδενός,
  [.β'] [..α] οὐ γὰρ βλέπεις εἰς πρόσωπον ἀνθρώπων,
 [β'] [.α] [..α] ἀλλ' ἐπ' ἀληθείας [..β] τὴν ὁδὸν τοῦ θεου διδάσκεις·
  [..β'] ἔξεστιν
  [.β] [..α] δοῦναι κῆνσον Καίσαρι [..α'] ἢ οὔ;
  [.β'] [..α] δῶμεν [..α'] ἢ μὴ δῶμεν;
 β[α] ¹⁵[.α] ὁ δὲ εἰδὼς αὐτῶν τὴν ὑπόκρισιν [.β] εἶπεν αὐτοῖς, [.β'] Τί με πειράζετε;
 [β] [.α] φέρετε μοι δηνάριον [.α'] ἵνα ἴδω.
 [β'] ¹⁶ οἱ δὲ ἤνεγκαν.
 β'[α] [.α] [..α] καὶ λέγει αὐτοῖς, [..β] Τίνος ἡ εἰκὼν αὕτη [..β'] καὶ ἡ ἐπιγραφή;
  [.α'] [..α] οἱ δὲ εἶπαν αὐτῷ, [..α'] Καίσαρος.
 [β] ¹⁷[.α] ὁ δὲ Ἰησοῦς εἶπεν αὐτοῖς, [.β] Τὰ Καίσαρος ἀπόδοτε Καίσαρι [.β'] καὶ τὰ τοῦ θεοῦ τῷ θεῷ.
 [β'] καὶ ἐξεθαύμαζον ἐπ' αὐτῷ.

In part A, in the temple, the questioning and challenging of Jesus begin with a question put by the chief priests, scribes and elders concerning Jesus' authority for doing the things he does. They had not believed John the Baptist, and they were rejecting Jesus. In part B, Jesus presents an allegorical parable ("told to/against *them*", 12.12) of the vineyard. Old Israel had rejected all whom God had sent to them: it would make the 'big mistake' of rejecting his Son also. The section ends on a climactic note of high drama, "And they sought how to seize him..." (see our table under Day Twenty-Three for the significance of this in the scheme of Days); it also sets up part B'. The leaders of Old Israel seek to "trap" Jesus "in a word", 12.13. (They fail. He was too good a match for them: they would have to find another way. This indeed is the leading subject of the following Day, the middle and pivotal Day of the Series, Day Twenty-Five.) The first questioners were 'sent' to Jesus by the chief priests, scribes and elders (we observe, therefore, the B,B' relationship of the two completing sections, and we observe also the historical present of Mark with which he most frequently begins a new section and so introduces new characters): they were the unusual alliance of 'heavies' of 3.6, who had wanted to destroy Jesus for a long time; they were Pharisees and Herodians. Their question, on Caesar and the tax, is the kind of question that the Herodians would more likely have wanted to ask than the Pharisees, but the manner of the questioning suggests that it is the Pharisees who put it to Jesus. Jesus replies, asking for a denarius, a Roman coin... The section and this overall B-construction to the first half ends with "their marvelling at him".

What follows is the completing of the Day's first half, with Section B':

Α α[α]¹⁸[.α] Καὶ ἔρχονται Σαδδουκαῖοι πρὸς αὐτόν, [.β] οἵτινες λέγουσιν
    ἀνάστασιν μὴ εἶναι, [.β'] [..α] καὶ ἐπηρώτων αὐτὸν [..α'] λέγοντες,
  [β] ¹⁹[.α] Διδάσκαλε, [.β] Μωϋσῆς ἔγραψεν ἡμῖν [.β'][..α] ὅτι ἐάν τινος
    ἀδελφὸς ἀποθάνῃ [..β] καὶ καταλίπῃ γυναῖκα [..β'] καὶ μὴ ἀφῇ
    τέκνον,
  [β'] [.α] ἵνα λάβῃ ὁ ἀδελφὸς αὐτοῦ τὴν γυναῖκα [.β] καὶ ἐξαναστήσῃ
    σπέρμα [.β'] τῷ ἀδελφῷ αὐτοῦ.
β[α] ²⁰[.α] ἑπτὰ ἀδελφοὶ ἦσαν·
    [.β] [..α] καὶ ὁ πρῶτος ἔλαβεν γυναῖκα, [..β] καὶ ἀποθνῄσκων
    [..β'] οὐκ ἀφῆκεν σπέρμα·
    ²¹[.β'] [..α] καὶ ὁ δεύτερος ἔλαβεν αὐτήν, [..β] καὶ ἀπέθανεν [..β'] μὴ
    καταλιπὼν σπέρμα·
  [β] [.α] καὶ ὁ τρίτος ὡσαύτως· [.β] ²² καὶ οἱ ἑπτὰ οὐκ ἀφῆκαν σπέρμα.
    [.β'] ἔσχατον πάντων καὶ ἡ γυνὴ ἀπέθανεν.
  [β'] ²³[.α] [..α] ἐν τῇ ἀναστάσει , [..α'] [ὅταν ἀναστῶσιν],
    [.β] τίνος αὐτῶν ἔσται γυνή;
    [.β'] οἱ γὰρ ἑπτὰ ἔσχον αὐτὴν γυναῖκα.

β'[α]²⁴[.α] ἔφη αὐτοῖς ὁ Ἰησοῦς, [.α'] [..α] Οὐ διὰ τοῦτο πλανᾶσθε [..β] μὴ εἰδότες τὰς γραφὰς [..β'] μηδὲ τὴν δύναμιν τοῦ θεοῦ;
[β] ²⁵ [.α] [..α] ὅταν γὰρ ἐκ νεκρῶν ἀναστῶσιν, [..β] οὔτε γαμοῦσιν [..β'] οὔτε γαμίζονται, [.α'] [..α] ἀλλ' εἰσὶν [..β] ὡς ἄγγελοι [..β'] ἐν τοῖς οὐρανοῖς.
[β'] ²⁶[.α] [..α] περὶ δὲ τῶν νεκρῶν [..α'] ὅτι ἐγείρονται [.β] [..α] οὐκ ἀνέγνωτε ἐν τῇ βίβλῳ Μωϋσέως [..α'] [...α] ἐπὶ τοῦ βάτου [...β] [....α] πῶς εἶπεν αὐτῷ ὁ θεὸς [....α'] λέγων, [...β'] [....α] Ἐγὼ ὁ θεὸς Ἀβραὰμ [....β] καὶ [ὁ] θεὸς Ἰσαὰκ [....β'] καὶ [ὁ] θεὸς Ἰακώβ;
²⁷ [.β'] [..α] [...α] οὐκ ἔστιν θεὸς νεκρῶν [...α'] ἀλλὰ ζώντων· [..α'] πολὺ πλανᾶσθε.

Β α[α] ²⁸[.α] Καὶ προσελθὼν [.β] εἷς τῶν γραμματέων [.β] ἀκούσας αὐτῶν συζητούντων,
[β] [.α] ἰδὼν [.β] ὅτι καλῶς ἀπεκρίθη αὐτοῖς, [.β'] ἐπηρώτησεν αὐτόν,
[β'] Ποία ἐστὶν ἐντολὴ πρώτη πάντων;
β[α] ²⁹[.α] [..α] ἀπεκρίθη ὁ Ἰησοῦς [..α'] ὅτι Πρώτη ἐστίν, [.α'] [..α] [...α] Ἄκουε, [...α'] Ἰσραήλ, [..β] [...α] κύριος ὁ θεὸς ἡμῶν [...α'] κύριος εἷς ἐστιν, ³⁰[..β'] [...α] καὶ ἀγαπήσεις κύριον τὸν θεόν σου [...α'] [....α] ἐξ ὅλης τῆς καρδίας σου [....γ] καὶ ἐξ ὅλης τῆς ψυχῆς σου [....δ] καὶ ἐξ ὅλης τῆς διανοίας σου [....ε] καὶ ἐξ ὅλης τῆς ἰσχύος σου.
[β] ³¹[.α] δευτέρα αὕτη, [.β] Ἀγαπήσεις τὸν πλησίον σου [.β'] ὡς σεαυτόν.
[β'] [.α] μείζων τούτων [.β] ἄλλη ἐντολὴ [.β'] οὐκ ἔστιν.
β'[α] ³²[.α] [..α] καὶ εἶπεν αὐτῷ ὁ γραμματεύς, [..β] Καλῶς, [..β'] διδάσκαλε, [.α'] [..α] [...α] ἐπ' ἀληθείας εἶπες [...β] ὅτι εἷς ἐστιν [...β'] καὶ οὐκ ἔστιν ἄλλος πλὴν αὐτοῦ·
³³ [..β] [...α] καὶ τὸ ἀγαπᾶν αὐτὸν [...α'] [....β] ἐξ ὅλης τῆς καρδίας [....β] καὶ ἐξ ὅλης τῆς συνέσεως [....β'] καὶ ἐξ ὅλης τῆς ἰσχύος [..β'] [...α] [....α] καὶ τὸ ἀγαπᾶν τὸν πλησίον [...α'] ὡς ἑαυτὸν [...α'] [....α] περισσότερόν ἐστιν [....β] πάντων τῶν ὁλοκαυτωμάτων [....β'] καὶ θυσιῶν.
[β] ³⁴[.α] [..α] καὶ ὁ Ἰησοῦς ἰδὼν [αὐτὸν] [..β] ὅτι νουνεχῶς ἀπεκρίθη [..β'] εἶπεν αὐτῷ,
[.α'] [..α] Οὐ μακρὰν εἶ [..α'] ἀπὸ τῆς βασιλείας τοῦ θεοῦ.
[β'] [.α] καὶ οὐδεὶς οὐκέτι [.α'] ἐτόλμα αὐτὸν ἐπερωτῆσαι.

Β' α[α] ³⁵[.α] Καὶ ἀποκριθεὶς [.β] ὁ 'Ιησοῦς ἔλεγεν [.β'] διδάσκων ἐν τῷ ἱερῷ,
  [β] [.α] [..α] Πῶς λέγουσιν οἱ γραμματεῖς [..α'] ὅτι ὁ Χριστὸς υἱὸς
     Δαυίδ ἐστιν;
     ³⁶[.β] [..α] αὐτὸς Δαυὶδ εἶπεν ἐν τῷ πνεύματι τῷ ἁγίῳ, [..β] [...α] Εἶπεν
     κύριος τῷ κυρίῳ μου, [...α'] Κάθου ἐκ δεξιῶν μου [..β'] [...α] ἕως ἂν
     θῶ τοὺς ἐχθρούς σου [...α'] ὑποκάτω τῶν ποδῶν σου.
     ³⁷[.β'] [..α] αὐτὸς Δαυὶδ λέγει αὐτὸν κύριον, [..α'] καὶ πόθεν αὐτοῦ
     ἐστιν υἱός;
  [β'] καὶ [ὁ] πολὺς ὄχλος ἤκουεν αὐτοῦ ἡδέως.
β [α] ³⁸[.α] Καὶ ἐν τῇ διδαχῇ αὐτου [.α'] ἔλεγεν,
  [β] [.α] Βλέπετε ἀπὸ τῶν γραμματέων
     [.β] [..α] τῶν θελόντων [..α'] [...α] ἐν στολαῖς περιπατεῖν [...β] καὶ
     ἀσπασμοὺς ἐν ταῖς ἀγοραῖς [...γ] ³⁹ καὶ πρωτοκαθεδρίας ἐν ταῖς
     συναγωγαῖς [...δ] καὶ πρωτοκλισίας ἐν τοῖς δείπνοις·
     ⁴⁰[.β'] [..α] οἱ κατεσθίοντες τὰς οἰκίας τῶν χηρῶν [..α'] καὶ προφάσει
     μακρὰ προσευχόμενοι,
  [β'] οὗτοι λήμψονται περισσότερον κρίμα.
β'[α] ⁴¹[.α] Καὶ καθίσας κατέναντι τοῦ γαζοφυλακίου [.β] ἐθεώρει πῶς ὁ
     ὄχλος βάλλει χαλκὸν [.β'] εἰς τὸ γαζοφυλάκιον·
  [β] [.α] καὶ πολλοι πλούσιοι ἔβαλλον πολλά· [.β] ⁴² καὶ ἐλθοῦσα μία
     χήρα πτωχη ἔβαλεν λεπτὰ δύο, [.β'] ὅ ἐστιν κοδράντης.
  [β'] ⁴³[.α] [..α] καὶ προσκαλεσάμενος τοὺς μαθητὰς αὐτοῦ [..α'] εἶπεν
     αὐτοῖς, [.β] [..α] 'Αμὴν λέγω ὑμῖν [..β] ὅτι ἡ χήρα αὕτη ἡ πτωχη
     πλεῖον πάντων ἔβαλεν [..β'] τῶν βαλλόντων εἰς τὸ γαζοφυλάκιον·
     ⁴⁴[.β'] [..α] πάντες γὰρ ἐκ του περισσεύοντος αὐτοῖς ἔβαλον,
     [..β] αὕτη δὲ ἐκ τῆς ὑστερήσεως αὐτῆς πάντα ὅσα εἶχεν ἔβαλεν,
     [..β'] ὅλον τὸν βίον αὐτῆς.

In part A, Sadducees (mentioned here only in the Gospel), come with a wonderfully complicated question on the resurrection. Jesus replies, with reference to Moses, and does not resist concluding intimidatingly, "much you are mistaken". In part B, one of the scribes, in approaching Jesus, is more sympathetic than cautious. Having questioned Jesus on the principal commandment, he concurs with his reply and receives something of a commendation, "You are not far from the kingdom of God". Part B' tells how Jesus, in his teaching in the temple, questions the scribes' understanding (consider 12.35, Καὶ ἀποκριθεὶς ὁ'Ιησοῦς ἔλεγεν...: part B' relates to part B, for "scribes") of the Christ as David's Son: he raises the issue between the Christ and David, as to whether the Christ is "Son" or

"Lord" of David: he is Lord of David, and all his enemies "will be put under his feet" (the quotation is from Ps.110.1). "The large crowd heard him gladly." In the two balancing/completing parts β and β‛, Jesus addresses the issue of true devotion: the scribes are devoted to themselves, not to God and his purposes (theirs is the "greater condemnation"; they are the Lord's enemies); and when Jesus is located opposite the treasury he sees a poor "widow" (χήρα is a verbal link between the two passages) who, in contrast, is utterly devoted to God. The second half of the Day's telling now begins:

A α   ¹[α] Καὶ ἐκπορευομένου αὐτοῦ <u>ἐκ τοῦ ἱεροῦ</u> [β] <u>λέγει</u> αὐτῷ [β‛] εἷς τῶν μαθητῶν αὐτοῦ,
    β   [α] Διδάσκαλε, [β] ἴδε <u>ποταποὶ λίθοι</u> [β‛] καὶ <u>ποταπαι οἰκοδομαί</u>.
    β‛   ²[α] καὶ ὁ Ἰησοῦς εἶπεν αὐτῷ, [α‛] [.α] <u>Βλέπεις</u> ταύτας τὰς μεγάλας <u>οἰκοδομάς</u>; [.β] [..α] <u>οὐ μὴ</u> ἀφεθῇ ὧδε [..β] <u>λίθος</u> [..β‛] ἐπὶ λίθον [.β‛] ὃς <u>οὐ μὴ</u> καταλυθῇ.

B α   ³[α] Καὶ καθημένου αὐτοῦ [β] εἰς τὸ Ὄρος τῶν Ἐλαιῶν [β‛] <u>κατέναντι</u> τοῦ ἱεροῦ
    β   [α] [.α] ἐπηρώτα αὐτὸν [.β] κατ᾽ ἰδίαν [.β‛] Πέτρος [α‛] [.α] καὶ Ἰάκωβος [.β] καὶ Ἰωάννης [.β‛] καὶ Ἀνδρέας,
    β‛   ⁴ [α] Εἰπὸν ἡμῖν [β] <u>πότε ταῦτα ἔσται</u>, [β‛] [.α] <u>καὶ τί τὸ σημεῖον</u> [.α‛] <u>ὅταν μέλλῃ ταῦτα</u> συντελεῖσθαι <u>πάντα</u>.

B‛ α   ⁵ ὁ δὲ Ἰησοῦς ἤρξατο λέγειν αὐτοῖς,
    β   [α] <u>Βλέπετε</u> [α‛] μή τις ὑμᾶς <u>πλανήσῃ</u>·
    β‛   ⁶[α] <u>πολλοὶ</u> ἐλεύσονται ἐπὶ τῷ ὀνόματί μου [β] λέγοντες ὅτι Ἐγώ εἰμι, [β‛] καὶ <u>πολλοὺς πλανήσουσιν</u>.

The second half begins with the above, section A, with Jesus going outside the temple. In the introductory section to the Day's telling (11.20-22) we discover some clear parallels of details and construction, which suggest that one has been written with the other in mind:

11.20-22   <u>Καὶ παραπορευόμενοι... εἶδον τὴν συκῆν... λέγει αὐτῷ,</u>
               Ῥαββί, <u>ἴδε</u> ἡ συκῆ... <u>ὁ Ἰησοῦς λέγει αὐτοῖς</u>...
13.1,2   <u>Καὶ ἐκπορευομένου</u> αὐτοῦ ἐκ τοῦ ἱεροῦ <u>λέγει αὐτῷ</u>...
               Διδάσκαλε, <u>ἴδε</u> ποταποὶ λίθοι... <u>ὁ Ἰησοῦς εἶπεν αὐτῳ</u>...

It is the temple now which is going to be destroyed. (Jesus cleared it, the Day previously: the judgement of God is upon it.) In part B, Peter, James, John and Andrew, as Jesus now sits opposite[25] the temple, question him, "When?" and "What will be the signs...?". In part B' Jesus prefaces his answers with a warning. His answers come in this half's overall Sections B (vv.7-17) and B' (vv.18-37): the first question is addressed in B, and the second in B'.

Section B clearly answers the first question: all three parts begin similarly:

13.7   "Οταν δε ἀκούσητε πολέμους
13.11   Καὶ ὅταν ἄγωσιν ὑμᾶς παραδιδόντες
13.14   "Οταν δε ἴδητε τὸ βδέλυγμα

Section B' answers the second question, and its three parts begin:

13.18,19 Προσεύχεσθε δε... αἱ ἡμέραι ἐκεῖναι θλῖψις
13.24   'Αλλὰ ἐν ἐκείναις ταῖς ἡμέραις μετὰ τὴν θλῖψιν ἐκείνην
13.32   Περὶ δὲ τῆς ἡμέρας ἐκείνης ἢ τῆς ὥρας

Section B is presented below:

A   α   ⁷[α] [.α] "Οταν δε ἀκούσητε [.β] πολέμους [.β'] καὶ ἀκοὰς πολέμων,
            [β] μὴ θροεῖσθε· [β'] [.α] δεῖ γενέσθαι, [.β] ἀλλ' οὔπω [.β'] τὸ τέλος.
    β   ⁸[α] [.α] ἐγερθήσεται γὰρ [.β] ἔθνος ἐπ' ἔθνος [.β'] καὶ βασιλεία ἐπὶ βασιλείαν,
            [β] [.α] ἔσονται σεισμοὶ [.α'] κατὰ τόπους,
            [β'] [.α] ἔσονται λιμοί· [.α'] ἀρχὴ ὠδίνων ταῦτα.
    β' ⁹[α] [.α] βλέπετε δὲ ὑμεῖς ἑαυτούς· [.β] παραδώσουσιν ὑμᾶς εἰς συνέδρια [.β'] καὶ εἰς συναγωγὰς δαρήσεσθε
            [β] [.α] καὶ ἐπὶ ἡγεμόνων καὶ βασιλέων σταθήσεσθε [.β] ἕνεκεν ἐμοῦ [.β'] εἰς μαρτύριον αὐτοῖς.
            ¹⁰ [β'] [.α] καὶ εἰς πάντα τὰ ἔθνη [.β] πρῶτον [.β'] δεῖ κηρυχθῆναι τὸ εὐαγγέλιον.

---

[25] For an anastrophe, or 'hook word' smoothing the transition between the two halves of this Day's telling, compare 12.41, κατέναντι τοῦ γαζοφυλακίου, and 13.3, κατέναντι τοῦ ἱεροῦ.

Β α ¹¹[α] [.α] Καὶ ὅταν ἄγωσιν ὑμᾶς παραδιδόντες, [.β] μὴ προμεριμνᾶτε
     [.β'] τί λαλήσητε,
     [β] [.α] ἀλλ' ὃ ἐὰν δοθῇ ὑμῖν [.β] ἐν ἐκείνῃ τῇ ὥρᾳ [.β'] τοῦτο
     λαλεῖτε,
     [β'] [.α] οὐ γάρ ἐστε ὑμεῖς οἱ λαλοῦντες [.α'] ἀλλὰ τὸ πνεῦμα τὸ
     ἅγιον.
  β ¹²[α] [.α] καὶ παραδώσει ἀδελφὸς [.β] ἀδελφὸν [.β'] εἰς θάνατον
     [β] [.α] καὶ πατὴρ [.α'] τέκνον,
     [β'] [.α] καὶ ἐπαναστήσονται τέκνα [.β] ἐπὶ γονεῖς [.β'] καὶ
     θανατώσουσιν αὐτούς·
  β' ¹³[α] καὶ ἔσεσθε μισούμενοι ὑπὸ πάντων [β] διὰ τὸ ὄνομά μου.
     [β'] [.α] ὁ δὲ ὑπομείνας εἰς τέλος [.α'] οὗτος σωθήσεται.
Β' α ¹⁴[α] Ὅταν δὲ ἴδητε τὸ βδέλυγμα τῆς ἐρημώσεως [β] ἑστηκότα ὅπου
     οὐ δεῖ, [β'] ὁ ἀναγινώσκων νοείτω,
  β [α] [.α] τότε οἱ ἐν τῇ Ἰουδαίᾳ [.α'] φευγέτωσαν εἰς τὰ ὄρη,
     ¹⁵[β] [.α] ὁ [δε] ἐπὶ τοῦ δώματος [.β] μὴ καταβάτω [.β'] μηδὲ εἰσελθάτω
     ἆραι τί ἐκ τῆς οἰκίας αὐτοῦ,
     ¹⁶[β'] [.α] καὶ ὁ εἰς τὸν ἀγρὸν [.β] μὴ ἐπιστρεψάτω εἰς τὰ ὀπίσω
     [.β'] ἆραι τὸ ἱμάτιον αὐτοῦ.
  β' ¹⁷[α] [.α] οὐαὶ δὲ [.β] ταῖς ἐν γαστρὶ ἐχούσαις [.β] καὶ ταῖς
     θηλαζούσαις [α'] ἐν ἐκείναις ταῖς ἡμέραις.

We noted above the indicators of basic structure. Here we note how the content of this Section B has its correspondence with Jesus' allegorical parable of the vineyard, in Section B of the first half of the Day's telling. Old Israel will continue to "beat" and "put to death" God's representatives, but the one enduring ("for Jesus' sake", v.9; "proclaiming the Gospel", v.10; through whom "the Holy Spirit speaks", v.11) "will be saved", v.13. Again, part A introduces the issues and the next two parts, B and B', complete the presentation.

Section B', presented below, is set up particularly by the anastrophe of "those days", at vv.17 and 19 (note: in Markan and rhetorical reversed orders: v.17: ἐν ἐκείναις ταῖς ἡμέραις; and v.19: ἔσονται γὰρ αἱ ἡμέραι ἐκεῖναι). Sections B and B' are linked, therefore, by an anastophe, which signals the end of one division and the beginning of another.

A α[α]¹⁸[.α] Προσεύχεσθε δε [.α´] ἵνα μὴ <u>γένηται</u> χειμῶνος·
[β] ¹⁹ ἔσονται γὰρ αἱ <u>ἡμέραι ἐκεῖναι</u> **θλῖψις**
[β´] [.α] [..α] οἵα οὐ <u>γέγονεν</u> τοιαύτη [..β] ἀπ' <u>**ἀρχῆς** κτίσεως</u> [..β´] ἦν <u>ἔκτισεν</u> ὁ θεὸς [.β] ἕως τοῦ νῦν [.β´] καὶ οὐ μὴ <u>γένηται</u>.
β[α] ²⁰ καὶ εἰ μὴ <u>ἐκολόβωσεν κύριος τὰς ἡμέρας</u>,
[β] οὐκ ἂν <u>ἐσώθη</u> πᾶσα σάρξ.
[β´] [.α] ἀλλὰ διὰ <u>τοὺς ἐκλεκτοὺς</u> [.β] <u>οὓς ἐξελέξατο</u> [.β´] <u>ἐκολόβωσεν τὰς ἡμέρας</u>.
β´[α] ²¹[.α] [..α] καὶ <u>τότε</u> ἐάν τις ὑμῖν εἴπῃ, [..β] ῎<u>Ιδε</u> ὧδε ὁ <u>Χριστός</u>, [..β´] ῎<u>Ιδε</u> ἐκεῖ, [.α´] μὴ πιστεύετε·
[β] ²²[.α] [..α] <u>ἐγερθήσονται</u> γὰρ [..β] <u>ψευδόχριστοι</u> [..β´] καὶ ψευδοπροφῆται
[.β] [..α] καὶ δώσουσιν [..β] <u>σημεῖα</u> [..β´] καὶ τέρατα
[.β´] [..α] πρὸς τὸ <u>ἀποπλανᾶν</u>, [..β] εἰ δυνατόν, [..β´] <u>τοὺς ἐκλεκτούς</u>.
[β´] ²³ [.α] ὑμεῖς δὲ <u>βλέπετε</u>· [.α´] <u>προείρηκα</u> ὑμῖν <u>πάντα</u>.

B α[α]²⁴[.α] [..α] Ἀλλὰ <u>ἐν ἐκείναις ταῖς ἡμέραις</u> [..α´] μετὰ τὴν **θλῖψιν** ἐκείνην
[.β] [..α] ὁ ἥλιος <u>σκοτισθήσεται</u>, [..α´] καὶ ἡ σελήνη οὐ δώσει τὸ <u>φέγγος</u> αὐτῆς,
²⁵[.β´] [..α] [...α] καὶ οἱ ἀστέρες ἔσονται [...β] <u>ἐκ τοῦ οὐρανοῦ</u>
[...β´] <u>πίπτοντες</u>,
[..α´] [...α] καὶ <u>αἱ</u> δυνάμεις [...β] <u>αἱ ἐν τοῖς οὐρανοῖς</u>
[...β´] <u>σαλευθήσονται</u>.
[β] ²⁶[.α] <u>καὶ τότε</u> ὄψονται τὸν υἱὸν τοῦ ἀνθρώπου [.β] ἐρχόμενον ἐν νεφέλαις [.β´] μετὰ <u>δυνάμεως</u> πολλῆς καὶ <u>δόξης</u>.
[β´] ²⁷[.α] <u>καὶ τότε</u> ἀποστελεῖ τοὺς <u>ἀγγέλους</u> [.β] καὶ ἐπισυνάξει <u>τοὺς ἐκλεκτοὺς</u> [αὐτοῦ] [.β´] [..α] ἐκ τῶν τεσσάρων ἀνέμων [..β] ἀπ' <u>ἄκρου</u> γῆς [..β´] ἕως <u>ἄκρου οὐρανοῦ</u>.
β[α] ²⁸ [.α] Ἀπὸ δὲ <u>τῆς συκῆς</u> [.α´] μάθετε <u>τὴν παραβολήν</u>·
[β] [.α] [..α] <u>ὅταν ἤδη</u> ὁ κλάδος αὐτῆς ἁπαλὸς <u>γένηται</u> [..α´] καὶ ἐκφύῃ τὰ φύλλα, [.α´] <u>γινώσκετε ὅτι ἐγγὺς</u> τὸ θέρος <u>ἐστίν</u>.
[β´] ²⁹[.α] οὕτως καὶ ὑμεῖς, [.β] <u>ὅταν ἴδητε</u> ταῦτα <u>γινόμενα</u>,
[.β´] <u>γινώσκετε ὅτι ἐγγὺς ἐστιν</u> ἐπὶ θύραις.
β´[α] ³⁰[.α] ἀμὴν λέγω ὑμῖν [.β] ὅτι οὐ μὴ <u>παρέλθῃ</u> ἡ γενεὰ αὕτη [.β´] μέχρις οὗ <u>ταῦτα πάντα γένηται</u>.
[β] ³¹ ὁ οὐρανὸς καὶ ἡ γῆ <u>παρελεύσονται</u>,
[β´] οἱ δὲ λόγοι μου οὐ μὴ <u>παρελεύσονται</u>.

Β΄ α[α]³²[.α] Περὶ δὲ [.β] τῆς ἡμέρας ἐκείνης [.β΄] ἢ τῆς ὥρας
[β] [.α] οὐδεὶς οἶδεν, [.β] οὐδὲ οἱ ἄγγελοι ἐν οὐρανῷ [.β΄] οὐδὲ ὁ υἱός,
[β΄] εἰ μὴ ὁ πατήρ.
β[α] ³³[α] βλέπετε [β] ἀγρυπνεῖτε· [β΄] οὐκ οἴδατε γὰρ πότε ὁ καιρός ἐστιν.
[β] ³⁴[.α] [..α] ὡς ἄνθρωπος ἀπόδημος [..α΄] ἀφεὶς τὴν οἰκίαν αὐτοῦ
[.β] [..α] καὶ δοὺς τοῖς δούλοις αὐτοῦ τὴν ἐξουσίαν, [..α΄] ἑκάστῳ τὸ ἔργον αὐτοῦ,
[.β΄] [..α] καὶ τῷ θυρωρῷ ἐνετείλατο [..α΄] ἵνα γρηγορῇ.
[β΄] ³⁵[.α] [..α] γρηγορεῖτε οὖν, [..α΄] οὐκ οἴδατε γὰρ πότε ὁ κύριος τῆς οἰκίας ἔρχεται,
[.β] [..α] ἢ ὀψὲ [..β] ἢ μεσονύκτιον [..γ] ἢ ἀλεκτοροφωνίας [..δ] ἢ πρωΐ,
³⁶[.β΄] [..α] μὴ ἐλθὼν ἐξαίφνης [..α΄] εὕρῃ ὑμᾶς καθεύδοντας.
β΄ ³⁷[α] ὃ δὲ ὑμῖν λέγω,
[α΄] [.α] πᾶσιν λέγω, [.α΄] γρηγορεῖτε.

Part A characterises "those days" as days of "distress" and as "shortened" for the sake of "the elect". Jesus also warns, as before in v.6[26], that others will come to mislead, if possible, the elect. For θλῖψις, see also v.24, the opening piece to the following part. Part B tells of the glorious finale which follows "the distress", the parousia and the angelic gathering up of the elect from every corner of the earth. People will be able to judge how near the event is, just as they know from the "parable" of the growth of a fig tree when summer is coming. All these things will happen in this generation: Jesus' word is to be trusted. Part B' amplifies and completes the lessons: it begins in a fashion that truly cements the parts: Περὶ δὲ τῆς ἡμέρας ἐκείνης ἢ τῆς ὥρας οὐδεὶς οἶδεν... The call is βλέπετε, ἀγρυπνεῖτε and it is reinforced with another parable. The illustration itself ends with ἵνα γρηγορῇ and a command, γρηγορεῖτε οὖν... Jesus may be talking only to Peter, James, John and Andrew, but his words are for "all" (so Mark presents): ὃ δὲ ὑμῖν λέγω, πᾶσιν λέγω, γρηγορεῖτε. We note: the teaching ends with words, γρηγορεῖτε and καθεύδοντας, which feature again in Day Twenty-six, the chiastically corresponding Day of the Series, as Jesus gives instruction to Peter, James and John in Gethsemane.

Clearly, the length of this Day's telling, in terms of its verses, has added to the difficulties of both establishing the Day's structure as

---

[26] Part A of this B' Section (vv.18-23) links, therefore, with the Introduction (vv.1-6), in this way also.

well as presenting it. We end our examination of Day Twenty-four with consideration of more minor matters of detail, but nevertheless, useful testings of this analytical approach. Two chiasms have been said to exist: one at 12.10,11 and one at 12.35-37, both proposed by Marcus[27].

The first is at 12.10,11: "The Rejected and Vindicated Stone", the quotation of Ps. 118.22-23 from the LXX (Ps.117):

"Have you not read this scripture:
"A stone which the builders rejected   A
this one was made the head of the corner   B
from the Lord this came to be   B'
and it is astonishing in our eyes"?   A'

We compare:

[β] [10][.α] οὐδὲ τὴν γραφὴν ταύτην ἀνέγνωτε,
[.β] [..α] Λίθον ὃν ἀπεδοκίμασαν οἱ οἰκοδομοῦντες,
[..α'] οὗτος ἐγενήθη εἰς κεφαλὴν γωνίας·
[11][.β'] [..α] παρὰ κυρίου ἐγένετο αὕτη,
[..α'] καὶ ἔστιν θαυμαστὴ ἐν ὀφθαλμοῖς ἡμῶν;

Marcus argues weakly that "parts B and B' speak of divine action of vindicating the stone", and that they are "framed by two human responses in parts A and A'." But he fails to recognise the Psalmist's two pairs of statements, where each pair is traditionally punctuated by a colon. His letter-designation of AB and B'A' in sequence destroys the rhythm of the verses. My judgement is that Mark has not diverted from his rhetorical method to incorporate the quotation, as with the last chiasm demonstrated, in 11.9,10. The quotation in structural terms is in two pairs of statements which are well described in Mark's context as [.β] and [.β'] parts, introduced by [.α].

The second is at 12.35-37: "David's Son and David's Lord": an arrangement around a quote from Ps. 110.1:

---

[27]   Marcus, *The Way of the Lord...*, pp.111f. and pp.130f.

THE FOURTH SERIES   263

    And answering, Jesus said, teaching in the Temple,   A
    How do the scribes say that the Christ is the Son of David?   B
    David himself said in the Holy Spirit,   C
    The Lord said to my Lord/Sit at my right hand,   D
    Until I put your enemies/under your feet.
    David himself calls him "lord"   C'
    How then is he his son?   B'
    And the large crowd heard him gladly.   A'

We compare:

Β΄α[α]³⁵[.α] Καὶ ἀποκριθεὶς [.β] ὁ Ἰησοῦς ἔλεγεν [.β΄] διδάσκων ἐν τῷ
    ἱερῷ,
[β] [.α] [..α] Πῶς λέγουσιν οἱ γραμματεῖς [..α΄] ὅτι ὁ Χριστὸς υἱὸς
    Δαυίδ ἐστιν;
³⁶[.β] [..α] αὐτὸς Δαυὶδ εἶπεν ἐν τῷ πνεύματι τῷ ἁγίῳ,
    [..β] [...α] Εἶπεν κύριος τῷ κυρίῳ μου,
    [...α΄] Κάθου ἐκ δεξιῶν μου
    [..β΄] [...α] ἕως ἂν θῶ τοὺς ἐχθρούς σου
    [...α΄] ὑποκάτω τῶν ποδῶν σου.
³⁷[.β΄] [..α] αὐτὸς Δαυὶδ λέγει αὐτὸν κύριον, [..α΄] καὶ πόθεν αὐτοῦ
    ἐστιν υἱός;
[β΄] καὶ [ὁ] πολὺς ὄχλος ἤκουεν αὐτοῦ ἡδέως.

    I judge again that Mark has not departed here from his usual αββ΄ rhetorical style: [β΄] is the completing response to [β], not [α] which here is an extravagant introductory statement, in its [.α] [.β] [.β΄] completion by Mark. Further to this, the line which follows his construction reads: β [α]³⁸ [.α] [..α] Καὶ ἐν τῇ διδαχῇ αὐτου [..α΄] ἔλεγεν... and it is another, similar introductory statement (for the next rhetorical unit) with a reversal of the common words which demonstrates the common functions of Β΄α [α]³⁵ [.α] and Β΄β [α]³⁸ [.α]. In the inner construction of [β] an identification of the same [.α] [.β] [.β΄] ordering is made, and within [.β] is another [..α] [..β] [..β΄], where we discover parechesis in the two lines of both [..β] and [..β΄]. Marcus at least recognises here (*cf.* his quote above, from Ps.118) that the quotation is two pairs of balancing statements. My alternative may lack his 'simplistic appeal', but it continues to display Mark's αββ΄ method at several levels of literary order; it pays attention to much more than a few verbal correspondences; and it qualifies the unit's fixing in its literary setting.

Day Twenty-five: 14.1-11:

Given that the first three Days comprise a sub-Series, this fourth Day's telling in Mark's final Series of seven Days occupies 'central' place. It behaves, as we might now expect, as a hinge, pivot or fulcrum to the material of the sub-Series of three Days each side of it. The Day relates two particular turning points, the plotting of Jesus' arrest and death, in which a disciple shares a part, in betraying him (see under Day Twenty-three, the table of conflict-climaxes), and the anointing of Jesus "for his burial" by a woman who will be remembered, "wherever the Gospel is proclaimed in all the world" (a unique clause in the Gospel narrative). In contrast to Judas Iscariot, literally "the one of the twelve", who will be remembered for his treachery, the woman who 'in one action anointed him Messiah, proclaimed his death and resurrection and made an act of total commitment to him as Lord'[28] is sadly unnamed.

The Day looks both backwards and forwards. Under Day Twenty-four I drew attention to the fact that the leaders of Old Israel set out to "trap" Jesus (12.13) but failed (12.13-34). They had to find another way. The Day's telling begins with their seeking how they might by stealth seize him and kill him: the Day's telling ends with the burden shifted onto Judas who now has to look for an opportunity to betray him. His chance comes the very next day.

The Day begins with what seems to be a simple and straightforward temporal reference[29], Ἦν δὲ τὸ πάσχα καὶ τὰ ἄζυμα μετὰ δύο ἡμέρας, but there is a problem, and it is not with the combining of the two feasts, for they had already become one[30]: it is with μετὰ δύο ἡμέρας. The key to understanding how Mark is counting, either inclusively meaning "the day before", or counting two whole days on, is found in Mark's references to Jesus' predictions that "after three days" he would rise (8.31, 9.31, 10.34). The three days are clearly Friday, Saturday and Sunday (see Days Twenty-seven, 15.1-47, and Twenty-eight, 16.1-8). He is counting inclusively. This Day's telling is located, therefore, on the day before the first Day of the Feast (14.12) which is Mark's Day Twenty-six

---

[28] Hooker, *The Gospel...*, p.330.
[29] See under Day Two for a listing of all Mark's Days which begin with temporal references.
[30] II Chron. 35.17; Josephus, *Antiquities*, XIV.2.1; XVII.9.3.

which follows this one. At first sight, the Day may appear structured to a chiasm, but discerning Mark's usual ABB' method we see how A (vv.1,2) is introductory to the Day, and B (vv.3-9) and B' (vv.10,11) complete the Day's telling and hold together for reference to 'place', to 'money' and to 'true discipleship'.

On 'place': B begins: Καὶ ὄντος αὐτοῦ ἐν Βηθανίᾳ ἐν τῇ οἰκίᾳ Σίμωνος τοῦ λεπροῦ κατακειμένου αὐτοῦ... (parechesis is observable in vv.2,3 but appears to function here more as an anastrophe to link vv1,2 and 3ff.); B' begins: Καὶ Ἰούδας Ἰσκαριὼθ ὁ εἷς τῶν δώδεκα <u>ἀπῆλθεν</u>... On 'money': the annoyance "of some" of the disciples with the woman was that the ointment could have been sold for over "three hundred denarii" and given to the poor (vv.4,5); and the chief priests promised Judas "silver" (v.11). The closing two parts β and β΄, which balance as first and second developments, do lend support to the view that Judas betrayed Jesus for the money. Though Matthew does not mention the "three hundred denarii" in relation to the ointment, he does, alone of the Synoptists, put the figure of "thirty" on the pieces of "silver" (Matt. 26.9,15). It would appear that both Mark and Matthew saw the monetary connection between the woman and Judas. On 'true discipleship': the greatest acts of generosity to Jesus express 'true discipleship'. Discipleship is not simply being listed among his followers, even his closest followers are capable of abusing his trust.

The literary structure of Day Twenty-five may be viewed as:

A α   ¹[α] Ἦν δὲ [β] <u>τὸ πάσχα</u> καὶ <u>τὰ ἄζυμα</u> [β΄] <u>μετὰ δύο ἡμέρας</u>.
  β   [α] καὶ ἐζήτουν <u>οἱ ἀρχιερεῖς</u> καὶ οἱ γραμματεῖς [β] πῶς αὐτὸν ἐν δόλῳ κρατήσαντες [β΄] ἀποκτείνωσιν·
  β΄ ²[α] ἔλεγον γάρ, [β] <u>Μὴ</u> ἐν τῇ ἑορτῇ, [β΄] <u>μήποτε</u> ἔσται θόρυβος τ<u>οῦ</u> λα<u>οῦ</u>.

B α[α] ³[.α] Καὶ ὄντος αὐτ<u>οῦ</u> [.β] <u>ἐν</u> Βηθανίᾳ [.β] <u>ἐν</u> τῇ οἰκίᾳ Σίμωνος τ<u>οῦ</u> λεπρ<u>οῦ</u>
  [β] [.α] κατακειμέν<u>ου</u> αὐτ<u>οῦ</u> [.β] ἦλθεν γυνὴ [.β΄] <u>ἔχουσα ἀλάβαστρον</u> <u>μύρου</u> νάρδ<u>ου</u> πιστικῆς πολυτελοῦς·
  [β΄] [.α] συντρίψασα τὴν <u>ἀλάβαστρον</u> [.α΄] κατέχεεν αὐτοῦ τῆς κεφαλῆς.

β[α]   ⁴[.α] [..α] ἦσαν δέ τινες [..α´] ἀγανακτοῦντες πρὸς ἑαυτούς, [.β] Εἰς
τί ἡ ἀπώλεια αὕτη τοῦ μύρου γέγονεν; ⁵[.β´] [..α] ἠδύνατο γὰρ
τοῦτο τὸ μύρον πραθῆναι ἐπάνω δηναρίων τριακοσίων [..α´] καὶ
δοθῆναι τοῖς πτωχοῖς·
[β]   καὶ ἐνεβριμῶντο αὐτῇ.
[β´]   ⁶[.α] ὁ δὲ 'Ιησοῦς εἶπεν, [.α´] [..α] ῎Αφετε αὐτήν· [..β] τί αὐτῇ κόπους
παρέχετε; [..β´] καλὸν ἔργον ἠργάσατο ἐν ἐμοί.
β´[α]   ⁷[.α] [..α] πάντοτε γὰρ τοὺς πτωχοὺς ἔχετε μεθ᾽ ἑαυτῶν, [..β] καὶ ὅταν
θέλητε [..β´] δύνασθε αὐτοῖς εὖ ποιῆσαι, [.α´] ἐμὲ δὲ οὐ πάντοτε
ἔχετε.
[β]   ⁸[.α] ὃ ἔσχεν ἐποίησεν· [.β] προέλαβεν μυρίσαι τὸ σῶμά μου [.β´] εἰς
τὸν ἐνταφιασμόν.
[β´]   ⁹[.α] ἀμὴν δὲ λέγω ὑμῖν, [.β] [..α] ὅπου ἐὰν κηρυχθῇ τὸ εὐαγγέλιον
[..α´] εἰς ὅλον τὸν κόσμον, [.β´] [..α] καὶ ὃ ἐποίησεν αὕτη
[..α´] λαληθήσεται εἰς μνημόσυνον αὐτῆς.

Β´α   ¹⁰[α] [.α] Καὶ 'Ιούδας 'Ισκαριὼθ [.α´] ὁ εἷς τῶν δώδεκα [β] ἀπῆλθεν
πρὸς τοὺς ἀρχιερεῖς [β´] ἵνα αὐτὸν παραδοι αὐτοῖς.
β   ¹¹[α] οἱ δὲ ἀκούσαντες [β] ἐχάρησαν [β´] [.α] καὶ ἐπηγγείλαντο
[.β] αὐτῷ [.β´] ἀργύριον δοῦναι.
β´   [α] καὶ ἐζήτει [α´] πῶς αὐτὸν εὐκαίρως παραδοῖ.

Day Twenty-six: 14.12-72:

The Day, the Gospel's third longest in the telling, begins Mark's final threesome/sub-Series of "Days". They are the most momentous of all his "Days". The hinge day of this Series, Day Twenty-five, in looking both backwards and forwards, may be considered to introduce the Passion narrative, but the Passion narrative as such actually *starts* here with the introductory section, 14.12-16, which begins with Mark's second reference to the Feast (see 14.1).

Of immediate interest, structurally speaking, is the description of "preparation" which has its clear parallel at the beginning of the first Day of the first sub-Series, 11.1-6[31]. The two sub-Series mirror each other, in their openings. The common details are substantial. The Markan ABA' structure to the "Jerusalem Days", where A is the first and A' is the second sub-Series around the middle Day B, is well demonstrated. We compare the Greek:

---

[31]   Neirynck identifies 11.1-7 and 14.12-16 as a 'Larger pericope Doublet', *Duality...*, p.135.

THE FOURTH SERIES 267

From 11.1-6:

α   ἀποστέλλει δύο τῶν μαθητῶν αὐτοῦ καὶ λέγει αὐτοῖς,
β   ‛Υπάγετε εἰς τὴν κώμην τὴν κατέναντι ὑμῶν.
γ   Καὶ εὐθὺς εἰσπορευόμενοι εἰς αὐτὴν εὑρήσετε πῶλον δεδεμένον ἐφ' ὃν οὐδεὶς οὔπω ἀνθρώπων ἐκάθισεν·
δ   λύσατε αὐτὸν καὶ φέρετε.
ε   εἴπατε, ‛Ο κύριος
ζ   Καὶ ἀπῆλθον καὶ εὗρον πῶλον δεδεμένον
η   καὶ λύουσιν αὐτόν... ἐκεῖ
θ   οἱ δὲ εἶπαν αὐτοῖς καθὼς εἶπεν ὁ Ἰησοῦς

From 14.12-16:

α   καὶ ἀποστέλλει δύο τῶν μαθητῶν αὐτοῦ [.α΄] καὶ λέγει αὐτοῖς,
β   ‛Υπάγετε εἰς τὴν πόλιν,
γ   καὶ ἀπαντήσει ὑμῖν ἄνθρωπος κεράμιον ὕδατος βαστάζων·
δ   ἀκολουθήσατε αὐτῷ,
ε   εἴπατε... ‛Ο διδάσκαλος καὶ ἐκεῖ ἑτοιμάσατε ἡμῖν.
ζ   καὶ ἐξῆλθον οἱ μαθηταὶ καὶ ἦλθον εἰς τὴν πόλιν καὶ εὗρον
[θ] καθὼς εἶπεν αὐτοῖς
[η] καὶ ἡτοίμασαν τὸ πάσχα.

Repeating phrases, words and endings are underlined. The details and the constructions of the stories follow each other more or less in order, up to the last lines. There is no doubting that one story owes its current form to the other, and there is every good reason to argue here that Mark created one to match the other in order to signal, in the same ways, beginnings to this Series' two threesomes of Days (11.1-13.37 and 14.12-16.8). To Schweizer, it is more likely 14.12-16 which Mark created because John's Gospel omits it[32]. To me, it is more likely 11.1-6. The account of 14.12-16 is much less repetitive in its detail than 11.1-6. Further, the details of 14.12-16 are important to the following reports in this Day's telling, whereas the details of 11.1-6 (which take up more than half Day Twenty-two's verses) appear to have as their primary purpose the aim of affirming that the prophecy of Zechariah is fulfilled.[33]

---

[32] Schweizer, *The Good News...*, p.294.
[33] See page 240 and my note 3, for an additional and very important link between these opening Days of these sub-Series: the allusions in both to the prophecy of Zechariah; in the first, Zech. 9.9 and in the second, 9.11.

The parameters of the Day are 14.12 and v.72[34], by way of the initial temporal reference and dating (see Day Twenty-five for a brief discussion), and because the following Day, which is consecutive, clearly begins at 15.1 with the words, Καὶ εὐθὺς πρωΐ... The literary-structure of Day Twenty-six is in the form of an ABB' scheme overall.

We examine the first section (14.12-31) designated A in the overall scheme for the Day. Part A (vv.12-16) introduces the Day's date and the matter of the disciples' preparation for Jesus to eat the Passover in an upper room which is made ready for them.

Part B (vv.17-25) tells how "when evening came" Jesus and the twelve shared the meal together (note ἔρχεται). At table the presence of the betrayer is the immediate issue: the two matters which complete the table-scene are Jesus' identification of his body and his blood of the 'covenant' with bread and wine; and that he will not drink wine again until "the day that" he drinks it "new" in the kingdom of God.

Part B' (vv.26-31) tells again of future events: on the Mount of Olives he tells them that they will be scattered, but that (1) after he is raised (2) he will go before them into Galilee (compare Day seven of this Series, the last Day of the Gospel narrative, at 16.7 for the telling of (1) and the reminder of (2)). The balancing concluding pieces link with the opening piece, through the word, σκανδαλισθήσεσθε. In the first, Peter claims he would not be like the others, but Jesus knows what will happen (as at the beginnings of this Day and Day Twenty-two, 11.1-11): he will deny him. In the second, Peter 'begins' to protest: what he says they all 'continue to say'.

I present the literary structure of Section A, 14.12-31:

---

[34] Heil views 14.1-52 as a nine-scene Markan whole, but because he fails to establish at the outset the beginning and end of a Markan presentation based on the beginning and ending of "Days" his "narrative structure" is immediately flawed. See John Paul Heil, "Mark 14.1-52: Narrative Structure and Reader-Response", *Bib.*, 71 no.3 (1990), pp.305-332.

THE FOURTH SERIES 269

A α[α]¹²[.α] Καὶ τῇ πρώτῃ ἡμέρᾳ τῶν ἀζύμων, [.β] ὅτε τὸ πάσχα ἔθυον,
[.β'] λέγουσιν αὐτῷ οἱ μαθηταὶ αὐτοῦ,
[β] [.α] Ποῦ θέλεις [.β] ἀπελθόντες ἑτοιμάσωμεν [.β'] ἵνα φάγῃς τὸ πάσχα;
[β'] ¹³[.α] καὶ ἀποστέλλει δύο τῶν μαθητῶν αὐτοῦ [.α'] καὶ λέγει αὐτοῖς,
β[α] [.α] ' Υπάγετε εἰς τὴν πόλιν,
[.β] καὶ ἀπαντήσει ὑμῖν ἄνθρωπος κεράμιον ὕδατος βαστάζων·
[.β'] ἀκολουθήσατε αὐτῷ,
[β] ¹⁴[.α] [..α] καὶ ὅπου ἐὰν εἰσέλθῃ [..α'] εἴπατε τῷ οἰκοδεσπότῃ
[.β] [..α] ὅτι ' Ο διδάσκαλος λέγει, [..α'] Ποῦ ἐστιν τὸ κατάλυμά μου
[.β'] [..α] ὅπου τὸ πάσχα [..β] μετὰ τῶν μαθητῶν μου [..β'] φάγω;
[β'] ¹⁵[.α] [..α] καὶ αὐτὸς [..β] ὑμῖν [..β'] δείξει
[.β] [..α] ἀνάγαιον μέγα [..β] ἐστρωμένον [..β'] ἕτοιμον·
[.β'] [..α] καὶ ἐκεῖ [..β] ἑτοιμάσατε [..β'] ἡμῖν.
β'[α] ¹⁶ καὶ ἐξῆλθον οἱ μαθηταὶ
[β] [.α] καὶ ἦλθον εἰς τὴν πόλιν [.β] καὶ εὗρον [.β'] καθὼς εἶπεν αὐτοῖς,
[β'] καὶ ἡτοίμασαν τὸ πάσχα.

B α[α] ¹⁷[.α] Καὶ ὀψίας γενομένης [.α'] ἔρχεται μετὰ τῶν δώδεκα.
[β] ¹⁸[.α] [..α] καὶ ἀνακειμένων αὐτῶν [..β] καὶ ἐσθιόντων [..β'] ὁ Ἰησοῦς εἶπεν,
[.β] [..α] 'Αμὴν λέγω ὑμῖν [..β] ὅτι εἷς ἐξ ὑμῶν παραδώσει με, [..β'] ὁ ἐσθίων μετ' ἐμοῦ.
¹⁹[.β'] [..α] ἤρξαντο λυπεῖσθαι [..β] καὶ λέγειν αὐτῷ εἷς κατὰ εἷς,
[..β'] Μήτι ἐγώ;
[β'] ²⁰[.α] [..α] ὁ δὲ εἶπεν αὐτοῖς, [..β] Εἷς τῶν δώδεκα, [..β'] ὁ ἐμβαπτόμενος μετ' ἐμοῦ εἰς τὸ τρύβλιον.
²¹[.β] [..α] ὅτι ὁ μὲν υἱὸς τοῦ ἀνθρώπου ὑπάγει [..β] καθὼς γέγραπται [..β'] περὶ αὐτοῦ,
[.β'] [..α] οὐαὶ δὲ τῷ ἀνθρώπῳ ἐκείνῳ [..β] δι' οὗ ὁ υἱὸς τοῦ ἀνθρώπου παραδίδοται· [..β'] [...α] καλὸν αὐτῷ [...α'] εἰ οὐκ ἐγεννήθη ὁ ἄνθρωπο ἐκεῖνος.
β[α] ²² Καὶ ἐσθιόντων αὐτῶν
[β] [.α] λαβὼν ἄρτον
[.β] [..α] εὐλογήσας [..β] ἔκλασεν [..β'] καὶ ἔδωκεν αὐτοῖς
[.β'] [..α] καὶ εἶπεν, [..β] Λάβετε, [..β'] τοῦτό ἐστιν τὸ σῶμά μου.
[β'] ²³[.α] καὶ λαβὼν ποτήριον
[.β] [..α] εὐχαριστήσας [..β] ἔδωκεν αὐτοῖς, [..β'] καὶ ἔπιον ἐξ αὐτοῦ πάντες.
²⁴[.β'] [..α] καὶ εἶπεν αὐτοῖς, [..β] Τοῦτό ἐστιν τὸ αἷμά μου τῆς διαθήκης [..β'] τὸ ἐκχυνόμενον ὑπὲρ πολλῶν·
β'[α] ²⁵ ' Αμὴν λέγω ὑμῖν
[β] [.α] ὅτι οὐκέτι [.β] οὐ μὴ [.β'] πίω ἐκ τοῦ γενήματος τῆς ἀμπέλου
[β'] [.α] ἕως τῆς ἡμέρας ἐκείνης [.β] ὅταν αὐτὸ πίνω καινὸν [.β'] ἐν τη βασιλείᾳ τοῦ θεοῦ.

Β̓ α[α] ²⁶[.α] Καὶ ὑμνήσαντες [.α´] ἐξῆλθον εἰς τὸ Ὄρος τῶν Ἐλαιῶν.
[β] ²⁷ [.α] καὶ λέγει αὐτοῖς ὁ Ἰησοῦς [.β] ὅτι Πάντες σκανδαλισθήσεσθε,
[.β´] [..α] ὅτι γέγραπται, [..β] Πατάξω τὸν ποιμένα, [..β´] καὶ τὰ
πρόβατα διασκορπισθήσονται·
[β´] ²⁸[.α] ἀλλὰ μετὰ τὸ ἐγερθῆναί με [.β] προάξω ὑμᾶς [.β´] εἰς τὴν
Γαλιλαίαν.
β[α] ²⁹[.α] ὁ δὲ Πέτρος ἔφη αὐτῷ, [.β] Ει καὶ πάντες σκανδαλισθήσονται,
[.β´] ἀλλ' οὐκ ἐγώ.
[β] ³⁰[.α] καὶ λέγει αὐτῷ ὁ Ἰησοῦς, [.α´] Ἀμὴν λέγω σοι
[β´] [.α] [..α] ὅτι σὺ [..β] σήμερον [..β´] ταύτῃ τῇ νυκτὶ
[.β] πρὶν ἢ δὶς ἀλέκτορα φωνῆσαι [.β´] τρίς με ἀπαρνήσῃ.
β´[α] ³¹[.α] ὁ δε ἐκπερισσῶς ἐλάλει,
[β] [.α] Ἐὰν δέῃ με [.β] συναποθανεῖν σοι, [.β´] οὐ μή σε ἀπαρνήσομαι.
[β´] ὡσαύτως δὲ καὶ πάντες ἔλεγον.

We continue with the Day's Section B (14.32-46). It is located wholly in Gethsemane. Section A (vv.12-31) has introduced two matters which have their fulfilment that night: the betrayal of Judas (from part B (vv.17-25), in section A) is enacted in the Day's section B (vv.32-46), and the scattering of the disciples and the denial of Peter (from part B' (vv.26-31), in section A) are enacted in section B' (vv.47-72). The Day is most certainly constructed to an ABB' sectional scheme.

A α[α]³²[.α] Καὶ ἔρχονται [.β] εἰς χωρίον [.β´] οὗ τὸ ὄνομα Γεθσημανί,
[β] καὶ λέγει τοῖς μαθηταῖς αὐτοῦ,
[β´] [.α] Καθίσατε ὧδε [.α´] ἕως προσεύξωμαι.
β[α] ³³[.α] καὶ παραλαμβάνει [.β] [..α] τὸν Πέτρον [..β] καὶ [τὸν] Ἰάκωβον
[..β´] καὶ [τὸν] Ἰωάννην [.β´] μετ' αὐτοῦ,
[β] [.α] καὶ ἤρξατο [.β] ἐκθαμβεῖσθαι [.β´] καὶ ἀδημονεῖν,
[β´] ³⁴[.α] καὶ λέγει αὐτοῖς, [.α´] [..α] Περίλυπός ἐστιν ἡ ψυχή μου ἕως
θανάτου· [..β] μείνατε ὧδε [..β´] καὶ γρηγορεῖτε.
β´[α] ³⁵[.α] καὶ προελθὼν μικρὸν [.α´] ἔπιπτεν ἐπὶ τῆς γῆς,
[β] [.α] καὶ προσηύχετο [.β] ἵνα εἰ δυνατόν ἐστιν [.β´] παρέλθῃ ἀπ'
αὐτοῦ ἡ ὥρα,
[β´] ³⁶[.α] καὶ ἔλεγεν, [.α´] [..α] [...α´] Αββα [...α´] ὁ πατήρ, [..β] [...α] πάντα
δυνατα σοι· [...α´] παρένεγκε τὸ ποτήριον τοῦτο ἀπ' ἐμοῦ·
[..β´] [...α] ἀλλ' οὐ τί ἐγὼ θέλω [...α´] ἀλλὰ τί σύ.

B α[α]³⁷[.α] καὶ ἔρχεται [.α´] καὶ εὑρίσκει αὐτοὺς καθεύδοντας,
  [β]   [.α] καὶ λέγει τῷ Πέτρῳ, [.α´] [..α] Σίμων, [..β] καθεύδεις; [..β´] οὐκ
        ἴσχυσας μίαν ὥραν γρηγορῆσαι;
  [β´] ³⁸[.α] [..α] γρηγορεῖτε [..α´] καὶ προσεύχεσθε, [.β] ἵνα μὴ ἔλθητε εἰς
        πειρασμόν· [.β´] [..α] τὸ μὲν πνεῦμα πρόθυμον [..α´] ἡ δὲ σὰρξ
        ἀσθενής.
  β[α] ³⁹[.α] καὶ πάλιν ἀπελθὼν [.β] προσηύξατο [.β´] τὸν αὐτὸν λόγον εἰπών.
  [β] ⁴⁰[.α] καὶ πάλιν ἐλθὼν [.β] εὗρεν αὐτοὺς καθεύδοντας, [.β´] ἦσαν γὰρ
        αὐτῶν οἱ ὀφθαλμοὶ καταβαρυνόμενοι,
  [β´] [.α] καὶ οὐκ ᾔδεισαν [.α´] τί ἀποκριθῶσιν αὐτῷ.
  β´[α] ⁴¹[.α] [..α] καὶ ἔρχεται τὸ τρίτον [..α´] καὶ λέγει αὐτοῖς, [.β] Καθεύδετε
        τὸ λοιπὸν [.β´] καὶ ἀναπαύεσθε;
  [β]   [.α] ἀπέχει· [.β] ἦλθεν ἡ ὥρα, [.β´] [..α] ἰδοὺ [..β] παραδίδοται ὁ υἱὸς
        τοῦ ἀνθρώπου [..β´] εἰς τὰς χεῖρας τῶν ἁμαρτωλῶν.
  [β´] ⁴²[.α] ἐγείρεσθε [.β] ἄγωμεν· [.β´] ἰδοὺ ὁ παραδιδούς με ἤγγικεν.

B᾿ α[α] ⁴³[.α] [..α] Καὶ εὐθὺς [..α´] ἔτι αὐτοῦ λαλοῦντος [.β] παραγίνεται
        Ἰούδας [.β´] εἷς τῶν δώδεκα
  [β]   [.α] καὶ μετ᾽ αὐτοῦ [.β] ὄχλος [.β´] [..α] μετα μαχαιρῶν [..α´] καὶ ξύλων
  [β´] [.α] παρὰ τῶν ἀρχιερέων [.β] καὶ τῶν γραμματέων [.β´] καὶ τῶν
        πρεσβυτέρων.
  β[α] ⁴⁴[.α] [..α] δεδώκει δὲ ὁ παραδιδοὺς αὐτὸν [..α´] σύσσημον αὐτοῖς
        [.α´] λέγων,
  [β]   [.α] Ὃν ἂν φιλήσω [.α´] αὐτός ἐστιν·
  [β´] [.α] κρατήσατε αὐτὸν [.β] καὶ ἀπάγετε [.β´] ἀσφαλῶς.
  β´[α] ⁴⁵[.α] καὶ ἐλθὼν [.α´] εὐθὺς
  [β]   [.α] προσελθὼν αὐτῷ [.β] [..α] λέγει, [.α´] ῾Ραββί, [.β´] καὶ
        κατεφίλησεν αὐτόν.
  [β´] ⁴⁶[.α] οἱ δὲ ἐπέβαλον τὰς χεῖρας αὐτῷ [.α´] καὶ ἐκράτησαν αὐτόν.

Section B (vv.32-46, above), in its three parts, displays typically Markan introductions to each: the first begins with two historical presents; the second begins with three; and the third begins with Καὶ εὐθὺς. In the first part A (vv.32-36), after the new setting and those with him are defined, Jesus first speaks to his three disciples and then, in prayer, to his father about his agony. The address to God is totally new in the Gospel, Ἀββα, ὁ πατήρ. Ἀββα, the Aramaic and intimate expression for "father" is nowhere else found in the Gospel (its use here, given the nature of Jesus' psychological state, is most appropriate). For "father" elsewhere, in respect to God, but nowhere else in the vocative, see 8.38, 11.25,26, and 13.32. The scene Mark paints allows the reader/listeners to witness the intimacy of the relationship Jesus has with the three and with his Father: it is a highly-charged moment which we are allowed to share.

Part B (vv.37-42) sees Jesus coming and going: three times he returns to the three. Each literary-part records a return of Jesus. It is a story beautifully, movingly and yet concisely told; and just as Jesus is beginning to accept that the three should be allowed their sleep, it ends dramatically with the betrayer coming near. (We note the verbal correspondences with the conclusion of Jesus' apocalyptic teaching of chapter 13, γρηγορεῖτε and καθεύδοντας, for which see under Day Twenty-four, page 261: we can so compare the last Day of the first threesome of Days of this Series with this Day, the first Day of the second threesome.)

Part B' (vv.43-46) opens with the telling of the arrival of Judas and a threatening crowd from "the chief priests, scribes and elders" (of Day Twenty-four's telling again, 11.27). The betrayal is told in the two balancing and completing parts. Jesus is seized.

We turn now to Section B' (14.47-72) which is linked to Section B by another anastrophe: we compare καὶ ἐκράτησαν αὐτόν, in 14.46, and καὶ οὐκ ἐκρατήσατέ με, in v.49. In part A (vv.47-54), in sub-part α Jesus is identified as a "robber" (see also 11.17 and 15.27 for λῃστὴν) in fulfilment of the scriptures (Isaiah 53.12[35]); in sub-part β Mark records the fleeing of Jesus' companions (in fulfilment of 14.27) and of the mysterious young man[36] who was nearly seized (v.51); and in sub-part β' the subjects for the remaining two parts, B and B' are introduced (in true Markan fashion, in A, his introductory piece), which in β'[α] is Jesus before the sanhedrin (part B), and which in β'[β] and [β'] is Peter in the courtyard of the high priest (part B').

Part B (vv.55-65) tells of Jesus before the sanhedrin. The opening piece α describes how the council sought any kind of witness against Jesus who remained silent in the face of false witness. The

---

[35] Marcus, *The Way of the Lord*..., p189: Marcus lists allusions to the Deutero-Isaian Servant Songs: 14.10,18,21,41-42, 15.1,10,15 (53.6,12); 14.24 (53.12); 14.61, 15.5 (53.7; 14.65 (50.6); 15.5,39 (52.15); 15.6-15 (53.6,12); I would add 14.48 (53.12).

[36] Compare 16.5: it appears to be indicated by Mark that the 'angel' who was later at the grave was first present at Jesus' arrest. We will return to this under Day Twenty-eight.

second piece β records the high priest's direct question, literally, "You are the Christ, the Son of the Blessed?"[37] Jesus gives a very direct answer. The high priest needed no other witness. Jesus is guilty of blasphemy. The third piece β' tells of the sentence: all condemned him to death; and then they began to mistreat him.

Part B' (vv.66-72) tells of Peter in the high priest's courtyard, in sub-part α, and later, outside in the forecourt, in sub-parts β and β', as he attempts to remove himself from the 'heat'. For each of the three sub-parts, read one 'denial', and note the common location for the last two parallel sub-parts, which also have in common the challenge: compare Οὗτος ἐξ αὐτῶν ἐστιν and Ἀληθῶς ἐξ αὐτῶν εἰ.

A α[α]⁴⁷[.α] [..α] εἷς δέ [τις] [..β] τῶν παρεστηκότων [..β'] σπασάμενος τὴν
<u>μάχαιραν</u>
[.β] ἔπαισεν τὸν δοῦλον τοῦ ἀρχιερέως [.β'] καὶ ἀφεῖλεν αὐτοῦ τὸ
ὠτάριον.
 [β] ⁴⁸[.α] καὶ ἀποκριθεὶς [.β] ὁ Ἰησοῦς εἶπεν αὐτοῖς, [.β'] [..α] Ὡς ἐπὶ
λῃστὴν ἐξήλθατε [..β] μετὰ <u>μαχαιρῶν καὶ ξύλων</u> [..β'] συλλαβεῖν με;
 [β'] ⁴⁹[.α] [..α] καθ᾽ ἡμέραν [..β] ἤμην πρὸς ὑμᾶς ἐν τῷ ἱερῷ
[..β'] διδάσκων [.β] καὶ οὐκ <u>ἐκρατήσατε</u> με· [.β'] ἀλλ᾽ ἵνα
πληρωθῶσιν αἱ γραφαί.
β[α] ⁵⁰[.α] καὶ ἀφέντες αὐτὸν [.α'] ἔφυγον πάντες.
 [β] ⁵¹[.α] [..α] Καὶ νεανίσκος [..α'] τις συνηκολούθει αὐτῷ
[.β] [..α] περιβεβλημένος σινδόνα [..α'] ἐπὶ γυμνοῦ, [.β'] καὶ
<u>κρατοῦσιν</u> αὐτόν·
 [β'] ⁵²[.α] ὁ δὲ [.β] <u>καταλιπὼν τὴν σινδόνα</u> [.β'] <u>γυμνὸς ἔφυγεν.</u>
β'[α] ⁵³[.α] Καὶ ἀπήγαγον <u>τὸν Ἰησοῦν</u> [.β] πρὸς <u>τὸν ἀρχιερέα</u>, [.β'] καὶ
συνέρχονται [..α] πάντες <u>οἱ ἀρχιερεῖς</u> [..β] καὶ οἱ πρεσβύτεροι
[..β'] καὶ οἱ γραμματεῖς.
 [β] ⁵⁴[.α] καὶ <u>ὁ Πέτρος</u> ἀπὸ μακρόθεν [.β] ἠκολούθησεν αὐτῷ [.β'] ἕως ἔσω
εἰς <u>τὴν αὐλὴν τοῦ ἀρχιερέως,</u>
 [β'] [.α] καὶ ἦν συγκαθήμενος [.β] μετὰ τῶν ὑπηρετῶν [.β'] καὶ
<u>θερμαινόμενος</u> πρὸς τὸ φῶς.
B α[α] ⁵⁵[.α] [..α] οἱ δὲ <u>ἀρχιερεῖς</u> καὶ ὅλον τὸ συνέδριον ἐζήτουν <u>κατὰ τοῦ</u>
<u>Ἰησοῦ μαρτυρίαν</u> [..β] <u>εἰς τὸ θανατῶσαι</u> αὐτόν, [..β'] καὶ <u>οὐχ</u>
<u>ηὕρισκον·</u> ⁵⁶[.β] πολλοὶ γὰρ ἐψευδο<u>μαρτ</u>ύρουν <u>κατ᾽ αὐτοῦ,</u>

---

[37] Marcus puts the case for restrictive apposition in 14.61, that is that there ought to be no comma between "Christ" and "Son of the Blessed", that the latter phrase qualifies the first and that they should not be read as two separate titles. Mark's rhetorical method, however, does not allow the expressing of anything so delicate as this: it demands a breaking down of sentences to phrases and phrases to words. It is a process which cannot be stopped! I read a ββ' pair: (β) Are you the Christ? (β') the Son of the Blessed? See, Joel Marcus, "Mark 14.61: "Are You the Messiah-Son-of-God?", *NovT*, 31, no.2 (1989), pp.125-142.

[.β'] καὶ ἴσαι αἱ μαρτυρίαι οὐκ ἦσαν.
[β] ⁵⁷[.α] [..α] καί τινες ἀναστάντες [..β] ἐψευδομαρτύρουν κατ' αὐτοῦ
[..β'] λέγοντες ⁵⁸[.β] [..α] ὅτι ' Ημεῖς ἠκούσαμεν αὐτοῦ λέγοντος
[..β] ὅτι 'Εγὼ καταλύσω τὸν ναὸν τοῦτον τὸν χειροποίητον [..β'] καὶ
διὰ τριῶν ἡμερῶν ἄλλον ἀχειροποίητον οἰκοδομήσω·
⁵⁹[.β'] [..α] καὶ οὐδὲ οὕτως ἴση [..α'] ἦν ἡ μαρτυρία αὐτῶν.
[β'] ⁶⁰[.α] [..α] [...α] καὶ ἀναστὰς [...β] ὁ ἀρχιερεὺς [...β'] εἰς μέσον
[..β] ἐπηρώτησεν τὸν 'Ιησοῦν [..β'] λέγων,
[.β] [..α] Οὐκ ἀποκρίνῃ οὐδέν; [..α'] τί οὗτοί σου καταμαρτυροῦσιν;
⁶¹[.β'] [..α] ὁ δὲ ἐσιώπα [..α'] καὶ οὐκ ἀπεκρίνατο οὐδέν.
β[α] [.α] [..α] πάλιν [..β] ὁ ἀρχιερεὺς ἐπηρώτα αὐτὸν [..β'] καὶ λέγει
αὐτῷ, [.β] Σὺ εἰ ὁ Χριστὸς [.β'] ὁ υἱὸς τοῦ εὐλογητοῦ ;
[β] ⁶²[.α] ὁ δὲ 'Ιησοῦς εἶπεν, [.β] 'Εγώ εἰμι, [.β'] [..α] καὶ ὄψεσθε τὸν υἱὸν
τοῦ ἀνθρώπου [..β] ἐκ δεξιῶν καθήμενον τῆς δυνάμεως [..β'] καὶ
ἐρχόμενον μετὰ τῶν νεφελῶν τοῦ οὐρανοῦ.
[β'] ⁶³[.α] [..α] ὁ δὲ ἀρχιερεὺς [..β] διαρρήξας τοὺς χιτῶνας [..β'] αὐτοῦ
λέγει, [.α'] [..α] Τί ἔτι χρείαν ἔχομεν μαρτύρων; [..β] ⁶⁴ ἠκούσατε τῆς
βλασφημίας· [..β'] τί ὑμῖν φαίνεται;
β'[α] [.α] οἱ δὲ πάντες κατέκριναν αὐτὸν [.α'] ἔνοχον εἶναι θανάτου.
[β] ⁶⁵[.α] Καὶ ἤρξαντό τινες ἐμπτύειν αὐτῷ [.β] καὶ περικαλύπτειν αὐτοῦ
τὸ πρόσωπον [.β'] καὶ κολαφίζειν αὐτὸν
[β'] [.α] καὶ λέγειν αὐτῷ, [..α'] Προφήτευσον,
[.β'] [..α] καὶ οἱ ὑπηρέται [..β] ῥαπίσμασιν [.β'] αὐτὸν ἔλαβον.
B' α[α] ⁶⁶[.α] Καὶ ὄντος τοῦ Πέτρου [.β] κάτω [.β'] ἐν τῇ αὐλῇ
[β] [.α] ἔρχεται μία τῶν παιδισκῶν τοῦ ἀρχιερέως,
⁶⁷[.β] [..α] [...α] καὶ ἰδοῦσα τὸν Πέτρον [...α'] θερμαινόμενον
[..β] ἐμβλέψασα αὐτῶ [..β'] λέγει,
[.β'] [..α] Καὶ σὺ [..β] μετὰ τοῦ Ναζαρηνοῦ ἦσθα [..β'] τοῦ 'Ιησοῦ.
[β'] ⁶⁸[.α] [..α] ὁ δὲ ἠρνήσατο [..α'] λέγων, [.β] Οὔτε οἶδα [.β'] [..α] οὔτε
ἐπίσταμαι [..α'] σὺ τί λέγεις.
β[α] [.α] καὶ ἐξῆλθεν [.β] ἔξω [.β'] εἰς τὸ προαύλιον·
OMIT [καὶ ἀλέκτωρ ἐφώνησεν]
[β] ⁶⁹[.α] καὶ ἡ παιδίσκη ἰδοῦσα αὐτὸν [.β] ἤρξατο πάλιν λέγειν τοῖς
παρεστῶσιν [.β'] ὅτι Οὗτος ἐξ αὐτῶν ἐστιν.
[β'] ⁷⁰ ὁ δὲ πάλιν ἠρνεῖτο.
β'[α] [.α] καὶ μετὰ μικρὸν [.β] πάλιν οἱ παρεστῶτες ἔλεγον τῷ Πέτρῳ,
[.β'] [..α] 'Αληθῶς [..β] ἐξ αὐτῶν εἶ, [..β'] καὶ γὰρ Γαλιλαῖος εἶ.
[β] ⁷¹[.α] ὁ δὲ ἤρξατο ἀναθεματίζειν [.β] καὶ ὀμνύναι [.β'] [..α] ὅτι Οὐκ
οἶδα [..β] τὸν ἄνθρωπον τοῦτον [..β'] ὃν λέγετε.
[β'] ⁷²[.α] [..α] καὶ εὐθὺς [..β] ἐκ δευτέρου [..β'] ἀλέκτωρ ἐφώνησεν.
[.β] [..α] [...α] καὶ ἀνεμνήσθη [...β] ὁ Πέτρος [...β'] τὸ ῥῆμα
[..β] [...α] ὡς εἶπεν [...β] αὐτῷ [...β'] ὁ'Ιησοῦς
[..β] [...α] ὅτι Πρὶν ἀλέκτορα φωνῆσαι δὶς [...α'] τρίς με
ἀπαρνήσῃ·
[.β'] [..α] καὶ ἐπιβαλὼν [..α'] ἔκλαιεν.

I comment on my note in the text above, 'OMIT': clearly [καὶ ἀλέκτωρ ἐφώνησεν] in v.68 has been added later, and not by Mark. Whilst it is supported by Codex Alexandrinus, it is not supported by Codices Sinaiticus and Vaticanus and many other witnesses. The reason is clear as to why it was added: Mark has failed, or an early copyist has failed to report the first cock-crow. The "second time a cock crew" is in v.72. We can be certain that the "first cock crow" is added where it is now by someone other than Mark, for three reasons. Firstly, we observe its bad positioning in the story-line:

β [α]   [.α] καὶ ἐξῆλθεν [.β] ἔξω [.βʻ] εἰς τὸ προαύλιον· [καὶ ἀλέκτωρ ἐφώνησεν]
[β]   ⁶⁹[.α] καὶ ἡ παιδίσκη ἰδοῦσα αὐτὸν [.β] ἤρξατο πάλιν λέγειν τοῖς παρεστῶσιν [.βʻ] ὅτι Οὗτος ἐξ αὐτῶν ἐστιν.
[βʻ]   ⁷⁰ ὁ δὲ πάλιν ἠρνεῖτο...

The story flows much better without it. Given the good story-telling position of the second cock crow immediately after the third denial (in [βʻ] of sub-part βʻ), its use here really does appear out of place, just after Peter changes location. My judgement is that Mark will have placed it after ὁ δὲ πάλιν ἠρνεῖτο to complete line [βʻ] of verse 70. The reasoning is based on an understanding of his rhetorical scheme of [.α] [.β] [.βʻ] and [.α] [.αʻ]. (Whoever added it where it is now did not know Mark's style.)

The logic, therefore, is that line β [α] is complete without the phrase: it reads:

β [α]   [.α] καὶ ἐξῆλθεν [.β] ἔξω [.βʻ] εἰς τὸ προαύλιον·

That is [.α] καὶ ἐξῆλθεν is introductory to the sentence, and in its own way it is complete. To it is added [.β] ἔξω which qualifies [.α] καὶ ἐξῆλθεν in the first place, and that phrase stands complete. To [.β] ἔξω is then added [.βʻ] εἰς τὸ προαύλιον which is further qualifying of [.β] ἔξω and therefore of [.α] καὶ ἐξῆλθεν [.β] ἔξω. It is a classic three-part Markan construction where the first part is introductory, the second is the first development and the third is the second and completing development. The phrase καὶ ἀλέκτωρ ἐφώνησεν does not belong at the end of this line β [α]. For very similar reasons the phrase does not belong at the beginning of the next line β [β]. Why it is judged that the phrase once sat, before copyists changed things, in line [β‛] after ὁ δὲ πάλιν ἠρνεῖτο is due to the following: 1) "denial" and "cock-crow" are elsewhere linked (14.30 and vv.71,72); 2) Mark places the second [ἀλέκτωρ ἐφώνησεν] in the [β‛] position in the sub-part β‛, the completing sub-sub-part to the story's last part; and 3) ἀλέκτωρ ἐφώνησεν after ὁ δὲ πάλιν ἠρνεῖτο, would be a proper [.α‛] qualifying/completing part to [.α], in Mark's method of presentation.

A third reason for judging that καὶ ἀλέκτωρ ἐφώνησεν is added in v.68 by another, is that it is arguable that Matthew and Luke identified the problem of the missing 'first-crowing' too, because they circumnavigated the problem by removing the word "twice" from Jesus' prediction: hence, "Before a cock crows you will..." If there ever was a first reference to 'cock crow', which a copier subsequently failed to copy, I judge it would fit appropriately only after ὁ δὲ πάλιν ἠρνεῖτο, in the first line of v.70.

Whatever the case, the Day concludes with the contritional tears of Peter. Thinking on what Jesus had said he would do, "he begins to weep". The implication of the Day's telling is that the last activities take place well into the night watches (a fire was lit, 14.54, around which people could warm themselves, in the cold night hours): Mark does not state which watch, but what he does say is that the events of the next Day begin early (see under Day One, for our discussion on the way Mark uses πρωΐ in a non-technical sense, of the fourth watch of the night, but co-incident, more or less, with sunrise).

Day Twenty-seven: 15.1-47:

The Day's telling begins Καὶ εὐθὺς πρωΐ... We identify a dramatic quickening of the pace of events. The form the Day's telling takes can be expressed as A:A', or in its longer, sectional form, as ABB':ABB' (see also Days Twenty-two and Twenty-four in this Series).

The first half of the Day's telling (21 verses) is told in three parts: part A (vv.1-5), Jesus before Pilate; part B (vv.6-14), Pilate before the crowd; and part B' (vv.15-21), Pilate pleases the crowd: Jesus is flogged, mocked and taken away for crucifixion. The second half (25 verses) begins with a historical present and a new location, Golgotha. It is told in three parts: part A (vv.22-32), Jesus is crucified at the third hour and is mocked; part B (vv.33-41), at the sixth hour, all is darkness and at the ninth hour he dies (women followers witness his death); and part B' (vv.42-47), as evening comes (just prior to the sabbath beginning), he is taken down from the cross and buried (two of the previously named women witness his burial).

The presentation of the Day's literary structure, which follows, demonstrates again the Markan rhetorical αββ style, which he has employed throughout his Gospel and applied at all the principal, lower levels of literary order. What is different, however, is that some significant verbal details are confined to this Day's telling alone in the Gospel: some, of course, will be due more to the nature of the content (the crucifixion) of the Day's telling than to deliberate planning on Mark's part, but one title and phrase which Mark clearly did deliberately use is his term "King of the Jews", for Jesus. In all the Gospel it is only presented in 15.2, 9, 12, 18 and 26 (in v.32 it is "King of Israel"). As he has shown careful control over his presentations in the first three Series of the Gospel regarding the 'secret of the person of Jesus', and demonstrated the same careful control in dispensing with 'the secret' in his third Series after 10.47,48 (the public and unrebuked affirmation of Jesus' messiahship)[38], it is more logical to conclude that Mark deliberately used this title of Jesus here than that this term was already lodged (solely) in the tradition of the crucifixion, prior to his receiving it.

Up until this Series, the only specific application of the word "King" attaches (improperly) to Herod, in 6.14. I said in my note 37, page 173, that it may have been a deliberate wrong use of the term by Mark in order to set Jesus' kingship as greater. In 11.1-11, Mark begs his audience to interpret his first Day's telling of this Series in the light of Zech. 9.9. He begins this Series (and first sub-Series) with telling us that Jesus is the 'coming King'. In 14.24, in the Day's telling which begins this sub-Series, Days Twenty-six to Twenty-eight, Mark begs his audience to interpret it in the light of Zech. 9.11. Jesus' blood seals the 'kingly covenant'. What has been

---

[38] See the discussion so far on the 'secret' and the third Series, page 234.

veiled until now, is spelt out here, in this Day's telling. It is the "King of the Jews" who is crucified.

Another word which is found here only in the Gospel, and only once unlike the phrase above, is located in 15.10, concerning Pilate:

ἐγίνωσκεν γὰρ ὅτι διὰ φθόνον παραδεδώκεισαν αὐτὸν οἱ ἀρχιερεῖς.

The word is φθόνον, meaning "envy", and it is immensely important because it explains why Jesus was crucified.[39]

It is worth first noting that we have already met with the singular use of two words in Mark's Gospel, in the previous Day's telling: in 14.36, 'Αββα ὁ πατήρ, and in 14.24, τῆς διαθήκης. These terms too are of great importance for understanding Mark's Gospel, which carries in its narrative so much allusion to the Old Covenant which is being replaced by the New. It is surely the case that Mark chooses to make very clear what he has been leading up to all the time. Jesus is truly the Son of God (see also 15.39 of this Day's telling), and his death seals the new covenant.

The same important function applies also, in 15.10, to Mark's use of "envy". Hagedorn and Neyrey[40] demonstrate emphatically in their paper that they have been right to develop a full 'anatomy of envy' "to indicate how pervasive and culturally plausible envy is in a document of conflict such as Mark's Gospel". They, and we should, consider Jesus' 'growing fame and reputation' for its attraction of envy and 'the growing attacks on Jesus'.[41] Here, in a single use of the word, Mark makes clear both the *source* of the conflict he has been telling about throughout his narrative, *and its outcome*. As a result of envy, Jesus is crucified.

In regard to the 'arrangement' of Mark's presentation, it has been suggested that Ps. 22 has influenced in particular the course of the telling of 15.22-16.8 (according to literary-structural analysis, 15.22-47 is the second half of this Day's telling, and 16.1-8 is the

---

[39] Anselm C. Hagedorn and Jerome H. Neyrey, " 'It was out of envy that they handed Jesus over' (Mark 15.10): The Anatomy of Envy and the Gospel of Mark", *JSNT* 69, (1998), pp.15-56.
[40] Hagedorn and Neyrey, "It was out of envy...", p.56.
[41] Additionally, Hagedorn and Neyrey would have us focus on 'envy which begins at home (Jesus' rejection at Nazareth)', 'the disciples' envy of a rival exorcist', 'envy among the disciples', Jesus' teaching on shunning honour and avoiding envy', 'secrecy and avoiding envy', 'refusing compliments', and 'the evil eye (of 7.21)'. "It was out of envy...", pp.47-54.

telling of the final Day of Mark's narrative). It may well be the case. Marcus[42] sees the parallels between the psalm and 15.20b-16.7:

	Psalm 22:	Mark:
Suffering	vv.1-21	15.20b-37
Worship of Gentiles	v.27	15.39
Kingdom of God	v.28	15.43
Resurrection	v.29	16.6
Proclamation to God's people	vv.30,31	16.7.

The comparison of 15.43 and v.28 is an interesting one, given the nature of this Day's unique but six times repeated disclosure of the person of Jesus. The verse of the Psalm can be read: "The Lord is King, and he rules the nations" (from the Good News Bible, which is bolder than most translations). It may have influenced Mark in his choice of this Day's title for Jesus, and the teaching that pertains to it, therefore, on the person of Jesus. Given that v.29 of the psalm resonates with resurrection notices, it may well be that Mark intended the interpretation to be this: that whilst they put to death, in the most awful way possible, *their* Lord and King, he was raised as the Lord and King of *all nations*. It is an interpretation that squares well with indicators of this in the Series (e.g. and so henceforth: 11.17, 13.27, 14.9), and it looks like another final sub-Series' clarification of the kind that we have been seeing above.

The literary structure of Day Twenty-seven is presented:

A α[α] ¹[.α] Καὶ εὐθὺς πρωι [.β] συμβούλιον ποιήσαντες [.β'] οἱ ἀρχιερεῖς
   [β] [.α] μετὰ τῶν πρεσβυτέρων [.β] καὶ γραμματέων [.β'] καὶ ὅλον τὸ συνέδριον
   [β'] [.α] δήσαντες τὸν Ἰησοῦν [.β] ἀπήνεγκαν [.β'] καὶ παρέδωκαν Πιλάτῳ.
β[α] ²[.α] καὶ ἐπηρώτησεν αὐτὸν ὁ Πιλᾶτος, [.α'] Σὺ εἶ ὁ βασιλεὺς τῶν Ἰουδαίων;
   [β] [.α] ὁ δὲ ἀποκριθεὶς αὐτῷ [.β] λέγει, [.β'] Σὺ λέγεις.
   [β'] ³[.α] καὶ κατηγόρουν αὐτοῦ [.β] οἱ ἀρχιερεῖς [.β'] πολλά.
β'[α] ⁴[.α] ὁ δὲ Πιλᾶτος πάλιν ἐπηρώτα αὐτὸν [.β] λέγων, [.β'] Οὐκ ἀποκρίνη οὐδέν;
   [β] [.α] Ἴδε [.β] πόσα [β'] σου κατηγοροῦσιν.
   [β'] ⁵[.α] ὁ δὲ Ἰησοῦς οὐκέτι οὐδὲν ἀπεκρίθη, [.α'] ὥστε θαυμάζειν τὸν Πιλᾶτον.

---

[42] Marcus, *The Way of the Lord...*, p.182.

Β α[α］ ⁶[.α] Κατὰ δὲ ἑορτὴν [.β] <u>ἀπέλυεν</u> αὐτοῖς ἕνα <u>δέσμιον</u> [.βʹ] ὃν παρῃτοῦντο.
 [β] ⁷[.α] ἦν δὲ ὁ λεγόμενος Βαραββᾶς [.β] μετὰ <u>τῶν στασιαστῶν δεδεμένος</u> [.βʹ] [..α] οἵτινες [..β] <u>ἐν τῇ στάσει</u> [..βʹ] φόνον πεποιήκεισαν.
 [βʹ] ⁸[.α] καὶ ἀναβὰς <u>ὁ ὄχλος</u> [.β] ἤρξατο αἰτεῖσθαι [.βʹ] καθὼς <u>ἐποίει</u> αὐτοῖς.
 β[α] ⁹[.α] <u>ὁ δὲ Πιλᾶτος ἀπεκρίθη αὐτοῖς</u> [.β] <u>λέγων,</u> [βʹ] [..α] <u>Θέλετε</u> [..αʹ] <u>ἀπολύσω ὑμῖν τὸν βασιλέα τῶν Ἰουδαίων;</u>
 [β] ¹⁰[.α] ἐγίνωσκεν γὰρ [.β] ὅτι διὰ φθόνον [.βʹ] <u>παραδεδώκεισαν</u> αὐτὸν <u>οἱ ἀρχιερεῖς.</u>
 [βʹ] ¹¹[.α] <u>οἱ δὲ ἀρχιερεῖς</u> ἀνέσεισαν <u>τὸν ὄχλον</u> [.αʹ] ἵνα μᾶλλον <u>τὸν Βαραββᾶν ἀπολύσῃ αὐτοῖς.</u>
 βʹ[α] ¹²[.α] <u>ὁ δὲ Πιλᾶτος</u> πάλιν ἀποκριθεὶς [.β] ἔλεγεν αὐτοῖς, [.βʹ] [..α] <u>Τί</u> οὖν [<u>θέλετε</u>] [..β] <u>ποιήσω</u> [..βʹ] [ὃν λέγετε] <u>τὸν βασιλέα τῶν Ἰουδαίων;</u>
 [β] ¹³[.α] οἱ δὲ <u>πάλιν ἔκραξαν,</u> [.αʹ] <u>Σταύρωσον αὐτόν.</u>
 [βʹ] ¹⁴[.α] <u>ὁ δὲ Πιλᾶτος ἔλεγεν αὐτοῖς,</u> [.β] <u>Τι</u> γὰρ <u>ἐποίησεν</u> κακόν; [.βʹ] [..α] οἱ δὲ περισσῶς <u>ἔκραξαν,</u> [..αʹ] <u>Σταύρωσον αὐτόν.</u>

Βʹ α[α] ¹⁵[.α] <u>ὁ δὲ Πιλᾶτος</u> [.β] βουλόμενος [.βʹ] <u>τῷ ὄχλῳ</u> τὸ ἱκανὸν <u>ποιῆσαι</u>
 [β] <u>ἀπέλυσεν αὐτοῖς τὸν Βαραββᾶν,</u>
 [βʹ] [.α] καὶ <u>παρέδωκεν</u> τὸν Ἰησοῦν [.β] φραγελλώσας [.βʹ] ἵνα <u>σταυρωθῇ.</u>
 β[α] ¹⁶[.α] [..α] Οἱ δὲ στρατιῶται <u>ἀπήγαγον αὐτὸν</u> [..β] ἔσω <u>τῆς αὐλῆς,</u> [..βʹ] ὅ ἐστιν <u>πραιτώριον,</u> [.αʹ] καὶ συγκαλοῦσιν ὅλην τὴν σπεῖραν.
 [β] ¹⁷[.α] καὶ <u>ἐνδιδύσκουσιν αὐτὸν πορφύραν</u> [.β] καὶ <u>περιτιθέασιν</u> αὐτῷ πλέξαντες ἀκάνθινον στέφανον· [.βʹ] ¹⁸[..α] καὶ ἤρξαντο ἀσπάζεσθαι αὐτόν, [..β] Χαῖρε, [..βʹ] <u>βασιλεῦ τῶν Ἰουδαίων·</u>
 [βʹ] ¹⁹[.α] καὶ <u>ἔτυπτον</u> αὐτοῦ τὴν κεφαλὴν καλάμῳ [.β] καὶ <u>ἐνέπτυον</u> αὐτῷ, [.βʹ] [..α] καὶ τιθέντες τὰ γόνατα [..αʹ] προσεκύνουν αὐτῷ.
 βʹ[α] ²⁰[.α] καὶ ὅτε ἐνέπαιξαν αὐτῷ, [.β] <u>ἐξέδυσαν αὐτὸν τὴν πορφύραν</u> [.βʹ] καὶ <u>ἐνέδυσαν αὐτὸν</u> τὰ ἱμάτια αὐτοῦ.
 [β] [.α] καὶ <u>ἐξάγουσιν</u> αὐτὸν [.αʹ] ἵνα <u>σταυρώσωσιν αὐτόν.</u>
 [βʹ] ²¹[.α] Καὶ <u>ἀγγαρεύουσιν</u> [.β] [..α] <u>παράγοντα</u> τινα Σίμωνα Κυρηναῖον [..β] <u>ἐρχόμενον</u> ἀπ' ἀγροῦ, [..βʹ] τὸν πατέρα Ἀλεξάνδρου καὶ Ῥούφου, [.βʹ] ἵνα ἄρῃ τὸν <u>σταυρὸν</u> <u>αὐτοῦ.</u>

A a[α]²²[.α] καὶ <u>φέρουσιν</u> αὐτὸν [.β] ἐπὶ <u>τὸν Γολγοθᾶν τόπον</u>, [.β'] ὅ ἐστιν μεθερμηνευόμενον <u>Κρανίου Τόπος</u>.
[β] ²³[.α] καὶ <u>ἐδίδουν</u> αὐτῷ ἐσμυρνισμένον οἶνον, [.α'] ὃς δὲ οὐκ ἔλαβεν.
[β'] ²⁴[.α] καὶ <u>σταυροῦσιν</u> αὐτὸν [.β] καὶ διαμερίζονται τὰ ἱμάτια αὐτοῦ, [.β'] [..α] βάλλοντες κλῆρον ἐπ' αὐτὰ [..α'] τίς τί ἄρη.
β[α] ²⁵[.α] <u>ἦν δὲ ὥρα τρίτη</u>
[β] ²⁶[.α] καὶ <u>ἐσταύρωσαν αὐτόν</u>. [.β] καὶ ἦν ἡ <u>ἐπιγραφη</u> τῆς αἰτίας αὐτοῦ [.β'] <u>ἐπιγεγραμμένη</u>, Ὁ βασιλεὺς τῶν Ἰουδαίων.
[β'] ²⁷[.α] Καὶ <u>σὺν αὐτῷ σταυροῦσιν</u> δύο λῃστάς, [.β] <u>ἕνα ἐκ</u> δεξιῶν [.β'] καὶ <u>ἕνα ἐξ</u> εὐωνύμων αὐτοῦ.
β'[α] ²⁹[.α] [..α] Καὶ οἱ παραπορευόμενοι ἐβλασφήμουν αὐτὸν [..β] κινοῦντες τὰς κεφαλὰς αὐτῶν [..β'] καὶ λέγοντες, [.β] [..α] Οὐὰ <u>ὁ καταλύων τὸν ναὸν</u> [..α'] καὶ <u>οἰκοδομῶν</u> ἐν τρισὶν ἡμέραις,³⁰[.β'] [..α] <u>σῶσον σεαυτὸν</u> [..α'] <u>καταβὰς ἀπὸ τοῦ σταυροῦ</u>.
[β] ³¹[.α] [..α] ὁμοίως καὶ <u>οἱ ἀρχιερεῖς</u> ἐμπαίζοντες πρὸς ἀλλήλους [..β] μετὰ τῶν γραμματέων [..β'] ἔλεγον, [.β] [..α] Ἄλλους <u>ἔσωσεν</u>, [..α'] <u>ἑαυτὸν</u> οὐ δύναται <u>σῶσαι</u>· ³²[.β'] [..α] [...α] ὁ Χριστὸς [...α'] <u>ὁ βασιλεὺς Ἰσραὴλ</u> [..β] καταβάτω νῦν <u>ἀπὸ του σταυροῦ</u>, [..β'] [...α] ἵνα ἴδωμεν [...α'] καὶ πιστεύσωμεν.
[β'] [.α] καὶ οἱ <u>συνεσταυρωμένοι σὺν</u> αὐτῷ [..α'] ὠνείδιζον αὐτόν.

B a[α]³³[.α] <u>Καὶ γενομένης ὥρας ἕκτης</u> [.β] σκότος <u>ἐγένετο</u> ἐφ' ὅλην τὴν γῆν [.β'] <u>ἕως ὥρας ἐνάτης</u>.
[β] ³⁴[.α] καὶ <u>τῇ ἐνάτῃ ὥρᾳ</u> [.β] [..α] <u>ἐβόησεν</u> ὁ Ἰησοῦς [..α'] <u>φωνῇ μεγάλῃ</u>, [.β'] [..α] [...α] <u>Ελωι</u> [...α'] ελωι [..α'] λεμα σαβαχθανι;
[β'] [.α] ὅ ἐστιν μεθερμηνευόμενον [.α'] [..α] [...α] <u>Ὁ Θεός μου</u> [...α'] <u>ὁ θεός μου</u>, [..α'] <u>εἰς τί ἐγκατέλιπές με</u>;
β[α] ³⁵[.α] καί τινες τῶν παρεστηκότων [.β] [..α] ἀκούσαντες [..α'] ἔλεγον, [.β'] [..α] Ἴδε [..α'] <u>Ἠλίαν</u> φωνεῖ.
[β] ³⁶[.α] [..α] δραμὼν δέ [..α'] τις [καὶ] γεμίσας σπόγγον ὄξους [.β] [..α] περιθεὶς καλάμῳ [..β] ἐπότιζεν αὐτόν, [..β'] λέγων, [.β'] [..α] <u>Ἄφετε</u> [..β] ἴδωμεν εἰ ἔρχεται Ἠλίας [..β'] καθελεῖν αὐτόν.
[β'] ³⁷[.α] [..α] ὁ δὲ Ἰησοῦς [..β] <u>ἀφεὶς φωνὴν μεγάλην</u> [..β'] <u>ἐξέπνευσεν</u>.
³⁸ [.β] [..α] Καὶ τὸ καταπέτασμα τοῦ ναοῦ ἐσχίσθη εἰς δύο [..β] ἀπ' ἄνωθεν [..β'] ἕως κάτω.
³⁹[.β'] [..α] [...α] Ἰδὼν δὲ [...β] <u>ὁ κεντυρίων</u> [...β'] ὁ παρεστηκὼς [..β] [...α] ἐξ ἐναντίας αὐτοῦ [...β] ὅτι οὕτως <u>ἐξέπνευσεν</u> [...β'] εἶπεν, [..β'] [...α'] Ἀληθῶς [...β] οὗτος ὁ ἄνθρωπος [...β'] <u>υἱὸς θεου</u> ἦν.
β'[α] ⁴⁰[.α] Ἦσαν δὲ καὶ γυναῖκες [.β] ἀπὸ μακρόθεν [.β'] <u>θεωροῦσαι</u>,
[β] [.α] [..α] ἐν αἷς καὶ <u>Μαρία ἡ Μαγδαληνη</u> [..β] <u>καὶ Μαρία η</u> Ἰακώβου τοῦ μικροῦ καὶ Ἰωσῆτος μήτηρ [..β'] καὶ Σαλώμη,⁴¹[.α'] [..α] αἳ ὅτε ἦν ἐν τῇ Γαλιλαίᾳ [..β] <u>ἠκολούθουν</u> αὐτῷ [..β'] καὶ διηκόνουν αὐτῷ,
[β'] [.α] καὶ ἄλλαι πολλαὶ [.β] αἱ συναναβᾶσαι αὐτῷ [.β'] εἰς Ἱεροσόλυμα.

Β'α[α]⁴²[.α] Καὶ ἤδη ὀψίας γενομένης, [.β] ἐπεὶ ἦν παρασκευή, [.β'] ὅ ἐστιν προσάββατον,
[β] ⁴³[.α] ἐλθὼν Ἰωσὴφ [ὁ] ἀπὸ ˙ Ἀριμαθαίας [.β] εὐσχήμων βουλευτής,
[.β'] ὃς καὶ αὐτὸς ἦν προσδεχόμενος τὴν βασιλείαν τοῦ θεοῦ,
[β'] [.α] τολμήσας [.β] εἰσῆλθεν πρὸς τὸν Πιλᾶτον [.β'] καὶ ᾐτήσατο τὸ σῶμα τοῦ Ἰησοῦ.
β[α] ⁴⁴[.α] ὁ δὲ Πιλᾶτος ἐθαύμασεν [.α'] εἰ ἤδη τέθνηκεν,
[β] [.α] καὶ προσκαλεσάμενος τὸν κεντυρίωνα [.β] ἐπηρώτησεν αὐτὸν
[.β'] εἰ πάλαι ἀπέθανεν·
[β'] ⁴⁵[..α] καὶ γνοὺς ἀπὸ τοῦ κεντυρίωνος [..α'] ἐδωρήσατο τὸ πτῶμα τῷ Ἰωσήφ.
β'[α] ⁴⁶[.α] καὶ ἀγοράσας σινδόνα [.β] καθελὼν αὐτὸν [.β'] ἐνείλησεν τῇ σινδόνι
[β] [.α] καὶ ἔθηκεν αὐτὸν ἐν μνημείῳ [.β] ὃ ἦν λελατομημένον ἐκ πέτρας, [.β'] καὶ προσεκύλισεν λίθον ἐπὶ τὴν θύραν τοῦ μνημείου.
[β'] ⁴⁷[.α] [..α] ἡ δὲ Μαρία ἡ Μαγδαληνὴ [..α'] καὶ Μαρία η Ἰωσῆτος [.α'] [..α] ἐθεώρουν [..α'] ποῦ τέθειται.

A discussion may be re-started here on the significant correspondences between this Day and its parallel Day in this Series, Day Twenty-three. For the main correspondence, that this Day's telling, in Day Twenty-seven, represents the fulfilling of the desires of Old Israel's leaders, stated in Day Twenty-three (specifically 11.18), see my table on page 244. For the suggestion that Mark may have deliberately paralleled Old and New sacrificial ways, of temple clearing and Jesus' death, see page 245. Here in this Day's telling, we do find the clearest possible connection, in 15.38, regarding the tearing of the temple curtain right at the moment of Jesus' death. In Day Twenty-three, 12.1-8, we read the parabolic equivalent to the actual event of Jesus' death. Days two and six of this Series do connect significantly, just as under Day Twenty-six's examination we saw how Days one and five of this Series do. These common themes and details, and those like them, demonstrate not only the balance Mark creates between his first and last sub-Series of this Series, but also how, by his balance of presentations, they explain each other.

We may also see how Days Twenty-six and Twenty-seven connect, that is days five and six of this Series. In 14.22-25, we read about Jesus' institution of the Lord's Supper, and in 14.24a, we read about the particularly significant identification of his blood with the (Kingly) "covenant" of Zechariah's prophecy, Zech. 9.11. His death of Day Twenty-seven is the shedding of his blood of the covenant "for many", 14.24b. We noted on page 245 how Mark makes the further verbal link between Jesus and the temple, on destroying the temple and rebuilding it in three days, 14.58 and 15.29. The prophecy of 14.27 is fulfilled on the same day, Day Twenty-six, in 15.40, but the absence of male disciples is confirmed in Day Twenty-seven, in 15.40,41. These common themes and details, and those like them, establish these Days as the first and second of the final threesome.

Under the examination of Day Twenty-five, 14.1-11, we saw how this middle day of the Series looked both backwards and forwards. In 14.8, Jesus is anointed for burial. In the telling of Day Twenty-seven, in 15.42ff., Jesus' body is placed in a tomb. In 14.10,11 Judas plots to betray Jesus; in Day Twenty-six, Jesus addresses the issue of betrayal, 14.18, and later in the telling Judas betrays Jesus, 14.43-46.

The final Day of Mark's telling in his Gospel narrative, Day Twenty-eight, has its correspondences with Day Twenty-six. We observed on page 268, the duality of 14.28 and 16.7; after he is raised, Jesus will go before the disciples into Galilee. Below, we will see a likely further correspondence, regarding "the young man" of 14.51,52. That Day Twenty-eight is the third day of the final threesome is established by the correspondence between the last pericope of the second day and the third day's three parts. In the opening parts of both, we read, in 15.42, about the onset of the "sabbath" with the evening, and in 16.1 about the passing of the "sabbath". In the third part of the one, in 15.46,47 we read about the laying of Jesus' body in the tomb, the stone that was rolled against its door, and the women who saw where he was laid. In the second part of the other, we read, in 16.2, about the women at the tomb, in 16.3,4 about the stone that was already rolled away from the door, and in 16.5,6, about the emptiness of the place where Jesus had been laid. In the third part of the last Day's telling, in 16.8, the women flee from the tomb.

Between days one and two of the sub-Series, we notice the connection between the lateness of the hour as the telling of the first Day ends, and the early beginning of the second Day. The final sub-Series is a threesome of Days best expressed again as in all the

Gospel's sub-Series by ABB': where A is the first Day which is introductory; Jesus is going to die; but he will be raised; where B is the second Day, the first development; Jesus dies and is buried; and where B' is the third Day, the second and concluding development; the tomb is empty because Jesus is risen.

Day Twenty-eight: 16.1-8:

This Day's telling is seen as the last of the Gospel narrative of "Days". Many commentators include this resurrection announcement within the Passion narrative section; some separate it[43]. But whether they think it is included or excluded from the Passion account most see it as concluding Mark's Gospel.

Given my literary-structural analysis, and the evidence for Mark's rhetorical scheme for his Gospel, based on Days and Series of Days, 16.1-8 may be judged: 1) as the third Day of his final threesome of days, Jesus' Passion and Resurrection[44] (14.12-16.8, Days Twenty-six, Twenty-seven and Twenty-eight); and 2) as his seventh Day of a seven-day presentation of "Jesus' Jerusalem Days", his fourth and last Series. What particularly confirms this is that Mark's *first* Series ends, on its last Day, with a 'raising of the dead' (see Day Seven, 5.21-43). Nowhere else in the Gospel is such to be found. The outer two Series of the Gospel conclude on the same story-lines, just as the inner two Series conclude on the same story lines (on healings of blind people).

V.1 is introductory, and v.2 begins the Day's account, with which Mark ends his Gospel Narrative on a note of tremendous climax. It is not without literary and theological significance that Mark presents this episode "very early on *the first day of the week... as the sun rose*"[45]. This last Day's telling, in the clearest possible way (compare all the other Days of his presentation), begins with the dawn of a new day, and a new week[46] (a new age).

---

[43] See my table of my four selected commentators, in my Summary of this Series which follows this presentation of Day Twenty-eight.
[44] Compare Matthew who includes a Saturday account (Mt.27.62-66).
[45] For a discussion of this, see under Day One, pages 79,80.
[46] Compare the Priestly story of creation, Gen. 1.1-2.4a: *creation* begins on the first day of the week.

Under the discussion of Day Twenty-seven, I drew attention to one connection that was to be made between the first and last Days of this last sub-Series, the "reminder" for the disciples (and the reader/listeners) of what Jesus had said (14.28), given at the tomb by the mysterious νεανίσκος to the women to relay (16.7). The νεανίσκος of 14.51,52 may be judged to be one and the same. That he was wearing a σινδόνα which he had to leave behind, and that Jesus' body was placed in one (15.46, in the Day's telling, prior to this) which he left behind does suggest some kind of a correspondence here. The 'young man' who was present at the tomb, significantly (to Mark, at least[47]) had been there at Jesus' arrest, though he was helpless to change the course of events over which Jesus had prayed, 14.35,36.

I present the literary structure of Day Twenty-eight:

A α   ¹<u>Καὶ διαγενομένου τοῦ σαββάτου</u>
  β   [α] Μαρία ἡ Μαγδαληνὴ [β] καὶ Μαρία ἡ [τοῦ] Ἰακώβου [β‛] καὶ Σαλώμη
  β‛   [α] ἠγόρασαν ἀρώματα [β] ἵνα ἐλθοῦσαι [β‛] ἀλείψωσιν αὐτόν.

B α[α]   ²[.α] <u>καὶ λίαν πρωῒ τῇ μιᾷ τῶν σαββάτων</u> [.β] <u>ἔρχονται ἐπὶ τὸ μνημεῖον</u> [.β‛] ἀνατείλαντος τοῦ ἡλίου.
  [β]   ³[.α] καὶ ἔλεγον πρὸς ἑαυτάς, [.β] Τίς <u>ἀποκυλίσει</u> ἡμῖν <u>τὸν λίθον</u> [.β‛] ἐκ τῆς θύρας τοῦ <u>μνημείου</u>;
  [β‛]   ⁴[.α] καὶ ἀναβλέψασαι [.β] θεωροῦσιν ὅτι <u>ἀποκεκύλισται ὁ λίθος</u>, [.β‛] ἦν γὰρ μέγας σφόδρα.
  β[α]   ⁵ καὶ <u>εἰσελθοῦσαι εἰς τὸ μνημεῖον</u>
  [β]   [.α] εἶδον νεανίσκον [.β] καθήμενον ἐν τοῖς δεξιοῖς [.β‛] περιβεβλημένον στολὴν λευκήν,
  [β‛]   καὶ <u>ἐξεθαμβήθησαν</u>.
  β‛[α]   ⁶[.α] ὁ δὲ <u>λέγει</u> αὐταῖς, [.α‛] Μὴ <u>ἐκθαμβεῖσθε</u>·
  [β]   [.α] [..α] Ἰησοῦν ζητεῖτε [..β] τὸν Ναζαρηνὸν [..β‛] τὸν ἐσταυρωμένον· [.β] ἠγέρθη, [.β‛] [..α] οὐκ ἔστιν ὧδε· [..β] ἴδε ὁ τόπος [..β‛] ὅπου ἔθηκαν αὐτόν.
  [β‛]   ⁷[.α] [..α] ἀλλὰ ὑπάγετε [..β] εἴπατε τοῖς μαθηταῖς αὐτοῦ [..β‛] καὶ τῷ Πέτρῳ [.α‛] [..α] ὅτι Προάγει ὑμᾶς εἰς τὴν Γαλιλαίαν· [..β] ἐκεῖ αὐτὸν ὄψεσθε, [..β‛] καθὼς εἶπεν ὑμῖν.

B‛ α   ⁸[α] καὶ <u>ἐξελθοῦσαι</u> [α‛] ἔφυγον <u>ἀπὸ τοῦ μνημείου</u>,
  β   [α] εἶχεν <u>γὰρ</u> αὐτὰς τρόμος [α‛] καὶ ἔκστασις·
  β‛   [α] καὶ οὐδενὶ οὐδὲν εἶπαν, [α‛] ἐφοβοῦντο <u>γάρ</u>.

---

[47] Matthew and Luke omit Mk. 14.51,52.

Section A is introductory, in its telling what the women did when the sabbath was over. It is a classically Markan rhetorical lead into section B, which tells what they find at 'the tomb'. Section B', well linking with section B in a classically Markan way again, reports the manner of their leaving 'the tomb'. (The last imperfect of the gospel narrative is clearly of continuous action.)[48]

A Summary of the Fourth Series of Seven Days:

The Seven Days are presented by Mark as two sub-Series of threesomes of Days (to the 'arrangement' of ABB') around a central, fourth Day of the Series, to form another overall Series' ABA' scheme, where A and A' represent the outer sub-Series around the middle Day B which behaves as a fulcrum, pivot or turning point. All four Series, therefore, in terms of their arrangement of Days are constructed in the same way. Additionally, we observe that all the opening Days of the Series are 'arranged' in the same way, in the form: A:A' (that is, in the longer annotation: ABB':ABB').

The Title to the Series, in the manner of the first three, with a view to brevity, can be stated simply as, "Jesus' Jerusalem Days: His Passion and Resurrection".

The first sub-Series of three Days are consecutive whereby: in the first, which is introductory, Jesus enters Jerusalem and the temple; in the second, he 'clears' the temple; and in the third, inside the temple, he faces various challenges, and outside the temple, he speaks of its coming destruction and the events that will occur at the last. The 'hinge', middle Day of the Series relates two particular turning points, the plotting for Jesus' death, in which a disciple shares a part in the plotting, and the anointing of Jesus for his burial by a woman who will be remembered, "wherever the Gospel is proclaimed in all the world". The balancing sub-Series of three days relates on the first Day, the Day the Passover is sacrificed, the passover meal which Jesus shares with his disciples, and his betrayal, arrest and trial before the Sanhedrin (Jesus will die, but he will be raised); the second tells of his trial before Pilate, his presentation to the people, his death by

---

[48] For a discussion of this Day and its relationship to the Passion and the longer ending, see Chapter 7.

crucifixion, and burial: and the third reports his having risen from the tomb.

In terms of rhetorical conventions, we observed on page 241 the *inclusio* of 'the Mount of Olives' in the first sub-Series. Correspondences and details were established throughout the three day analyses: for a summary, see pages 243,244. The second sub-Series was established by correspondences of theme and detail: see in particular pages 282,283. The middle Day's rhetorical function was discussed on page 264 and 266. A discussion on a possible Series' seven-day chiasm is found on pages 244-246. Such an alternative summary of Mark's scheme was rejected principally because Days one and five of the Series (Days Twenty-two and Twenth-six) were emphatically constructed each with the other in mind, as introductory Days to new sub-Series. On pages 261 and 272, we noted the major correspondences between Days three and five of the Series. Each side of the central Day their common details help smooth the transition, after the manner of ancient rhetoric, from the first to the second sub-Series.

The structural scheme of this Series of seven Days is indeed best described by ABA', but here, we pick up the force of the impressive clarifications of the second sub-Series of three days (see pages 277-279), particularly of Days Twenty-six and Twenty-seven. The final Day, Day Twenty-eight, is, nevertheless, the crowning of the three. It was out of envy that the Old Covenant leaders handed Jesus over to the Gentiles to put him to death. Jesus died both as "Son of God" and "King of the Jews". His death sealed a New Covenant with the world, but it was his resurrection which affirmed him Lord and King of all nations.

We set these summaries against those of the first sub-Series. Jerusalem welcomes *its* Messiah. The fig tree episodes (which spelt judgement for Old Israel and its leadership) coupled with the temple clearing (of the Old Covenant sacrificial means of being made right with God), and the answers Jesus gave to the challenges put to him, which Mark follows with Jesus' telling of the temple's destruction, all spelt the end of Judaism.

The middle day's 'future' anticipation is the preaching of the Gospel throughout the world, while Jews plot against Jesus.

The dynamic of this, the last Series is represented by ABA', where:

- A communicates what will be the demise of the Old Covenant;
- B communicates the future preaching of the Gospel in the 'world', against the then plotting of the Jews; and
- A' communicates the events which establish the New Covenant.

In terms of Aristotelian Greek Tragedy: A is the 'complication'; B is the 'turning point'; and A' is the 'dénouement'. It reflects the rhetorical scheme of the First Series (pages 145-147). For further discussion on the comparison with Series One, see the end of this Chapter.

At this juncture, we usefully compare the limits of the Series' three parts (A,B,A') with those of the 'sections' of the commentators I have chosen to follow:

	A	B	A'
From the above	11.1-13.37	14.1-11	14.12-16.8
Taylor[49]	11.1-13.37		14.1-16.8
Nineham[50]	11.1-12.44	13	14.1-15.47 16.1-8
Schweizer[51]	11.1-13.37		14.1-16.8
Hooker[52]	11.1-13.37		14.1-15.47 16.1-8

Clearly, the delimiting of the first sub-Series of three consecutive Days coincides with all of them for its beginning, and with all but Nineham's at its close. My separating of the middle Day, from 14.12-16.8, as it behaves as a fulcrum or pivot to the whole Series' presentation, appears to suggest that my reading is very different, but in 14.1-11, for all of us, the Passion narrative is introduced. For me, however, it also looks back (two Days' tellings of conflict, particularly the failure of the leaders of Old Israel to "trap" Jesus "in his words", lead to the necessity of their plotting[53]). What I discern to be Mark's structure, therefore, is not so very different at this level of literary order from theirs.

It remains to gather up the information of the introductory pieces of the seven Days' tellings of this Series to summarise the

---

[49] Taylor, *The Gospel...*, pp.110,111,450-610.
[50] Nineham, *Saint Mark*, pp.287-435,437-448.
[51] Schweizer, *The Good News...*, pp.226-363.
[52] Hooker, *The Gospel...*, pp.28-29, 255-387.
[53] See under Day Twenty-five for a fuller discussion.

number of days which Mark's presentation covers in all, of the Jerusalem stage of Jesus' mission. Clearly, the three Days of the first sub-Series are consecutive *in his telling*. At the beginning of Day four (14.1), the central Day in the Series, his introductory information is different in form and style. It requires interpreting by recourse to 14.49, because Jesus says at his arrest, "Daily I was with you in the temple teaching and you did not seize me". We observe that the first sub-Series covers three days of Jesus' appearances in the temple, but only the second and the third qualify as days of his "teaching" there. The question is now: do these two Days constitute "daily"? As we understand the term today, they clearly do not. The story-line of this Series and the presentation of the three consecutive days requires that we interpret that Jesus spent other days teaching in the temple which Mark has not reported. It follows that Day Twenty-four (11.20-13.37) is not necessarily representative of the last day that Jesus was teaching in the temple. Days likely pass, therefore, between the telling of days three and four of this Series.

Days Twenty-five (14.1-11), Twenty-six (14.12-72) and Twenty-seven (15.1-47) are clearly consecutive (see my discussions of the introductory pieces of these Days). On the activities of the Saturday following the Friday of Jesus' crucifixion, Mark simply summarises what the women do after the passing of the sabbath (at sunset). He does this in his introduction to Day Twenty-eight (16.1-8, see 16.1). We can be certain, therefore, that the Days' tellings of Twenty-seven and Twenty-eight cover three, inclusive of the Friday, the Saturday and the Sunday (refer also: 8.31, 9.31, 10.34).

To the seven Days of Mark's telling, therefore, we have only to add two or three days between the third and the fourth Days, and a day between the sixth and the seventh Days of his telling. The Jerusalem stage of Jesus' mission, which Mark told in just seven Days, may be judged to be about ten or eleven days in all. We observe that this Series which is by far the longest in Mark's telling represents, nevertheless, the shortest stage in Mark's presentation of Jesus' mission.

A Tabular Summary of the literary-structure of the Fourth Seven Days:

DAYS: number identified	1	2	3	4	5	6	7
number identified in Gospel	22	23	24	25	26	27	28
chapters and verses	11.1-11	11.12-19	11.20-13.37	14.1-11	14.12-72	15.1-47	16.1-8
SERIES' STRUCTURE	A			B			A'
DAYS: in literary-terms, in series	A	B	B'	A	B		B'
DAYS' sections	A A'	A	A A'	A	A B B'	A A'	A
DAYS' sectional sub-divisions	A B B' A B B'	A B B'	A B B' A B B'	A B B'	A B B' A B B' A B B'	A B B' A B B'	A B B'
DAYS' number of verses	11	8	94	11	61	46	8
SUB-SERIES' number of verses		113				115	
SERIES' number of verses				239			

Addendum to the analysis of "The Fourth Seven Days":

It can be said at the outset that many of the propositions for the examination of the text of 11.1 to 16.8 were rehearsed in the presentations of the analyses of the first three Series. It is only in the telling of this Series, however, that Mark employs a number of rhetorical devices to signal the beginnings of his new Days' tellings. These are found at 11.12, 11.20, 14.1,12, 15.1 and 16.1,2:

At 11.12	Αα[α]¹²[.α] Καὶ τῇ ἐπαύριον
11.20	Αα ²⁰[α] Καὶ παραπορευόμενοι πρωΐ
14.1	Αα ¹[α] ⁷Ην δὲ τὸ πάσχα [α´] καὶ τὰ ἄζυμα μετὰ δύο ἡμέρας.
14.12	Αα[α]¹²[.α] Καὶ τῇ πρώτῃ ἡμέρᾳ τῶν ἀζύμων, [.β] ὅτε τὸ πάσχα ἔθυον,
15.1	Αα[α]¹[.α] Καὶ εὐθὺς πρωι
16.1,2	Αα ¹Καὶ διαγενομένου τοῦ σαββάτου.... Βα[α]²[.α] καὶ λίαν πρωΐ τῇ μιᾷ τῶν σαββάτων [.β] ἔρχονται ἐπὶ τὸ μνημεῖον [.β´] ἀνατείλαντος τοῦ ἡλίου.

All are discussed under the Days they begin, or referenced there if they were discussed under other Days because they added to the discussion of other Day beginnings. In every other way, historical presents and many imperfects, introductory presentations to sections (parts, sub-parts, and so on), correspondences between words (phrases and constructions), and thematic correspondences which are intra- and inter-sub-Series (in terms of their Days, Day-sections, parts and so on), all serve again in combination to disclose his compositional method and style.

Finally, we may consider from the table the range of verses of Mark's Day reports. The shortest Days in the telling are Days Twenty-three (11.2-19) and Twenty-eight (16.1-8) with 8 verses each. The longest Day, in the telling, of the Series (and of the Gospel) is Day Twenty-four (11.20-13.37) with 94 verses. I identify here a factor of difference of just less than 12 which is the largest of all the Series. This observation leads to two likely conclusions: that Mark was much more interested in creating structural balance to his Series and Days than he was in achieving a balance of their size; and that he had much more tradition to hand than in the earlier Series, which he wished to accommodate.

A Comparison of the First and Fourth Series of Seven Days:

Now we have completed our separate examination of the literary-structure of the last Series of the Gospel, we can determine what if any relationship Mark deemed it to share with the first Series. Their titles again are: Series One: "Jesus' first Days of Mission, confined to

Galilee and the Region of its Sea"; and Series Four: "Jesus' Jerusalem Days: His Passion and Resurrection".

Under the examination of Days Seven and Twenty-eight we paid attention to the fact that these alone in the Gospel tell stories about the raising of the dead. They are the concluding Days of the first and last Series. Days One and Twenty-two, which begin the Series exhibit correspondence too, in 1.21 and 11.11: for entry into a town, and into the synagogue/temple. We have noted above that the middle Days of the two series (Days Four and Twenty-five) correspond for the plottings against Jesus (3.6; 14.1,2; vv.10,11). In the fifth Days of each (Days Five and Twenty-six), Judas Iscariot is introduced (emphatically) as the 'betrayer' (in 3.19) and he 'betrays' Jesus (in 14.43ff.). The third days of both Series (Days Three and Twenty-four) raise the issue of Jesus' authority, by scribes (in 2.6f.) and answered by Jesus (in 2.8-10); and by chief priests, scribes and elders (in 11.27,28), though this time Jesus does not have to answer (11.29-33).

An impressive number of correspondences can be identified between the two Series, but then again we might expect such because they cover between them 410 verses of the 641 of the Gospel narrative (nearly two-thirds of the material). What is particularly impressive, however, is the way in which many of the common themes and details correspond *in order*, just like those we have mentioned already above. In 1951, Farrer saw this.[54]

He discerned a steady cyclic development in Mark's Gospel, and judged the structure of the Gospel to be:

1.1-6.56	Two double cycles, which he called, "Little Gospel"
	1.1-2.12; 2.13-3.12 / 3.13-6.6; 6.7-6.56
7.1-9.1	One double cycle: "Continuation of Little Gospel"
	7.1-37; 8.1-26 (8.27-9.1)
9.2-16.8	Two double cycles: "Fulfilment of Little Gospel"
	9.2-10.31; 10.32-13.2 / 13.3-14.31; 14.32-16.8

The passage 8.27-9.1 is set in parenthesis because, rather oddly (for all his painstaking efforts) he was not able to place it with any sense of certainty. What he was assured of, however, was that the book is a unity; that it is composed in series and 'cycles'; that the whole

---
[54] Austin M. Farrer, *A Study*...

scheme comprises a chiasm; and that, whatever his sources, Mark dominated them. The literary-structural analysis I have been doing supports these statements. Farrer likewise attempted a literary-analysis, but his approach differs from mine in that the object of his study was to follow "the symbolical and interpretative element in the Gospel to the farthest point"[55]. My aim has been only to identify Mark's signifiers of his Gospel plan and of his structures at every level of his literary presentation. The real point of difference between Farrer's results and mine stems from the fact that he identified healing miracles as the prime indicator of Markan ordering whereas I identify the importance of Days.

What is supportive of my analysis (and my view, therefore, that Mark created his first and last Series of the Gospel in parallel) is the number of correspondences which Farrer sees follow the same order, between 1.21 to 5.43[56] and 11.1-16.8 which are the limits of the outer two Series set by literary-structural analysis. Below, I list his observations[57]:

2.23-3.6	synagogue, David... destroy him crisis in the synagogue	11.1-19	temple, David destroy him crisis in the temple
3.1	withered	11.20	withered
3.6	Pharisees and Herodians	12.12,13	Pharisees and Herodians
3.7-12	left synagogue ascended mountain initiated disciples	13.1-3	left temple ascended Mount of Olives with the twelve
3.22-26	false prophets/kingdom	13.5-8	false prophets/Christs/ kingdom
3.28-30	the Holy Spirit	13.9-11	the Holy Spirit
3.31-35	mother and brothers... dissociation	13.12,13	brother, father, child, parents... dislocation
4.1-20	the sower/endurance	13.13-20	endurance

---

[55] Farrer, *A Study...*, p.10.
[56] What is particularly contradictory about Farrer's approach is that he sees the correspondences up to and between 5.21-43 and 16.1-8 but continues with an attempt to complete the first series at 6.56 (knowing there are no more parallels) on the basis of completing two double cycles.
[57] I summarise them from Farrer, *A Study...*, pp.159-168.

4.26-29	harvest	13.24-27	harvest
4.35-41	sleeping/wake	13.32-37	sleep/watch/wake
5.25-34	woman who touched Christ	14.3-9	woman who anointed Christ
5.21-43	Jairus' daughter's resurrection	16.1-8	Jesus' resurrection

We can identify twelve correspondences of references (approximately twenty verbal/thematic correspondences) which are in order, verse to verse, from his study. We may observe that parallels found in 3.7-4.41, Day Five, lie diagonally opposite in Mark's scheme those which are found in 13.1-37, Day Twenty-four which is Day three of its Series. One parallel only lies in *Day to Day* order: it is 5.21-43 and 16.1-8. We can add to this those that have been mentioned in the analyses of Chapter 3 and this chapter. In day to day order (Series One and Series Four):

1.21	synagogue	11.11	temple
2.5-10	forgive	11.25,26	forgive
2.6-10	authority/reasoning	11.27-33	authority/reasoning
3.6	a plot against Jesus	14.1,10,11	a plot against Jesus
3.19	Judas Iscariot: betrayer	14.43ff.	Judas Iscariot: betrayal
3.29	liable	14.64	liable
4.35-41	sleeping/wake	14.32-42	sleep/watch/(wake)
5.1-20	Jesus' victory over great evil	15.1-16.8	(Jesus' victory over great evil)
5.20	all marvelled at Jesus	15.5,44	Pilate marvelled.

These are found in Days one, three, four, five, six and seven of both Series. Other correspondences which are not in day to day order include:

1.40	leper	14.3	Simon, the leper
2.7^1	blasphemy	14.64^2	blasphemy
$2.19,20^1$	the bridegroom taken	$14.46\text{-}15.47^2$	Jesus' arrest...
2.22^1	wine	14.25^2	vine
$3.28, 4.12^3$	forgive	$11.25,26^4$	forgive
$3.23, 4.2\text{-}34^3$	teaching crowd in parables	$12.1,12^4$	teaching crowd in parables
	explaining to disciples	$13.3,28^4$	explaining to disciples
$3.28\text{-}30^3$	the Holy Spirit	12.36^4	the Holy Spirit
5.20	all marvelled at Jesus	12.17	they marvelled at Jesus.

THE FOURTH SERIES

Those that are denoted [1], however, occur in the last Day of the Series' first sub-Series while those that are denoted [2] (their parallels) occur in the first Day of the second sub-Series.

Those that are denoted [3] occur in the first Day of the second sub-Series, and those that are denoted [4] (their parallels) occur in the last Day of the first sub-Series.

That is they *are* ordered: they correspond cross-diagonally opposite each other around the central Days of the Series. This can hardly be a coincidence. With certainty, we may say that Mark deliberately wrote these connections into his narrative scheme in this way. With certainty too, we may say that he built his skeletal plan and matrix with seven days across the page and four Series down the page. In Chapter 8, we will view this feature.

The number of references of common material has increased to about thirty, and the verbal and thematic details to approximately forty. Ten of these references demonstrate sequence, Day to Day (Series to Series). Sixteen of these hold relationship in diagonal pairings around the central Days. Clearly, Mark has balanced some of his material vertically Day to Day, and some diagonally Day to Day, between these Series. He has balanced sub-Series' material vertically too (that is the contents of the first sub-Series of both Series have their correspondence, likewise the second sub-Series of both Series). For a first sub-Series' example of one of these consider references to Jesus' "authority": 1.22,27, 2.10, against which compare 11.28,28,29,33. In regard to the middle Days and the last sub-Series, we can compare usefully the ways in which the two Series crescendo and climax.

After the middle Day's disclosure of a threat to Jesus' life, in the first Series, in the concluding sub-Series, we read firstly how all "Old Israel" gathers to Jesus who at that time lays down the foundations for a "New Israel". In the course of these Days he demonstrates great power and authority, stilling a raging storm, 'doing battle' with and (amazingly) succeeding over a whole 'legion' of evil spirits, healing an 'incurable' and showing himself to be victorious over death. The same crescendo and climax are seen in the turning point and latter half of the Fourth Series. After Jesus is anointed for burial, and one of his own has plotted with the leaders of "Old Israel" to betray him, he lays down the foundations of the "New Israel" (in the last supper,

Gethsemane, through his capture and trial before the sanhedrin); on the Day of his death he 'does battle' with evil; and, at the last, he is victorious over death. Both Series conclude in ways that first-time listeners to the Gospel, with experience of first century rhetorical method, would have "marvelled". Using Farrer's terms, we may say that 11.1-16.8 'fulfils' 1.21-5.43.

Again, as for Series Two and Three, for suggesting a *formal* relationship, there is the literary-structural argument in the sense that these two outer series comprise significantly more verses than the middle two. They are 171 verses and 239 verses respectively (compare 119 and 112 verses for the two middle Series in turn). There is also the rhetorical argument that the two Series exhibit similar interpretations of a 'complication', a 'turning point' and a 'dénouement'. In both Series the 'complication' is the clash between the 'old' and the 'new'; the 'turning point' includes plottings; and in the 'dénouement' is the resolution, the 'old' is going, the 'new' is come.

We might consider, therefore, another kind of thematic summary, still more stimulating:

| First sub-Series: | Turning point: | Second sub-Series: |
| Jews and the Old Covenant | Jews/Gentiles | the New Covenant and Gentiles |

It is the case that this reflects the last Series of the Gospel (see page 288), but does it reflect the first?

The first sub-Series of the First Series establishes the beginnings of Jesus' mission in Jewish territory, to Jews, and raises immediately, on the first Day, Old Covenant leadership inadequacies (1.21,22). It ends in demonstrating that Jesus is replacing the Old Covenant means of being made right with God (2.5-7,10); Jesus will die (2.20); and the Old Covenant will be no more (2.21,22). The turning point concludes and climaxes with leaders under the Old Covenant (Pharisees) and leaders under the domination of Rome (Herodians) plotting together to kill Jesus (3.6). Mark is telling us that both Jews and Gentiles would be responsible for Jesus' death. The second sub-Series begins with Jesus' choosing a New Covenant leadership from the massive and totally Jewish assembly (3.7-19). Jesus' mission proceds to Gentile country, where he shows himself powerful enough to defeat the world's evil. It ends in Jewish territory again, where Jesus shows himself to be victorious over death.

My summary thematic presentation *is* reflective of Mark's own presentational approach, for both of the outer two Series of his Gospel narrative. This immediately raises the question, "Do the central Series reduce thematically in the same way?" We re-read the literary-structural analyses of my Chapters 4 and 5.

In Series Two, the first sub-Series tells of events in Jewish territory, and its second Day records an open-air 'banquet' for Jews. The turning point is set in Gentile/Jewish territory and displays a Jewish/Gentile issue. The second sub-Series is set in Gentile territory for its first two days, but ends in Jewish territory on the third. The second Day reports an open-air 'banquet' for Gentiles. It is clearly the case that Mark has employed this same scheme in Series Two. (One Series remains to be judged.)

In Series Three, the first sub-Series may be said to be set in Jewish/Gentile territory, but it clearly associates Jesus with the Jews: in the first Day's telling, he is "the Christ"; and in the second Day's telling he is the one who fulfils Jewish end-time expectations. Mark sets the middle Day and turning point of his Series in ambiguous territory, apparently deliberately (10.1). It suggests both Jewish ("Judea") and Gentile ("beyond the Jordan": the Decapolis?/ Gerasene?) territories. And the Day's telling raises an issue of tension between Jews and Gentiles which Jesus addresses with reference to the "beginning of creation". The second sub-Series begins in the same territory as that of the middle Day's telling. Only at the second sub-Series' close is it clearly based in Jewish territory (compare the last Day of the first Series). In the second Day's telling of this second sub-Series the word "Gentiles" features significantly (this Day's detailed disclosures of Jesus' suffering at the hands of the Gentiles, we may note, are fulfilled on the parallel day in the final Series). This Series also follows the same plan.

In Chapter 8, we will be able to gather up the results of all these analyses, and see the full matrix of the Gospel which Mark devised before he wrote a single word of his Gospel. Here, for the first time, we can at least summarise the primary structure of the Gospel's narrative. The two outer Series are set in parallel, around two middle

Series which parallel. Mark's overall scheme for 1.21-16.8, therefore, can be described as a chiasm: ABB'A', where:

A	represents	Series One;
B		Series Two;
B'		Series Three;
and A'		Series Four.

The analysis of the text of 1.1-16.8 is now complete, but for summary presentations. Mark's Prologue and Gospel Narrative are defined. A rigorous literary-structural analysis has been undertaken, and that analysis has been informed and interpreted both by the rules of ancient rhetoric in general, and by what has been discovered of Mark's use of such rhetorical conventions in particular.

Now we must give consideration to the fact that Greco-Roman Literature, the Aristotelian Greek Tragedy Play, and much Old Testament writing, all end with 'Epilogues'[58]. Rhetorical considerations require that we must go this one step further. 16.1-8 is no 'Epilogue' in ancient rhetorical terms. It has not the characteristics of an 'Epilogue'. 16.1-8 is fully integral with Mark's narrative; it is the seventh Day's telling of the last of four Series of seven Days. After all that has been discovered in 1.1-16.8, which accords with the rules of ancient rhetoric, it is inconceivable that Mark cheated rhetorical convention and his audience's expectations at the last by not producing an 'Epilogue'.

We can entertain two possible approaches: 1) we could assume that it is lost and try to create one ourselves, which would reflect his Prologue and complete his Gospel's presentation in the manner he suggests in his Narrative; or 2) we could risk an analysis of the longer ending, which most scholars today say is not Mark's, to see if there is anything which looks remotely like an Epilogue that he might have created (the other endings do not look too promising). I opt for 2). I will give consideration also to some of Mark's key words and phrases from his Prologue and his Narrative: such as "creation", "gospel", "world", "Gentiles", "covenant", and "Jesus of Nazareth", as well as his predilection for "twos".

---

[58] See the section of my Introduction, "The Cultural and Historical Context of the Gospel".

Chapter Seven
The Days Following (16.9-16, 19-20a):

The longer Ending: 16.9-20:

Anyone who labels this longer ending 'Markan' and views it, therefore, as an original 'Epilogue', stands against a great weight of scholarly opinion[1]. Principally, the arguments go: it is absent from the most reliable, early manuscripts; it does not square with the preceding passage, 16.1-8; and its language is different from the rest of the text. We will consider these three basic points and then the issue of dependency, before proceeding to a literary-structural analysis.

1) The absence from reliable, early manuscripts:

The longer ending, 16.9-20, is clearly missing from the fourth century Codices Vaticanus and Siniaticus, which are in every other way deemed to be the 'reliable, early manuscripts'. Presented in three columns and by two hands, and in four columns and by three hands, respectively, they are the only two copies remaining of fifty that were made by Eusebius of Caesarea with the help of his friend Pamphilus (from a collection of earlier manuscripts to which they had access). An historical note of some consequence tells how they supplied Constantine at his request in the year 331 with fifty copies of the

---

[1] But see: B. Mariani, "Introduction", *Introduction à la Bible*, Eds. A Robert & A. Feuillet, Desclée & Co., Tournai, Belgium, 1959, p.73, and K.W Clark, "The Theological Relevance of Textual Variation in Current Criticism of the Greek New Testament", *JBL* 85 (1966), pp.9-12, who consider the question insoluble; E. Linnemann, "Der (wiedergefundene) Markusschluss", *ZThK* 66 (1969), pp. 255-259, whose hypothesis is that Mt 28.16f. + Mk. 16.15-20 was the original ending (the argument against his view is that his hypothesis is based on too many arbitrary assumptions); and W.R. Farmer, *The Last Twelve verses of Mark*, Cambridge University Press, Cambridge, 1974, who considers the question "still open" after attempting an explanation of the differences of style and vocabulary - when compared with the rest of the Gospel, on the basis that Mark in his epilogue handles the traditional material *differently* (the critical judgement of his work is that he did not present a strong enough case).

Greek Bible;[2] "fifty copies of the sacred scriptures" were "to be written on fine parchment in a legible manner and in a convenient portable form by professional scribes thoroughly accomplished in their art." It was Eusebius who says, "They were produced in threefold and fourfold forms." It follows, then, that our two most cherished manuscripts for Mark's Gospel, with characteristics of very fine vellum and size which conform to Constantine's request, were copies made at the same time, and in the same place, and from the same earlier manuscript collection.

Eusebius himself commented on the longer ending[3], and many scholars interpret what he had to say as indication that the longer ending was not Markan. When asked about the differences between Matthew 28.1 and Mark 16.9 on the timing of the resurrection, he replied:

"They can be solved in two ways." (The first way here only) "The person not wishing to accept this chapter (the passage under consideration) will say that it is not contained in all copies of the Gospel according to Mark. Indeed the accurate copies conclude the story according to Mark in the words of the young man seen by the women and saying to them Do not be afraid... for they were afraid. For the end is here in nearly all the copies of Mark. What follows is found but seldom, in some copies but by no means in all..."[4]

It is emphatic, even excessively so[5]. The longer ending was *not to be found* among his *best* Greek manuscripts. Nevertheless, manuscripts, which did include the longer ending, did exist, and he knew them. Clearly other manuscripts and other families of manuscripts did exist also at that time. He cannot have had access to them all[6]. Further, if Trocmé[7] *et al.* are right about the Gospel's place

---

[2] Eusebius, *Life of Constantine*; Bruce M. Metzger, *The Text of the New Testament: Its Transmission, Corruption and Restoration*, Clarendon Press, Oxford, 1968, p.7; also *IntDB*, p.751.

[3] Jerome's letter to Hedibia (Jerome, *Letter*, 120.3).which deals with the same issues, a generation or so later, appears to be reiterating Eusebius' understanding. It is not judged to be a separate witness.

[4] This record comes from a lost work known to us as *Gospel Questions and Solutions Addressed to Marinus*, which was found last century. See Johannes Quasten, *Patrology, Volume 3. The Golden Age of Greek Patristic Literature: from the Council of Nicaea to the Council of Chalcedon*, (Utrecht, 1960) repr. Newman Press, Westminster, Md., 1986, p.337.

[5] We probably have all heard about the preacher's sermon margin notes which say, "Shout louder here, argument weak."

[6] The family of Italy and Gaul, from which came Codex Bezae; and the family of

of composition, the *exemplar* would have started its life in Rome and likely have been there at that time (if it still existed then), and not immediately available to Eusebius in Caesarea. What manuscripts he did possess which included other endings did not survive[8] so we cannot assess his method of evaluation, nor his choice therefore, of the ones on which he based Codices Vaticanus and Sinaiticus. It is troubling to note, furthermore, that his judgement on other issues is questionable. Eusebius was not exactly free from error in his critical judgement of early material on the Eastern Church on which he wrote most, and what little he wrote on the Western Church does suggest that he knew much less about it, and its documents.[9]

In a wonderfully titled book, *The Last Twelve verses of the Gospel According to S. Mark Vindicated against Critical Objectors and Established* (1871)[10], Burgon appealed to patristic evidence which is, in fact, much earlier than the manuscript evidence of Eusebius. We can too. V.20 of the longer ending was known to Justin (*Apology*, 1.45) in about AD155. Vv.14,16,19 were known to Tatian (*Diatessaron; the Persian Gospel Harmony*) in about 165. Irenaeus knew v.19 (*Against Heresies*, 3.10.6) in about 180, and he knew that it came from Mark's Gospel, for he writes, "At the end of the Gospel Mark says And so the Lord Jesus after he had spoken to them, was taken into heaven, and sat down at the right hand of God". Hippolytus, whose life and work spanned the turn of the second century, knew v.16 (*Apostolic Constitutions*, 6.15) and vv.17,18 (*Ap. Con.*, 8.1). We can conclude, therefore, that manuscripts of the Gospel with the longer ending *were* circulating in the second century. What we cannot conclude is that any Gospel manuscript which finished at 16.8 was circulating as early as this.

We cannot know what happened to Mark's own *exemplar* and its earliest copies. Certainly plenty of evidence does exist which shows that the leaves of early manuscripts did become worn or torn,

Carthage, from which came Codex Washingtonianus.
[7] Trocmé, *The Formation...*, p.242.
[8] No manuscript exists today from before the fifth century which includes the longer ending: see for fifth century examples: Codices Alexandrinus (A), Ephraimi Syri (C), Washingtonianus (W), and the 5th/6th century Bezae (D).
[9] "Eusebius", *The Oxford Dictionary of the Christian Church*, ed. F.L. Cross, 3rd Ed. Oxford University Press, 1997.
[10] J.W. Burgon, *The Last Twelve Verses of the Gospel According to S. Mark Vindicated against Critical Objectors and Established*, G. Bell & Son, Oxford and London, 1871.

and that outer leaves became totally separated[11]. In such a manner, 16.9-20 could have been lost, and the re-discovering of it later because the Gospel had been memorised is quite feasible (see my Introduction, for the mnemonic qualities of ancient rhetoric). Less feasible to some, however, is that this last leaf contained these verses only. But it may be the case that Mark wrote his Prologue on one leaf, and gave his Epilogue similarly a separate page. Clearly it is not for us to know, and the reasonable counter argument to all of this, of course, is that the *exemplar* would have been copied before it disintegrated.

Other possibilities also can be entertained. Farmer raises one. He asks, "Were there conditions obtaining in Alexandria under which the last twelve verses could have been omitted from copies of Mark deliberately?"[12] He argues cogently from patristic documents that the discrepancies between the endings of the Gospels were causing innumerable problems. The timing of the resurrection was one of them, and in this matter, Matthew's Gospel was viewed as the tradition. Vv.17,18 were causing a particular problem too. It was not anything to do with the resurrection as such, but to do with spiritual gifts and their exercise. The church attempted to deal with their troublesome influence by containment[13], but there is no evidence that they succeeded with this approach. Expurgation of vv.9-20 *may* have been the church's only considered recourse.

In summary of this section, we must simply conclude that there is, therefore, no sure evidence against Markan authorship of the longer ending based on its absence from 'reliable, early manuscripts'. Scholars who maintain that the last twelve verses of Mark's Gospel are written by someone other than Mark cannot appeal to manuscript evidence.

---

[11] For example: Luke's Gospel, Bodmer Papyrus XIV, P75 (175-225AD) V. Martin & R. Kasser (eds.) Cologny-Genève 1961.
[12] Farmer, *The Last...*, p.59.
[13] Farmer, *The Last...*, pp.66-72. Farmer quotes from *The Ante-Nicene Fathers*, vii, pp.479-481. Farmer observes also the Alexandrian attempt to introduce a 'cut' in Homer's work.

2) It does not square with the preceding passage, 16.1-8:

The break itself, between 16.8 and v.9, has been an issue which many have attempted to resolve by recourse to the argument that vv.9-20 were added later, and not too cleverly at that. But the break is justifiable simply, given my analysis of 1.21-16.8, on literary-structural grounds because at 16.8 the narrative (organised from 1.21-16.8 on the basis of a presentation of "Days" in four "Series of seven Days") ends. Further, in the last Day's report, 16.1-8, Mark's application of his ABB' rhetorical structure is identified again as completed. If Mark had written anything beyond 16.8 it *would have shown* a disjunction of some kind with 16.1-8.

The argument that Mary Magdalene is introduced afresh in v.9 as though she were not already on stage[14] evaporates. The Day of resurrection is begun to be retold in a new way (and with several repetitions: see not only the mention of Mary Magdalene, but also that of the day and also the timing of Jesus' resurrection). We note the obvious: Jesus was not 'on stage' himself in Day Twenty-eight's telling; but now he is, in v.9. The 'Epilogue', if that is what vv.9-20 represent, is, therefore, introduced with a recapitulation of details, but for a new purpose. If this is of Mark, then we must judge that he established both an appropriate break in his text, and a new beginning. Regarding what may have been his purpose, we can deduce from the longer ending that it may have been to inform his audience about Jesus' appearances and his final commands. For a possible 'Epilogue', these do not seem out-of-place aims.

Mark's last presentation in his twenty-eight Day narrative did, of course, communicate to his audience the Gospel's most amazing happening of all. Its ending, with the report that the women fled from the tomb and told no-one anything because they were afraid (16.8), would have been totally understable. (That there is no resumption of the theme of fear and silence in v.9 *is* a further sign of disjunction, but it is no signal that Mark himself is not writing.) To Hooker, "It is Mark's final irony. In the rest of the story, Jesus has commanded men and women to say nothing about the truth they have glimpsed, and they have frequently disobeyed. Now that the time has at last come to

---

[14] D.C. Parker, *The Living Text of the Gospels*, Cambridge University Press, Cambridge, 1997, p.138.

report what has happened, the women are silent!"[15] Whether or not this is truly ironical, we may judge later. What is raised here is a question of approach, for Hooker goes on to represent the views of many when she says that the longer ending "does not attempt to deal with the problems caused by Mark's abrupt ending (the women's silence and the unfulfilled promise to the disciples that they would see Jesus in Galilee) and it shows no reliance on vv.1-8."[16]

To me, the focus is wrong. The last sub-Series of the Gospel narrative, 14.12-16.8, provides us our text in the first place for interpreting the longer ending, not 16.1-8. Further, before we can say whether or not this is truly Mark's 'Epilogue' we will have to interpret it in the light of all that he has written previously, in his Prologue, his Series and sub-Series. The first task is my business here; the second will follow at the end of this chapter.

From the longer ending, we note that the first post-resurrection appearance, to Mary Magdalene, takes place in Jerusalem on the day of the resurrection (16.9). In the Passion Narrative, Mark is concerned to tell us that she and other women who had "followed and served" Jesus in Galilee[17] were present, when no male disciple was anywhere at all to be seen, because they had all "scattered" and "fled" (see 14.27,50). The women (Mark tells us these things because his choice of scripture fulfilment necessitated this: as a result no male disciple could be present) were witnesses to Jesus' crucifixion, 15.40f., and to his burial, 15v.47; they prepared themselves to go to the tomb and anoint the corpse, 16.1; and they only were witnesses to the empty tomb, 16.2-7. The men who had followed with Jesus (beginning in Galilee, like the women) were nowhere to be found at these times. Mary Magdalene and the other women, at least, were still in Jerusalem on the day of Jesus' resurrection.

The logic of the story-line of the longer ending is that Mary Magdalene first had to find the others who had been with Jesus before she could report to them Jesus' appearance to her. It is the case also that she, and the other women who had been at the tomb with her, would have had to have found the disciples before they could report the message they had been given by the "young man" at the tomb.

---

[15] Hooker, *The Gospel...*, p.387.
[16] Hooker, *The Gospel...*, p.389.
[17] Compare 1.31 for another woman serving Jesus.

Mark says in v.8 that the women said nothing to "anyone because they were afraid". We can interpret from the Gospel's final sub-Series, the Passion Narrative, that they could not report immediately either to "the disciples" as they were no longer in the city, or to "Peter", who, after his humiliation (in 14.70) is nowhere stated to be present on the day of Jesus' crucifixion. The last time we heard of Peter, he was a broken man. He was left "weeping", in the Gospel account of 14.72. Not surprisingly, perhaps, when Mary reaches them with the message of Jesus' appearance (16.10), she finds all "those who had been with him (Jesus) mourning and *weeping*". Further, the women's earlier message had been for "the disciples and Peter" (16.7) and not just for "anyone" (16.8). The ending of the last Day (16.1-8) of Mark's telling may be interpreted, therefore, as one of apparent irony only, not one of "Mark's final irony"[18].

The 'longer ending' indeed does not tell, as does the shorter (and much later) ending[19], that the women broke their silence and so gave their message. What it does tell, in 16.10, is that Mary Magdalene had to "go" to report. We ask, "Go where?" According to 14.28 and 16.7, the answer is somewhere on the way to Galilee. In 14.28, it would seem that Jesus expected his disciples to go to Galilee, after their "scattering" (see 14.27). 14.28 does not look like a disguised command of Jesus to his disciples to go there, nor could it have been a command of any such kind when, as it is expressed by Mark, their "scattering" would be a fulfilling of the scripture. The logic of the story-line, therefore, is that before the women were able to report the young man's message, from the tomb, to Peter and the disciples, Jesus' appeared to Mary Magdalene, with the result that she had the message of his appearance to tell as well as the message of the young man (*cf.* Mt.28.5-9). In the longer ending, the message of Jesus' appearance eclipses the message of the young man. (The message of the young man (16.7), in its repetition of Jesus' earlier statement to the disciples now looks more like a literary device on Mark's part, than a matter of true record[20].) The drift of the longer ending is freed

---
[18] See page 303 for Hooker's reference to the phrase.
[19] Found in L Ψ 099 0112 274^{mg} 579 k sy$^{hl\,mg}$ and in some MSS. of sa bo aeth.
[20] Compare Mark's handling of the story of the withered fig tree. It appears likely that he created 11.11 for his purpose of creating a break (a Day's break, in this instance) so that he could introduce his next Day's telling with the first episode of the fig tree incident. The tradition of Jesus' entry into Jerusalem may well have connected with his clearing of the

from 'journey' and 'day' concerns; it can concentrate on the real point for Mark's audience: the believing of those who had seen the risen Jesus.

The longer ending, therefore, tells how the risen Jesus was three-times his own witness, and how the disciples twice reacted *reasonably,* but *unbelievingly,* to reports of his being seen. (We observe that the empty tomb does not feature in this account.) Vv.9-11, vv.12-13, and v.14 tell of appearances of the risen Jesus. The first two tell of the reports which are then given and the reponses they attract. In the third, in which Jesus appears to the eleven, we are told of Jesus' extreme annoyance that the reports were not believed. In fact, three times the audience of the writer of the longer ending hears that the reports of witnesses to the risen Lord were not believed (vv.11,13,14).

The empty tomb was not in itself evidence of resurrection (Matthew picks that one up: see 28.11-16 for a possible alternative reason for its being empty). The message of a young man in a white robe was evidence of a kind[21] (but with Mark's account we are left wondering who he was anyway; when we read Mt. 28.2 and Lk. 24.4ff. we helpfully find *angelic* developments). But the fact that Jesus appeared to certain people who could be identified, that could be called evidence, though it was still evidence which could be rejected. Hence, therefore, we observe the force of the risen Jesus' remonstrating with his disciples, in 16.14, which has its precursor in 8.17f.; and his most severe remonstration is not for his disciples alone but for *all* who would deny[22] the veracity of the report of witnesses to a face-to-face meeting with him, after his resurrection.[23]

The longer ending records that Mary Magdalene did report Jesus' appearance to her to his disciples. If we interpret that Mary

---

temple. Likewise, the fig tree incident may have been one whole story in the tradition. The teaching that attaches to the second episode (11.20-25) looks to be a Markan additon.

[21] Likely the same mysterious young man of 14.51f.: compare the first and last days of the final threesome of days of the gospel and note the verbal similarities: in 14.51f., νεανίσκος... περιβεβλημένος σινδόνα, and in 16.5, νεανίσκον... περιβεβλημένον στολὴν λευκήν; for further references to σινδόνα see 15.46, in the passage of the entombing of Jesus. See also under the examination of Day Twenty-eight.

[22] It is a feature of Mark's Gospel that the disciples' place in the company of Jesus is exemplary to the listener.

[23] We note how the Prologue is not just written to inform but to draw the listener into taking a stand: it would appear that the longer ending fulfils a similar role.

Magdalene delivered her report immediately, we interpret wrongly. We now ask, "How could she have done?" We can only deduce that the first section of the longer ending (vv.9-11) covered several days, as she sought out Jesus' disciples, either in Galilee, or on their way to Galilee (Jerusalem to the Sea of Galilee is about 87 miles). Likewise, the second section of the longer ending (vv.12,13), we may deduce, is intended to convey what happened after a further interval of time, and in a place quite different from Jerusalem. The second appearance takes place as "*two* of them were walking... going into (the) country". And we note, "they went away from there" (the place of the meeting) to report. Of the greatest support for Markan authorship of this piece is Mark's repeated motif of "twos" in his Prologue and in each of his Gospel narrative Series. (So many scholars readily argue dependency on Lk. 24.13-35, and ignore this connection. See pages 64,65.)

It would appear that the "country" of Galilee is the setting for the second section's story. The third section of the longer ending (16.14), in that case, would be similarly set. The timing of the appearance of Jesus to the eleven would be possible, therefore, anytime after the two had been able to return to the group and report. The longer ending, given the sifting of its inherent logic (taking into account information from the Passion Narrative), reports events which cover (like the Prologue) a number of days, and which take place in settings on the way to Galilee and in Galilee.

The longer ending is clearly condensed and abbreviated, but it is in the style of the Gospel as a whole in that respect[24]. (Brevity particularly in "an Epilogue" is a quality which Aristotle commends[25].) When the longer ending is interpreted in the light of the contents of the last sub-Series of the Gospel (Days Twenty-six, Twenty-seven and Twenty-eight) it is observed that it not only attaches well to what has been told before it, but also what has been told before it prefaces it and, therefore, interprets it. The longer ending, or its first section at least, is looking like it is Mark's composition. What we have seen above demonstrates, whoever the writer is, that the story lines and details that we have focused upon

---

[24] David Hall (*The Gospel Framework*..., p.54) draws attention to this characteristic of abbreviation in the gospels as a whole. One of his attacks on Schmidt's thesis is based on this.
[25] Aristotle, *Ars Rhetorica*, III.19 1420^b: consider his example, "I have done. You have heard me. The facts are before you. I ask for your judgement."

are complete without temporal and geographical details of journeyings (such would have cluttered the presentation; and such, we might judge, were unnecessary anyway given the twice repeated location in the final sub-Series). Essentially therefore, the writer has been able to focus upon the two important issues that follow on from Jesus' death and resurrection: the need of the church to believe the witnesses of the risen Christ; and the need of the church to preach the good news everywhere (vv.15,20a). For the moment we have given attention only to the first of these.

3) Its language is different from the rest of the text:

Over the years, much has been written about the differences of the vocabulary, style and grammar of the longer ending over and against that of the rest of the gospel[26]. Farmer[27] judges that the most exhaustive studies have been made by scholars who have wished to disprove authenticity. He argues that they have been selective of the evidence. In singling out Morgenthaler's 'word-statistical' research on the longer ending[28] for special attention, Farmer demonstrates that it does not lead to 'clear results', as claimed. On the use of καί and δέ in the longer ending, for example, Morgenthaler notes that καί is used 'on average' half what it is elsewhere in Mark, and δέ is used over twice as often. Morgenthaler notes that these frequencies do vary in different parts of the Gospel, but still concludes that this feature 'certainly speaks for the unauthenticity' of vv.9-20. Farmer points out that Morgenthaler's own statistical results show that the use of καί is greater in the first half of Mark than the second, while the use of δέ is greater in the second half. Farmer[29] judges that the use of καί and δέ in the longer ending is in keeping with these tendencies in the Gospel.

---

[26] E.g. and so henceforth: Wellhausen, *Das Evangelium...*, 1909; Taylor, *The Gospel...*, 1952; and W.G. Farmer, *The Last...*, 1974.
[27] Farmer, p.79.
[28] Robert Morgenthaler, *Statistik des Neutestamentlichen Wortschatzes*, Gotthelf Verlag, Zürich, 1958
[29] Farmer, *The Last...*, p.81.

Many scholars[30] have concluded with Morgenthaler that "A style is written here (in vv.9-20) completely different than appears elsewhere in Mark's Gospel." It is clearly the case that only one of the nine sentences begins with καί. For comparison's sake, Morgenthaler looked at the section 15.46-16.8, and noted that eight out of the sixteen uses of καί begin sentences. Farmer, however, looked at 15.35-45, and noted that out of the fourteen uses of καί only two begin sentences. He further observes that καί is used twelve times after 15.39 before it is used a second time to begin a sentence. Farmer counters, therefore, "It is the case that καί is used with greater frequency to begin sentences in Mark, especially in the early chapters. But it is not true that the use of καί and δέ in 16.9-20 is 'completely different than appears elsewhere in Mark's Gospel'."[31]

Fascinatingly, it would appear that this is not all there is to the matter. What scholars have continued to overlook is the rule of ancient rhetoric on the Epilogue which states that its style *should be different* from what precedes it. Aristotle's final and emphatic point on the Epilogue[32] may be translated: 1) "The end of the whole ought to be free from conjunctions, to make the hearers aware that our discourse is at its close"; 2) "Asyndeton is appropriate for the end of the discourse since this is an *epilogos* not a *logos*"[33]; and 3) "For the conclusion, the disconnected style of language is appropriate, and will mark the difference between the oration and the peroration"[34]. It would appear that the writer of the longer ending was aware of this rule. The lack of καί introductions to sentences is no reason to judge that it was not Mark who was writing.

Farmer examined all the verses. We note his conclusions: "Evidence for non-Marcan authorship seems to be preponderent in verse 10. Verses 12, 14, 16, 17, 18 and 19 seem to be either

---

[30] My selected commentators, Taylor, Nineham, Schweizer and Hooker, all agree on this matter. And Paul Ellingworth, "The Dog in the Night...", p.127, says, "The frequency of the non-καί sentences increases sharply in the alternative endings of Mark, confirming that they are not part of the original Gospel."
[31] Farmer, *The Last...*, p.83.
[32] *Ars Rhetorica*, III.19 1420^b (*Aristotelis Ars Rhetorica*, ed. Rudolfus Kassel, Walter de Gruyter, Berlin, 1976).
[33] *Aristotle on Rhetoric: A Theory of Civic Discourse*, tr. George A. Kennedy, Oxford University Press, New York/Oxford, 1991, p.282.
[34] W. Rhys Roberts,"Rhetorica", *The Works of Aristotle, Translated into English*, tr. ed. W.D. Ross, Vol. XI, Clarendon Press, Oxford, 1924, III.19 1420^b.

basically, or in balance neutral. Evidence for Markan authorship seems to be preponderent in verses 9, 11, 13, 15, and 20."[35] For Parker[36], who addresses these matters in less than a single page, the significant feature is that "as many as seventeen words in this short passage of twelve verses are either not found in Mark 1.1-16.8, or are used here in a non-Markan sense." For him, "the argument about style and word usage is cumulative."

On word usage, in particular, we have seen in the analysis of the final sub-Series of the Gospel narrative how Mark is still introducing there new words and phrases. The ones that were identified on pages 277,278 are: "covenant", "Abba", "envy", "King of the Jews", and King of Israel". We judged that he had chosen deliberately to set these new words in his final sub-Series because he was sharpening his audience's focus on the strands of his earlier narrative which have their fullest interpretation in the Passion account. It follows that if Mark did write the longer ending, or much of it, he could have continued with the same in writing an Epilogue. Additionally, the subjects that we find in vv.9-20 are new to the Gospel's telling, and include post-resurrection appearances, and final commands. New themes require new vocabulary. Still on evidence of word usage, we also noted how Mark's Days' tellings in his final Series began in ways that were different from those of his earlier Series (see page 290). An Epilogue's sectional beginnings, we might judge, would require introductory descriptions that were different from the Narrative's text, but similar maybe to the Prologue's text. Already we have seen the introductory function of v.9. We shall consider below the supposed non-Markan words of Μετὰ δὲ ταῦτα (v.12) and Ὕστερον δὲ (v.14) in their *story* context, for that is the only way to assess them properly.

Firstly, we may observe John's use of the first of these phrases, Μετὰ δὲ ταῦτα. In his Gospel it is much in evidence. Only once does it have the sense of "immediately following" (in Jn. 19.28). Only once does it have the sense of "very soon after" (19.38). Elsewhere in John's Gospel, it has the sense of "next", "next in what is related", and what is more, it infers a passage of days between the pericope which precedes it and the one which it introduces. New

---

[35] Farmer, *The Last...*, p.103.
[36] D.C. Parker, *The Living Text...*, pp.141,142.

sections and sub-sections begin[37] in John's Gospel at Jn. 2.12, 3.22, 5.1, 6.1, 7.1 and 21.1. Interestingly, we note, in regard to the last of these references (21.1), the setting leaps to "the sea of Tiberias" without any explanation at all. In Mark's Gospel, by way of contrast, we have explanation of what will be the setting of "Galilee" (in 14.28, 16.7), but no mention of the place when the stories are being told. The phrase, Μετὰ δὲ ταῦτα, in the longer ending behaves as in the majority of cases in John's Gospel, but it does not look as if it is dependent on John. We may observe, in 1.14 of Mark's Gospel, by way of introduction to the third section of the *Prologue*, something very similar to it, Καὶ μετὰ τὸ , which is followed by an aorist passive infinitive. A passage of days takes place there, before the introductory phrase to 1.14-20. We have also by way of comparison, in 16.19, μὲν οὖν... μετὰ τὸ , followed by an aorist active infinitive. The use of Μετὰ δὲ ταῦτα at v.12 in the longer ending cannot be considered non-Markan. It functions in the way that the passage requires, given its setting in a threesome of events which covers several days in the telling.

The second of the two introductions may read as "Finally..." or "At the last...", as in Matthew's use of ὕστερον at 4.2, 21.30,32,37, 22.27 (*cf.* Luke, in his parallel, 20.32), 25.11 and 26.60. The writer of the longer ending, therefore, uses the word which is the one most appropriate. In the threesome of stories, it introduces the last of the three scenes (v.14). In terms of the Gospel as a whole, of course, it introduces the last of all its scenes. If it is Mark who has written this longer ending, or the greater proportion of it, then it may be said that he has chosen for the opening of his last presentation-piece of the Gospel a word he has not used before in all its verses. It would have to be acknowledged also that he has chosen the most suitable word available to him.

In terms of the continuing story-line of the Gospel narrative and the longer ending, we might read, therefore, "*At the last*, he appeared to the eleven as they sat at table..." (v.14) When interpreted in the light of the Passion Narrative, 14.11-16.8, the scene clearly reflects that of the last supper, beginning at 14.17,18. Also, the prediction of Jesus, in 14.25, is now about to be fulfilled: "Truly I tell you, No

---

[37] See Palmer, *Sliced Bread...*, pp.87ff.

more will I drink the fruit of the vine, until *that* day when I drink it new in the Kingdom of God." This is the scene of his ascension, according to the longer ending, and we may interpret that it is then that he enters the Kingdom of God[38]. Again it has to be argued that the longer ending is interpreted correctly against the back-drop of the Passion Narrative. Similarly, the lack of a place-name for this scene in the longer ending is not problematic because Mark has stated twice already that they would see the risen Jesus in Galilee[39]. Further, with Mark's use of ἐκείνης in 14.25, we have a verbal connection of sorts with ἐκείνη, in v.10, and ἐκεῖνος, in vv.13,20, which others say are not 'used absolutely' at all in 1.1-16.8. To Farmer[40], this fact is one of the features that sets v.10 aside as non-Markan. I note, however, that it is 'used absolutely' in 7.20: there ἐκεῖνο is clearly the singular subject of the verb.

Given the analysis of the literary-structural method of Mark for his narrative based on "Days", we do find changes of place at the beginnings of the second and third parts of many of his three-part presentations, but because they are confined to introducing new events on the same, particular "Days" we do not find conjunctions of the kind that we meet here in the longer ending which reports a series of events which take place over a series of days. Indeed, both, in the Prologue and in the longer ending, we discover conjunction-constructions which are not used anywhere else in the Gospel at major *sub-structural* points. Consider 1.9, "And it came to pass in those days, came Jesus..."; and 1.14, "And after John was delivered, came Jesus...". The literary-constructional requirements of both Prologue and the longer ending are different from the rest of the Gospel, because they each cover a number of days within their three-fold structures.

It would seem, therefore, that it is not enough for scholars to describe these sub-structural introductions in the longer ending as non-Markan simply because they had not been used before in the gospel. Their function in the longer ending is to introduce the second

---

[38] See 14.62, also 8.38, 9.1: for Mark's understanding of the Kingdom of God, as coming from heaven, while Jesus sits at the right hand of power.
[39] The first is at 14.28 and the "reminder" is at 16.7 (on the first and third days in the telling of Mark's last sub-Series of days).
[40] Farmer, *The Last...*, pp.85,86.

THE DAYS FOLLOWING 313

and third closing sections to the gospel and so report events which took place over several days. There is no reason why Mark himself could not have employed the terms. The matter of authorship of the longer ending, to Farmer, is still an open question[41]. Given the above, authorship cannot be settled by reference to differences with 1.1-16.8, in regard to its vocabulary, style and grammar.

4) Dependency:

On the issue of dependency, Parker begins by stating that the longer ending is "best read as a cento or pastiche of material gathered from the other Gospels and from other sources"[42]. He says he will go through the longer ending "verse by verse", but in practice he groups some together. On vv.9-11, he speaks of the 'universal tradition', as found in Mark 16.2, as the initial source for the writer of the longer ending. He says that Jesus' appearance to Mary Magdalene is Johannine tradition. He says that vv.10,11 are based on Luke 24.10b-11 (with John 20.18 as another parallel). He says that the reference to "mourning and weeping" is "an expansion of the tradition" and adds a note, "the oldest version, the Freer Gospels, lacks the second verb, so that this expansion can be shown to have grown by stages". He starts his argument, and launches into it as if the issue of unauthenticity is beyond question. Many commentators do the same and assume that the longer ending is dependent on Luke 8.2 for the statement that Jesus saved Mary Magdalene from "seven demons", on John 20.11-18 for Jesus' appearance to Mary Magdalene, on Luke 24.11 for the failure of the disciples to believe her report (note: of the empty tomb), on Luke 24.13-35 for a much shorter story about "the two" (the stories, I note, conclude in different ways), on Matthew 28.19, Luke 24.46-49 or Acts 1.8 for a commissioning of the disciples (and in the case of the Lukan parallel, a heavenly co-operation, for which compare 16.20b), on Acts 2.4, etc. for speaking in new tongues, and on Acts 28.3-6 for picking up snakes.

---

[41] Farmer, *The Last...*, p.109.
[42] Parker, *The Living Text...*, p.138.

No case is put by any of the four commentators, to whose work I have been principally referring, for believing dependency is this way about. The principle has been established already above. If the longer ending is to be assessed for authenticity, it has in the first place to be interpreted by the Passion Narrative, and in the second by Mark's Gospel as a whole. Only when that has been done might we be able to say that we have established a sure result. Up till now I have been following, in the main, only the first path, and it has been a worthwhile journey. Connections abound which suggest the authenticity of the majority of the verses of the longer ending. But putting aside this methodolgy for the moment, there is still a case to be put for thinking that the longer ending is authentically Markan, and that dependency is that of Matthew and Luke upon it, for their endings of their gospels as for the rest of their gospels.

Matthew tells how before the women (Mary Magdalene was one of them) could report their message (the same as in Mark) from the tomb, Jesus met with them on their way (Mt. 28.8,9 cf. Mk.16.8,9). In his v.8, Matthew, it appears, simplified Mark's v.8 and made it less difficult to handle, in terms of continuing story. It might be said that in his v.9, Matthew dispensed with the longer ending's opening phrase, Ἀναστὰς δὲ πρωῒ πρώτῃ σαββάτου, and replaced 'Mary Magdalene' with the 'two women' for a clearer correspondence with the previous passage on the 'two' (not the Markan 'three') women at the tomb, 28.1-7. We could say that he thus demonstrated again as elsewhere *his* predilection for pairs, see 8.28, 21.2,5, and so on). Matthew then created his v.10 from Mark's v.7 and his own earlier development of it in his own v.7, and created in near juxtaposition, therefore, a pair of messages about seeing the risen Jesus in Galilee (the first from the angel, the second from the risen Jesus) for the women to deliver to the disciples. It appears very much like a clarifying of the geographical setting of the longer ending, as does also Matthew's rather mundane, repetitive mention (by comparison) of Galilee again, in his v.16. In vv.11-15, it may be argued that Matthew addressed a flaw in Mark's witness of the empty tomb (Jesus' body could have been stolen by his disciples), and that he then rejected the longer ending's ascension scene in order to present an already exalted Christ who, in this state, re-visited the eleven (and presumably could visit them and the church again and again) from heaven[43]. The longer ending's Jesus, in contrast, lacks this (later added) facility because he takes a one way route to heaven to return only on the Day appointed. In the scene of Jesus' post-resurrection meeting with his disciples, Matthew records "some doubted"[44], and it does look as though it might have had its origin in the longer ending's v.12, ἐφανερώθη ἐν ἑτέρᾳ μορφῇ. Further, Matthew's v.17 expunges totally any reproach Jesus may have had for his disciples (the longer ending's vv.11-14) which does look like a typically Matthaean gospel development of Mark, in presenting Jesus' disciples in a better light. Also Matthew's 'great commission' (vv.18-20a) looks more refined than the longer ending's vv.15,16, so the longer ending could have supplied him with the idea. Lastly, Matthew's final statement (v.20b) looks like a development of the longer ending's final statement because it reads as an unmistakable promise to the continuing church of Jesus' continuing presence. The longer ending could be interpreted as limited to the time of the apostles.

Luke tells events in detail which the longer ending tells only briefly. Luke reads the longer ending as if it only covered one day, and represents it that way (Lk.24). Further, it would not be untypical of Luke to develop a story based on 16.12,13, and to develop a "commissioning scene" based on 16.14-20 in order to set the two in parallel, for his own literary purposes[45]. At some stage, of course, Luke was persuaded to write a second book: the longer ending could have suggested it to him, but in regard to Mk.16.17,18 it looks more like the dependency is the other way about. Lastly, the reference to Mary Magdalene's 'seven' demons (Mk. 16.9, cf. Lk. 8.2) discloses a numerological/numerical interest which may be judged to be not untypically Markan[46].

---

[43] For example of which, see Saul's conversion in Acts 9 (and its two further tellings, in chapters 22 and 26).
[44] See the end of Mt. 28.17, "but some doubted".
[45] See Palmer, *Sliced Bread...*, pp.83f., for parallels between Lk. 24.13-32 and 33-53, and for much evidence of Luke's ability to create stories as well as re-tell stories with new purposes.
[46] Compare: the woman with the issue of blood..., and Jairus' daughter, both 'twelve' years (5.25,42) and the feedings of the five- and four-thousands (6.30-52 and 8.1-21), for a variety of numbers.

A case could be put, therefore, for a dating of the longer ending, 16.9-20, earlier than Matthew's and Luke's Gospels, and for these Gospels to be dependent upon it, that is, the majority of its verses[47].

A Summary Statement of Today's Predominating Views on 16.9-20:

Issues of dependency in regard to the synoptic gospels, Mark's Gospel and longer ending content and style considerations, and most importantly manuscript evidence have all been judged in this century to establish that the Gospel was intended to end at 16.8, as it does in Codex Vaticanus and Codex Siniaiticus and a number of later manuscripts. The inclusion of the shorter ending[48] between the gospel and the longer ending in some manuscripts has also served to support the view that the longer ending was added later, and not by Mark. Further to this, while many scholars have recognised that a number of the themes and details of the longer ending have their contact with the gospel as a whole, this fact has been used to justify "the abrupt ending".

Some of the longer ending material on the role of the disciples has its clear mention in chapter 3. "Preaching" and "believing" in the longer ending *are* much covered elsewhere[49]. That Jesus would be raised from the dead *is* severally stated in the narrative, and that he would be seen by his disciples in Galilee after his resurrection is twice stated.[50] The otherwise closing statement that the women did not report what they were told to report "because they were afraid" has had its objectors. The answer that they have received, and properly so, is that the response of fear to a report of his resurrection,

---

[47] Kümmel (*Introduction...*, p.100) argues that Matthew and Luke demonstrate uneasiness that Mark could not end at 16.8: but their divergence beyond shows that Mark already ended there. My reading above, however, takes account of Matthew's and Luke's different approaches to the work of writing their gospels; Kümmel's does not.

[48] See note 19.

[49] We observe that "baptism", outside of the Prologue, is only mentioned metaphorically (10.38,39).

[50] We note, however, that Jesus' violent death is predicted three times in direct manner, and a number of other times indirectly (see, for example 2.20), but no-one suggests that Mark did not intend Jesus' death to be included. Indeed, Jesus' death and resurrection are three-times predicted together (see 8.31; 9.31; 10.34).

is entirely in keeping with responses found elsewhere in the gospel, to the healings and miracles of Jesus. Likewise, the objection that a gospel would not end with γάρ has been met with examples of paragraphs ending this way[51]. It is the case that since 1903, when Wellhausen first suggested that Mark intended to end his gospel at 16.8, objections to his proposal have been addressed to the satisfaction of most scholars and commentators.

This compounding of the justification that the gospel was always intended to end at 16.8, because the longer ending material is much to be found already in the Gospel, tends to the following kind of views:

i) The story ends with the invitation to all to "go to Galilee", the place of discipleship, and that "if you want to see Jesus then follow where he leads. This is the end of Mark's story because it is the beginning of discipleship"[52];

ii) "Readers or hearers of Mark know the disciples did see Jesus; they also know that they themselves experience his powerful presence...; we have always to return to the beginning in Galilee... It is a continual pilgrimage".[53]

iii) "The *modern reader* will not be misled by the call (16.7) to follow Jesus who has gone before. Discipleship is following in the way of Jesus..."[54] (I interpret this writer to mean that Mark's *first audiences* of 1.1-16.8 also were not misled.)

Clearly, these similar views are representative of the inevitable end of currently accepted scholarship on the issues addressed in 1) to 4) above. Rather, my studies of these issues lead me to judge that the longer ending *is* the place to look for what may be Mark's original 'Epilogue'. Contrary to Painter, I do not think that the longer ending is "clearly secondary"[55]; I cannot say that it does not do "anything to illuminate Mark"[56]; and I cannot accept that "Whoever compiled this ending does not display Mark's dramatic skills."[57] We turn now,

---

[51] For examples: see Lightfoot, *Locality and Doctrine...*, pp.1-48, and *The Gospel Message...*, pp.80-97; and Hooker (*The Gospel...*, p.391) who cites Menander's *Dyscolos*, lines 437-8. Others are still adding to the list.
[52] Hooker, representing the views of others (*The Gospel...*, p.394).
[53] Best, presenting his own view (*Mark: The Gospel...*, pp.132f).
[54] Painter, *Mark's Gospel...*, p.216.
[55] Painter, *Mark's Gospel...*, p.215.
[56] Painter, *Mark's Gospel...*, p.216.
[57] Painter, *Mark's Gospel...*, p.215.

therefore, to the text of the longer ending and subject it to the same literary-structural analysis that the text of 1.1-16.8 has undergone.

Literary-structural Evidence:

Below, I present the literary-structure of the longer ending, 16.9-20, as it exists now. It clearly demonstrates two halves consisting of three-part presentations of the kind we have encountered elsewhere in Mark's Gospel. It is in the form A:A', or in its expanded form it reads: ABB':ABB'. All three sections of the first half are linked by resurrection appearances, reportings and their being met with "disbelief". Again the important common words have been underlined.

In the first half, section A (vv.9-11) introduces, by first report, the theme for the other two sections, and focuses on Jesus' "first" appearance, to Mary Magdalene: she reports to "those who had been with him..."; they *disbelieve*. Section B (vv.12,13) records "next" the appearance of Jesus "to two of them" who then report "to the rest" who *disbelieve*. Section B ʿ (v.14) records "at the last", Jesus' appearance "to the eleven", and his upbraiding them for *disbelieving* those who had seen him. There is no direct speech in any of these reports up to this point; they are compact third-person reports of the writer.

In the second half, section A (vv.15,16), as it stands now, includes direct speech: Jesus sends the eleven out into the world to preach the gospel: a pair of sayings, on those "*believing*" and those "*not believing*" occupy the two balancing, closing parts β and β ʿ. Section B (vv.17,18) tells of "signs" which will follow those who "believe", and these are listed. Section B' (vv.19,20), as it stands now, is itself again in three parts, which record Jesus' ascension (in the first), his heavenly seat (in the second) and the eleven's mission and his working with them with "signs" accompanying (in the third).

We consider:

A α ⁹ [α] [..α] Ἀναστὰς δε [..α˙] πρωῒ πρώτη σαββάτου [β] ἐφάνη πρῶτον
Μαρίᾳ τῇ Μαγδαληνῇ, [β˙] παρ᾽ ἧς ἐκβεβλήκει ἑπτὰ δαιμόνια.
β ¹⁰[α] ἐκείνη πορευθεῖσα [β] ἀπήγγειλεν τοῖς μετ᾽ αὐτοῦ γενομένοις
[β˙] πενθοῦσι καὶ κλαίουσιν·
β˙ ¹¹[α] κἀκεῖνοι ἀκούσαντες [β] [.α] ὅτι ζῇ [.β] καὶ ἐθεάθη [.β˙] ὑπ᾽ αὐτῆς
[β˙] ἠπίστησαν.

B α ¹²[α] [.α] Μετὰ δὲ ταῦτα [.β] δυσὶν ἐξ αὐτῶν [.β˙] περιπατοῦσιν
[β] [.α] ἐφανερώθη [.α˙] ἐν ἑτέρᾳ μορφῇ [β˙] [.α] πορευομένοις
[.α˙] εἰς ἀγρόν·
β ¹³[α] κἀκεῖνοι ἀπελθόντες [α˙] ἀπήγγειλαν τοῖς λοιποῖς·
β˙ [α] οὐδὲ ἐκείνοις [α˙] ἐπίστευσαν.

B˙ α ¹⁴[α] Ὕστερον δὲ [β] ἀνακειμένοις αὐτοῖς [β˙] τοῖς ἕνδεκα
ἐφανερώθη,
β [α] καὶ ὠνείδισεν [β] τὴν ἀπιστίαν αὐτῶν [β˙] καὶ σκληροκαρδίαν
β˙ [α] ὅτι τοῖς θεασαμένοις αὐτὸν ἐγηγερμένον [α˙] οὐκ ἐπίστευσαν.

A α ¹⁵ [α] Καὶ εἶπεν αὐτοῖς, [β] [.α] Πορευθέντες [.α˙] εἰς τὸν κόσμον
ἅπαντα [β˙] [.α] κηρύξατε τὸ εὐαγγέλιον [.α˙] πάσῃ τῇ κτίσει.
β ¹⁶ [α] [.α] ὁ πιστεύσας [.α˙] καὶ βαπτισθεὶς [α˙] σωθήσεται,
β˙ [α] ὁ δὲ ἀπιστήσας [α˙] κατακριθήσεται.

B α ¹⁷ [α] Σημεῖα δε [β] τοῖς πιστεύσασιν [β˙] ταῦτα παρακολουθήσει·
β [α] ἐν τῷ ὀνόματί μου [β] δαιμόνια ἐκβαλοῦσιν, [β˙] γλώσσαις
λαλήσουσιν καιναῖς,
β˙ ¹⁸ [α] [.α] [καὶ ἐν ταῖς χερσὶν] [.α˙] ὄφεις ἀροῦσιν.
[β] [.α] κἂν θανάσιμόν τι πίωσιν [.α˙] οὐ μὴ αὐτοὺς βλάψῃ,
[β˙] [.α] ἐπὶ ἀρρώστους χεῖρας ἐπιθήσουσιν [.α˙] καὶ καλῶς ἕξουσιν.

B˙ α ¹⁹ [α] Ὁ μὲν οὖν κύριος Ἰησοῦς [β] μετὰ τὸ λαλῆσαι αὐτοῖς
[β˙] ἀνελήμφθη εἰς τὸν οὐρανὸν
β [α] καὶ ἐκάθισεν [β] ἐκ δεξιῶν [β˙] τοῦ θεοῦ.
β˙ ²⁰[α] [.α] ἐκεῖνοι δὲ ἐξελθόντες [.α˙] ἐκήρυξαν πανταχοῦ,
[β] [.α] τοῦ κυρίου συνεργοῦντος [.α˙] καὶ τὸν λόγον βεβαιοῦντος
[β˙] διὰ τῶν ἐπακολουθούντων σημείων.

The longer ending, as it stands now, has the appearance of a Markan composition. That is the first thing we can say about it. The second is that it is most economical in its presentation. In each of its sections it is not at all wasteful of words. As a candidate for an 'Epilogue' (after the manner of ancient rhetoric) it is suitably succinct and to the point. But now we must ask if it is possible that another writer has re-worked it, and included material which is strange to Mark. In section 1) of this chapter, we noted the possibility that the whole of the longer ending was expunged from the text because vv.17,18, of all the verses, were problematic to the church in patristic times. In section 2) the longer ending was interpreted by a re-reading of the Passion Narrative, 14.11-16.8. No connection between vv.17,18 and the Passion commended themselves. In section 3) attention was paid to key features of the vocabulary, style and grammar of the longer ending. We may here consider the fact that of the seventeen words/phrases which are not found elsewhere in Mark, or are handled differently, eight[58] appear in these two verses. In section 4) I noted, in regard to dependency, that it was more likely that vv.17,18 were constructed by reference to Luke's writings than the other way about. Additional to these considerations, there is the principle in writing today, that 'one does not introduce new material into one's conclusion'. It may be that it was one of the rules of ancient rhetoric[59]. Vv.17,18 (and 20bc, therefore), on "signs", *do* represent 'new material'. Any possible link with 6.7-13 is tenuous. Further to this, these verses contradict what Mark expresses in 8.12 ("no sign will be given" this generation). Equally, the reference in 13.22, is not exactly positive about "signs and miracles", in the church's mission programme. No, the force of the first half of this longer ending is emphatically on "believing" the reports of Jesus' appearances after his death. "Believing" and "being baptised", in the second half's telling of the longer ending, alone reflect this and the Prologue's similar revelations, if, that is, we read correctly that "baptism" will continue to be a sign of "repentance". "Preaching", here, is the fundamental task of the 'eleven', and it is reflective of the same, simple introduction of Jesus' mission, in the Prologue (1.14).

It is true that as they stand the 'signs passages' balance each other in their current positions and as such have *the appearance* of Markan arrangement. But a simultaneous, double removal of vv.17,18 and vv.20bc immediately creates a better balance between the introductory phrases Καὶ εἶπεν αὐτοῖς and Ὁ μὲν οὖν κύριος Ἰησοῦς μετὰ τὸ λαλῆσαι αὐτοῖς, which have the appearance of

---

[58] παρακολουθήσει, γλώσσαις λαλήσουσιν καιναῖς, ὄφεις, θανάσιμόν, τί (separated from the conditional particle), πίωσιν, βλάψῃ, καὶ καλῶς ἕξουσιν.
[59] One of the purposes of the Epilogue was to "review *what you have already said*", another was "to magnify or minimize your leading facts", *Ars Rhetorica* III.19. See also note 25, on the issue of brevity.

intended balance, in the normal Markan positions of B and B'. By removing from the existing second half those passages which speak of "signs" that will follow "the ones believing", and "signs" that "accompanied", we observe a number of interesting results:

A α ⁹ [α] [..α] Ἀναστὰς δε [..α'] πρωῒ πρώτῃ σαββάτου [β] ἐφάνη πρῶτον Μαρίᾳ τῇ Μαγδαληνῇ, [β'] παρ' ἧς ἐκβεβλήκει ἑπτὰ δαιμόνια.
β ¹⁰[α] ἐκείνη πορευθεῖσα [β] ἀπήγγειλεν τοῖς μετ' αὐτοῦ γενομένοις [β'] πενθοῦσι καὶ κλαίουσιν·
β' ¹¹[α] κἀκεῖνοι ἀκούσαντες [β] [.α] ὅτι ζῇ [.β] καὶ ἐθεάθη [.β'] ὑπ' αὐτῆς [β'] ἠπίστησαν.

B α ¹²[α] [.α] Μετὰ δὲ ταῦτα [.β] δυσὶν ἐξ αὐτῶν [.β'] περιπατοῦσιν [β] [.α] ἐφανερώθη [.α'] ἐν ἑτέρᾳ μορφῇ [β'] [.α] πορευομένοις [.α'] εἰς ἀγρόν·
β ¹³[α] κἀκεῖνοι ἀπελθόντες [α'] ἀπήγγειλαν τοῖς λοιποῖς·
β' [α] οὐδὲ ἐκείνοις [α'] ἐπίστευσαν.

B'α[α]¹⁴ [.α] Ὕστερον δὲ [.β] ἀνακειμένοις αὐτοῖς τοῖς ἕνδεκα [.β'] ἐφανερώθη,
[β] [.α] καὶ ὠνείδισεν τὴν ἀπιστίαν αὐτῶν [.α'] καὶ σκληροκαρδίαν
[β'] [.α] ὅτι τοῖς θεασαμένοις αὐτὸν ἐγηγερμένον [.α'] οὐκ ἐπίστευσαν.
β[α] ¹⁵ [.α] Καὶ εἶπεν αὐτοῖς, [.α'] [..α] Πορευθέντες εἰς τὸν κόσμον ἅπαντα [..β] κηρύξατε τὸ εὐαγγέλιον [..β'] πάσῃ τῇ κτίσει.
[β] ¹⁶[.α] [..α] ὁ πιστεύσας [..α'] καὶ βαπτισθεὶς [.α'] σωθήσεται,
[β'] [.α] ὁ δὲ ἀπιστήσας [.α'] κατακριθήσεται.
β'[α] ¹⁹ [.α] Ὁ μὲν οὖν κύριος Ἰησοῦς [.β] μετὰ τὸ λαλῆσαι αὐτοῖς [.β'] ἀνελήμφθη εἰς τὸν οὐρανὸν
[β] [.α] καὶ ἐκάθισεν [.α'] ἐκ δεξιῶν τοῦ θεοῦ.
[β'] ²⁰[.α] ἐκεῖνοι δὲ ἐξελθόντες [.α'] ἐκήρυξαν πανταχοῦ.

The literary-structure, by this removal, becomes that of a three-section presentation, where all the sections now contain resurrection appearances, reportings, and a focus on matters of belief. It results in the word ἐκεῖνοι appearing in a repeated and emphatic position at, or very near the beginning of the last line of each section. The amendment further, and most interestingly, restores what were very likely the syllable-sounds to the endings of the last two parts of the Gospel, so echoing the way the Gospel begins[60], τοῦ θεοῦ and

---

[60] For this feature, turn to the examination of the Prologue, and also to the examinations of the opening Days to the two middle Series, and of Day Twenty-four, the longest in the telling of all Days (13.1/3 where the same οῦ sound would appear to confirm the beginning of

πανταχοῦ[61]. The questionable παρ' ἧς ἐκβεβλήκει ἑπτὰ δαιμόνια occupies a [β'] setting, and appears to sit in true Markan fashion quite comfortably in the text. It can be maintained that it is Markan for its reference to "demons", and its numbering of them. "Seven", as elsewhere used in the Gospel, in first century understanding, represented 'fulfilment' and 'completion'. It would not have been beyond Mark's intention to affirm and emphasise Jesus' power to defeat evil, in this way and here too. It is a sure indicator that Jesus has fully and completely defeated evil now, by his dying and his rising[62].

It would appear, therefore, that we have a case for considering this reduced longer ending to be Mark's original Epilogue. It reflects Mark's method of structuring better than the longer ending as a whole does. Even though there is not much balance between the two B sections for size, there is nothing new in that. (Compare, for example, Day Twenty-eight's presentation.) This case will be strengthened, of course, if it can be shown that the Prologue and this Epilogue behave similarly as framing pieces to the Gospel's narrative.

Prologue (1.1-20) and reduced longer-ending (16.9-16,19-20a) compared:

In my presentations of both Prologue and longer ending I have given some attention to the fact that they both do more than present a story-line: they both engage the listener in identifying with the disciples. Now we can see how both Prologue and reduced longer ending each break down structurally into three parts. We have noted above how they each employ introductory pieces to their parts which are not found elsewhere in the Gospel. We have just seen that there is a common employment of parechesis, at the beginning of the Prologue and in the concluding of the reduced longer ending. In my summary on the Prologue, I estimated that it covered fifty days or thereabouts, as a minimum. We may judge that the period the reduced longer ending covers is at the very least seven days (see page

---

the second half in the presentation).
[61] The word πανταχοῦ is used by Mark previously in 1.28.
[62] For the connection between the dying of Jesus and the defeat of evil, see my summaries at the end of Chapter 6.

307). We note that Church tradition, after Luke, suggests forty days, and forty days, of course, has its parallel in the Prologue's forty days of Jesus' time in the desert. Clearly, the reportings of these two framing elements contrast with those which make up the gospel narrative (1.21-16.8). These both cover a number of days each, whereas the other primary elements cover one Day at a time. Thematically and in some verbal details we do find significant correspondences between the Prologue and this reduced longer ending. They are listed:

1) The mission of the one coming before Jesus is spoken about in the Prologue: the mission of those coming after Jesus is spoken about in the reduced longer ending.
2) In the Prologue, disciples are called to follow and a promise is made by Jesus regarding their future function; in the reduced longer ending, they are commissioned and sent out.
3) In the Prologue, the heavens open and the Spirit descends on Jesus; in the reduced longer ending, Jesus himself ascends into heaven.
4) The little-used term in the Gospel, of "Lord", is applied to Jesus in both the Prologue and the reduced longer ending, see 1.3 and 16.19 for a variant, "Lord Jesus".
5) The phrase "preaching the gospel" is common also to both: in 1.14, it is what Jesus is doing "in Galilee"; in 16.15, he is commanding his disciples to do the same; and in 16.20a the reduced longer ending indeed concludes with their preaching "everywhere".
6) The word "baptism" is common to both: in both Prologue and reduced longer ending, it is understood to have salvific importance for all people.
7) "Belief" is also important in both: in the Prologue, at 1.15, Jesus says, "Repent and believe the gospel of God"; in the reduced longer ending, at 16.16, he makes a two-fold statement, "The one believing and being baptised will be saved: but the one who disbelieves will be condemned"[63].
8) Three geographical names and settings of the Prologue are interpreted in the reduced longer ending from the passion: Jerusalem, Judaea and Galilee.
9) In the Prologue, Jesus calls two sets of two brothers to be his disciples; in the reduced longer ending, he appears to two disciples.

It can be said, therefore, that the Prologue of twenty verses and the reduced longer ending of nine-and-a-half verses connect in these ways. What remains to be done is to give consideration to some of

---

[63] We note that Luke, in his parallel opening and closing sections to his Gospel makes much of "believing and disbelieving", see Palmer, *Sliced Bread...*, pp.82ff.

Mark's key words and phrases, and to consider his use of them throughout his Gospel as they reflect his development and completion of his themes, and his 'arrangement' of them in his Prologue, Narrative and Epilogue. If the reduced longer ending is Mark's Epilogue, it will demonstrate a sympathetic use of them.

We observe firstly an important and most significant difference between the Prologue and the possible Epilogue. It is that the Prologue emphasises in several ways that Jesus' mission is to the Jews. It is they who are repenting and preparing themselves for his mission. It is Old Covenant scripture and Jewish expectations which are being fulfilled. And it is Jewish territory, principally, in which Jesus is set. In the proposed Epilogue, it is the same territory in which the stories are set, but the mission of the disciples is now to the "world" and to "all creation", with the result that they "preached everywhere". Clearly, this difference between the Prologue and the proposed Epilogue can be judged to be a feature which well expresses the thrust of Mark's narrative. It is a story which has begun with the Jews, but which ends with the "world".

This description of this framing well establishes the paradigm for the narrative itself, for which for each of its Series, Mark presents Jesus' mission: in its first sub-Series, to the Jews in respect to the Old Covenant; at the turning point, in respect to Jewish/Gentile tension which focuses upon him; and in the second sub-Series, in respect to the New Covenant and to Gentiles.

We have seen, under the examination of the Passion Narrative in Chapter 6, how the word, "covenant" is used only once in the Gospel, in 14.24, but that Mark's use of the term, where it does appear, spells out the truth for the very first time, that Jesus' death establishes the (New) Covenant. Up till then, the Gospel's first three Series' second sub-Series had been pointing to this truth, only by allusion and in veiled terms. The reference in the Epilogue, in 16.15, to the "world" and to "creation" puts it beyond any doubt that the New Covenant is not just for the Jews but for the world, for Gentiles. The word "world" is first found in 8.36 (in the first Day's teaching of Jesus on discipleship, in Series Three). Significantly, it is next found in 14.9 (the middle Day and turning point of the Fourth Series). Here the "world" and the "gospel" are linked by "preaching", which is what we find in the Epilogue at 16.15. The Epilogue is in harmony with the Fourth Series, which at its centre and 'turning point' reveals (in true ancient rhetorical style) the significance of what is taking place. Earlier use of the word "creation" is found in 10.6 (the turning point of Series Three), and in 13.19 (in the apocalyptic teaching of Jesus, of Day three in the final Series). There is more than a hint in the Prologue and the Narrative that Mark understands Jesus' mission as that of establishing a New Creation. In the Introduction, we noticed the possibility that his 'arrangement' and 'style' had been influenced by the Genesis accounts of creation and new creation, in Gen. 1-11 (pages 24,25). His Gospel opens in Genesis' style. The Prologue begins the telling of 'twos' in the Gospel (*cf.* animals entering the ark, and see pages 64,65) and the proposed Epilogue (16.12) completes the telling of "twos". The narrative of the Flood for its 'Twenty-seventh Day' (Gen. 8.14ff.) which marks the moments of the completion of God's judgement of the world and its evil (v.21), and of his work of new creation (see particularly v.17) parallels exactly Mark's Twenty-seventh Day's telling of Jesus' death. (In 13.30,31, in the context of "this generation", Jesus' "words" - *cf.* Gen. 1.3,6,9 and so on - contrast with the passing away of "the heaven and the earth".) The proposed Epilogue's reference to "creation", in 16.15, is indicative of the opportunity the world now has for 're-creation', and it is synonymous with what the Gospel as a whole indicates.

The word "gospel" is, of course introduced in the opening line of the Prologue. In pages 30,31 of the Introduction, we considered political and historical issues which might have caused Mark to begin writing. We interpreted there that the late 60's, and the year 70 in particular, were "bad news" for the Jews, but that he had "good news" to share with the world, with both Jews and Gentiles. God had made a New Covenant with the world, which was more than a replacement for the Old Covenant which was suffering its demise. The Prologue makes clear in the first instance, in 1.14,15, that the "gospel" was for the Jews. The next mentions of the word "gospel" are not until 8.35 (in the first Day's telling of the first sub-Series of the Third Series, which goes on to tell, in the second day, about Old Covenant fulfilments pertaining to the Jews) and 10.29 (in the first Day's telling of the second sub-Series of Series Three, which goes on to tell, in its second day, about New Covenant foundations laid down at the hands of the Gentiles). Both read "for the sake of me and the gospel". The next use of the word "gospel" appears in 13.10 (in Jesus' apocalyptic teaching): it is to be preached to all the "Gentiles/nations". In 14.9 (the turning point of Series Four), it appears again, as we noted above: it will be "preached" in all the "world". The word "gospel", then, is found extra to the Prologue, at significant structural points in the Series' tellings, and in the apocalyptic teaching of Jesus. Its use in the proposed Epilogue is entirely in keeping with Mark's employment of the word elsewhere. His emphasis, at the last, in 16.15, that the "gospel" is for all the "world" and for all "creation" is entirely in keeping with his development and his completing of his Gospel.

We have begun to see already above the significance also of the word "Gentiles" in Mark's Gospel. We noted in the summaries at the end of Chapter 6 that the first allusion to Gentiles is at the turning point of Series One, in regard to the Herodians (who are under Roman authority) and their plotting with Pharisees (under the Old Covenant) against Jesus, 3.6. Gentiles and Gentile country are also only alluded to in the First Series' second sub-Series. In the Second Series, after the turning point mention of the Greek woman, Gentile country and Gentiles are alluded to again, but more strongly than before (notably again in the second sub-Series). It is not until 10.33 and 10.42, in Series Three's second sub-Series, that we encounter uses of the word itself. Most significantly, the first mention of the word "Gentiles" links them with the suffering and death of Jesus (*cf.* 3.6, for the first hint of this): Jesus will be handed over to "the Gentiles" who will mock, spit, whip and kill him. Gentiles indeed do all these things to Jesus, according to report in Series Four's second sub-Series, on the same sixth Day of that Series. Further, at the scene and at the moment of Jesus' death, it is a Gentile, "a centurion", 15.39, to whom understanding is given. (I have pointed out before that on the sixth Day of the First Series, Jesus demonstrates that he is victorious over great evil. That Day's telling anticipates this. On that Day, evil is expressed as "Legion", a Gentile word with the same characteristic as that of "centurion".) Further employments of the word "Gentiles" appear in the Fourth Series' first sub-Series, in 11.17 (the Temple was always intended for "all Gentiles/nations": Jesus replaces the temple with himself, 14.58, 15.29, and rights a wrongful practice), and in the apocalyptic discourse again, in 13.8, 13.10 (in the first, in relation to wars soon to be engaged, and in the second, as above, in relation to the "preaching of the gospel"). The word "Gentiles" from that point becomes eclipsed by the more inclusive word, "world" (for which, see above; it is indisputably inclusive of both Jews and Gentiles). The use of the word "Gentiles", only towards the end of the Gospel narrative, sharpens the focus on what we can call Mark's scheme, by which the "gospel" is presented firstly to the Jews, but which by the involvement of Gentiles becomes the "gospel" for the "world". The proposed Epilogue well concludes this scheme.

Finally, we consider Mark's use of the phrase, "Jesus of Nazareth" (lit. "Jesus the Nazarene"). In the Prologue, Jesus is presented as the one who "came from Nazareth", 1.9. The term "Jesus of Nazareth" is first found in 1.24 (in the First Day's telling of the narrative). It is last found in 16.6 (in the Last Day's telling). It serves in one sense as an *inclusio* in the narrative. It is found also in 10.47 (in the last Day's telling of Series Three): here Mark makes it plain that "Jesus of Nazareth" is accorded messianic status. It is also found in 14.67 (in the first Day's telling of the last Series' second sub-Series), where it corresponds with the final use of the term, in 16.6, as an anastrophe (in the last Day's telling of the same sub-Series). In 16.6, "Jesus of Nazareth" who was crucified is risen; he is not there in the tomb. In the proposed Epilogue, Jesus is not actually named at all until the final scene, where just as he is "taken up" into heaven, in 16.19, he *is* named, and titled, "the Lord Jesus", for the first and only time in the whole Gospel. (The longer ending's use of this term is not as strange, or as foreign to Mark, as scholars have supposed, given the setting, and given also the earlier uses of the former title for Jesus.) In other words, in the narrative, Mark presents Jesus as "Jesus of Nazareth". In the Prologue, Mark tells us where he has come from, and titles him simply "Jesus". In the proposed Epilogue, Mark tells us where he is going, and addresses him "the Lord Jesus", just at the point of his going up to heaven. There is evidence of Markan intention here, and of a Markan systematic use of titling for Jesus. The Epilogue's reverencing of Jesus with the title "Lord", at the last, and at such a moment, is entirely in keeping with the story-line of the Gospel which in its Prologue, in the scripture quotation in 1.3, identifies Jesus with the "Lord" of prophecy. (For other references to "Lord" as it pertains to Jesus in the narrative, consider for possibilities: 2.28, 5.19, 7.28, 11.3, 12.37.)

With these word-studies I conclude my presentation of the evidence for viewing my reduction of the longer ending as the original Epilogue of Mark's Gospel. Presented below, in conformity with chapters 3 to 6, are summaries of the common, basic literary-structural features of these components of the Gospel:

A Tabular Summary of the literary-structures of the Prologue and the revised longer ending, the original Epilogue:

DAYS: before and after	P. Prologue	E. Epilogue
chapters and verses	1.1-20	16.9–16, 19-20a
Sections: for comparison with the narrative text	A	A
Sectional sub-divisions	A B B'	A B B'
Number of verses	20	9 1/2

Conclusion:

To the arguments, since Wellhausen[64] in 1903 raised objections to the longer ending and proposed that Mark ended his Gospel at 16.8, I have introduced new information which has come from a literary-structural analysis of the text itself, and I have introduced illuminating references to rules of ancient rhetoric which have been long neglected. It is true to say that if Mark had written more, it must have been an account about an appearance (or appearances) of the risen Jesus, to the disciples, and set in Galilee. The *reduced longer ending*, seen in the light of its relationship to the reports of the last

---

[64] J. Wellhausen, *Das Evangelium Marci*, Reimer, Berlin, 1903.

threesome of "Days" of the gospel narrative (in particular), satisfies these three criteria. Furthermore, in regard to Mark's overall Gospel plan and purpose, the *reduced longer ending* completes what the Prologue begins and what the Gospel narrative develops.

As a result of literary-structural analysis and attendant investigations of the Gospel of Mark, 1.1-16.20, I, therefore, conclude that the *reduced longer ending*, 16.9-16,19-20a, is the original 'Epilogue", which Mark himself did indeed write to complete his Gospel.

If we now ask the question, "Did Matthew and Luke know Mark's original Epilogue?" we can at least answer that this reducing of the content of the longer ending *takes nothing away* from the possibility that they did. Only, in regard to Luke's second book, and as to what inspired him to write it, have we been considering the possibility that he knew the "longer ending" in its entirety, with vv.17,18 and v.20b. But, as we have argued in 4), it is more likely that it was the other way about, that Luke's second book inspired the *editor* of the longer ending to add to it.

What is fascinating to consider, is that new arguments *can be added* now to the discussion under section 4) above (on page 314). We were there reviewing the possiblity of Matthew's and Luke's rehandling of the longer ending. Given the reduced longer ending, it is not the removal of vv.17,18 that particularly raises new issues, but the removal of v.20b that does. The ending of Mark's 'Epilogue' reports the ascension of Jesus, and the eleven's leaving to preach everywhere. (We have considered already Matthew's possible reasons for rejecting the ascension scene.) It may well be that Matthew reacted to Mark's ending (or Matthew's church did) which clearly could be interpreted, without v.20b, that Jesus 'is not here anymore'. Without v.20b, there is no 'accompanying Jesus'. The argument might go this way that Matthew replaced the ending of vv.19,20a with one which assured the church of Jesus' continuing presence (see Mt. 28.20b).

Finally, given my arguments and my conclusions, for believing that Mark's Epilogue is now 'found', I present what I consider is a likely re-construction of the events which led to its becoming 'lost' in the Longer Ending. It is mostly *suggested* by the historic documents and the manuscripts to which we have access today:

Mark's Gospel, 1.1-16.16,19,20a, was circulating in the churches from the early seventies. It was the first compilation of its kind. It was received gladly, but it attracted a number of criticisms, chief among which was that its Epilogue *could be* interpreted that "Jesus was no longer present in his church"[65]. This and other deficiencies prompted the contributions of both Matthew and Luke. In additon, these two writers had much more teaching tradition to share than Mark had included.

Sometime after Luke's second book was written, Mark's Epilogue was revised, by addition only of vv.17,18 and v.20bc. It was carried out by someone who was sympathetic to his style, but who was not aware of his parachesis, or who thought it comparatively unimportant. The amendment attempted to resolve the chief deficiency, as described above. It attempted also to give the church a warrant for experiencing signs and miracles in its mission work. Material for the amendment came from the editor's reading of the Acts of the Apostles, and a legend on drinking poison without harmful effect (16.18, a second reference to which is not found anywhere in the New Testament[66]).

Mark's Gospel with this longer ending (vv.9-20) began to circulate in the early part of the second century. During this phase of the Gospel's life, patristic sholars began noticing and addressing the difficulties caused by differences between the longer ending and Matthew's Gospel in matters of the timing of Jesus' resurrection (by then Matthew's Gospel was being viewed as the tradition)[67]. Vv.17,18, also began to attract criticism for the trouble that they were causing in the church (regarding spiritual gifts and their exercise). Attempts to contain this trouble failed. It was decided eventually by the Church leaders in Alexandria that the longer ending should be expunged altogether[68].

---

[65] Compare Mt.28.16-20 (for which see my earlier arguments), and Luke's second book for the "Acts of the Holy Sprit". Consider also that Mark expected Jesus' early return. Matthew does likewise, and his emphasis on obedience (28.20) is as important as the other changes he makes to Mark's ending.

[66] But mentioned by Papias (Eus. *HE*, 3.39) of Barsabbas and in a well-known legend concerning St. John (Acts of John, xx, cf. M.R. James, *The Apocryphal New Testament*, Clarendon Press, Oxford, 1924), and in many stories attested by Theophylact (v. H.B. Swete, *The Gospel according to St. Mark*, 3rd Ed. Macmillan, London, 1913, p.406).

[67] See notes 3 and 4 of this Chapter.

[68] Refer to note 13 of this Chapter.

Copies of the reduced Gospel, 1.1-16.8, began to be made and to be circulated. A few copies of the Gospel with its amended Epilogue existed. They were not destroyed. They simply lay in storage. No copies of the original Gospel were being made by then. Copies had been so well read that they had disintegrated with use, and they were beyond further useful reference. In various centres throughout the mission field, collections of manuscripts began to be made.

In the fourth century, Eusebius had access to one such collection of manuscripts. Most of his copies, and his best copies at that, were of 1.1-16.8, but he did have some copies of the version with the longer ending. In the year 331, Constantine requested "fifty copies of the sacred scriptures". Eusebius, naturally, made copies of the best manuscripts available to him. *Gospel Questions and Solutions Addressed to Marinus*[69] and Codices Vaticanus and Siniaticus are testimony to this.

A century later, in Alexandria, the "longer ending", the edited original Epilogue, was discovered in the much older manuscripts, and vv.9-20 were added back. Codex Alexandrinus is testimony to that. Elsewhere, by then other endings were being written and attached, with the result that copies began to be made and to circulate with more than one ending. Other manuscripts are evidence of this.

In summary of the analyses and conclusions of this Chapter, contrary to the great weight of scholarly opinion, it does appear that Mark did write an epilogue, and that the Epilogue which is original to Mark is discovered in the longer ending. It is that of 16.9-16,19-20a. It is as important to Mark's Gospel as his Prologue. It completes its framing, and it completes, therefore, Mark's presentation.

---

[69] See note 4 of this Chapter.

Chapter Eight
The Gospel Matrix of Days and Series of Days:

The Results of Literary-structural Analysis:

We gather up the results of the literary-structural analyses of the preceding six chapters and, for the first time, take a look at the Markan Matrix. The Table below summarises my findings in regard to the schematic arrangement of Days and Series of Days in the Gospel Narrative, 1.21-16.8.

Table 1: The Primary Schematic Structure of the Gospel Narrative:

a	1	2	3	4	5	6	7	8	9	10	11	12	13	14	15	16	17	18	19	20	21	22	23	24	25	26	27	28
b	1	2	3	4	5	6	7	1	2	3	4	5	6	7	1	2	3	4	5	6	7	1	2	3	4	5	6	7
c	A	B	B'		A	B	B'	A	B	B'		A	B	B'	A	B	B'		A	B	B'	A	B	B'		A	B	B'
d	A		B		A'			A		B		A'			A		B		A'			A		B		A'		
e	A							B							B'							A'						
f	1		172					2		119					3		112					4		239				

Key:
  a Days of the Gospel narrative;
  b Days of the Series of seven days;
  c Days in sub-Series of threes;
  d Series of Days: the three sections of each;
  e Series of Days of the Gospel narrative;
  f number of verses of the four Series.

The information for this table is found in the written and tabular summaries of chapters 3 to 6. Clearly, what is demonstrated is a regular and systematic presentation on Mark's part in his construction of the Series, in the number of Days they comprise, and in the arrangement of the Days within the Series. In terms of the Series'

THE GOSPEL MATRIX 333

numbers of verses, the middle two Series balance for size (compare verses 119 and 112) and the outer two reasonably balance as the larger presentations (172 and 239 respectively).

Again, from the written and tabular summaries, but this time taken from chapters 2 to 7, we can establish Mark's Series' theme plan and basic structure for the whole of his Gospel:

Table 2: The Markan Matrix: His Series' Theme Plan and Basic Structure:

Prologue:
1.1-20

SERIES A: Jesus' First Days of Mission, confined to Galilee and the region of its Sea:

Day 1	Day 2	Day 3	Day 4	Day 5	Day 6	Day 7
1.21-38	1.39-45	2.1-22	2.23-3.6	3.7-4.41	5.1-20	5.21-43

Sub-Series: A: 1.21-2.22   B: 2.23-3.6   A': 3.7-5.43

SERIES B: Days of Increase in the Mission of Jesus:

Day 1	Day 2	Day 3	Day 4	Day 5	Day 6	Day 7
6.1-29	6.30-52	6.53-7.23	7.24-30	7.31-37	8.1-21	8.22-26

Sub-Series: A: 6.1-7.23   B: 7.24-30   A': 7.31-8.26

SERIES B': The Days of Jesus Journeying to Jerusalem:

Day 1	Day 2	Day 3	Day 4	Day 5	Day 6	Day 7
8.27-9.1	9.2-29	9.30-50	10.1-16	10.17-31	10.32-45	10.46-52

Sub-Series: A: 8.27-9.50   B: 10.1-16   A': 10.17-52

SERIES A': Jesus' Jerusalem Days: his Passion and Resurrection:

Day 1	Day 2	Day 3	Day 4	Day 5	Day 6	Day 7
11.1-11	11.12-19	11.20-13.37	14.1-11	14.12-72	15.1-47	16.1-8

Sub-Series: A: 11.1-13.37   B: 14.1-11   A': 14.12-16.8

Epilogue
16.9-16, 19-20a

For summaries of the "Days" in Series and the "Four Seven-Day Series" presented separately and more comprehensively, and framed by both Prologue and Epilogue, see the two charts at the end of this chapter, on pages 363,364. These presentations elucidate Mark's Gospel theme plan and afford a horizontal reading (across the page) and a vertical reading (down the page) which, with annotations, well demonstrate the overall form and contents of the Gospel. The charts display what we might describe as Mark's "rhetorical plan". Fascinatingly, however, this is not all there is to the matter. In my summaries of Chapters 6 and 7, I found that it could be presented still more simply and more meaningfully:

Table 3: The Gospel's Primary Thematic Scheme:

    The Prologue: The Gospel appears to be for the Jews

    The scheme for each of the four Series:

    The first sub-Series: Jews and the Old Covenant
    The turning point: Jews/Gentiles
    The second sub-Series: The New Covenant and Gentiles

    The Epilogue: The Gospel is for the World.

I risk stating this *so* simply. Some will say that there is mention of "Jews" here, and allusions to "Gentiles" there. Yes, but the above does, nevertheless, reflect Mark's thematic thrust for the three parts of each of his four Series' presentations, and it does reflect the effect that his narrative has upon the difference between the themes of his Prologue and his Epilogue. Additionally, in the outer Series, as I have identified in my summaries of the four Series, Series A and A' display Markan 'arrangement' after the manner of an Aristotelian understanding of the structure of a Greek Tragedy: the first sub-Series is the 'complication', the middle day is the 'turning point', and the second sub-Series is the 'dénouement'. The middle two Series, B and B', however, simply display the same balance of contents structurally. It is tempting to describe them in Aristotelian fashion, but I judge that would be to force the argument. Clearly, issues of "rigidity" and "flexibility" on Mark's part arise with such summaries as these.

THE GOSPEL MATRIX 335

According to Best[1], both Farrer and Carrington envisaged "rigid planning" on Mark's part, though they came to very different conclusions. Farrer[2] suggested a scheme based on numerology in relation to miracles and five-paragraph sectionalising. Carrington[3] pursued the possibility that the order of the material was dictated by the liturgical needs of the church. The Markan matrix which is presented here (Prologue, four Series of seven Days, Epilogue) might properly be described as "rigid", and Mark's presentational method, for its ABB' form, is one that might be termed "rigid", but the evidence shows flexibility, nevertheless, on Mark's part as he composed his Day-reports. His "rhetorical" and "rigid" plan did not strait-jacket him. We consider this feature in the next few summary tables:

Table 4: Number and Order of Verses of "Days":

	Day 1	2	3	4	5	6	7
Series A	14th 18 verses	24th 7	10th 22	19th 12	2nd 70	12th 20	8th 23
B	5th 29	8th 23	7th 27	24th 7	24th 7	11th 21	28th 5
B'	18th 13	6th 28	13th 19	15th 16	16th 15	17th 14	24th 7
A'	20th 11	22nd 8	1st 94	20th 11	3rd 61	4th 46	22nd 8

The range of verses is from 5, for the seventh Day of Series B, to 94, for the third Day of Series A'. The factor of difference is nearly 19. On this basis alone, it would be improper to call Mark's compositional approach "rigid". Even when we consider the numbers of verses of Days within the Series themselves (as we perhaps should,

---

[1] Best, *Mark: the Gospel as Story*, p.107.
[2] Farrer, *A Study in St Mark...*
[3] P. Carrington, *The Primitive Christian Calendar: A Study in the Making of the Markan Gospel*, Cambridge University Press, Cambridge, 1952.

judging their weight within the local setting of each Series and not the Gospel as a whole) the ranges are still more variable and the factors of difference are still greater than we might have expected them to be in a planned presentation:

	Range:	Factor of difference:
Series A:	7 to 70 verses	10
Series B:	5 to 29	just less than 6
Series B':	7 to 28	4
Series A':	8 to 94	just less than 12.

From these results of analysis, because the factors of difference are less for the two middle Series, we may judge that Mark exercised greater control over these Series than the outer two.

Table 5: Number and Order of Verses of Sub-Series of three-somes of Days and of Verses per Series of Seven Days:

Series:	A A : B : B'	B	A' A : B : B'	Totals:
A	6th 47	12	2nd 113	2nd 172
B	4th 79	7	8th 33	3rd 119
B'	5th 60	16	7th 36	4th 112
A'	2nd 113	11	1st 115	1st 239

Again we discern a Series' range overall of 112 verses for Series B' and 239 verses for Series A', and a sub-Series range of 33 verses for the second (A') of Series B and 115 verses for the second (A') of Series A'. Mark's "rhetorical plan" has not strait-jacketed him: where he has had more material to present, his rhetorical method has been flexible enough to cope with it. As was discussed in the summaries of the analyses of each Series, it is necessary to conclude that Mark was not as interested in quantitative balance of composition as he was with completing his constructions, whether at the level of ABA' (for sub-Series A, pivotal Day B, sub-Series B'), or at the level of ABB' (for the sub-Series: Day A, Day B, Day B'), or at the level of his Day compositions (which we will summarise below). Though we have noted above already that the inner two Series compare well for overall size and the outer two also, it is not so much in terms of their number of verses, but rather in terms of their contents, thematic and detailed, that balance is perceived in turn between the inner two Series, the outer two Series, and also the Prologue and Epilogue:

Table 6: Fundamental Correspondences between the Series' Days, Prologue and Epilogue:

P J							
A k t	1	2 m	3 I x (y)	4 H	5 G t x (z)	6 n	7 F
B A s	1	2 B	3 w	4 C	5 s w	6 D	7 E
B' A r	1	2 B	3 v	4 C	5 r v	6 D p	7 E
A' k q	1	2 m	3 I u (z)	4 H	5 G q u (y)	6 n p	7 F
E J							

In this table, I have attempted to represent: by same capital letter annotation, the primary correspondences between Days in the balancing Series; by same lower case letter, significant further correspondences Day to Day; and by bracketed, lower case letters, the principle diagonal relationships of Days. The table attempts to summarise those correspondences that we observed in the Series' summaries (see the concluding presentations of chapters 5, 6 and 7). The two charts presented on pages 363 and 364 display some of the salient points of contact between the Series and the Days. Mark has employed rhetorical techniques whereby correspondences establish: in the first place, the beginnings and ends of his Series; in the second, the beginnings of his Series' sub-Series; in the third, 'transitional smoothings' in Days three and five of his Series, around a central Day four; and in the fourth, relationships between his outer Series which are of a diagonal kind. Further, consider my extended list of Farrer's identifications, of progressive and corresponding details in the comparison of the First and the Fourth Series of Seven Days (in chapter 6): many do not correspond Day to Day. Mark has exercised freedom too, and has not been bound to balancing every detail and sub-theme in his scheme. But what it clearly suggests is that as he composed one Series, he had the other to hand as he did so. He was guided by it, but he did not feel required to follow it slavishly. It is, of course, impossible to summarise here all the many correspondences, and the functions of them all. My analyses of the Days themselves will have to be gone through again and again.

In the same vein, we can consider the structures of Mark's Days, Prologue and Epilogue, as taken from the summary tables in chapters 2 to 7:

Table 7: The Structures of the Gospel's Component Parts:

P A						
A 1 A/A'	2 A	3 A/A'	4 A/A'	5 AA'/AA'	6 A/A'	7 ABB'
B 1 A/A'	2 ABB'	3 ABB'	4 A	5 A	6 A/A'	7 A
B' 1 A/A'	2 AA'/AA'	3 ABB'	4 A	5 A	6 A	7 A
A' 1 A/A'	2 A	3 A/A'	4 A	5 ABB'	6 A/A'	7 A
E A						

Mark has not "rigidly" stayed with the same presentational pattern for each component part of his scheme, though we can discern that his Prologue and his Epilogue follow the same arrangement as each other, and most significantly, perhaps, also his first Day's tellings of each of his Series. He has begun his four Series "rigidly", but he has not kept "rigidly" to repeating the same throughout. He has kept, however, to his ABB' rhetorical method throughout, by which he created his scheme's component parts to a variety of forms:

      Style 1   A   13 times used
              2   A/A'   10
              3   AA'/AA'   2
              4   ABB'   5

I use above the same annotation as in the summary tables at the end of chapters 3 to 7. Each of the letters above represents an ABB' form. Style 1 is, therefore, Mark's simple style, ABB', which he has used most of all. (Style 4 is the same, but it is identified separately for its greater scale.) The remaining styles are compound versions:

      Style 2   ABB'/ABB' (in an A/A' sequence)
              3   ABB':ABB'/ABB':ABB' (in an AA'/AA' sequence)
              4   ABB':ABB':ABB' (in an ABB' sequence).

We now chart Mark's rhetorical styles, for each level of Literary Order, and we discern both 'repetition' and 'variety'. At the lower levels of Literary Order, we observe Mark's fundamental employment of his rhetorical style: denote it ABB' or αββ', no difference is intended to be expressed, save that the lower case Greek is used in my presentations of the results of my literary-structural analysis for each Day once the sectional and the sub-sectional divisions of the Days are defined.

The following table employs the annotational method I used throughout my examinations of the text in chapters 2 to 7. It demonstrates how at the lower levels of literary order, Mark does employ two alternatives to his αββ' method: αβγδε, which is a listing of parts; and αβγγ'β'α', which is a chiasm of parts. He in fact uses these very sparingly indeed. Only at level five (A/A', AA'/AA') and at the lower levels of 8 downwards ([α] [α'], etc.) does he regularly exhibit a further method of ordering, which is that of a simple parallelism of parts (see page 24, for similar examples from the Genesis creation account).

Table 8: The Gospel's Literary Orders:

1	P:A:B:B'A':E	The Gospel: comprising Prologue, Gospel Narrative and Epilogue
2	A : B : B' : A'	The Series of the Gospel Narrative
3	A : B : A'	Series, in sub-division
4	(ABB') (-) (ABB')	Days in Series of sevens
5	A; A/A'; AA'/AA'; ABB'	Days' sections
6	ABBˋ	Days' sectional sub-divisions
7	αββˋ; αβγγˋβˋαˋ	sub-sectional divisions
8	[α] [β] [βˋ]; [α] [αˋ]; [α] [β] [βˋ] [αˋ]	parts
9	[.α] [.β] [.βˋ]; [.α] [.αˋ]; [.α] [.β] [.γ].... [.ε]	sub-parts
10	[..α] [..β] [..βˋ]; [..α] [..αˋ]; [..α] [..β] ... [..ι]	sub-sub-parts
11	[...α] [...β] [...βˋ]; [...α] [...αˋ]	sub-sub-sub-parts

We briefly open up a discussion on Mark's presentational methods. Undoubtedly, his preferred method of presentation is that of αββˋ (and at other levels: [α] [β] [βˋ] and so on) where α is the introductory part, β is the first development, and βˋ is the second and concluding/completing development. It is found in profusion, and there is much indication that he filled out his presentation to achieve it, again and again: consider two examples:

11.1 [α] Καὶ ὅτε ἐγγίζουσιν εἰς ʽΙεροσόλυμα
   [β] εἰς Βηθφαγὴ καὶ Βηθανίαν
   [βˋ] πρὸς τὸ Ὄρος τῶν Ἐλαιῶν...,
and
12.35 [.α] Καὶ ἀποκριθεὶς [.β] ὁ Ἰησοῦς ἔλεγεν [.βˋ] διδάσκων ἐν τῷ ἱερῷ...

The [α] [αˋ] method of presentation (at literary level order 8, and below, [.α] [.αˋ] and so on) is used regularly by Mark, but its use is particularly associated with introducing direct speech in [α] and reporting the speech itself in [α'], and with the beginnings and endings of sections where an emphasis is intended (for good examples of this, see the three sections of the Prologue). Only twice in the whole of the Gospel does Mark use his [α] [α'] method of presentation at literary level order 7 where it is, therefore, designated α:α'. It is found at 11.9,10 where it introduces (in α) and presents (in α') a chiasm, and in 11.11 where it provides a balancing pair. It is at the point of Jesus' entry into Jerusalem, where Mark demonstrates a preference to accentuate the telling of the shouts of the crowd with a different form of construction, for maximum effect.

He used 'chiasms' very sparingly indeed. Contrary to Dewey, Marcus *et al*, who read many chiasms, or concentric structures in Mark's Gospel, in the details and in the 'medium-structures' (we shall call them), my literary-structural examination of the text has revealed only two, 5.3-5 (αβγγ'β'α', the description of the demoniac's state) and 11.9b,10 ([α] [β] [β'] [α'], the welcoming shouts of the crowd in Jerusalem). In the planning of his Series, however, Mark did employ chiasm in that he established a middle, pivotal Day as his 'turning point', around which he created sub-Series of three Days, in balance. In the planning of the Gospel's framework, he also employed chiasm, centring two balancing middle Series, around which he placed two balancing outer Series, all of which he framed with the Prologue and the Epilogue. Chiasm is one of Mark's literary tools, but his employment of it is near-restricted to the higher levels of literary order, and not the middle or lower orders.

As with chiasms so also Mark used 'listings' very sparingly: I find them only:

in Series A, at 3.16-19: [..α] ... [..ι] the appointing of the 'twelve';
at 4.3b-8: [.α] ... [.ε] the parable of the 'sower';
at 4.14-20: [.α] ... [.ε] the interpretation of the parable;
in Series B, at 7.21b,22: [..α] ... [..ζ] six plural and
[..α] ... [..ζ] six singular terms (on 'what defile').

Five listings, in four references, are all that Mark created.

In the analysis of the Gospel text (my Chapters 2-7) I identified a number of rhetorical devices which Mark employed as signifiers of his structuring, in opening new Days' tellings and in organising his Days' reports into sections. They were discussed as they arose out of the text and were summarised at the conclusions of the presentations of the Series in which they were identified. (See particularly the Addendums of the first, second and fourth Series.) We review only one of these devices here, that of parechesis, Mark's repetitions of the ου sound.

Examples are found at:

Prologue:	1.1-3	the opening of the Gospel;
Series B:	6.1	the opening;
Series B':	8.27	the opening;
(Series A'	12.36	quote from Ps110.1 in Day 24;
	13.1/3	the opening of Day 24's second half;
	14.2/3	the opening of Day 25);
Epilogue:	16.19b,20a	the closing of the Gospel.

It may be recognised, of course, that the genitive absolute wherever it is used repeats the ου sound, but the identification of parechesis depends on other than this in the above cases. The genitive absolute is found at 16.1, the beginning of a new Day's telling (the last in Mark's presentation), but the ου sound there is not developed by Mark: he does not intend his audience to differentiate it there from other sounds. Parechesis is a feature of Mark's presentation with which he, literally, begins and ends his Gospel, and with which he identifies for his audience the two openings to his middle Series. In the longer, concluding Series A', he retains one usage which he finds in a quotation from the Psalms (12.36), he introduces one (which we may note is not complete, for reasons of v.2's separating of the sounds) to begin the second half of his longest presentation of a Day (Day Twenty-four, 11.220-13.37, 94 verses), and includes another (which is not complete, for reasons of v.1's omission of the sounds) at the beginning of the middle Day's telling (Day Twenty-five, 14.1-11). It may be judged that Mark's creation of parechesis, where it is complete, is wholly consistent. It so proves to be an important rhetorical device, which we can find amongst historical presents, imperfects, three-step progressions, opening formulae, etc., in his well-equipped (rhetorical) tool box. Without it, we would be without major supporting evidence of structural division. Fundamental to completing the exercise of gathering up the results of literary-structural analysis is a consideration of what Mark understood to be the total number of days Jesus' mission covered. In his telling of only four Series of Seven Days, there is indication that he presented his work so as to suggest that he was telling only the most significant. At the conclusion of the analysis of each of the Series, I explored the introductory pieces to each of the Days which are the only points in the Gospel narrative where Mark included information of this kind. Because the Prologue and the Epilogue each cover a number of days, their full texts had to be considered also. The following is a summary of estimates made:

> Prologue: fifty days;
> Series A: many weeks;
> Series B: several weeks;
> Series B': several weeks;
> Series A': ten/eleven days minimum;
> Epilogue: seven days minimum.

Due to the fact that Mark has not attempted to define the passing of days with the same exactitude in all cases (as in 1.13, 8.1/2, 9.2, 11.12, 20, 14.1, 12, 15.1, 16.1/2), and due to the fact that some of these may be more symbolic, or typological than historical (e.g. 1.13: "forty days"; and also 9.2: "And after six days"), we should not attempt to add up the days and the weeks of Jesus' mission with a calculator, and pretend that we have a view on Mark's understanding of how long it actually took. Rather, this is as far as this exercise should properly go. We may estimate only that Mark might have understood the story he tells (in Prologue, twenty-eight Days, and Epilogue) to have covered possibly twelve months, or so[4].

---

[4] Schmidt suggests a minimum of one year: *Der Rahmen...*, p.190. He and Hall (*The Gospel Framework...*, p.55) make much of 2.23-28, for its suggesting a harvest time in the year previous to the Passover. Without it, they both say that Mark's telling could have covered only a few months. *IntDB* Vol. 2, on "Harvest", p.527, suggests a date up to the end of June: that would suggest an occurrence for this scene, nine to ten months before the Passover.

For Mark's travelogue of Jesus, see my map on the opposite page which plots the Gospel's mentions of geographical places according to Days and framing sections.

In the light of all these results, we now revisit the issues that were addressed in the Introduction, the issues, that is, that have been taxing Markan scholarship for the whole era of modern biblical critical studies.

Fundamental Questions in the Study of Mark's Gospel, Re-visited:

In my Introduction, I presented the case that fundamental questions remained unanswered in regard to Mark's Gospel, even though the methodological tool-box of biblical critics was full to overflowing. A brief survey of the findings of scholarship on Mark's leading idea, and on his theological, literary and compositional abilities shows that there is the widest possible range of views, and much contradiction. Though many had been examining Mark's Gospel by many different approaches, an analysis of the text of Mark's Gospel, that is *the text alone*, was still needed, if progress was to be made on these issues.

Now that my literary-structural analysis of the text is completed, and that the results of it have been gathered together, the fundamental questions can be re-visited to see if there is indication, or not, of its being helpful. For the purpose of this critique, I consider the five aspects of the practice of ancient rhetoric, as presented in my Introduction: 'invention', 'arrangement', 'style', 'memory' and 'delivery'. I have two reasons for taking this approach. Though my analysis of Mark's text has been fundamentally literary-structural from the beginning, it has been informed increasingly by the rules of ancient rhetoric as Mark more and more demonstrated himself to be an exponent of the ancient writing art. A full rhetorical analysis appears now possible: it will be furthered itself, therefore, by this kind of concluding examination. Additionally, it must be the case that any assessment of Mark's skills and abilities is only appropriately made with true regard to the practice and purpose of rhetoric in the first century. My analysis does demonstrate that Mark was well

schooled in ancient rhetoric[5]. His skills and abilities in literary and theological matters cannot be properly compared with twentieth century scholarship, in the first instance.

'Invention':

'Invention' in ancient rhetoric is the first stage of composition when thoughts and arguments are marshalled, and when basic themes are chosen. The 'leading idea', or the purpose of the book is established at this stage. 'Invention' was the conceptual stage in the process of composition. Decisions had to be taken on the subject to be elaborated, and how it was going to be promoted.

Table 3 above may be said to disclose what Mark chose primarily for his literary and theological task. And it will have been one task. The theme of his book was "Good News". His book would demonstrate how, in the beginning, it was presented to the Jews, but in the end, it was for presenting to the whole World. The Prologue would cover the former, the Epilogue the latter, and in his narrative between, he would develop a series of presentations which would begin with the Jews and Old Covenant issues; they would develop through a turning point concerned with both Jews and Gentiles; and he would end them with the Gentiles and New Covenant issues. (My reading of the Acts of the Apostles well demonstrates something very similar: the scheme is 'Jerusalem/Antioch/Rome'[6]). The "bad news" that he would counter would be the Fall of Jerusalem, the destruction of the temple, and what appeared to be the end of Judaism. He would re-interpret it as Good News not only for the Gentiles, but also for the Jews.

---

[5] Best, *Mark: the Gospel...*, p.107; see also Kennedy, *New Testament Interpretation...*, p.102: in discussing whether or not Mark may have used the methods of the rhetoricians, they say that we must allow that even if Mark had not attended a school where rhetoric was taught and it is most unlikely that he had, some of the broader principles of composition would have percolated down from these schools to the general public. My analysis shows that we can be more certain than this.

We recall Tolbert's arguments (*Sowing the Gospel...*) for the two major formative influences of Greco-Roman rhetoric and popular culture, on Mark. See my Introduction, pages 20,21.

[6] Palmer, *Sliced Bread...*, pp.49-86.

His exchange of the word "world" for "Gentiles" in the concluding of his last Series, and his use of the word "world" in his Epilogue would show that the New Covenant was for all, not just the Gentiles. He would show how both Jews and Gentiles were complicit in the death of the story's central character. Through this death, his audience would be shown that God established a New Covenant with them. In presenting Jesus, at the point of his dying, as the Son of God, he would demonstrate that for the "world" it was an act of new creation like that at the time of Noah. The creation account would have its reference and allusion. He would show that God had dealt with evil in the world in this new way.

For his supporting arguments, he would explore possibilities in the Old Covenant scriptures, particularly the Genesis account of creation, and 1 and 2 Kings for the earlier prophets, but also the Psalms and the Prophets as well, which he would use by allusion and direct quotation, and maybe by reference too.

For his presentation of his argument, he would choose to tell his story in Series of "Days", as in the creation account[7]. The 'twenty-seventh day' in his account would replicate that in the account of Noah[8], as a day of new creation. The book would be expressive of the "Day of the Lord"[9], a day of both judgement and salvation. A telling in Days would be understood not only by the Jews, but also by the Greeks who had their epic[10] about their origins, which was told in Days.

---

[7] See my Introduction, pages 23-25, and Chapter Seven, page 325, but also page 144: Mark does not present a 'week' of days as such for each Series; rather he presents a 'stage'/'phase' in the mission of Jesus, which is 'completed' by his telling of specifically 'seven' Days.

[8] See Gen. 8.14-9.17.

[9] See note 4 in the examination of the Third Series and Day Fifteen, and discussion in the text on the suggestion of Best, and in particular of Marcus who considers the Gospel to be "The Way of the Lord". For "the Day of the Lord" and "the Day of Judgement", see Isaiah, Jer., Lam. Ezk., Hos., Joel, Amos, Zeph. and Zech.; for "the coming of the great and dreadful day", see Mal. 4.5.

[10] Homer's *Iliad*. It has been viewed as the 'Old Testament' of the Greek's (A. Sinclair, p.xiii) because it is judged to have presented to an ancient people their origins - in ancient myths, legends and, as a result of archeological discoveries, much history too. We may judge from the contents of his Gospel that Mark's theological work similarly and creatively combines these three elements too, for the purpose of presenting the origins of what was expected to be (and what has proved to be) a new, universal nationhood. See also my Introduction, pages 25,26.

'Arrangement':

'Arrangement' was as important and creative a process as 'invention'. In actual practice, each influenced the other in the work of composition. The task was to establish order so that the themes, their content, and their development could be expressed clearly. There were standard skeletal outlines to choose from, but developments of these were possible. Once established, the outline would normally have been hidden so that the story unfolded smoothly.

Tables 1 and 2 represent Mark's 'arrangement'. Tables 4 to 8 qualify his 'arrangement' with descriptions of the end results of his compositional process. He chose for his narrative, 1.21-16.8, a scheme of four Series of seven Days; and for each of his Series, he chose two sub-Series of three Days which would lie each side of his middle Day and 'turning point' of the Series. It is likely that Mark lifted this Series' scheme simply 'off the peg'. It is representative of Homer's scheme for his *Iliad* (Books 2-8; 9; 10-23: three Days; one Day; three Days)[11], and we can deduce, therefore, that it had been used many times over in the intervening eight centuries. In creating his four Series in the form of ABB'A', it is again likely that he chose it from a stock of standard outlines. Both these 'arrangements' are described today as chiastic[12].

Table 2 demonstrates Mark's use of this 'arrangement' for presenting *four stages* in Jesus' Mission. As we have seen in the summaries of Chapter 6, the outer two Series balance, by way of a prefiguring in the former, and a fulfilling in the latter. The summaries of Chapter 5, demonstrate the balance between the two middle Series. Mark demonstrates employment of 'chiasm' (like Homer[13]) in his larger constructions. His use of them elsewhere, in what I describe as the lower levels of literary order, is restricted to two (see page 341).

---

[11] See my Introduction, page 25.
[12] For earlier designations for 'chiasm', see Ian H. Thomson, *Chiasmus*..., pp.12-16.
[13] For examples of balance we have: from Homer's first book, 'the treatment of Chryses', and from his last book (the twenty-fourth) 'the treatment of Priam'; and from the same books in turn also, 'the burning of the Achaian ships' and 'the burning of Hector's body'. From book three, 'the meeting of Menelaos and Paris', compare from book twenty-two, 'the meeting of Hector and Achilles'. And from book six, 'the arming of Paris', compare from book sixteen, 'the arming of Patroclos'. Homer's chronological scheme makes the balancing "absolutely explicit". See page 25 again.

Because Mark creates a compound of the two chiastic forms, and creates a 'four times seven' scheme, we have to consider if he intended that his scheme carried meaning[14]. As we have seen already, under Day Thirteen, in Series Two, Mark does well demonstrate an interest in numerology (see 8.16-21). He sets the numerical details of the 'feedings' in such a fashion as to create a numerological conundrum which requires solution by those who are listening (for my solution, see under Day Thirteen). As 'seven' is a sacred number in many of the world's religions, and as it stands for 'fulfilment' and 'completion' in Hebrew-usage[15] we, who have not been encouraged in the modern Western world to think in these terms, do have to consider seriously Mark's reason for using it in his rhetorical plan. Given also the meaning of 'four' which is another sacred number expressing 'universality' in many of the world's first century religions (in Hebrew-terms expressive of the 'four winds' and, therefore, the four points of the compass), we do have to consider the possibility that Mark intended a 'deep meaning' for his 'four' by 'seven' narrative scheme. Such symbolical arithmetic translates, 'the fulfilment for the world of the divine plan'. It does at least accord with the leading idea expressed above.

Finally, we observed in the summaries of Chapters 3 and 6, and in the summary above (page 334), that the three-part arrangement of Mark's outer Series can be read as the 'complication', the 'turning point', and the 'dénouement' of the Greek Tragedy play. It is another form which he could have lifted simply 'off the peg'.

'Style':

'Style' was also a matter of choice to the rhetor. There were many methods he had to choose from to present his material in the course of his composition. Mark's first choice is unmistakably an ABB' presentation. See Table 1, for his application of this in his sub-Series of Days. See Table 7, for his use of it for structuring his Gospel's

---

[14] Consider Rev. 18.11ff.: "the merchants of the *earth* will weep and mourn"; no-one will buy any of their 'twenty-eight' items of trade. Or consider the 'twenty-eight' days of the lunar month: here the possibility that Jesus, or his mission, is likened to "the *lesser* light to govern the night" (Gen. 1.16) is not too likely; compare the "sun of righteousness" (Mal. 4.2).
[15] *Int.DB*, 1961, Twelfth reprinting 1981, p.564.

main components: Prologue, Days and Epilogue. Compounds of the same are used in a variety of ways. See Table 8, for its use at levels of literary order, 4 down to 11.

Again we have to ask if he meant any significance in using it. We might see in these 'threes' another 'divine number'. 'Threes' abound in Mark's Gospel: consider the mentions of "Peter, James and John", Jesus' three days in the tomb, etc., etc.). Next to the number 'seven', the number most frequently used in connection with sacred matters is 'three'. This number naturally suggests "the idea of completeness - of beginning, middle and end".[16] Or it might be that Mark adopts the scheme simply because of its use elsewhere, as in the Genesis 'creation account', and 1 and 2 Kings[17]. The latter is perhaps more likely.

Very occasionally only (see above, pages 340,341) does Mark diverge from this 'style', with listings (five), and chiasms (two). In his composite Day structures (A/A', AA'/AA'), he combines it with simple parallelism, and employs the same also in his lower orders.

'Style' too refers to the matter of a rhetor's choice of grammar, syntax, and the selection of balancing/connecting words. At the end of Chapters 3 to 6, I have summarised those features of 'style' that Mark chose to employ to signify new Days. Elsewhere, we have seen how Mark has a whole armoury of rhetorical conventions to hand. He uses parechesis, anaphoras, anastrophes, historical presents, imperfects, inclusios, dualities, non-καί sentence-beginnings, three-step progressions and so on to define the components of his composition and signal their inter- and intra-relationships.

'Style' like 'arrangement' was important: as a matter of aesthetic; also for its mnemonic value; and for its persuasive effect. Mark's use of much parataxis and koine Greek will have been a choice he made in order to ensure 'popular' attention to his presentation.

'Memory' and 'Delivery':

We take 'memory' and 'delivery' together. 'Arrangement' and 'style' will have assisted the reader's memorising of the story, for natural and

---
[16] *Int.DB*, Vol. 3, p.564.
[17] See my Introduction, pages 19, 20 and 25.

purposeful delivery[18], taking account of breathing rhythms, the need for movements of quiet, reflective presentation, and others for dramatic crescendo and climax. Mark had to produce his "Gospel" for public performance, in an oral-aural culture. It is proper that we remind ourselves of this fact.

Mark's Literary and Compositional Abilities:

For Mark's audience, therefore, there is order in the presentation, but it is not tedious. In the Introduction, we asked, "How was a Gospel to function" in a first century world of few readers and of few book-owners? We may deduce that Mark's plan and method were much influenced by the requirements then. If any literature was to stand a chance of popular success, it had to have a good story-line. It also had to be written in such a way that it could be well presented orally. It needed, therefore, a rhythmic, repetitive structure and an engaging style. We may judge that Mark's Gospel had 'the story' and the technical qualities for popular listening then.

Mark has been credited in the past, with creating a new, literary genre, Gospel, but we note Bultmann's judgement which has been supported by many over the years, that "Mark is not sufficiently master of his material to be able to venture on a systematic construction himself."[19] Meagher, much more recently, has judged Mark's Gospel to be "a clumsy construction", that it has "an air of great ordinariness" and that it "is not egregiously bad... nor memorably good" as a literary work[20]. It would seem that not a few judgements of Mark's literary and compositional abilities will need to be revised. Mark should be credited not only with creating a new literary genre, but also with taking from Greco-Roman rhetorical

---

[18] In her article on "The Gospel of Mark as an Oral-Aural Event: Implications for Interpretation", *The New Literary Criticism and the New Testament*, eds. Edgar V. McKnight and Elizabeth Struthers Malbon, Trinity Press International, Valley Forge, Pennsylvania, 1994, Joanna Dewey usefully reminds us that Mark's composition would only take an hour and a half to two hours to read. She describes it as a "quite customary duration for oral performances... Furthermore, good storytellers could easily learn the story of Mark from hearing it read or hearing it told." (p.146) But she goes on to conclude that "in oral-aural cultures before there is any written text, or when a written text is recycled back into oral circulation, *there is no fixed text* that is used in oral performance." (p.157) This must be a matter for conjecture, surely?
[19] Bultmann, *The History...*, p.350.
[20] See note 26 in the Introduction.

technique all that he needed to 'create' a connected narrative[21] which would popularise, in the first century cultural milieu, his church's message.

Contrary to what many scholars have said, Mark's Gospel does have the appearance of being a kind of 'day-to-day' account of the story of Jesus, as from his baptism and focused on his mission, passion and resurrection[22]. The Gospel does appear to consist of Days as if taken from a diary, and as such this would seem to be expressive of Mark's intention, to present his story of Jesus, from its beginning to its end, as a heavenly story which is, nevertheless, well-earthed in the human space- (Palestine) and time-frame (Days). That Mark gave his serialised story an artificial structure, as Schmidt suggested long ago, cannot be in doubt: the many correspondences of his themes and details in his matrix clearly demonstrate that his presentation is schematic.

It would seem that his primary literary purpose was to create a 'connected narrative' which would tell the Good News of Jesus Christ, the Son of God. In his Prologue, Mark tells how Jesus came to begin his mission and begin calling followers to himself. In his first Series, he describes the first days of Jesus' mission and demonstrates the authority and power of Jesus and his ability to draw crowds to himself: he also shows how his presence and activities stirred up the leaders of Old Israel against him, and how Jesus laid the foundations for New Israel which would grow from small beginnings to be big in the world. In the second Series, Mark demonstrates how Jesus' mission extended, and how, by recourse to numerological presentation, Gentiles were not excluded from the New Israel in formation; further, the crowds stayed longer with him and were larger in number. In the third Series, he demonstrates that the Messiah necessarily took the way of suffering, death and resurrection, in order to establish New Israel. Jesus had much to teach his would-be followers about the way they should live too. In the fourth Series, Mark tells of the events in Jerusalem that led up to and included Jesus' passion and resurrection by which, in his own person, he replaced the institution of the old temple (which in AD70 was

---

[21]   See Luke 1.1,2: "connected narrative" would seem to be a Lukan description of Mark's work.
[22]   See note 81 in the Introduction, and the discussion in the text.

destroyed[23]) and its sacrificial means of being made right with God, and so replaced the foundations of Old Israel with those of New Israel. The Epilogue tells how the disciples came to be restored to Jesus (after having deserted him) and, after Jesus' ascension how they began continuing Jesus' mission in the world. Mark's Good News is clearly for both Jew and Gentile.

Just as he introduced his Gospel with the words, "The beginning of the Good News..", so too the Gospel ends with a continuation of the story, for which Jesus' followers/disciples bear the burden, until the Day of judgement which no-one knows but 'the Father', when Jesus will return in power and glory. Mark's interest in the coming "Day", is exhibited particularly in 13.7-37, and reflects much of the visionary statements of the O.T. prophets. His reasons for writing in "Days" may be judged to be both literary and theological.

Mark's Gospel is at once both an evangelistic appeal, which would provoke commitment on the part of the hearers, and an educational tool, which would raise issues and encourage question and answer. And to the evangelistic appeal a warning is attached. The Gospel announces the coming Day of the Lord, and of judgement that will attend it. God himself has communicated with humankind in the person of his Son, in whom is 'the fulfilment of the divine plan for the world'. Jesus' mission, passion and resurrection are disbelieved at peril.

We may judge it likely that Mark's reasons for writing when he did were to do with the fact that eye-witnesses of the life of Jesus were dying out (see the Introduction, pages 28 to 31), but were also much to do with the two events of the fall of Jerusalem and the destruction of the temple which, in themselves, will have promoted the view that Judaism had no future. If we are right that Mark had been writing soon after AD70 (see above) it could be argued that he seized (or was given) his opportunity to promote the new universal faith out of the 'ruins' of its forebear, and provide this 'good news' for the universal[24] church's dissemination.

---

[23] I hold to the view, with Hooker (*The Gospel...*, p.303), that Mark was writing soon after the fall of Jerusalem and the destruction of the temple in AD70. 13.21-23 suggests it is so, for the 'false signs' that will further be. See also 14.58, 15.29 and v.38 for an identification of Jesus with the temple.

[24] It is presently the case that many commentators and scholars are content to think of Mark as writing for a 'particular' community (see Hooker, *The Gospel...*, p.4) as a pastor and

To us today, who have never before been so fully introduced to the writing of a gospel to the rules of ancient rhetoric, it seems at first incredible that anyone would write as Mark did, creating such a matrix as has been uncovered here. Amazing too is the way in which Mark employed a style of presentation at so many levels of literary order simultaneously. Not least surprising, however, is that these features of his work would appear to have lain hidden over so many centuries. We may now marvel at Mark's literary and compositional abilities, but if we are tempted to describe him as some special 'literary artist', we should be aware that his composition is simply equal to that of many first century writers, whose schooling initially had been in Homeric rhetoric[25].

Mark's Theological Abilities:

In my Introduction, I noted the wide range of opinion that there is on Mark's theological abilities. To Bultmann, Mark was simply a collector or hander on of traditions, "not a theologian"; whereas, to Marxsen and Schweizer, in turn, he was a profound interpretor, whose theology may also be used on the contemporary scene. (See pages 13-15 of the Introduction, for these and other views too.) Literary-structural analysis has made the difference on a number of previously open issues in regard to Mark's Gospel; we ask now, "In what ways, if any, might it influence our attitudes to Mark as a theologian?"

Literary-structural analysis clearly establishes that Mark exercised full control over his presentation. Tradition did not control him. The evidence demonstrates that Mark was the writer of his Gospel and not simply the editor of tradition. It follows, therefore,

---

theologian. Literary-structural analysis which exhibits the influence of ancient rhetoric shows him to be more likely a writer/theologian (whether a 'disciple of Peter or not') who was commissioned like Luke was (Lk.1.3). Mark's universalistic leading idea contains no distinctively local appeal, and his naming of only Jairus, Bartimaeus and Simon the leper, out of all those to whom Jesus ministered, hardly can be said to display knowledge of any local church's membership. He was likely writing in Rome and could even have witnessed the return of Titus with the spoils from the temple. (See note 72 in the Introduction for Trocmé's support of Rome as the place of Mark's writing, but also for the emphasis again that the Gospel was for 'his church's own use').

[25]   See Introduction, note 42, A. Stock.

that he himself exercised full control over the Gospel's theological developments and that he was solely responsible for his 'leading idea' which is both literary and theological. He has to be credited, therefore, with selecting and developing Old Testament texts and with applying titles to Jesus where he thought they were appropriate to his Gospel scheme.

In the past, a number of scholars have confidently separated so-called "tradition" from Mark's so-called "editorial hand" or "construction" (though they have displayed little agreement). The process was hazardous enough, but given that the stamp of Mark's rhetorical method and purpose can now be seen on all the Gospel material, the separating of what is tradition from what is editing will be a task which few will dare to tackle. The bottom line is that Mark is to be credited with full compositional control over the tradition and the theology of his Gospel. It follows, therefore, that if we discover any lack of "a coherent and consistent theology"[26], it is down to Mark himself, or it is down to us, either for misreading Mark, or for expecting too much refinement in what is, when all is said and done, the first writing ever of a Gospel. And his Gospel, of course, was written not for the purpose of twentieth century study, but for first century proclamation of the Good News of Jesus *Christ* the *Son of God* (1.1). It was Good News which *in the beginning* was presented to the Jews, but *in the end* was to be presented to the world. The Good News was that God had made a new Covenant with the world. Jesus' death and resurrection sealed the New Covenant, and it signalled a time of new creation for the world. The Good News countered the 'Bad News' of Jerusalem's fall, the temple's destruction, and the apparent demise of the Old Covenant, so much so, given Mark's theme plan, that one wonders if there would have been any 'Good News' at all without the Jewish War.

Under 'Invention' above, I am satisfied that I have captured the salient theological features of Mark's leading idea for his Gospel. In this regard, we consider Wrede's work of 1901, principally because it has continued to be influential throughout the biblical-critical era. His judgement was that Mark's leading idea was the constructing of his Gospel on the basis of a dogmatic theory of a messiahship which was to be kept secret until after his resurrection. On page 234, I join

---

[26] Best, *Disciples...*, pp.46f.

forces with Wrede, and address the problem with which Mark had to grapple in his presentation. Jews and Gentiles could not knowingly crucify the *Messiah* and *Son of God* in order to establish a New Covenant between God and the world. Equally, it could not be that they had no opportunity of knowing who Jesus was during his Mission. Mark's problem *and* his solution are immediately apparent.

In the third Series, these matters are given an airing by Mark. After the confession, "You are the *Messiah*", silence is demanded (8.30). After the mountain disclosure of Jesus *'my beloved Son'*, silence is demanded until after the resurrection (9.9). Telford, in his work on *The Barren Temple and the Withered Tree* (p.262) says of 10.46-12.37 (which bridges the third and fourth Series), that "it is in many respects damaging" to Wrede's thesis, "The Secrecy motif rather than presenting Jesus as the concealed Jewish *Messiah*, serves to present him as the concealed *Son of God*." Given these observations, we may make another, of the greatest importance. It would appear that Mark presents Jesus to the *Jews* as their *Messiah*, and that he presents Jesus to the *Gentiles* as the *Son of God*.

We do a short word-study. It completes an examination of Mark's key words, begun on pages 323-328:

For "The Christ"/"Son of David"[27], as designations for Jesus, see 1.1, 8.29, 9.41, 10.47,48, 11.10, 12.35-37, 14.61,62, and 15.31,32.

In 1.1, its use has no specific attachment, either to Jews, or Gentiles as such; in 8.29* and 9.41, it is for the disciples to know; in 10.47,48, Bartimaeus knows; in 11.10, Jerusalem's crowds know; in 12.35-37, the temple crowds know; in 14.61,62, the high priest wants to know, and Jesus tells all the Sanhedrin; and in 15.31,32, chief priests and scribes mock (they really did not know, they could not believe Jesus for his answer).

For "Son of God" (and variations) as a designation for Jesus, see 1.1,11, 3.11, 5.7, 9.7, 12.6 *bis.*, and 15.39.

In 1.1,11, its use has no specific attachment, either to Jews, or Gentiles as such; in 3.11, Jews *and* Gentiles are present and hear, "You are the Son of God" (3.7,8 define the crowd mix; *cf.* 3.8 and

---

[27] The titles for Jesus, in Day Twenty-seven, of "King of the Jews" (15.2,9,12,18 and 26) and "King of Israel" (15.32) attach further messianic status to Jesus. See my page 241. The Royal Psalms (for example, especially Ps. 2, to which Mark refers in Day Twenty-seven's telling) were interpreted "in later times as thoroughly messianic": *IntDB*, Vol. 3, p.361.

10.1 for "beyond the Jordan"; and 3.8 and 7.24 for "Tyre and Sidon"; in both the connecting stories, Gentiles are present, and the issues are Jewish/Gentile ones); in 5.7, Gentiles hear, "Jesus, Son of God of the Most High" (it is Gerasene and "pig" country); in 9.7*, it is like 1.11, but it is for Peter, James and John only to know, until after the resurrection (9.9); in 12.6, the use of "son" is parabolic and allegorical, for the temple crowd; in 15.39, Jesus' dying provokes the Gentile "centurion" to affirm Jesus "a Son of God".

It is significant that the references in 8.29, to Peter's identification of Jesus as "the Christ", and in 9.7, to the reference to Jesus as "my beloved Son" (hence, my asterisks above), occupy the first and second Days respectively of Series Three. The central point of Mark's gospel scheme has just been passed.

Both Jews and Gentiles were complicit in Jesus' death, but to Mark they do 'associate' with Jesus in these particular ways. It is astute of Mark. The connection between the Jews and the Messiah is supported by Old Covenant scriptures (he could appeal to these). He had, however, to create the connection between the Gentiles and Jesus. But it was easy to do. Caesar Worship[28], and Emperor Worship[29] were such that the *sacramentum* of the Roman Soldier was "Caesar is Lord"; Caesar was a "Son of God". Mark chose to affirm to Gentiles that Jesus was the one to "follow". Additionally, we observe, in 12.13-17, that Pharisees (leaders under the Old Covenant) and Herodians (leaders of Israel under Roman authority) together try to trick Jesus over paying tribute to Caesar.

We have noted already, in Chapter 2, that literary-structural analysis defends the phrase "Son of God" textually, in the opening verse of the Gospel, 1.1. In this opening line of his Gospel, Mark is telling us something more than we have understood before. His Gospel is for both Jews and Gentiles. He has written it so that both, in their different ways, may know the Good News about Jesus. The secrecy motif[30], of Jesus' Messianic status and of his status as Son of

---

[28] *IntDB*, Vol. 1, p.479.
[29] *IntDB*, Vol. 2, pp.98,99.
[30] The *restricting of information* (on the Kingdom, on who Jesus is, and on what he has been doing, or will be doing) is found in the Gospel only in the Days of the first three Series:

Series One:	<u>1</u>	2	3	4	<u>5</u>	6	<u>7</u>
Series Two:	8	9	10	11	<u>12</u>	13	<u>14</u>
Series Three:	<u>15</u>	<u>16</u>	17	18	19	20	21

God, which Wrede identified, is not Mark's leading idea as such, but it attends it very closely.

To put it succinctly: the findings of literary-structural analysis, informed by the rules of ancient rhetoric, demonstrate Mark's profound, creative theological ability. He may not have written his Gospel to everyone's abiding satisfaction[31], but it was the first to be written, and as such its importance to the Church's *understanding* about its beginnings is without parallel.

The Agenda for Future Work:

Clearly, this literary-structural exercise demonstrates that there is now much further work to be done. A re-appraisal of all critical methodologies and of much Markan scholarship appears to be required. Of the tools of critical investigation, it is plain that structural and rhetorical criticism have proved much more valuable in this exercise than source, form and redaction criticism. The Commentaries of Taylor, Nineham and Schweizer, which were chosen for their different approaches, and with that of Hooker, for their scholarship and insight, proved most valuable in the process of examining the text, but their usefulness lay more in their detailed consideration of Mark's writing than in their understanding of how the Gospel was put together. Because of this discovery of the Gospel's form, it does mean that much Markan scholarship will need to be re-visited and re-assessed. And much that is presented

---

All the underlined Days contain a secrecy command of Jesus. Only the double-underlined Days contain a command to keep quiet about his identity specifically (at 1.25,34, 3.12, 8.30, 9.9). Additionally, Days 5, 17 and 20 which are italicised contain expressions which inform Mark's audience that it was for the disciples alone, and not the crowds, to know certain things, such as the meanings of the parables, and the matters about Jesus' suffering, death and resurrection, before events took place. Others, who had been *healed*, had been told not to say anything, at 1.44, 3.12, 5.43 (witnesses to the raising), 7.36 (witnesses to the healing), and 8.26. These are to be found in the telling of Days 2, 5, 7, 12 and 14, some of which are represented by a single underline, that is where they do not contain other 'secrecy' statements.

[31] Consider: 1) the first re-writing of his Gospel with additions, by Matthew; 2) in turn, Luke's second re-writing of his Gospel and of Matthew's simultaneously; 3) the amendments to, and then the expurgation of the original epilogue; 4) its neglect over the centuries, as it was viewed as subordinate to Matthew's and Luke's; and 5) the judgements of scholars over the last one hundred years, concerning Markan inconsistencies.

immediately above, based on the results of literary-structural analysis, will require a great deal of further consideration too.

Effort, in the past, has been expended on an ever-increasing range of tasks: it may be that it can be more focused now. Also, what has been done here for Mark, requires to be done for other writers. Clearly, all books that were produced in the latter half of the first century, whether or not they found their way into the canon of Holy Scripture, require similar structural and rhetorical analysis. The work has been begun, of course, and I have made my own contribution too, before now, on the Gospels, Acts and the Revelation to John[32], but the development of the study of book-structures is a matter of the greatest importance if we are to understand the theology of these writers[33], and, therefore, what it is that their books represent. It is plain, as a result of this exercise, that we should suspend all judgement on any writer's purpose or leading idea, theology, compositional and literary skills, until we have established his book-framework and his rhetorical style. We need not be hesitant: all the writers of these books did have a plan, and a presentational method.

On Mark's Gospel, we may judge that the following jobs specifically are waiting to be done:

1) On Reading Mark now:

Principally, for the purpose of reading Mark now, the work of textual criticism can be developed. What is not of Mark, and what is of Mark, from the many mss., because of the uncovering of his rhetorical method, can be more easily assessed than before. In the analysis, for example, of Day Twenty-six, in 14.68, the phrase, "and the cock crowed" in the Nestle-Aland text (which is not supported by Codices Vaticanus and Sinaiticus) simply does not fit Mark's [.α] [.β] [.β'] scheme. (See under Day Twenty-six for my interpretation that

---

[32] Palmer, *Sliced Bread...*, 1988.
[33] Others who are saying the same, from their standpoints, are: N. Perrin, "The Evangelist as Author: Reflections on Method in the Study and Interpretation of the Synoptic Gospels and Acts", *BR* 17 (1972), pp.5-18; Stephen H. Smith, "The Literary Structure...", 1989; Greg Fay, "Introduction to Incomprehension...", 1989.

the phrase once had its place at v.70.) It is simply one of those phrases which some mss. witness to and others do not.

Translation is the next job of work on my list, if Mark's Gospel is to be read and heard as it was meant, by more than ancient-Greek scholars. It would be a hugely challenging task to repeat Mark's α β β˘ rhetorical style (if not to the eleventh level of literary order, at least to the ninth or tenth), but it would be respectful of his endeavours.

Presentation comes next. The Gospel is deserving of a complete revision, of paragraphs, annotations, headings and sub-headings. Readers today should have access to its structure, and, therefore, have opportunity to read according to it. Literary-structural analysis further demonstrates that the Gospel has its own lectionary scheme built in: no other reading schemes are needed now, save that for church purposes of Sunday public-readings and for group study there remains a need to allot the Gospel's elements for successive reading.

2) Understanding Mark now:

If Mark is to be understood by the many, the above would go a long way. In addition, a new commentary based on the Greek analysis, would be useful. Clearly, a 'true' translation would be usefully incorporated. And the commentary would have to be an exegetical commentary: an ordinary one would not do! It would have to take account of the kind of exegesis Mark intended by his balances of intra- and inter-Series' tellings of Days and themes and details of Days, and his constructions of his Series. The commentary would necessarily have to engage the reader in issues of midrash and historiography too. Matters of tradition and history will be required to be re-addressed in the context of first century story-telling and literary-method. And such matters as David Friedrich Strauss raised in the nineteenth century, on myth and history in the Gospels[34], will have to be revisited too.

New study courses for individual, group, sunday school and church use will be required. And in this age, when fewer people than

---

[34] David Friedrich Strauss, *Das Leben Jesu, kritisch bearbeitet*, 2 vols., 1st ed. Tübingen, 1835-36, 4th ed. Tübingen, 1840; Eng. Tr. by George Eliot, *The Life of Jesus Critically Examined*, SCM Press, London, 1973.

before are reading for long sittings, and when communication is more visual than written or spoken, the assistance of not just a chart, but an art-work, or a series of pictures, even a tape-slide presentation, would be entirely proper. Structured literature clearly lends itself well to artistic reproduction; see the following page for my own attempt.[35]

3) Sharing Mark now:

In the assessment of Mark's purpose above, we judged that the Gospel was fundamentally an evangelistic appeal and an educational tool. We have addressed the second of these two features, now we address the first, its evangelistic appeal. Often, copies of Mark's Gospel are distributed today at evangelistic meetings, or amongst members of uniformed youth organisations and sunday schools, primarily because it is the shortest Gospel, but also because it has inner momentum. Its benefit also may be judged to be that it does not include any long 'speeches'.[36] In its presentation of four stages in the mission of Jesus, and its disclosure of the nature of his mission and its meaning for the world, it is to be recommended still today... but in the presentation which will reflect its form, and in the new 'illuminated' translation which will be the uncut, Markan, vigorous version that it was always meant to be.

Mark's Gospel was prepared for the popular market, with a little re-packaging...

---

[35] I devised my own some time ago now, after I (nearly) discerned the basic framework, and it has been useful in both church and group work. It also translated well to a coffee-table sized jig-saw in thick card. (For the purpose of presenting it here it has been amended.)

[36] Compare Eusebius' early record which seems to bemoan the fact: Mark "adapted his teachings to the needs of the moment and did not make an ordered exposition of the sayings of the Lord.", *HE* iii.39.15, also Bettenson, *Documents...*, p.27.

MARK'S GOSPEL

	1st sub- Series of 3 Days			Pivotal Day	2nd sub- Series of 3 Days		
P.	Prologue: 1.1-20 The Days Beginning; John's mission; Jesus' baptism and 40 days; Jesus' mission						
A	Day 1: 1.21-38 In Capernaum: in synagogue, teaching, casting out unclean spirit; and healing...	Day 2: 1.39-45 Healing of leper; Jesus' fame spread	Day 3: 2.1-22 Healing of paralytic, forgiving sins, teaching parabolically; conflict with scribes	Day 4: 2.23-3.6 Conflict with Pharisees over the sabbath; a plot to kill Jesus	Day 5: 3.7-4.41 Appointing of the twelve, teaching in parables, conflict with scribes	Day 6: 5.1-20 Healing of demoniac; Jesus' fame spread	Day 7: 5.21-43 Healing of incurable; and raising of dead
B	Day 8: 6.1-29 In home town: Jesus' identity? mission of disciples; report: Death of John the Baptist	Day 9: 6.30-52 Feeding of 5,000 Jews; Jesus walks on the sea	Day 10: 6.53-7.23 Pharisees' challenge on unclean/unwashed hands	Day 11: 7.24-30 Jew/Gentile issues: Jews first; Gentiles second	Day 12: 7.31-37 Healing of deaf man	Day 13: 8.1-21 Feeding of 4,000 Gentiles; Pharisees ask for a sign	Day 14: 8.22-26 Healing of blind man (in two stages)
B'	Day 15: 8.27-9.1 In Caesarea Philippi: Jesus' identity; Jesus' prediction, teaching on discipleship/kingdom	Day 16: 9.2-29 Jesus with Two in glory; prediction; healing of boy (issues: faith and prayer)	Day 17: 9.30-50 Jesus' prediction. Servanthood; Entry into life/the kingdom of God	Day 18: 10.1-16 Pharisees question Jesus. Discipleship hinges on receiving the kingdom of God	Day 19: 10.17-31 Eternal life/entering the kingdom of God; the issue of riches	Day 20: 10.32-45 Jesus' prediction. Two want to be with Jesus in glory; servanthood	Day 21: 10.46-52 Healing of blind man who follows Jesus
A'	Day 22: 11.1-11 Jesus' entry into Jerusalem (as messiah/king) and temple	Day 23: 11.12-19 Fig tree cursed; Jesus' clearing of temple; chief priests and scribes seek to destroy Jesus	Day 24: 11.20-13.37 Fig tree withered; teaching in/out temple; Jewish leaders seek to seize Jesus	Day 25: 14.1-11 A plot to kill Jesus: Jesus' anointed for burial	Day 26: 14.12-72 Last Supper; Jesus' arrest and trial before the sanhedrin; Peter's denial	Day 27: 15.1-47 Trial before Pilate; Death of King of Jews and burial	Day 28: 16.1-8 Raising of dead announced; women flee from tomb
E.	Epilogue:16.9-16,19-20a The Days of Jesus' three appearances and ascension; the mission of his disciples						

"Days" in The Markan Matrix:

The Four Seven-Day Series of The Markan Matrix:

		1st sub-Series of 3 Days	Pivotal Day	2nd sub-Series of 3 Days
P.	**1.1-20: The Days beginning**	1.1-20		
A	**1.21-5.43: Jesus' first Days of Mission, confined to Galilee and the region of its Sea:**	1.21-2.22 — Where and how Jesus first became known, and where and how his fame spread; he shows his power and authority, and arouses conflict	2.23-3.6 — Conflict with Pharisees; a plot to kill Jesus	3.7-5.43 — "Old Israel" gathers to Jesus who lays foundations for "New Israel"; he demonstrates immense power and authority, over evil and death
B	**6.1-8.26: Days of Increase in the Mission of Jesus:**	6.1-7.23 — Where and how Jesus' fame further spread; his identity is an issue; Jesus feeds 5,000 Jews, and clashes again with Pharisees and scribes	7.24-30 — Jew/Gentile issues: Jews 1st; Gentiles 2nd	7.31-8.26 — Jesus continues establishing "New Israel", but in Gentile country; he feeds 4,000 Gentiles; clashes again with Pharisees
B'	**8.27-10.52: Days of Jesus' Journeying to Jerusalem, to the Cross and Glory:**	8.27-9.50 — Jesus' identity; he is the Christ; will suffer, die and rise again, and come with the kingdom in glory; he teaches on discipleship, life/kingdom	10.1-16 — Discipleship hinges on receiving the kingdom	10.17-52 — Jesus teaches on life/kingdom and discipleship, his suffering, death and rising again, status in glory; he heals a blind man who "follows"
A'	**11.1-16.8: Jesus' Jerusalem Days: his Passion and Resurrection:**	11.1-13.37 — Jesus enters Jerusalem as messianic king and enters the temple, which he clears, and where he teaches on judgement, life…; conflicts deepen	14.1-11 — A plot to kill Jesus; he is anointed for burial	14.12-16.8 — Jesus' last meal before the new one in the kingdom; his arrest, trials, crucifixion as King of the Jews, death, burial, and victory over death
E.	**16.9-16,19-20a: The Days following**			

Bibliography:

Achtemeier, Paul J., "Toward the Isolation of Pre-Markan Miracle Catenae", *JBL* 89 (1970), pp.265-291
Achtemeier, Paul J., "The Origin and Function of the Pre-Markan Miracle Catenae", *JBL* 91 (1972), pp.198-221
Aharoni, Yohanan & Avi-Yonah, Michael, *The Macmillan Bible Atlas*, Rev. Ed., Macmillan Publishing, New York & Collier Macmillan Publishers, London, 1977
Allen, R.E. (ed.), *Concise Oxford Dictionary of Current English*, Clarendon Press, Oxford, 8th ed. 1990.
Bailey, K.E., *Poet and Peasant: A Literary Cultural Approach to the Parables*, Eerdmans, Grand Rapids, 1976
Bandstra, Barry L., *Reading the Old Testament: An Introduction to the Hebrew Bible*, Wadsworth Publishing Co., International Thomson Publishing Inc., 1995
Barclay, Wm., *Mark*, Daily Study Bible, St Andrew Press, Edinburgh, 1954
Barthes, Roland, "Introduction to the Structural Analysis of Narrative", *Image - Music - Text*, ed. & tr. Stephen Heath, Hill and Wang, New York, 1977
Beach, C., *The Gospel of Mark: Its Making and Meaning*, Harper & Bros., New York, 1959
Belo, Fernando, *A Materialist Reading of the Gospel of Mark*, Maryknoll, New York, 1981
Best, Ernest, *Mark: the Gospel as Story*, T. & T. Clark, Edinburgh, 1983
Best, Ernest, *Disciples and Discipleship: Studies in the Gospel according to Mark*, T. & T. Clark, Edinburgh, 1986
Bettensen, H. (ed.), *Documents of the Christian Church*, Oxford University Press, London, 2nd ed. 1963
Bilezikian, Gilbert G., *The Liberated Gospel: A Comparison of the Gospel of Mark and Greek Tragedy*, Baker, Grand Rapids, 1977
Blass, F. & Debrunner, A., *A Greek Grammar of the New Testament and other Early Christian Literature*, tr. & rev. R.W. Funk, University of Chicago Press, Chicago, 1957
Blomberg, Craig, "Midrash, Chiasmus, and the Outline of Luke's Central Section", pp.217-259, *Gospel Perspectives (Studies in Midrash and Historiography)* Vol. III, eds. France & Wenham, JSOT Press, Sheffield, 1983

Bowman, J., "The Gospel of Mark: The New Christian Passover Haggada", *StPB* 8 (1965)
Brown, Colin (ed.), *The New International Dictionary of New Testament Theology*, The Paternoster Press Ltd., Exeter, 1975
Bultmann, Rudolf, *Die Geschichte der Synoptischen Tradition*, Göttingen, 1931, *The History of the Synoptic Tradition*, tr. John Marsh, Basil Blackwell, Oxford, 1972
Burgon, J.W., *The Last Twelve Verses of the Gospel According to S. Mark Vindicated against Critical Objectors and Established*, G. Bell & Son, Oxford and London, 1871
Buth, Randall, "Mark's use of the Historical Present", *Notes on Translation* 65 (1977), pp.7-13
Carrington, P., *The Primitive Christian Calendar: A Study in the Making of the Markan Gospel*, Cambridge University Press, Cambridge, 1952
Carrol, Robert, Book Review: Leach & Aycock, "Structuralist Interpretations of Biblical Myth", *RS*, 21/1 (1985), pp.116-118
Clark, David J., "Criteria for Identifying Chiasm", *LB* 35 (1975), pp.63-72
Clark, K.W., "The Theological Relevance of Textual Variation in Current Criticism of the Greek New Testament", *JBL* 85 (1966), pp.9-12.
C.E.B. Cranfield, "The Gospel of Mark", *IntDB*, Abingdon, Nashville, 1962
C.E.B. Cranfield, *The Gospel According to St. Mark*, gen. ed. C.F.D. Moule, The Cambridge Greek Testament Commentary, Cambridge University Press, Cambridge, 1959, rev. 1977
Cross, F.L.& Livingstone, E.A. (eds.), *The Oxford Dictionary of the Christian Church*, 3rd Ed., Oxford University Press, Oxford, 1997
Culpepper, R.A., "An Outline of the Gospel According to Mark", *R&E* 75 (1978), pp.619-622
Deeks, David, "The Structure of the Fourth Gospel", *NTS* 15 (1968-69), pp.107-129
Dewey, Joanna, *Markan Public Debate: Literary Technique, Concentric Structure, and Theology in Mark 2.1-3.6*, SBLDS 48, Scholars Press, Chico CA, 1980
Dewey, Joanna, "The Gospel of Mark as an Oral-Aural Event: Implications for Interpretation", *The New Literary Criticism and the New Testament*, eds. Edgar V. McKnight and Elizabeth Struthers Malbon, Trinity Press International, Valley Forge, Pennsylvania, 1994
DeWitt Burton, Earnest, *Syntax of the Moods and Tenses in New Testament Greek*, 3rd ed., T. & T. Clark, Edinburgh, 1955
Dibelius, M., *Die Formgeschichte des Evangeliums*, 5th ed. ed. G. Bornkamm, J.C.B. Mohr, Tübingen, 1966
Di Marco, Angelico, "Der Chiasmus in der Bibel: 1. Teil", *LB* 36 (1975), pp.21-97

Di Marco, Angelico, "Der Chiasmus in der Bibel: 3. Teil", *LB* 39 (1976), pp.37-85
Dodd, C.H., "The Framework of the Gospel Narrative", *ExpT* 43 (1932), pp.396-400.
Drury, John, "Mark", *The Literary Guide to the Bible*, Eds. Robert Alter & Frank Kermode, Collins, London, 1987, pp.402-417
Drury, John, "Mark 1.1-15: An Interpretation", in *Alternative Approaches to New Testament Study*, ed. A.E. Harvey, SPCK, London, 1985
Ellingworth, Paul, "How Soon is 'Immediately' in Mark?", *BT* 29 (1978), pp.414-419
Ellingworth, Paul, "The Dog in the Night: A Note on Mark's non-use of KAI", *BT* 46 (1995), pp.125-128.
English, Donald, *The Message of Mark: The mystery of faith*, BST, The Bible Speaks Today, Inter-Varsity Press, Leicester, 1992
Fanning, Buist M., *Verbal Aspect in New Testament Greek*, Clarendon Press, Oxford, 1990
Farmer, W.R., *The Last Twelve Verses of Mark*, Cambridge University Press, Cambridge, 1974
Farrer, Austin M., *A Study in St. Mark*, Dacre Press, Westminster, 1951
Farrer, Austin M., "On Dispensing with Q", *Studies in the Gospels*, Ed. Nineham, Blackwell, London, 1955
Faw, C.E., "The Outline of Mark", *JBR* 25 (1957), pp.19-23
Fay, Greg, "Introduction to Incomprehension: The Literary Structure of Mark 4.1-34", *CBQ* 51 (1989), pp. 65-81
Fenton, John C., "Inclusio and Chiasmus in Matthew", *Studia Evangelica*, International Congress on New Testament Studies, ed. Kurt Aland, et al., Akademie-Verlag, Berlin, 1959 Vol. 73, pp.174-179
Fischel, Henry A., "Story and History: Observations on Greco-Roman Rhetoric and Pharisaism", *AOS, Middle West Branch, Semi-Centennial Volume*, ed. Dennis Sinor, pp.59-88, 1969
Fowler, R.M., *Loaves and Fishes. The Function of the Feeding Stories in the Gospel of Mark*, SBLDS 54, Scholars Press, Chico CA, 1981
Funk, R., *Language, Hermeneutic, and the Word of God*, Harper & Row, New York, 1966
Gamba, Giuseppe G., "Considerazioni in margine alla poetica di Mc.2.1-12" *Salesianum* 28 (1966), pp.324-349
Gamble, Harry Y., *Books and Readers in the Early Church: A History of Early Christian Texts*, Yale University Press, New Haven and London, 1995
Gerhardsson, Birger, *Memory and Manuscript: Oral Tradition and written Transmission in Rabbinic Judaism and Early Christianity*, tr. Eric J. Sharpe, C.W.K. Gleerup, Uppsala, 1961

Gnilka, J., "Das Evangelium nach Markus", 1-2, *EKK* 2/1-2, Neukirchen (1978-79)
Goulder, M.D., *The Evangelists' Calendar (A Lectionary Explanation of the Development of Scripture)*, SPCK, London, 1978
Goulder, M.D., "The Chiastic Structure of the Lucan Journey", *TU* 87 (1963), pp.195-202
Güttgemanns, E., *Offene Fragen zur Formgeschichte des Evangeliums*, Christian Kaiser Verlag, München, 1970
Hagedorn, Anselm C. & Neyrey, Jerome H., " 'It was out of envy that they handed Jesus over' (Mark 15.10): The Anatomy of Envy and the Gospel of Mark", *JSNT* 69 (1998), pp.15-56
Hall, David R., *The Gospel Framework: Fiction or Fact? (A critical evaluation of Der Rahmen der Geschichte Jesu)*, Paternoster Press, Carlisle, 1998
Harris, William, *Ancient Literacy*, Harvard University Press, Cambridge, Mass., 1989
Hawkins, J.C., *Horae Synopticae, Contributions to the Study of the Synoptic Problem*, Clarendon Press, Oxford, 2nd ed. 1909
Heil, John Paul, "Mark 14.1-52: Narrative Structure and Reader-Response", *Bib* 71, 3 (1990), pp.305-332
Hengel, Martin, *Studies in the Gospel of Mark*, SCM Press, London, 1985
Hengel, Martin, *Judaism and Hellenism*, tr. J. Bowden, Fortress Press, Philadelphia, 1974
Hirsch, E., *Frühgeschichte des Evangeliums. Das Werden des Markusevangeliums*, J.C.B. Mohr, Tübingen (1940) 2nd ed. 1951
Hooker, Morna D., *Beginnings: Keys that open the Gospels*, SCM Press, London, 1997
Hooker, Morna D., *The Gospel according to St. Mark*, Black's New Testament Commentaries, A. & C. Black, London, 1991
Isaaksson, A., *Marriage and Ministry in the New Temple*, C.W.K. Gleerup, Lund, 1965
Jenkins, Luke H., "A Markan Doublet", *Studies in History and Religion: Presented to Dr. H. Wheeler Robinson*, ed. Ernest A. Payne, Lutterworth, London, 1942
Jeremias, J., *Infant Baptism in the First Four Centuries*, tr. by D. Cairns, SCM Press, London, 2nd ed. 1971
Jeremias, J., *The Prayers of Jesus*, tr. J. Bowden *et al*, SCM Press, London, 1967
Jeremias, J., *New Testament Theology*, tr. J. Bowden, SCM Press, London, 1971
Juel, Donald, *Messiah and Temple: The Trial of Jesus in the Gospel of Mark*, SBLDS 31, Scholars Press, Missoula, Montana, 1977

BIBLIOGRAPHY 369

Keck, L.E., "The Introduction to Mark's Gospel", *NTS* 172 (1966), pp.352-70
Kennedy, G.A., *New Testament Interpretation through Rhetorical Criticism*, University of North Carolina Press, Chapel Hill, NC, 1984
Kingsbury, J.D., *The Christology of Mark's Gospel*, Fortress Press, Philadelphia, 1983
Koch, Dietrich-Alex, *Die Bedeutung der Wundererzahlungen für die Christologie des Markusevengeliums*, BZNW 42, Walter de Gruyter, Berlin, 1975
Kolenkow, Anitra Bingham, "Beyond Miracles, Suffering and Eschatology", *1973 Seminar Papers*, ed. George MacRae, SBLSP 109 (1973) pp.155-202
Kuhn, Heinz-Wofgang, *Ältere Sammlungen im Markusevangelium*, Studien zur Umwelt des Neuen Testaments 8, Vandenhoeck & Ruprecht, Göttingen, 1971
Kümmel, W.G., *Introduction to the New Testament*, SCM Press, London, 1979
Lambrecht, J., "Jesus and the Law: an Investigation of Mark 7.1-23", *EphThL* 53 (1977), pp.24-79
Lambrecht, J., *Marcus Interpretator: Stijl en Boodschap in Mc.320-4.34*, Desclée de Brouwer, Brugge-Utrecht, 1969
Lang, Friedrich G., "Kompositionsanalyse des Markusevangeliums", *ZThK* 74 (1977), pp.1-24
Leach, Edmund, *Genesis as Myth and Other Essays*, Cape, London, 1969
Leach, Edmund & Aycock, D. Alan, *Structuralist Interpretations of Biblical Myth*, Cambridge University Press, Cambridge, 1983
Lightfoot, R.H., *The Gospel Message of St. Mark*, Clarendon Press, Oxford, 1950
Lightfoot, R.H., *Locality and Doctrine in the Gospels*, Hodder & Stoughton, London, 1938
Linnemann, E., "Der (wiedergefundene) Markusschluss", *ZThK* 66 (1969), pp.255-259
Lohmeyer, E., *Das Evangelium des Markus*, Vandenhoeck & Ruprecht, Göttingen, 11th ed. 1951, Orig. 1937
Mack, Burton L., *Rhetoric and the New Testament*, Fortress Press, Minneapolis, 1990
Malbon, E.S., "Galilee and Jerusalem: History and Literature in Marcan Presentation", *CBQ* 44 (1982), pp.242-248
Marcus, Joel, *The Way of the Lord: Christological Exegesis of the Old Testament in the Gospel of Mark*, T. & T. Clark, Edinburgh, 1993
Marcus, Joel, "Mark 14.61: Are You the Messiah-Son-of-God?", *NovT*, 31, 2 (1989), pp.125-142
Mariani, B., "Introduction", *Introduction à la Bible*, eds. A. Robert & A. Feuillet, Desclée & Co., Tournai, Belgium, 1959

Marxsen, W., *Introduction to the New Testament,* tr. G. Buswell, Blackwell, Oxford, 1968
Marxsen, W., *Mark the Evangelist,* (1956), tr. J. Boyce, Abingdon Press, Nashville, 1969
Matera, Frank J., *What are they saying about Mark?,* Paulist Press, New York/Mahwah, 1987
Matera, Frank J., "The Prologue as the interpretative Key to Mark's Gospel", *JSNT* 34 (1988), pp.3-20
Meagher, J.C., *Clumsy Construction in Mark's Gospel: A Critique of Form- and Redaktionsgeschichte,* Toronto Studies in Theology 3, Edwin Mellen, New York, 1979
Metzger, Bruce M., *The Text of the New Testament: Its Transmission, Corruption and Restsoration,* Clarendon Press, Oxford, 1968
Minette de Tillesse, G., *Le secret messianique dans l'Évangile de Marc,* LD 47, Éditions du Cerf, Paris, 1968
Morgenthaler, Robert, *Statistik des Neutestamentlichen Wortschatzes,* Gotthelf Verlag, Zürich, 1958
Moulton, J.H. & Milligan G., *The Vocabulary of the Greek Testament* (London, 1914-29), Eerdmans, Grand Rapids, 1972
Mourlon Beernaert, Pierre, "Jésus controversé: Structure et théologie de Marc 2.1-3.6", *NRT* 95 (1973), pp.129-149
Neirynck, Frans, *Duality in Mark: Contributions to the study of the Markan Redaction,* Rev. Ed., Leuven University Press, Leuven, 1988
Nineham, D.E., *Saint Mark,* The Pelican Gospel Commentaries, Penguin, Harmondsworth, 1963
Noble, D.F., *An Examination of the Structure of Mark's Gospel,* PhD Thesis, University of Edinburgh, 1972
Osburn, Carroll D., "The Historical Present as a Text-Critical Criterion", *Bib* 64 (1983), pp.486-500
Painter, John, *Mark's Gospel: Worlds in Conflict,* Routledge, London and New York, 1997
Palmer, David G., *Sliced Bread: The Four Gospels, Acts & Revelation: Their Literary Structures,* Ceridwen Press, Cardiff, 1988
Parker, D.C., *The Living Text of the Gospels,* Cambridge University Press, Cambridge, 1997
Parunak, H., "Oral Typesetting: Some uses of Biblical Structure", *Bib* 62 (1981), pp.153-168
Perelman, Chaim & Olbrechts-Tyteca, L., *The New Rhetoric: A Treatise on Argumentation,* University of Notre Dame Press, Notre Dame, Ind., 1969
Perrin, N., "The Evangelist as Author: Reflections on Method in the Study and Interpretation of the Synoptic Gospels and Acts", *BR* 17 (1972), pp.5-18.

BIBLIOGRAPHY 371

Pesch, Rudolf, *Das Markusevangelium 1. Teil: Einleitung und Kommentar zu Kap. 1.1-8.26*, Herders Theologischer Kommentar zum Neuen Testament II, Herder, Freiburg, 1976
Petersen, N.R., *Literary Criticism for New Testament Critics*, Fortress Press, Philadelphia, 1978
Petersen, N.R., "The Composition of Mark 4.1-8.26", *HThR* 73 (1980), pp.185-217
Quasten, Johannes, *Patrology, Volume 3. The Golden Age of Greek Patristic Literature: from the Council of Nicaea to the Council of Chalcedon* (Utrecht 1960) repr. Newman Press, Westminster, Md., 1986
Räisänen, Heikki, *The "Messianic Secret" in Mark*, tr. Christopher Tucket, "Studies of the New Testament and Its World", ed. John Riches, T. & T. Clark, Edinburgh, 1990
Rhoads, D. & Michie, D., *Mark as Story. An Introduction to the Narrative of a Gospel*, Fortress Press, Philadelphia, 1982
Richardson, A., *The Miracle Stories of the Gospels*, SCM Press, London, 1941
Riches, John.K., *A Century of New Testament Criticism*, The Lutterworth Press, Cambridge, 1993
Rienecker, Fritz, *A Linguistic key to the Greek New Testament: Matthew-Acts*, tr. & rev. Cleon L. Rogers, Jr., Bagster & Sons, London, 1977
Robbins, Vernon K., *Jesus the Teacher (A Socio-Rhetorical Interpretation of Mark)*, Fortress Press, Philadelphia, 1984
Ryken, Leland & Longman III, Tremper (eds.), *A Complete Literary Guide to the Bible*, Zondervan Publishing House, Grand Rapids, Michigan, 1993
Schmidt, K.L., *Der Rahmen der Geschichte Jesu, Literarkritische Untersuchungen zur ältesten Jesusüberlieferung*, Trowitzsch & Sohn, Berlin, 1919
Schmithals, W., "Das Evangelium nach Markus", 1-2, *ÖTK* 2/1-2, Güttersloh (1979)
Schreiber, J., "Die Christologie des Markusevangeliums. Beobachtungen zur Theologie und Komposition des zweiten Evangeliums", *ZThK* 58 (1961), pp.154-183
Schweizer, Eduard, *The Good News according to Mark*, tr. Donald H. Madvig, John Knox Press, Atlanta, 1970
Schweizer, Eduard, "Die Frage nach dem historischen Jesus", *EvTh* (1964), pp.403-419
Schwyzer, Eduard, *Griechische Grammatik*, vol. ii, *Syntax und syntaktische Stilistik*, ed. Albert Debrunner, C.H. Beck, Munich, 1950
Scott, M.P., "Chiastic Structure: A Key to the Interpretation of Mark's Gospel", *BThB* 15 (1985), pp.17-26
Smith, Stephen H., "The Literary Structure of Mark 11.1-12.40", *NovT* 31, 2 (1989), pp.104-124

Souter, Alexander, *A Pocket Lexicon to the Greek New Testament,* Clarendon Press, Oxford, 1976
Standaert, Benoît, *L'Évangile selon Marc: Commentaire,* Lire la Bible 61, Les Éditions du Cerf, Paris, 1983
Stock, A., "Chiastic Awareness and Education in Antiquity", *BThB* 14 (1984) pp.23-27
Stock, A., "Hinge Transitions in Mark's Gospel", *BThB* 15 (1985), pp.27-31
Strauss, David Friedrich, *Das Leben Jesu, kritisch bearbeitet,* 2 vols., 1st ed. Tübingen, 1835-36, 4th ed. Tübingen, 1840; tr. George Eliot, *The Life of Jesus Critically Examined,* SCM Press, London, 1973
Swete, Henry Barclay, *The Gospel According to St. Mark,* 3rd Ed., Macmillan, London, 1913
Talbert, Charles H., *Literary Patterns, Theological Themes, and the Genre of Luke-Acts,* SBLMS 20, Scholars Press, Missoula, Montana, 1974
Tannehill, Robert C., "The Disciples in Mark: The Function of a Narrative Role", *JR* 57 (1977), reprinted in *The Interpretation of Mark,* ed. W.R. Telford, SPCK, London, 1985
Taylor, Vincent, *The Gospel according to St. Mark,* Macmillan, London, 1952
Telford, William R., *The Barren Temple and the Withered Tree,* JSNT Suppl. Series 1, JSOT Press, Sheffield, 1980
Thackeray, H. St. John, *The Septuagint and Jewish Worship: A Study in Origins,* 2nd edn., The Schweich Lectures, Oxford University Press, London, 1923
Thiel, R., *Drei Markus-Evangelien,* (AKG, 26), Walter de Gruyter, Berlin, 1938
Thomson, Ian H., *Chiasmus in the Pauline Corpus,* JSNT, Sheffield Academic Press, Sheffield, 1995
Tolbert, Mary Ann, *Sowing the Gospel: Mark's World in Literary-Historical Perspective,* Fortress Press, Minneapolis, 1989
Trocmé, Étienne, *The Formation of the Gospel According to Mark,* tr. P. Gaughan, SPCK, London, 1975 (first pub. in Fr. 1963)
Vanhoye, A., *La Structure Littéraire de l'Epître aux Hébreux,* Desclée de Brouwer, Paris-Bruges, 1976
Vermes, G., *Jesus and the World of Judaism,* SCM Press, London, 1983
Via, Dan O., *The Parables: Their Literary and Existential Dimension,* Fortress Press, Philadelphia, 1974
Via, Dan O., *Kerygma & Commedy in the New Testament: A Structuralist Approach to Hermeneutic,* Fortress Press, Philadelphia, 1975
Watt, I., "The First Paragraph of the *Ambassadors*: An Explication", in *Contemporary Essays on Style: Rhetoric, Linguistics, and Criticism,* eds. G. Love & M. Payne, Scott Foresman & Co., Glenview, Ill., 1969, pp.266-283

Wellhausen, J., *Das Evangelium Marci,* Reimer, Berlin, 2nd ed. 1909, orig. 1903
Wendling, E., *Die Entstehung des Marcus-Evangeliums,* J.C.B. Mohr, Tübingen, 1908
Wilson, T. McL., "Mark", *Peake's Commentary on the Bible,* Matthew Black & H.H. Rowley (eds.), Nelson, Sunbury-on-Thames, 1977, pp.799-819
Williams, J.G., *Gospel against Parable. Mark's Language of Mystery,* Sheffield Academic Press, Sheffield, 1985
Wrede, W., *The Messianic Secret,* tr. J.C.G. Greig, James Clarke & Co., Cambridge and London, 1971
Zerwick, Max & Grosvenor, Mary, *A Grammatical Analysis of the Greek New Testament,* Biblical Institute Press, Rome, 1981

Texts:

Nestle-Aland, *Novum Testamentum Graece,* Deutsche Bibelstiftung, Stuttgart, 27th ed. 1993
Brenton, Sir Lancelot C.L., *The Septuagint with Apocrypha: Greek and English,* Regency Ref. Lib., Zondervan Publishing House, Grand Rapids, Michigan (orig. pub. S. Bagster & Sons, London, 1851)
Codex Vaticanus, Roma, Bibl. Vatic., Gr. 1209
Codex Sinaiticus, London, Brit. Mus., Add. 43725
Codex Alexandrinus, London, Brit. Mus., Royal 1 D. VIII

Ancient Authors and Writings:

The Acts of John (tr. ed. M.R. James, *The Apocryphal New Testament,* Clarendon Press, Oxford, 1924)
Aristotle, *Poetics*
Aristotle, *Ars Rhetorica* (*The Art of Rhetoric,* tr. J.H. Freese, Loeb Classical Library, Harvard University Press, Cambridge, Mass., 1926; also: *Aristotelis Ars Rhetorica,* ed. Rudolfus Kassel, Walter de Gruyter, Berlin, 1976; *Aristotle on Rhetoric: A Theory of Civic Discourse,* tr. George A. Kennedy, Oxford University Press, New York/Oxford, 1991; and "Rhetorica" by W. Rhys Roberts, *The Works of Aristotle, Translated into English,* tr. ed. W.D. Ross, Vol. XI, Clarendon Press, Oxford, 1924)

Cicero, *De inventione*
Demetrius, *On Style*
Eusebius, *Historia Ecclesiastica* iii.39.15
Eusebius, *Life of Constantine*
Eusebius, *Gospel Questions and Solutions Addressed to Marinus* (See J. Quaston, *Patrology, Volume 3. The Golden Age of Greek Patristic Literature: from the Council of Nicaea to the Council of Chalcedon*, (Utrecht, 1960) repr. Westminster, Md., 1983)
Hermogenes, *On Invention* (ed. H.Rabe, *Rhetores Graece* Vol. 6, Bibliotheca Scriptorum Graecorum et Romanorum, Teubneriana, Leipzig, 1913)
Herodotus, *The Histories*
Homer, *Iliad* (tr. by W.H.D. Rouse, with Intro. and Appreciation by Andrew Sinclair, Heron Books/Thomas Nelson, London; also tr. by Robert Fagles, with Intro. and Notes by Bernard Knox, Viking Penguin, 1990 & The Softback Preview, 1997)
Homer, *Odyssey*
Jerome, *Letter to Hedibia*
Josephus, *Contra Apionem*, 2.204, *Antiquities*, IV.211; XIV.2.1; XVII.9.3, *The Jewish War* (tr. G.A. Williamson, Rev. Ed., Penguin, Harmondsworth, 1980)
Justin Martyr, *Apology*, 1.67
Lucian, *De conscribenda historia* (tr. D.A. Russell, in *Ancient Literary Criticism: the Principal Texts in New Translations*, eds. D.A. Russell & M. Winterbottom, Clarendon Press, Oxford, 1972)
Philo, *Ad Gaium*
Rhetorica ad Herennium (tr. Harry Caplan, Loeb Classical Library, Harvard University Press, Cambridge, Mass., 1954)
Theon, *The Progymnasmata* (see Christian Walz, ed., *Rhetores Graeci*, 5 vols., Cottae, Stuttgart, 1832-36)
Virgil, *Eclogues, Georgics* and *Aeneid*
Xenophon of Athens, *Memorabilia*